CULTURAL IDENTITY IN MINOAN CRETE

Neopalatial Crete – the 'Golden Age' of the Minoan civilization – possessed Palaces, exquisite artefacts, and iconography with preeminent females. While lacking in fortifications, the island was cloaked with ritual symbolism, an elaborate bureaucracy logged transactions, and massive storage areas enabled the redistribution of goods. We cannot read the Linear A script, but the libation formulae suggest an island-wide *koine*. Within this cultural identity, there is considerable variation in how the Minoan elites organized themselves and others on an intra-site and regional basis. This book explores and celebrates this rich, diverse, and dynamic culture through analyses of important sites, as well as Minoan administration, writing, economy, and ritual. Key themes include the role of Knossos in wider Minoan culture and politics, the variable modes of centralization and power relations detectable across the island, and the role of ritual and cult in defining and articulating elite control.

Ellen Adams is Lecturer in Classical Art and Archaeology at King's College London. She has conducted research based at the University of Cambridge (PhD), the British School at Athens (PhD and Leverhulme Study Abroad Award), and Trinity College Dublin (IRCHSS PostDoctoral Award). She has been involved in fieldwork in Britain, Greece, Bulgaria, and Cyprus.

CULTURAL IDENTITY IN MINOAN CRETE

SOCIAL DYNAMICS IN THE NEOPALATIAL PERIOD

ELLEN ADAMS

King's College London

CAMBRIDGE
UNIVERSITY PRESS

CAMBRIDGE
UNIVERSITY PRESS

University Printing House, Cambridge CB2 8BS, United Kingdom

One Liberty Plaza, 20th Floor, New York, NY 10006, USA

477 Williamstown Road, Port Melbourne, VIC 3207, Australia

4843/24, 2nd Floor, Ansari Road, Daryaganj, Delhi – 110002, India

79 Anson Road, #06–04/06, Singapore 079906

Cambridge University Press is part of the University of Cambridge.

It furthers the University's mission by disseminating knowledge in the pursuit of
education, learning, and research at the highest international levels of excellence.

www.cambridge.org
Information on this title: www.cambridge.org/9781107197527
DOI: 10.1017/9781108178525

© Cambridge University Press 2017

First published 2017

Printed in the United Kingdom by TJ International Ltd. Padstow Cornwall

A catalogue record for this publication is available from the British Library.

ISBN 978-1-107-19752-7 Hardback

CONTENTS

FIGURES

TABLES

PREFACE

On Saturday, 2 July 2016, I took a break from thinking about an island on the south-eastern margins of Europe and joined a pro-EU march in the capital of an island situated in the diagonally opposite north-western corner. Forty-eight per cent of the population of Britain (plus those who had come to regret their decision) were still in shock from the result of the EU referendum just a few days earlier. Appallingly – and yet not entirely surprisingly – the Brexiters had won: the people of Britain had instructed their government to trigger Article 50, which would expel the UK from the EU. It was typical 'layer' weather – ideally you'd have three, to pile on or shed as required, in response to the rather icy fresh breeze, teasing rain, and sections of full sun that gloriously baked the tens of thousands below. Possession of both sunscreen and an umbrella, and an undying fascination with what the heavens send (combined with an appropriate dry retort), is typically British; the identity being embraced (or mourned), however, was wholeheartedly European.

The fallout from the result was equally shocking, involving the unapologetic retraction of promises made by the Leave campaigners, the tortured realization by the Remainers that the measured, for many realistic, promotion of the EU (rather than an impassioned celebration of it) had badly backfired, the shameful sneering of UKIP's Nigel Farage in the European Parliament (he had seven times attempted to become a British MP, and seven times failed – so settled with becoming an MEP for the entity he despised), Shakespearean backstabbing among the governing Tory party, and a Labour opposition that was bent on self-implosion rather than doing any actual opposing. The European dream was, for us at least, broken.

There is a good case to make for viewing Minoan Crete as the first European civilization, as we generally understand the term; unsurprisingly, coffee-table works such as *Knossos: At the Threshold of European Civilisation* are keen to exploit this idea.[1] The Minoans built vast, complex buildings, had writing, produced incredibly sophisticated art, and managed their lives in a surprisingly (and perhaps deceptively) familiar fashion, from their bureaucracy to flushing toilets. If a shared European identity is to be constructed from the remains of the past, both in antiquity and today, then this culture is important and relevant to all of us.[2] Like Britain, Minoan Crete had a very distinctive cultural identity, but could not effectively (and *splendidly*) function without significant interaction with other landmasses, both near and far. And, as Britain discovered so sharply in June 2016, the apparent homogeneity of its elite culture masked considerable variations within, of age, class, and region; these demographics generally escape us in the essentially prehistoric Cretan material, but the regional variations at least are clear.

In Greek myth, Europa is the Phoenician princess seized from the shores of the East by Zeus, disguised as a bull, who rapes and settles her on the shores of Crete. The message seems to convey the *ex oriente lux* narrative of European civilization, while the abuse involved renders the choice of Europa as an emblem of Europe a rather odd one.[3] Greatness was forced upon the continent; unity arose from violence. Europa was deposited on Crete, where she bore her three sons, including Minos – who, of course, lends his name to the great Bronze Age culture. Bulls abound in Greek myth associated with Crete – Minos' wife, Pasiphae, lusted after and seduced the bull sent by Poseidon, god of the sea, the result being the doomed Minotaur; Minos' competition in love was eventually killed by Heracles. Minoan art reveals an obsession with the bull, from bull leaping to remarkable stone libation vessels shaped as bull's heads, and it is not unreasonable to interpret the 'Horns of Consecration' symbol as those of a bull. It is debatable whether such myths contain kernels of historical truth, but it remains the case that the island produced modern Europe's first literate civilization.[4]

This book is the result of many years of thinking about Crete. I first formally studied the island as an undergraduate under Sofia Voutsaki, who became my main PhD supervisor; I am very thankful for her sound advice. I am also grateful to the supportive graduate community at the Faculty of Classics, Cambridge, and the AHRB for financial support during my MPhil and PhD. I have spent highly productive periods at the British School at Athens, as Cary Student from 2000 to 2001, and later with the support of a Leverhulme Trust Study Abroad award from 2003 to 2005. The Taverna at Knossos served as a useful base on several trips over the years, and I am appreciative for the numerous discussions held there. I thank the Irish Research Council for the Humanities and Social Sciences for a two-year postdoctoral award, and the Department of Classics at Trinity College Dublin for incredible support during the planning of this book; I would like to thank Hazel Dodge, Christine Morris, and Sofia Voutsaki for their advice on the proposal. Finally, this monograph would not have been possible without two sabbaticals taken during my time at King's College London, and I would like to thank the Department of Classics for being such a fantastic place to work.

I have published a number of articles on Neopalatial Crete, and taken the readers' responses to heart; they have helped to shape this book for the better, I hope. The two readers of this book gave many insightful, constructive, and supportive notes for improving the work, and I trust I have done them justice. Andrew Shapland not only read the manuscript in its entirety, but also when it was at first draft stage; this is very much appreciated. Peter Warren was kind enough to read Chapters 1 and 2, and Fritz Blakolmer read Chapter 9; the comments were excellent, as were the offprints provided. Christine Morris and Todd Whitelaw helped me source relevant papers not available in London, and thanks are due to Christine, Alan Peatfield, and Evangelos Kyriakidis for helping with queries related to peak sanctuaries. I am particularly grateful to Beatrice Rehl for fielding my numerous queries, and to the production team for its work and support.

The argument has been made that too little has been excavated and published for anyone to ask theoretical questions in a synthetic manner.[5] I disagree. Minoan Crete is one of the most researched areas in the world, if not *the* most explored one. It has, if anything, too much data for one researcher to absorb, even for a restricted time-frame like the Neopalatial period. But we have a responsibility to present our findings to the outside world, both academia and the general public, and we need to tack constantly between data and holistic interpretation in order to reach some kind of (temporary) understanding of the past. The spirit of this synthesis is that it will by no means produce a definitive version of the past, and that it is subject to change; indeed, it is hoped that it provokes as many questions as it answers.

More justification is required for the use of published material alone. The simple reason here is that, if it is unpublished, then it may as well still be in (or on) the ground – in fact, it may be *better* if it were. Minoan archaeology has a notable backlog of unpublished fieldwork, with plenty that has been dutifully disseminated. It is also necessary to make decisions at every point about what to include or not in a synthesis, especially when dealing with sites like Knossos, which was mainly explored at the birth of scientific archaeology and has some significant taphonomic problems. There simply has not been the space to set out and justify the rationale for certain decisions, which I acknowledge produces frustrations on all sides (see below, p. 253, fn. 69).

My interest in Crete began at the age of thirteen, during my first foreign holiday with my mother, stepfather, and sister. It fascinated me, and the spacious and timeless Heraklion Museum sparkled with its exhibits (even before the recent splendid renovation). It also spurred me to start going on a local dig not long after. I would like to thank them, and my father and stepmother, for support over many years. This book is dedicated to the memory of my stepfather; Phaistos, on the book's cover, was understandably his favourite site.

CHAPTER ONE

INTRODUCTION

ACCORDING TO ARTHUR EVANS, AND MANY SINCE, THE NEOPALATIAL period is the 'Golden Age' of the Minoan civilization of the Cretan Bronze Age.[1] Palaces carpeted the island, and highly skilled workers crafted exquisite artefacts. Lacking in fortifications, the island was cloaked with ritual symbolism, forming a powerful ideology. An elaborate bureaucracy logged transactions, while massive storage areas enabled redistribution. While we cannot read the Linear A script, the libation formulae suggest an island-wide koine. Within this cultural identity, considerable variation appears in how people – notably the elites – organized themselves on an intra-site and regional basis. This book explores and celebrate this rich, diverse, and dynamic culture through site analyses and the key control networks of administration, writing, the economy, and ritual. Key themes include the role of Knossos in wider Minoan culture and politics, the variable modes of centralization and power relations detectable across the island, and the role of ritual and cult in defining and articulating elite control.

This book investigates the social strategies of the Neopalatial period, mainly through the distribution of a wide range of elite features and, by extension, practices. 'Social strategies' is a deliberately vague term, in recognition that such practices may incorporate a variety of aspirations and intentions, depending on the make-up of the social groups involved and the situations they are partici-pating in. Exploring strategies of social differentiation will produce insights into the power relations of elites, both established and aspiring.[2] It also negotiates the 'spatial dynamics' of the age, acknowledging the considerable regional and temporal variations across Crete during this period. Therefore, not only are the distribution patterns of elite features and functions through the landscape analysed, but diachronic changes are also taken into account where possible, in order to map the aspirations, successes, and failures of strategies of social differentiation.

The nature and degree of the centralization of certain elite features and functions are analysed on the site and regional levels. At the site level, we will consider whether the owners and users of central buildings (where present in sites) monopolized certain practices, or simply engaged in them on a greater scale than others. On the regional level, we will examine whether these settlements fall into well-defined categories, which might reflect a site hierarchy. While settlement hierarchies do not necessarily reflect political ones, the categorization of sites can shed light on how the regions and island functioned as a whole. Central to this issue is the role of Knossos on an island-wide level, and the extent and nature of its control beyond its immediate hinterland. The role of ceremony is a key factor in understanding these power relations, and the organization of ceremony and the economy are compared. The role of ritual in the Minoan world is one of the most hotly debated problems for the period, and therefore takes a central place in this book.

NEOPALATIAL CRETE

In ceramic terms, the Neopalatial period is MM (Middle Minoan) III to LM (Late Minoan) I; in absolute terms, it is ca. 1700–1450 BC. This section introduces the chronological frameworks and key aspects of the material and visual culture. It outlines the various temporal resolutions applicable to the different types of evidence, and the challenges faced in drawing them together. Neopalatial Crete has one of the most finely tuned ceramic structures developed in prehistory, but the problems with tagging this onto architectural, artefactual, and iconographical material are considerable. We will also overview the characteristic elements of Neopalatial elite culture, which stand as markers for 'Minoan' identity.

Crete is the fifth largest Mediterranean island, strategically placed as a stepping-stone between the central and eastern Mediterranean. While an island, it was by no means insular during this period, and enjoyed wide-ranging external relations. Its shape – 245 km long and only 50 km wide at the most – means that, as the crow flies, no part was far from the sea (Figure 1.1). However, it is a very mountainous island, with fifteen mountain ranges, three of them more than 2,000 m high.[3] Such division enabled the creation of islands within the island, and the articulation of regional identities. The White Mountains on the west of the island are presumed to explain the lack of

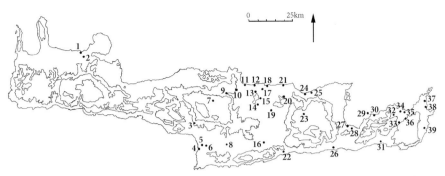

1.1 Map of Crete with main Neopalatial settlements (ritual sites in Figure 6.1). 1) Chania; 2) Nerokourou; 3) Apodoulou; 4) Kommos; 5) Ayia Triada; 6) Phaistos; 7) Zominthos; 8) Mitropolis-Kannia; 9) Sklavokambos; 10) Tylissos; 11) Gazi; 12) Poros; 13) Knossos; 14) Vathypetro; 15) Archanes; 16) Protoria; 17) Prassos; 18) Amnissos; 19) Galatas; 20) Kastelli; 21) Nirou Chani; 22) Chondros; 23) Plati; 24) Malia; 25) Sissi; 26) Myrtos-Pyrgos; 27) Priniatikos Pyrgos; 28) Gournia; 29) Pseira; 30) Mochlos; 31) Makrygialos; 32) Achladia-Riza; 33) Ayios Georgios/Tourtouloi; 34) Klimataria; 35) Petras; 36) Zou; 37) Vaï; 38) Palaikastro; 39) Zakros.

archaeological sites in the region (with due exceptions, especially on the north coast). The Psiloritis, Dictaean, and Thryphti Mountains also serve as formidable landmarks that shape and restrict the communication routes across the island. Despite such internal divisions, and the vital role of the sea in communication, Crete's coast offers a useful boundary for this study. As we shall see, many aspects of Minoan culture are unique to the island, or have a limited distribution further afield.

With crucial exceptions, such as the plethora of conical cups,[4] the distinctive elements of Neopalatial culture tend to be drawn from elite culture. The concentration on elite culture is not only necessary because of the traditional focus on the upper echelons of society, but it also includes the most striking and distinctive elements of the period. It is not the case that this characteristic material and visual culture can be mapped onto a clear, geographically well-defined, collective identity, and further exploration of the variation within indicates local responses to this *koine*.

The palatial form itself is uniquely Minoan, with the large rectangular Central Court and West Court (see Chapter 3 for more detailed analyses of elite features). Ashlar masonry was often used in the construction of elite buildings, with the addition of gypsum, and/or wall paintings. Elite architectural forms include Lustral Basins, sunken rooms entered by a dog-legged or L-shaped series of steps, and Minoan Halls, units provided with light-wells and polythera (multi-door) systems that allow great flexibility in terms of the movement of people, light, and air. Prestige and ritual objects are often made from imported raw materials such as gold or ivory, and are of exquisite craftsmanship. The economic basis to this appears to have been agricultural, visible by the presence of storage rooms (notably magazines) and large ceramic storage jars, or *pithoi* (singular *pithos*: see also 4.8B). Flourishing harbour sites indicate intensive trade, combined with considerable manufacturing. All was organized with a complex administrative system, which deployed the (undeciphered) Linear A script to write down the Minoan language. There is, in contrast to the rich settlement evidence, an unfortunate lack of burial data for Neopalatial Crete.

The 'Neopalatial period' is an architectural or cultural term describing the construction of the second Palaces at Knossos, Malia, and Phaistos, and first Palaces elsewhere. It therefore also provides a chronological unit, traditionally set ca. 1700–1450 BC. Important critiques of this term have been raised given our increased understanding of the chronological variation in the use of the Palaces during this period – there was no neat construction and destruction horizons marking the beginning and end (see following section). Furthermore, the term 'Palace' itself has been reconsidered – it can mean either the architectural form of a particular building that is set around a Central Court, or the institution that the building housed and represented. Or, it can stand for 'elite'; in this book, the term 'palatial' is reserved for sites that possess a building with a recognized Central Court. Concerns have been raised about assumptions projected back from the modern use of the word (see Chapter 3). It is sensible to capitalize the term 'Palace' in order to signal the specificity of this term, both historigraphically (following Evans' view of a Palace-Temple around a courted residence) and culturally (as set during this period of the Cretan Bronze Age).[5] Similarly, the decision has been taken to capitalize the label 'Villa'.

CHRONOLOGICAL FRAMEWORKS

Several chronological frameworks are in use for the Cretan Bronze Age, depending mainly on the material under study. The structure deployed has a profound effect on the narrative created. Clarke stated: 'Archaeological data are not historical data, and consequently archaeology is not history.'[6] This has not been the view widely held in Minoan studies, where many have striven to create a historical narrative. The wide range of sources, combined with the lack of decipherable written evidence, means that several different chronological resolutions (and therefore histories) are available.

Platon set up the Prepalatial, Protopalatial, Neopalatial, and Postpalatial divisions in response to the ceramic phases, which, although more precise in resolution, did not invite a broader, cultural narrative.[7] However, not all 'new' Palaces were built at the beginning of the Neopalatial period; some of these Palaces, such as Galatas, did not replace an 'old' (Protopalatial) version, and not all Palaces were in use throughout the entire epoch. Such is the situation that it has been suggested that the traditional Protopalatial and Neopalatial periods should be united into a single 'palatial' period, with various rebuilds occurring across the island at different times.[8] Linking structures and ceramics remains a fine balancing act, although most scholars use both systems concurrently.[9]

Crete offers one of the best defined chronological frameworks in prehistory, due to painstaking analyses by ceramic experts for more than a century. Where possible, the chronology will follow ceramic phases, namely MM III (A and B), LM IA and LM IB. Absolute (calendar) dates are of less importance in this study, and are heavily debated, particularly concerning the eruption of the island of Thera,[10] which, in ceramic terms, occurred in late LM IA.[11] Figure 1.2 indicates the discrepancies between the more traditional (low) chronology based on the Egyptian calendar and imports,[12] and the more recent (high) chronology based on scientific techniques such as dendrochronology and radiocarbon dating.[13] For the purpose of this book, we will focus on the relative framework. It would, however, be useful to establish the duration of each phase, for which absolute dates are required.[14] The higher chronology suggests that LM IB in particular was a longer period than indicated by the lower chronology (around seventy to ninety years).[15] Even if this were clarified, many of the types of evidence we are exploring, such as frescoes and seals, cannot be easily attached to a specific phase.[16] While the remainder of this section explores some of the issues raised by pottery specialists, most of the data considered in this book are non-ceramic.

The ceramic framework has been set in place since Arthur Evans and his right-hand man, Duncan Mackenzie,[17] defined it over the course of their excavations at Knossos. Scholars have come to differentiate between ceramic *styles* and ceramic *periods*,[18] and Evans himself understood the limitations of a ceramic framework: 'All such stratigraphical demarcations are of their nature somewhat arbitrary and any idea of Minoan civilization as divided into so many distinct compartments must be dismissed from the minds of students. All is, in fact, transition.'[19] In other words, societies do not 'switch' from one era to another overnight, and our tidy categories provide a basic guide to a much fuzzier reality.[20] Two recent works have provided essential surveys of the early and late parts of the Neopalatial period, one on MM III, and one on LM IB.[21] They have both produced vital information concerning the comparative developments of sites across the island. At the same time, they highlight the need to separate stylistic and chronological labels, due to site and regional variations.[22] At some sites, subdivisions within these phases are discernible, but it remains a great challenge to cross-reference these across the island.

Evans originally divided this earlier period into MM IIIA and MM IIIB. However, Betancourt has argued that it is too difficult to distinguish MM IIIA

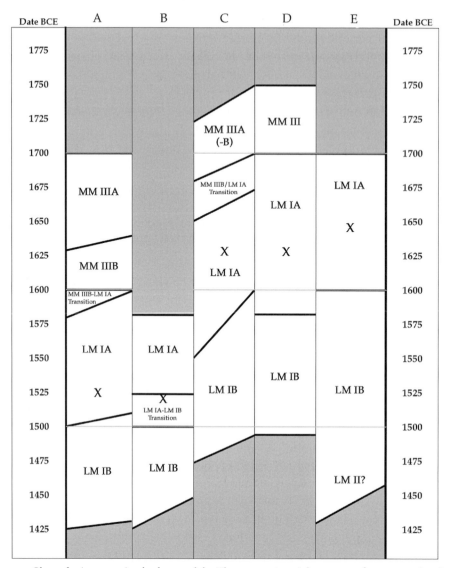

1.2 Chronologies: ceramic, absolute, and the Theran eruption. Adams 2007a, figure 2, reprinted with permission, courtesy *American Journal of Archaeology* and Archaeological Institute of America. A) traditional low chronology (Warren and Hankey 1989); B) updated traditional low chronology (Warren 1998; 2010); C) high chronology (Manning 1995); D) modified high chronology and low Egyptian chronology (Rehak and Younger 2001, 391); E) simplified recent high chronology (Manning et al. 2002; Manning and Brock Ramsey 2003; see also Hammer et al. 2003; Hammer 2005).

as a separate period,[23] while Warren and Hankey suggest that MM III as a whole may have been a relatively short period anyway. They developed a MM IIIB-LM IA 'transitional' phase;[24] generally, however, scholars prefer to keep MM IIIB as a distinct period.[25] The more detailed our understanding of MM III becomes, the clearer it is that there was no single, sudden 'start' to the architectural Neopalatial period.[26] Even within the same site, even within the same *building* (such as the Palace at Knossos), there is not necessarily a single destruction and rebuilding that marks the divide between the Proto- and Neopalatial eras, as has been traditionally assumed.[27] Macdonald and Knappett advocate a realistically vague definition for the beginning of the Neopalatial period as 'either at the start of or somewhere in the earlier part of MM III'.[28] It remains a major challenge to apply the finely tuned ceramic phases to these architectural structures.

Macdonald and Knappett suggest three main (architectural) trajectories experienced by sites during MM III.[29] As always, Knossos stands in a category of its own, continuing to develop and prosper at a rate not matched by others. Phaistos and Malia, and other semi-palatial sites with important central buildings, such as Petras, Myrtos-Pyrgos, and Gournia, experienced a setback. Some sites, however, established new palatial or high-status buildings, including Galatas and Chania, along with other harbour towns, such as Palaikastro and Mochlos. Sites responded to the broad 'Protopalatial' destruction horizon in different ways.

The technical innovations in the slip and firing that marks LM I came in gradually, beginning in MM III.[30] The relative prosperity of LM IA and LM IB has been much discussed since the publication of Driessen and Macdonald's (1997) work *The Troubled Island*. They argued that the Theran eruption brought about a period of recession, if not depression, in Minoan culture. LM IA was, therefore, the Golden Age for the Minoan world, rather than LM IB. However, many sites were clearly flourishing during LM IB, and sites experienced very different trajectories.[31] The physical impact of the Theran eruption on Crete is heavily debated, from minimalist positions to more weighted – links between environmental events and cultural change are problematic to establish.[32] The initial physical damage was probably not that substantial, although we should not discount additional psychological impact.[33] While harbour sites in the north-central area of Crete appear to have suffered (but were not completely destroyed),[34] we know that the palatial site of Zakros, on the eastern coast, prospered precisely in the LM IB period. It is plausible that trade disruptions resulted in fluctuations in economic prosperity across the island.

Identification of a deposit as LM IB as opposed to LM IA is dependent on the presence of particular styles, such as the Marine Style, although LM IA motifs continue.[35] Marine Style ceramics are disproportionately selected for publication, a practice that has led to the misleading impression that they were common. In fact, the style is 'quite rare',[36] outside Knossos at least (and Archanes and Poros).[37] The recent volume on LM IB ceramics highlights well the tension between the desire to link various sites into a homogenous, Cretan narrative, and the recognition that, stratigraphically, certain sites present an idiosyncratic picture.[38] These surveys have clarified both the evidence for subdivisions within the period on a site-by-site basis, and the evidence for a single destruction horizon at the end of it across the island. Of the sites most closely analysed in this book, several have revealed no evidence for LM IB subdivisions, including Nerokourou, Phaistos town, Ayia Triada, Sklavokambos, Tylissos, certain areas of Knossos, Archanes, Vathypetro, Nirou Chani, Galatas town, Kastelli Pediada, Malia town, Myrtos-Pyrgos, Gournia, Pseira, Makrygialos, Petras, and Epano Zakros Villa.[39] Other sites that have some evidence for subdivisions within LM IB include: Chania Kastelli hill, Phaistos Palace, Kommos, Mochlos, Palaikastro (two destruction levels, with no diagnostic differences between the assemblages), and Zakros.[40] Even if one recognizes separate phases of LM IB at some sites, we are not in a position to confirm correlations between sites across the island.[41]

Perhaps more importantly, the traditional picture of a single destruction horizon at the end of LM IB (brought about by Mycenaean warriors, initially through Knossos) has been brought into question. Excavators have suggested that the final destructions at Chania, Malia, Kommos, Mochlos, and Palaikastro occurred later than those at Knossos and north-central Crete, while the one at Petras may have occurred earlier, although this has been questioned and modified.[42] Stylistic elements continue from LM IB to LM II, so, for example, LM II coarse wares from the Unexplored Mansion at Knossos resemble those of LM IB Nirou Chani.[43]

Ceramics offer the finest resolution, and this is ultimately based on Evans' and Mackenzie's work at Knossos. Finley, writing from outside the discipline, made the link between this ceramic framework and Knossocentrism as long ago as 1968, stating that how the former 'is too neatly symmetrical is almost self-evident. It also has an empire-building note to it, for the scheme, worked out from the ruins at Knossos, was imperiously extended to the whole of Crete, though it is now certain that at least some of it will not work at all for other sites, such as Phaistos. And why should it? That the whole of Crete was monolithic in its culture and politics is a gratuitous (and now demonstrably false) assumption.'[44] Evans' technical, and apparently objective, method of organizing his material into temporal phases enabled a coherent narrative that has had significant implications regarding the role of Knossos and the island's socio-political homogeneity.

THE ROLE OF KNOSSOS: CULTURAL TO POLITICAL

Since Evans' publication of *The Palace of Minos* (1921–35), the palatial site at Knossos has been the traditional type-site against which other Minoan sites are compared, with a stress on similarities rather than differences (Figure 1.3).[45] Evans' vision of the Minoans took its lead from Knossos and

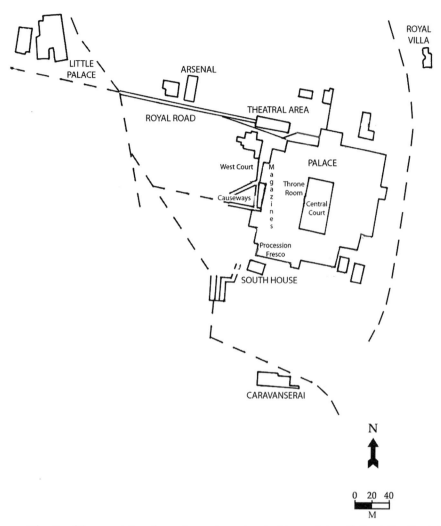

1.3   The site of Knossos. Adams (2010, figure 3), reprinted with permission. © *Cambridge Classical Journal*.

set out a remarkably standardized world: 'The culture as a whole is cast in the same mould and shows an essential unity ... Throughout a space of time extending, at a moderate estimate, over two thousand years – the course of the Minoan civilization is singularly continuous and homogeneous.'[46] The ceramic framework established by Evans and Mackenzie is one reason why Knossos has become the type-site for Minoan culture, and why an implicit assumption remains that all innovations began at this site. Many scholars have emphasized the role of Knossos in the dissemination of all elite features – even though there is no evidence that Knossos invented them.[47] The first known Lustral Basin, for example, comes from a non-palatial building at Malia.[48]

One of the key themes of this book is the slippage in describing elite culture as 'Knossian' or 'Minoan'. Cultural influence is too often seen as political control, even by the excavators of sites who might have been expected to stress their independence. They believe that the island became Knossian over the course of the Neopalatial period, culturally, ritually, and probably economically and politically. Knossos is the most impressive and important Neopalatial site, and clearly a very influential force. Whether the Knossian elite imposed its political might via these cultural trappings needs to be demonstrated rather than assumed – local sites may have had much more agency, choosing to emulate the larger site. Most accounts highlight the 'prestigious position' of Knossos, even if it 'may never have been an official "capital" of Minoan Crete'.[49] But many scholars suggest that, over the Protopalatial and Neopalatial periods, the island became increasingly centralized under Knossos,[50] and that Knossos was indeed its capital in the Neopalatial period.[51] The Final Palatial situation, where Knossos did control a substantial part of the island, should not be projected back onto the earlier one.

It is still true that 'most writing about Minoan archaeology is pitched at the level of the civilization as a whole, rather than of individual polities within it'.[52] Cherry states that cultural imperialism need not imply political domination, and innovations may not always have come from Knossos.[53] The peer–polity interaction model is important, as it allows for individual polities to exist within a cultural *koine*. Bennet has argued that 'in periods when a single [administrative] center has existed, such a system has been imposed from outside',[54] or the system was 'probably unstable'.[55] In other words, the 'natural' state for Crete is to be fragmented, unless externally administered. The location of these polities' boundaries and the nature of inter-site relations remain poorly understood, however.

Warren has recently made an explicit search for a Knossian 'state', but with the subtle distinction between natural, political, social, economic, cultural, and religious borders.[56] It is useful to consider these different spheres separately.[57] For example, Knossos has been perceived as the ceremonial or cosmological centre of the island,[58] which emphasizes the non-economic and apolitical aspects of control and/or influence. The current state of affairs appears to be that most agree that Knossos had cultural, ideological, and possibly religious influence over a broad area, if not the entire island, but it is becoming increasingly questioned whether this was political.[59]

Inter-site relationships have often been voiced in terms of either political dependency or autonomy. However, interdependency (rather than dependency versus independence) and a relational understanding of power are here the preferred terms and approach.[60] Power relations arise from social interaction, rather than existing as a precondition of action. Similarly, Warren speaks of a hierarchical dependency between first-order sites and others, although he argues that 'hierarchy and dependency do not necessarily imply control'.[61] The approach taken here considers a wider understanding of power, which incorporates all social strategies and dynamics, not only the ability to make (political) decisions and mobilize resources. The term 'social complexity' avoids the overtly *political* implications of the 'state'.[62] On both the regional and site levels, politico-economic control is extremely difficult to identify, but we may be able to detect different modes of centralization.

MODES OF CENTRALIZATION IN NEOPALATIAL CRETE

Aside from Knossos, there are other palatial sites and central places, Villas, farms, harbours, and ritual sites (peak sanctuaries and caves). This variability would suggest further that there were different degrees and mechanisms of centralization at work as well. Chapters 3 to 6 focus on the distribution patterns of elite features and intra-site analyses based on these. This brings insights into the nature and extent of centralization at sites, and various types of political organization. In later chapters, this can be extended by further island-wide studies of administration, the economy, and iconography.

In the previous section, we surveyed the terms 'Knossian' and 'Minoan'. There is a similar slippage between 'palatial' and 'elite'. The relationship between power and the trappings of wealth is not clear-cut; the presence of a decision-making body cannot necessarily be assumed from demonstrations of economic wealth or elaborate display.[63] The term 'palatial' may refer to the elite organizational group, or to manifestations of elitism. A problem with identifying elites is that it is often part of their nature to make themselves exempt from close scrutiny by others.[64] For Neopalatial Crete, the make-up of the 'central authority' is unclear, whether it comprised an individual or a group.[65]

Elite features may be concentrated in the Palaces, but they are certainly not monopolized by them, and it is important that, in an over-enthusiastic reaction to traditional views, this is not confused with the fragmentation of political power. Indeed, the trappings of elite material culture may be *expected* to be more widely distributed than the spatial seat of the political governing authority because of emulation. If this is the case, then it would be incorrect to assume that a wide distribution of elite artefacts necessarily reflects a non-hierarchical model and a more egalitarian society.[66] Aspiration to social status and power should not be confused with the articulation of them.

THE ROLE OF RITUAL AND CULT IN NEOPALATIAL CRETE

The themes discussed so far relate to cultural and political influence, but it is highly probable that rituals (and religion) are also central to Neopalatial political geography. Cult is often seen as a separate, distinct aspect of life in the modern West. However, Evans believed that the secular and religious spheres were so deeply intertwined as to be inseparable, a view many scholars have followed since.[67] Ritual played a central role in all spheres of life in the Minoan world, which is one of the main reasons why it is so difficult to define and, ironically, to identify. Bell's common-sense plea to archaeologists to make their lives simpler by adhering to a basic definition of rituals as 'those activities that address the gods or other supernatural forces' is refreshing and tempting, but part of the problem is that not all rituals were of this nature.[68] Archaeological evidence for rituals may indicate non-religious practices, performances, and ceremonies, which need not be directed to other worlds. Furthermore, the distinction between deity, priest, or other important human is very unclear in the Minoan iconography (Chapter 9). Apparent ritual practices in settlements are discussed in Chapters 3, 4, and 5, while ritual sites are explored in Chapter 6; ritual uses of Linear A are discussed in Chapter 7, while the possibility of ritualized feasting is explored in Chapter 8. It infuses all areas of Minoan life.

It is argued that Minoan ritual serves to bind people together with a shared cultural symbolism and sense of collective identity, while, at the same time, it creates, legitimizes, and challenges social differentiation.[69] The ritual process appears to smooth over this apparent contradiction, cementing the wider social group, while asserting social differentiation, both 'real' and aspired.[70] During the past twenty-five years, there has been a growing interest in the social role of religion in legitimizing the Minoan elite's position,[71] or the 'significance of performances for materializing ideologies'.[72] This is a sound approach, but there is a danger of producing a functionalist interpretation of the role of ritual, without due recognition of the other experiences of ritual performance. Embodied aspects, or the archaeology of the senses, may be added to the mix to lend a more experiential quality to ritual.[73]

Evans' view of religion was based largely on iconographical data gathered from 'the length and breadth of Crete' and beyond.[74] He moved readily from a particular example to generalized interpretations, presenting Minoan Crete as a coherent ideological entity, and blurring regional and contextual variations. This is partly due to the need to take a broad chronological resolution for such material. Also, the island's population was brought together by a shared system of practices (and/or beliefs), as indicated by the Linear A 'libation formulae'. However, religion and ritual is now recognized as a dynamic force, with a complex tension between change and continuity, where traditions are invented and veils of stasis mask variations. Cult and ritual undoubtedly contributed to a wider sense of 'Minoan-ness', but it is becoming clearer that this was articulated in more localized ways. This continues the trend Nilsson set when he highlighted the differences between the Minoan and Mycenaean religions; increasingly, scholars seek a more detailed, localized understanding of ritual practice and its socio-political impact.[75]

Evans' influence looms over the particular distinction between the study of Minoan ritual practice and religious belief. He, characteristically, was interested in both. At the dawn of Minoan archaeology, he drew together iconographical evidence for rituals focused on trees and pillars.[76] He was also keen to reconstruct the practices that may have been performed in the architectural spaces he was excavating. For example, the label 'Theatral Area' suggests a performative ritual; these areas, notable at Knossos and Phaistos, comprised steps for observers facing a road or court.[77] For Evans, 'the historic imagination calls up a vision of solemn processions, of divine effigies and of Priest-Kings, borne aloft on portable thrones, and followed by their worshippers and acolytes, wending their way along this *Via Sacra* between the lesser and greater Palace Sanctuaries'.[78] Evans organized Cretan dances here in 1903, and remarked it would be well-suited for the kind of boxing matches depicted in the art. Scholars such as Picard and Warren have developed this idea of 'ritual action' as a crucial part of Minoan religion.[79] This follows Bell's theory of a practice approach to ritual, and is a useful one for archaeologists to adopt, given that one may hope that such practices left material traces.[80] Equally important has been Evans' views on Minoan religion, the deities, and personnel (see Chapter 9).

ORGANIZATION OF THIS BOOK

Chapter 2 explores two key background areas to the study: the discovery of Neopalatial Crete, and the Protopalatial period that preceded it. Minoan archaeology has a long history, and it has witnessed many major political overhauls that have inevitably impacted practice. This volatile history, and relatively recent absorption into the Greek nation-state, has significant implications for the island's claim to have produced the first European civilization. The central role of Sir Arthur Evans in this narrative is explored in more depth. The Protopalatial background is important in terms of why the Palaces emerged on Crete in the first place. The circumstances that triggered this heightened social complexity are heavily debated, and we set this discussion against an overview of the Palaces, sites, and culture. The chapter ends with a consideration of what the Protopalatial period may have looked like to those living in the Neopalatial era. Archaeologists often forget this perspective.

Chapter 3 introduces and explores distinctive aspects of Neopalatial architecture and artefacts in more depth. It also raises the distinction between *elite* architecture in general, and *palatial* features in particular. We naturally begin with the 'Palaces', itself a problematic term, but one well established in the literature. Courts and other public open areas, such as Theatral Areas, are also discussed, as iconographical evidence suggests that they were the setting for major events. Urban shrines (or temples) are briefly discussed. Formulized spaces such as halls and Lustral Basins are considered next. In these cases, it is extremely difficult to determine whether they are cultic or otherwise ceremonial, but they certainly appear to be 'special'. Certain ritual artefacts that are characteristic of Crete during this time are then overviewed, notably figurines, libation tables, Horns of Consecration, and the Double Axe symbol. This chapter seeks to outline the overall distributions of these broad categories; much of the data will be explored at an intra-site level in the following chapters.

Chapter 4 focuses on the palatial sites (with Central Court buildings, or Palaces), particularly Knossos, Malia, Phaistos, and Zakros. The same structure is followed for each, for ease of comparison. We begin by exploring how each Palace was approached, in particular their entrance systems. This not only adds an experiential quality to the structures, but also serves to highlight that these complexes were not homogeneous, and visitors may have had access to a small section of them. The various functions of each Palace are then analysed, noting similarities and differences between them. Where possible, the Palace is then set into its urban context; however, the evidence for the surrounding towns is varied. This is an essential expansion of the discussion on their functions; they did not exist in vacuums. Finally, these palatial towns are set in their immediate hinterland, with a discussion of the regional picture. There are also sections on Galatas and Petras in this chapter, as they are both, in architectural form, clearly following the palatial model. The division of settlements between this and the following chapter is made on these grounds, but there are some clear central buildings and important non-'palatial' settlements, such as Archanes and Chania (or their Palaces are not fully discovered). One reason for singling out the form of the Central Court so strongly is that it is such a distinctive feature of the Minoan Cretan civilization.

Chapter 5 explores the wide variety of other settlements, including some semi-palatial ones, such as Gournia and Ayia Triada, which appears to have taken a palatial role in the Mesara for much of the Neopalatial period. In order to highlight the regional variation, the data are set out according to area: north-central Crete, the west of the island, the Mesara, the south coast, the Mirabello Bay area, then eastern Crete. Around twenty excavated sites are discussed, demonstrating out the great range of types of (flourishing) sites during this period. One of the most striking variations is in the form of central building (or absence of one, as the case may be). Some sites possess a clear non-palatial focal building, such as Myrtos-Pyrgos, while others, notably Palaikastro, are extremely prosperous but have not yet yielded a central building.

Chapter 6 provides an overview of the rich ritual landscape: peak sanctuaries, ritual caves, and idiosyncratic sites such as Kato Syme. The identification of such sites is not always clear, and the certain examples are not evenly distributed across the island. In order to aid mapping this chapter onto the previous two, the sites are organized according to region. We begin again with the area around Knossos and north-central Crete more generally, before exploring the west, the south, then the east. Certain areas, such as the Mirabello Bay area, lack ritual sites, while sacred caves are particularly rich and concentrated in the central region. This variety is highlighted when set against the palatial and non-palatial sites; no model for the relationship between settlements and ritual sites works for the entire island.

Chapter 7 juggles several strands of communication, including literacy and administration. Linear A is undeciphered, and it is not even clear whether the language is Indo-European. However, the ideograms and the numerical system shed light on the nature of these documents. Linear A tablets were part of a much wider system of non-written documents, which can be subdivided according to form and function. We also explore evidence for the Knossian 'replica rings', as scholars have relied on these rather heavily for reconstructing the island's political geography, and the Zakrian 'look-alike' sealings. The final section deals with writing in the ritual sphere, notably the Linear A libation formulae found across the island.

Chapter 8 presents the economic evidence, focusing on agricultural storage, 'redistribution', and craft specialization. We begin with an overview of the economic landscape and settlement patterns, particularly as provided by survey evidence. This requires considerations of the practicalities of moving around the landscape, such as journey times (rather than distances). The question of whether Minoan society was a 'redistributive' one, and, if so, its nature and extent, is tied to the issue of centralization. After overviewing the evidence for storage patterns, we focus on settlements with known central buildings in order to compare their storage facilities. The theme of production and craft specialization is hindered by the difficulties in establishing workshops; however, there is clear evidence in some places. A close link between production and harbour (trade) sites is noted.

Chapter 9 explores a variety of data under the central theme of self-representation and identity, or Cretan 'Minoan-ness'. The main focus is on iconographical evidence. We begin with analysing depictions of the human form in terms of Minoan self-identity. It is acknowledged that the different media – frescoes, seals, figurines, and stone vases – provide different insights into this question. The challenge of identifying humans and deities in Neopalatial art is explored, turning then to how the 'Minoans' viewed themselves and wished to be viewed. The second half of the chapter takes three types of 'others' that those living on Neopalatial Crete could set themselves against: first, the limited evidence of the mortuary sphere, second, relations with the divine – with caveats due to possible misidentifications – and third, beyond the shores of Crete in the Aegean and eastern Mediterranean.

Chapter 10 concludes the book, and attempts to draw together these detailed analyses to address the main themes outlined previously.

CHAPTER TWO

THE BACKGROUND TO NEOPALATIAL CRETE

THE DISCOVERY OF THE MINOANS

The Formation of Modern Crete

The link between nation-building and archaeology is particularly fraught in the case of Crete.[1] Greece became an independent nation-state in 1830 with its extraction from the Ottoman Empire, and once more served as the easternmost frontier of what we now call Europe. It was not until 1913 that Crete joined the mainland, after an unsettled period from 1898 as an autonomous state of the Ottoman Empire; it lay under a High Commissioner with the support of the four Great Powers (Britain, Italy, France, and Russia), while the Ottoman Sultan retained sovereignty.[2] This uneasy compromise meant that some crucial issues, such as financial control of how certain taxes were spent, was open to interpretation.[3] Furthermore, this confused state of affairs stimulated the need for a clear island identity, which archaeology could help to define. Prior to the 1913 unification with Greece, the possibility of *enosis* was also a delicate subject, desired by Christian Cretans, but contrary to the interests of most Muslim Cretans, the Great Powers, and the Ottoman Empire.

Until the situation had settled, Cretans were extremely wary of major excavations being conducted on the island, lest, as according to Ottoman law, the important finds would be transported to Constantinople.[4] Joseph Hazzidakis, the president of the Herakleion Syllogos, stalled activity at Knossos for this reason. However, part of the process of entering the Greek nation-state was to establish a Cretan museum. The link between museums and the rise of the nation-state is increasingly recognized;[5] ordering and mapping the world in a demarcated, purpose-designed space is an important strategy in controlling the past and the nationalistic message. Historical narratives could be promoted, suppressed, and even invented. In 1883, the Herakleion Syllogos (under Hazzidakis) began organizing the collection of antiquities in what was to become the Herakleion Archaeological Museum – the building itself was not constructed until 1904–12.[6] It was set up by Cretans for Cretans (and the outside world), in contrast with so many of the excavations of major sites, which were foreign-led.

Hazzidakis and Stephanos Xanthoudides were also responsible for the drafting of the antiquities law in 1899, which gave Cretans ownership of antiquities, and prevented the transportation of finds from the island. This also made it easier for foreigners to gain permission to dig on Crete, allowing the age of the Big Dig to begin, and for major investment into archaeological work.[7] Foreign involvement was courted – Prince George himself was the patron of the British-organized Cretan Exploration Fund, which had the explicit aim of resourcing and staking out British rights to areas for excavation. Meanwhile in Britain, Sir Arthur Evans' close association with Oxford's Ashmolean Museum provided an important arena for articulating the importance of Crete on the global stage. When he first visited Herakleion in 1894, one of his intentions was to obtain artefacts for the Ashmolean,[8] where he had been Keeper since 1884. It was during this trip that he decided to purchase land at Knossos, a feat not completed until 1900.[9]

It took time for the implications of his findings to be absorbed. Sherratts states: 'Here was the first complex, literate society on the soil of what would later be called Europe: a major influence not only on the Greek mainland but (either via mainland intermediary or possibly more directly) on the Bronze Age of south-east and central Europe, and arguably therefore the "birthplace" of European civilisation as a whole.'[10] Crete was now fully absorbed into the European sphere.

Evans' work captured the public imagination in many ways, fuelled by his media contacts. Even Sigmund Freud was quick to comment on this in a letter of 4 July 1901: 'Have you read that the English excavated an old Palace in Crete (Knossos), which they declare to be the real labyrinth of Minos? ... This is the cause for all sorts of thoughts too premature to write down.'[11] Freud considered himself the great puzzle-solver of the mind, an Oedipus of the consciousness, which fitted the analogy of the labyrinth well. His comments also indicate how the Minoans were seen as possibly the origins to something modern; in order to understand ourselves, we needed to understand them.

Today, the Minoans are Hellenized in schools, despite the distinctiveness of Minoan culture (and the fact that the Linear A script represents a non-Greek language), which might otherwise allow the opportunity of producing a local island identity.[12] Minoan culture is less charged in *nationalistic* terms than later Greek antiquity,[13] but it forms part of the primary school syllabus in Greece and is regularly referenced in popular culture,[14] including in tourist advertising. The best of both worlds is sought, whereby the bounded island becomes part of the national state, but on its own terms. As a bridge between East and West, there is little contradiction in also having a separate identity.

History of Excavations

There has been interest in the archaeology of Crete since the Renaissance.[15] Minos Kalokairinos first made soundings at the Knossian Palace in 1878, striking the ground in the area of the west magazines. He worked hard to bring the site to the world's attention, and indeed triggered a competition among foreign worthies who sought to excavate at the site.[16] Twenty-two years later, on 23 March 1900, Arthur Evans began work at the site; this followed the 1899 Cretan antiquities law, which offered greater protection against the export of archaeological finds, and therefore made it easier for foreigners to get permission to excavate. The British also conducted work at Psychro and Zakros (David Hogarth), Palaikastro (Richard Dawkins and John Myres), and Praisos (Robert Bosanquet), while the Italians excavated in the south-west, at Phaistos (Luigi Pernier) and Ayia Triada (Federico Halbherr). The Americans worked mainly in the east, at Kavousi and Gournia (Harriet Boyd Hawes), Vasiliki, Pseira and Mochlos (Richard Seager), and Vrokastro (Edith Hall). Cretan archaeologists were also active, such as Stephanos Xanthoudides at Chamaizi and Joseph Hazzidakis at Tylissos. In more recent years, Greek activity has extended to the Palaces of Zakros, Petras, and Galatas (as well as other probable palatial sites, such as Archanes and Chania).

These major projects were all initiated during the first decade of the twentieth century, and they set the narrative for Minoan studies; much work conducted today is centred on clarifying and re-examining the details of these projects.[17] The speed of many of these digs had consequences for their quality: Hogarth's 'forceful' work at Psychro, for example, would not be condoned today.[18] The tightening up of export laws appears to have been one reason for this improvement in practices (although, under the Cretan antiquities law, Evans was allowed to take duplicates back to Britain, namely, the Ashmolean Museum).[19] Percy Gardner wrote:

> Turkey and Crete are copying the laws of Greece in such matters. All that the western nations are now allowed to gain by work in the East is knowledge. We have reached the scientific stage of discovery. And since knowledge has thus been put in the place of actual spoil, it is natural that excavation has been conducted in a more orderly and scientific way, find spots and circumstances of finding being recorded with great

exactness . . . And we must now accept the changed circumstances, and do what we can for historic and artistic progress, without hope of results in the form of works of ancient art for our museums.[20]

This suggests that scholars were *forced* into paying proper attention to contextual information.[21] The quality of fieldwork has become notably more scientific. Techniques range from residue analysis, archaeozoology, and environmental studies to physical anthropology. Recording is also much more precise, including GIS, while non-invasive techniques such as geophysics are increasingly deployed.

Survey has a long tradition on Crete. Pendlebury extensively surveyed the island, especially the Lasithi area; his distance maps are still of great use.[22] In later decades, intensive surveys of a known site became more common, such as Hood's archaeological survey of Knossos, or his wider travels that covered considerable swaths of relatively unknown areas.[23] Other approaches have focused on the island-wide coverage of a particular type of site, such as work on peak sanctuaries or the road systems.[24] The most recent trend has been to undertake intensive surveys; eastern areas, such as the Bay of Mirabello, must be among the most intensely surveyed regions of the world.[25]

Minoan archaeology has also become distinguished by intense specialization, be it on a site, types of site, a particular type of data, or a particular period of pottery. This level of expertise is impressive and daunting in equal measure, and serves as the bread and butter of any synthesis. As in many parts of the world, synthetic approaches to Minoan archaeology are hindered by the presence of too much and too little data.[26] This contradictory position pales into insignificance when the sheer volume of unpublished data is considered, but an overwhelming amount of material remains available. The discipline has also opened up to theoretical developments in other related fields.[27] The present synthesis is an attempt to incorporate highly variable data with the understanding that many adjustments will be required with further excavations (or, more specifically, publications).

Arthur Evans, 'the First Stepping-Stone of European Civilization', and Cretan Identity

Sir Arthur Evans' four-volume tome, *The Palace of Minos at Knossos* (1921, 1928, 1930, 1935), concerned not only Knossos but also the Minoan civilization as a whole, and, with Knossos as type-site, it set the agenda for all further Minoan studies: it was Evans who described Crete as 'the first stepping-stone of European civilization'.[28] Evans' key role in writing the history of Minoan Crete has led scholars to ask whether he was its discoverer or inventor.[29] 'Minoan' replaced 'Mycenaean' in Evans' initial reports produced soon after he began excavating at the site, and was firmly in place by the time the first volume of *The Palace of Minos* was published.[30] He stated: 'By the Greeks themselves the memory of the great Age that had preceded their own diffusion throughout the Aegean lands was summed up in the name of Minos.'[31] For Evans, the term 'Minos' could indicate a dynastic title, like pharaoh, rather than an individual monarch.[32] This side-stepped the issue of origins and when and whence the 'Minoans' arrived to Crete, although this was a question that he considered.[33] Rather than a term intended to label the Bronze Age of Crete chronologically,[34] it came to refer to the culture and even the population as an ethnonym.[35]

It has been argued that Evans was deeply influenced by his Victorian and Edwardian environment, and that he looked for and found a palatial structure in Crete that would mirror the British monarchy. But he also referred to these structures with Central Courts as 'Palace-Temples', the seat of power for the Priest-King.[36] This differed from the Edwardian terminology, although British monarchs are also the head of the Church of England.[37] It was also distinct from the civilizations discovered in the Near East, where temples were clearly spatially demarcated from Palaces. Evans desired to distinguish the Minoan culture from these in order to highlight its role, rather than that of classical Greece, as the first European civilization.[38]

The Minoan culture was defined in opposition to other known cultures both in time and space, particularly classical Greece, the Near East, and (eventually) Mycenaean Greece. Evans wanted to emphasize not only Crete's distinctiveness, but also its legacy, both in terms of the later classical Greeks[39] and of all of European civilization. Throughout Evans' work, there is a tension between the desire to present the Minoans as non-, or even anti-, classical Greek,[40] and the emphasis on the cultural debt owed to the Minoans by those same Greeks, who 'cannot be adequately studied without constant reference to their anterior stages of evolution'.[41] For him, the Minoan culture was the 'cradle of European civilization'.[42] Europe now had a prehistory that could be set against that of the Near East.[43] It was not therefore the first millennium BC classical Greeks who laid the foundations for the modern, Western nation-states, but the second millennium BC Minoans.

When Evans was excavating at Knossos, Greek history, and therefore Western history, was still felt to begin in 776 BC, the year of the first Olympiad. Greek speakers were believed to have come from the north during the Dorian invasion – a very different direction of influence from that of Crete, which further drew inspiration from the East. Then the 1952 decipherment of 'prehistoric' and even 'prehellenic' Linear B as an early form of Greek surprised everyone, including the decipherer, Michael Ventris. This proved that Greek was spoken in the Aegean during the second millennium BC, undermining the Dorian theory.

Evans's anti-classicism agenda is clear, and must stem from more than being turned down for an Oxford fellowship.[44] Classical archaeology was itself a very young discipline in Britain and elsewhere; it was not a formal part of the classical curriculum until well into the twentieth century.[45] It had to mark its territory against the traditional philological and literary studies. At the same time, the archaeology of the first millennium BC–AD needed to protect its interests against the lure of the Bronze Age: during the late Victorian era in Britain, before Evans began work at Knossos, the excavations at Troy and Mycenae had impressed the world.[46] In 1909, Waldstein wrote:

> There exists now a new danger to classical study and especially to the study of Classical Archaeology. It may be, if not submerged, at all events depressed by the powerful waves of prehistoric study beating against the shores of ancient Greece and Rome. In previous days the danger to the study of Greek literature and art came from the study of Philology, of language as such. The danger threatening the study of ancient art and religion, which is essential to the understanding of Hellenism, now comes from the prehistoric and ethnological point of view.[47]

Waldstein's paper begins in a polite, gentlemanly tone, but the author's distress is clear from the outset. While he applauds the recent success in pushing back Greek history to Neolithic times, the reader is aware that there is a 'but . . . ' on its way. The new threat attacks his standing and livelihood, and the search to understand the primitive origins of the Greeks serves, in his view, to boil down the Greek genius to a simplistic essence. Besides, the Aegean Bronze Age was not really classical, but belonged with anthropology, and was best kept separate. We may compare this with his earlier work of 1885, which include an essay on 'the province, aim, and methods of the study of Classical Archaeology'. Here, we see a rather modern historiographical approach to the topic, and there is a regret that classical archaeology is 'still considered as a subordinate department of classical philology'.[48] Aegean prehistory is not yet granted the attention that it was to receive in 1909; presumably Waldstein spent the intervening years observing this great storm building.[49]

According to Evans, the classical Greeks misremembered the earlier civilization in the myths of the Minotaur, in a 'childish wonder at the mighty creations of a civilization beyond the ken of the new-comers. The spade of the excavator has indeed done much to explain and confute them'.[50] In other words, he, as a modern Briton, was more in control of the 'facts' than the ancient Greeks, who were almost to be pitied for their ignorance. However, he was prepared to reference the ancient Greeks if this aided his fund-raising efforts for the Crete Exploratory Fund: in *The Times* (31 October 1900) he portrays one of his recent finds as a 'beautiful life-size painting of a youth, with a European and almost classically Greek profile' who 'gives us the first real knowledge of the race who produced this mysterious early civilization'. The message is clear: these people were distinctive, but still the first Europeans.

The implications of finding the first great European civilization were potentially profound, not merely in terms of European history, but also in terms of

Europe's identity. When Evans began excavating at Knossos, Crete had only just shaken off the shackles of full Ottoman control and had not yet become part of the Greek nation-state. Crete's role, semi-independent and caught between the East and the West, is therefore an interesting one. For Evans, ancient Crete was not Hellenic, but nonetheless the kernel of European identity – and a shared history is fundamental to the development of a strong sense of identity. The search for origins was therefore a natural part of the process of forming a European identity that overarched the emerging national ones. This approach is still pursued in some quarters today.[51] In order to emphasize the distinctiveness of Minoan identity, and the role of the culture as the seed of 'Europeaness', Evans focused on island-wide homogeneity, especially as led by 'his' site at Knossos.

Orientalism was most notably described by Said as 'the Western style for dominating, restructuring and having authority over the Orient'.[52] This built upon earlier ideas, for example by Reinach (1893), which sought to emphasize Europe's independence from Asian influence or diffusionism, as *le mirage oriental*. This may be compared to Evans' slightly later work on 'The "Eastern Question" in Anthropology'.[53] Both thought that Eastern influence was not the explanation for the rise of European civilization, and there is known correspondence between the two men.[54] Evans critiqued the influence of biblical training and the classical tradition in propagating this mirage.

However, the notion of *ex oriente lux* existed in the ancient world in the shape of the Europa myth. Europa was the Phoenician/Asian princess who was seized from the shore of the East and brought to Crete by Zeus in the form of a bull – a notable Minoan symbol. The myth of King Minos, Europa's son, has been more of a focus in 'Minoan' studies, Evans noting that he was the 'son of Zeus by Europa, herself, perhaps an Earth-Goddess'.[55] She lent her name and blood to Europe, but was not herself European in origin. V. Gordon Childe, briefly a student of Evans, describes the idea of 'the irradiation of European barbarism by Oriental civilisation' along similar lines.[56] According to Childe, the Minoans did not blindly borrow from the East, even if they were indebted to them. Instead, they revealed signs of European individualism and enterprise, or Western modernism.[57] Likewise, Evans insisted that the Minoans did not borrow heavily from other cultures during their development; this would undermine their contribution to the world stage.[58]

THE PROTOPALATIAL BACKGROUND

The Minoan culture extends far beyond the ca. 1700–1450 BC timeframe studied here. This Neopalatial 'Golden Age' might be considered as emblematic of the wider Minoan story, but that is not the approach taken here. Setting aside the possibility that we should no longer arbitrarily divide the palatial period into two across the island,[59] the chronological focus on these 250 years allows for a more in-depth treatment of the wide range of data and variability across the island. A section on the Protopalatial period (ca. 1900–1700 BC) is not intended to act as the necessary background to 'explain' the subsequent one; origins in themselves do not account for later developments.[60] This kind of evolutionary, cause-and-effect approach is one of the key consequences of Darwin's influence (or the misuse of his ideas) in archaeology.[61] *Who* the Greeks were depended very much on where they came from, and so it was not inappropriate that many early discussions of prehistory were published in the *Journal of Hellenic Studies*.[62] The idea that the explanations can be located in looking back to foundations remains a tempting one for many today,[63] but this removes much of the potential agency from the actors performing such activities. It suggests that the outcome was inevitable – although the prior circumstances remain the backdrop, they do not, in themselves, offer only one consequence. This is also a very passive view of evolution; the Darwinian approach is much more dynamic, and based on the battles of 'natural selection'.[64]

Therefore, we do not assume that events and processes are inevitable.[65] Nor do we assume that the rationales for particular activities are rooted in the past, even acknowledging the power of tradition. Traditions can change radically, and they can be invented – they frequently were during the Neopalatial period. A fresh look at the inhabitants of the Neopalatial period that considers their view of their past, present, and future will highlight the considerable dynamism of the period. And neither should evolutionism be blurred with the idea of inevitable development and progress towards greater enlightenment, perhaps most strikingly illustrated by Service's ladder of human development from bands, tribes, and chiefdoms to states.[66]

Rather than provide an evolutionist study of trajectories based on a narrative of inevitable cause and effect, the Protopalatial background is important when considering how people during the Neopalatial period encountered their recent past, a phenomenon that continued during the Neopalatial period, as buildings were rebuilt, altered, and destroyed, incorporating these earlier buildings and objects into their daily lives. Here we focus on what the Protopalatial period looked like. The story of the Protopalatial period is that of state development, the mobilization of significant resources, and the construction of monumental buildings, including the 'Palaces'. The distinction between social complexity, including 'elite' features, and the 'palatial' process is increasingly recognized.[67]

State Formation

One of the most influential contributions to the study of civilization (and a particular civilization) and culture (and a particular culture) was produced in Renfrew's 1972 work, *The Emergence of Civilization*. The title reveals an emphasis on origins, and an evolutionary approach to defining and explaining the rise of specific complex societies, especially those with urban centres. This partly stems from the definition of 'civilization' as 'the self-made environment of man, which he has fashioned to insulate himself from the primaeval environment of nature alone', a situation arguably best seen in urban societies.[68] Renfrew's model rested ultimately on the emergence of a redistribution economy, based on increasing crop specialization, which necessitated the rise of an elite in order to organize it. These chiefs were then able to transfer any surplus into resources for craft specialization. The assumption is that such an emerging elite had altruistic inclinations, one that few would support today.[69]

Renfrew emphasized endogenous process, in response to previous diffusionist ideas that had emphasized influence from the East (see also above). While many facets of his argument still convince – such as the stance that no single cause can explain or result in the emergence of civilization – the work has had the honour of receiving substantial critiques since its publication.[70] A combination of internal and external factors is likely to have been active in the case of the Aegean; Eastern influence may be recognized without insisting that the Cretans borrowed blindly. For example, there are clear signs of contact with Egypt during the Protopalatial period, but the Cretans did not adopt Egyptian motives of kingship, or, in Watrous' words, 'Egypt offered the Minoans a stimulant rather than a model for imitation or adaptation, in contrast to what happened at Byblos.'[71] One issue with Renfrew's approach is that the notion of civilization is not so closely linked to the historically specific construction of the Minoan Palaces. This leads to a rather homogenous, universal view of these complexes; in fact, as we will see, there was considerable variety in their functions, local purposes, and island-wide role, and these, moreover, changed dramatically over time. Furthermore, it has recently been argued that state formation on Crete post-dates MM IB, and therefore also post-dates the construction of the first Palaces.[72]

'Civilization' and its sometime replacement 'state' are terms defined in opposition to other, lesser, stages of complexity, set on a ladder of political entities (band, tribe, chiefdom, then state).[73] The term 'state' has also received much attention since Cherry described the 'emergence of state-type institutions'.[74] In a later work, he argues that the process occurred as 'revolution' in the case of Minoan Crete, namely, a sudden change rather than a gradual development.[75] Other scholars have sought Early Minoan precedents to the Middle Minoan palatial societies.[76] Renfrew emphasizes the developments between Early Minoan (EM) I and EM II, but cannot really explain the lack of clear, apparent development in EM III.[77] The debate centres on how to frame the historical narrative (the manner of change), rather than the explanation behind why it happened.[78]

A state might be distinguished by the use of writing, a clear social hierarchy, and centralized organized processes and practices, including bureaucracy and religion. Centralization is key to this definition, and this may be demonstrated, in different ways, in several areas of Neopalatial Crete. This does not mean that they are necessarily *static*, however: both personnel and regulations may change within a basically stable institution. Many different types of state, past and present, have been identified.[79] While it is important not to be too focused on the mechanics of statehood, they have formed the framework for previous discussions of Minoan politics across the island, and so it is useful to explore them.

Unlike the later Neopalatial period, there is a general consensus concerning the fragmentation of the island into separate Protopalatial polities,[80] despite the similarities in palatial form at the three main sites at Knossos, Phaistos, and Malia (and Petras, to the east) and the wide distribution of architectural forms, finds, and practices, such as peak sanctuaries. This is based on regional clusters of material culture, such as pottery, mortuary architecture, and scripts. For example, Cadogan has reconstructed a Knossian state from natural boundaries and 'cultural indicators', mainly pottery, although communication routes to the Mesara region were straightforward.[81] A workshop in the Mesara provided Kamares pottery for Phaistos and also Knossos.[82] Analysis of the Malian polity suggests that contact between particular sites like Malia and Myrtos-Pyrgos could be targeted, and not necessarily include all of the land in between.[83] Furthermore, it is becoming increasingly clear that different regions of Crete experienced different trajectories to social complexity in its Neopalatial form, some regions prospering from trade for example, but others from agriculture.[84] This serves as a more sophisticated compromise to previous accounts that emphasized agriculture.[85]

Protopalatial Palaces, Ritual Sites, and Culture

Most of the evidence is covered or destroyed by later Neopalatial complexes, but the basic palatial form (four wings around a Central Court, with an additional West Court), is developed at various points of this period. From the late Prepalatial period onwards, dramatic settlement size increases (and accompanying population growths) can be discerned.[86] Elements of the Neopalatial and even Final Palatial periods have been projected back onto this epoch. Traditional accounts may distinguish between 'Minoan' and 'Mycenaean' Crete, but less attention is paid to the different Minoan architectural phases.[87] However, more recent approaches attempt to use only the Protopalatial remains.[88] These are careful to recognize not only the distinction between these architectural eras, but also the diversity within them.[89] Malia and Phaistos have provided us with the most secure Protopalatial

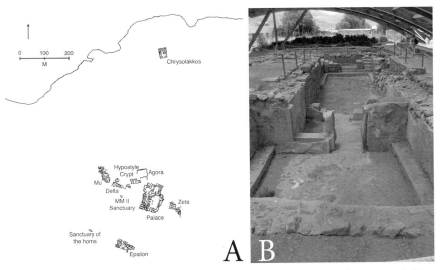

2.1 A) The site of Malia (drawn by author, after Pelon 1992, plan 1). B) Malia, Hypostyle Crypt (photograph by author).

evidence,[90] and, if anything, their Palaces are slightly larger than that at Knossos.[91] Furthermore, the first Knossian court building seems to have been built later than the Malian one (Figure 2.1).[92] While Knossos was to become the most impressive Palace, it is less likely that it was the original great innovator.

Protopalatial Palaces were built in existing towns, so would have involved substantial land clearance. It is difficult to establish whether the palatial form developed over many years or was planned and built at one point. Evans believed that the process was gradual, with several insulae being set up around the Central Court at Knossos, although others, such as MacGillivray, have since argued that it was planned as a coherent unit from the start.[93] Tomkins sets the pendulum back to Evans' view, arguing that the 'palatial' form developed over time from several buildings shaped by a communal urban identity.[94] A similar distinction may be seen in terms of whether particular functions were centralized immediately or over time. General functions, such as agricultural storage and administration, may have gradually become concentrated on the Palaces, or they may have been established there from the start.[95] As with the architectural layout, this cannot be conclusively determined. The Neopalatial Palaces and sites were planned and constructed over a period of time, and experienced very different cultural biographies.

Perhaps surprisingly, the earliest evidence for a Palace comes from Malia, which was, by no means, to become the grandest Neopalatial Palace. The Protopalatial Malian Palace appears to have had a single storey, and was possibly less impressive than the later version. Soundings under the later Palace indicate that the Protopalatial complex covered more or less the same area, with the layout of certain areas, such as the east magazines, dating back to this period.[96] There is little agreement among the French excavators concerning the role of the Palace and its relationship with the town. Van Effenterre believed that the outlying, monumental buildings, of which he excavated the Hypostyle Crypt and Agora,[97] each served specific functions under the umbrella of palatial administration, while Poursat argued that the town, of which he excavated Quartier Mu, was more independent.[98] The excavators also identified the Hypostyle Crypt as the meeting place for the town council, which has a modern democratic tone (Figure 2.1).[99]

The earliest evidence for 'palatial' features such as a Lustral Basin or Minoan Hall is found in the non-palatial MM II Malian buildings, set in the area called Quartier Mu.[100] The buildings may have been under the control of the Palace, despite being spatially distinct, but they give the impression of being a prosperous, self-contained unit. Furthermore, these innovations at Malia call to question the assumption that such features are 'Knossian'. Quatier Mu also had features indicating the storage of liquids as seen in the east magazines of the Palace and the Hypostyle Crypt. The same functions therefore appear to be reduplicated across the site. Parts of the buildings were of dressed sandstone blocks, and clay archive documents in Cretan Hieroglyphic were also found in the area, as were clay human and animal figurines. Workshops were found nearby, for seal-engraving, pottery, and metalworking. The area does not appear to have been rebuilt during the Neopalatial period.

The Palace at Phaistos has given archaeologists the most information regarding this period, since the west facade of the later Palace was constructed several metres to the east.[101] The Protopalatial facade was built of substantial ashlar orthostates, designed to impress, and the roughly north–south orientation of the Central Court was set in place. The layout therefore followed the precedent set by Knossos and Malia, and would have involved careful planning, a substantial number of builders and a major disruption to the site's organization, including the construction of large-scale terracing. In the northern area was located a six-roomed shrine, where much archival material was found, but most space appears to have been set aside for storage. The rooms were mostly small, and movement between them comprised many twists and turns.

Unlike other buildings that were left in a ruined condition, the West Court was covered over with a thick layer of concrete-like material, and was therefore completely out of sight, presumably to be gradually forgotten (see cover image for Protopalatial West Court). This fill also covered the *kouloures*, large, circular, lined pits that may have been used for storage of grain, cisterns, rubbish pits, large planters for trees, or blind wells.[102] Similar Protopalatial pits were found under the West Court at Knossos. However, even if they did not function as granaries, an association with agriculture may have been made as the magazines were located just behind the west facades.

The lack of evidence to the south of the Knossian Palace suggests that the Central Court may not have been surrounded on all sides,[103] and therefore served as a liminal zone between Palace and town as the West Courts did. Approaches to this complex were carefully staged, such as the Royal Road, leading from the west. It is also clear that the top of the hill was levelled in order to construct this vast complex. The MM II West Court covered MM IA houses, so the process of clearing the site for palatial use was ongoing. While the evidence for the palatial building is unclear, it has been argued that the bulkiness of the building, and the extensive use of coloured stone for decorative purposes, changed to more intricate designs and representational wall paintings in the Neopalatial period.[104] As later, the town flourished around and beyond these complexes. The 'Town Mosaic' from Knossos (several faience plaques that are believed to have covered a wooden chest) is suggestive of what settlements looked like during this period. Houses have more than one storey, with windows on upper ones; presumably the lowest one is for storage.

If the functions of the Neopalatial Palaces are debated, those of the Protopalatial era are even more unclear. MacGillivray described Protopalatial Knossos as intended to be a 'place of worship and . . . storehouse for wealth – rather like an early temple, but also as the dwelling of the ruling family – like the contemporary Palaces in the Near East'.[105] It has, however, been questioned whether the Palaces had a central role in a hierarchical society at all.[106] Such is the size and complexity of these structures that it is likely that they were the seats of power, to some extent at least. The scale of these complexes could vary considerably; most notable here is the MM II palatial site at Petras. The Protopalatial period is richly represented at the site, and a Palace was first constructed in MM IIA, destroyed in MM IIB preserving a hieroglyphic archive.[107] As such, it is the only known Protopalatial Palace in eastern Crete; however, this is considerably smaller than those from the central region.

As in the subsequent Neopalatial period, settlements could be very prosperous without possessing a Palace. Monastiraki is an important, but non-palatial settlement, placed in the Amari Valley, on the route between the Mesara and Rethymnon. It was large, around 20 ha, and an open-air area, possibly a court, has been revealed alongside evidence for substantial buildings. Three archives of sealings and a clay house model have been found, dating to within the Protopalatial period; the site was probably closely linked to Phaistos.[108] Destroyed by fire and abandoned in MM II, it would have been a ghost town for those later passing by. A series of destructions are visible at the end of MM II, such as at Knossos, Malia, Phaistos, and Monastiraki, but this was not a single destruction horizon, and what we describe as the Neopalatial period did not begin in the same way across the island.

2.2 Phaistos, Central Court looking to the area of the Kamares Cave (photograph by author).

The ritual landscape is one area that changed considerably from the Protopalatial to Neopalatial periods, in a way that was presumably entrenched in the experience and memory of the later inhabitants of Crete. Indeed, far more 'peak sanctuaries' date to the Protopalatial period than later, and no new ones were established during the Neopalatial era. They are located in high (not necessarily 'peak') locations. Three clusters of (known) peak sanctuaries have been defined.[109] The most common and easily identifiable finds at these sites are clay figurines. Remains of walls and possibly terracing have been found at Juktas dating to the Protopalatial period, but the later architecture was much more monumental and complex. A deep chasm in the bedrock was used for depositing pottery, which was mostly Protopalatial (see Figure 6.2B).[110] Ash, animal bones, and pottery shapes associated with feasting (such as conical cups and cooking pots) have been found. It is notable that the Central Court (or slightly to the west) at Knossos is aligned towards this site to the north. Ritual caves were also important during this period, notably the Kamares Cave, which lends its name to the pottery ware, and is directly visible from the Central Court at Phaistos (Figure 2.2).

The evidence from the peak sanctuary on Petsophas, to the east of the island, is important, not least because it has been unusually well published. Rutkowski describes an open area surrounded by terraces, and the finds included human figurines (male and female), body parts, animal figurines (such as cattle, sheep, goats, birds, and beetles), and miniature vases.[111] The smaller, more rural peak sanctuary at Atsipades has provided important information on a site that fell out of use in MM II, unlike Juktas and Petsophas.[112] In addition to pottery, male and female human figurines, animal figurines, and evidence for feasting, the site is notable for its abundance of clay body parts and pebbles, brought in from the valley below.[113] In short, while the category of 'peak sanctuary' still holds, there are different types, from regional to local ones, although variations in finds may not indicate different cults.[114]

Two different writing systems were used: Cretan Hieroglyphic and Linear A. There are indications of regional preference, with Linear A script concentrated in the Mesara region and Hieroglyphic inscriptions more common in north-central Crete and further east.[115] These scripts may represent different languages and therefore possibly dissimilar ethnic identities. There were differences in practice as well as possibly language; Linear A was written on flat-page documents, while Cretan Hieroglyphic was inscribed on two- and four-sided bars and seal stones.[116] Roundels were associated more with Linear A administration, and medallions with Hieroglyphic, although both shared other types of documents.[117] However, the discoveries of Protopalatial Linear A at Knossos and a Cretan Hieroglyphic sealing at Phaistos demonstrate at least an awareness of other practices. There is a conclusive shift to Linear A used across the island in the Neopalatial period, which, if Knossos was the main cultural and administrative force on the island, may be surprising, as this site mainly used Hieroglyphic in the Protopalatial period. Linear A was used on more materials and kinds of objects in the Neopalatial period, marking a further shift in use.

In terms of the arts, the Protopalatial period witnessed a high level of craftsmanship. For example, some pieces of jewellery survive, such as the bee pendant from the Chrysolakkos building at Malia, decorated with filigree and granulation. The two swords found in the Palace at Malia also attest to the high quality of workmanship during this period. The Kamares Ware pottery is the most distinctive ceramic feature of Protopalatial Crete. A deposit of ceramics from the Palace at Knossos might indicate a hierarchy in terms of users; most pieces are coarse and simply made, while fewer better-quality ones were produced, leading to a single fine Kamares goblet at the top of a pyramidal structure.[118] Petrographic analysis indicates that Kamares Ware originated from the Mesara region, so this was an import into the area.[119]

Finally, the Protopalatial period has yielded much more evidence for mortuary rites than in the succeeding one. There was some regional variation in this, house tombs in the Bay of Mirabello area, for example, with some rich grave goods such as a silver kantharos in Tomb I at Gournia. Chamber tombs were used at some sites such as Knossos, while the distinctive Chrysolakkos tomb from Malia was reconstructed in MM IB with an ashlar facade.[120]

In contrast, tholoi dating to the Prepalatial period continued to be used in the Mesara area.[121] These were particularly rich, and some of the Protopalatial deposits included clay figurines as found on peak sanctuaries.

Overall, the evidence for the Protopalatial period is difficult to assess, precisely because of the high level of activity in following ones that covered it. While the Palaces may not be very well understood, there were certainly substantial central buildings in at least three sites that were to become important Neopalatial centres. Evidence for other major settlements exists, but they were not as widely distributed throughout the landscape as later. Diversity in administrative practice, mortuary practices, and the arts have all been used to suggest that the island was internally divided into several prosperous polities. That is our understanding of the Protopalatial period: it is also pertinent to consider this era from the point of view of the Neopalatial one.

The Past in the Past: Looking Back at the Protopalatial Period

I have argued before that we should consider not just what happened in the era before one's area of study, but also how the people in the past may have encountered, understood, and even misinterpreted their own past.[122] The use of the past in the past has been a topic of study for many years in Greek archaeology, and has recently been given a breath of fresh air with considerations of 'social memory';[123] although people also misremember and actively seek to make breaks from the past as well.[124] Their past is the past remembered, so, in this case, those living in the Neopalatial period would have constructed memories of the Protopalatial one that may conflict with our picture of 'what actually happened'.[125] The latter case is well illustrated by site distribution maps, which indicate those in use during a particular chronological phase. The inhabitants could be well aware of sites that had fallen out of use, but which still formed a focal point in the landscape: this approach views the world as a palimpsest.[126] In other words, the *memory* of the use of a site can play a powerful role in the formation and articulation of identity, rather than approaches that simply focus on the *use* of a site.

Malia provides a good example for exploring how people in the Neopalatial period perceived their predecessors (Figure 2.1).[127] Quartier Mu was burned to the ground at the end of the Protopalatial period and left in ruins.[128] If the owners or inhabitants of Quartier Mu really were independent, even challengers of the Palace,[129] then the Neopalatial abandonment of the site would have served as a reminder of the ultimate failure of this kind of challenge.[130] None of the later buildings appears to have possessed the range of activities as seen in Protopalatial Quartier Mu. Was the complex left in ruins as a memorial to such folly?

The north-west quarter of the Palace at Malia appears to have been turned into an open space in the Neopalatial period.[131] This corner of the

Palace faces the Protopalatial Agora and Hypostyle Crypt, which also fell out of use. The so-called Agora to the north-west of the Palace, an open square ca. 30 by 40 metres, would presumably have still been visible. Whatever activities occurred in this area remain unknown, but it is intriguing that such a substantial space located close to the Palace became disused in this manner. In the town, the MM II town 'shrine'[132] and the Sanctuary of the Horns[133] were left abandoned, and there is no known equivalent Neopalatial example of an urban shrine with the possible exception of the shrine located in the south wing of the Palace.[134] Possibly this more independent practice was brought within the palatial sphere. These 'ghost-spots' had the ability to trigger memories and perceptions of the past (individual, group, and social) in settlements in the Neopalatial period (Figure 2.1).[135] This represents Gosden and Lock's recent 'historical' past, as opposed to the more distant 'genealogical' past.[136]

Genealogical past is less clearly associated with memory, although any distinction between 'real' and 'imagined' memory is problematic.[137] One rare Neopalatial example is found at Mochlos, where the layout of a new building (B2) constructed at the beginning of LM IB was determined by a much earlier Prepalatial building.[138] An open space was constructed above Prepalatial remains, showcasing and commemorating them. A female skull was found in the basement in the south-west corner of the LM IB B2 Building, visible through a window.[139] While the 'ritual' nature of the area and 'Pillar Crypts' nearby in B2 is unclear,[140] the special treatment of these earlier remains does suggest a certain respect for them. At Knossos, a store of Neolithic pottery was found with LM I sherds in an 'artificial cave' in the so-called Pillar Crypt of the Southeast House at Knossos (see Chapter 3, Figure 3.1).[141] This cavity was then sealed, possibly an example of Bradley's 'remembering by forgetting',[142] and the binding of the mythological past with contemporary material (possibly like a foundation deposit).[143] Overall, however, there is little to suggest that these earlier Knossian remains were commemorated in any way, and it is possible that the inhabitants of this area were so forward-looking that they were less concerned with antiquities.

CONCLUSION

This chapter presents vital background to our analysis in a variety of ways. The history of the discovery of Neopalatial Crete needs to be set against the politics of the period: this affected not only the ability for foreign investment in fieldwork, but also the nature of how the culture was interpreted. Archaeology offered this island the means for some stability in a turbulent world, with so many stakeholders in terms of governance and collective or national identity. This extended to the role the island appears to have had in shaping European identity, as its first complex civilization. Such grand narratives deserved the Big Digs of the early twentieth century, which remain the foundations of our understanding of the Minoan world. Increasing specialization, however, has provided a dataset that deserves to be the envy of the world.

Issues concerning the rise of the Minoan civilization are also relevant to the main case study, if only to remind ourselves that the Neopalatial outcome was not inevitable. There is clear evidence for social differentiation in the Protopalatial period, and predecessors of some kind beneath the main Palaces. However, architectural innovations, as far as we can see, were conducted at Malia, which also appears to be slightly earlier and larger than the contemporary Knossian counterpart. This was reversed in the Neopalatial period, with Knossian influence in the surrounding landscape by no means being replicated by the Malian elite. Finally, we attempted to consider the Protopalatial remains from the point of view of those in the Neopalatial period. They would doubtless have been aware of these vestiges, but what is one of the most surprising aspects of the Neopalatial period (in comparison with Protopalatial practices, and those of the surrounding Aegean and eastern Mediterranean) is a *lack* of engagement with their past.

CHAPTER THREE

ELITE ARCHITECTURE AND ARTEFACTS

INTRODUCTION

The narrative of Minoan culture has been skewed towards elite elements. It is this level of cultural expression that is most distinctive, and appears as the strongest articulation of the island's collective identity. This stance neglects the silent majority, but it remains the case that our knowledge is biased towards the upper echelons of Neopalatial society. This chapter explores various elements of elite living, from the palatial form and other architectural features to ritual and/ or prestige artefacts.[1] It is argued that a broader consideration of 'elite' aspects is more beneficial than deploying the term 'palatial' for features found beyond the 'Palaces' themselves.[2] The functions and meanings of these spaces and objects may not always be clear, which can lead to a level of discussion restricted to noting their presence or absence. However, as they form the core of the distinctive Neopalatial culture, and illustrate so well the confusion between the ritual and socio-political spheres, they deserve an in-depth discussion.

These analyses essentially rely on distribution patterns, which can be explored on several scales, from building, site, and region to island-wide and beyond. The relationship between activity areas and artefacts (formal patterns) and activity systems (structural patterns),[3] or, in other words, the relationship between the spatial and the social, is central to our understanding of the Palaces in their urban context, and Knossos in the island context. These distribution patterns can be interpreted in a variety of and occasionally opposing ways. For example, Evans' view of the Palaces as the residences of rulers on which the inhabitants of other buildings were dependent has recently been reassessed.[4] The deployment of the term 'heterarchy' explores both horizontal and vertical social divisions (in contrast to 'hierarchy'), while 'faction' refers to political groups that compete on a comparable footing. Similar in approach, with an emphasis on vertical competition, they are not interchangeable concepts.[5] In terms of the emphasis on competition, there are some similarities between intra-site factions and regional peer polities, but a clear difference in scale.[6]

A wide distribution of elite architectural features, artefacts, and administrative evidence does not necessarily reflect a fragmented social structure or factionalism. It may also indicate emulation, the influence and imitation of a hierarchical elite. But it is also the case that the apparent *centralization* of certain features and activities need not demonstrate the *monopolization* of such elements. The Palaces, while distinctive and demanding close comparison, need to be set within their urban and regional context, which is the aim of Chapter 4.

Evans' view that religion held a central role in Minoan society has been highly influential, and with good reason. This chapter demonstrates how the dividing line between religious and secular is genuinely difficult to determine in the material and visual culture. Elite practice and symbolism is often ascribed to be 'ritual' or 'cultic', but this is a world where there seems to be significant slippage between that and the secular – although this may frustrate the post-Enlightenment, scientific project to rationalize and quantify everything. Ritual is best not analysed in isolation, precisely because it is the sphere in which all cultural and social concerns are created, reproduced, and negotiated. It held a central role for both the expression of a wide range of identities and the articulation of socio-political power, including the aspiration to power. However, the possibility of theocratic leadership should not be overemphasized without demonstrating such a phenomenon.[7]

We will consider first the pinnacle of 'Minoan-ness', the so-called Palace. Leaving aside the issue of the most appropriate label for these complexes, there is no doubt that this form, restricted to the island of Crete, is the most striking statement of Minoan cultural identity. Open-air courts play a key role in the architecture and, we assume from iconographical evidence, practices were performed in and around these structures. This chapter considers the distribution and nature of halls and the so-called Lustral Basins throughout Neopalatial settlements. These features of Minoan elitism have a much wider distribution than the palatial complex, and so can shed light on a larger (although still elite) section of the population. While examples may occur outside Crete (e.g., Akrotiri on Thera/Santorini), they are clearly a fundamental part of the island's high culture during the Neopalatial period.

These kinds of features are frequently and misleadingly referred to as 'palatial' architecture. It is not clear that architects always derived their inspiration from Palaces – the first known examples of a Minoan Hall (a distinctive type of hall) and Lustral Basin come from a non-palatial building. There is further slippage between 'Knossian' and 'Minoan'. McEnroe recently suggested the term 'palatialization' to describe the spread of these features across the island instead of 'Knossification', which implies that all were looking directly at Knossos when emulating these forms (Knossocentric).[8] However, given the wide distribution, it is probably prudent to deploy the more general term 'elite'.

These features also reveal the common problem in Minoan archaeology in distinguishing the mundane, utilitarian, and practical from ritual, particularly religious, cult. Identifying ritual sites in the landscape is not always straightforward (Chapter 6), but identifying ritual in the settlement context is much more problematic. Settlement ritual foci are difficult to define partly because of the lack of figurines found in these contexts.[9] These mark the clear ritual sites in the landscape very notably, especially peak sanctuaries, but their general absence in settlements means that we lack a comparable criterion to mark ritual space.

Even where there is some consensus in defining a space as 'ritual', clarifying whether this was a 'religious' ritual (involving other worlds) or not (e.g., socio-political ceremonies) is challenging. The construction of some specific architectural units implies the formalization and possibly the ritualization of certain practices.[10] For example, Lustral Basins may represent the consecration of certain chthonic beliefs. It is therefore a rather different category from architectural elaboration, which may simply reflect economic wealth. As well as providing information on regionalism, there are also important chronological distinctions across the island concerning when these features were used.

Likewise, there is often some confusion between objects of ritual or prestige. In order to explore this, we will take four types in turn: figurines, libation tables and vessels, Horns of Consecration, and the Double Axe. Whether in material form or visual representation, each of these categories poses particular challenges for interpretation. While architectural trends through time may roughly be charted within the Neopalatial period, due to association with ceramic assemblages, the iconographical evidence is much broader in nature. We need to extract the Neopalatial evidence only, rather than drawing from the Final Palatial material to supplement the earlier material.

Labels inherited from the early archaeologists can also prove misleading. One example is the 'Pillar Crypt' (Figure 3.1). The construction of this cultic category resulted in all pillared rooms being defined as ritual, without this explicitly being demonstrated. Evans excavated what appeared to be 'ritual' Pillar Crypts (with upper pillared rooms) in the Palace, Southeast House, South House, Royal Villa, and Hogarth's House B at Knossos, but it is highly debatable whether the feature is 'architecturally distinctive' as he and others believed.[11] The example from the Southeast House at Knossos contained

3.1 Knossos, Southeast House 'Pillar Crypt' (photograph by author).

a 'curious' six-footed stand of painted plaster with a framed basin-like feature.[12] A Double Axe sign was engraved on an upper block of the pillar, and a gypsum block (see Figure 3.1; left of pillar) contained a socket that may have been used for such a device.

Some of these spaces (in the Royal Villa, South House, and Little Palace) had an additional, separate staircase to the upper floor, which was, strictly speaking, unnecessary for a house of this size – the special attention to access may indicate a ceremonial or special function. However, many appear to be storage rooms.[13] A considerable problem is that these buildings were reused at a later date, so we do not have the Neopalatial artefacts to shed light on practices, and the function of such spaces could change over time. Overall, while many have been tempted to view this architectural form as ritual,[14] each case needs to be assessed individually.

Another significant early mislabelling occurred in the west wing of the Palace at Knossos. Here, a recent review of the evidence for Evans' 'Central Palace Sanctuary' (CPS) has found that 'there is nothing in the CPS to declare a cult activity'.[15] This is particularly worrying, as the assumption of a major sanctuary here has led to sweeping observations regarding the ritual nature of palatial west wings and the occurrence of harvest festivals. The 'Temple Repositories' in the west wing indicate storage, probably of ritual objects, but this does not prove that ritual occurred in this area. The East Pillar Crypt in the Palace at Knossos was used as a storeroom during its last stage, but the high concentration of Double Axe mason's marks may indicate an original ritual function;[16] the evidence is ambiguous. Similarly, it has been argued elsewhere that the so-called Domestic Quarters are cultic, while others present a more secular view of the Palaces.[17] Scholars want to distinguish ritual and secular space and artefacts, but this remains a highly problematic challenge in the Neopalatial context.

Renfrew's checklist for identifying ritual does not distinguish between religious and secular rituals, which he himself recognizes.[18] Public, formalized, and large-scale ritual areas may be identified with more confidence, while domestic rituals are generally more difficult to do so. Offerings, worship, and 'focal point' (to name some of his criteria) can be aimed at a divinity or a human, or some other kind of force or concept: in other words, traces of these may indicate political or religious practices, or the distinction between the two may be very blurred. Previously, I have preferred to employ the term 'ceremonial' for 'ritual' in a more general manner.[19]

Certain methodological questions arise when identifying ritual. How many ritual artefacts are required to indicate ritual space? And does a ritual assemblage indicate ritual practice in that area, or storage? The relationship between activity areas and activity artefacts is not only historically specific, but also likely to vary within societies.[20] Are rituals always repeated, meaningful actions, or can a one-off action also be imbrued with symbolic meaning and ritualized? The assemblage of children's bones from the Stratigraphical Museum excavations have been argued to indicate ecstatic religion, for example, but the uniqueness of this case renders them difficult to fit into a general Minoan narrative.[21] In the attempt to create order out of a muddled picture, this study has leant towards patterns and standardizations rather than the idiosyncratic.

DEFINING THE PALACES

The Palace of Minos serves more as an outline of Evans' view of this newly discovered civilization than an excavation report of Knossos. It, along with Evans' earlier papers, set out the terminological framework for future discussions – including the role of the Minoan 'Palaces'. The term 'Palace' has been argued to be a product of many factors, including early twentieth-century Edwardian assumptions regarding the bearers and nature of power, the effect of Near Eastern archaeology on Minoan studies during this time, the impact of the decipherment of Linear B with its *wanax* (the Mycenaean male leader who presumably inhabited a 'Palace'), and the influence of Homer and the figure of 'King Minos' in Greek mythology.[22] Yet the term 'Palace' was not always Evans' preferred one. He viewed these complexes as more ambiguous than this;

'Palace-temple' better sums up his interpretation of these immense complexes that were governed, of course, by a 'Priest-King'.[23] On one level, this ambiguity exists in English: bishops as well as kings live in 'palaces'.

It is, however, true that either 'king' or 'Priest-King' bears the assumption that the building was inhabited by a dynastic monarchy, which was headed by a male individual, which in turn legitimizes the term 'Palace'.[24] The use of 'Palace' is often blamed on the 'social and political climate of Victorian and Edwardian Britain, its Empire and naval power',[25] although Buckingham Palace (among the others) are *not* the seat of Britain's socio-political power. An alternative suggestion is that the Palaces were not residential units at all, but the locale of competition between factions based in other buildings.[26] Arguably, a desire to see independent competing groups (or 'parties') based outside these Palaces reflects the modern British political scene much more, centred on Westminster.[27] The notion of extreme fragmentation into factions across Crete has not convinced all.[28] Proving residential functions (such as beds made of organic material) is virtually impossible, so there is no way of demonstrating this either way.

It has recently been suggested that these structures be renamed 'Court Compounds', as it is not loaded towards a particular socio-political interpretation, and because it recognizes that the Central Court is the key criterion of a 'Palace'.[29] For consistency, the term 'Palace' is retained here, and the aim of this section is to explore the range of meanings it may have, as well as variation in form. Perhaps what we call these complexes is a moot point, if the use of such a label leads to the personification of these buildings – comments such as 'the Palace at Knossos exerted much influence ... ' pepper the literature. Obviously, the implication is that the people who controlled these buildings achieved this effect, but by setting the building as agent, one circumnavigates the need to explore the actual people responsible. Herva views the building as an agent.[30] But there is an important difference between acknowledging that architectural space is active, organic, and can shape human relations, and claiming that it possesses agency. The latter stance undermines the fact that these are manmade constructs. There may have been elements of animism in the Minoan world, but this is impossible to demonstrate despite hints, such as apparent engagements with trees and baetyls (Chapter 9). Here, we focus on how the Palaces were used and how they appear to have been viewed.

There are four main ways in which Minoan Palaces have been distinguished from other buildings: by their functions, size, degree of architectural elaboration, and architectural form (see Figure 3.2 for an outline). Functionally, they have been interpreted as redistribution centres because of the substantial storage space for agricultural goods and the evidence for administration,[31] centres of production or craft specialization,[32] and ritual and

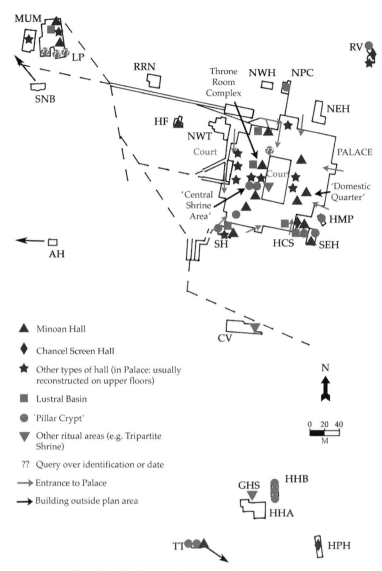

3.2 Knossos, formalized architectural ceremonial units. Adams 2004a, figure 3, reprinted with permission, *Journal of Mediterranean Archaeology* and © Equinox Publishing ltd 2004.
Abbreviations: AH: Acropolis House; CV: Caravanserai; GHS: Gypsades House Shrine; HCS: House of the Chancel Screen; HF: House of the Frescoes; HHA: Hogarth's House A; HHB: Hogarth's House B; HMP: House of the Monolithic Pillars; HPH: High Priest's House; LP: Little Palace; MUM: Minoan Unexplored Mansion; NEH: Northeast House; NPC: North Pillar Crypt; NWH: Northwest House; NWT: Northwest Treasury; RRN: Royal Road North; RV: Royal Villa; SEH: Southeast House; SH: South House; SNB: Stratigraphical Museum Excavations North Building; TT: Temple Tomb.

political foci in the urban and regional context.[33] The probable multi-functionality of these complexes is brought out by Halstead's description of them as a combination of Buckingham Palace, Whitehall, Westminster Abbey, and Wembley Stadium.[34]

It is vital to examine whether there is a monopoly or merely a concentration of certain functions and practices in the Palaces. Functions should be referred to as 'palatial' only if they appear to occur solely within the Palaces, or outlying buildings controlled by them. For example, the west magazines of Palaces are generally interpreted as storage space for agricultural produce, which in turn suggests some form of redistribution. This is supported by the lack of space for agricultural storage in the second-tier buildings at Knossos, but the case is different at Malia, where the urban buildings do contain facilities for agricultural storage.[35] Similarly, it will be argued that elite features should not be regarded as 'palatial' unless they appear to be monopolized by the Palace, otherwise, they are simply 'elite'. It is therefore imperative to set these complexes in their urban context, although no Minoan town has been excavated in its entirety.[36]

Minoan Palaces have been described as a city-within-a-city, which is an apt term for the larger and more complex examples.[37] The Palaces formed a striking focal point within the urban landscape, to the extent that many roads ultimately led to them.[38] Perhaps this strong focus meant that the centre took on an exemplary role, as Geertz suggested concerning the Negara, where court-and-capital 'is not just the nucleus, the engine, or the pivot of the state, it *is* the state'.[39] It is partly because of the focal nature of these complexes that scholars have been willing to view them as ceremonial centres, enticing outsiders in ritualized processions. The lack of temples in the Minoan world has often been noted, leading N. Marinatos to suggest that 'what have been termed "Palaces" are, in reality, the monumental sacred buildings that we are looking for'.[40] The extent to which the Palaces were religious centres is much debated – few, like Rutkowski, have suggested that it was a basically secular institution, and that 'the principal cult places were situated not inside the settlements but in natural spots out in the country',[41] while more have emphasized their religious nature.[42]

The second and third criteria to distinguish Palaces from other buildings are size and architectural elaboration. The Palaces are clearly the largest buildings found on Neopalatial Crete, both in general and within their respective settlements. The Palace at Knossos is by far the largest at around 13,000 m^2; fittingly, the surrounding settlement is also the largest on Crete. They also tend to be the most architecturally elaborate buildings in their settlements, although the Malian (mostly mudbrick) example highlights that this criterion is not clear-cut.

The most distinctive feature of the Palaces, apart from their size, is their architectural form.[43] The distinctive rectangular Central Court, around which were set four wings, with a West Court, is a design unique to the island and one of the most distinctive traits of 'Minoan-ness'. It need not mean that they functioned the same, however. Indeed, we should be wary of the modern maxim of 'form follows function'.[44] The Central Court is a clear marker of difference, both from non-Cretan contexts, and from the weaker sections of the society within the island; there is, however, considerable variation between our examples (see Chapter 4). The Palaces possessed a variety of functions, and we do not have clear evidence that the Central Court was used in the same way across the island. Furthermore, this standardization in form has resulted in the tendency to treat the complexes as monolithic entities, existing in direct contrast to 'the town'. The West Court is therefore viewed as an open, liminal zone between these two distinct entities, in contrast to the enclosed Central Court.

COURTS AND THEATRAL AREAS

The Minoans would have spent a lot of time outside, as do Cretans today. Built courts, occasionally lined with verandas, provide the ultimate outside architecture. Great attention could be paid to the facades of neighbouring buildings (including Palaces) as a backdrop for these spaces.[45] They may be a public, urban space, or semi- or fully enclosed by a complex. The most famous courts are the palatial Central Courts, which were probably multi-functional. Their uses included the pragmatic, as an access point between the four surrounding wings, and the symbolic, as the '"glue" that gave special meaning to the surrounding structures'.[46] Possibly they also were the stage for bull-leaping performances,[47] for which there is no direct evidence. Graham's comment that these courts served as 'the organizing nucleus of the plan, at once dividing and uniting parts of the Palace' is remarkably similar to the approach to ritual taken here, with its ability to both cement group identity and enforce social differentiation. However, as he notes, the courts were also the 'focus of much of the daily activities of normal Palace life'.[48]

The standardization of the orientation of the Central Courts suggests that the movement of the sun and astronomical observations were incorporated into the design. They are rectangular spaces (close to 1:2) with the long axis oriented along a roughly north–south orientation, tilting slightly towards the east as you pass from Phaistos, Knossos to Malia; at Zakros, the axis falls thirty-seven degrees to the east.[49] Shaw suggests that this discrepancy may be due to the moon rather than the sun influencing the layout of Zakros, as at certain times of year, the moon would rise this far south.[50] Goodison has illustrated the potential role of the sun in a series of striking images taken from the Throne Room, Knossos, which opens onto the Central Court.[51]

The floor surfaces were well maintained, and could include features that have been described as 'altars' (e.g., at Malia and Zakros).[52] Porticoes ran along some facades, such as on the north and east sides of the Central Court at Malia, or the east and west facades at Phaistos. The north facade at Phaistos comprises a stately symmetry of half columns and niches (see Figure 3.3). At Knossos, a shallow portico was set in front of the south facade, and there may have been one to the east.[53] The layout of the west facade at Knossos led Evans to

3.3 Knossos, Central Court looking to Juktas peak sanctuary (photograph by author).

reconstruct a 'Tripartite Shrine', one of his many reconstructions that is now questioned.[54] The possibility of balconies on the upper stories of stoas is intriguing, where people could observe and be observed, as suggested by Knossian frescoes.[55] It has been suggested that a square is formed when the ritual areas of the west wings are incorporated, which works particularly well at Knossos and Malia. This might provide a 'fundamental ritual of power – presented in its two forms: the indoor and the outdoor',[56] an intriguing idea that is difficult to support through the architecture alone.

Knossos' Central Court is the largest, at around 53 × 28 m, while those at Malia and Phaistos are both around 51 × 22 m, and the Zakrian example is around 30 × 12 m.[57] Elsewhere, it has been argued that how the Central Courts were approached set the tone for how the palatial elites wished the complex as a whole to be perceived.[58] All four courts could be directly accessed from outside, but the manner and mood varied greatly. At Knossos, one could enter from the large, imposing twelve-columned hall from the north, to be channelled up a sloping, narrow ramp.[59] The effect is intimidating and disempowering, as visibility is restricted; there is no way of viewing the events occurring in the court from outside the complex. Upon entering the Central Court, one is confronted by Mount Juktas in the distance, the only Neopalatial Palace with such visibility with a peak sanctuary (providing the south wing was not built above the sightline: Figure 3.3).[60]

3.4 Malia: kernos (in foreground), south entrance (in background) (photograph by author).

Two entrances led straight into the Central Court at Malia; these were flat, straight, and wide, so when the doors were open people could see into the court. A benched room with the famous circular vessel with a series of depressions, presumably for offerings ('kernos'), was located close to the south entrance in the west wing (Figure 3.4).[61] The kernos was large, around 90 cm in diameter, and had a large hollow in the centre with twenty-four smaller ones running around the rim. It may have been a kind of game board, or a libation table for agricultural first fruits. The situation is different again at Phaistos, where a flat, straight, and wide corridor-entrance linked the Central and West Courts. Finally, at Zakros, the south entrance gave direct access to the Central Court, although its turn would have prevented those outside the Palace from seeing into the Central Court. This would not have mattered, however, since the Palace lay on lower ground to the town, which overlooked the Palace and its court. Arguably, the Central Court at Zakros is not only the smallest of these four, but also the least intimidating and most difficult to control visual access to.

These four main examples are not the only Central Courts known in Neopalatial architecture. The one at Galatas is slightly larger than the one at Zakros, at 35 × 15 m. The 'semi-Central Court' at Gournia is also mid-range, at around 40 × 15 m, while that at Petras is considerably smaller at under 18 × 8 m from MM IIA until the LM IA destruction, while the LM IB court was

3.5 Knossos, Theatral Area (photograph by author).

somewhat reduced to 15 × 5 m, due to the construction of a large stoa.[62] Non-palatial central buildings also possessed courts, such as Archanes, Nirou Chani, Vathypetro,[63] Myrtos Pyrgos, and Makrygialos. These appear to be roughly around 5–7 m wide × 13–16 m long (where known), which is comparable to the court at Petras. Ayia Triada had two substantial courts of around 45 × 12 m and 62 × 40 m, and the south court at Kommos (J/T) was around 38 × 29 m.[64] Kastelli has evidence for the formalized use of outside space with a 'processional way',[65] while other sites, such as Chania and to a lesser extent Tylissos, are too problematic to assess because of modern towns on top of them. Courts could be associated with ritual elements – Horns of Consecration were found in the court at Nirou Chani[66] and Vathypetro,[67] while ritual use has been suggested for the exedra in the court at Archanes.[68] They may have been the setting for certain ceremonies, but they would also have been the locale for various daily activities, including basic access.

The palatial West Courts were places potentially used for ritual, and some, most notably Knossos and Phaistos, were linked to Theatral Areas (Figure 3.5; see also book cover).[69] It is assumed that these low steps enabled spectators to sit or stand while observing performances in the West Court and/or Royal Road and processions to the Palace.[70] They probably had a performative and ritual role, although in the case at Phaistos it is notable that the grandeur of this space was much reduced when the (Protopalatial) ground level was raised by more than a metre, burying the bottom set of steps and the earlier causeways.

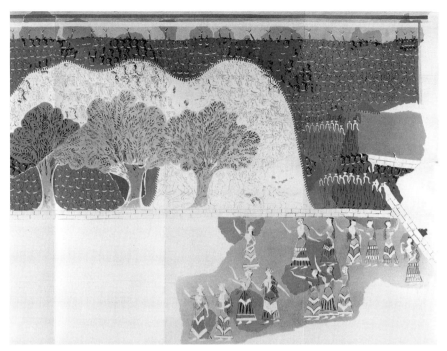

3.6 Reconstruction drawing of the miniature 'Sacred Grove and Dance' painting indicating original fragments. Arthur Evans Fresco Drawing J/3. © Ashmolean Museum, University of Oxford.

The raised causeway at Phaistos cuts into and runs up the structure (a feature also seen at Protopalatial Knossos), suggesting movement to and from the stepped area. Graham stated that it was 'evidently designed for some kind of spectacle or performance', which is rather ambiguous as this could suggest that he envisaged it as the set for the performance rather than the stand for the audience.[71]

The Sacred Grove and Dance Fresco from Knossos offers iconographical evidence for these spaces (Figure 3.6).[72] As Palace and town meet, so too do the built environment and nature, as (heavily reconstructed) trees are placed at intervals. The causeways and stepped platforms for the audience (assumed from the raised head levels) may suit the West Courts and Theatral Areas more than the Central Courts. These causeways have been described as 'red carpets', leading grandly and diagonally across these open spaces.[73]

West Courts were not as universal a feature as Central ones, however, or the evidence for them is not always clear. The west facade at Zakros, for example, does not appear to be designed as such a monumental front.[74] An L-shaped set of four steps led from the urban court at Gournia up into the Palace; activities occurring here may be reminiscent of the palatial ones. There is a hint of a similar series of steps in the court at Ayia Triada, but this is poorly preserved.[75]

Urban Shrines

Overall, urban shrines are notable for their absence in Neopalatial Crete; this is particularly odd, perhaps, as there are some convincing Protopalatial examples, such as at Malia.[76] Neopalatial palatial towns do not appear to have constructed urban buildings for ritual purposes (i.e., shrines or sanctuaries), with the exception of the West Bench Sanctuary Complex at Phaistos (Rooms 8 and 9; 10 and 11), which was part of the palatial complex but only accessible from outside it, from the West Court.[77] It seems that the Palaces and courts centralized or even monopolized communal ritual activity.

Some non-palatial towns have produced possible evidence for urban shrines. The south-west section attached to Building V at Palaikastro (Rooms 1, 2, and 13) dates to the late Neopalatial period and LM III.[78] This was the findspot of the remarkable 'Palaikastro Kouros', which was apparently deliberately smashed and scattered when the building was destroyed. It is this object that most strongly hints at a Neopalatial shrine. Some shrines have been suggested for the Bay of Mirabello area. Although the LM IIIB shrine building at Gournia was constructed in the late Neopalatial period, we cannot project back this function to the earlier time. At nearby Mochlos, late Neopalatial Building B2 at Mochlos has been interpreted as the ritual centre for the entire region.[79] The late Neopalatial Building AC at Pseira has been called a shrine, but it was more or less empty of finds; it did, however, yield fragments of at least one female figure in moulded plaster.[80] These possible examples share a timeframe (LM IB) and are located in an area without a full palatial structure, and with no known Neopalatial peak sanctuary. It may, therefore, demonstrate localized responses to ritual needs, while deploying clearly recognizable island-wide 'Minoan' objects.

FORMAL HALLS

Grand halls of various kinds are widely distributed throughout Crete. Hall systems offered a setting for a potentially diverse set of reasons. Such spaces may have been used in the shaping of client–patron relationships or in the governance of the local area. In the case of governance, the politics conducted within them may not be necessarily of a hierarchical nature, but of factional competition.[81] Their standardization, formal nature, and attention to detail suggest that some kind of ceremonial activity could have occurred there, but rarely do the contents of these structures shed light on the practices that occurred within. However, their grandeur is part of the reason why, for example, statements such as 'the Knossian Palace was a religious centre' are commonly made.[82] The suggestion that halls were often located on upper floors for better light and air is convincing, although little architectural evidence has been preserved for this.

3.7 Phaistos, Minoan Hall in the northern part of the north wing (photograph by author).

Halls may be placed near to entrances for convenience,[83] or they might be strategically placed at the heart of a complex, so visitors would be led past impressive areas before arriving at their destination.[84] There is no universal relationship between accessibility, political significance, and cultural notions of public/private. It is tempting to grade them in terms of public/private depending on their distance from an entrance, but their use could have changed over the course of a day, year, or decade to the extent that the public/private dichotomy is rendered unhelpful.

The Minoan Hall represents a highly formalized unit which became particularly popular in north-central Crete in the Neopalatial period (Figure 3.7).[85] Around thirty-four examples have been found. The standardized layout suggests a ceremonial function,[86] but it also disguises the variability in terms of location within that building's structure. The flexibility of the architecture as well gives weight to the belief that these spaces were multi-functional. It comprises three sections on an axial alignment: hall, fore-hall, and light-well, separated by pillars or pier-and-door partitions, which allow maximum flexibility in terms of access, light, and air. Few finds have been found in them to assist interpreting their function. The House of the Frescoes at Knossos and Building A at Achladia yielded some evidence for commensal activities. Driessen initially interpreted these spaces as living rooms or reception rooms, rather than cult ones, although he considered a more ceremonial function later.[87]

Changing construction techniques, with an increased use of wood and thinner walls, allowed the adoption of pier-and-door partitions. Privacy could be controlled in two ways; one permanent, concerning how far the hall was located from the entrance, and one variable, in that the doors could be closed, open or somewhere in between (with just one or two doors shut).[88] A part of a Minoan Hall could be turned into a corridor by closing one or two sides. Some variations may be due to the necessary alterations for incorporating Minoan Halls into an existing building.[89]

The Minoan Hall is particularly popular in north-central Crete,[90] and found throughout the sites of Knossos (Figure 3.2) and Malia (Figure 3.8).[91] Its presence outside the Palaces in six other buildings at Knossos and four other buildings at Malia is a reminder that such spaces were *elite*, and not solely palatial. Possibly the architects of the Palaces inspired other builders or provided a training ground for them, but the commissioners of these units were reasonably widespread.[92] The Palace has the largest number of halls of any building at Knossos, with eight still visible and seven more reconstructed on upper floors;[93] seven of the visible halls are Minoan Halls (Figure 3.8). There may, therefore, be some justification to the idea that the form had particular Knossian and palatial connotations. Within the Palace at Knossos, the distribution of halls is even, with concentrations in the west and east wings. One can distinguish four groups: entrance halls; upper halls accessed from outside the Palace; upper halls accessed from inside the Palace; and unique forms, namely the Throne Room complex and the Domestic Quarter complex.[94]

The most striking example of a so-called residential area is the 'Domestic Quarter' at Knossos (Figure 3.2). Evans named the main hall after the masons' marks depicting Double Axes, and defined certain sections as more or less private depending on how accessible they were.[95] The series of pier-and-door partitions and columns made this a very flexible space, with light potentially coming from the west light-well, and the east and southern areas, which look over the Kairatos Valley. When pairs of Minoan Halls occur, the larger is considered to be designed for a male, the smaller for a female (or even a 'Queen').[96] Recently, McEnroe has suggested that the 'Queen's Megaron' at Knossos was a bedroom, but others have argued that the Palaces were not residential at all.[97] They could have been meeting places, or ceremonial.

Domestic or Residential Quarters are so called because of the belief that they were private, an assumption based on their distance from the main entrances (see Chapter 4, Figure 4.2A).[98] In the case of Knossos, the Domestic Quarter lay far from the two main monumental entrances at the north and west of the Palace.[99] However, these halls would have been fairly accessible by the east bastion and the south-east entrance.[100] Several important urban buildings were located on this side of the Palace; their inhabitants may have accessed this wing of the Palace for governance and administrative purposes. The functions

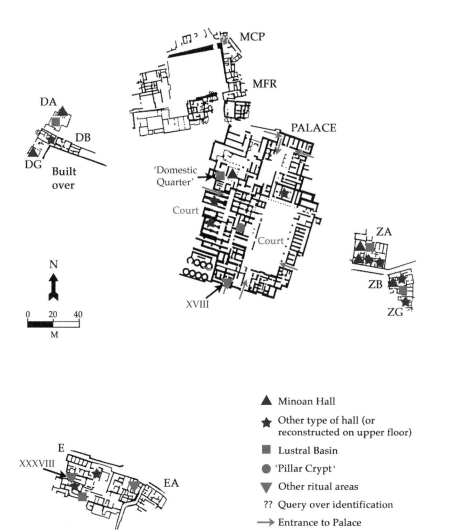

3.8 Malia, formalized architectural ceremonial units. Adams 2004a, figure 7, reprinted with permission, *Journal of Mediterranean Archaeology* and © Equinox Publishing ltd 2004. DA: Delta Alpha; DB: Delta Beta; DG: Delta Gamma; E: Epsilon; EA: Epsilon Alpha; MCP: Maison de la Cave au Pilier; MFR: Maison de la Façade à Redans; ZA: Zeta Alpha; ZB: Zeta Beta; ZG: Zeta Gamma.

of residency and meeting place in this wing are not mutually incompatible, especially given the number of storeys in the area.[101] Meetings of political significance would not always required the ceremonial pomp and circumstance offered by the two main entrances to the north and west.

Many of the grand mansions at Knossos have more than one hall, and the Little Palace has three juxtaposed (Figure 3.2).[102] A comparison of the location of Minoan Halls varies greatly, from being entrance halls and thoroughfares (e.g., South House and Temple Tomb) to isolated (e.g., House of the Frescoes and the

3.9 Knossos, House of the Chancel Screen, Chancel Screen Hall (photograph by author).

Southeast House). Such variety suggests that the form comprised a multi-functional architectural fashion rather than being mono-functional. No ritual artefacts were found in any of these Minoan Halls, including those that were uninhabited after the Neopalatial period (i.e., not 'contaminated' by later use). Conical cups and vases with Double Axes were found in the Minoan Hall from the House of the Frescoes, but these do not, in themselves, indicate ritual.

The Chancel Screen Hall is found only in the Royal Villa, the House of the High Priest at Knossos, and the House of the Chancel Screen (Figure 3.9).[103] Comparable examples have also been found at Kastelli and Archanes, but it appears to be a specifically Knossian feature.[104] It is difficult to ascribe either a ritual or secular function. Fotou follows Evans' view that the niche was for a seated person, rather than an object, although the latter case would suggest more strongly a ritual use.[105] The one in the Royal Villa provides the only entrance into a space that is traditionally referred to as a 'Pillar Crypt' (and upper floor), although a ritual function is not often demonstrated for these spaces. This particular example had intriguing basins and a channel cut into the floor, presumably for the pouring or overspill of liquids.[106] Ritual artefacts have only been found in the House of the High Priest,[107] but they all clearly served as a ceremonial focal point of some kind.

The 'Throne Room' at Knossos may well date to the Neopalatial period, although what we see today is a reconstruction of the Final Palatial hall; likewise the nearby Lustral Basin may be early Neopalatial (see Chapter 4, Figure 4.1).[108] The Throne Room is named after the later seat set against the north wall, with benches set around, and it had a matching anteroom. It seems reasonable to follow Evans in ascribing importance to the person sitting in the seat, although the term 'throne' does carry unproven overtones of royalty.[109] The idea that the Throne Room may have provided the setting for epiphany rituals has proved popular, and may be supported by certain visual theatricalities, such as how the dawn light strikes the throne at certain times of the year.[110] Elsewhere in Neopalatial Crete, benched halls, such as Hall 10 at Archanes[111] and Hall 12 at Nirou Chani,[112] are also fairly common; see also Rooms 4 and 4a at Ayia Triada. The latter is of some importance, as a female bronze figurine was found a few centimetres above the floor of the area with a raised dais.

The 'Domestic Quarter' in the north-west area of the Palace at Malia is somewhat isolated from both the Central Court and the entrances to the Palace, which may support a residential function.[113] A Lustral Basin was located close to it (Figure 3.11). Halls have been reconstructed above the west magazines, which could have been accessed from the west entrance. The 'banquet hall' to the north of the Central Court was so called because storage and service areas appear to be located around it.[114] Zeta Alpha contained four halls, and is the only building at Malia to have two Minoan Halls (Figure 3.8).[115] Zeta Beta has an unusual Minoan Hall: not only is it 'lopsided', but it also leads directly into a workspace.[116] Epsilon does not possess a Minoan Hall, while it has two other types of hall (columnar and impluvium). As at Knossos, there is some variety concerning the location of the Minoan Hall in terms of the entrance of the building it was in. Thus, while halls are widely distributed across the site, they do not conform to a pattern (Figure 3.8).

Other palatial sites have not yielded such widespread evidence for Minoan Halls (and, indeed, other types of hall); in these cases, there appears to be much more centralization. A Minoan Hall was found in the north-west section of the Palace at (early LM IA) Galatas. The two halls in the east wing were probably for feasting.[117] At the LM IB Palace at Phaistos, the preservation problems render it difficult to judge how accessible the two 'residential' areas to the north and east were (which included Minoan Halls), although there are possible entrances into the areas (see Chapter 4, Figure 4.12).[118] A kind of Minoan Hall served as the entrance from the broad stairway on the west side. The halls above the west wing at Phaistos would have provided an excellent setting for Palace–town interactions.[119] This may further have been the case for the Domestic Quarters in the north and east wings at Knossos and Malia.

A Minoan Hall was located in the east wing of the Palace at Zakros, but it is the collection of halls on the ground floor of the west wing that is particularly impressive here (see Chapter 4, Figure 4.13). The flexibility was such that the spaces could be opened up into one area, or closed off into up to six separate

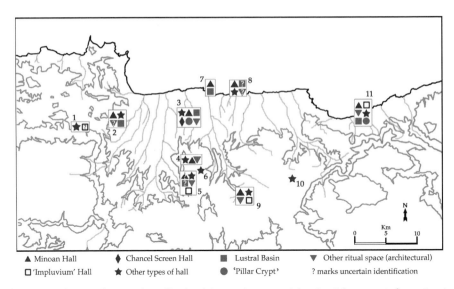

3.10 North-central Crete, formalized architectural ceremonial units. Adams 2006, figure 8, reprinted with permission, courtesy *American Journal of Archaeology* and Archaeological Institute of America.
1: Sklavokambos; 2: Tylissos; 3: Knossos; 4: Archanes; 5: Vathypetro; 6: Xeri Kara; 7: Amnissos; 8: Nirou Chani; 9: Galatas; 10: Kastelli; 11: Malia (the site of Sissi is located to the east).

spaces. This may have heightened the theatricality of the wing, and Platon described the main part as the 'Hall of Ceremonies'.[120] Access into the so-called Domestic Quarter in the east wing of the Palace at Zakros was fairly straight-forward from the main north-east entrance. Perhaps arbitrarily, the cluster of halls in the west wing is described as reception rooms rather than residential,[121] although security was presumably tight in the area (due to the substantial deposits of prestige artefacts and archives).

In non-palatial settlements, there is also great variation in how halls are oriented and their size. They could serve as entrance halls, such as at Nirou Chani, Malia Zeta Alpha, and Archanes-Tourkoyeitonia, where they also faced onto courts (Figure 3.10).[122] But they could also be set back from the entrance, allowing more control over access, as occurs in Buildings A and C at Tylissos. In some cases, such as Chania Kastelli Hill, the Minoan Hall takes a central position, which Driessen compares to the Mycenaean Megaron.[123] In the Villa at Ayia Triada, a very complex series of formal spaces includes two Minoan Halls set at right angles. While this feature is certainly part of elite architecture, it is not specifically palatial. Furthermore, variations of the feature were incorporated into less grand buildings, such as House BC at Pseira to the east, or Nerokourou to the west.[124] Some non-palatial Minoan Halls were also set back as far as possible from the entrance, but in certain cases they appear to have served as meeting points.[125]

While pier-and-door partitions are present at Palaikastro, the site is notable for the so-called Palaikastro Hall (or impluvium hall).[126] This is a rectangular room with four columns set in a square in the centre, in which a basin could have collected rainwater. It occurs in Blocks B (House 1–22), D, and G, and possibly a further one elsewhere. A Lustral Basin was found close to those in B and G, similar to the common pairing seen elsewhere with Minoan Halls. Impluvium halls have been found in other parts of Crete, such as at Maison Epsilon at Malia, the Palace at Galatas, Vathypetro, and possibly Sklavokambos.[127] Again, there is variation concerning the proximity of the impluvium halls to entrances: at Vathypetro and Sklavokambos they were entrance halls. The Minoan Hall was rejected at Palaikastro, however, apart from one possible one in Block M that was swiftly dismantled (in LM IA, and before the impluvium halls were built; see Chapter 5). Driessen has interpreted this as a short-lived Knossian intervention at the site.[128]

As a category, halls represent well the problems of identifying the function of formal spaces. Without the preservation of artefacts *in situ* to inform us of the activities conducted therein, we are almost restricted to noting the presence/absence of such architectural features, in addition to formal variation such as positions within the building. This survey has revealed, in historiographical terms, how scholars have ascribed various functions, from residential, governance, and reception to ritual, for spaces that may also simply be declarations of elite social status; the practical design in terms of comfort may have been the strongest reason for installing this feature. Across time and space, these rooms may have served all such functions, and more than one simultaneously. There is nothing to suggest that these areas were 'palatial', however, as Knossos and Malia have revealed a wide distribution of them – and they occur in non-palatial sites. Furthermore, despite the concentration in north-central Crete, there is nothing to suggest that they signalled 'Knossos'.

LUSTRAL BASINS

Lustral Basins are sunken rooms entered by a dog-legged or L-shaped series of steps (Figure 3.11).[129] The reason for the introduction of this architectural unit and its accompanying practices on Crete is unknown.[130] It has also been argued that Lustral Basins were used for bathing, but the absence of drains makes this interpretation unlikely.[131] It is possible that some form of oiling took place in Lustral Basins, but scholars differ concerning the extent to which this was *ritual*.[132] The formalized nature of these units suggests ceremonial activities of some sort, and their lowered floor level could imply a focus on chthonic deities.[133]

The north-west and south-east Lustral Basins in the Palace at Knossos were filled in during an earlier part of the Neopalatial period (MM III), and they contained 'oil flasks' – which may indicate ritual anointing.[134] Their

3.11 Malia, Palace, Lustral Basin (photograph by author).

proximity to entrances (a reconstructed entrance in the case of the south-east example) suggests further that these purification rites were performed by those entering and leaving the complex. Purification 'is one method of negotiating transitional zones' such as entrances, 'particularly where there is a sharp gradient between profane and sacred'.[135] When they fell out of use during the Neopalatial era, this presumably indicates that cultural perceptions of threshold rites also changed (these architectural units were still in use throughout Crete). Most of these later Lustral Basins lie at some distance from the entrance to the building.

The best evidence for the function of these units comes not from Crete, but from Akrotiri, namely Xeste 3.[136] Bathing appears to have occurred in the clay tubs in Room 2, so this function is less likely to be reduplicated here; the well-preserved wall paintings from the Lustral Basin area (over two floors) suggest a rite of passage. They depict three girls on the north wall and a structure with Horns of Consecration on the top of the east wall. The structure is often referred to as an 'altar';[137] it is notable that a red liquid, presumably blood, is dripping down the Horns of Consecration. Sacrifice is not depicted on Cretan iconography until the Final Palatial period, such as the Ayia Triada sarcophagus, but this does seem to be a reference to a blood libation.[138]

The central girl sits facing the viewer's right on a rock. She holds her right foot with her right hand, and her forehead with her left. Blood drips from her right foot, echoing the Horns of Consecration (which she faces). Behind her, a standing female approaches the right, behind the rocks and towards the Horns of Consecration. This figure holds a necklace outstretched in her left hand, suggesting some kind of offering out. She also appears to be older and more fully breasted than the other figures. The third female stands in front of and facing the seated figure, but twists her head back so that she is also looking at the Horns of Consecration. She seems to be fixing or raising a veil over herself. Our understanding of Minoan age signifiers suggests that she is the youngest, with a partially shaved head.[139] The three different age distinctions, presence of blood, and focus on the Horns of Consecration (seemingly a ritual symbol: see below), has led to the suggestion that this is a rite of passage for menstruating girls.[140] While this evidence is not Cretan, there is a cross-reference in that the Lustral Basin from the Palace at Zakros also depicts Horns of Consecration.[141]

At Knossos and Malia, Lustral Basins occur both in the Palaces and in other urban buildings (Figure 3.2). Three Lustral Basins have been found in the Knossian Palace, from different ceramic phases.[142] The one set in the Throne Room complex, in use later on in the Neopalatial period, lies at some distance from any entrance.[143] While there were significant locational and chronological variations, Graham has argued that the associated activities failed to change because of the 'naturally conservative character of religious practice'.[144] However, there is little that is 'naturally conservative' about religious practice; rituals, both religious and non-religious ones, are continuously being constructed and subject to change.[145] The architectural *formalization* of specific rituals should not lead to the assumption that they were static. Three Lustral Basins have been uncovered within urban structures at Knossos, in the South House, the House of the Chancel Screen, and the Little Palace. All of these were closely associated with a Minoan Hall, and none of them was located particularly close to the main entrance. The floors of all were raised (filled in and brought up to the standard floor level) during LM IA (before the building fell out of use in the South House, probably at this time in the Little Palace),[146] or left as built when the entire building was abandoned (House of the Chancel Screen).[147]

The single example from the Palace at Malia was located in the slightly secluded north-western area, or the 'Domestic Quarter' (Figure 3.11). There are three other certain Lustral Basins at Malia (Delta Alpha, Zeta Alpha, and Epsilon), and a further possible example in Zeta Beta.[148] These Lustral Basins tended to be located close to the Minoan Hall, but not close to the entrances, apart from that in Epsilon. Practices at this site differ from those at Knossos, as none of the four certain examples of Lustral Basins appears to have been attached to purification rites by the entrance of the building, although they were all (with the exception of the one in Epsilon) associated with a Minoan Hall. Furthermore, there is no positive evidence that they had their floor raised (Table 3.1).[149] It appears that the Malian palatial and second-tier elites did not want to reject or alter the rites associated with these structures.

TABLE 3.1 *The identification and changes in use of Lustral Basins in north-central Crete. Adams 2007a, Table 2, reprinted with permission, courtesy American Journal of Archaeology and Archaeological Institute of America.*

	Type or variation	Location and in association with	Change over Neopalatial period	Contents	References
Tylissos A	Lustral Basin	Far from entrance, access from Minoan Hall (or originally Room 2: Driessen 1982, 36)	Floor raised during LM IA, followed by remodelling of surrounding walls	No published objects	Hazzidakis 1934, 17–18; Platon 1967, 238–9; Driessen 1982, 34–6; Gesell 1985, 135; Graham 1987, 264; Platonos 1990, 151
Tylissos C	Lustral Basin	Far from entrance, access from Minoan Hall	Floor raised during LM IA	No published objects	Hazzidakis 1934, 40–1; Platon 1967, 238–9; Driessen 1982, 38; Gesell 1985, 136; Graham 1987, 264; Platonos 1990, 151
Knossos Palace, North-west	Lustral Basin	By entrance, access from Minoan Hall	Destroyed MM III – then new construction built on top	Oil flasks; stone vases	Evans 1921, 405–14; Gesell 1985, 90; Platonos 1990, 147–8; Rutkowski 1986, 132
Knossos Palace, South-east	Lustral Basin	By possible entrance, access from Minoan Hall	Destroyed MM III – then floor raised or covered with debris	Oil flasks	Evans 1921, 575–6; 1928, 330–1; Platon 1967, 241; Gesell 1985, 92; Driessen and Macdonald 1997, 147; Platonos 1990, 148; Rutkowski 1986, 132
Knossos Palace, Throne Room	Lustral Basin	Far from any entrance	Unchanged	N/A later use (deposit of Neopalatial artefacts from floor above)	Evans 1935, 928–34; Gesell 1985, 88–9; Niemeier 1987; Platonos 1990, 147
Knossos South House	Lustral Basin	Central/set back; access to Minoan Hall after floor was raised	Floor raised during LM IA before the building fell out of use	Oil flasks; incense burner; conical cups	Evans 1928, 378–80; Driessen 1982, 39–41; Gesell 1985, 96; Driessen 2003, 32; Graham 1987, 264; Platonos 1990, 150

(continued)

Knossos Little Palace	Lustral Basin	Far from entrance, hall system nearby including Minoan Hall	Raised: higher LM III floor. Hatzaki 2005, 75, 199: probably filled in during LM IA	Unclear chronology. Possibly Neopalatial: fragmentary faience vessel, crystal discs and bronze curls (e.g., Hatzaki 2005, 186–7)	Evans 1928, 519–25; Gesell 1985, 93–4; Driessen and Macdonald 1997, 60; Platonos 1990, 150; Hatzaki 2005, 50–2
Knossos House of the Chancel Screen	Lustral Basin	Reconstructed corridor from the entrance/Minoan Hall	Unchanged (building out of use at end of LM IA)	No published objects	Evans 1928, 393; Gesell 1985, 95; Platonos 1990, 150
Amnissos	Lustral Basin	Unclear relationship with Minoan Hall	Floor raised during LM IA, then building fell out of use	No published objects	Platon 1967, 238–9; Driessen 1982, 27, 71 n. 164; Gesell 1985, 68; Platonos 1990, 151
Malia Palace	Lustral Basin	Far from any entrance, in "Domestic Quarter"	Unchanged	No published objects	Pelon 1980, 109–10; Van Effenterre 1980, 363–64; Gesell 1985, 105; Platonos 1990, 149–50
Malia Epsilon	Lustral Basin	Far from entrance, close to columnar (not Minoan) Hall	Unchanged	Fragment of stone square libation table; miniature stone lamp; bronze objects	Deshayes and Dessenne 1959, 102–3; Gesell 1985, 108; Platonos 1990, 151
Malia Delta Alpha	Lustral Basin	Central, close to Minoan Hall	Unchanged (Driessen 1982 suggests it was raised, but no positive evidence)	Cups and small vases in upper fill	Demargne and Gallet de Santerre 1953, 45–6; Driessen 1982, 49–50, 63–4 n. 12; Gesell 1985, 108; Platonos 1990, 152
Malia Zeta Alpha	Lustral Basin	Central, close to Minoan Halls	Unchanged (fill from destruction: Driessen 1982 suggests from a raised wooden floor)	Stone vases and pottery in fill of ash and burnt matter	Demargne and Gallet de Santerre 1953, 71; Driessen 1982, 51–2, 63–4 n. 12, 70 n. 150; Platonos 1990, 151–2

(continued)

TABLE 3.1 (continued)

	Type or variation	Location and in association with	Change over Neopalatial period	Contents	References
Malia Zeta Beta?	Lustral Basin? Imitation, built raised?	South, by entrance. Access from slanting Minoan Hall	Southern part of the house a later (LM IA?) addition	No published objects	Deshayes and Dessenne 1959, 21–2; Driessen 1982, 52–3, 63–4 n. 12, 71 n. 163; Driessen and Macdonald 1997, 190: 'slightly sunken'
Knossos Palace, Queen's Megaron?	Lustral Basin? Imitation, built raised?	Not by any entrance, in the 'Domestic Quarter'	Raised? Built raised?	N/A later use	Evans 1930, 381–7; Platon 1967, 239; Graham 1987, 102, 257, 264; Platonos 1990, 148.
Knossos Royal Villa?	Lustral Basin? Imitation, built raised?	Anteroom from entrance corridor; Minoan Hall on other side of anteroom	Raised? Built raised?	N/A later use	Evans 1928, 402; McEnroe 1982, 5. No Lustral Basin: Platonos 1990, 153
Knossos Southeast House?	Lustral Basin? Imitation, built raised?	Set back from entrance, Minoan Hall nearby	Raised? Built raised?	No published objects	McEnroe 1982, 5
Nirou Chani?	Lustral Basin? Imitation, built raised?	Southeast corner, entered from East Court	Raised? Built raised?	N/A On 'raised' floor: four large bronze double axes; stone blossom bowl; pottery	Xanthoudides 1922, 6, 12–13; Platon 1954, 449–50; McEnroe 1982, 5; Gesell 1985, 116–17; Rutkowski 1986, 132. No Lustral Basin: Platonos 1990, 153
Vathypetro?	Lustral Basin?	Far from entrance, alongside but with no access to the Minoan Hall	Raised?	No published objects	Driessen and Sakellarakis 1997, 70. No Lustral Basin: Platonos 1990, 153

The Palace at Phaistos had five Neopalatial Lustral Basins, but one (70) belongs only to the MM IIIA period; some belong to the LM IB rebuild (see Chapter 4, Figure 4.12). Lustral Basins 19 and 21 are notable for their close proximity, an unusual feature in Minoan architecture. A further extraordinary feature is the large bench or platform to the east of Lustral Basin 83 in the north of the Palace.[150] Neighbouring Ayia Triada, in contrast, did not possess one at all. The Palace at Galatas has not (yet) yielded a Lustral Basin.[151]

The example from the Palace at Zakros is important, as it has rare fresco evidence, although not as rich as the (earlier) Theran example. Horns of Consecration are depicted on altar bases. The paving of the nearby Harbour Road entrance is remarkably similar to that of the west entrance at Knossos, which had Lustral Basins at entrances during the earlier part of the Neopalatial period. This is one way in which the architects of the LM IB Zakrian Palace may be deliberately alluding to Knossos (see Chapter 4). A second Lustral Basin was placed in the west wing, just to the west of the hall complex. It is tempting to think of the Throne Room complex at Knossos in this light; this was apparently the only Lustral Basin operating in the Knossian Palace during the later part of the Neopalatial period.

The coupling of Minoan Hall and Lustral Basin is common in the Neopalatial period, and this is found at Knossos, Malia, Tylissos, Amnissos, possibly Vathypetro,[152] Nirou Chani,[153] and Archanes[154] in north-central Crete (Figure 3.10; Table 3.1). Lustral Basins and nearby Minoan Halls are also found at Chania to the west and Zakros to the east, so this is another widespread 'Minoan' feature with a particular concentration in the area around Knossos. Intriguingly, while standard plans of these Neopalatial buildings suggest that these features were used at the same time, it may be the case that the Lustral Basins were often filled in before the structure was adapted to incorporate a Minoan Hall.[155]

During LM IA, several sunken Lustral Basins in non-palatial buildings had their floors backfilled, raising them to the surrounding level (e.g., Tylissos Buildings A and C, Knossos South House and Amnissos: Table 3.1).[156] These adaptations occur particularly in the broad Knossian area, as noted by Platon.[157] Elsewhere in Crete, such as in the Palaces at Zakros and Phaistos, Lustral Basins were constructed in LM IB – quite the opposite practice. The fact that some Minoan Halls were incorporated into standing Neopalatial buildings has important consequences; Driessen suggests that some Minoan Halls were introduced in LM IA after the Lustral Basin fell out of use, for example, in the South House at Knossos.[158] This kind of observation, albeit extremely difficult to demonstrate, clearly affects observations on the relationship between the two features, and is a further reminder not to perceive the Neopalatial period as a homogeneous architectural block.

The raising of the floor of Lustral Basins represents an isolated action or moment that has been preserved in the archaeological record.[159] It has been attributed to changes in bathing habits,[160] but changes in ritual practices are more likely, particularly if we are correct to view the iconographical evidence as suggestive of a rite of passage.[161] Or, these units may have initially been used for ritual, and then for less formalized and symbolic washing after their floors were raised. In any case, it represents a break from tradition, even though these 'traditions' were relatively recently introduced. If they were ceremonies attached in particular to women, as the Theran frescoes suggest, did this represent a shift in gender values? Why did the rites performed in them, presumably on a regular basis, become defunct? The raising of the floor signifies a denial of the authority (either socio-political or religious) associated with these elitist rites. However, the memory of particular rituals continued to carry some influence beyond the performance of them. Some spaces appear to have been designed to imitate filled-in Lustral Basins – while this phenomenon remains unclear, this is an intriguing possibility.[162] Finally, it is notable that not *all* Lustral Basins had their floors raised – this break from tradition was a selective phenomenon.

This discussion has intended to explore how a tight chronological resolution can be played off against issues of temporality in order to produce a more experiential understanding of past societies. It is not just the case of whether a particular Lustral Basin was in use at a certain time that is of interest, but also what light this may shed on how the inhabitants of these buildings intended to reach out to other worlds and times through the articulation of their authority through these rites – assuming that they provided the locale for female rites of passage.[163] The Lustral Basins' rites would have required repeated attention to maintain them. A further variation in practice can be seen at other sites, such as Phaistos and Zakros, which built Lustral Basins in LM IB – after many had been raised in the area around Knossos. This 'Neopalatial' phenomenon is varied across time and space, and, therefore, we should not be surprised if it is varied in meaning also.

RITUAL AND PRESTIGE ARTEFACTS AND SYMBOLS

The slippage between ritual/mundane, palatial/elite and Knossian/Minoan holds for objects as well as spaces. It is not necessarily easier to identify artefacts as ritual than architectural spaces, and, indeed, it is important to avoid circularity – identifying a space as ritual on account of one or more objects that have been categorized as ritual because of their 'ritual' context, and so on. Artefacts may be stored for dedication elsewhere, thus misleading the archaeologist who views them as the remains of *in situ* practice. One should not fall foul of the 'Pompeii premise'.[164] This assumes that artefacts are found frozen in mid-use, rather than victim to various natural and cultural post-depositional processes.

Some modern categories range across ritual and non-ritual, prestigious and lowly values. For example, chalices may well be prestige artefacts, if also 'clearly

3.12 The Bull's Head Rhyton from the Little Palace, Knossos. © Ashmolean Museum, University of Oxford.

ritual'.[165] One limited solution around this is to cover both under the term 'ceremonial'.[166] Rhyta (singular 'rhyton') have both domestic and ritual functions.[167] They are defined as having two openings that allow liquid to flow through the 'extra' hole; they therefore come in a variety of shapes.[168] In addition to sometimes being strainers or funnels rather than ritual objects,[169] they vary greatly in material and quality, from clay to stone, metal or faience. Conical rhyta were a common shape, while the animal heads (notably bulls) were clearly very prestigious objects. Perhaps the most famous is the Bull's Head Rhyton from the Little Palace at Knossos (Figure 3.12); a similar object was found in the Palace at Zakros. The smaller, secondary hole was located at the animal's mouth.

The modern distinction between non-functional ritual and the practical secular sphere is a product of post-Enlightenment rationalism.[170] Simple conical cups, normally regarded as cheap and dispensable, could also be used in ritual practices. This is apparently the case in the 200 conical cups found in Hogarth's House B at Knossos, inverted and covering the remains of vegetable matter.[171] Double Axes were usually utilitarian, but this form developed a symbolic function (see later). A further aspect of Neopalatial ritual to bear in mind is the notable regionalism across the island, even between neighbouring sites such as Knossos and Malia.[172] For the remainder of this chapter, we take four types of ritual evidence and investigate the interpretive issues they raise.

Figurines

The most common figurines by far are the terracotta human and animal ones found at ritual sites, particularly in the Protopalatial period.[173] The numerous terracotta figurines dedicated at sanctuaries were non-elite and presumably relatively easy to acquire. Bronze figurines were also plentiful in the Neopalatial period; this may indicate social differentiation between the dedicators (Figure 3.13). While there is a consensus that these objects are ritual, more precise interpretations are evasive. Human figurines were either full figures or body parts. The body parts mostly represented in peak sanctuaries are legs, arms and heads.[174] Peatfield highlights the female figurine from Traostalos, with a notably swollen leg.[175] This indicates how, as in later cultures, bodily concerns related to health as well as ideal forms. A full figurine may have been intended as a votive offering, representing either worshippers or the deity. The former is more likely; cult images, usually assumed to be larger, such as life size, appear to be absent in the Minoan world. It is also possible that the complete anthropomorphic figurines depicted ecstatic participants.[176]

The ritual function of these figurines is confirmed from their presence at ritual sites, such as peak sanctuaries,[177] but as a category they cover a very wide range in terms of investment, from the basic clay ones, to the Knossian faience 'Snake Goddesses' and the ivory Palaikastro kouros (Chapter 9). Notably, these very prestigious examples are found in settlement contexts, not ritual sites. In fact, the picture changes remarkably from the Protopalatial period, when terracotta figurines were in abundance in extra-urban sanctuaries. They still occur in the Neopalatial era, but are essentially 'replaced by a few statuettes of divine or elite figures, made of precious materials, faience and ivory'.[178] We return to depictions of the human body in Chapter 9.

They are distinctive in certain postures as well as findspot. There is a perhaps surprising lack of such objects at prosperous sites, such as Knossos or Nirou Chani, both of which have yielded examples of Horns of Consecration and Double Axes.[179] However, the elaborate 'Snake Goddesses' were found in the Palace at Knossos, and other palatial sites, such as Malia, produced them. Figurines typical of ritual sites occur in many kinds of settlements, normally as isolated examples or few in number; Archanes is an important exception, and has produced significant numbers of them. This may have been due to ritual activity at the site itself,[180] or because it was a production centre for the nearby site at Juktas. Overall, we may assume that the practice of depositing human and animal figurines was

3.13 Bronze figurine with hand to the forehead. © Ashmolean Museum, University of Oxford.

observed by a wide section of society at ritual sites in the landscape, and this was not absorbed and monopolized by elites in large settlements. Some differentiation may be discerned, however, in terms of the quality and wealth of the votives.

Libation Tables and Vessels

'Libation tables' did not have the flat surface we would expect from the label, but were rectangular or circular tables with a sunken receptacle, presumably to receive liquids or food.[181] Kernoi – or vessels with several receptacles – could have been used for multiple libations (Figure 3.4). However, these, like most other objects reviewed here, need to be contextualized: some may have been gaming boards.[182] Such games could have been ritualized, however, as sports appear to have been.[183]

Libation tables are found mainly at ritual sites, but also occur in settlements;[184] for example, a wide range of buildings at Knossos and Malia possessed them. The palatial sites of Knossos and Zakros were particularly rich in them. The fact that they are concentrated in Palaces supports a link between palatial and ritual sites.[185] Nirou Chani is notable for the volume of clay tables stacked together. Stone ones could be inscribed with Linear A, and, although the evidence is limited, there seems to be certain repeated formulae on some (Chapter 7, also Figure 7.7). The largest number of them comes from the ritual site at Kato Syme, followed by Juktas. Their deposition at peak sanctuaries appears to be a particularly Neopalatial phenomenon (not apparently occurring earlier),[186] although they cannot be dated to a particular ceramic phase.

Some Neopalatial objects have been interpreted as altars, on the basis that 'the cult needs an altar' – religious ritual is inconceivable without them to some.[187] Without supporting evidence, such as literary sources, it is extremely difficult to identify an altar as opposed to a table or any other type of more mundane structure. There are alcoves, or chancel screens, that may have had a ritual focus in three buildings at Knossos (see earlier). There may be representations of altars, such as the structure with a Horns of Consecration on top, depicted in a fragment from a steatite pyxis from Knossos. However, there is too much of a tendency to see structures such as benches as 'altars'.

Horns of Consecration

These objects (and this symbol) are named after their visual similarity with bulls' horns (Figure 3.14A; see also Figure 9.3B).[188] There is a consensus that this was a ritual symbol, with a long history dating to EM III–MM I at least.[189] Evans stated that 'sacral horns could mark any residential building belonging to a Minoan lord who also performed sacerdotal functions'.[190] While the specifics of this statement are impossible to prove, there may be an underlying ambiguity between the sacred and political. Horns of Consecration have become part of a wider narrative on the role of the bull in Minoan society, and how humans engaged with animals. Bull-leaping represents the control of this most powerful (and economically useful) creature. The bull is the most popular animal of prey on seal images – attacked by lions, griffins, man, the 'Minoan Genius', and even 'weaker' animals, such as an octopus.[191] In the Neopalatial period, the bull comprised more than 44 per cent of seal motifs found at Knossos.[192] A recent proposal has revisited Hazzidakis' idea that they were a symbol of the sun, based on a similarity with the Egyptian symbol of the horizon (with the sun represented in the base of the curve).[193]

The MM II examples from the sanctuaries at Malia, Phaistos, and Knossos suggest a link with the emergence of the Palaces.[194] In the Neopalatial period, they also occurred in the elaborate buildings of non-palatial settlements, such as Archanes and Nirou Chani. Furthermore, unlike libation tables, which were ritual equipment, or the Double Axes, which were portable objects to be carried and dedicated, Horns of Consecration appear to have a specifically architectural association.[195] Their further association with peak sanctuaries, as deduced by the Peak Sanctuary Rhyton from Zakros, the clay model of Horns of Consecration from Petsophas, and the stone example from Pyrgos, may, furthermore, support an interpretation based on the mountains themselves.[196] Examples are usually found as single specimens, not the rows often reconstructed (such as Evans' view of the south entrance). In terms of distribution, this is a pan-Cretan symbol, perhaps with a concentration at Knossos. For example, monumental (architectural) Horns of Consecration have been found at Knossos and nearby Juktas.[197] Medium-size and miniature examples occur across central and eastern Crete, with a concentration around Knossos.[198]

Double Axe

The Double Axe was used as a practical tool, but it was also a clear ritual symbol (Figure 3.14B). A recent experimental study has shed light on the production and use of these tools,[199] while the cultic function and meaning continue to evade us. Nirou Chani produced four extraordinarily large bronze specimens, while miniature versions in precious metals (gold, silver, and lead), steatite, and terracotta also occurred in ritual contexts and sites. Hogarth, upon discovering many Double Axes in the ritual cave at Psychro, articulated well the contrast scholars make between utilitarianism and ritual: 'The axes are all *simulacra*, being either too small or of too thin a bronze to have served any useful purpose'.[200] While some votives may also have been used as practical objects, those with little 'functional' value are more readily assigned to the realm of ritual.

Representations of these votives also occur in the iconography,[201] although there are fewer Neopalatial examples than later. When depicted with humans, it is always women carrying them, so this does not appear to be an attribute of a male thunder god, based on the Near Eastern model.[202] The Neopalatial

3.14 A) Colossal stone 'Horns of Consecration' (restored) from the Southwest Palace area at Knossos. The ridge of Juktas is shown between the horns (Evans 1928, 159, figure 81). B) Bronze ritual Double Axe and socket of black steatite from Psychro (Evans 1921, 438, figure 315).

iconography does not support a sacrificial function, and Marinatos argues that its association with women renders this idea less likely.[203] It may have a votive role with, as three of the four sealings and seal we have depicting women carrying Double Axes are also associated with garments. Clothing would have not survived if they were left as dedications.

At other times, their appearance on pottery or as mason's marks is of less clear cultic use.[204] The 'basket-shaped' vase from Pseira, for example, has four friezes of elaborate Double Axes.[205] Seager states that the 'curious shape and the abundant use of the Double Axe show that this vase was probably intended for ritual use'.[206] It is its unusual and rather impractical shape that is suggestive of 'ritual' use; in contrast, the amphora decorated with Double Axes and bulls' heads from the same site has clearer potential for practical use.[207] The difficulty in identifying this symbol's meaning has led to continued variation in inter-pretations, united in the idea that it is some kind of symbol of religious power.[208]

CONCLUSION

In addition to exploring a selective but representative range of Neopalatial features, this chapter has revealed some of the challenges faced in Minoan archaeology, including the slippage between elite and palatial, Knossian and

Minoan, and ritual and secular. There is a clear concentration of elite features in the palatial sites and the Palaces themselves, but they do not monopolize them. There is also a disproportionate number of features in north-central Crete, but they do occur elsewhere. This overview of island-wide distribution sets the scene for closer analyses of the settlements, both strictly palatial, and those without a Palace.

We labour under the terms of the early archaeologists. In the rush to correct any misinterpretations that may have arisen in consequence, some of the early ideas may have been dismissed out of hand – without any more concrete foundation laid down to replace them. This chapter has also demonstrated how different types of material (architectural, artefacts, iconographical) need to be assessed differently – no other type of material can match the fine chronological resolution of ceramics, for example, and certainly not iconography. Weaving them all into a coherent narrative, therefore, requires a fine balancing act, but patterns emerge readily enough.

CHAPTER FOUR

PALACES AND THEIR CONTEXT

INTRODUCTION

As previously discussed, much ink has been spilled concerning whether these complexes should be called 'Palaces', 'Palace-Temples', or 'Central-Court buildings'. 'Palace' is maintained here on the grounds of simplicity: we are, after all, analysing the 'Neo*palatial*' period, and this feature is the most distinctive one of that era. 'Central-Court building' is more ambiguous regarding function and occupant(s), as it focuses on form. However, ambiguity extends to the form as well, as there is a series of structures that do not quite reach full Palace status in architectural terms, despite containing numerous functions often considered 'palatial'. These, such as Gournia, will be considered in the following chapter along with other major, non-palatial settlements. We focus here on the four unambiguous examples, Knossos, Malia, Phaistos, and Zakros, with a further consideration of Galatas and Petras.[1]

The outcome of the debate itself ('what should we call these structures?') is rather less serious than the implications of its existence in the first place. This discussion carries the inherent assumption that they all functioned and were perceived in the same way across the island, and so it is appropriate to assign a single, fixed label. This impression, however, is simplistic; one aim of bringing all clear examples into one chapter is to highlight their chronological, functional, and contextual variations. The central buildings at these sites share very distinctive architectural features, notably the Central Court, but it becomes more difficult to generalize about them when they are set in their urban and regional context. Furthermore, they flourished at different times within the Neopalatial period, which has obvious implications for understanding island-wide dynamics.[2]

Some buildings were very short-lived, such as LM IA Galatas and the LM IB Palaces at Zakros and Phaistos, while Knossos was in continual use until LM IIIA2, with the evidence for some phases, notably LM IB, 'cleared up' in subsequent periods. The best evidence for Malia comes from LM IA, and there is some debate about when the complex was destroyed. Zakros is the only Palace here with any significant (unplundered) deposits. Both Malia and Phaistos are frustratingly empty; the former was apparently pillaged,[3] while the latter may have never been fully functioning. Architecturally, the Neopalatial period is very diverse in terms of these structures. It is not so much the case of there being One New Palace; this is the era of many Palaces.

This chapter also incorporates a more experiential methodology in order to move beyond 'label', 'form', and 'function'. Approaches that perceive buildings as theatres for social discourse are becoming more common.[4] Consideration of the physical impact for people moving towards, through, and around buildings is more difficult to acknowledge when we rely significantly on the bird's-eye view of 2-D plans.[5] We will focus on the entrance systems. As N. Platon stated: 'There is an ancient axiom that the entrance to a building sets the mood of the visitor. Feelings of awe, wonder, puzzlement, even terror can be motivated by the combination of approach, entrance, and facade.'[6] We will consider not only the ritualized nature of approaching the Palaces, but also the more everyday and mundane elements concerning interactions between Palace, town, and beyond.[7]

Archaeology has traditionally focused on functionalist approaches, such as the overall function of a building (e.g., defining a 'Palace' and its occupants; see also Chapter 3), or the individual functions or activities that occurred within buildings (e.g., storage or ritual). This chapter will also explore the evidence for functions and practices within each of these structures in a standardized, comparable manner, covering size and elaboration, elite (or ritual) architectural features, administration, storage, production, and notable assemblages.

While the focus of this chapter is understandably on the central buildings (not least because excavators have focused on them), we will also consider the urban context as much as possible. This is the only way of establishing which (if any) of the features and functions were monopolized (as opposed to merely centralized) in the Palaces. It is important to recognize that these were not monolithic entities existing in a vacuum. Finally, we will consider the regional context, and the question of whether we can establish the range and nature of the influence of the people based in these structures.

KNOSSOS

Knossos was the largest Cretan site from the Neolithic period. In EM II, it possessed a central authority, who organized communal activities and a building programme. It controlled the gateway port of Poros, reaching out to shores beyond Crete in a manner that would intensify throughout the Late Bronze Age.[8] However, it does not appear, on present evidence, to have been the earliest or largest Protopalatial (MM I–MM III) Palace.[9] Overall, while Knossos may have played a formative role in state development, there is little suggestion that it was the main political site on Crete before the Late Bronze Age. Neopalatial Knossos clearly exceeds the size and population of other Cretan sites at around sixty-seven hectares and 14,000–18,000 people.[10]

The statement that we 'do not have a clear history of the Palace because its history was never clear' is honest, rather than defeatist.[11] The complexity of the site befits its importance, and our confusion is testament to its greatness. The Palace was thriving during the earlier part of the Neopalatial period (Macdonald's 'New Palace' and 'Frescoed Palace'), although the LM IB evidence is unclear.[12] LM IB Marine Style pottery was found as strays in later deposits in the east wing, but there is little clear stratigraphical evidence.[13] The lack of LM IB evidence in the Palace does not necessarily indicate that it was 'ruined' or in diminished use,[14] but could be due to the fact that the material was removed.[15] The LM IB 'dump' in the area of the South House may be the remains of occupation in the Palace, discarded during the LM II–III reorganization.[16] Other Neopalatial buildings subsequently occupied, such as the Little Palace and Royal Villa, present similar problems. The 'grand mansions' located near the Palace (the South House, the Southeast House, and the House of the Chancel Screen) were not rebuilt after the LM IA earthquake;[17] possibly the area became taboo, or significant LM IB resources were required for projects elsewhere.[18] However, the buildings close to the north wing of the Palace continued in use (for example, the Northwest Treasury). LM IB deposits are found slightly further from the palatial centre.[19]

Arthur Evans' role at Knossos was discussed in Chapter 2. A further aspect of Evans' legacy is his physical reconstructions, or, as he called them, reconstitutions.[20] They were partly necessary to reinforce the building, which was built on a steep slope, as it was excavated. However, there is no doubt that, some decades after he first began work at the Palace, Evans decided to rebuild beyond the required minimum. He intended to bring the Palace back to life for the education (as well as entertainment) of the public.[21] Concrete was poured into four areas in particular: the South Propylaeum, the north entrance passage, the Domestic Quarter, and the Throne Room.

Comparing photographs of the original excavation with how the areas look today is startling. In the case of the Throne Room, a photograph from 1900

4.1 Reconstruction of the Throne Room at Knossos, © Ashmolean Museum, University of Oxford.

shows the throne and benches, with walls preserved to shoulder height. The 1930 post-reconstruction photograph reveals how a first floor was added on top (as can be seen today).[22] In 1901, a reconstruction drawing imagined the reality that Evans later created (Figure 4.1: note Lustral Basin to the left). A consequence of his moulding of the site in newly invented reinforced concrete was to transform it, according to D'Agata, into a '"mythic" subject, or at any rate a generator of myths'.[23] The evidence for how and why Evans reconstructed certain areas is not so clear. The notebooks help, and he employed architects (Theodore Fyfe, Christian Doll, and Piet de Jong), so trained and expert advice was available,[24] but the dividing line between the excavated remains and Evans' vision is unclear.[25] The concrete poured into the site did more than simply support the excavated remains; it enabled Evans to rebuild them for a modern audience.

Approaching the Palace

Considerable community or collective organization is demonstrated by the paved roads, possibly laid on a grid plan,[26] which served to channel inhabitants and visitors through the site.[27] Many of the roads led to the West Court of the Palace, which allowed an uninterrupted view of the vast complex. The west facade was huge, and may have appeared fortress-like, although the windows that were apparently set on the upper floor would have broken the sense of impenetrability.[28] The manner in which the facade was comprised of recesses and projecting blocks would have also broken up the view.[29] There is a strong tendency, in considerations of the function of the complex, to perceive it as a unified, homogeneous block; however, this is not how it was experienced.

Preziosi states that 'despite the great size of this megastructure, one is seldom very far from an entrance either to the periphery or to the Central Court'.[30] Although the evidence is not equally clear around the Palace, it has been argued that there are five certain entrances, and five further possible ones (Figure 4.2A).[31] Spaces that appear to be 'porter's lodges' suggest some degree of control concerning access.[32] We can expect that different users used different entrances, and that only particular, limited sections of the Palace were accessed, depending on status and occasion. At Knossos, all zones are directly accessed from one entrance only. The proximity of the north and north-east entrances is misleading, as in fact they led into different areas.[33] The Palace was carefully designed, with certain structural 'mirrorings', most notably the north and south entrances, and the north-west bailey and the south-east entrance. These highlight the careful design of the complex, and that the interface between Palace and town was carefully orchestrated.[34]

The north entrance comprised a vast columned hall, with a narrow ramp leading up from its south-west corner, previously argued to be a strategy of intimidation.[35] With the construction of the east and west bastions during the Neopalatial period, this passage became narrower, producing a greater bottleneck.[36] The famous relief fresco of a bull has been reconstructed on the upper storey of the west bastion; it is difficult to see how it could have been visible from the passage, however. When you emerge onto the vast Central Court, Mount Juktas, with its peak sanctuary, looms ahead of you (provided the original level of the south wing did not obscure this: Figure 3.3).[37] No other entrance at Knossos appears to lead directly into any kind of court; one reason may be that access was carefully controlled from the outside, and if visitors moved into a court with several exits, this would be more difficult.

The kind of theatricality of the north entrance can also be seen in the west entrance, where one moves from the West Court, with its directional causeways or 'red carpet', to the relatively narrow corridor that winds its way into the Palace (Figure 4.2B).[38] The room, possibly a porter's lodge, set besides this corridor was where Evans pictured the Priest-King receiving visitors, with a fresco of a bull situated nearby. The corridor acts as a funnel into the Palace, and one is accompanied by life-sized figures painted on and proceeding along the walls (but these may well belong to the Final Palatial period).[39] If there were a continuous file of figures into the South Propylaeum, then they would have numbered around 536 in total.[40] This reinforced and celebrated the notion of ceremonial procession (some of the figures bear gifts, and certain individuals appear to be marked out as 'special', seated ready to receive the gifts).[41]

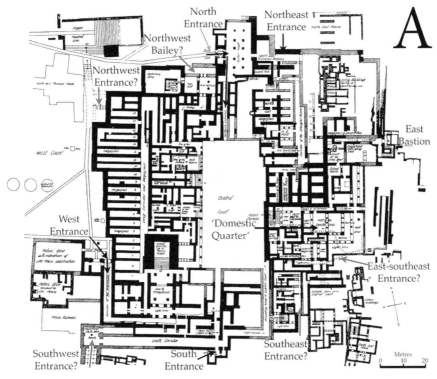

4.2 A) Knossos, Palace entrances. Adams 2007b, figure 1, reprinted with permission, *Oxford Journal of Archaeology* and © 2007, John Wiley and Sons. B) Knossos, west entrance to West Court, with causeways (photograph by author).

The south and west entrances enter the heavily reconstructed South Propylaeum; the evidence for this area is unclear.[42] Other poorly preserved areas include the entrance into the north-east magazines; Evans suggested that a small room here was used to exchange goods.[43] He reconstructed a further entrance at the north-western area to the halls on the first floor, but Graham moderated this to suggest a ramp for animals to deliver produce to the west magazines level.[44] This would explain how vast amounts of goods could be physically carried into the Palace, and this activity would be tucked away from the main, ceremonial entrances.

Entering the Palace was clearly an intimidating experience, especially through the main, funnelling entrances that have also yielded evidence for iconography (the north, west, and south entrances). While direct access to the Central Court was possible, it is the most secluded of Central Courts in terms of visibility. In some senses this is the most inward-looking Palace, since no part of the complex is accessible only from outside (without further communication with the rest of the complex), in contrast to the other three main Palaces.

The Functions of the Palace

The size of the Knossian Palace (including the number of storeys) and the degree of architectural elaboration was unequalled in the Minoan world.[45] The complex appears to have hosted a unique fresco programme, most notably of bull imagery, which dates from the Neopalatial period onwards. This has led to the suggestion that the bull was the symbol of power for the 'sovereign' at Knossos, although the figure behind this power might not be a king.[46] This symbol may stem from the economic importance of cattle management,[47] but such investment in large-scale wall paintings indicates a move towards the use of the animal as a social statement. The Palace is particularly rich in halls, especially Minoan Halls, but less so in Lustral Basins (Chapter 3, Figure 3.2).

The wealth of material from the Knossian Palace is particularly impressive given the fact that it was in use after the Neopalatial period, and was therefore heavily disturbed. Two deposits of prestige and ritual artefacts were located in the west wing (the Temple Repositories and the Stone Vase Deposit) and one in the east wing (the Treasury of the Shrine: see Figure 4.3).[48] These contained 'special' artefacts, which may have had a cultic use in addition to the social prestige they conveyed. For example, the (MM III) east wing deposit contained, among other items, miniature gold-plated bronze Double Axes, gold-plated bronze curls, fragments of ivory figurines, a faience bull's head, and a rock-crystal bowl.[49] Since figurines are such an important element of ritual sites, it may be expected that these indicate ritual, although the actual practices remain evasive.

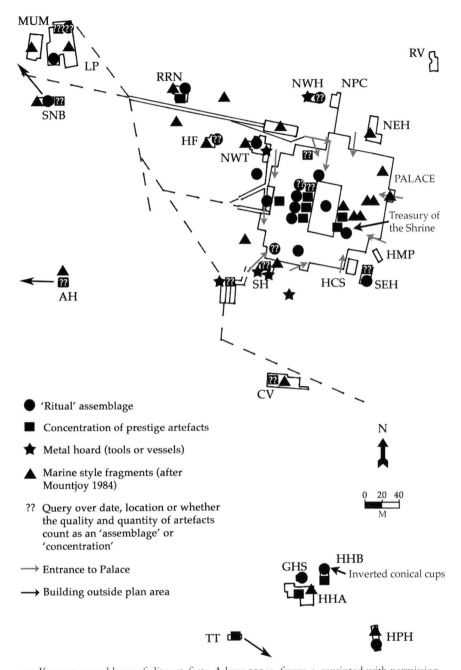

4.3 Knossos, assemblages of elite artefacts. Adams 2004a, figure 4, reprinted with permission, *Journal of Mediterranean Archaeology* and © Equinox Publishing ltd 2004.

Abbreviations: AH: Acropolis House; CV: Caravanserai; GHS: Gypsades House Shrine; HCS: House of the Chancel Screen; HF: House of the Frescoes; HHA: Hogarth's House A; HHB: Hogarth's House B; HMP: House of the Monolithic Pillars; HPH: High Priest's House; LP: Little Palace; MUM: Minoan Unexplored Mansion; NEH: Northeast House; NPC: North Pillar Crypt; NWH: Northwest House; NWT: Northwest Treasury; RRN: Royal Road North; RV: Royal Villa; SEH: Southeast House; SH: South House; SNB: Stratigraphical Museum Excavations North Building; TT: Temple Tomb.

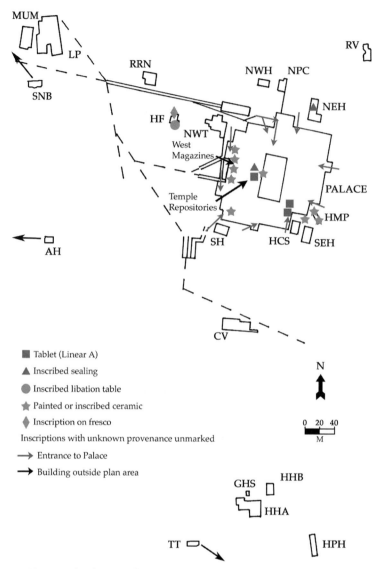

4.4 Knossos, distribution of Linear A script. Adams 2004a, figure 5, reprinted with permission, *Journal of Mediterranean Archaeology* and © Equinox Publishing ltd 2004.
Abbreviations: AH: Acropolis House; CV: Caravanserai; GHS: Gypsades House Shrine; HCS: House of the Chancel Screen; HF: House of the Frescoes; HHA: Hogarth's House A; HHB: Hogarth's House B; HMP: House of the Monolithic Pillars; HPH: High Priest's House; LP: Little Palace; MUM: Minoan Unexplored Mansion; NEH: Northeast House; NPC: North Pillar Crypt; NWH: Northwest House; NWT: Northwest Treasury; RRN: Royal Road North; RV: Royal Villa; SEH: Southeast House; SH: South House; SNB: Stratigraphical Museum Excavations North Building; TT: Temple Tomb.

At Knossos Linear A tablets have been found only in the Palace, and they all date to the earlier part of the Neopalatial period (Figure 4.4, Chapter 7). Linear A administrative evidence from the rest of the site is surprisingly rare.[50]

The tablet from the Temple Repositories was not found *in situ* as part of an archive, although a vast number of sealings were also found in this deposit. The tablets in the south-east of the Palace are not associated with other administrative material. Linear A signs on many of the pithoi from the west magazines were probably some kind of marker identifying the contents.[51] Most sealings found in the Palace date to a latter destruction (Final Palatial period).[52] Sealings, unlike administrative Linear A, are found throughout the Neopalatial town.

While the Palace was a great consumer of prestige objects, it is less clear whether they were made within it. A few scattered tools indicate that some production or maintenance activities took place in the Palace, but no Neopalatial workshops have been identified here (Figure 4.5). The overall amount of space for agricultural storage in the Palace is substantial, with the three largest areas being the west magazines, the north-eastern magazines, and the royal magazines (Chapter 8).[53] While avoiding the temptation to project back the later Final Palatial evidence, the distinctive layout of the west magazines provides indirect evidence for their use as storerooms. Eighteen such storerooms lie along a corridor, initially established in MM IIIB.[54] Taking the average capacity of a large LM I pithos (550 litres), and assessing that there was space for around 420 such containers, Christakis has calculated a potential for the storage of 231,000 litres in this part of the Palace alone, while emphasizing the tentative nature of such sums.[55] Nor does this amount include the ninety-three *kaselles*, or cists, cut into the floors. His work indicates that storage continued to be an important function throughout the Neopalatial period, refuting the theory that storage for staples decreased from the Protopalatial to the Neopalatial period.[56] In summary, there is a clear concentration of ceremonial areas, administration, space for agricultural storage, and the consumption of prestige goods in the building. It remains to be seen how these are distributed throughout the town.

The Knossian Town

A valuable survey has been conducted by Hood and Smyth, which will be augmented by the Knossos Urban Landscape Project (KULP).[57] Studies of individual buildings, both overviews by Evans and more detailed recent contributions, also shed important light.[58] Around twenty structures at the site are known well enough for discussion, which can be categorized into broad groups, including grand mansions and specialized buildings.[59] Linear A markings were found on the (stacked up) frescoes from the House of the Frescoes, which also yielded a libation table with a Linear A inscription (Figure 4.4). Overall, the distribution of non-administrative examples of Linear A throughout the town was wider than the administrative ones.[60]

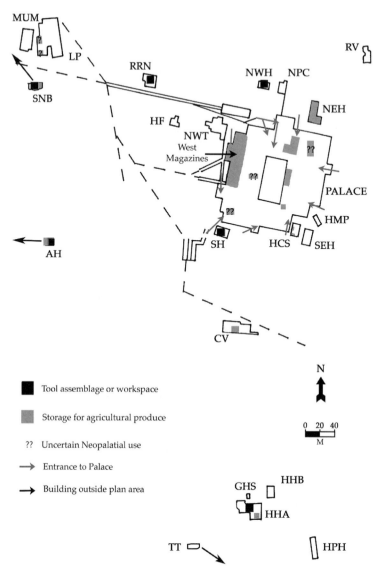

4.5 Knossos, storage of staples and assemblages of tools. Adams 2004a, figure 6, reprinted with permission, *Journal of Mediterranean Archaeology* and © Equinox Publishing ltd 2004.
Abbreviations: AH: Acropolis House; CV: Caravanserai; GHS: Gypsades House Shrine; HCS: House of the Chancel Screen; HF: House of the Frescoes; HHA: Hogarth's House A; HHB: Hogarth's House B; HMP: House of the Monolithic Pillars; HPH: High Priest's House; LP: Little Palace; MUM: Minoan Unexplored Mansion; NEH: Northeast House; NPC: North Pillar Crypt; NWH: Northwest House; NWT: Northwest Treasury; RRN: Royal Road North; RV: Royal Villa; SEH: Southeast House; SH: South House; SNB: Stratigraphical Museum Excavations North Building; TT: Temple Tomb.

However, the fact remains that most Knossian buildings have produced no evidence whatsoever of literacy on the part of their inhabitants.

While the Palace is by far the largest structure, the Little Palace is also considerable, at around 1,395 m².[61] The Little Palace stands alone and, above all other Neopalatial buildings, blurs the line between Palace and town.[62] A cluster of buildings covers 300–450 m² (the Northeast House, the Minoan Unexplored Mansion, the Northwest Treasury, and the Temple Tomb), each being rather idiosyncratic in layout and function. The next cluster is more homogeneous, at 220–45 m²; this includes the Royal Villa, the House of the Chancel Screen, the South House, the Southeast House, and Hogarth's House A. Other structures have areas of less than 145 m², and include the House of the Frescoes, the North Pillar Crypt, the House of the Monolithic Pillars, and the Acropolis House: these are also less standardized in layout and function.[63]

This 220–45 m² group comprises the 'grand mansions' of the site, although the Little Palace and the House of the Frescoes are also elite structures.[64] These structures have ashlar masonry, frescoes, and gypsum (see also the Caravanserai).[65] In addition to their standardized size, these grand, apparently domestic structures have a set architectural ceremonial assemblage of Minoan Hall and Lustral Basin (and possibly the poorly defined Pillar Crypt, but see Chapter 3, Figure 3.2), but no other notable ritual areas or deposits. Nor have they presented considerable evidence for agricultural storage, although this is problematic in cases that were later occupied. The Royal Villa, the Southeast House, and the House of the Frescoes appear to have no storage areas for agricultural produce (Figure 4.5). This was limited in the South House and the House of the Chancel Screen, and potentially greater in the Little Palace.[66] This suggests that, despite the grandeur of these buildings, they had limited self-sufficiency.[67]

The assemblage of silver vessels from the South House indicates that rich deposits were not confined to the Palace, and several other bronze hoards have been found at the site (Figure 4.3).[68] The most common prestige goods found throughout the town were stone vases.[69] In terms of production, the South House is the only grand mansion that has revealed such evidence: a tool-kit of bronze instruments (Figure 4.5). This indicates the ability to produce and repair artefacts, even if it was not performed in this space. While there is variation in layout, the overall impression is one of considerable formalization of ceremonial activities. This suggests competition among those responsible for commissioning these buildings, although there may have been some dependency on the Palace for staples.

In contrast, some of the 'specialized buildings' (most notably the Caravanserai and the Northeast House) tended to have substantial space set aside for agricultural produce, although others had none (e.g., Hogarth's House B and the Royal Road North Building).[70] The simpler buildings (such as the Acropolis

Houses and Hogarth's House A) have produced some pithoi. Inhabitants of buildings who had not taken up this elite assemblage (e.g., Minoan Hall and Lustral Basin) tended to perform idiosyncratic and less formalized ritual practices. For example, the Stratigraphical Museum North Building has evidence for LM IB child sacrifice and/or cannibalism,[71] and the inverted conical cups from Hogarth's House B may have had a ritual purpose. They have also yielded most of the evidence for production, such as ivory and stone-working in the Royal Road North Building. The ideological symbols shared between the Palace and the Royal Road North Building include bull frescoes (these are the only buildings to have produced them), Horns of Consecration, figurines, rhyta, and libation tables, and they would suggest a special relationship.[72] The Royal Road North Building may have been a kind of extension of the Palace, providing production areas away from the formal spaces of the Palace.[73]

The Neopalatial Palace was not only the largest building in all of Crete, but also the most architecturally elaborate, with a unique fresco programme, and a concentration (though not a monopoly) of ceremonial features, Linear A evidence, and agricultural storage (Figures 3.2, 4.3, 4.4, 4.5). The fresco programme emphasized group participation and perpetual enactment, which must have promoted a strong sense of collective, Knossian identity.[74] Many important and standardized town houses have been excavated, which are notable for their rich ceremonial features, but possess fewer indicators of economic and administrative control. The wide distribution of elite features, such as Minoan Hall and Lustral Basin, demands a reassessment of whether they were 'palatial', or more simply 'elite' or 'Minoan'. Apart from certain features, such as the palatial bull iconography or the Chancel Screen Hall, elite elements are too widely distributed throughout the island to be viewed as purely 'Knossian'. There may have been an 'unusually intense level of hierarchical socio-political competition' at the site, with a strong second tier of factions, but they were not necessarily self-sufficient, and may have relied on the Palace for staples.[75] In turn, this group would have put pressure on the Palace's inhabitants to increase conspicuous consumption. With power comes the fear of losing it, and maybe those positioned at the highest, palatial level changed from time to time; evidence for hierarchy does not imply a static structure.

The Regional Picture

It is crucial to set this site not just in the regional context, meaning the immediate hinterland, nor even just that of the entire island, but of the Aegean and beyond. For now, we focus on the immediate surrounding region, and I have asked this question before: 'why did the site (and Palace) at Knossos not absorb all of the wealth in the region, as in the case of the Mycenaean Palaces?'[76] Knossos had an important visual and ceremonial link with the peak

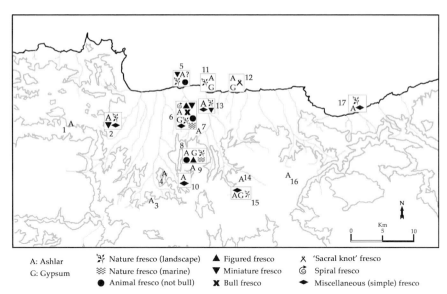

4.6 North-central Crete, architectural elaboration (ashlar, gypsum, and frescoes by type). Adams 2006, figure 5, reprinted with permission, courtesy *American Journal of Archaeology* and Archaeological Institute of America.
1: Sklavokambos; 2: Tylissos; 3: Galeni; 4: Vitsila; 5: Poros; 6: Knossos; 7: Skalani; 8: Archanes; 9: Xeri Kara; 10: Vathypetro; 11: Amnissos; 12: Nirou Chani; 13: Prasa; 14: Voni; 15: Galatas; 16: Kastelli; 17: Malia (with the recently excavated site of Sissi to the east).

sanctuary at Juktas, which, towering over the region, could signal Knossian power very effectively. It is in this wider region that we can see being 'Knossian', or 'being excessively Minoan' occurred with great intensity. That this emulation fans out towards the coast suggests that this land mass was very outward looking, as is common for island communities (Chapter 9).

Ashlar masonry is commonly used in the region, while gypsum is used more selectively, and nowhere can match the fresco programme of the Palace at Knossos (Figure 4.6).[77] Many sites in the surrounding area incorporated Minoan Halls and Lustral Basins into their elite buildings (Figure 3.10).[78] The distribution of prestige/ritual assemblages is more uneven, with some substantial deposits, such as the animal and human figurines from Archanes and the stacks of libation tables and bronze Double Axes from Nirou Chani.[79]

The evidence for administration and production/storage is considered in more detail in subsequent chapters. However, it is of note that magazine-like storage areas are found in the central buildings at other sites, such as Tylissos, Archanes, and Nirou Chani, so this is not solely a 'palatial' feature, although the form in itself may have carried elite connotations. Perhaps the Knossian elite endorsed the adoption and articulation of elite features by other (lesser) local groups, as this articulated and reinforced Knossos' pre-eminence in the process. Knossos was obliged, in turn, to increase the intensity of intra-site conspicuous consumption.[80] This picture of mutually beneficial ideological emulation and investment does little to solve the issue of political centralization.[81] The difficulty in establishing the extent of Knossian political control is well tested by the case of Galatas, excavated in recent years.

GALATAS

One case that illustrates the difficulties involved in assessing who initiated certain developments, and with what motivations, is the very short-lived Palace at Galatas (Figure 4.7). This was built in MM III and fell out of use in mid-LM IA; it appears to have been squatter-occupied in mature LM IA, and was later abandoned before the end of LM IA.[82] For example, the column hall

4.7 Galatas, plan of the Palace and surrounding buildings, from Rethemiotakis and Christakis (2011, 207, figure 2). Permission from authors.

(14) became a cooking area,[83] although the Minoan Hall in the north wing and various other spaces remained in use during LM IA.[84] Elsewhere on the site, Building 2 was built in MM IIIB and destroyed in the LM IB period,[85] while Building 3 underwent reuse in this period. Recent excavations have discovered a structure (Building 6) to the south of the Palace, which contained a Minoan Hall and Lustral Basin.[86] Overall, the settlement experienced a very different trajectory from the Palace, apparently flourishing during LM IA and LM IB; the nature of elite behaviour and power in the site therefore changed considerably.

The evidence for administration is limited, although seals have been found in the Palace and Building 2. Excavations are incomplete, but it is clear that this site witnessed a short burst of investment, in contrast with the steadily increasing developments at Knossos. It did not enjoy the longevity of the Malian Palace, which was arguably not as well constructed, being substantially mudbrick. Extensive use of ashlar and gypsum occurred at Galatas, while the Central Court was finely paved.[87] Horns of Consecration, from different periods and buildings, have been found,[88] and a 'baetyl' and exedra were recovered to the south of the Palace.[89] However, the west wing did not follow the standard plan of magazines, as seen in other Palaces; instead, storage, food preparation, cooking, and dining areas were juxtaposed in the east wing. The Palace was remarkably empty, as is unfortunately so common (see also Malia and Phaistos). However, a shrine model with a seated female figure inside was found in Building 6 (MM III period).[90]

The ceramics are Knossian in type, but probably from the Archanes area, in contrast to the local style in the Protopalatial period.[91] Some scholars are tempted to associate Knossian-style pottery with Knossian power.[92] It has been suggested that the Knossians set up Galatas as a frontier site, which they then lost interest in after pushing further south.[93] It may seem odd that the Knossians would establish a Palace as a frontier, because of the well-formed assumption that Palaces are *central* sites, circled by a catchment area, and not peripheral ones. However, Zakros perhaps served as a similar frontier institution, albeit one of a more maritime nature.

However, it is, at present, impossible to demonstrate this. The presence of gypsum from Knossian quarries in the monumental north wing cannot be used to demonstrate Knossian control. Whitelaw points out that the *pictorial* fresco fragments from Galatas are the earliest known – so it is perhaps perverse to use them as evidence of Knossian influence (Figure 4.6).[94] Rather than throwing doubt on Knossian dominance in the craft, it is still assumed that Knossian artisans were ultimately responsible.[95] Rethemiotakis initially argued that the Horns of Consecration used as building material in the LM IB Building 2 probably originally came from the Palace, and 'provided direct links with Knossos'.[96] But this symbol is found throughout Crete, and is not specifically Knossian.

Some have viewed this failed attempt at sustaining a functioning Palace as an indication rather of frustrated local ambitions.[97] Perhaps this elite did not have Knossos' full blessing to build this complex, or perhaps they fell out of favour.[98] The inability of the site's elite to maintain this investment, which apparently sprang from nowhere and faded to a much more mediocre standard of living afterwards, suggests an elite with aspirations that it was unable to sustain. It may well be that the Knossian elite had an interest in Galatas, but it is not yet demonstrated that they had considerable or full control. Rethemiotakis' position has modified to allow for the possibility that an ambitious local elite emulated Knossos to an extent that it was deemed confrontational.[99] The shift visible here is on the part of the excavators; a willingness to allow the picture to become fuzzier, messier, and therefore more human. It is difficult to see where this local elite sprang from, given the apparent low population of the region before the Palace was established.[100] The preliminary results of the Galatas survey indicate that the number of large sites around Galatas rises significantly in the Neopalatial period.[101] Nonetheless, it does not seem so certain that an elite was imposed on the site by Knossos. Then again, the issues of agency and motivation may be moot given the extent to which the elite at Galatas aspired to imitate Knossos, and perhaps become Knossian.

MALIA

Stylianos Xanthoudides discovered the site in 1915, and, since 1920, the French School at Athens has excavated it. The site is coastal, with the Selena mountains lying to the south. Few sites of substance lie in the immediate area, with the exception of Sissi (see below). However, the construction of the Aposelemis Dam (south of Chersonesos, west of Malia) has necessitated rescue excavations; Greek archaeologists are discovering a series of Neopalatial sites, including a building with fifty-two rooms at Sphendyli.[102]

In the original excavation publications, the material is listed under the headings of (Protopalatial) 'première époque' and (Neopalatial and later) 'seconde époque', which renders it difficult to establish sub-phases within the Neopalatial period. Van Effenterre has divided the ceramic material into three Neopalatial styles – i) linear and spiral, ii) floral, and iii) marine – which can be broadly attached to the Knossian ceramic styles.[103] However, there is some difficulty in distinguishing between MM III and LM IA in the Palace and Quartier Epsilon, and the distinction between LM IA and LM IB is not always clear.[104] The full use of the Palace in LM IB has been debated, and it ceased functioning either in late LM IA/early LM IB or at the end of LM IB.[105] Whether the other buildings continued in use or not in LM IB seems to depend more on location (Epsilon and the Zeta Quarters appear to have continued in use, but not the Delta Quarter).[106]

Approaching the Palace

Sherd coverage in the immediate area appears to have contracted or decreased from the Protopalatial to the Neopalatial period.[107] It also seems that the Neopalatial settlement shifted from the coast to concentrate around the Palace.[108] The system of paved roads was Protopalatial, and may have remained in use during the Neopalatial period, when blocks encroached upon it.[109]

The Palace at Malia was well planned, although there were no 'mirrorings' of entrances. It had five certain entrances and with a further, debated one (Figure 4.8A).[110] On the whole, the architectural layouts of Minoan Palaces formed distinct zones, with one zone per entrance.[111] The north and south entrances may have had porter's lodges. The main entrance appears to have been the northern one,[112] with a well-paved road leading up to it (Figure 4.8B, with pithos). It led to a court, from which several options were available. The sharp angle turning south at the north entrance would have prevented easy visibility from the causeway into the north court. As storerooms and production areas were located nearby, the north-east entrance enabled a separate access system, so that the ceremonial feel of the north entrance would not be 'contaminated' by those involved in the basic economic activities. This provides a good example of how various types of users may have accessed and experienced the same area of a Palace very differently. Similarly, the west entrance may have been used for transferring goods rather than the movement of people, as the doorway was partly blocked, rendering full access problematic.[113]

While the Central Court lies at the heart of the Palace, access to it was direct from both the south and the south-east. A ritual area appears to have been located in area XVIII, which does not appear to have further access into the Palace. Terracotta feet (from a figure) were found in it, and a small stone 'altar'.[114] Perhaps this provided the opportunity for people to approach identities or powers associated with the Palace, without gaining full right of entry. Given that Malia had a tradition of urban shrines (dating to the Protopalatial period),[115] this may have been a practice that the Palace decided to appropriate into the palatial complex.

The Functions of the Palace

The construction of the Palace at Malia is not as impressive as that at Knossos.[116] Three quarters of the walls were constructed with rubble and mudbrick, and were no more than two or three storeys throughout. Floors were not generally paved;[117] gypsum is absent or very rare.[118] The Central Court was re-laid several times, and a spherical stone object, possibly a baetyl, was placed in the north-west corner.[119] The small structure in the centre may

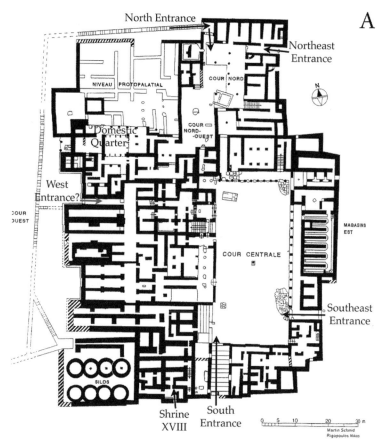

4.8 A) Malia, Palace entrances. Adams 2007b, figure 2, reprinted with permission, *Oxford Journal of Archaeology* and © 2007, John Wiley and Sons. B) Malia, north entrance looking west with pithos (photograph by author).

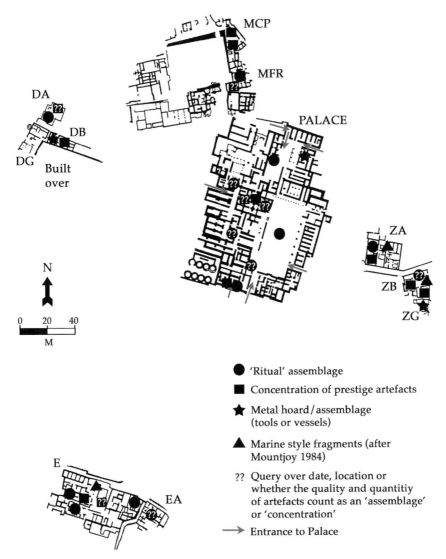

4.9 Malia, assemblages of elite artefacts. Adams 2004a, figure 8, reprinted with permission, *Journal of Mediterranean Archaeology* and © Equinox Publishing ltd 2004.
DA: Delta Alpha; DB: Delta Beta; DG: Delta Gamma; E: Epsilon; EA: Epsilon Alpha; MCP: Maison de la Cave au Pilier; MFR: Maison de la Façade à Redans; ZA: Zeta Alpha; ZB: Zeta Beta; ZG: Zeta Gamma.

have been a sacrificial hearth.[120] Non-figurative wall paintings have been found in the building, particularly in area VII. A possible ritual space in the two-pillared room or 'Pillar Crypt' in the west wing (VII 4) lies opposite the baetyl discovered in the Central Court (Figure 3.8).[121] Isolated prestige artefacts (in particular, stone vases) are found throughout the Palace, rather than in concentrated deposits (Figure 4.9).[122] One notable example is the stone triton found just to the north-east of the Palace.[123] As well as a scatter of tools, there

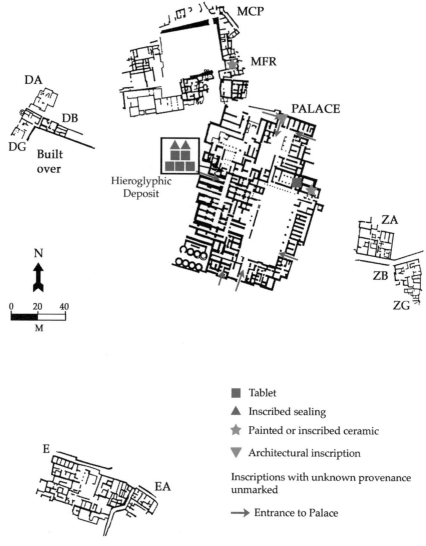

4.10 Malia, distribution of Linear A script. Adams 2004a, figure 9, reprinted with permission, *Journal of Mediterranean Archaeology* and © Equinox Publishing ltd 2004.
DA: Delta Alpha; DB: Delta Beta; DG: Delta Gamma; E: Epsilon; EA: Epsilon Alpha; MCP: Maison de la Cave au Pilier; MFR: Maison de la Façade à Redans; ZA: Zeta Alpha; ZB: Zeta Beta; ZG: Zeta Gamma.

appear to be two workshops of luxury goods in the Palace at Malia, one for ivory (IV 9–10) and one for stone vases (XVII 2). The palatial elite therefore had direct control over some of the production of elite artefacts.[124]

At Malia, the only evidence for literacy comes from the Palace, apart from a sherd with a hieroglyphic sign on it from the Maison de la Façade à Redans (Figure 4.10). The Hieroglyphic Deposit from III 8 in the Domestic Quarter contained five Linear A tablets, and a further one was discovered under the

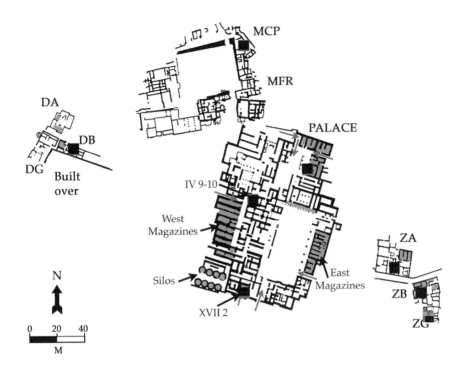

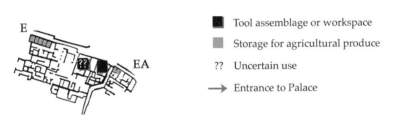

■ Tool assemblage or workspace

▨ Storage for agricultural produce

?? Uncertain use

→ Entrance to Palace

4.11 Malia, storage of staples and assemblages of tools. Adams 2004a, figure 10, reprinted with permission, *Journal of Mediterranean Archaeology* and © Equinox Publishing ltd 2004.
DA: Delta Alpha; DB: Delta Beta; DG: Delta Gamma; E: Epsilon; EA: Epsilon Alpha; MCP: Maison de la Cave au Pilier; MFR: Maison de la Façade à Redans; ZA: Zeta Alpha; ZB: Zeta Beta; ZG: Zeta Gamma.

stairs close to the 'banquet hall'.[125] No non-administrative, or ritual/ideological, uses of Linear A have been recovered from the Palace or from the rest of the town. The main storage areas in the Palace were the north magazines, the west magazines, the east magazines, and the silos (Figure 4.11).[126] If they were filled, the Malian silos would have provided the annual ration for more than 1,000 people.[127] The east magazines were also used for the storage of solid foodstuffs, as well as liquids.[128] This use of the east wing is notably different from the other

Palaces explored in this chapter. The north magazines may have served the hall in that area, as a banqueting hall. Likewise, the west half of the west wing comprises halls and storage areas, which could have been accessed directly from outside via the west entrance. Overall, the storerooms cover 1,400 m² and 15.7 per cent of the ground floor.[129]

The Malian Town

Müller's survey of the wider region has indicated that no substantial sites lay nearby (but see Sissi below).[130] Individual houses have been excavated in the town area around the Palace, and around twelve are published well enough for comment.[131] Linear A has not been found in the town (Figure 4.10). Epsilon is the largest building after the Palace (ca. 1370 m², possibly single storey).[132] Zeta Alpha and Zeta Beta are large (420 and 310 m², respectively), which is partly due to their storage areas, but Epsilon Alpha and Delta Alpha also had storage areas, and yet are much smaller (180 and 165 m², respectively).[133] The final group consists of simple houses of around 130 m² (Maison de la Cave au Pilier, Maison de la Façade à Redans, and Ayia Varvara). Some elite buildings, such as Zeta Alpha, employed ashlar masonry, but others, such as Epsilon, had little of it.[134] Evidence for painted stucco has been found in the Zeta and Epsilon Quarters, but this is non-figurative and simple. Little correlation can be discerned among size, location, and architectural elaboration.[135] The distribution of prestige artefacts is also wide, and consists mainly of stone vases (Figure 4.9).

Zeta Alpha and Delta Alpha are the only buildings that would conform to the Knossian 'grand mansion' group, with Minoan Hall and Lustral Basin (Figure 3.8). However, they differ in that they possess storage areas, and so are presumably self-sufficient, and they do not follow the standard Knossian size.[136] These formal similarities appear to allude to the style and practices of the urban elite group in the more spectacular site. There are further similarities between Maison Zeta Alpha and the Tylissos buildings (particularly Building A), such as size, a broad distinction between living/ceremonial and service/storage areas, and the presence of a Minoan Hall with Lustral Basin located nearby. Elsewhere at Malia, Epsilon provides an excellent example of a certain group of people who eschewed this set pattern, and adopted certain cultural features for their own requirements. Therefore (at least in comparison with Knossos), functions were relatively decentralized at Malia, and the grander houses formed more of a diverse group.[137] This diversity may indicate that the inhabitants of these buildings were factional elites, marking out different practices as distinctive identities.

There are urban buildings with magazines for agricultural storage, including Epsilon and Zeta Alpha (Figure 4.11). This feature is not 'palatial', therefore (or confined to Palaces). The adoption of a specific architectural design for storage indicates long-term organization based in a distinct area of the complex. There are only two buildings without any evidence for storage at all: Delta Gamma and the Maison de la Façade à Redans. Presumably, the occupants of the majority of buildings were self-sufficient. On the whole, the evidence for production is very widespread, and includes some of the grander buildings.[138]

In summary, the Neopalatial town has revealed no clear groupings or patterns concerning the non-palatial buildings, in terms of specific distribution patterns of data or how they correlate.[139] The features exclusive to the Palace are the courts and its size, and apparently administration. No palatial fresco programme promoted a strong sense of collaborative and collective identity. Other functions appear to be widely distributed throughout the site, including storage for agricultural produce and production, although the only evidence for ivory-working comes from the Palace. Formalized architectural features were adopted, but there was no regular architectural assemblage to which the inhabitants of the more elaborate, and presumably 'elite', buildings chose to conform. Evidence for the use of Linear A is generally absent in the town, but evidence for agricultural storage, production, and the use of prestige goods is widespread, with no clear correlations among size, architectural elaboration, or ceremonial practices.

The Regional Picture

It has been argued that there is not only centralization of elite features on the regional level at Malia, but also apparent monopolization (Figures 3.10, 4.6).[140] The recent excavation at Sissi demands that this generalization be qualified, although it remains to be seen exactly how. The poorly preserved Building F opened out to a large court around 10 × 20 m, the limits of which are not fully excavated.[141] It points towards Mount Selena to the south (possible significance unknown), around 15° off north. The north side has a bench set against the wall with several circular depressions carved in the west facade of the court, which is made of ashlar masonry. Buildings BA and BC provide examples of more basic but nonetheless well-built buildings where various manufacturing activities took place; a stone blossom bowl was found in the latter. The excavators present the intriguing idea that Knossos invested in Sissi in order to undermine Malian authority; this remains a hypothesis and fieldwork is ongoing.[142]

Overall, however, there remains a void of sites around Malia, in comparison with Knossos. It seems very unlikely that the Malian elite was *more* successful in terms of the centralization of both power networks and the articulation of wealth. Instead, it failed to promote the palatial institution on the site or regional level to anything like the same degree. Nor are there any important ritual sites linked to the palatial town. This is surprising, given that Malia was a flourishing Protopalatial site. The evidence is ambiguous, and scholars' interpretations are therefore changeable.

For example, Poursat has pointed out that scientific tests have not been conducted to demonstrate the provenance of possible Knossian imports, and, in any case, this would not necessarily imply Knossian political dominance.[143] He notes here the apparent absence of marine activity (i.e., imports) at Neopalatial Malia, which might be considered a reduction in power and autonomy. But later he states that: 'It is hard to escape the conclusion that Malia was a dependency of Knossos in this period, whether vassal or satellite.'[144] The LM IA rebuilding of the Palace at Malia could be said to resemble that of Knossos, which might be taken to indicate a new Knossian second-order centre.[145] While there is no way of proving or disproving this political involvement by Knossos, it is difficult to see how the evidence presented leads to this conclusion. For example, if Knossos was involved in the site, one might expect that this would be a useful additional harbour for Knossos, so the lack in maritime activity is odd. The Knossian-style grand houses might indicate imitation as much as imposition from outside. The few LM prestige goods, and the lack of frescoes and archival documents, may be due to preservation factors. Perhaps if there were rich artefacts and evidence for administrative control, it would be credited to Knossos. However, nothing changes the fact that Neopalatial Malia did not fully build on its prosperous Protopalatial background.

PHAISTOS

When we turn to Phaistos, we begin to really see how variable the palatial trajectories were – for much of the Neopalatial period, this Palace lay abandoned. There appears to be some initial reuse of the building after the great earthquake that ended the Protopalatial phase (Levi's third Protopalatial phase, or MM IIIA) or during MM IIIB.[146] There was an MM IIIA 'ceremonial building' associated with palatial functions in the west wing and north-east area, although whether this formed a central building is a matter of debate.[147] Today, one may view the Protopalatial West Court and causeways (see cover photograph). Remarkably, a substantial amount of *astraki* (*calcestruzzo* or concrete) was placed over them, so this was not a Neopalatial feature; this deposit may have been made in several layers rather than just one.[148]

Levi believed that his Protopalatial phase III was immediately followed by the rebuilding of the New Palace.[149] This degree of continuity is not clearly borne out by the evidence, and there was a long hiatus between the two main complexes.[150] The Second Palace at Phaistos does not appear to have been completed until mature LM IA or early LM IB, after a gap in occupation or a very long period of building work.[151] Most outside areas had not been completed by the time of the LM IB destruction.[152] We shall focus on this later period (LM IB), at the end of which the Palace fell out of use.[153] As with the Neopalatial Palace, the house at Chalara and probably that at Ayia Photini were constructed in the beginning of LM IB.[154]

The Protopalatial period has generally been emphasized at Phaistos, probably because it does not appear to have been so great an administrative centre in the Neopalatial era.[155] The main excavation reports are Levi for the Old Palace period and Pernier and Banti for the Neopalatial one.[156] Recent (and ongoing) fieldwork is clarifying the picture, and recent overviews of Italian participation in Cretan archaeology have been published.[157] The Palace at Phaistos was initially excavated from 1900, under the supervision of the Italian archaeological school. As an Italian site, it originally offered a counter to the British Knossos, and a challenge was set against Evans' Knossocentric interpretations of Minoan culture, culminating in Levi's revisions of the chronological framework.[158] Pace suggested the existence of a single sovereign with seats at both Knossos and Phaistos, an idea picked up by British scholars and based on the Near Eastern or Egyptian kings.[159] La Rosa has since returned to Evans' ceramic subdivisions, and Italian interpretations of the Neopalatial Mesara in south-central Crete have focused on apparent Knossian elements of Ayia Triada.[160]

Approaching the Palace

Preziosi states that, 'in contrast to the clustering pattern . . . for Knossos and Mallia . . . the organization of Phaistos is simpler and more block-like'.[161] The south-east areas of the Palace cannot be reconstructed, however, due to substantial erosion down the hill. As far as we can reconstruct the Palace, one entrance leads into each zone, and there is evidence for five certain entrances and four possible ones (Figure 4.12).[162] The three main entrances, at the north-east (53), the Propylaeum (67), and Corridor 7 have evidence for porter's lodges. The north-east entrance led into the east court (90) and the north court (48) via a corridor, and into which the possible north entrance (87) also led.

The Palace exemplifies the theatrical qualities of Minoan architecture, such as the great Propylaeum (66–9) leading from the Theatral Area in the West Court.[163] In a sense, the grandeur and open feel of this area is misleading, as access points beyond it are few and narrow, one of which leading to a single room or possible porter's lodge. The Palace was quite unusual in having direct access between the Central Court and the West Court (Corridor 7).[164] This entrance was wide and flat, allowing visibility without physical access when the doors were open, as we saw at Malia. It had both ceremonial and economic use, as it offered direct access to the Central Court, and had the means to exchange goods between outside the Palace and the west magazines (via Space 31).[165]

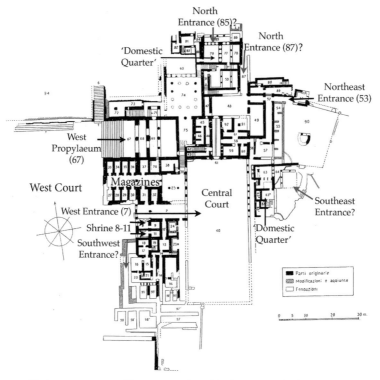

4.12 Phaistos entrances, with areas mentioned in the text marked. After Adams 2007b, figure 3, reprinted with permission, *Oxford Journal of Archaeology* and © 2007, John Wiley and Sons.

Just south of Corridor 7 at the Palace of Phaistos is Shrine 8–11, which is only accessible from outside and looks out onto the West Court.[166] Gesell labelled Room 8 the preparation room, and Room 10 a bench sanctuary, with store-rooms behind both areas. Room 8 may have been more open, as it did not have a pivot hole indicating some kind of door,[167] and Room 10 contained a libation table and figurines.[168] A similar situation was seen at Malia, whereby there is the opportunity to enter ritual space associated with palatial authority without gaining access into the main Palace itself.

The Functions of the Palace

The Palace is somewhat empty of finds, and was not particularly well preserved by a clear destruction.[169] The lack of finds does not appear to be due to later occupiers cleaning out the Palace;[170] plundering might explain the lack of prestige artefacts, but not the scarcity of pithoi or ceramics of daily use. However, the inside of the Palace appears to have been finished despite this emptiness, and many rooms had been decorated with painted plaster. Notably, especially in comparison with Ayia Triada, there are no figurative frescoes either in the MM IIIA or LM IB Palace,[171] although rooms 77–9, 81 did have wall paintings.[172] The intention of certain functions may be discerned from the architectural plan, however (e.g., magazines for storage: Figure 4.12).

The paving of the Central Court belonged to the First Palace, being reused later (Figure 3.3). While there was no further embellishment here, a significant amount of ashlar masonry was employed in the Neopalatial Palace. It has been suggested that Court 74 was a reception area,[173] or an official area,[174] and that Area 23–4 was a kind of the Throne Room.[175] The Palace has yielded a significant number of halls and Lustral Basins (Chapter 3, Figure 3.7). A substantial part of the west wing would appear to comprise magazines (Figure 4.12). Altogether, around 219 m^2 (3.1 per cent of ground floor) was set for food storage, although the remains of only eleven LM IB pithoi were found in the Palace.[176] In order to sustain the palatial group, many more pithoi would be required. In Militello's recent summary of the administration at Phaistos, he notes that a few tablets (PH 1 in 101 outside the Palace and PH 3 on the window sill of Lustral Basin 70) and sealings (from under Rooms 10 and 11) can be dated to Levi's third Protopalatial phase (MM IIIA).[177]

The Phaistian Town and Region

While the Phaistian town is very poorly understood, recent publications have shed light on pockets of it, including the house at Ayia Photini and the mansion or farm at Chalara.[178] For the MM III period, there are four known groups of houses, to the west and south of the Palace, the Chalara area, and on the western hill.[179] It may even be the case that the LM I urban remains were as rich as the Protopalatial ones, although these do not lie in the immediate vicinity of the Palace.[180] The building at Ayia Photini was not constructed particularly elaborately, such as with hewn blocks of stone, stone thresholds, paved floors, or stuccoed walls, but it contained pithoi.[181] Militello notes an LM IB tablet from Room Iota at Ayia Photini (PH 31), together with PH Zb 4–5.[182] La Rosa described this as a sacred context.[183] Chalara was more elaborately constructed, and contained pithoi, with a considerable overall storage potential.[184] Despite these examples, too little is known of the surrounding town to really set the Palace in its urban context.

Sustainable Neopalatial political restoration at Phaistos appears to have been unachievable, and aspirations were unfulfilled.[185] A similar argument was made for the case of LM IA Galatas earlier. The shift from Phaistos to Ayia Triada in the early Neopalatial period could indicate Knossian dominance.[186] La Rosa notes that the situation at Phaistos is not very compatible with the picture of LM IB decline as presented in the *Troubled Island*.[187] The rebuilding of the Palace at Phaistos in LM IB could represent local elites re-emerging or further

Knossian control.[188] To contrast the overall ceremonial tone of Phaistos too sharply with the administrative centre at Ayia Triada might be misleading given the state of the evidence.[189] The relationship between Phaistos and non-palatial Ayia Triada is explored more fully in the following chapter.

ZAKROS

This terrain is different from the area around Petras, or the other main site in the east, Palaikastro.[190] At Zakros, gorges cut into a landscape that is not so arable. It is a site that might look out to the sea more easily than into the land. Zakros was initially a harbour town, rather than a town organized around a Palace.[191] The site had neither peninsula nor offshore island, so ships were probably anchored near the shore or pulled up onto it.[192] It has one of the safest bays of eastern Crete, although the surrounding terrain renders the spot isolated.[193]

While there are paths between the buildings, there does not appear to be a clear grid system or deliberate, regular organization. Also, the buildings had to contend with the steep contours of the hill. Buildings may be aligned along a road, but they were often more haphazardly oriented. This lack of alignment indicates further that the Palace was supplanted onto the pre-existing organic town. Platon believed that the richer urban elites were situated closer to the Palace while the poorer were further away, but this division is unclear.[194]

The site was inhabited from EM onwards, and larger buildings were constructed during MM. Stratigraphically, MM III is difficult to find at the site.[195] The Palace at Zakros was built in mature LM IA or LM IB,[196] but no palatial predecessor has yet come to light.[197] It fell out of use at the end of LM IB, and two stratified destructions may be discerned from this period.[198] It therefore shares a similar history to the Palace at Phaistos, with the difference that it is not clear whether there was a Palace structure underneath this late Neopalatial one, as there was at Phaistos.[199] We will therefore focus on the later part of the Neopalatial period here.

The British School explored Zakros briefly at the beginning of the century (1901), but Hogarth failed to locate the Palace. Instead, he explored around twelve houses on the north-east or south-west hills, thus avoiding the flood-waters of the lower land where the Palace lies. House A revealed an important deposit of sealings and a Linear A tablet. A Greek team under the direction of N. Platon explored the site intensively from 1961 onwards, when the Palace was found and excavated.

Approaching the Palace

The short-lived Palace at Zakros does not possess the block-like features of some of the longer-established examples, and 'porter's lodges' do not appear to

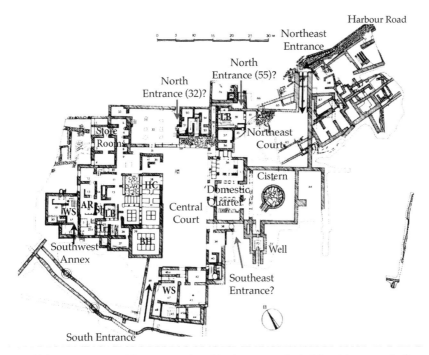

4.13 Zakros entrances, with areas mentioned in the text marked. After Adams 2007b, figure 4, reprinted with permission, *Oxford Journal of Archaeology* and © 2007, John Wiley and Sons. AR: Archive Room; BH: Banquet Hall; HC: Hall of Ceremonies; LB: Lustral Basin; Sh: Shrine?; Tr: Treasury; WS: workshops (or areas with production).

be a feature of this complex.[200] Neither were the entrances designed to 'mirror' each other, although the architectural limits are unclear, particularly in the south and east (Figure 4.13). This is the only Palace that does not have an entrance from the west.[201] The west annex was mainly used for production, possibly including dyeing fabrics, and it does not appear to have any further access into the rest of the Palace.[202] The Central Court could be accessed fairly directly from the south, via a crooked corridor. Visibility into the Palace would not have been possible from just outside it, as is the case at Malia and Phaistos. However, the Palace was set at the foot of a hill; there would have been points in the town above where the activities of the Central Court would have been visible.[203] To the west and north-west of the Palace were paved courts that appear to have gone out of use when covered by earth in the last phase, when a late drain was also installed.[204]

There were probably two ways to enter the Palace from the north, with townspeople coming through the possible entrance in 32, but the main access being via the main north-east entrance. This entrance opens from the harbour road into and overlooking the north-east court, which then led to the Lustral Basin, the west wing, or the Central Court via a corridor. The floor of

4.14 A) Zakros, north-east entrance, leading down into Palace (photograph by author); B) Zakros, view of Palace from town (photograph by author).

this route was paved with a 'red carpet' (or central stones) guiding visitors (Figure 4.14A).[205]

The Functions of the Palace

The Palace contained many riches, due to the fact that it appears not to have been plundered or occupied after its LM IB destruction. However, it was not one of the most elaborately built Palaces. Local materials were used, particularly limestone and mudbrick, while wood was available from cypress forests; no gypsum was available.[206] A limited amount of ashlar masonry was employed, concentrated on the facades of the Central Court and features such as the intriguing Spring Chamber in the eastern area, which was a 2 m deep well (Figure 4.13). This, along with the Great Cistern with a 5 m diameter, indicates special attention to water features at this site. It is notable that the area of the Palace is prone to flooding, in addition to its being a harbour site. These features make this Palace distinctive, but it is difficult to see whether these were used ritually in addition to drawing water.[207] Well-preserved olives were found in the well, which may have been offerings.[208] The hypothesis that some kind of water deity was a patron here remains appealing.

The west wing includes the archive area, a 'Treasury' (with rich prestige artefacts), a splendid hall system, and an area that the excavator, Nicholas Platon, interpreted as a shrine, centred on Room 23, which then served to support the notion of a theocratic government in Neopalatial Crete (Figure 4.13).[209] A Lustral Basin was found nearby in Room 24, but the finds from the benched Room 23 do not point conclusively to ritual, consisting of a piriform rhyton, two bronze plates that were originally part of a box, a grindstone and pottery, including cups with Double Axe decoration.[210] The treasury (25) contained a more significant ritual deposit, with many outstanding rhyta, including those shaped as bulls' heads and a lioness, a spectacular rock-crystal rhyton, chalices, ivory inlays, and bronze Double Axes.[211]

The 'Hall of Ceremonies' was a large (12 × 10 m) room with access to the so-called shrine area and the Central Court (Figure 4.13). It was subdivided, with a light-well to the north-west, and was well decorated, with decorative panelling on the floors (although wall paintings have not survived).[212] The stone Bull's Head Rhyton and the Peak Sanctuary Rhyton were found fallen from above the Hall of Ceremonies and the 'banquet hall', along with other rhyta and vessels, faience and ivory objects, sealings, and two Linear A tablets.[213] Imported raw materials for elite objects were also found, namely, three ivory tusks and six bronze ingots. The banquet hall was so called because of the number of wine vessels it contained.[214]

Elaborate halls were also found in the (poorly preserved) east wing, which the excavator interpreted as residential or living quarters, although the positive evidence for this is unclear. The justification for defining these rooms as living quarters for the royal family rests on their grandeur and comparisons with similar areas in the other main Palaces – however, this argument is ultimately circular.[215] A second Lustral Basin was found in the north-eastern area, close to the harbour road entrance. It was linked to the eastern hall system (36–7). This Lustral Basin revealed a fresco with Horns of Consecration on altar bases.

Many Linear A tablets were found in the west wing, in the 'Archive Room' (16), which the excavator states 'undoubtedly belonged to the shrine' (Figure 4.13).[216] However, we cannot demonstrate a religious authority over the complex's administrative system. The Archive Room had three high mudbrick compartments built against the south wall, supporting shelves that held the tablets.

Storerooms were also positioned in the north-western area, although these did not follow the same magazine plan as the other great Palaces (Figure 4.13). Around 165 m², or 5.7 per cent of the ground floor, was set aside for storage, and more than eighty-three pithoi have been found (along with other containers).[217] Huge, two-man bronze saws and other tools were found in the west wing. The presence of these saws suggests that damage had occurred to the building before the final destruction.[218]

There was much more evidence for production at Zakros than the other Palaces, notably in the south wing and the annex to the west (Figure 4.13). Evidence for the production of various kinds of commodities and objects was found, such as perfume, crystal, ivory and faience objects, and possibly bronze vessels and stone vases. The south wing also contained a hall, and a nearby corridor possessed wall paintings of plants; cooking equipment was also found in the area.[219] A kitchen was located in the north wing, pointing towards the hospitality that must have occurred in the complex.

The Zakrian Town

The quality of the construction of town buildings is much lower than the Palace, whereas at Knossos and Malia some of the buildings shared features with their respective Palaces. Zakros therefore witnessed a sharper divide between Palace and town (Figure 4.14B). It has been suggested that the centralized LM IB Palace suppressed the rather more liberal distribution of prestige goods and administration that had occurred in LM IA.[220] There was considerable variation in building size. The Strong Building had around eighteen spaces on its ground floor and an upper storey, while the Building of the Tower had just seven in its ground floor. The Strong Building is notable for having three separate zones, each accessed by its own entrance; the same functions appear to have been repeated in each of these 'apartments'.[221]

Overall, however, there was a standard kind of floor plan, with small storage/utility rooms arranged around a larger one that opened onto the street.[222] The settlement spread out to the south-west on the Ayios Antonios hill, where Hogarth's House A had two phases, LM IA and LM IB. The large collection of sealings and a Linear A tablet suggest that book-keeping and the movement of commodities occurred here. House B in this area was large, at 400 m², and had two entrances and staircases, a polythyron, and a possible treasury, as well as evidence for agricultural production, including wine.[223]

A great amount of obsidian has been found scattered throughout the Palace and town.[224] Small fragments of unworked steatite and partly worked pieces of prismatic objects from the same material were found scattered throughout the site, particularly in the Palace.[225] While agricultural resources (such as wine presses) have a broad distribution across the site, they do not occur in every unit. This leads to the suggestion that some people were reliant on installations that others owned, resulting in unequal access to resources or the need for some kind of bartering system.[226]

The Regional Picture

Zakros was surrounded by 'Villas' further afield, such as at Epano Zakros, Azokeramos, and Chiromandres.[227] Epano Zakros was a substantial, frescoed building, with agricultural installations and many pithoi, one of which had a Linear A inscription with twenty-six signs. Most sites appear to be farmhouses, converted from the Protopalatial 'watchtowers'.[228] While some kind of settlement hierarchy may be reconstructed for the area,[229] a main interest concerning Zakros is its relationship with Knossos.

The excavators have argued that the Palace at Zakros was an LM IB Knossian placement on the previously prosperous, but non-palatial, town.[230] Features cited in support of this include the architectural features, ceramics, administration, and stone rhyta. These cultural features are suggested to reflect 'a certain political supremacy from the centre', meaning Knossos.[231] It certainly might, but modern parallels imply that the link between culture and politics is not as clear-cut as this. It is not easy to reconstruct the various mechanisms of emulation across the island. Knossian architects and craftsmen may have been commissioned: the question is by whom. One example would be the rosso antico lamps with bent leaves, found in both Pseira and Zakros.[232] These were not necessarily both from Knossos; both objects may have been made in Zakros, by craftspeople trained in or influenced by Knossian ones. Thus we see how difficult it is to trace the relationships between Minoan centres on the basis of exchange goods alone.[233]

How can we demonstrate Knossian power, rather than mere influence, at the site? Two parallels with the Palace at Knossos are particular to this site. First, the paving of the north-east entrance is remarkably similar to that of the west entrance at Knossos (Figures 4.2B, 4.14A).[234] The short strip of paving at Zakros at this entrance provides a sharp contrast with the cobbled surface of the harbour road, whereas the Corridor of the Procession at Knossos leads more naturally from the causeway of the West Court. The Zakrian example would seem to involve the more 'token' insertion of this particular motif. It remains unclear, however, whether this was intended as an imposed 'coat of arms' or emulation of an admired, distant neighbour.

Furthermore, there is a Lustral Basin apparently in association with this entrance, with a wall painting of Horns of Consecration on altar bases. However, this Lustral Basin is not contemporary with other palatial examples at entrances. The Lustral Basins associated with entrance systems at Knossos and Phaistos fell out of use in MM III (or possibly early LM IA in the case of the south-east Lustral Basin at Knossos). There was no contemporary functioning Knossian entrance Lustral Basin when this one was built. Elsewhere, I have suggested that this apparent adoption of a Knossian practice or even religious ritual that had already fallen out of date might not indicate confident Knossian presence and/or power at Zakros.[235] Rather than being a symbol of Knossian power, this embrace of neglected past rites may indicate panic, confusion, and insecurity on the part of Knossian and/or local elites. In other words, when we witness the recommencing of rites associated with neglected authorities, they may not always indicate the straightforward manifestation of political control as generally assumed, but instead a more desperate attempt in troubled times to be *recognized* as having power. It is clear that, while this Palace may share some Knossian features, it does not possess the Knossian system.

PETRAS

Metaxia Tsipopoulou has conducted fieldwork at Petras since 1985.[236] In terms
of layout, it does not resemble the other main eastern Neopalatial settlements,
such as Gournia, Palaikastro, or Zakros.[237] However, the estimated size of
the settlement (2.5 ha) and population (500) is comparable to Gournia.[238]
The Palace was located on top of a hill, which was levelled before construction
began. This therefore contrasts with the Palace at Zakros, which lies at the foot
of the surrounding town. Zakros is not one of the more intimidating Palaces,[239]
while Petras could have made a striking impression, despite being so small.[240]
The two palatial towns also differ in that there is a sharper contrast in wealth and
prestige between Palace and town at Zakros than Petras.[241] This is perhaps
surprising, as the Petras Palace had a longer history, rather than being inserted
into a pre-existing town, and its elite had longer to build up resources to signal
social differentiation.

The actual establishment of the Palace is difficult to pinpoint, but it lies
between the MM IIB and the LM IA destructions.[242] Its largest, most important period is Protopalatial, rather than Neopalatial;[243] this in itself defies the
traditional model of ever-increasing development. These terms are somewhat
misleading in this case, however, as the first phase runs MM IIA–LM IA, while
the second renovated structure is LM IB: once again we are reminded of the
idiosyncratic trajectories of Minoan Palaces. The small, then reduced, Central
Court (see Chapter 3) led its excavator to argue for its palatial status.[244]
The Neopalatial Palace covered around 2,400 m², with four main areas,
including the Central Court. In the earlier phase, the large north magazines
offered significant storage space with thirty-six large pithoi (two with Linear
A inscriptions); they probably contained oil when the structure was destroyed
in LM IB.[245] Access to the storerooms appears to have been more open than in
other Palaces – it seems that the north magazines were even accessed from
outside the complex.[246] In LM IB, pithoi were also stored in the Central Court.
There was a west wing and an open space to the east.

It lacks many elite architectural features, such as a Lustral Basin or Minoan
Hall, and it also lacks certain elite architectural elements, such as the use of
monumental orthostates or fine frescoes – this absence is typical for the region
as a whole.[247] Two Linear A tablets were recovered from the building, hinting
at the administrative organization of goods.[248] Several hundred conical cups
were found in the space. However, it has not yielded notable prestige objects,
nor evidence for their manufacture. It fails, therefore, to conform to the general
pattern whereby northern and eastern coastal sites engaged in production, such
as Mochlos, Poros, and Zakros (see Chapter 8).

Two further complete Neopalatial buildings have been excavated, House I.1
(until LM IA) and House II.1 (until the end of LM IB: this is the only area with

clear LM IB destruction evidence).[249] As in the other palatial sites explored, different areas of the settlement experienced different trajectories. House I.1 contained an infant buried in a jar. House II.1 lay beyond House I.1 from the Palace, and possibly contained an atypical Minoan Hall from mature LM IA.[250] It had some facilities for storage, but not enough to be self-sufficient, and some 'ritual' objects, such as rhyta, bull figurines, and Horns of Consecration.[251] The building also revealed evidence for Linear A (a nodulus and inscribed sherd) and textile production. A (LM IA) lentoid seal with combat scene (two men with swords) has been found in the settlement, outside the Palace.

This is a small palatial site, with a small Palace. There is some concentration of functions in the central building, but the two excavated houses have also yielded objects of high social status. The site is unusual in having a Protopalatial Palace, and it is possible that its Neopalatial successor was not as secure and powerful (possibly like Malia), although this is conjecture. This case study is important for demonstrating how a Palace could function on a small, regional scale.

CONCLUSION

These monumental buildings speak of ultimately hierarchical societies, even if there was a strong second tier in the pyramid. They were the ceremonial and, most likely, economic centres of the settlements; the archival deposit retrieved from Zakros supports this suggestion. The combination of ideological, administrative, and economic centralization points to a strong political position within the settlement and beyond. Hierarchies may be as dynamic as any form of social structure, and control may have passed through different individuals, but that the mechanisms of power was focused on these central buildings is undeniable.

Despite the formal and functional differences between these four (or six) Neopalatial Palaces, the category of 'Palace' still holds good. Broad similarities occur between the west wings of the Palaces, but it is the Central Court that remains the most striking distinction of this Cretan phenomenon, possibly designed with square form created by the juxtaposition of the Central Court and the west wing.[252] The west wings tend to have a split function, with halls and storage to the west, and confined ritual spaces to the east. The Palace at Zakros demonstrates an archival/administrative use for this space. The east wings were more variable, organized according to local needs, and could consist of halls, meeting rooms, living quarters of various kinds, or storage.

There are also clear differences in investment, elaboration, and iconography. Knossos is not only bigger, but it is also far better built, with a distinctive fresco programme, and we can only dream of the riches it once held to judge from the quality of the Zakrian artefacts. The attention to water features at Zakros raises

the possibility that the Palaces worshipped or paid attention to different proper-
ties or even deities. Not only were the Palaces different in nature, but they also
all had different relationships with their surrounding towns (although we
cannot assess the situation at Phaistos so well).

There appear to be different kinds of non-palatial buildings at Knossos,
reflecting diversity in class, wealth, comfort, and specialism. The standardized
package of elite buildings at Knossos is little seen elsewhere; Delta Alpha and
Zeta Alpha at Malia are intriguing exceptions, but they have some differences,
such as being self-sufficient with storage areas. Possibly, the variety in elite
expression among the more elaborate mansions at Malia indicates a greater
concern with factional competition than with hierarchical conflict.
The slightly more 'elite' non-palatial buildings at Zakros do not compare;
here, the contrast between Palace and all urban buildings is particularly striking.
Competition within other social tiers at these sites therefore varied, with
standardization of grand mansions at Knossos, increased variability at Malia
and greater, rather more impoverished, homogeneity at Zakros. This may
suggest that the mechanics of competition (or factionalism) varied considerably
between the second-tier elites, as well as between the Palace and non-palatial
inhabitants.

At Knossos, this competition appears to have led to the homogeneity of
ceremonial practices (an argument not dissimilar to that of peer–polity interaction, but now at the intra–site and class levels).[253] We might expect factional
elites to possess more self-sufficiency in terms of storage, perhaps having
a surplus to redistribute among their clients, but instead there appears to have
been some level of economic dependency on the palatial elite. The factional
model assumes a certain degree of autonomy for each faction, even as they
compete among themselves for economic resources. In contrast, the variation
in the ceremonial practices of the more elaborate buildings at Malia could
represent the manifestation of different collective identities such as factions.
The self-sufficiency of the inhabitants of these buildings indicates that they
were in a stronger position to act as patrons. However, the site as a whole failed
to promote an investment in resources in the hinterland. Much of the town at
Zakros has been excavated, but there are no indications in the layout that the
town was divided into distinct groups, possibly headed by its own elite as in
factions.

All Palaces had substantial areas set aside for storage (especially Knossos and
Malia), but there is some apparent variation concerning how much this was
centralized within the Palace, with Knossos perhaps the only site able to impose
dependency on the surrounding (elite) inhabitants. There is no reason to
believe that the palatial elite provided staples for the urban elite on altruistic
grounds; rather, this process provided the opportunity for conspicuous
consumption.[254] However, the trappings of power are not unique to the

Palace, being visible throughout the (excavated) site. In contrast, the palatial elite at Malia functioned with the dignity that being a long-lived palatial institution allowed, but does not appear to have imposed such control. The urban buildings here appear to have been reasonably self-sufficient.

Given the variation in urban and regional context, as well as function, the similarity of the palatial form is perhaps surprising. Despite the different local requirements, these elites were loyal to this Cretan form, and they deliberately tapped into this island-wide identity, made, perhaps, in contrast to various 'others' (Chapter 9). The greatest distinction between these sites, in terms of the evidence left for us, is the chronological variation. As far as we can see, the heydays of the Knossian and Malian Palaces fell in LM IA, although the LM IB evidence is simply unclear. Galatas was built and abandoned in a very short period of LM IA. Yet the Neopalatial constructions at Phaistos and Zakros were mostly LM IB, and possibly never fully inhabited at the former. The urban context of each Palace was dramatically different in formal, spatial, and functional terms, while the chronological floruits were also extremely variable. To explore the impact of this, we need to explore regional overviews in the next chapter, and expand the discussion to other settlements.

CHAPTER FIVE

OTHER SETTLEMENTS AND REGIONAL GROUPINGS

I N THE PREVIOUS CHAPTER, WE SAW THAT THE MINOAN PALACES, THE most distinctive feature of Neopalatial Crete, cannot be understood without being set in their regional and island-wide context. But it is only when the full range of settlements is taken into account that we can begin to appreciate that Minoan elite (and indeed non-elite) culture is an incredibly varied phenomenon, including some elements that are not always anchored in the palatial sphere. Settlements differ in many ways: they range in size, location (notably coastal versus inland), the presence or absence of a (non-palatial) central building, the economy (e.g., based on agriculture, production, and/or trade), ritual practices, and overall monumentality and investment. This is before we note the diversity in excavation practice and state of publication. Perhaps the only feature that appears to link these Neopalatial sites, with very few exceptions such as Poros, is the perplexing lack of mortuary evidence.

This chapter focuses on sites that have been (reasonably) well excavated and published. Since the publication of *The Troubled Island*,[1] island-wide changes within the Neopalatial period have been impossible to ignore. We begin in north-central Crete, in order to flesh out the areas around Knossos and Malia, before moving west, then back round to the south-west and the Mesara plain. We then move east along the south coast, up towards the Ierapetra isthmus area, and finally explore the far eastern area. Some of the material is explored in more depth in later chapters, such as evidence for agricultural storage and administration. Ritual sites are considered in Chapter 6.

NORTH-CENTRAL CRETE

This region has been discussed in the previous chapter, as it hosts three Palaces: Knossos, Malia, and Galatas. Around them are located many other sites, which prospered during all or part of the Neopalatial period; Knossos, or its ritual site at Juktas, appears to lie at the centre of this thriving area. There are settlements that engaged in elite conspicuous consumption to the west and east of this region, such as Tylissos and Kastelli respectively. It is not necessarily the case that Knossian influence fades over distance; the routes behaved as conduits for people, objects, and information, with local centres acting as nodes. Important harbour sites also exist in the area.

Harbours around Knossos

Evans first suggested that Poros-Katsamba, which lies at the mouth of the Kairatos River, was the port of Knossos.[2] There is some evidence that the area was relatively flat and sandy in pre-modern times, which would have been suitable for the beaching of ships.[3] As discussed in Chapter 8, this trading post was also a centre of manufacturing.[4] Evidence for the wealth derived from such activities can be seen, for example, in the LM IA floral frescoes from buildings in the Psychoyoudakis plot.[5] There is not much surviving administrative evidence to explain how these activities were organized, although many seal stones have been found at the site.[6] The site is unusual in that it has yielded significant mortuary evidence.[7] Gazi lies on the western side of this region, and Evans and Hazzidakis suggested it served as a port for Tylissos.[8]

Further to the east, near the mouth of the Karteros River, lies the small town of Amnissos. The river leads, via different branches, to Archanes and Galatas. It is likely that a road led to Knossos from it.[9] A beach nearly 2 km long runs between two rocky headlands, and the islet of Monocharako would have served as a projecting reef, or may even have been attached to the mainland.[10] The sea level is now higher than in Minoan times, as is the case at other parts of the northern coast. The most important structure known here is the Villa of the Lilies, named after its frescoes. It has been described as 'a sort of royal bathing resort',[11] which is an unnecessarily specific label, and fails to account for the likely trading function of the site. The Villa was used in LM IA, with limited LM IB evidence.[12] It yielded a Minoan Hall and Lustral Basin, the latter of which was abandoned in the second phase of the building's life.[13] This 'package' has been seen at

Knossos, and, like those grand mansions, the Villa of the Lilies appears to contain no storage or production areas.

Nirou Chani

Another harbour site, to the east, was excavated by Xanthoudides in 1918–19, and re-examined by Platon in the 1940s (Figure 5.1A). The mansion has been interpreted in many different ways: a cult centre or residence of a religious functionary;[14] a private residence;[15] the seat of a local ruler;[16] and a trade distribution centre of ritual artefacts.[17] During the excavation, Xanthoudides referred to the building as 'the little Palace'.[18] This site demonstrates well the problems with ascribing specific labels to structures; it may have served as all or none of these suggestions. It is also a site that illustrates the problematic blurring between 'palatial' and 'elite'. Xanthoudides lists the following as parallels with the Palaces at Phaistos and Knossos: the wall paintings, the division of the building into different parts according to function, the court with structure, the corridors and recesses, the hall with light-well and pier-and-door partitions (Minoan Hall), the magazines with pithoi, and the plastered benches set against walls.[19] However, these are features adopted by elite Minoan architecture, and not just the Palaces.

The site lies around 14 km from Poros, and is surrounded by a coastal settlement.[20] The harbour consisted of a projecting reef, and the Vathianos River also provides a potential route inland. The mansion was built either in late MM III or early LM IA, and burned down in LM IB.[21] There is a well-laid court to the east of the building, with a structure on the southern side (Figure 5.1B). Xanthoudides compared this to the Theatral Areas at Phaistos and Knossos, while Evans drew a parallel with the raised dais in the Central Court at Malia.[22] At around 620 m², the mansion is nearly three times the size of many of the elite houses at Knossos, but significantly smaller than either the Little Palace at Knossos or Epsilon at Malia, and comparable to Buildings A and C at Tylissos. It was mostly built with ashlar masonry, and had gypsum dadoes. The south-central part of the building was particularly rich in wall paintings, which Evans reconstructed as 'sacral knots'.[23]

The building had four entrances, with a particularly fine one from the court leading straight into the Minoan Hall (Figure 5.1A). Given the considerable number of ritual artefacts found here, it is perhaps surprising that it does not have a Lustral Basin, although Gesell has suggested that Room 7 was a remodelled one.[24] Four large bronze axes were found in this room, while numerous altars were found stacked in Rooms 17 and 18. Their number and manner of storage suggest that the altars were meant to be transported for use elsewhere; similarly, the size of the axes was too large for internal use.[25] No seals, sealings, or administrative documents have been

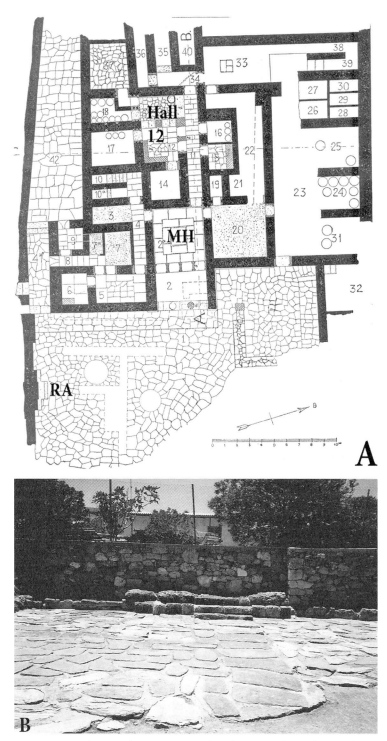

5.1 A) Nirou Chani, with areas mentioned in the text marked (after Xanthoudides 1922, Plan A). MH: Minoan Hall; RA: raised area (see 5.1B); B) Nirou Chani court and raised structure (photograph by author).

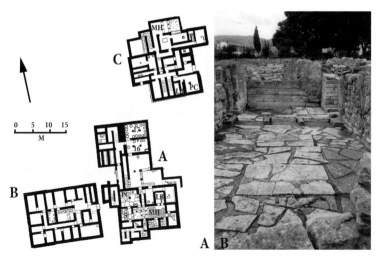

5.2 A) Tylissos, with areas mentioned in the text marked (after Hazzidakis 1934, Pl. XXXIII).
LB: Lustral Basin; MH: Minoan Hall; PC: 'Pillar Crypt'; B) House A, Minoan Hall (photograph
by author).

found at the site, and there is no evidence for production. Many pithoi were
found in the building, one of which contained carbonized seeds, and five
mudbrick bins contained beans and vetch seeds. Food and drink were
presumably consumed on or near the premises, and Koehl has compared
Hall 12 with the later *andreia*, where 'communal meals were taken by the
initiated males of each city'.[26] Such a specific parallel is impossible to
demonstrate, but the structure does appear to be the setting for feasting,
possibly of a ritual nature.

Tylissos

Tylissos lies under a modern town. While no Central Court has been found
here, it has produced remarkable elite buildings (Figure 5.2A). The source of its
ancient (as modern) wealth may be its location on a good route running
between Knossos and the west, including Sklavokambos; it is also a rich area
agriculturally. Gazi possibly served as its harbour (see above). Hazzidakis
excavated three buildings in 1909–13, which Platon re-examined in
1953–5.[27] Buildings A and C were built at the end of MM IIIB and destroyed
by fire in LM IB.[28] Traces of Protopalatial occupation have been recovered,
and the Neopalatial evidence was disturbed by later activity, especially in
Building C. Miniature frescoes were found here, but their exact provenance is
unclear.[29] Gypsum was not used at the site.[30]

Building A was a substantial building (ca. 620 m²), built of ashlar masonry and
multi-storied. The south area contained a Minoan Hall, which appears to have

functioned as both a focal point and a thoroughfare, with its numerous exits (Figure 5.2B). There was also a Lustral Basin, the floor of which was raised in LM IA. The pillared room to the north-west has been labelled a ritual 'Pillar Crypt'. However, as in many such cases, the evidence is unclear; the bronze figurine from the area probably fell from an upper floor, and there is little to justify the ritual label.[31] Area 5 contained enormous bronze cauldrons, gold foil, two Linear A tablets, and several sealings, in addition to bronze ingots and other bronze objects (Figure 5.2A). The northern area contained storerooms, notably Spaces 16 and 17. Room 15, the columned entrance hall, contained tools as well as pithoi.[32] In addition, Building B may have been a storage annex for Building A, with the two buildings possibly linked by a bridge; however, only three pithoi were actually found in it.[33] Such an arrangement may possibly imitate the Knossian pairing of the Little Palace and Unexplored Mansion. Building B contained no distinctive ceremonial areas, save a hall-like space in the centre.

Building C was similar to Building A in some ways, with its Minoan Hall and Lustral Basin, and possible Pillar Crypt (Figure 5.2A).[34] Its layout was very different, however, with the Minoan Hall set against the northern edge of the building, and the Lustral Basin to the south; this again was raised during the Neopalatial period. On the eastern side, spaces appear to have been set aside for storage, although few pithoi were found. No Linear A tablets or evidence for production was found here. If these 'Pillar Crypts' were used ritually, then this would be a distinctively Knossian feature and practice. However, this identification is questionable, and the Minoan Hall/Lustral Basin pairing (even when they are not in use simultaneously) is widespread beyond central Crete, and is therefore arguably a Minoan, rather than a Knossian, feature.

Archanes

Archanes lies on the east flank of Mount Juktas, and the Kairatos River passes Knossos on towards Poros. Because a thriving modern town now lies over the site, only restricted areas have been excavated. Initially, Evans conducted excavations there, much of which is unknown.[35] The main area excavated, Tourkoyeitonia, was renovated in LM IB after damage, and flourished in this final part of the Neopalatial period (Figure 5.3).[36] To the south was found a 'Theatral Area', with stepped altar and Horns of Consecration. This may have been related to the Tourkoyeitonia building,[37] as might the seven (probably LM IB) Linear A tablets found to the south-west.[38] Substantial storerooms were found in the Tourkoyeitonia building (Rooms 32 and 33),[39] and a cistern located nearby suggests a centrally organized water system.[40]

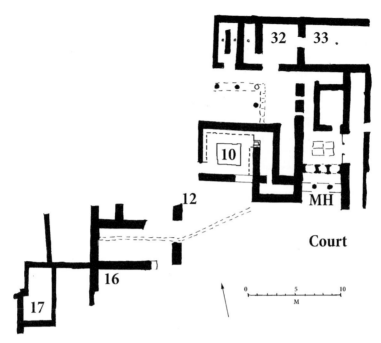

5.3 Archanes-Tourkoyeitonia plan (drawn by author, after *Archaeological Reports* 2000–1): MH: Minoan Hall.

The remains uncovered do not follow a palatial form, although a fine courtyard leads into the entrance Minoan Hall (as at Nirou Chani); the ashlar walls are very monumental, and three storeys have been reconstructed. The tripartite nature of the north side of Courtyards I and II resembles the north side of the Central Courts at Galatas and Phaistos. The width of this area is around 17 m, slightly larger than the width of the Central Court at Galatas. Four incurved altars block the east side of the entrance, and the hall had a wall painting of a woman holding a branch and a gypsum floor.[41] A separate hall area (10) contains many notable features. The centre of the room was covered by a rectangular pavement of bluish marble slabs, while a raised dais in the centre of the north wall had a depression and channel in the floor.[42] This feature is reminiscent of the Chancel Screen Hall at Knossos, particularly the one in the House of the High Priest, but the layout is idiosyncratic.

A room on the upper floor contained a vast, unique table, thirty plaster tripod offering tables, and two plaster Horns of Consecration. Furthermore, the site has yielded an astonishing number of figurines; one assemblage fell from above in Room 12, one was found in Room 16 with Horns of Consecration, and chryselephantine figurines fell from the upper floor of Room 17.[43] The wealth of ritual objects found here may be connected to its proximity to the peak sanctuary on Mount Juktas. Other prestige objects found in the building include gold sheet, a silver earring, and stone vases.

Vathypetro

The Villa, or separate buildings, was part of a small settlement located around 15 km south of Herakleion and 4 km south of Archanes. Marinatos excavated it in 1949–53 and 1955. It has not been fully published, but a recent re-examination has clarified some of the architectural and chronological issues.[44] Driessen and Sakellarakis argue that the West Building was relatively open and elaborate in the earlier LM IA phase, with access later restricted (Figure 5.4A). The East Building also belongs to this second phase.[45] The West Building is well-made, with ashlar masonry and evidence for wall paintings. Although representations of Tripartite Shrines exist, Vathypetro has the only known physical example of one at the end of a Minoan Hall (24–5), with a fragment of a Horns of Consecration found nearby (Figure 5.4B).[46] From the inside of the building, the recess is reminiscent of the Chancel Screen Halls at Knossos.[47] Room 3 contains a four-columned structure, perhaps serving as an impluvium hall. Space 17 may be a raised Lustral Basin.[48] The building had good storage space and pithoi (Rooms 10 and 40), but it did not yield evidence for Linear A.[49] The East Building was a service or industrial complex, possibly an annex to the grander one, in the nature of Building B at Tylissos or the Unexplored Mansion at Knossos.

Not all of the site was in use throughout the Neopalatial period, and there appears to be some degree of deterioration in living conditions. In this case, the later inhabitants would have been moving around the rubble of the grander period. Other, nearby settlements, such as Archanes, flourished in this later period, to add to the relative sense of decline and lost prosperity.[50] It is this kind of nuance that the increased understanding of Neopalatial dynamics allows.

Kastelli

The Pediada plain was densely inhabited during the Neopalatial period, especially 'along routes and axes that lead to the major Palaces of Phaistos and Malia, but mainly to Knossos', which Panagiotakis suggests reflects more intensive relations with Knossos.[51] Kastelli's inland location allowed trade via land if not sea, and the agricultural wealth of the area is notable. The central building found here was destroyed in LM IB, having been rebuilt in the Neopalatial period. This building was well built, with ashlar masonry and a Minoan Hall, which had a stone-built platform built across it. Rethemiotakis has noted the similarities with this design and the Chancel Screen Halls at Knossos.[52] The building was approached via a 'processional way', and contained some elite materials, such as ivory and rock-crystal inlays. A clay token with Linear A inscribed on it has been reported.[53]

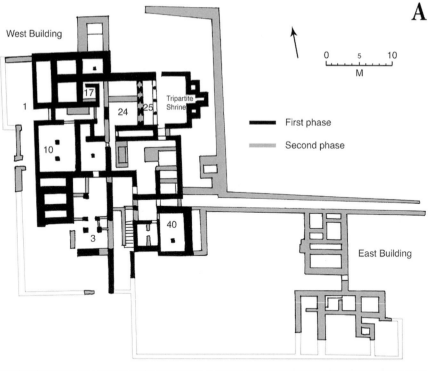

5.4 A) Vathypetro plan (drawn by author, after Driessen and Sakellarakis 1997, figure 5). B) View of Minoan Hall, from the area of the Tripartite Shrine (photograph by author).

The Regional Picture

These sites were prosperous, local focal points, demonstrating a high-level conspicuous consumption, at which Knossos excelled.[54] Their elites were able to generate substantial resources and to engage in high-level consumption (Figures 3.10, 4.6). It does not make sense to apply Thiessen polygons to the region; for example, if Archanes were to be taken as a local centre with its own polity, then a line would be drawn between Knossos and Juktas.[55] However, it is unnecessary to state that Knossos 'owned' Archanes. Evans suggested that Archanes was a 'summer Palace ... of the Priest-Kings', presumably of Knossos, whereas the most recent excavators of the site have been keen to stress its independent nature, 'Archanes, with its own centre and periphery... ', and they refer to it as a Palace.[56] It has recently been argued that Archanes is 'too rich, too large and too close to Knossos to function as a second-tier center distributing power from and sourcing goods to Knossos',[57] but it must be stressed that *nowhere* on Crete is as anything like as rich or large as Knossos.

Many of the sites would be considered 'Villa' sites, although this term has long been recognized as problematic because of the diversity in terms of location, elaboration, and function. These sites include Amnissos and Vathypetro, among others.[58] The label 'Villa' conveys the sense of localized, relative social differentiation.[59] The sites that appear to be Villas tend to be located in the Temenos region around Knossos; those further afield are more likely to be regional centres, such as Kastelli.

Power relations and site hierarchies are fluid in the Minoan world, and, given the manner in which the prosperity of sites waxed and waned within the Neopalatial period, very dynamic. Most sites and buildings in this region were occupied during MM III–LM IA, but not all continued in use in LM IB.[60] The Palace at Galatas fell out of use during LM IA,[61] and it is unclear whether the Palaces at Knossos and Malia were fully functioning in LM IB, although many other buildings at the sites had positive evidence for LM IB occupation (see Chapter 4).[62] The central building at Archanes-Tourkoyeitonia was clearly in use in LM IB,[63] as were those in other regional centres, such as Kastelli[64] and Tylissos.[65] In terms of the harbour sites,[66] positive LM IB evidence has been revealed at Nirou Chani[67] and Poros;[68] the Villa of the Lilies at Amnissos was abandoned in LM IA, although there was occupation in other parts of the settlement.

THE WEST

While the west of the island has not yielded numerous sites, it is not an empty landscape, and some of the 'blanks' may be due to lack of investigation rather than actual absence of material. Chania is a remarkable site, while others, such as Nopigia, Nerokourou and Stylos, help to fill in the landscape.[69] These all lie on the northern part of the area; to the south, the colossal White Mountains provide much less welcoming terrain. Nerokourou was a Villa with a Minoan Hall and an upper story. It was damaged by bulldozing, but revealed evidence for three architectural phases.[70] 'Reduced circumstances' have been noted for the last stage, comparable with Vathypetro.[71]

Chania

Clearly an important site, and probably a palatial one, the location of the central building here remains unproven. Windows have been explored in what is now a flourishing town. Despite these logistical difficulties, several Neopalatial architectural phases can be discerned.[72] Elite architecture has been found, but it is debatable whether it was 'palatial', as the excavator suggested.[73] Andreadaki-Vlazaki justifies this label on the grounds of the following evidence: 'the Linear A archives, the palatial features in the architecture, the emphasis on ceremonial and cult areas, the scenes on seal impressions, and the mason's marks'.[74] Important Linear A archives have been found at the site, which amount to more than 100 fragments of clay tablets, 124 roundels, and twenty-eight nodules.[75] Certainly, the Linear A archive suggests an important site, but, like Ayia Triada, it may not be palatial, in possessing the form of a Palace. These features do not, in themselves, demonstrate the presence of a Palace, but the location, Linear A archives, and link with Kydonia in the Linear B tablets do make the theory attractive. Nor can the iconography help establish whether there was a Palace here. The Master Impression from Chania (Chapter 9) appears to be a strong statement of power and authority, although the nature of this is unclear.

House I in the Ayia Aikaterini area was an impressive elite complex, with two storeys, a Minoan Hall, storerooms, and Linear A tablets, but it cannot be described as a Palace architecturally (yet): Figure 5.5.[76] The Master Impression comes from this area. Most of the Linear A tablets, however, came from the Katre no. 10 plot, which possibly served as an administrative centre.[77] The Daskalogianni excavation revealed a large complex, with significant storerooms in magazine style, a Lustral Basin, a Minoan Hall, and architectural elaboration such as ashlar masonry, plastered walls, and an impressive entrance.[78] The only Lustral Basin found in west Crete so far comes from this site, which was destroyed by earthquake in LM IA, when the area was filled.[79] A substantial hall was found nearby, with an associated platform. A number of conical cups were found in the building, in pits or sunken floors. Some were associated with animal bones, and this has been ascribed to a series of events involving feasting.[80] The excavator believes that the end of the LM IB

5.5 Chania, Ayia Aikaterini Square, looking east towards Minoan Hall (photograph by author).

period here fell later than in central Crete, as may be the case at other sites, such as Mochlos, Palaikastro, Malia, and Kommos.[81]

THE MESARA

During the Protopalatial period, site numbers increased from seven to thirty-eight settlements,[82] and it seems clear that the Palace at Phaistos provided the main focal point for the region. The Phaistos survey has established that the immediate hinterland of the Palace reached its greatest size in MM IB–II (at least 55 ha).[83] There were possible parallel developments between Phaistos and Ayia Triada during the Protopalatial period, with common interests and complementary functions, but MM IB–II Ayia Triada was probably a satellite centre of Phaistos.[84] It is clear that the history of Phaistos is entwined with that of Ayia Triada. The number of Neopalatial settlements in the area appears to have dropped and reduced in size, becoming farm-sized; the Kommos area witnessed a similar picture.[85] However, some areas of less desirable land were taken over for agricultural use. Given that there seems to have been a population decrease, there may have been political rather than demographic reasons for this, with the emergent elite demanding a surplus.[86]

Sites other than Phaistos, Ayia Triada, and Kommos flourished in the Mesara during the Neopalatial period, such as the 'Villa' from Mitropolis-Kannia on the eastern side and some distance north of the coast. It would therefore have benefitted from lying close to the main route between the Mesara and Knossian area.[87] It was in use throughout the period, and destroyed by fire in LM IB, with parts reused in LM III. It had ashlar masonry and undecorated plaster, and there is little Neopalatial evidence for ritual, unlike the figurines deposited during later use, and no evidence for administration. It did, however, contain a substantial amount of space for food storage, around one third of the ground floor.[88] Pitsidia is another fine Villa set around a central hall, and the building was large enough to require two separate staircases. It was built over LM IA structures, and destroyed at the end of LM IB.[89] During the Neopalatial era, the role of Knossos also looms in the background (or, for some scholars, the foreground). We will consider two sites in detail, Ayia Triada and Kommos, before turning to the regional picture and relations with Knossos.

Ayia Triada

Like Phaistos, the early excavations at Ayia Triada were published posthumously by those not involved in the excavation.[90] There have been several phases of excavation under the Italian School, including 1902–14 (Halbherr), 1934–6 (Pernier), the 1970s (Laviosa and Levi), and 1977–99 (the Italian School, including La Rosa).[91] It has been suggested that, in the Bronze Age, the coast lay further inland and so closer to the site.[92] Ayia Triada was easily reached from Phaistos via the route along the Ieropotamos River, and it had easy access either towards Kommos or towards the north-west (Figure 5.6). Watrous points out that the 'Villa' has been variously identified as a Palace, a grand Villa, or even a royal summer residence for the ruler at Phaistos.[93] Banti rejects the latter idea,[94] and points out that it is based on the apparent wealth (e.g., rich finds, wall paintings) of Ayia Triada in comparison to Phaistos, a situation which is probably a result of circumstances of survival.[95]

The chronological fine-tuning of recent work has allowed a far more complicated picture to be painted than the earlier excavators could have envisaged.[96] The Villa Reale (Royal Villa) was founded at or before the end of MM III,[97] coinciding with the interruption of building activity in the Palace at Phaistos, i.e., the break following Phaistos phase III.[98] MM III ceramics are plentiful at Ayia Triada, the architectural remains less so, but it seems that the site really transformed in MM IIIB.[99] In contrast to the evidence from the Palace at Phaistos, La Rosa describes a destruction layer that occurred during LM IA; Puglisi also describes two LM IA phases and one dating to LM IB. Immediate reoccupation of the site is assumed after this destruction (by earthquake and fire).[100] Recent research has established five distinct ceramic phases from the end of MM III to the end of LM I.[101]

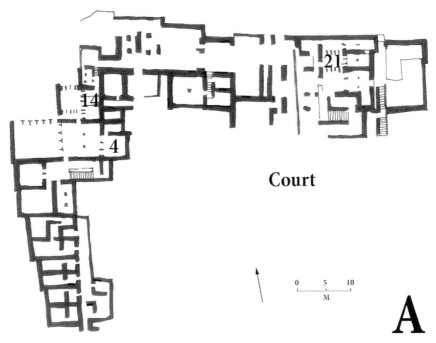

Court

0   5   10
M

A

5.6 A) Ayia Triada, Neopalatial 'Villa' plan, with areas mentioned in the text marked (drawn by author, after Halbherr, Stefani, and Banti 1980, pull-out; Watrous 1984, figure 1; Driessen and Macdonald 1997, figure 7.58). B) Ayia Triada view, with court to left (photograph by author).

The Muraglione was built only at an advanced stage of LM I; against it was then set the Casa del Lebete.[102] This picture apparently runs against that of the *Troubled Island*;[103] there is no visible evidence for the Theran eruption having a direct impact on the region, and Ayia Triada continued to flourish after the event.[104] There was no single LM IB destruction horizon across the site.[105] The Villa was destroyed before some other units, such as Casa del Vassoio Tripodato. It was later disturbed by an LM III complex, but it has yielded much evidence for a flourishing Neopalatial central building.

There were courts at the site (Figure 5.6A), but no palatial Central Court – the 'Royal Villa' is, at best, half a Palace according to the architectural definition (as is the case at Gournia). However, some have used this terminology, such as Evans ('Palace' or 'small Palace'), Van Effenterre ('villa royale' or 'manoir'), and Platon ('palais d'été'); Graham ('seasonal residence for the rulers of Phaistos'): the sense is of a lesser estate of a VIP, who was probably based elsewhere.[106] The 'elsewhere' in this case was initially assumed to be Phaistos, but now some feel that this would be Knossos (see later).

The L-shaped complex appears to be one structure, rather than two separate ones,[107] and it had an upper storey (Figures 5.6A, 5.6B). There may have been an LM IB Propylon serving as a monumental entrance to it.[108] The two wings appear to be different in nature, however. Militello, in an assessment of the administrative evidence, argued that the north-west quarter was open to the public, while the east was more private and residential.[109] It was extremely finely built, with rich wall paintings. The surviving hall systems are particularly impressive, and its contents are unusually rich. Around 41 per cent (723 m²) of the ground floor was for storage (increasing in the LM IB period) and evidence for around eighty-eight pithoi and pitharakia survives – there is evidence for the accumulation of staple surpluses.[110] The Villa contained the most impressive Linear A archive (along with the Casa del Lebete; see Chapter 7).

Important cultic activities probably occurred in the complex, a hypothesis supported by the frescoes.[111] In particular, the small area 14, located close to the halls in the west area, has been associated with cult; among the frescoes is a woman identified as a goddess or priestess.[112] It is unclear whether these areas are specifically cultic.[113] Objects that may be defined as ritual are often fallen from the upper story, and therefore difficult to match with the architecture.[114] Most notable are the stone vases, such as the Boxer Rhyton, and also some figurines from the south-west area. Certain architectural features, such as the Lustral Basin, are absent at the site.[115] Some portable objects, such as libation tables, have also not been found. Hall 21 was a fine Minoan Hall, and Hall 4, with its benches and fine architectural detail, would have served as a good meeting place.[116] Residential areas were probably based on the upper floor.[117] The surrounding settlement is very small, which renders the grandeur of the Villa all the more striking. There is the suggestion of military might as well, with a concentration of weapons in the south-western quarter of the building.[118]

The Casa del Lebete was considerably smaller than the Villa, and poorer architecturally in terms of construction and design; it contained only one nondescript hall.[119] Given the small size of the structure, however, the storage potential is exceptional, providing eighty-two months' worth of food for five adults.[120] The Casa del Lebete contained a deposit of Linear A tablets in Room 7, with a heap of broken pottery, a bronze tripod basin, and a clay bathtub, as well as some fine LM IB decorated pottery, one imitating LH (Late Helladic) IIA ware.[121] It may have been some kind of extension of the Villa.[122] A 'Bastione' functioned as a storage area, and beyond this lay the village.[123] The Tomba degli Ori and adjoining area may have been used for funerary practices.[124] A ritual function has been stated for the LM IB Complesso della Mazza di Breccia, located in the area of the necropolis.[125] Overall, this is a small site with a remarkable combination of well-built buildings.

Kommos

This harbour site flourished during the Neopalatial period, and experienced a different trajectory from both Phaistos and Ayia Triada (Figure 5.7). Fieldwork at Kommos has been Canadian-led since 1976, and has been exemplarily published.[126] Evidence for contact with the east is present, although this peaks after the Neopalatial period.[127] The east–west road separates the civic buildings from the domestic structures, and serves as the main thoroughfare (more than 2.6 m wide).[128] Architecturally, the Neopalatial site is most marked by Building T, built in the early (MM III) part of the era. The facade is remarkable, and contains the largest known stone blocks from Bronze Age Crete.[129] The impressiveness of the facade is highlighted by the very few entrances into the complex, which also makes it difficult to access, even unwelcoming.[130] This structure has been described as 'palatial'.[131] It faces a rectangular court (nearly 29 m by more than 39 m), although it lacks the strict palatial plan. Its excavators point out that Building T is more than three times the size of the Palace at Gournia and almost four times that of Petras, and yet the surrounding town is not that large.[132] The court's surface comprised a 20 cm layer of sea pebbles, occasionally combined with plaster.[133] The stoas, to the north and south of the court, were unusually deep (around 5.2 m and 3.25 m).[134] The western side is poorly preserved, but special attention was given to other areas, such as the northern facade with the north stoa.

The eastern wing is poorly understood. LM III Building P, built in the same area, appears to have been ship sheds, but this structure had much more suitable earth floors than the plaster floors of Building T. Building T received major

5.7 Kommos (photograph by author).

damage during the Neopalatial period, with reuse concentrated in the stoas, particularly to the south of the court with the LM IA kiln.[135] This previously grand space was therefore put to industrial use. The site has not yielded an overwhelming amount of Neopalatial ritual ceramics and/or figurines; those that have been found generally date to before or after the Neopalatial period – for example, the shrine in X7 dates to LM II.[136] Early LM IA plaster tables from the south stoa area may have been ritual or serving trays.[137] Overall, this is an enigmatic and unusual site, with evidence for use throughout the Neopalatial period, if witnessing major changes in function.

The Regional Picture (and Knossos)

Our focus remains on the 'Great Minoan Triangle' of Phaistos, Ayia Triada, and Kommos.[138] Located so close together, their very different trajectories were clearly intertwined. Their floruits vary widely, and they illustrate how the unit of 'Neopalatial period' presents a misleading impression of homogeneity.[139] The LM IB destructions at Phaistos and Ayia Triada fit the traditional account, but before this all is in flux. Not only does it seem that power shifted between Phaistos and Ayia Triada, but also, during one early part of the Neopalatial period, when Kommos' Building T was in use, neither of these two inland sites had a functional monumental building.[140] The intriguing suggestion that Kommos Building T served as a 'Palace' for commercial purposes, rather than the standard religious and residential ones,[141] is helpful in that it opens the concept of 'Palace' to being much more fluid and dynamic than the standardized architectural form would suggest. However, the excavators also point out that the stark contrast between the substantial, elaborate Building T and the moderate town around it may imply that it served as a hub established by those controlling the Mesara more widely.[142]

There is a consensus that non-monumental Ayia Triada was a satellite site of Phaistos during the Protopalatial period (MM IB–MM II),[143] but Neopalatial regional dynamics were clearly more complex. The establishment of the Villa at Ayia Triada in MM III paints a totally different picture, and there is less agreement about the implications of this. Historiographically, the views of the Italians have changed considerably regarding the relationships between the Mesarian sites. Halbherr viewed Phaistos as above Ayia Triada on the settlement hierarchy.[144] This interpretation was made on the assumption that the Palace at Phaistos would have been a fully functioning institution through the Neopalatial period.[145] Banti, responsible for publishing the initial excavations many decades later, also argued that Phaistos had the primary role in the region.[146] While there are those who have supported this view in more recent years,[147] the long period of abandonment in the Palace is highly problematic.

Initially, La Rosa took the view that 'it seems unlikely that the ascendancy of Haghia Triadha occurred at the expense of, or without the consent of, the managers of the Palace [of Phaistos]'.[148] He argues for interdependence rather than decentralization – although it seems that Ayia Triada flourished independently *after* the Neopalatial period, in a power transfer. Later, La Rosa suggested that LM IB Phaistos was the ceremonial centre, but Ayia Triada remained the administrative and economic centre.[149] More recently still, he has argued that Ayia Triada was heavily influenced (or controlled) by Knossos during the periods that Phaistos was out of use. Moreover, even when the new LM IB Palace was built at Phaistos, it was still of 'limited function'.[150] This would suggest that the main seat of the region did not simply pass between the two sites, but that the relationship was even more complex.

Others have suggested that the LM IA Theran eruption triggered a period of Knossian control over much of Crete.[151] Watrous states that, stylistically, the finest LM I clay vessels found at Ayia Triada appear to be imports from Knossos,[152] but Van de Moortel, on the basis of the pottery, has not been able to detect positive evidence for this hypothesis.[153] Cucuzza concluded from the masons' marks that LM IA architectural renovations on the Royal Villa and the Casa Est were carried out by two teams, one local, one Knossian, but this still does not demonstrate Knossian political involvement.[154] La Rosa suggested that the restoration of Phaistos and the new foundation at Zakros represent the weakening of the control of the central band of the island and the opening of an eastern option for Knossos.[155] In other words, Knossos transferred its trading interest from the south-west to the east. In LM IB, great investment was poured into the nearby site of Phaistos, which would presumably indicate the weakening of Knossian power, if the abandonment of Phaistos indicates Knossian strength in LM IA. However, Ayia Triada is also flourishing in LM IB, so we do not appear to be witnessing tipping scales, with the power shifting from one to the other.

Not all agree with the idea that Ayia Triada was essentially a Knossian site; local agents, for example, could have shaped regional dynamics.[156] It has been suggested that there was a collective rather than a hierarchical structure in the Mesara;[157] this would fit in either with the idea of Knossian interference in the region or its independence. However, there is no need to interpret these monuments as evidence for non-hierarchical social structures; at the end of the day, access to them was clearly controlled, and this implies unequal opportunities and hierarchy.

THE SOUTH COAST

Myrtos-Pyrgos

The site benefited from a coastal position near the mouth of the river Myrtos, while an inland route led north to the Lasithi mountains, and, beyond that, Malia.[158] Gerald Cadogan excavated the LM I 'country house' in the 1970s, which is perched on a small, steep hill overlooking the nearby coast (Figure 5.8). This construction follows a curious MM III hiatus,[159] and it burned down in LM IB. It was finely built with the use of gypsum and coloured stones in the courtyard, but it did not possess some other standard elite features, such as a Lustral Basin.

The entrance is via a veranda, as at Sklavokambos.[160] It had a pleasant hall with gypsum bench, and a shrine may have been located on the upper floor. This 'shrine' assemblage includes clay tubular stands, two clay nodules, two Linear A tablets, a faience conch shell, a bronze rosette, and pieces of two early reworked Egyptian stone vases.[161] One of the Linear A tablets records ninety units of wine, which implies feasting. By being in a position to organize such large amounts, the Villa's inhabitants could also reassert their social position. The storage facilities (Rooms 8 and 9) contained pithoi and jars, but these were not of a significant size.[162] Less is known of the

5.8 Myrtos-Pyrgos, view from court to 'Villa' (photograph by author).

surrounding settlement, but a street system followed the hill's contours to the Villa.

Makrygialos

Sites in the eastern region tend to be located to the north or east. Makrygialos, on the south coast, is therefore unusual, but not completely isolated.[163] Like Myrtos-Pyrgos, it was excavated in the 1970s, by Costis Davaras. In form and function, Makrygialos has been compared to Gournia (Figure 5.9).[164] The central building has yielded evidence for a single LM IB phase.[165] It is an oddity: the quality of construction is rather modest, but it is sizable (ca. 630 m^2) and has a small 'central' court (6 × 12.5 m), which provides access to the building via the south-east entrance corridor. While this is much smaller than the main Palaces, it was adorned with porticoes and an 'altar' on the north side.[166] A sizable hall with central column (16) lay in the east wing, while Room 10 in the north wing was the only one with a paved floor. As tripod cooking vessels were found here, it may have been a banquet room; the space appears to have been surrounded by storage rooms (7–9, 22), which would support this identification. However, the overall storage potential was moderate, and unable to support any notable surplus.[167]

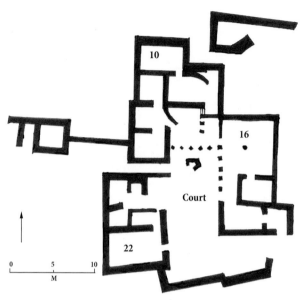

5.9 Makrygialos 'Villa' (drawn by author, after Davaras 1997, figure 2 and Mantzourani 2012, figure 12.1).

Room 22 in the west wing had benches, and may have functioned as a further meeting room. Not many prestige artefacts were reported, and the site (like Myrtos-Pyrgos) is not fully published. The pottery is being re-examined. Much of it was imported, so it may shed light on the consumption, rather than the production, of this material.[168] A female bronze figurine was found, possibly with her genitals represented.[169] This would be a rare example of attention being drawn to the sexuality or nurturing roles of the female body. There is, however, little overall to suggest that this building, destroyed in LM IB, was a 'cult-villa'.

The Regional Picture

To the west of Myrtos-Pyrgos lay other settlements that may have been of similar rank; two separate buildings were found near Chondros, and one at Kephali Lazana had ashlar masonry.[170] Further west still, on the way to Galatas or the western Mesara, lies Skinias, a single-phase LM IB building of ca. 250 m², which yielded more than 900 vases, including 650 conical cups.[171] This scattering of semi-prosperous habitation may have been linked by the rich site at Kato Syme, the great, if isolated, ritual focal point in the area (Chapter 6). At some distance to the east, beyond the Ierapetra Isthmus, lies the rather isolated site of Makrygialos. Both Myrtos-Pyrgos and Makrygialos are settlements that possessed a central building, rather than a series of elite structures. However, there is little sense of regional identity or territoriality in this part of

Crete. To the east, in particular, it is difficult to carve the island up according to terrain or cultural markers.

MIRABELLO BAY AREA

This region has been extremely well explored, particularly by the Americans. Recent survey projects at Vrokastro, Kavousi, and Gournia have located a number of LM I sites.[172] However, there was also some reduction in the number of sites from the Protopalatial period, which suggests centralization or depopulation. For example, Vrokastro witnessed an overall reduction in site numbers, with no indication of an increase in site size (Chapter 8).[173] The region does not possess a full Palace. The half-Palace at Gournia provided the most important focus in the region, but there were many other flourishing towns as well, particularly Pseira and Mochlos. Other important settlements in the area not discussed in detail include Priniatikos Pyrgos.[174] Smaller sites have also been excavated, such as the farmstead at Chalinomouri, described as a rural outpost of Mochlos.[175]

Gournia

Gournia was another of the sites excavated at the dawn of Minoan archaeology, with work beginning in 1901. It stands out for two main reasons: the excavator was a woman, Harriet Boyd (Hawes), and she excavated most of the town, rather than simply focusing on the central building (Figure 5.10). She also produced her discoveries in a very prompt and (for the time) thorough publication in 1908. Costis Davaras and Jeffrey Soles conducted further work in the 1970s–1980s, while the most recent activity has been Vance Watrous' fieldwork, ending in 2014. The settlement is located in an area with some arable land and a permanent source of water, and it is in a strategic position at the junction of the north–south and east–west roads.[176] The nearby coast provided a fair-weather harbour. The harbour area possessed walls with towers, what appears to be a large ship shed, and a road that links coast to town.[177]

The residential area of Gournia was only around 2.5 ha.[178] Most of the material dates to the LM IB destruction, and Hawes believed that the entire 'Palace' was LM only, although very recent investigations have pushed this back to MM IIIA.[179] Its central building is often referred to as a 'Palace',[180] although not all agree with this title.[181] A contrast is often made between sites like Gournia and the 'Big Four' (Knossos, Malia, Phaistos, and Zakros), but there is no reason why a site should not be second rank in an island-wide context *and* locally perceived as palatial. This complex is much smaller than the main Palaces and there is no evidence for extensive administration; however,

5.10 Gournia, view of town (photograph by author).

the 2012 excavation revealed a fragment of a Linear A tablet, and seals and sealings were found in the west wing.[182] Notably, its 'central' court unites the building with the town, as West Courts would usually do, and the court does not follow a purely rectangular plan (Figure 5.11).[183] Strictly speaking, it is not architecturally a 'Palace', but it contains palatial elements.

A small court lay to the west of the Gournian 'Palace' (Figure 5.12). Just outside the south–west area of the central complex lay a further, very small space, which contained a kernos and baetyl.[184] Architects sought to make the structure distinctive; ashlar masonry was added to the most visible areas of the Palace (e.g., the south facade) in LM IB.[185] The steps leading up at this point may have deliberate echoes of the Theatral Areas of the grander Palaces, and Horns of Consecration were found in the north portico. It possessed halls and a Lustral Basin, while storage areas and possibly workrooms were located in the west wing.[186] The changes introduced in LM IB have been described as a 'Knossian remodeling' that occurred in line with similar interventions at MM IIIA Galatas, LM IA Ayia Triada, and LM IB Zakros.[187]

The streets, following the contours of the hill, were paved with cobbles and equipped with gutters, which implies some degree of civic organization. Very few elite (or 'palatial') features were found in the town, and they appear to be concentrated on House Ha, the structure located to the south of the 'Palace' on

5.11 Gournia, view to Palace (photograph by author).

the west side of the court. It has been suggested, partly due to their ashlar facades and location, that Houses Ha and Hb were an extension of the central building, linked by a floor (or bridge) covering the paved road dividing them.[188] However, the nature of this road suggests that it was exposed to the elements. Rhyta appear to be distributed throughout the town, but it is not clear whether they all had a ritual function. The ritual use of an LM III 'shrine' to the north of the Palace should not be projected back to the Neopalatial period. Overall, the level of investment in elite features throughout the town is much lower here than in most of the main palatial sites, including Malia, located not far to the west.

Evidence for industries, such as bronze-working and textiles, is fairly evenly spread throughout the site.[189] For example, seventeen buildings revealed evidence for bronze-working (the tools at least – whether it occurred at that spot is a different matter), eighteen structures for ceramic production, fourteen houses for textile production, and fifteen houses for stone vase making.[190] Such intense activity in manufacturing may be due to the site supplying the immediate hinterland and further afield in the Mirabello area. Evidence for trade, such as stone balance weights, supports this view. The LM IB period may have become more centralized in economic terms, however, with the consumption of elite objects focused on the Palace.[191]

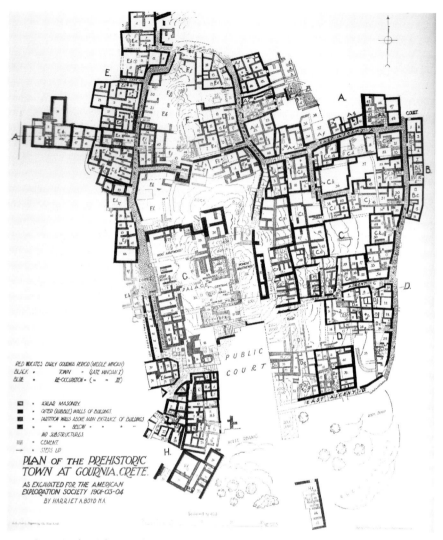

5.12 Gournia plan (after Boyd Hawes 1908, 27).

Pseira

Richard Seager explored Pseira at the beginning of the twentieth century, while Philip Betancourt and Costis Davaras have done so more recently.[192] The small island was heavily landscaped in order to maximize agricultural use,[193] and its position lent itself to trade. Opposite the island, situated on the mainland, was another port at Tholos. The street system indicates communal projects, but there is no clear central building (Figure 5.13). The standard plan indicates the LM IB town with around sixty buildings, although an earlier LM I phase is discernible on the ground.[194] Furthermore, two separate LM IB phases have been identified.[195] Evidence for literacy is limited (merely two

5.13 Pseira town (photograph by author).

pithoi inscriptions),[196] although it was likely to have been a flourishing trading post.

The Plateia Building is the largest on the site (ca. 360 m²), but it is probably misleading to describe it as a reduced Palace.[197] While it is slightly larger than the Villa at Myrtos-Pyrgos, the latter site has a much clearer contrast between the Villa and the surrounding settlement. However, the location of the Plateia Building is notable, fronting the public court with megalithic masonry and a portico (as at Gournia, and other sites), and so are the frescoes. These features support the notion that the structure belonged to a successful set of people, and that a semi-ranked society occupied the site – egalitarian overall, but with some rather more equal than others. An alternative suggestion is that it was a communal building, with a focus on ritual meals.[198] A kernos was found in the plateia.[199] The similarities with the central building at Gournia in terms of the relationship with the court should not detract from the fact that these sites and buildings are of different ranks in terms of investment and elaboration.

Building BC (the 'Building of the Pillar Partitions') also stands out, with its Lustral Basin and pier-and-door partition. Building AC may have been a shrine; it produced frescoes of ladies in the Knossian style,[200] and a collection of rhyta fell from the upper storey of AF.[201] There seems to be a wide distribution of ritual objects, such as rhyta and triton shells, throughout the site. Stone vessels were made at the site, and there is evidence for an obsidian workshop,[202] but all pottery was imported. Betancourt notes that the domestic ceramics from Area B shared shapes and fabrics with other sites of the area,

5.14 A) Mochlos islet, view from mainland (photograph by author; B) Mochlos, Building B2 (photograph by author).

namely, Gournia and Mochlos.[203] The only Knossian pottery found is LM IB, not earlier or later, and representation of the Knossian Special Palatial Tradition is a tiny fraction of the total known from the site, at 0.01 per cent.[204] This may be relevant in assessing Knossian influence at the site.

Mochlos

Seager excavated the islet of Mochlos near the beginning of the twentieth century, and Soles and Davaras began new fieldwork in 1989, particularly on the coastal areas, but also on the island (Figure 5.14A).[205] The coastal plain had a sandstone quarry, serving Gournia as well as Mochlos.[206] The islet, where most of the town was based, was probably connected to the mainland in Minoan times. It flourished throughout the Neopalatial period, particularly in LM IB, and also enjoyed off-island contact.[207] Narrow lanes linked the buildings, and no clear central structure has been found. Building B2, one of the larger ones, had ashlar masonry and possessed a Minoan Hall and benched hall (Figure 5.14B).[208] It has been suggested that this complex was constructed partly in order to honour ancestors, with the framing of Prepalatial remains where offerings could be made.[209] Such practices may have occurred, but it remains unclear whether this makes Mochlos a 'religious centre', to which people in the surrounding countryside made pilgrimages.[210]

Workshops were situated on the coast opposite the islet, a further example of the common relationship between harbours and manufacturing (see Chapter 8). Soles suggests that an extended artisan family occupied each building,[211] and minor shrines associated with the workshops may indicate a request for divine protection for their work.[212] The pottery from this area and Chalinomouri suggest that areas of Mochlos were still occupied after the LM IB destruction at Pseira.[213] Indeed, certain ceramic shapes occurring here (and at Pseira) overlap with central Cretan LM II, but there are no pure LM II shapes that would prove this definitively.[214] It may simply be that 'LM IB' should be viewed as a longer period than previously thought. This uncertainty regarding which period assemblages fit into, and whether there is a clear, even horizon across the island, demonstrates further that our idea of a single, coherent, and homogeneous 'Neopalatial period' needs to be broken down. It is also a reminder of the limitations we have in attaching ceramic phases to socio-political developments.

The Regional Picture

As in the case of Ayia Triada, the lack of a strict palatial form may not have prevented central buildings in the area being perceived as 'palatial' in terms of authority. In contrast with the sites on the south coast with clear central buildings, the coastal towns of Mochlos and Pseira give a more egalitarian impression with several prosperous buildings. But in terms of town planning, architectural features, and artefacts, they do not differ widely from Gournia. Watrous has painted a picture of local abandonments and destructions, probably caused by violence on a local level, during the Protopalatial period.[215] Out of this, Gournia emerged the 'winner', the centre for the Mirabello region. The palatial elements of the Gournia settlement may suggest an ideological hold over the wider area. Soles has argued the case for a small Gournian polity,[216] but it is impossible to demonstrate political and economic control.

   Soles has emphasized the close relationship between Gournia and Mochlos; for example, both use the same sandstone in architecture and a similar pottery style.[217] In contrast, Betancourt, excavator of Pseira, has emphasized the island's Knossian links, arguing that the island was essentially a seaport for the latter.[218] His reasons are based on cultural changes, 'deep-seated alterations in basic ways of living and thinking'.[219] But in fact they are grounded on the presence of certain types of material culture. The conical cup is adopted, replacing the carinated cup favoured at Pseira in the Protopalatial period. But the latter is unpopular throughout Neopalatial Crete, and not just Knossos – tastes changed across the island. Actual Knossian imports should not be of surprise, as they presumably bore some kudos for their owners. This includes the Knossian-style rhyta, which in themselves do not demonstrate that a specifically Knossian practice was being performed at the site. The presence of bull imagery may be significant, given the persuasive argument that this was a symbol of Knossos, but this point is unclear as it occurs on non-Knossian pottery.[220] Emulators would also seek frescoes based on the Knossian style, but their presence does not prove Knossian control. Likewise, elements of elite architecture at the site, such as pier-and-door partitions and the Lustral Basin, are Minoan, not specifically Knossos.

   These architectural elements cannot be used to suggest Knossian influence or control. There is nothing to suggest that a distinctively Knossian mind-set was operating at the site, although Knossian traders may still have had an interest in the harbour. Knossian characteristics found at sites such as Gournia have also been ascribed to emulation along the lines of peer–polity interaction.[221] In contrast, rhyta hoards are not a feature at Mochlos, and there is less imported LM IB Knossian pottery.[222] The latter may be because of the presence of a thriving pottery industry at the site. It may also suggest more resistance to buying into the Knossian (or north-central Cretan) package than seen at Pseira, or both. The overall focal point of the region is undoubtedly Gournia, however, which is the only one with an unambiguous central building. While this was not a fully-fledged Palace in form, it may still have been considered palatial from the perspective of those living in the region.[223]

THE EAST (NORTH AND CENTRAL)

The east of the island is well explored in both excavations and surface surveys, such as the Minoan Roads Network project.[224] The latter discovered a series of defensive structures or farmsteads over certain routes (Chapter 6; see also Chapter 8). Zakros and Petras have already been discussed; a further wealthy, but non-palatial, site lies at Palaikastro.

Palaikastro

Robert Carr Bosanquet excavated a substantial area from 1902–6; this was another major turn-of-the-century British excavation on Crete. Mervyn Popham and Hugh Sackett reintroduced excavations in 1962–3, with further fieldwork by Sackett and Alexander MacGillivray from 1986. Current fieldwork is under way under Carl Knappett, Alexandra Livarda, and Nicoletta Momigliano. A local site sequence has been developed at this site, where Period VIII = MM IIIA, Period IX = MM IIIB, Period X = LM IA, and so on; some re-dating of the pottery from up to LM IB corrects earlier accounts.[225] Earthquake damage occurred at the end of MM IIIB, and a 7 cm deposit of ash is thought to originate from the (LM IA) Theran eruption.[226] The latest LM IB phase may match early LM II at Knossos.[227] Later (LM III) occupation has disturbed some areas.

At the end of the Protopalatial period, the town witnessed widespread destruction after which the road system (with drainage) was improved; further alterations were made in LM IB (Figure 5.15). This clear town plan represents communal activity, whether centrally organized or by consensus. During the Neopalatial period, buildings tended to have ashlar facades on the streets, with an apparently agreed uniformity.[228] By the time the site was destroyed in LM IB, the town covered around 30 ha., and it was the second largest town on Crete after Knossos.[229] The reasonably regular street grid

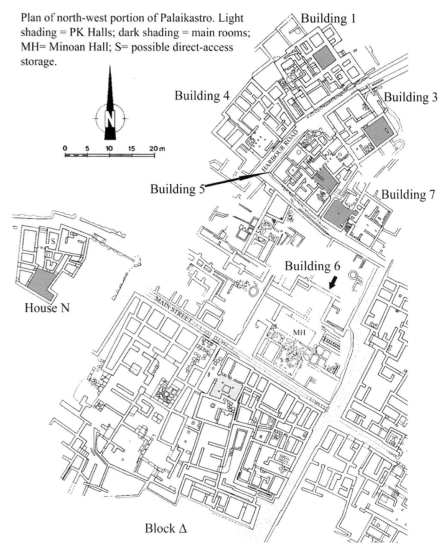

Plan of north-west portion of Palaikastro. Light shading = PK Halls; dark shading = main rooms; MH= Minoan Hall; S= possible direct-access storage.

Building 1

Building 4

Building 3

Building 5

Building 7

House N

Building 6

MH

Block Δ

5.15 Palaikastro plan (Cunningham 2007, figure 11.1). Reproduced with permission of the British School at Athens.

produced even blocks for subdivision, although it is not always straightforward to isolate discrete houses in the older excavations.[230]

The area excavated so far is thought to be the elite quarter of the town. The average size of houses at Palaikastro was 215 m², which is comparable to many of the elite mansions at Knossos. In contrast, the average floor plan for houses at Gournia was 80 m². Fourteen buildings had wall paintings, although fewer had halls or Lustral Basins.[231] Block E produced evidence for substantial food preparation, a deposit of 980 conical cups, and some prestige objects such as the agrimi rhyton and a steatite cup with four Linear A signs.[232]

However, there is as yet no central building, with or without the palatial form; extensive geophysical work has been conducted at Palaikastro looking for traces of such a complex, with inconclusive results. The nearby site at Zakros serves as a warning that excavators may initially miss the main central focus of a site. Reasons have been presented for Palaikastro having an as-yet undiscovered central building or area: there is little evidence so far for the collection of agricultural surplus at the site, which would support feasting and payment for communal work, and there is no public open space, which is fundamental for Minoan life elsewhere.[233] Ultimately, it is felt that the second largest town known on Crete must have had some kind of central building, which might be expected to be a Palace.

In MM IIIA, a hall with polythyron was built in the Southeast Building of Area 6 or Block M (Figure 5.15).[234] Its interpretation as a full Minoan Hall has been doubted, as it is not axially aligned and other minor discrepancies.[235] When this area was destroyed by earthquake at the end of MM IIIB, the hall was not rebuilt, and reoccupation was limited. Later, in LM IB, the block was apparently unoccupied, although two wells were dug in the area. The abandonment of this prime space in the town is noteworthy, and this has been ascribed to the initial demonstration of Knossian allegiance with the construction of a semi-Minoan Hall, followed by a total rejection of this association in LM IB.[236] Instead, elites at the site constructed the 'Palaikastro Hall', comprising a sunken central basin with four columns set around it; three of the four excavated have a Lustral Basin nearby. This is a fascinating attempt to unite architecture and politics, but there are three problems. The Knossian nature of the Minoan Hall has been emphasized, although it is a more general Cretan phenomenon – indeed, the first known example comes from Malia.[237] There is a concentration of these forms in north-central Crete, however. Second, if a Minoan Hall is rendered specifically Knossian, then it is unclear why a Lustral Basin should not also be, and the people of Palaikastro were eager to build them. Third, architectural units very similar to the 'Palaikastro Hall' have been found in north-central Crete, at Maison Epsilon at Malia, the Palace at Galatas, Vathypetro, and possibly Sklavokambos (see Chapter 3).

Ritual objects, and perhaps shrines, were distributed throughout the site, such as baetyls, rhyta, Horns of Consecration, and Double Axes.[238] The destructions from the LM IB town produced rhyta in sixteen of the thirty excavated buildings, the highest known density.[239] The 'Palaikastro Kouros' was a gold-and-ivory figure found broken and scattered in and around Building 5, in the area bordering Buildings 1, 3, and 4. It is an extremely impressive piece (see Chapter 9).[240] In LM IA, Building 1 was constructed, the first building with ashlar masonry on all four sides.[241] It has been suggested that Building 1 was some kind of ritual complex, partly due to the presence of the Palaikastro Kouros,[242] although this has also been used to justify the label of 'shrine' to

5.16 Klimataria-Manares (photograph by author).

Building 5.[243] Overall, this is an extremely prosperous site that engaged with Minoan elite culture at all levels. This renders the lack of central building all the more notable.

Villas of Eastern Crete

The east of the island is littered with 'Villas', which is a wide-ranging category.[244] Nicholas Platon excavated most of these in the 1950s, before he turned his attention to Zakros. On the whole, they are not isolated buildings, but set within settlements.[245] They provide a second tier of settlements between the main coastal ones (Petras, Palaikastro, and Zakros) and the farmsteads picked up in surveys (Chapter 8).

Ayios Georgios (Tourtouloi) is incompletely excavated, and appears to have been built in LM IA and destroyed in LM IB.[246] The site has yielded evidence for more than forty rooms, frescoes, twelve pithoi, wine presses, and a stone table. Both Nikolaos and Lefteris Platon viewed it as a farmhouse, heavily engaged in agricultural activity, but also as some kind of local authority.[247] It is possible that the complex comprised more than one building,[248] although, on balance, the original interpretation that it was a single building seems more likely.[249] Achladia is another impressive example.[250] Located 12 km from Siteia, it has been compared to the Villas at Tylissos in the way the buildings cluster together.[251] The site has yielded a Minoan Hall, eleven pithoi, and a wild goat rhyton. Zou has revealed evidence for possible pottery production, a fragment of an animal head rhyton, and a terracotta tripod table.[252]

Klimataria is an unusual case, as it appears to have been isolated rather than part of a larger settlement (Figure 5.16).[253] It was discovered during the construction of the island's main east–west road along the north coast, and bulldozers destroyed the central part; this coincidence presumably reflects a similar strategic rationale for the site's location in Minoan times. A recent re-evaluation concludes that it was a 'country villa' standing alone.[254] Overall, many broad similarities exist between the houses in the settlement at Petras and those in the surrounding countryside like Achladia, such as industrial activities and portable finds, although ritual artefacts are not abundant in either context. In comparison with the 'Villas' of central Crete, they were smaller, less monumental, and with less evidence for storage, administration, and ritual.[255]

The Regional Picture

Petras has already been discussed, but this town was surrounded by satellite sites, such as Klimataria, Ayia Photia, Piskokephalo, Achladia, and Zou, with a third tier of farmsteads. A surface survey in the Ayia Photia area indicated a slight increase in sites from the Protopalatial to Neopalatial period, with six small, isolated farmhouses.[256] Various hypothetical routes may be reconstructed in the area, with the coastal one probably the most important.[257] The Protopalatial/ Neopalatial Palace represents a clear ideological choice to invest in the most distinctive feature of 'Minoan-ness', and yet the standard of architecture is not particularly 'palatial'. The consensus is that the site was the central focus in an independent polity,[258] with no suggestion of Knossian involvement. If it is the case that 'Knossian' features do not necessarily indicate Knossian control, then their absence need not mean a complete lack of interest by the major Minoan site. However, the slight evidence for the production and consumption of prestige goods would suggest poor external relations, both within and beyond the island.

'Villas', such as Vaï, lie in the Palaikastro area, and this major settlement had its own peak sanctuary at Petsophas. The settlement pattern is different from that at either Petras or Zakros; the former had more substantial Villas in the surrounding area than Palaikastro, while the latter was more concentrated on both the regional and site level.[259] Defining territorial boundaries is not straightforward. One possibility is that Petras was a centre to the north, Makrygialos to the south, and Zakros-Palaikastro to the east.[260] Overall, we might reconstruct three or four clusters of settlements around the main sites of the region, with a three-tiered settlement hierarchy.[261] But there is also the case of the LM I town of Papadiokampos, which lies between the Mirabello area and Siteia Bay (with Petras), and enjoyed a 'local taste' in ceramics.[262] Overall, the far eastern area of Crete possesses sites of different rank and nature, but it is not clear how they should be set territorially.

CONCLUSION

There is a certain logic to dividing the island as done here, not least as it follows the geography of the mountain ranges. Regional trends in settlement type lend a distinctive flavour to each region. However, it is not easy, or even possible, to divide each of these regions into a clear pyramidal structure or settlement hierarchy. Furthermore, it has been argued that particular sites have a strong relationship with Knossos, and were even controlled by this site's elite. While this is by no means impossible, one should be wary of assuming this from the presence of 'Knossian' forms and features. Firstly, upon further inspection, these often prove to be more generally 'Minoan', or at least part of a concentrated trend in north-central Crete. Secondly, objects, architectural designs, and even practices can spread and be emulated without indicating socio-political control. It is undeniable, however, that Knossos was the largest and most prosperous site by far on Crete; it is highly likely that its influence rippled through the island in some form, even if not necessarily political.

Many of these sites have revealed that the category of 'Palace' is not clear-cut. It is unexpected that the second largest site (Palaikastro) should fail to reveal one, while a much smaller site to the south (Zakros) should have produced such a rich example. If we define a Palace on strict architectural terms, we are then left with a number of semi-palatial sites: there are clear central buildings that do not possess this architectural layout. Furthermore, the appearance of many 'palatial' features in all kinds of non-palatial buildings indicates the slippage between this term and 'elite' more generally. In order to explore this confusing picture further, we need to turn to a further type of locale across the island: ritual sites.

CHAPTER SIX

THE RITUAL LANDSCAPE AND EXTRA-URBAN SANCTUARIES

INTRODUCTION

In previous literature, some scholars have concentrated on ritual spaces within settlements.[1] Others have focused on extra-urban sanctuaries, specializing further on either caves used for ritual purposes (such as Psychro) or the so-called peak sanctuaries (such as Juktas). This chapter opens with an overview of these two categories, before considering in more detail the considerable challenges involved in dealing with this evidence.[2] This includes ruling out sites that are too poorly understood or published to be securely identified as a ritual site. The main aim of this chapter is to take a regional, localized view of the selected ritual sites, regardless of the category they have been assigned to. This will enable further analysis of their common characteristics and divergences, particularly with regard to distribution patterns and how they relate to local (important) settlements. In this way, we will gain a more nuanced view of the regional settlement patterns seen in the previous two chapters, and shed further light on the role of ritual in Minoan society.

To begin, this categorization involves central methodological issues. First, it may lead to the assumption the groups represent different practices, beliefs, and socio-political roles.[3] The topographical and environmental variations between windy peak sanctuaries and caves that encroach deep into the earth are bound to result in different experiences; nonetheless, comparable sequences of rites may have been followed, and the same deities/supernatural entities involved. It is notable that offerings were placed in the crevice at Juktas, which may be a nod to cave practices,[4] and caves were often located at high altitudes:

this could suggest a degree of blurring. The frequent high altitude of ritual sites, combined with a (presumed) fascination with the underworld, suggests that these were liminal zones, nodal points for contact with other worlds.

Second, the formation of these categories occasionally poses a rather different problem, in that features found at one site are automatically transferred to others within that category, under the assumption that they would all function the same.[5] This produces a form of circular reasoning, and weakens rather than strengthens interpretative nuance. This is particularly problematic when a 'type-site' is set up, a standard against which all other sites are compared. Juktas, for example, is the peak sanctuary extraordinaire, but it is also atypical.[6]

Peak Sanctuaries

The term 'peak sanctuary' was first used by Sir John Myres in relation to Petsophas, located on the peak of the hill overlooking Palaikastro.[7] At 215 mamsl (metres above mean sea level), this peak sanctuary has one of the lowest altitudes; others are much higher, over 1,000 mamsl. Arthur Evans, when at Juktas, then adopted the term for the wider category.[8] As with the term 'Palace', the label given for this group of sites has been critiqued in recent years,[9] and the criteria (or less static 'elements' as defined by Peatfield)[10] revisited and refined. The two main criteria are topography and finds;[11] as yet, too little is known about the practices performed at the majority of these sites for detailed comment.

Peatfield's topographic criteria are followed in the present study. These were: a high altitude (close to, but not necessarily on a summit); a prominent location in the surrounding terrain; that the worshippers could see the sanctuary from their settlements, and vice versa; that the sanctuaries were accessible and close to inhabited areas; and inter-visibility between peak sanctuaries.[12] They were not, therefore, places of long-distance pilgrimage, far from major settlements in either visibility or mobility terms. Indeed, visibility was more important than being located on the actual summit of the hill or mountain – hence the unease with the term 'peak' sanctuary. There is much variation – for example, in the range of altitude – and there are some exceptions. It is unclear, for example, which major settlement Kophinas might be associated with; it lies more than a day's walk from Phaistos, but the unexplored remains at Protoria may hold the answer.

Terracotta figurines are the most common and distinctive finds; indeed, they are essential for the definite identification of peak sanctuary. They could be in the form of animals, humans, or body parts.[13] The human figurines were often set in distinctive postures, and were apparently of the worshippers themselves (Figure 3.13).[14] Part of a terracotta face from Petsophas may have been from a life-size figure, which may in turn have represented a deity.[15] The votive limbs appear to be comparable to the later classical practice of requests or thanks for healing.[16] Animal figurines were mainly of domestic animals that were important to Minoan economy and husbandry, such as cattle, sheep, goats, dogs, and pigs, but there were also agrimi (wild goat) and dung beetles.[17] Peak sanctuaries tend to be found within vegetation zones that could support arable and/or pastoral farming (and inhabitation more generally), and this attention to livestock (and their protection) is unsurprising.[18] Pebbles are also a common find.[19] This is perhaps less expected; a worshipper may have left one as a token of his or her visit and dedication.

The dedications became much more valuable over time, in terms of both raw materials and craft skill. Neopalatial finds include bronzes (including figurines), jewellery, and stone offering tables (some of which had Linear A 'formulae' inscribed on them: see Chapter 7). Stone discs may have served as 'improvised offering tables' for the first fruits (aparchai).[20] Defining an object as a 'votive' because of its presence on such a site may be circular reasoning, but this remains the most straightforward interpretation. The presence of lamps opens up the possibility of night-time rituals,[21] and perhaps feasts continued until late in the evening. Vessels for drinking, cooking, and eating were commonplace, indicating the considerable social roles facilitated by such worship.[22] The ceramics also give the best indications of the date of activity at these sites, and here the story becomes particularly intriguing.

Peak sanctuaries were established as popular, local community shrines before or during the Protopalatial period,[23] so it is all the more surprising that such broad similarities occur island-wide (if mainly in central and eastern Crete). Faure's extensive fieldwork led to the identification of more than fifty 'peak sanctuaries', although his criteria were not explicitly laid out.[24] Rutkowski brought the number down to thirty-seven on stricter principles, while Peatfield reduced it further still to twenty-five.[25] Nowicki has argued that these Protopalatial peak sanctuaries form two or three separate clusters, with some apparent exceptions; Davaras has convincingly argued, however, that Thylakas (one such exception) was misidentified as a peak sanctuary.[26] Furthermore, these clusters may have radiated from a central, flagship site: Juktas in central Crete and Petsophas to the east. It appears, therefore, to be significant that both of these continued in use throughout the Neopalatial period.

A significant fall occurred in the number of sanctuaries in use crossing over into the Neopalatial period (MM III) and beyond.[27] Peatfield lists Juktas, Petsophas, Traostalos, Vrysinas, and (MM III) Kophinas and Gonies as certain Neopalatial sites.[28] We can add (MM III) Kastelli-Liliano to this list (Figure 6.1: see later for some uncertain cases). That some were used during MM III but not beyond indicates further how arbitrary our division between 'Protopalatial' and 'Neopalatial' is. These later sites generally had buildings, which were apparently open air with one or more rooms;[29]

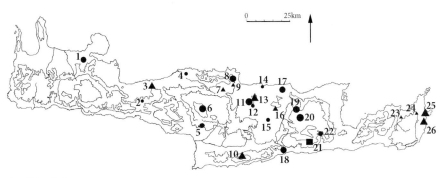

6.1 Ritual sites

Triangle: peak sanctuary; Circle: sacred cave; Square: other (Kato Syme). Large symbol: clear use throughout period; small symbol: unclear use, or fell out of use during Neopalatial period. 1: Mameloukos; 2: Patsos; 3: Vrysinas; 4: Melidoni; 5: Kamares; 6: Ida; 7: Gonies; 8: Trapeza; 9: Pyrgos; 10: Kophinas; 11: Chosto Nero; 12: Stravomyti; 13: Juktas; 14: Amnissos; 15: Arkalochori; 16: Kastelli-Liliano; 17: Skotino; 18: Tsoutsouros; 19: Phaneromeni; 20: Psychro; 21: Kato Syme; 22: Selakanos; 23: Prinias; 24: Modi; 25: Petsophas; 26: Traostalos.

furthermore, structural features such as benches were built, and also terraces. Juktas, Kophinas, Petsophas, Traostalos, and Vrysinas yielded evidence for burning, ash and bones.[30] In addition to providing evidence for feasting and possible sacrifice, these may also indicate fire signals across the landscape; this, however, remains a hypothesis, as only Juktas and Traostalos have yielded positive evidence for such ashy layers.[31]

Ritual Caves

While caves carpet (or burrow) the Cretan landscape, few have positive evidence for ritual use, and these are concentrated in the central area.[32] The lack of evidence for ritual caves in east Crete is not down to an absence of exploration; Faure investigated 120 caves in east Crete, and did not find evidence of prehistoric ritual use.[33] In contrast to the peak sanctuaries, accessibility from major settlements varied considerably. Access to some ritual caves, such as Skoteino, was not particularly strenuous, but others, such as the Idaean Cave, would require a pilgrimage-type journey. While sacred caves might suggest reaching out to chthonic deities, they could still have powerful vistas over the landscape, as well as being visible from the surrounding area. The Kamares Cave, for example, is a distinct black dot visible today from the Central Court of the Palace at Phaistos.

Cool and damp, and often containing stalagmites, stalactites, and pools of water (which the sun and candlelight could reflect on), caves can be ideal settings for rituals.[34] As caves may be used for many other reasons, such as inhabitation and animal pens, ritual use needs to be confirmed by (votive) artefacts. There are a number of reasons why a pot may come to be left (dropped?) in a cave, although fine wares are unlikely to be brought to animal pens. The kinds of pots found suggest libation and cooking and eating.[35] Clay human figurines have been found only at Psychro, and no clay body parts at all, apart from one possible example from the same site;[36] this is a key criterion to identifying peak sanctuaries.

Peatfield states that the wide range of deposits in ritual caves could mean that 'the caves do not represent any single cult, while the peak sanctuaries do'.[37] Faure attempted to divide the ritual caves into four different types of worship centred on initiation, childbirth, agriculture, and pastoralism, but the evidence is too sparse to demonstrate this.[38] Tyree has divided the Neopalatial caves into five groups according to their cult objects,[39] but again there are significant problems with incomplete excavations, publications, looting, and stratigraphy: the lack of systematic and comparable analyses across a representative number of sites renders such approaches problematic.

The number of these ritual sites increases from the Protopalatial period, in contrast to the widespread abandonment of peak sanctuaries. Tyree's recent list of caves contains nine caves; they coincide with those taken here with two exceptions: Tsoutsouro is included in Figure 6.1, whereas Melidoni is considered a possible case.

Identifying Extra-urban Sanctuaries: Challenges and Criteria

In comparison with identifying ritual areas in settlements, it is usually much more straightforward to detect extra-urban sanctuaries – providing that sufficient material has been retrieved and published. Renfrew's methodological criteria for identifying ritual (in particular religious ritual, engaging with supernatural powers) have been applied in order to confirm the ritual nature of Atsipades and Psychro.[40] Ironically, perhaps, these are two sites where ritual activity was never in doubt; what is much harder to judge are sites such as peak sanctuaries with unclear continued use into the Neopalatial period, or a cave initially thought to be ritual, but then was re-interpreted as a hoard site.

The reasons for exclusion are varied, such as in cases where only sherds were reported (so non-cultic use is possible).[41] For example, Stous Athropolithous has long been described as a sanctuary, and has produced Neopalatial conical cups and pithoi. However, no Neopalatial votives or comparable structures have been recorded (the figurines are Protopalatial, with one possible Neopalatial example).[42] Its ritual use during the Neopalatial period is therefore undemonstrated. Figurines would be required to identify a peak sanctuary, but caves did not tend to have them. The cave at Amnissos yielded pottery only for the Neopalatial period, and I have discounted it from the discussion (although it is marked on the map for information).[43] The cave at Melidoni has clearly revealed evidence for Neopalatial use in terms of pottery, but it is unclear whether ritual use is demonstrated.[44] The deposit of pottery was made in a secluded chamber, accessed by a steep descent – this was not an accidental assemblage. The site is marked on Figure 6.1, but as a smaller symbol, and the evidence is considered too preliminarily published to be presented in the discussion.

Likewise, Stravomyti, on the western slope of the southern part of the Juktas range and at around 400 mamsl, has also yielded Neopalatial evidence. Marinatos excavated the site and believed it was used ritually, with some kind of altar at the entrance, but the evidence basically comprises fifteen pithoi.[45] Faure suggested that the water in the depth of the cave, which produces thick concretions, could help to create a religious atmosphere,[46] but the evidence at present is too slight to include this with the certain ritual sites. Although it is true that pottery may have played a more important part in cult than we have acknowledged,[47] a cautious approach is taken here. These sites are included, but in smaller scale on Map 6.1, in case further observations come to light.[48] A further problematic site is Patsos, which has, in the past, been defined as a ritual cave. This cavity in fact has no Bronze Age evidence, but there is a nearby area where the remains of Minoan pyres and handle-less cups were found.[49]

Arkalochori, which lies just 3 km from the palatial site at Galatas, was long considered ritual, but recently 'demoted' to a hoard site.[50] A small 'altar' was mistakenly ascribed to the site,[51] and the cave lacks figurines, stone libation vessels, or cultic vases. A considerable amount of metal was found in the cave, with both usable tools and votives (miniatures or too thin to use); some of the Double Axes (of gold, silver, and bronze) were inscribed with Linear A script. The deposit resembles a hoard left on a single occasion, rather than the remains of repeated ritual practice. Rethemiotakis has associated the assemblage with the Palace at Galatas, which he suggests was involved in the circulation of metals and votives; the hoard could be the result of a political crisis.[52] This is indeed a more convincing interpretation – or, it seemed so until a recent paper by Lefteris Platon advocated a ritual use once more.

In the case of sites such as Amnissos, ritual use is undemonstrated, because the finds consist only of ceramics. With Arkalochori, the *lack* of pottery suggested the absence of cult. However, Platon reports unpublished notes (by his father, Nikolaos Platon), which state that the stepped path leading to the cave was littered with conical cups, that some Neopalatial pottery was found in the cavity, and that there were four main deposits of metal offerings – which could suggest more than a one-off placement.[53] In the same volume, Tyree points out that this is a cavity, not a cave, and the excavator, Marinatos, noted only small quantities of Neopalatial pottery.[54] This example perhaps best illustrates that we cannot (and should not) expect to reach a definitive list of ritual sites, but we individually need to consider each example on a case-by-case basis.

This site is not topographically a cave, but still could be a ritual site. The finds are definitely special, prestigious, and of a ritual nature. But we encounter a problem seen in settlement contexts; this could be a storage area, rather than ritual space. Finally, in terms of practice, it is noteworthy that some stress is placed on whether this was a single deposit or several. The implication appears to be that it is more likely to be a ritual space if it were a repeated action. However, this assumption is questionable, as foundation deposits demonstrate.[55] The practice of feasting is as yet unproven.

A similar case is Selakanos, located at 930 mamsl, in the south part of the Lasithi region. The finds include ten bronze Double Axes, dated by Faure to LM I,[56] and various other bronzes. A further Double Axe from the area was inscribed. Since it is not clear that these were dedications rather than a hoard, this case is also in doubt. These are clearly 'special' deposits, even treasure troves. A poor compromise is reached in that both these caves are left out of the discussion on ritual, while indicated on the map at a smaller scale.

In terms of generating a synthesis, a recurring problem is the preliminary nature of the recording of these sites. This tends to be less of an issue for more recently discovered sites, such as the peak sanctuary found at Gournos Krousonas.[57] As the latest material dated to MM IIIA, it is not included on Map 6.1. Rethemiotakis has also excavated an MM IIIA and early MM IIIB peak sanctuary at Kastelli-Liliano.[58] As this is more securely positioned in the Neopalatial period, it is on the map, at a smaller scale.[59] However, some recent discoveries are recorded so briefly, that the date (Protopalatial and/or Neopalatial period) is not recorded.[60] In these cases, we need to await further information before incorporating them into a synthesis.

Some sites, recorded in brief many decades ago, are even more difficult to assess. Nowicki has recently explored the problems with identifying old discoveries.[61] Some, like Ziros Plagia and Korphi tou Mare, are impossible to locate today, but there is evidence that there was a ritual site in the vicinity. Others, like Ambelos and Etiani Kephala, appear to have been misidentified topographically. The situation with the peak sanctuary at Gonies-Philioremos is unclear, but it was in use at the beginning of the Neopalatial period.[62] The presence of a building here suggests a Neopalatial date – although there is a danger of circularity when deploying this argument.[63] This is the only Neopalatial peak sanctuary that has not yielded evidence for Linear A libation formulae. The building at Pyrgos (Tylissos) would appear to date activity to the Neopalatial period,[64] and use here also trails off over the course of the Neopalatial period.[65] Finally, the case of Vrysinas provides a further caveat. Preliminary reports emphasized Protopalatial pottery at the site, but full examination revealed that, in fact, Neopalatial pottery predominated.[66] As the vast majority of these sites are briefly mentioned in reports, the overall picture will likely need to be revised in the future.

When synthesizing such data, one is torn between caution and comprehensiveness, and there are degrees of certainty. Further subdivisions may be required: for example, Rutkowski and Nowicki divided caves into those certainly used ritually, those probably or possibly used in this way, and those that should be discounted. This is necessarily subjective and subject to change – Arkalochori figures in their 'certain' group, but is rejected as ritual here. While also drawing from Watrous' list of sanctuaries,[67] Amnissos and Arkalochori (listed by him) are not considered ritual here. Inclusion on Figure 6.1 has been decided on the basis of current evidence as consistently as possible; sites were not chosen to support a preconceived theory. Ambiguous sites are depicted smaller, as are sites that are MM III only.

EXTRA-URBAN SANCTUARIES

The following survey is mainly organized by region. The exception is the section on the four isolated ritual caves that, by definition, lie at some distance from major settlements. They also form a natural extension to the previous section on the north-central region, forming the eastern and western boundaries of the area (such as we can reconstruct them). Other sites, such as Kato Syme and Kophinas, are similarly isolated but placed in their regional section (for which they comprise most of the Neopalatial evidence). Following the north-central region, we turn to the west, south, then east.

North-Central Crete: Juktas and Surrounding Area

Juktas lies at 811 mamsl, overlooking the Knossian plain, and around 13 km to the south-west of the palatial site.[68] Arthur Evans investigated the peak sanctuary, and Karetsou's excavations highlighted the importance of this site. Anemospilia lies on the route to the sanctuary, and the MM III Alonaki Building is nearby, forming a 'unique triad in the heart of north-central Crete'.[69] Anemospilia and Alonaki were abandoned after MM III earthquakes, the former in MM IIIA, the latter in MM IIIB: this was followed by extensive building at the established sanctuary on the peak,[70] which was used throughout the Neopalatial period (Figure 6.2A). It is the most monumental ritual site, with a processional way, platform, and stepped altar.[71] A five-room building with decorated walls was constructed nearby, with evidence for feasting.[72]

Juktas is the only Neopalatial peak sanctuary in Crete to have produced seal stones and sealings, although some caves did.[73] It also produced many figurines (human and animal), models of human body parts, stone offering tables, sheet bronze votive tools, and a painted terracotta fragment of a house model. Eleven

6.2 Juktas. A) with Archanes below (photograph by author); B) the chasm (photograph by author).

of the stone vessels were inscribed with Linear A formulae.[74] Also found were several gold items, including a pendant decorated with a scorpion, snake, and spider, a gold beetle, a gold agrimi horn,[75] and a gold shell bead. Karetsou argued that the 'character and quality of the finds have a palatial character'.[76]

Evans suggested that there was a special relationship between Knossos and Juktas, the latter towering over the settlement.[77] There are also traces of a road between the two sites, running via Sillamos, Vasilies, and Protopalatial Anemospilia. Knossos and Juktas are the only two sites to have revealed monumental Horns of Consecration, which suggests a ceremonial connection.[78] This claim is justified by the visual connection between Juktas and the Central Court of the Palace at Knossos: the north–south orientation of the Central Court and west wing looks straight towards Juktas (Figure 3.3). The Juktas massif can be seen from a wide area, including Tylissos to the west[79] and Galatas to the southeast. It had no settlements located on it, and may have been sacrosanct.[80]

On the regional level, Juktas lies at the centre of the area in which caves were used ritually (Figure 6.1). The cave at Chosto Nero lies at 780 mamsl, on the western slope of the southern part of the Juktas range. In the front of the cave is a 12 m wide platform, and pools had formed within it. Pottery, miniature ceramic vases, and clay animal figurines were found.[81] These have been dated to MM III or LM I.[82] This change in practice (from peak to cave) appears to occur in a very literal manner at Tylissos, where the ritual focus moved from the Pyrgos peak sanctuary to the Trapeza cave, situated on the northern slope of Pyrgos, around 500–600 m from the summit and around 150 m below it, at an altitude of 685 mamsl.[83] The settlement of Tylissos is visible from the cave; only one Neopalatial bronze human figurine was found in the sanctuary, with Neopalatial sherds.[84]

The Skoteino Cave overlooked the communication route between Knossos and Malia. A recent speleological study has confirmed that it is environmentally suited towards ritual rather than inhabitation.[85] Neopalatial artefacts comprise decorated bowls, fruit stands, offering vessels, and a kernos, in addition to a bronze votive Double Axe.[86] Large numbers of handle-less cups and fragments of pedestalled chalices were found,[87] with many tripod cooking pots. Three bronze figurines were found at Skoteino, which Davaras dated to the Neopalatial period.[88] Considerable deposits of animal bones and ashes have been found, but these are impossible to date.

Rethemiotakis suggests that Kastelli-Liliano was the central peak sanctuary of the Pediada Plain, although the 'peak' is actually a low hill just south of and visible from Kastelli. Furthermore, as it fell out of use in MM III, ritual activity may have transferred from the landscape to the central building at Kastelli.[89] The finds include fragments of human and animal figurines, and Rethemiotakis notes that they were made with clay similar to that of ceramics excavated at Kastelli.[90] A clay shrine model and the feet of a human figure were preserved.

Psychro, Phaneromeni, the Idaean, and Kamares Caves

Psychro Cave lies at 1025 mamsl, just 200 m above the Lasithi plain; a substantial terrace provides a platform overlooking it.[91] Flooding would have been a problem in the plain before the Roman or Venetian drainage systems were installed, but grain would have grown well there (this is too high an altitude for the olive).[92] Small settlements tend to hug the low slopes of the surrounding Lasithi massif. After being used for inhabitation, cult use began during MM IB–II in the upper cave, and spread to incorporate the lower cave in MM III (Figure 6.3).

More than 200 bronze knives and daggers (both votive and 'real') were found, with personal toilet items such as bronze razors and tweezers and an unique bronze chariot (model?).[93] Many bronze Double Axes (mostly votive) were inserted into crevices in the stalagmites. Bronze human and animal figurines have been found, as have clay figurines; male figurines had hands on their chest or were saluting, while women had hands under or on their breasts, or were also saluting.[94] Miniature ceramic vessels, seals, glass, and crystal beads were also recovered, and some stone offering tables had Linear A formulae.[95] There is evidence for feasting (including meat), braziers, conical cups, ashes, and pithoi in the upper chamber, along with an 'altar'. Around this structure were found libation tables, and lamps.[96] Different rites may have been performed in the upper and lower chambers, with the evidence for feasting focused in the upper chamber while most of the weapons were found in the lower one.[97]

Phaneromeni Cave lies above and south of Avdou in the Lasithi Range. This is a remote, mountainous area, overlooking the route between Malia and the Pediada plain.[98] Three stone offering tables were found here, as well as Double

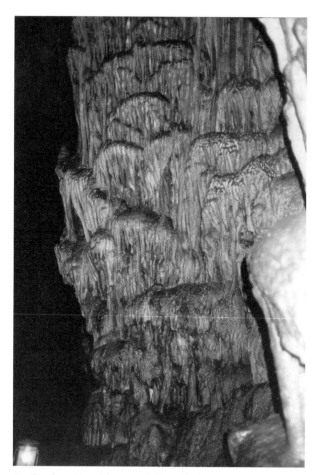

6.3 Psychro Cave (photograph by author).

Axes (one gold, two bronze) and two bronze human figurines. Later activity has confused the Neopalatial picture in terms of reconstructing cult practice.[99]

The Idaean Cave was set at an even higher altitude (around 1540 mamsl), and 125 m above the Nida plain. Like Psychro, it had two main levels, an upper and lower chamber. It has also had a long history of archaeological interest,[100] but its later use in antiquity has obscured the Neopalatial picture. There is limited evidence for both Protopalatial and Neopalatial activity. The Neopalatial finds include two stone kernoi, an engraved bronze Double Axe, votive bronze daggers (similar to those from Arkalochori), crystal beads, a number of seals, and a large conical rhyton;[101] no terracotta figurines have been retrieved from the site.[102] The pithoi found would presumably indicate feasting, as indicated by ashes and animal bones (possibly Neopalatial).[103]

The Kamares Cave lent its name to the well-made MM II pottery that was first found here.[104] The cave experienced a sharp decline in the wealth of offerings in the Neopalatial period – however, a recent study of the material has demonstrated that Neopalatial presence (and deposition) was greater than previously realized.[105] Drinking vessels are particularly well-represented here, as are transport and storage containers; the presence of some tripod cooking pots indicate feasting, as at other extra-urban sanctuaries. Ritual paraphernalia was generally missing from the cave; its ritual use is assumed from the isolated location and visual relation with Phaistos – the cave opening is visible from the Palace's Central Court (Figure 3.3).[106] The Neopalatial use of the cave also appears to reflect activity at the palatial site – including a drop in LM IA, when the Palace was abandoned.[107] The shared trajectory does not seem coincidental, and the fortunes of the two sites waxed and waned together.

The West: Vrysinas, Patsos, and Mameloukos

The peak sanctuary at Vrysinas lies several kilometres south of Rethymnon, on a summit at 858 mamsl and with good views of the surrounding area. Davaras explored it in the 1970s, and the site is currently under investigation by Tzachili.[108] Terraces were constructed, but the site is badly eroded.[109] The site yielded considerable amounts of pottery (with far more Neopalatial than Protopalatial material, as revealed in modern investigations)[110] and clay figurines (human and animal, notably bovine).[111] It is notable that activity at the site ends in LM IA.[112] Some figurines were unusually large (date unclear), and the lower part of a bronze male figurine was found. Miniature Double Axes and knives, clay Horns of Consecration and libation tables, one with a Linear A inscription, were found.

We end with two examples that appear to be certain ritual sites, but are (as yet) poorly understood. Patsos Cave is more like a rock shelter than a cave – Rutkowski and Nowicki describe it as a 'spring sanctuary'.[113] It has certain cave-like qualities (including a stalactite) so is marked as such here. Finds include clay and bronze figurines (human and animal), a small amount of LM I pottery, and fragments of a bronze Double Axe, knife, and stone libation table.[114] The cave Mameloukos (Trypa) is close to Perivolia, on the west slope of the Perivolia mountain. A kernos and clay bull figurine (MM III–LM I) and LM I sherds suggests ritual use.[115]

The South: Kato Syme, Tsoutsouros, and Kophinas

Kato Syme is rather inaccessible, especially in the winter, but it has a rich spring, which presumably drew the Minoans to the spot (Figure 6.4).[116] The site is open air (not a cave), set in a natural amphitheatre (not a peak) at 1130 mamsl. This important site therefore defies the strict categorization between peak and cave. The long life of the site, until the Roman period, causes problems in defining the Neopalatial activity. After Protopalatial activity at the site, a walled enclosure was

6.4 Kato Syme (multi-period site) (photograph by author).

built, containing a large podium, which a road led up to. This appears to have been the focus of sacrifices, feasting, and libations. Building U was an early Neopalatial large building with fourteen rooms, which was replaced by an open air complex and then Building S by the end of the Neopalatial period.[117] Votives included a large number of libation tables (several inscribed with Linear A), as well as human figurines, especially male ones (bronze and terracotta).[118] Miniature weapons, including a Double Axe, stone seals, lamps, and kernoi were also found.[119] Drinking and cooking vessels were recovered; chalices were particularly common. The variety in the quality and size of the chalices and libation tables may reflect different socio-economic groups of worshippers.[120]

Tsoutsouros Cave is another long-lived extra-urban site, stretching to the Roman period. There is Neopalatial evidence here (and indeed Protopalatial), particularly in the form of terracotta and bronze human figurines.[121] Unusually, the latter are female; one bronze figure with flared skirt wears crescent-shaped headwear (possibly resembling horns). In contrast to certain other sites, such as Kophinas to the west, the pottery is not so much catered for eating and drinking, but for worship; notable are the miniature vases.[122] Lacking at this site are bronze daggers, which we have seen at other caves (such as Psychro and the Idaean Cave). Indeed, similarities are noted with peak sanctuary cult, and more accessible caves such as Skoteino.[123]

Kophinas Cave lies at 970 mamsl, some 250 below the highest point of the mountain.[124] While visible from a wide area, including north-central Crete, the Kophinas peak is only just discernible from the Palace at Phaistos. The area of the sanctuary itself is less visible, even from the Mesara (including Protoria).[125] An extensive series of buildings was found at the site, which was surrounded by a peribolos wall. Also found were human figurines (mostly male), arm fragments that appear to be wearing boxing gloves,[126] animal figurines (mostly bovine), bull's head rhyta, bronze votive daggers, a clay boat model, seals, and twenty-four stone offering tables.[127] Figurines were placed in the cracks of the rock, as well as inside the peribolos.[128] Linear A formulae have been found here. The Neopalatial pottery formed mostly handle-less cups, with bowls and trays with appliqué decoration.[129] The site was active during the early Neopalatial period, namely MM IIIB.[130] Cups are the most common vessel, with a good proportion of tripod cooking pots.

The East: Petsophas and Traostalos

The peak sanctuary at Petsophas provided the first material on peak sanctuaries at the beginning of the twentieth century. It is located close to the site at Palaikastro, on a low but steep and notable hill to the south of the prosperous town (Figure 6.5). Coincidentally, it was also one of the few peak sanctuaries that continued in use in the Neopalatial period, complete with a building and deposition of Linear A formulae. The stratigraphy for the figurines is, however, unclear. Most appear to be Protopalatial, especially those with Kamares decoration, but others appear to be Neopalatial, such as the female figurines with hair in a bun and long side-locks.[131] The richer Neopalatial material includes Linear A inscriptions.

The peak sanctuary at Traostalos stands at 515 mamsl, and dominates the surrounding area. During the Protopalatial period, the site could look out to other peak sanctuaries, including Ziros, Viglos, Modi, and Petsophas, among others, as well as the sea to the east. Davaras initially investigated the site in the early 1960s, and Chryssoulaki has recently renewed work there.[132] Three makeshift buildings were constructed, and there is evidence for fierce burning from regular bonfires. The site was rich in votives: clay figurines, both human and animal, with good evidence for healing offerings (seated figure with

6.5 Palaikastro and Petsophas, intervisibility (photographs by author).

swollen leg, male head with protruding thyroid gland), bronze figurines, stone libation tables, and stone discs. Evidence for Linear A script also came from this site.

DISCUSSION

The sites have been discussed by region in order to allow certain patterns to emerge. There are some island-wide phenomena however, in addition to the wide distribution of libation formulae (see Chapter 7). There was a marked increase in the wealth of objects, such as the deposition of bronze figurines in addition to (or instead of) clay ones, and a dramatic increase in votives of rare raw materials, such as gold. Furthermore, structures were frequently built. The number of peak sanctuaries fell across the island, and their abandonment may be surprising given the oft-assumed increasing ritualization of Minoan settlement life. This process continues within the Neopalatial period, as seen at MM III Kophinas, Gonies, and Kastelli-Liliano. The five clear Neopalatial peak sanctuaries cover Crete fairly evenly, although there is an eastern pairing with Petsophas and Traostalos, and an apparent absence in the Bay of Mirabello area.

The uneven degree of fieldwork and publication means that any comparative analysis of the finds must be tentative.[133] Peak sanctuaries always have figurines; sacred caves do not. Libation tables are widespread throughout Crete, but Double Axes tend to be found in the central region, including Kophinas and Kato Syme to the south.[134] There is little correlation between altitude (mamsl) and types of finds (although altitude as experienced is relative to the surrounding area, rather than sea level). For example, Chosto Nero and Phaneromeni lie at 780 mamsl and in rather isolated areas, but the assemblages at each site differ considerably. The range of artefacts at Phaneromeni and Skoteino (much lower, at 230 mamsl) is, in contrast, similar, and there are certain physical similarities.[135] However, they differ considerably in terms of isolation. This is a complex picture from which to draw general socio-political interpretations.

The Social Role of Extra-urban Sanctuaries: Previous Scholarship

Evans had long emphasized the close relationship between Knossos and Juktas, but Cherry first emphasized island-wide connections between Palace and peak sanctuary, arguing that: iconographic representations of peak sanctuaries are only found in Palaces; Palaces and peak sanctuaries have the same cult apparatus; and Linear A is common to Palaces and peak sanctuaries.[136] These observations played an important part in uniting the two categories of site for interpretive purposes, but they also have limitations.[137] For example, Linear A ritual formulae also occur in caves and at Kato Syme, and are in fact rare in palatial sites (which used Linear A for administrative purposes, as did other non-palatial buildings). The cult apparatus is not as shared as one might assume; figurines, for example, are not widespread throughout settlements, palatial or otherwise (with notable exceptions, such as Archanes). There is little to suggest that the ritual equipment used at peak sanctuaries was kept in Palaces.[138] Most importantly, these observations would appear to hold for the Neopalatial period, and not earlier, when the considerable majority of peak sanctuaries were in use.

Peatfield has sought to explain the notable chronological shift in the use of peak sanctuaries with reference to the *changing* relationship between Palace and peak.[139] Palatial elites appropriated certain peak sanctuary rituals in the Neopalatial period, so they became institutionalized with buildings, Linear A inscriptions, and much wealthier dedications. Sanctuaries not part of this development fell out of use. Juktas and Knossos fit this model particularly well, with the visual connection from the Palace, and the traces of a Minoan road linking the two sites, but others less so. In fact, this is the only canonical Palace with visibility of a peak sanctuary.[140] Petsophas is associated with Palaikastro, which, as yet, has not revealed a Palace, while MM III Kophinas and Neopalatial Vrysinas are not associated with any (known) major settlement. Some Palaces, such as Malia or Phaistos, do not appear to have had an associated peak sanctuary. These sites have mainly, but not entirely, been found on Crete,[141] whereas the palatial form is (so far) limited to the island. This would suggest that the association was not felt to be binding. In general, we cannot distinguish between LM IA and LM IB use in ritual sites, as we could for settlements.[142] However, it appears that some fell out of use during the Neopalatial period (or MM III); this suggests that the shift in the ritual landscape was an ongoing process, and that we should not reconstruct a sharp divide between the Proto- and Neopalatial periods.

Finally, we should surely take into account other types of extra-urban sanctuary as well, *especially* given our limited understanding of Minoan religion.

There is also no standard pattern for caves used ritually in terms of the relationship they have with the nearby major settlements. Some were located at some distance from large settlements, necessitating a significant pilgrimage, which was presumably part of the ritual process. It has been suggested that the increase in the use of caves and the abandonment of most peak sanctuaries was connected with the seismic disturbances at the end of the Protopalatial period, which brought people to chthonic cult.[143] However, this does not explain why this type of cult is particularly notable in central Crete.

One aspect which has not yet been discussed, and may seem out of place in a 'ritual' chapter, is warfare. We are long past viewing the second-millennium BC Cretans as flower-power Minoans – or are we? A recent survey of Bronze Age Crete sought to reposition power as a 'triadic balance between religion, war and political/economic administration'.[144] While I would not want to join the rank of authors who have failed to mention the topic,[145] there *is* a strange lack of evidence for war, fortifications, and military control in Neopalatial Crete. Structures have been found along Bronze Age roads, and it has been suggested that they were guardhouses manned by warriors, but these seem to be Protopalatial; later periods reoccupied many of them, but put them to different functions.[146] Type A swords date from MM II, notably the blades or rapiers from Malia.[147] Peatfield suggests that these were 'part of the paraphernalia of elite religious ideology'.[148] Similarly, the Double Axe was a functional object as well as a ritual symbol.

Ritualized competition and games appears in the iconography, or 'agonistic art' (e.g., the Boxer Rhyton from Ayia Triada).[149] Combat scenes are also present, especially towards the end of LM IB (going into LM II).[150] Note that the Kophinas figurines appear to have boxing gloves depicted. War scenes may be sought, but they are few and far between; the iconography is more concerned with fights between men and animals.[151] That has been assigned to a *Pax Minoica* under the control of Knossos – but advocates of this have not so far explained how the Knossians achieved this.[152] The underlying suspicion is that ritual is the answer. It is notable that weapons have been found in many sacred caves and the hoard at Arkalochori – while not necessarily a ritual site as such – is a rich deposit of them.

It nonetheless appears to be the case that the Neopalatial elite (palatial or otherwise) appropriated the pre-existing ideological framework and shaped it to their needs. With reference to the two roles of ritual to unite and divide societies, we see here a widespread communal practice reshaped to justify the elite's hierarchical position over the surrounding landscape. While attention may have traditionally been focused on the most finely crafted prestige objects,[153] it is now clear that eating and drinking were of great importance at sites such as Neopalatial Juktas, Vrysinas, and MM III Kophinas. The abundance of cooking pots indicates that these were not just 'picnic' sites, but the locale of the preparation of food, presumably feasts. Ritual, therefore, was deeply embedded in social activities. More can be said about regional variations within these general observations.

Regional Patterns

Inevitably, we begin with the north-central, Knossian region. In the wider surrounding area, there were several other peak sanctuaries in use during the Protopalatial period, such as Pyrgos (Tylissos), Keria, and Karphi, while Gonies and Kastelli Liliano appear to have fallen out of use after MM III.[154] Could these other sites simply not compete? Perhaps it became taboo for open-air sanctuaries in high places to be used ritually in the area overlooked by Juktas, when Knossos chose to invest all its resources into a single, landmark site. Indeed, if the relations between Knossos and Juktas were as strong as is commonly believed,[155] then the situation appears to be that Knossos was able to overlook its sphere of influence from this ritual site; it became an extension of Knossian power. This 'special relationship' does not necessarily mean that Knossos *monopolized* activity at the ritual site, but it did provide an excellent platform for demonstrating Knossian authority. Archanes may have capitalized on the wider importance of Juktas, for example, in the production of figurines. Rather than being a liminal extra-urban sanctuary, Juktas is therefore the focal point for the north-central region.

While there is a dearth of other peak sanctuaries in this area, the majority of sacred caves are found here. Rutkowski noted certain physical similarities between Skoteino and Phaneromeni.[156] Neither of these caves appears to have been used ritually in the Protopalatial period, although Protopalatial pottery has been found at Skoteino. It is possible that Skoteino was some kind of boundary marker, not necessarily political, but significant in some way. It lies in the area where the three palatial territories converge as reconstructed by Whitelaw, and Warren suggests that the caves of Ida, Arkalochori, and Skoteino 'may also be seen marking western, southern, and eastern limits of Knossian religious territory'.[157] The cave falls on the border between Knossos and Malia in Bevan's Protopalatial reconstruction.[158]

There are good indications that sanctuaries were used to mark boundaries in Classical Greece, both in the newly established colonies and on the mainland.[159] In a world without maps, territory could be marked with processions and pilgrimages between urban centre and sanctuary. Watrous has used de Polignac's theory concerning the historical placement of Greek sanctuaries as boundary markers during the rise of the polis as support for the same phenomenon occurring in the Protopalatial period.[160] The current lack of systematic analyses of the material from such sites results in a heavy reliance on dots on modern maps. However, a recent study suggests that the Skoteino Cave was a local sanctuary used by people living in the northern Pediada.[161] The perhaps surprising lack of interest from either palatial site to the west or east leaves it less likely that this was a boundary site.

This is in contrast to the more isolated and yet richer caves on Dikte (Psychro) and Ida. A diverse range of artefacts was found at both sites, although Psychro is clearer as post-Minoan use at the Idaean Cave has confused the Neopalatial evidence. Rutkowski also noted physical similarities between the two caves.[162] Both caves are also located at high altitudes, far from the sea and large settlements, with glorious views over the landscape. They are located in what may well have been no-mans' land. While the Lasithi plain was inhabited, no large sites have been found.[163] Plati lies around fifteen minutes west of Psychro, and its Neopalatial remains are poorly preserved – the only published vase is an LM IA ewer.[164] This area (Block A) comprises parts of buildings aligning a road, which is preserved at 2.2 m wide and 28 m long. It may have served as a stopping point for those visiting Psychro.[165] Similarly, Zominthos may have been involved with the administration of the Idaean Cave. An LM IA building has been found here, of substantial size (ca. 1600 m²), with a polythyron.[166] It contains a potter's workshop and evidence for food pre-paration, along with some ritual artefacts such as two bronze figurines and a terracotta bull rhyton.[167] Presumably, it catered for those making a pilgrimage to Ida. At 1,187 mamsl, it is somewhat isolated, while providing a vital stop for pilgrims.

It takes several hours to reach Psychro from either Knossos or Malia.[168] This is a very different kind of pilgrimage and commitment than one would expect with a Protopalatial peak sanctuary. In 1996, Watrous declared that: 'the sanctuary at Psychro may have been for Malia at this time what Juktas was for Knossos.'[169] However, he later reviewed some of Hogarth's material from the Herakleion Museum. Due caveats are required given the unsystematic nature of the material's collection (and later recording), but this analysis confirms that ceramics (mostly for liquids: cups, jugs, and amphorae) from both Malia and Knossos were being brought to the cave.[170] There was an important shift from a mostly Malian presence in the initial Neopalatial periods up until LM IB, when Knossian vases became predominant.[171] Again caution is required, as pots do not necessarily mean people, but in this case it is a reasonable assump-tion. This may mirror the apparent Knossian engagement across the island in LM IB, as has been advocated at Ayia Triada and Zakros. Watrous associated the cessation of peak sanctuaries throughout the Neopalatial period with this phenomenon, suggesting that Juktas became the extra-urban shrine of Knossos to such an extent that this suppressed activity elsewhere, and that Psychro also came under Knossian control.[172]

The large, isolated ritual sites may be compared with later Greek Panhellenic sanctuaries.[173] These historic sites have evidence for civic and individual competition in the form of athletic, musical, and theatrical competitions, and the establishment of treasuries. In the eighth century BC, rich objects, which had previously been deposited in graves, were dedicated in such sanctuaries.[174] Panhellenic sanctuaries were politically neutral (at least at face value), which enabled such competitive practices. Despite its unclear Neopalatial evidence, the Idaean Cave fits this comparison particularly well, as do Kato Syme (which has been compared to Delphi)[175] and perhaps Psychro.[176] The predominance of Knossian material at Psychro does not negate this idea; it merely demonstrates that users of Knossian pottery were particularly active in leaving ceramics at the cave.

In this light, the markedly reduced use of the ritual cave at isolated Kamares is intriguing, given that caves became commonly used for ritual in central Crete. If Knossos had become a political power in the western Mesara in the Neopalatial period (particularly LM IA perhaps), then it might have been expected that its elite appropriated this ritual. However, it was Ayia Triada, not Phaistos, that flourished for the most of this time, and it is this site that is believed to have been 'Knossian'. Possibly, the Kamares Cave was seen to be too much associated with Phaistos to be allowed to continue to be used, and we see a clean slate imposed on ritual activity in the area.

The previous section has indicated that there were several ritual sites in the landscape that received rich votives and, in most cases, structural investments and permanent buildings. But the sudden drop in the use of peak sanctuaries might also give the impression that there was *less* attention to the ritual landscape. This would contradict the general impression that control was heavily ritualized in the Minoan world, instead of extensive fortifications and other forms of military control. However, the grand open-air spaces within and nearby the Palaces would appear to form a good arena for mass rituals. The rise in the use of ritual caves, including those that took a lot of time and effort to reach, also demonstrate the importance of the ritual landscape.

CHAPTER SEVEN

LITERACY, ADMINISTRATION, AND COMMUNICATION

T HIS WAS A LITERATE WORLD, WITH A WRITING SYSTEM THAT WE
cannot read – but then, neither presumably could have most of those
living in Neopalatial Crete.[1] Literacy, and the increasing standardization of
it,[2] appears to have played some role in the legitimization of the elites.[3]
The overall administration was sophisticated, with some types of documents
recognizable elsewhere in the eastern Mediterranean, others specific to
Crete.[4] 'Communication' is a far wider topic, incorporating all manner
of symbols and images, so there is some overlap with Chapter 9.[5] This
chapter therefore explores a range of themes concerning the various communication mechanisms that bound together Minoan life, especially among
the elite.

After introducing the Linear A script, we will consider what we know (or
rather, what we do not know) about the language it represents. The administration will be considered from the point of view of writing, sealing, and labelling.
Two Neopalatial phenomena deserve further discussion. The first are the 'replica
rings', misnamed but of great interest for the insights they shed into inter-site
communication, possibly of a diplomatic nature, between very different types of
site. The second are the so-called look-alike sealings, found particularly at
Zakros. We will also explore non-administrative uses of Linear A script.
In particular, libation tables with inscribed formulae also indicate the desire to
communicate with other worlds, and 'materializing the relations between the
elite and the divine world'.[6]

THE LINEAR A SCRIPT

Crete was the first area of modern Europe to adopt a writing system. High levels of complexity can be achieved without literacy, such as in the Inca state in Peru,[7] but writing transforms the temporal and spatial modes of knowledge externalization and communication. Literacy, or the ability to read and write a conventional script, both reflects and reinforces social differentiation through education. Writing can be seen as mysterious or even magical to those uninitiated in the rites of reading. Homer (*Iliad* Book 6) sang of a tablet with 'murderous symbols' inscribed on it; in this context, these signs had the power to sentence the bearer to death. These markings are not described as writing as such, and the poet does not appear to fully understand the nature of writing and its power to give instructions across time and space. This illustrates an important point: writing not only enables economic control by elite bureaucracies in addition to other forms of 'knowledge transfer', but literacy also bestows social prestige upon those able to unlock these cryptic signs.

While writing may be displayed as an intimidation strategy for those not 'in the know', most writing was hidden from general view. Few, presumably, had access to administrative archives, and some inscribed objects were taken out of sight and circulation, such as those thrown into the Psychro Cave or deposited in mortuary contexts. The intended audiences of Neopalatial writing were far-ranging; it enabled communication between elites, a public display of the elite's superiority (over the illiterate), or interaction with other worlds in the ritual sphere. Before exploring these issues in more detail, let us consider what we know about this undeciphered script.

Linear A findspots are concentrated on Crete, but it occurs in small numbers beyond its shores, such as in the Cyclades, the Greek mainland, the western coast of Anatolia, and the Near East.[8] It was not the only Bronze Age Cretan script, nor the first. Cretan Hieroglyphic was developed around 2000 BC; this was syllabic, with ideograms and numbers. Linear A, which was to become the sole Neopalatial script, was developed slightly later than Cretan Hieroglyphic, and they were used simultaneously in the Protopalatial period.[9] Linear A was apparently developed in south-west Crete. Occasionally both are present in the same archive, such as in Room III8 in the Palace at Malia, where MM IIIB Linear A and Cretan Hieroglyphic documents were found together. Linear A deposits are spread throughout the Neopalatial period, with very few examples of the script known from after it.[10] It is possible to date the administrative evidence to particular ceramic phases, unlike the ritual deposits, which are usually assigned 'Neopalatial' more generally. Linear B (the script used for Mycenaean Greek) postdates Linear A; the Mycenaeans borrowed the Linear A signs despite the fact that they were poorly suited to represent Greek. There is general consensus that the two languages are not related. It is possible, with due caution, to compare the two scripts.[11]

Linear A is syllabic. The syllabary includes seventy-five signs that appear more than five times in the texts. Logograms represented objects, identifications that are confirmed by using Linear B equivalents. A system of numbers was developed based on a decimal system, which the Linear B script adopted.[12] It can be difficult to distinguish script from non-script, for example mason's marks or the graffiti on pithoi.[13] In the case of mason's marks, Owen defines 'real' Linear A inscriptions as a series of at least three signs, which can be compared to existing inscriptions.[14] On the whole, however, potter's marks and mason's marks have little connection with writing. 'In a figurative sense the signs are like the words of a language whose grammar or syntax is provided by the contexts of the signs'; such as its location on architectural stone.[15]

The standard typology for the script rests on the distinction between administrative and non-administrative uses. The former category is subdivided according to type of document (e.g., tablet or 'roundel'), the latter according to material (e.g., stone vessel or metal object). This is a convenient, modern classification that can be misleading. For example, signs painted or inscribed on pottery (such as pithoi) that label products could be included with the administrative documents, which would be part of the W-series in *GORILA*,[16] but instead they are placed in the Z-series. On a more abstract level, the distinction between the secular 'business' and ritual spheres is not perhaps as clear-cut as this typology suggests. Archives are often found in association with ritual areas, such as in the west wing at Zakros (Figure 7.1), while inscribed stone vessels have also been found in settlement contexts (not ritual sites), such as at Prassos.

Linear A has been found inscribed on stone (notably libation tables) and metal, and painted on pottery and wall paintings. It has also been found in a variety of contexts: Palaces, sanctuaries, tombs, and houses. These observations become all the more striking when compared with the distribution of Linear B, which was purely palatial and administrative (although we do not know what was written on perishable materials). Scholars have concentrated on three aspects of the Linear A script: the decipherment, the administrative and economic function, and its cultic use, particularly the libation formulae. This chapter will focus on the latter two areas, following a brief discussion of previous attempts at decipherment.

The Language of Linear A

Language is generally seen as a key component of ethnicity, due to its role in communication and forming identities.[17] It is unclear whether Cretan Hieroglyphics and Linear A were used to represent two different languages, or were simply different scripts to represent the same tongue. Numerous

7.1 Zakros Palace, archive area in west wing (photograph by author).

attempts have been made to decipher Linear A, or to establish the guiding linguistic principles.[18] It has been identified as Greek, Lycian, Luwian, Semitic, Sanskrit, and Etruscan, but only by means of pseudo-scientific methods; the fact remains that not enough documents have survived to allow a convincing decipherment.[19] Since most administrative documents of any length are lists, there is little information about the language's syntax.

Some scholars have attempted to apply the Linear B values onto the same Linear A signs, but this process can be used to 'demonstrate' links to both (non-Indo-European) Semitic and (Indo-European) Lycian.[20] The influence of the language through the subsequent Mycenaean period can be seen in the survival of pre-Greek names, notably those ending in –ssos (e.g., Knossos, Tylissos, Amnissos, and Prassos). It is not always clear whether anthroponyms or toponyms are being referred to in the texts; this is partly a frustration of there being so few examples.[21] Papers concerning individual inscriptions tend to concentrate on the signs themselves, rather than the archaeological context.[22] There is not enough evidence, however, to conduct an internal decipherment, and no Rosetta Stone equivalent exists.[23] However, the contexts of the documents can still convey much information, and it is on them that we focus.

ADMINISTRATION

The Linear A tablets may not be deciphered, but they give rich insights into Minoan administration and the movement of goods, and 'the purpose of any administration is to keep track of the incoming and outgoing movements of goods'.[24] Three major categories have been discerned: inventories of stored products; incoming items and labour; and outgoing items and personnel.[25] As such, this section shares themes with the storage of staples in the following chapter. 'Administration' also refers to the organization of people, governance, and even law.[26] Two tablets from Ayia Triada list around 500 people, a significant number, and comparable to those listed on the later Linear B tablets of Knossos and Pylos.[27]

The administrative system relied on a far wider body of documents beyond the written ones, with a complex series of sealing devices. Linear A studies are often conducted separately from the wider sealing network, and it can be difficult to integrate the two strands. In support of this modern division, tablets and sealed documents appear to have been stored separately in the Neopalatial context, leading to the assumption that they represent different stages of the administrative process.[28] For example, at Ayia Triada, it is possible that the tablets recorded the transactions that the sealings and roundels represented.[29] This is particularly the case as the tablets concerning the same subject were found in different rooms, suggesting that 'most documents do not give evidence for on-the-spot recording of economic processes'.[30]

The lack of evidence is highly problematic, most notably in the palatial sites, such as Knossos and Malia. Clay documents need to be fired in order to be preserved. Since this was not done deliberately by either sun or kiln, we require buildings to have been destroyed by fire. Where the destruction involved an intense fire, such as Myrtos-Pyrgos (two LM IB Linear A tablets, no sealings) and Palaikastro (only one (LM IA) tablet), we might have expected more to have survived if the building served as an administrative centre. Weingarten has provided a comprehensive list of settlements lacking sealings.[31] She suggested that the presence of sealings at so few sites indicated that four major administrative centres centralized administration (i.e., Ayia Triada, Zakros, Chania, and Knossos, via Sklavokambos and Tylissos). This hypothesis has received limited acceptance.[32] We will first explore what the Linear A tablets indicate, and then examine the wider sealing activity.

The Linear A Tablets

Linear A tablets occur as page-shaped tablets and bars. The evidence for Linear A tablets comes mainly from the LM IB destructions, although this may reflect accidents of preservation.[33] In any case, this hinders gauging change within the Neopalatial period.[34] Ayia Triada, the prosperous non-palatial site in the Mesara, has produced the largest number of Linear A tablets at 147, Chania, the probable palatial site to the west, has now produced 100, while the eastern site of Zakros with its LM IB Palace has produced thirty-one (Table 7.1).

TABLE 7.1 *Administrative documents in Neopalatial Crete. Wa and Wc are listed whether inscribed or not; Wb, Wd, We, Wf and misc. are listed here if inscribed. After Schoep 2002, 21, Table 1.2 (in turn adapted from Hallager 1996, 25, Table 2); with additions: del Freo 2008; 2012; Watrous 2015, 434–8.*

Sites	Wa	Wb	Wc	Wd	We-Wf	Wy Misc Wg	Tablet
Archanes							7
Gournia		2	2		12		1
A. Triada	936	76	22	11	53	5	147
Chania	20	57	118	6	3	3	99
Knossos	14	36	14	3	55	3	6
Malia		1	5				6
Petras						1	3
Phaistos	4	4	11	1	8	7	26
Palaikastro					3	1	1
Pyrgos			2		1		2
Sklavokambos			2		37		
Tylissos	1		2		2		2
Zakros	7	492	1	53	7		31

The evidence from other non-palatial sites is also generally dated to LM IB, while the limited palatial evidence (from Knossos, Malia, and Phaistos) tends to be earlier; the smaller Palaces at Zakros and Petras are the exceptions. A similar variability occurs in the intra-site evidence, with some sites having apparently concentrated deposits (such as Myrtos-Pyrgos), and some more widely distributed (such as Ayia Triada). Here the nature of preservation may again be the major factor, as well as major differences in the original volume of finds.[35]

Table 7.1 indicates some isolated finds of tablets at flourishing sites, such as Palaikastro, where the archives may be undiscovered. It is likely that the Linear A clay tablets performed a temporary function before a more permanent record was made – but on a perishable material.[36] It may be the case that settlements kept small archives, such as at Tylissos and Myrtos Pyrgos.[37] At Myrtos-Pyrgos, neither of the two tablets was found in a primary context, but certainly PYR 1 and possibly PYR 2 appear to belong to an assemblage of artefacts including clay tubular offering stands, a faience conch shell, and a bronze rosette.[38] It has been suggested that this assemblage was ritual, either a shrine or a treasury for ritual activity taking place elsewhere.[39] Many of these clay documents come from secondary or tertiary contexts. The administrative function of these tablets may have become obsolete, while they became social prestige objects, perhaps with symbolic or mystical overtones. Were all sites with such evidence administrative centres? Or were they being administered from elsewhere? Knossos was an administrative centre, although we lack strong direct evidence, while Myrtos-Pyrgos is a good example of how difficult it is to answer this important question. Weingarten believed that the two tablets signify literacy only, and not autonomy, while others are willing to accept it as an administrative centre.[40]

The observation that the numbers recorded in the Linear A tablets are considerably smaller than both Linear B and, perhaps more surprisingly, Cretan Hieroglyphics, has economic implications.[41] Presumably the estates and number of people involved are also smaller, or the Linear A documents certify a different stage of the administrative process. A further difference is that the Linear A tablets do not indicate a focus on a particular commodity, as occurs on the Linear B tablets.[42] Zakros differs in this respect; here, eleven of the sixteen tablets from the Palace magazines have single commodity sections.[43] Generally, the collection of commodities listed is more varied, which is possibly due to a less specialized bureaucracy. With one possible exception, and again in contrast to Linear B, Schoep states that 'there are no extant inventories of raw materials and/or finished objects'.[44]

While we should not apply Linear B values to Linear A signs in an attempt to unlock the language,[45] there are some signs which, from their position, may be applied to Linear A. 'KU-RO' refers to the 'total' of various sections of lists, while 'KI-RO' appears to refer to deficits.[46] Therefore, records were made of debts carried over rather than simply noting transactions as they occurred. The latter is important, as it indicates the ability to control resources over time as well as space, and enables us to think beyond the basic question of how spatially centralized organization was.[47] Transaction signs are frustratingly difficult to assign to transactional terms. Schoep notes that they 'can vary considerably depending on whether incoming (taxes, levies or tributes, gifts, finished products, payment of loans etc.) or outgoing (payments, rations, offerings, loans or the transmission of goods within the central administration) commodities are concerned' – but we cannot generally clarify this further, not even establishing whether the commodities were incoming and/or outgoing.[48]

Schoep also notes that it is difficult to find any pattern in the ratio of goods assigned to individuals.[49] Therefore, each individual on HT 27 and HT 89 was allotted ca. 2.4 and 2.2 litres of wheat and 2.7 and 2.2 litres of figs, whereas on KH 7 each individual took 4.8 litres of grain. This information cannot be analysed in detail, since we do not know the number of dependents reliant on such rations, or the length of time it was intended to last. Alternatively, there are up to 4,148 units of grain (assuming no duplicates) in the thirty-nine relevant tablets from Ayia Triada.[50] This would support 20,740 women workers for a month, or 1,728 for a year.[51] From the surviving evidence, there is little to distinguish between the tablets from the central Villa Reale and the nearby Casa del Lebete, by 'subjects, scale, and procedures for recording'.[52]

Hallager has discussed in detail Tablet HT 24, which was found in Corridor 9 of the Villa along with forty-five noduli (tokens) on the windowsill between Corridor 9 and Room 27.[53] The total on the verso of the tablet would be 4.5

'Talent' (135 kg); i.e., forty-five units of wool. The clear conclusion from this is that forty-five units of wool were given or received by someone outside the Villa, in exchange for the noduli, and the transaction was registered in the tablet. That they were located close to an entrance to the Villa would support this thesis, as this would have been the obvious point of exchange. Watrous suggests that agricultural products were collected at the Villa to be redistributed and used to support various professions, from scribe to smith, carpenter to cook. The Villa was, therefore, the centre of an extensive estate.[54] Later, he argues that Ayia Triada's administrative purview 'was not limited to this immediate area west of Phaistos, but was actually regional in scope'.[55] Although the evidence from Ayia Triada is impressive, the actual territory involved in producing the amount of wheat, oil, and wine mentioned in the tables may only have been about 15 km^2.[56] While this site is the most rewarding in terms of extracting information about the logistics of the Neopalatial administration, consideration of the full set of Minoan administrative documents indicates regional preferences across the island.

Other Administrative Documents: Form, Distribution, and Seals

Minoan administration possessed a range of documents that operated without text, although some of these (especially the roundels) could also have inscriptions (Table 7.1).[57] On the whole, however, sealings 'were in the first place authenticated documents',[58] or, in other words, their seal-impression lent authority to the documents or items they sealed or labelled, which have not themselves been preserved. The terms for the various forms will be discussed later in this chapter, and we follow the convention for inscribed documents as set out in *GORILA* (W-series): see Table 7.1. Functionally, these can be divided into three main types (Figure 7.2). Some are ***free-standing*** records, which are not attached to any other document or item (the roundel and the nodulus, pl. noduli), so serving as some kind of receipt or token. The flat-based nodules and the less common direct sealings were ***pressed*** against another document or item, as revealed by the impression underneath; here the seal authorized the object or transaction.[59] ***Hanging*** nodules could also be fastened to items or pegs as a kind of label. Some types would have formed part of a 'working' administration, and served as a temporary record of ongoing interactions, and some would have provided a final, permanent record. Tablets and noduli are likely to have assisted with temporary records, but hanging nodules with permanent ones (as they secured perishable documents).[60]

Single-hole nodules (Wa) and two-hole hanging nodules (Wd) would have been attached to an object or peg via a cord fastened through the hole. Single-hole nodules could be suspended, while the cord ran horizontally through the clay document in two-hole nodules. Wa documents are the most numerous

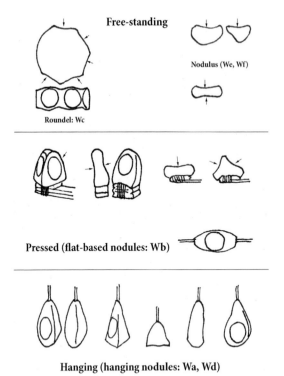

7.2 Types of Minoan administrative documents (drawn by author, after Hallager 1996, figure 2).

type of Linear A document to have survived, and can possess a seal impression as well as an inscription (usually a single sign). Wd documents tended to have seal impressions but had very few inscriptions. It is believed that they sealed and labelled commodities; they may have secured written documents as well.

Flat-based nodules (Wb) also served as labels; from the impressions of their flat sides, it appears that they were set against and sealed folded parchment, with the thread wrapped around the seal to doubly secure it. The pieces of parchment were extremely small, usually a maximum of 6 × 6 cm,[61] or the impression from the parchment that we have is simply a strip cut to secure the document.[62] It is unclear whether this type of document could have been diplomatic correspondence. Exceptions from this standard small size include the Master Impression from Chania, which sealed a larger packet, or KH 1559 (CMS V Suppl. 1A nos. 128–37), which sealed a folded piece of leather of around 10.8 × 2 cm, and was stamped twelve times by ten different seals.[63] Notably, these are usually sealed but rarely carry inscriptions; therefore, the authorization of the seal (whether it represents a person, office, or product and so on) appears to be more important than the individual labelling of the attached.

Roundels (Wc) are specific to the Linear A administration. A roundel was a clay disc with one or more seal impressions stamped on its rim; it also usually had one or more Linear A signs inscribed on either or both faces; the inscriptions are usually logograms and rarely numerals. Here we witness a cross-over between seal-impresser and scribe. This was a record or token, not attached to another item. If the logogram indicated the commodity, then the sealings could indicate a transaction – for example, the storeroom administrators dispatched a unit.[64] Noduli (We and Wf: they are categorized in terms of dome-noduli and disc-noduli, but functionally appear to be the same) were also free-standing documents, but less frequently inscribed. Sealings or direct object sealings (Wg) were pressed against an object other than strips for documents; these are quite uncommon in the Linear A administration, although they do occur at Chania. Incised pottery (Zb: thirty-six examples) and painted pottery (Zc: four examples) could have been administrative in that they described the contents of the pot, which is often a pithos. Boskamp suggests that the graffiti on the inscribed pithoi in the magazines at Knossos were simple marks (albeit classifiable as 'script'): 'not trade marks or workshop marks, but perhaps rather a sort of quality certificate'.[65]

Administrative documents have been found only in settlement sites, with the largest (LM IB) archives at Ayia Triada, Chania, and Zakros. These sites, along with Knossos and Phaistos, are the only sites that have produced all types of documents.[66] The Knossian evidence is disappointing, although this is certainly a matter of poor preservation rather than a reflection of the historical picture. One early deposit at Knossos is the assemblage of noduli (seals that do not seal) in the Temple Repositories along with the nodules.[67] These administrative documents were a stored archive, but no longer serving their original function.[68]

Administrative documents were not always found in the central building: Knossos and Ayia Triada revealed documents in impressive surrounding structures, while House A at Zakros was less distinguished.[69] Such structures may have served as outposts for the central authority, and it is not necessary to interpret a scattered distribution with factions or any form of social decentralization. It is highly likely that Chania was a palatial site, but the precise location and layout of the Palace remains unknown. The administrative documents were widely distributed across various buildings. Whether this 'may hint at an additional, private level of administration' is debatable,[70] as this distribution may still represent communication and control by the central elite. Administrative control is not always indicated by spatial concentration, and equalifinality remains an issue in social interpretations.

In contrast to the Linear A tablets, the use of seals and sealings is much more widespread throughout the landscape.[71] Seals themselves may serve as conspicuous jewellery, as seen hanging on the wrist of the (Final Palatial) Cup-bearer Fresco from Knossos. They could be made of precious or semi-precious stone (as well as more standard stone); some were very colourful, and some

were exquisitely engraved or mould-made with rich iconographical representations (see Chapter 9). A distinct engraving could represent the person, his or
her rank, or his or her office in an abstract manner.[72] When pressed into
a malleable material such as clay or wax, the impression could act as an
authorization or declaration of ownership. It is also possible that they had
apotropaic or magical functions. Some sealings were marked by more than
one seal (multiple sealings), a sphragistic practice common at LM IB Zakros, for
example, and a few had Linear A signs inscribed on them as well.

The shapes of the seals become more standardized in the Neopalatial period,
namely, cushion, lentoid, and amygdaloid seals; roughly 1,800 Neopalatial seals
survive.[73] There are around 900 'talismanic' seals (a name based on Arthur
Evan's belief that they were amulets rather than of sphragistic use), but only
around two dozen impressions from them – this would indeed suggest that they
did not form a core part of the administrative repertoire.[74] Around 130 ring
impressions have been found, possibly but not necessarily of gold.[75] Most
sealings come from the fire destructions that ravished Crete at the end of LM
IB, and more than 1,800 survive from these.[76] Cult scenes have been found
particularly at Ayia Triada, with some more from Chania and few from
Knossos.[77] However, Weingarten notes that many of the most active seal
owners at LM IB Ayia Triada possessed mediocre or basic seals, only three
high-use (and preserved) examples are of the highest quality.[78]

Knossian 'Replica Rings'

A series of 'replica ring' sealings have been found at five or six Cretan sites,
including Ayia Triada, Zakros, Sklavokambos, Gournia, Knossos, and possibly
Chania. They were all found in LM IB contexts on Crete, but also in LM IA
Thera.[79] Hallager identifies fifty-three impressions from ten such rings.[80]
However, this includes examples that have been found only at one site, such
as CMS II.6 no. 17 from Ayia Triada. The current analysis focuses on the four
certain examples, used at more than one site (Figure 7.3). These often depicted
bull-leaping scenes. The Knossian elite may have appropriated the image of the
bull, as it is at Knossos where we find wall paintings of bull-leaping and
a particular concentration of the motif.[81] Otherwise, one of the impressions
shows a combat scene. It is notable that these 'replica ring' examples do not
include cultic scenes found on gold rings or their impressions.

The term 'replica ring' is very misleading, but has been maintained here, in
order to correspond with previous works.[82] It refers to sealings from different
sites that were stamped with the same sealing device (generally speaking,
a golden ring around 3 cm long). This name is misleading as it was the *same*
ring that stamped the separate sealings, rather than replica ones; those made
from similar rings will be discussed later. Betts' seminal work from 1967 both

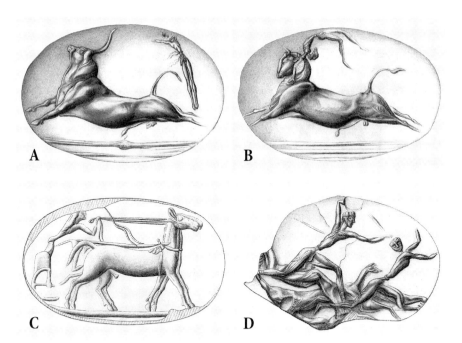

7.3 'Replica rings': Images courtesy of the CMS Heidelberg.
  A) CMS II.6 no. 43 (Ayia Triada: three flat-based nodules); see also CMS II.6 no. 161 (Gournia: one nodulus); CMS II.6 no. 259 (Sklavokambos: two flat-based nodules); CMS II.7 no. 39 (Zakros: one nodulus).
  B) CMS II.6 no. 44 (Ayia Triada: one flat-based nodule); see also CMS II.6 no. 162 (Gournia: one flat-based nodule); CMS II.6 no. 255 (Sklavokambos: one flat-based nodule).
  C) CMS II.6 no. 19 (Ayia Triada: two flat-based nodules); see also CMS II.6 no. 260 (Sklavokambos: four flat-based nodules); CMS V Suppl. 3 no. 391 (Akrotiri: three flat-based nodules).
  D) CMS II.6 no. 15 (Ayia Triada: five flat-based nodules); see also CMS II.8 no. 279 (Knossos: two single-hole hanging nodules).

set this topic on the agenda, and generated some of the persistent confusion. He believed that representatives of the ruler travelled from site to site with a replica of the ruler's mark, so several identical rings were in circulation.[83] This would make sense if the rings were made with steatite moulds,[84] but closer analysis indicates that the sealing devices were handmade, and therefore unique.[85]

Most scholars have also followed Betts' suggestion that these rings were made at Knossos,[86] or that the sealings originated from a single site, most probably Knossos. This conclusion was initially made on the basis of the likely importance of Knossos as a bureaucratic centre, and the assumption that prestigious objects such as gold rings would originate from there. Scientific analyses indicate that the clay of most of the 'replica' documents has a north-central provenance, pointing towards Knossos. In this work, Goren and Panagiotopoulos tested all nodules, including the pieces from Knossos

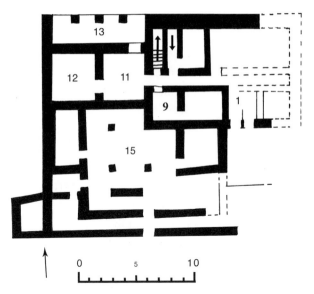

0   5   10

7.4 Sklavokambos (drawn by author; after Marinatos 1948, figure 4; Fotou 1997, figure 8).

which belonged to single-hole nodules.[87] This implies that there was a single ring from one centre (Knossos) and it was the sealings that travelled (with the documents or objects they were attached to), rather than various individuals with identical rings.[88]

They serve as proof of communication between the sites, which might otherwise have been assumed; however, they do not necessarily indicate Knossian *control*. This kind of evidence falls particularly foul to the chance of preservation, so what we have is surely the tip of the iceberg. Nonetheless, I intend to take a close look at the relevant sites from a comparative point of view. Communication between sites did not result in standardization in administrative practices, providing yet another example of structural variations within the apparent homogeneous picture of Neopalatial Crete.

The similarities with the (later) Taureador Fresco at Knossos concerning the compositions and poises of the figures of the first two examples are notable, although here both figures curve round to follow the shape of the ring. Likewise, the bull is unrealistically stretched out to follow the horizontal line; both seals depict the line of the ground. In the first example, it is notable that stamped noduli (the free-standing documents) made their way to the Palaces, whereas flat-based nodules that secured documents ended up at the Villa Reale and Sklavokambos (Figure 7.4). The nodules presumably indicate communication, possibly diplomatic, between sites. There is more than one example of Figure 7.3A at Ayia Triada and Sklavokambos. The same person or office needed to communicate in different documents to these non-palatial sites, while also sending out noduli to the other (palatial) sites. The noduli are more difficult to interpret; if they were tokens, such as receipts, then they may indicate actions owed, fulfilled, or desired. Aside from these 'replica ring' sealings, these Palaces yielded very little evidence for such documents. However, the second bull-leaping scene comes entirely from flat-based nodules, from all four sites apart from Zakros (Figure 7.3B). All of the nodules with these two examples have a single impression on them (even if there is more than one such nodule at the site), which indicates a single (Knossian) authority for the contents of the documents.

The chariot scene (Figure 7.3C) is also designed to follow the shape of the ring, with the bent figure leaning over the back of the horses, which are elongated to fit the space. This example was found in the two non-palatial (even if central) buildings at Ayia Triada and Sklavokambos; furthermore, it also occurs at Akrotiri on Thera, an intriguing non-Cretan and earlier (LM IA) example. All examples are flat-based nodules, so sealed a document. Impressions from this ring occur more than once at all of these sites, and in the same assemblage, so one individual or officeholder was keen to lodge repeated statements with the receivers. Normally the impression occurs on its own, but in one example from Ayia Triada, the impression was joined by a bull-leaping scene (CMS II.6 no. 41).

The combat scene (Figure 7.3D) is a graphic portrayal of a fight, where a man is striking his fallen foe. This provides a rare example from the assumed 'mother' site, Knossos, in the form of two single-hole hanging nodules, of a type known from Ayia Triada where the other example of this scene occurs.[89] However, the examples from Ayia Triada occur on five flat-based nodules. Three of these possess only this impression, but the other two have a further impression of a cult scene (CMS II.6 no. 4), where a female kneels at a stone and twists round to look back at floating objects.

Overall, the majority of these impressions appear on one-seal, flat-based nodules,[90] used to secure, seal, and authorize non-perishable documents (such as parchment). These served a very different administrative purpose from roundels, disc-shaped nodules, or single-hole hanging nodules.[91] In fact, these rings may not fall under 'administration' at all, but rather represent diplomatic relations between certain individuals.[92] Goren and Panagiotopoulos draw attention to the surprising observation that no other contemporary seal-using administrations in the eastern Mediterranean created such a wide distribution of documents impressed by the same ring.[93] It is worth undertaking a comparative and holistic analysis of these Cretan sites. Knossos itself is too problematic to discuss, given the dearth of LM IB evidence,[94] so we focus on the other four: Ayia Triada, Zakros, Sklavokambos, and Gournia.

It is often remarked that the Villa at Ayia Triada has many Knossian features, and was influenced if not controlled by the site (see Chapter 5).[95] Ayia Triada provides the richest administrative evidence,[96] with 1,200 sealings, but it is now extremely difficult to match artefacts to findspots.[97] The provenance of the Linear A tablets is not always clear;[98] however, they were also found outside the main Villa, unlike the sealings, which were more centralized. Within the Villa Reale, the sealings were clustered in batches; most were kept separate from the tablets, and not in areas of production and storage. The site has yielded the full range of administrative documents, with tablets (147), roundels (22), noduli (53), flat-based nodules (76), two-hole nodules (11), single-hole nodules (936), and miscellaneous (5): Table 7.1. There were also four inscribed pieces of pottery (pithoi). Most of the sealings (nearly 80 per cent) are hanging nodules, or labels that do not seal as such, and these were mostly unsuitable for heavy items or long distance transport.[99]

Weingarten has noted that seventeen seal holders (out of nearly 150 seal devices used) were responsible for more than 80 per cent of all sealings.[100] The owner of one seal (AT 125) was responsible for a quarter of all sealings, or 259 of those surviving, while AT 13 and AT 95 were also unusually prolific. The use of Linear A signs was also restricted to a certain number of seal holders (twelve of the seventeen 'elite' administrators).[101] This suggests that a few resident seal holders were responsible for most of the administration. In sum, while the site provides strong evidence for inter-site relations in terms of the 'replica rings' sealings, it also demonstrates a very pyramidal structure and centralization of seal use in the central building.

Two deposits from Zakros were found in the Palace and House A. There is spatial decentralization of sealings, and apparently less of an 'administrative elite' at Zakros, indicated by a wider spread of sealing motifs. The sealing deposit from House A contains 1,070 seal impressions on 554 objects, the vast majority of which (490 or 88 per cent) are nodules with impressions of parchment documents on them.[102] Around half these impressions portray monsters, hybrids, and fabulous creatures.[103] The Palace yielded thirty Linear A tablets, one nodulus, one two-hole hanging nodule and two flat-based nodules. The Palace has not produced many sealings, and their findspots and current locations are not always clear. The Treasury appears not to have been secured with sealings.[104] However, it is a nodulus, probably from the Archive Room with the Linear A tablets (Room XVI: see Figure 7.1), that has produced the site's definite 'replica ring' example.[105] Therefore, while House A yielded the vast majority of sealings, the Palace demonstrates communication with other sites, namely, Gournia, Sklavokambos, and Ayia Triada.

The building at Sklavokambos was excavated by Marinatos in the 1930s, preliminarily published then re-examined by Fotou (Figure 7.4).[106] This structure would have been the first one of the settlement encountered from the east. Various ritual artefacts were also found, such as a stone conical rhyton and a clay ox head found fallen from above the hall.[107] The deposit of sealings (thirty-seven flat-based nodules and two noduli) from Sklavokambos fell from the upper floor of the entrance leading to the north-eastern hall; a terracotta human foot also fell from this area. Areas 11 and 12 provided storage areas, and contained whole and broken pithoi.[108] The storage and administrative evidence combine to suggest that this was an organizational centre for commodities, presumably from the Psiloritis region towards the main centres of consumption.[109] It may have also served as a more localized marketplace. One of the nodules was impressed by three seals (CMS II.6 nos. 267–70); this is the only multiple-sealed free-standing nodule found outside Zakros.[110] Furthermore, two of the seals closely resemble the distinctive Zakros creatures. This may also represent communication between the distant sites.

Gournia has revealed very little evidence for administration (Chapter 5). The recent excavations revealed a Linear A tablet from Room 16 of the Palace, in an LM IB deposit.[111] One (probably LM IA) roundel with a Linear A inscription came from House Cf 25, with fourteen LM IB sealings (mostly noduli).[112] House Fg 30 yielded a series of eight noduli impressed with the same seal, and deposited inside the inverted lid of a vase.[113] Both of the 'replica ring' sealings came from the Palace, mirroring the situation seen at Zakros.

These sites and buildings cover the full range of Minoan settlement types. The examples come from the fully-fledged (if small) Palace at Zakros, the non-palatial central building at Ayia Triada, the semi-Palace at Gournia, and the 'Villa' at Sklavokambos. The L-shaped structure at Ayia Triada (ca. 2,200 m^2) is around half the size of the Palace at Zakros, but it is larger than the semi-Palace at Gournia,[114] and considerably larger than the Villa at Sklavokambos. This variation in size is further seen in terms of architectural elaboration. The Zakrian Palace possesses both Lustral Basins and Minoan Halls, while the Villa Reale has Minoan Halls. Both buildings are very well made, with notable wall paintings from the Villa Reale. The 'Palace' at Gournia contained ashlar masonry, as well as a Lustral Basin identified in the northern area, and a large, central hall with pier-and-door partitions. The building at Sklavokambos possessed minor elite elements, such as ashlar doorjambs, but no formal elite features, such as a pure Minoan Hall (although the hall was entered via a pier-and-door partition, rather than subdivided by it).

They all have evidence for the storage of agricultural goods, but to varying extents. According to Christakis, the area set aside for storage ranges from around 720 m^2 in the Villa Reale at Ayia Triada to 165 m^2 in the Palace at Zakros, 116 m^2 in the semi-Palace at Gournia, and 42 m^2 at Sklavokambos (see Chapter 8).[115] Just 6.5 per cent of the ground floor at Zakros and Gournia was set aside for this function, in comparison with 10.6 per cent at Sklavokambos and 41 per cent at Ayia Triada. In each context, despite their clear differences when set side by side, each building with 'replica ring' sealings was the focal point of that settlement.

Considerable evidence for literacy occurs at Ayia Triada and Zakros, not so for the other two. The seals were stamped on devices of different shapes and functions, which by extension may indicate decentralization or independent bureaucratic systems.[116] The administrative assemblages from these four sites vary greatly, with a majority of single-hole nodules at Ayia Triada, flat-based nodules at Zakros (House A) and Sklavokambos, and noduli from Gournia (Table 7.1). There are few flat-based nodules (6 per cent) at Ayia Triada, so we are witnessing a different level or kind of administration from Zakros.[117] Given that noduli were not attached to objects, and probably served as dockets, then the preserved evidence from Gournia indicates a very different mode of organization from the hanging objects from Ayia Triada, or the pressed sealings from Zakros and Sklavokambos. Communication occurred between sites that were organized differently.

It is perhaps too defeatist to state that these impressions can 'tell us nothing about the governance of the island'.[118] They are too tantalizing a source to dismiss so quickly. Their shared provenance in the north-central part of Crete suggests not that they were in communication with one another, but that they were receiving correspondence from the same person or office at Knossos. The problem comes back to the relations that the sites had with Knossos. This same evidence has been used to argue for a 'Neopalatial Knossian-controlled Minoan thalassocracy',[119] or, in contrast, for four administrative areas within Crete.[120]

'Look-Alike' Seals and Sealings

Many further 'duplicates' or 'look-alikes' have been found within the same site – twenty-five from Zakros, three from Ayia Triada, and one from Knossos.[121] As for so many terms coined some time ago, 'look-alike' has come under fire. It does not distinguish between images that look identical (minor differences can be indistinguishable to the naked eye), those that look similar, and those that fall under a general theme. It is true that the term should be further qualified, but it remains a productive area of study. The term 'local replicas' is useful in that it is distinct from the sealings discussed in the previous section (found at different sites, but from the same ring), and also indicates that these are made from different devices. 'Replica' can mean copy or reproduction, often on a smaller scale, and does not have to be cast from the same mould.[122] One example is the Zakros ring (CMS II.7 no. 8) that imitates a larger Knossian example (CMS II.8 no. 268) – if we assume that the latter came first (Figure 7.5A, 7.5B).

While Pini believes that 'we should not put too much weight on the apparent similarities,'[123] they remain striking and deliberate enough to warrant further thought. There are clear differences in the detail, but the overriding similarities in theme and composition are not coincidental. They would appear to represent a special relationship of some kind between the wearers or owners, which may be of an administrative nature, or indicate declarations of shared identity. 'Spot the

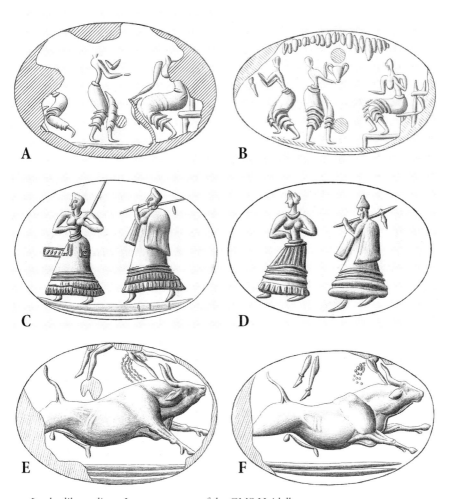

7.5 Look-alike sealings: Images courtesy of the CMS Heidelberg.

    A) CMS II.7 no. 8
    B) CMS II.8 no. 268
    C) CMS II.7 no. 16
    D) CMS II.7 no. 17
    E) CMS II.7 no. 37
    F) CMS II.7 no. 38

difference' is straightforward to play with the drawn images here, but as sealings they would be much more difficult to distinguish. The second and third pairs of sealings were made from metal rings (Figure 7.5C, 7.5D, 7.5E, 7.5F). All four rings were used in the same phase at Zakros.

Altogether, more than 1,000 seal impressions at Zakros were made by 214 seal devices.[124] Nearly 85 per cent of known multi-sealed documents (more than one impression from different seals) were found at Zakros, with complicated variants. This is not seen at other sites with good administrative evidence,

namely, Ayia Triada and Chania.[125] As most of these examples come from
House A at Zakros, it is worth exploring this structure further. Hogarth initially
described this as a chieftain's house (before the Palace was found), but it is now
considered a customs house, or a point at which transactions could occur away
from the grandeur of the Palace.[126] House A rests on an earlier structure, and
was well-built with Cyclopean blocks and painted plaster. It is located around
100 m to the north-west of the Palace, on the summit of a hill overlooking the
harbour. The path to the House led to the harbour road (running off to the east)
and a route around the hill of Ayios Antonios (running to the west), but it is
nonetheless quite tucked away to serve as a customs house.[127]

House A yields evidence for food preparation and consumption (including
a wine press) and, in the room furthest away from the entrance (VIII), five large
pithoi, nine amphorae, and many conical cups. In a rough estimate, Christakis
calculates that this house would have provided sustenance for five adults for
twenty-two months.[128] On the whole, evidence for the processing of foodstuffs and staples comes from the town area, while workshops for precious
materials are situated in the Palace.[129] However, 60 per cent of the bronze tools
came from the Palace, so these were rare in the town and House A is unusual in
that respect:[130] the building was destroyed at the end of LM IB, burying
a bronze sword and tools. The sealings appear to have been kept in some
kind of container on the upper floor (VII). House A is unlikely to represent
an archive, as it has just one roundel and one tablet,[131] so it was a working
bureaucracy. What is particularly notable is the evidence for 'look-alikes'.[132]

'Look-alike' sealings have similar images or compositions; they were not
made with the same seal as with the 'replica rings'. The implications of these
'look-alikes' are unclear. Some argue that this concentration of 'look-alikes'
simply indicates craftsmen repeating themselves,[133] but they may also indicate
two different seal users with the same rank or authority.[134] It is suggested that
different seals represent different people;[135] alternatively, they may represent
different posts. In the latter case, some motives, such as bucrania and butterflies,
may represent different roles.[136] They may represent other ties, such as
kinship.[137] This explanation plays down the administrative role, and it is
convincing to think of seals as playing a positive role in affirming identity.
However, they are found on essentially administrative documents – records of
transactions. Wiener has suggested that the documents represent specialized
communication involving sea transport, concerning either traders or even the
military/navy.[138] The lack of look-alikes from sites otherwise rich in administrative evidence is notable. The concentration in an apparently self-sufficient,
non-palatial building is a further reminder that administration occurred outside
these central complexes. This is particularly notable in a site where there is such
a sharp divide between Palace and town concerning production and the
organization of resources.

7.6 Dictaean Libation Table with Linear A inscription, © Ashmolean Museum, University of Oxford.

WRITING IN THE NON-ADMINISTRATIVE SPHERE: THE Z-SERIES

Inscribed artefacts assigned to the Z-series of Linear A typology mostly, but not entirely, refer to the ritual sphere. The most numerous objects here are the forty inscribed stone vessels (Za), the majority of which were libation tables. These artefacts mainly come from ritual sites, which suggests 'un lien entre l'écrit et le sacré'.[139] The 'tables' were four-sided or circular, with one (or more) central circular depression(s), which have been classified into eight main types according to shape.[140] The reference to libations follows Evans' initial comparison of the Dictaean Libation Table with Egyptian tables (Figure 7.6).[141]

Inscribed and painted ceramics (Zb and Zc) are normally categorized with non-administrative uses of Linear A, but they might fit with the 'W' series (see earlier). Inscriptions on stucco (Zd: four examples)[142] and architectural inscriptions (Ze: five possible examples)[143] may indicate graffiti, be relevant to the construction process, or have some kind of apotropaic function. The latter would indicate some link with ritual.[144] Owens suggests that the common position of the Ze examples next to entrances, and the similarity with certain mason's marks (e.g., the double-axe, trident, star, and branch), point to a phylactic or apotropaic role.[145]

Metal inscriptions (Zf: seven examples) tend to be elite objects and of very high craftsmanship, and they have been found only in non-settlement contexts, such as cemeteries. An inscribed silver pin and a gold ring were found in different chambers of the same tomb at Mavro Spelio, Knossos. This was the largest tomb in the necropolis, and clearly rich.[146] Another silver pin came from Platanos. The exact provenance is not mentioned by the excavator,

7.7 Libation formulae (drawn by author; data after Schoep 1994, Table 1; see also Driessen and MacGillivray 1989).Circle: 08-59-28-301-54-57 (A-TA-I-301-WA-JA); Diamond: 10-06-77-06-41, 28-39-06-80, 41-26-04 (U-NA-KA-NA-SI, I-PI-NA-MA, SI-RU-TE); Square: 57-31-31-60-13 (JA-SA-SA-RA-ME); Star: 59-06-28-301-10-37-55 (TA-NA-I-301-U-TI-NU); Cross: 57-07-67-69 (JA-DI-KI-TU); Triangle: 28-01-[(I-DA-[)1) Vrysinas; 2) Apodoulou; 3) Platanos; 4) Kophinas; 5) Juktas; 6) Knossos; 7) Prassos; 8) Archanes Troullos; 9) Arkalochori; 10) Psychro; 11) Kato Syme; 12) Petsophas (and one example at Palaikastro).

Xanthoudides, but Alexiou and Brice suggest that it comes from a Neopalatial burial in the area outside the disused Tholos Tombs A and B.[147] Further examples include a bronze bowl that probably came from Kophinas,[148] and inscribed votive Double Axes from the cave at Arkalochori.[149] The prestige value of these metal artefacts supports the link between literacy and the elite, and the suggestion that writing was used as a deliberate manifestation of the power of the elite. Inscriptions on metal, stucco, and architecture (prestigious and elite materials) have been found only in the central region of the island.

Libation Formulae

'Libation formulae' are syllable groups that occur on more than one surviving example across the island (Figure 7.7).[150] There are problems with this term: the inscriptions are much more fragmentary than the label suggests, and there is no way of demonstrating that liquids were involved. Evans used the term 'dedicatory formula', which is appropriately more vague.[151] It is their context, elaboration, and 'special' nature that points to a ritual use. A second function may be as 'ready tools for the manipulation and legitimation of political authority', as in the Etruscan case.[152]

They are mostly found on stone libation tables, but also other stone objects such as the ladle from Archanes–Troullos, and other materials such as the silver pin from Platanos. Only a very small proportion of all known 'libation tables' were inscribed.[153] Libation tables are much smaller than their name suggests, with some exceptions, such as the Dictaean Libation Table (Figure 7.6). Because they were so often broken into even smaller pieces, a feat that requires considerable force, scholars have suggested that they were 'killed'.[154] However, some have survived intact in ritual sites (e.g., IO Za 6 at Juktas and PK Za 9 at Petsophas), and some from 'non-ritual' contexts (so presumably not yet ritually deposited) are also broken (e.g., KN Za 10 at Knossos). Such breakages may therefore be natural.

They usually come from un-stratified contexts in ritual sites or unclear contexts in settlement sites, so can be dated only broadly to the Neopalatial period.[155] They have been found in Neopalatial peak sanctuaries and the cave at Psychro, and do not generally occur in settlements of regions without peak sanctuaries, such around Malia, Chania, Phaistos, and the Ierapetra Isthmus.[156] Juktas has offered examples of all six known formulae, mostly found in a disturbed context with other votives.[157] Up to fifteen inscriptions were found here, mostly on libation tables, but also on other stone vessels and a terracotta object. Thirteen inscriptions originate from Petsophas,[158] while just one fragment comes from Vrysinas. The Dictaean Libation Table has been mentioned, while the site to the south, Kato Syme, has yielded many libation tables, twelve of which are inscribed.[159]

They have not been found in Palaces, but an inscribed libation table fragment came from the House of the Frescoes at Knossos. They are more often found in non-palatial settlements, such as Apodoulou, Prassos[160], and Palaikastro, and on a ladle from Archanes-Troullos.[161] The 'Villa' at Apodoulou produced three in a rich deposit that included metal Double Axes (gold and bronze) and a terracotta rhyton. It has been suggested that this assemblage belonged to an independent sanctuary or a house shrine,[162] but it may have been a storeroom for activities occurring elsewhere. The storage of these objects in settlement contexts suggests some degree of circulation before being deposited at ritual sites and taken out of circulation. Other types of ritual stone vessels, such as the kernoi found in funerary contexts, do not have such inscriptions.[163]

There is no standard place for the inscription on the vessel. It is 'remarkable that, despite the ominous volume of relevant bibliography, very little can be said with certainty on the meaning and/or importance of the "formula"'.[164] There is a limit to how far we can read these objects or evoke their original role in certain performances. It has been suggested that the rare inscribed examples could act as 'a sort of label for the entire batch',[165] or more simply that it represented a better-educated and upper-class dedicator. They also express an elite cultural *koine*, providing one of the strongest indications that Minoan culture and identity was felt across the island, above and beyond any regional socio-political variations.

There was certainly something special about this set of artefacts. These small stone memorials (to other people or gods, or both) were made at different places, rather than originating at a common source,[166] so it was the phrases rather than the objects that circulated around the island.[167] This contrasts with the 'replica rings' above, with the single provenance for widely circulated documents. A permanent record was made for posterity and/or other worlds,[168] and the act of taking these artefacts out of circulation could also serve as the construction of timelessness.[169] Adam describes the externalization of knowledge through representation (art and writing) as a way of making time stand still (as with ritual and monuments).[170] The libation formulae illustrate well these '*created* acts of time transcendence'.[171] They represent the attempt to control time on a grand scale in terms of audience (mortal and immortal), geography (they occur across the island), and time itself (deliberately deposited in a manner to take the artefacts out of circulation, and therefore rendering them both timeless and immortal).[172]

CONCLUSION

The contexts in which the Linear A script has been found indicates that the literacy was wide-ranging in terms of economic and ceremonial impact and control. A Minoan *koine* is suggested by the libation formulae, and the 'replica rings' indicate inter-site communication, but within this there was considerable variation. Regionalism in the style of writing has been noted,[173] and inscriptions on metal, stucco, and architecture have been found only in the central region of the island. Regionalism in administrative practices also appears to be strong, notably the multi-sealed flat-based nodules and 'look-alikes' at Zakros.

Knossos is unique in having an example of each kind of administrative and non-administrative use of Linear A. The administrative evidence is centralized in the Palace, but non-administrative uses of Linear A are distributed throughout the site.[174] Other sites that have both administrative and non-administrative examples of Linear A are important settlement sites, namely, Ayia Triada, Phaistos, Tylissos, Malia, Petras, Palaikastro, and Zakros. Chania has produced a great wealth of administrative documents, but not evidence for non-administrative use, as has Myrtos-Pyrgos – but this appears to be a ceremonial context. Several 'Villa' sites have not produced objects in the Linear A script, but have other non-inscribed administrative documents, for example, Nerokourou, Vathypetro, Sklavokambos, Makrygialos, and Achladia. Harbour towns such as Mochlos, Poros, and Amnissos have not produced any, or very few.[175]

The Ierapetra Isthmus region appears to have largely rejected both the symbolic and/or ritual use of writing, and its administrative use. It is misleading to work *ex silentio* when such a small number of data is involved.[176] But this large number of null cases might imply that Linear A was not a universally used and understood phenomenon. The surviving LM IB evidence suggests a local level of administration (recorded in the Linear A tablets) and an inter-site one (revealed by sealed documents).[177] But the parchments that these widespread documents sealed do not survive. They may be diplomatic rather than administrative, in the sense of tracking goods and personnel. Or, they may represent communications (between peers or between different ranks) rather than control by one party.

CHAPTER EIGHT

THE ECONOMY

THIS CHAPTER CONSIDERS THE BASIC TRIAD OF THE ECONOMY – THE 'open systems of production, distribution, and consumption of material things and social services' – but follows the modern tendency to focus on the political economy, or the socio-political *organization* of land, labour, and resources.[1] Bronze Age economies have traditionally been divided into reciprocal, redistributive, and market systems. These models are useful, but not mutually exclusive, and the terms need to be further qualified. Nor are these mechanisms purely economic, as the recent volumes on feasting and redistribution have highlighted. Earle, in line with his general substantivist approach, positions the economy firmly in the social matrix.[2]

Much work has been done on various aspects of the Minoan economy, including the collection, storage, and (re)distribution of staple goods, craft specialization, trade, and exchange. This chapter focuses on the elites' control over these activities, and the various types of centralization. It begins by assessing the evidence for the political geography, including time distances for journeys between sites, survey evidence, settlement patterns, and population. It then turns to the evidence for the storage of staples (including surpluses), explicitly analysing the central places (which may not necessarily involve the Palaces).[3] Surpluses are often thought to enable professional craft specialization; in reviewing the evidence for that, we note the tendency for workshops to occur in harbour sites.

This is a world with writing, but no coinage, that ultimate objective mark of monetary value. Does this mean that no standardized exchange occurred? There is clear evidence for the measurement of commodities, from a system of weights to units in Linear A, and even the standardized weights of copper ingots.[4] This enables barter and mutually acceptable exchanges, and the weight and quality of the commodity could be guaranteed by a stamp.[5] Thus, commodities were exchanged without the need for an external scale of measurement provided by money (which is an enabler, or representational, rather than useful in itself). Regular quantities or set types of artefacts could serve as a standard for further exchange, including the 'votive models' of tools and weapons, such as those found at Juktas and Arkalochori.[6] These objects had inherent value as a recyclable material, as well as in the finished product. However, the existence of a weighing system does not shed light on the nature of the economy, such as the extent and nature of redistribution, or how free a market there was.

THE ECONOMIC LANDSCAPE AND POLITICAL GEOGRAPHY

One can detect in the current literature some slippage between the political economy and political geography.[7] Whether it was the land or the labour that the elite controlled is mostly a moot point.[8] Economic catchment areas are distinct from political units,[9] and even if an elite does manage to maintain a strong sense of territoriality over a large terrain, there may not be boundaries in the sense that we draw them on maps.[10] We may acquire a more nuanced picture of Neopalatial Crete if we remember that administration can indicate targeted communication or control *over* distance, as well as *of* space and land (note the 'replica rings' in Chapter 7).[11] That is why the political geography must include equal weight to ritual and other types of control networks, in addition to the fundamental control of foodstuffs and other aspects of the economy.

Spatial distribution maps are useful in 2-D publications, but the Cretan landscape does not resemble the flat plains of such maps, and a consideration of walking times (and shipping times around the coast) fleshes out the practicalities of organizing movements of people, goods, and, indeed, information. This is best measured in time rather than space: 'Distances are useless. Times alone matter,' stated Pendlebury.[12] The importance of viewing distance in terms of time rather than space is indicated by the fact that he took two and a half hours to reach Juktas from Knossos, but only three hours to reach Arkalochori from Vitsila, a much greater distance as the bird flies (Figure 8.1).[13] Bevan's more recent approach covers the entire island and incorporates computed predictions to produce a more thorough overview, especially with the incorporation of sea voyages.[14] With those taken into account, both Chania and Zakros can be reached from north-central Crete in a journey with a single overnight stop.[15]

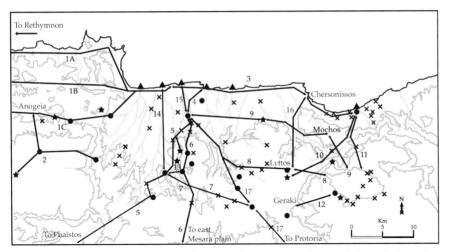

8.1 Pendlebury's (1939) walking times for selected routes in north-central Crete (unless other-wise noted). Adams 2006, figure 2, reprinted with permission, courtesy *American Journal of Archaeology* and Archaeological Institute of America.
1A) Heraklion to Rethymnon, 18 hrs; 1B) Heraklion to Rethymnon, 15 hrs; 1C) Heraklion to Rethymnon, 14 hrs; 2) Idaean Cave to Anogeia, 4.5 hrs; Idaean Cave to Kroussonas, 4.5 hrs; 3) Heraklion to Chersonissos, 4.5 hrs, Chersonissos to Malia, 1.5 hrs; 4) Schäfer's (1991) route from Amnissos to Knossos; 5) Evans' (1928) Great Road south from Knossos to Phaistos: Pendlebury, 12 hrs; Knossos to Juktas (Pendlebury), 2.5 hrs; 6) Knossos to Archanes, 1+ hr; Archanes to Mesara plain, 5 hrs; 7) Vitsila to Arkalochori, 3 hrs; 8) Knossos to Lyttos, 5 hrs; Lyttos to Lasithi, 4 hrs; 9) Knossos to Skotino, 3 hrs; Skotino to Mochos, 3.5 hrs; Mochos from Lasithi, 2.5 hrs; 10) Rethemiotakis (1990) route from Malia to Liliano; 11) Malia to the Lasithi Plain, Malia from Krasi, 3.5 hrs; 12) Plati to Geraki, 2.75 hrs; 13) approach to Vathypetro from the west (Driessen and Sakellarakis 1997); 14) Evans' (1928) route from Vitsila to the coast; 15) Knossos to Poros, 50 mins; 16) Lyttos to Chersonissos, 3.5 hrs; 17) association of the hoard at Arkalochori with Galatas (Rethemiotakis 1999b) and route to Protoria (Warren 2004).

The evidence from intensive surface surveys is also useful for exploring economic landscapes, highlighting the geography, topography, and availability and control of agricultural resources. This technique was born in the heyday of processualism, and shares the tendency towards economic determinism with the region taken as a study area, as opposed to a single site-based approach.[16] We are encouraged to explore regions by our modern administrative divisions and widespread use of maps and GIS: this spatial parcelling has become deeply ingrained.[17] The study of economic landscapes has not adapted so well to the post-processualist trends of the 1980s onwards – phenomenological studies of the ritual landscape, involving monuments and walkways, are more relevant.[18] Or, in other words, the economic landscape is more quantitative, the ritual more qualitative, despite the 'critical self-consciousness' that surveyors have developed.[19] By necessity, survey data create a broader narrative, more of a *longue durée* then the tighter chronology available from the excavated record. Scholars have studied how historical and archaeological data may be incorporated according to these different rhythms, drawing in particular from Braudel and the Annales school.[20] The methodological issues involved in integrating survey and excavation data remain under-theorized.[21]

The Cretan surveys demonstrate the dramatically different settlement trajectories that occurred across the island. Driessen attributes this to 'local environmental or geopolitical conditions'.[22] Most palatial centres did not have sufficient agricultural land in their hinterlands to support their populations – notable exceptions are Phaistos and Ayia Triada in the Mesara Plain, and Galatas in the Pediada Plain. There was a drop in the number of sites around Phaistos from the Protopalatial to Neopalatial periods. The Kommos survey revealed thirty-two Protopalatial sites with a small decrease after,[23] and the western Mesara survey (a small area just around Phaistos) located twenty-five then a slight Neopalatial fall.[24] The Neopalatial extent of Phaistos may be around 55–60 ha.[25] Perhaps more notably, these other sites are small, with only Ayia Triada exceeding 2.5 ha.[26] This means that there are no second-order centres that might be expected of a territorial state, although by no means has the entire region been investigated. To the south, the Ayiofarango survey revealed a steady decline in number of sites.[27]

Outside the Mesara, the other Palace that could be self-sufficient was Galatas, but its settlement patterns differed greatly. A recent survey has discovered that, not only did the number of sites increase dramatically in the Neopalatial period, but also that they were fairly large.[28] Knossos probably drew agricultural resources from the Pediada area, and may have been the source for the major increase in population. This in turn could suggest more Knossian political involvement in the area. However, Müller's survey (covering 40 km² around Malia) has revealed a considerable drop in sites from around eighty in the Protopalatial period to nine in the Neopalatial era.[29] Malia was, on present evidence, functioning in a void of significant sites, with the exception of Sissi. Further publication and excavation is required to ascertain the nature of these sites, and Cunningham and Driessen ask: 'one has to wonder if there was not even some kind of coerced relocation of inhabitants – a forced depopulation of the largest and closest rival' – namely, Knossos.[30] It is intriguing to think that they may have been rehoused in the Pediada Plain.

It is extremely difficult to judge whether the Lasithi Plain is 'Malian' in the Neopalatial period, as has been argued for the Protopalatial era.[31] The plain would indeed be a rich source of grain if exploited.[32] Watrous detected a drop in the number of sites in the Lasithi Plain during the Neopalatial period from MM III to LM I, which he attributed to emigration, namely to Knossos and Malia,[33] and argued that the settlement patterns 'suggest that the area was an active member in a larger economic system, centered at the palatial sites'.[34] A drop in number has, however, been contested, and it is certainly challenging to detect these specific ceramic phases using survey evidence.[35] Furthermore, as we have seen, the population around Malia appears to have decreased at this time – so perhaps they went to the Pediada. There is no evidence (yet) that ashlar, ostentatious buildings were built in the Lasithi area. The Neopalatial remains at Plati are poorly preserved (see Chapter 6).[36]

To the east, the Bay of Mirabello has been noted for its lack of Neopalatia evidence for features from peak sanctuaries to ceremonial uses of Linear A, but it is very well surveyed. The town of Gournia would have relied on staples brought from other areas;[37] however, sites in Gournia's immediate hinterland were abandoned.[38] The size of the town itself did not increase. A survey of the wider area around Gournia revealed a very slight decrease in numbers between the Protopalatial and Neopalatial periods; some of the locations of sites changed.[39] Pseira is unusual in that the population would have struggled to have supported itself on the available land on the island.[40] In the Vrokastro region, a notable decrease in site numbers occurred during the Neopalatial period, and no evidence for nucleation.[41] This lack of apparent land intensification has been taken to indicate that the area was not part of the Gournian polity, as it does not demonstrate the need to provide a surplus.[42] A slight drop in number occurs in the Kavousi region further east still, from around sixty Protopalatial sites to around fifty during the Neopalatial period, with some population nucleation.[43]

Further east around Petras, the number of sites peaked during the Neopalatial period.[44] Villa sites surrounded the palatial site at Achladia-Riza, Ayios Georgios/Tourtouloi, Klimataria, and Zou to the east, and Vaï to the west (equidistance between Petras and Palaikastro); they in turn played a central role for their much smaller settlements.[45]

Karoumes Bay lies between Zakros and Palaikastro, and slightly nearer to the latter. Linked to the hinterland by a gorge, the bay also offers a decent anchorage. The land is poor for agriculture, but a survey has revealed a dense network of sites, generally isolated buildings, some with megalithic masonry, and with various other structures.[46] These sites flourished in LM IA, while occupation was sparser in LM IB.[47] Those that did continue in use had less storage capacity and less evidence for dining, although decorated *pithamphoras* have been found.[48] The later pottery appears to come from both Palaikastro and Zakros, although more came from the former. There may have been an 'open market' for ceramics in the east of the island.[49] The administrative evidence at Zakros supports the notion that the palatial elite was organizing staples grown beyond the immediate environs.[50] The Protopalatial 'watch-towers' may have been adapted into Neopalatial farmhouses, peppering the hinterland.[51] Zakros was also a trading centre, and possibly some resources came in from the sea.

Such surveys have picked up a wealth of information about farms or rural households that probably contributed towards the transfer of agricultural goods towards the local centre. The mechanisms behind such exchanges remain unclear, and probably varied across time and space. Christakis, on the basis of cross-cultural comparisons, suggested that this movement was controlled by 'force and tribute; establishing a presence in another region either within an existing center or by setting up one's own (colonies); even purchasing or exchanging segments of territory'.[52] These are all valid suggestions for which historical examples may be given. They are all, however, fundamentally economic and secular in nature, and the ceremonial clout of certain centres (particularly palatial ones), probably alters the Minoan case.[53]

The nature and make-up of an island-wide settlement hierarchy may shed light on the political economy. Numerous Neopalatial sites have been detected on Crete, categorized according to size and type, and then placed on an island-wide pyramidal hierarchy, sometimes applying models from other fields and disciplines. Categories divide and order; models represent and generalize. How categories and models are constructed, and whether they focus on the economic, ceremonial, or political spheres, will clearly affect the final picture. The general category of 'palatial site' does not allow for the special role that Knossos is often deemed to have on Crete. There is, therefore, a curious mismatch between archaeological narratives that seek a central seat of administration, and the site categories that play down any particular site's individuality.

Sites can be grouped in a number of ways. One obvious categorization is by size – Rackham and Moody divided them into hamlets, villages, small towns, and large towns.[54] Alternatively, five levels have been applied to the Minoan case studies, with the smallest further subdivided into 'small village', 'hamlet', and 'single house/farm'.[55] On Crete, one key distinction lies between palatial, non-palatial, and other ranks of towns, while 'Villas' are often classified as a coherent group.[56] But sites may also be considered in terms of function – the harbour town of Mochlos, for example, appears to have been organized very differently from a sizable town set in a rich agricultural area, such as Kastelli. Another distinction is made between settlements and the myriad kinds of ritual sites found across the island.[57] The apparently even distribution of palatial and ritual sites across the island also lends weight to the strong, cohesive sense of Minoan identity. However, a closer analysis reveals that the relationship between Palace and ritual site was not the same across the island; non-palatial Palaikastro enjoyed a nearby peak sanctuary at Petsophas, whereas palatial Malia does not have a clear ritual site.[58]

The non-palatial central buildings have been traditionally classed as 'Villas', which, like 'Palaces', is a problematic term due to the diversity in their location, elaboration, and function.[59] At the least, a distinction should be made between urban mansions and 'country houses'. McEnroe has explored Neopalatial houses in detail. His typology rests on 'types of rooms, arrangements of rooms, constructional details, and size'.[60] Type 1 is the most elaborate, with elite features such as a Minoan Hall, and elaborately constructed. It is notable that *all* 'Type 1' Villas in his Tables 1 and 2 are found in north-central Crete.[61] Achladia in the east is designated to Type 2 on the island-wide scheme, but in a more local context may have been perceived as 'Type 1' (i.e., it was relatively impressive for that area). A relational approach to such buildings defies a single definition according to function or type.

Problems remain with drawing up solid boundaries for past polities, even though we may still feel that a sense of territoriality existed.[62] Monica Smith has summed up the issue well: 'the cartographic depictions of ancient states and empires convey the impression of comprehensive political entities having firm boundaries and uniform territorial control.'[63] Smith's alternative is to deploy network models rather than bounded-territory models; a third way is to think in terms of different modes of centralization.[64] It is true to say that our notion of territory is very black and white, extending into the sea and air, and it is impossible to see how this rigidity can be applied to days before maps.[65] It is clearly inappropriate to attempt to apply the same model across all of Crete. For example, central place theory was constructed from an economic stance, as the need for regular hubs was assumed for the provision and redistribution of produce and services. From this, economic patterns were assumed to reflect political realities. The hubs, or central places, are apparently identical, and there is little indication of how their internal organization would impact regional dynamics, and vice versa. Thiessen polygons are less orientated towards economic factors, but they still demand the simplistic carving up of landscapes.[66] The peer–polity interaction model ultimately depends on such boundary-generating approaches, with a similar assumption that 'peer' means identical in nature and structure.[67] The very application of these models rest on assumptions that may be anachronistic.

We need some kind of grasp of population in order to appreciate basic human economics, and all estimates rely on underlying assumptions regarding the relationship between people and space. Branigan estimated a rural population of around 82,000 and 60,000–80,000 town dwellers, with around 11,000 living at Knossos.[68] Taking a nuclear family as the basic household unit, and factoring the zoning of settlements, with different densities of inhabitation, Whitelaw arrives at an estimate of 14,000–18,000 people at Knossos.[69] This, unsurprisingly, appears to have had the largest population on the island. This kind of concentration of population is notable, and would have required a sophisticated organization of staples (see later in this chapter).

Combining this with estimates of agricultural catchment areas can give us some idea of how a region might be sustained,[70] although food could always be imported, particularly into the centres with the means to mobilize resources by land and sea. Underlying a strong emphasis on such catchment areas surrounding central places does seem to be an assumption of large-scale redistribution. However, the survey evidence indicates that, beyond any issue with the concept of 'redistribution' in the Bronze Age context,[71] settlement patterns varied considerably across Neopalatial Crete. Translating economic organization into political terms is highly problematic and requires as much scaffolding as interpreting the ritual landscape. By highlighting an area immediately around a centre, there is the assumption that, even if all of the produce did not physically go into the centre, it was in some way controlled by it. Possibly it did move in this way, but political communication and control can also be targeted across much wider distances.

Polanyi's three mechanisms of reciprocity, redistribution, and market exchange are often presented as mutually incompatible, but we may detect elements of each of these kinds of transactions in the Minoan world.[72] This culture has often been referred to as 'redistributive', and there is clear evidence for such activities. Earle divides redistribution into four different institutional forms: levelling mechanisms (such as progressive tax); householding (pooling, or Domestic Mode of Production); share-out (co-ops); and mobilization.[73] These are different in nature as well as scale or institutionalization. It is therefore unsurprising to conclude that the use of the term 'redistribution' demands further qualification, and that the Aegean political economy differed from other modes of redistribution, such as that in Mesopotamia.[74] Some no longer view redistribution as holding a dominant position in the Minoan economy, but believe that the presence of sizable areas for storage indicates an upwards mobilization of resources rather than an altruistic sharing of them.[75] While the simplistic use of the term is highly problematic,[76] there is no need to discard it completely, and it does not need to imply the pooling of resources by an altruistic elite. In order to explore this further, we need to consider the excavated evidence for agricultural storage.

COLLECTION, STORAGE, AND REDISTRIBUTION OF STAPLE GOODS

Storage, even of 'mundane' agricultural goods, has been of interest to Minoan scholars since Evans investigated the west wing of the Palace at Knossos in 1900, following the promising lead of Kalokairinos (Figure 8.2A).[77] Such facilities for storage suggest the production of a surplus, which is necessary or desirable for a number of reasons: insurance; seeds for future crops; fodder; to demonstrate or gain social differentiation; and to provide forms of payment and remuneration.[78] Renfrew stressed that the Palaces were redistributive centres.[79]

Halstead argued that the storage of agricultural goods in the Palaces was reduced from the Protopalatial to the Final Palatial periods, whereas the control of prestige raw materials and craft specialization became more concentrated in

8.2 A) Knossos west magazines (photograph by author); B) Malia east magazines (photograph by author).

them, as 'social storage'.[80] However, it is unlikely that staple storage became *less* important in the Neopalatial period, even if wealth storage become more so. The Protopalatial evidence is too poor to determine that 20–30 per cent of the Palaces were assigned to storage facilities,[81] and there is no reason to state that there was a drop in this during the Neopalatial era. Focusing on the latter period, one key question is whether the Palaces were the sole locales of redistribution, or whether this occurred in other buildings, in both towns and smaller settlements.

The Neopalatial evidence of storage is not always clear. Not all areas that appear to be designed for storage contained their maximum number of storage vessels; some were remarkably empty of them. We do not know what was contained in those Neopalatial buildings that were used in the Final Palatial period. However, pithoi have the archaeological advantage of being difficult to move, so in some cases it appears that a lack of pithoi reflects the original situation.[82] Working from the available data, and closely with Christakis' excellent studies, we will consider the various types of centralization that appear to be visible in the Neopalatial settlements. This will incorporate evidence for pithoi and recognizable storage spaces (such as the magazines), and some evidence from the Linear A texts.

Minoan administration records the mobilization of resources, including deficits, but it remains unclear where such resources were stored and how they were actually mobilized.[83] For example, goods do not need to be physically stored within Palaces in order to be controlled by them. TY 3 from Building A at Tylissos refers to an amount of olive oil that would have required about 60–70 pithoi (more than 20,000 litres) – an amount the building itself could not hold.[84] The evidence from Ayia Triada also suggests that the inhabitants of the Villa Reale controlled goods, but not that all was actually stored there.

A variety of sites will be discussed beyond the palatial ones, including 'Villa' sites in the landscape and settlements without a clear central building (on present evidence). This will provide the necessary data for assessing how centralized the distribution of agricultural produce was, and whether this occurred similarly across the island. It is more difficult to assess whether this changed over time, since the sites flourished at different times, and LM IA Malia is compared with LM IB Phaistos, for example. In the cases where areas designed for storage did not reveal artefactual evidence for such, the functions may have changed. At Phaistos, the Palace may have been destroyed before full storage potential was fulfilled, while in the case of Malia, Galatas, and Gournia, pithoi may have been removed at or after the destruction of the Palaces.[85] However, two areas need to be considered. First is the ability to house a surplus, and second is the indication that domestic units are reliant on others – suggesting redistribution. After outlining the levels of storage, from apparently none through to self-sufficiency, we will take a regional view as made possible by the survey data.

Five Levels of (Non-palatial) Storage

Christakis has calculated that an adult would require at least 300–400 litres worth of produce a year.[86] Most of the buildings he has analysed have little or no evidence for storage at all. Arguably, smaller domestic units may have had more use for organic, destructible storage containers (such as collapsible bags), which could be put to temporary use and the space assigned for other functions when necessary. Since these houses tend to be urban, the inhabitants presumably had access to regular, small amounts of supplies nearby, not necessarily from the central building.[87]

Many other urban houses contained a limited amount of storage of up to 1,000 litres; this would be just a few months' reserve for a household of five.[88] This pattern occurred in small, basic domestic units in palatial towns (e.g., House Ac at Gournia), more elite ones in palatial towns (e.g., Da and Za at Malia, the House of the Chancel Screen at Knossos), or houses in towns without a known, clear central building (e.g., Buildings B and C at Tylissos). Again, some dependence on outside sources is to be assumed here. Most LM IB domestic units would appear to have 'restricted subsistence autarky',[89] which implies some reliance on external provisions.

The third group consists of buildings with the capacity to store larger amounts, from 1,200 to 2,000 litres, which would have been able to provide for a household of five for eight to thirteen months; presumably these were self-sufficient, but carried no surplus.[90] These include central buildings (e.g., Myrtos-Pyrgos) and large urban buildings (e.g., Building 5 at Palaikastro). Other buildings in this group were involved in production (e.g., House A at Zakros, which also contained sealings).

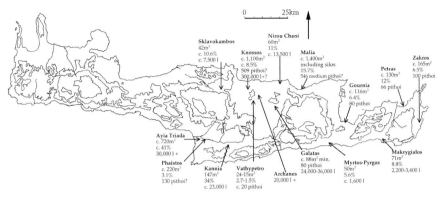

8.3 Storage facilities of central buildings within settlements, namely, the Palaces at Phaistos, Knossos, Galatas, Malia, Petras, and Zakros, the mansions or 'Villas' at Ayia Triada, Kannia, Sklavokambos, Vathypetro, Archanes-Tourkoyeitonia, Nirou Chani, Myrtos-Pyrgos, Gournia (or 'Palace'), and Makrygialos (drawn by author, showing ground floor area, percentage of ground floor, and capacity by pithoi and litres where calculated: after Christakis 2008).

Buildings able to store 2,000 to 4,000 litres also included a mix of central buildings (e.g., Makrygialos) and other large buildings in settlements with (or without) a central building, such as the Little Palace at Knossos, Epsilon at Malia, House B at Zakros, and House B at Palaikastro.[91] In some cases, such as House B at Zakros, the high transportability of the pithoi suggests that the 'storage' here was a temporary stage in the production process.[92] From Figure 8.3, only Myrtos-Pyrgos and Makrygialos are considered central buildings that do not belong in the final group following.

The last category of non-palatial central buildings contained a very significant capacity for storage from 5,000 litres upwards, and includes Sklavokambos, the Villa Reale at Ayia Triada, Mitropolis-Kannia, LM IA Vathypetro, Nirou Chani, and Archanes-Tourkoyeitonia.[93] Other important (apparently non-central) buildings include Building A at Tylissos and the Casa Est at Ayia Triada. It is generally the case that these buildings housed large pithoi, so storage was at its most permanent, in that these cannot be moved without considerable difficulty. This was supported further by clear storage architecture (notably magazines), which indicate that long-term, institutionalized storage was designed for the building from the outset.

However, the Palaces still possessed significantly more facilities for storage, and were main storage centres in the Neopalatial period (as had been assumed for the Protopalatial era).[94] In the elite buildings of non-palatial settlements, there seems to have been 'a dramatic reduction of storage potential in their final years of use'.[95] Christakis convincingly demonstrates that there is no solid evidence for a shift from Palaces to Villas in terms of agricultural storage at the beginning of or during the Neopalatial period. Most palatial pithoi were large, with high capacity, low transportability, and low accessibility, the exception being those at Malia, which were unusually small.[96] Several mechanisms of economic mobilization can occur at the same time; doubtlessly the Palaces organized much exchange, but did not monopolize it. In smaller buildings, the pithoi tended to be smaller as well, for higher transportability and greater flexibility.

Central Buildings and Evidence for Redistribution

Figure 8.3 presents the storage facilities of most Neopalatial central buildings, whether they were palatial or not; the outlines in Chapters 4 and 5 indicate how different these buildings are in terms of size and architectural elaboration.[97] When set in their urban context (in terms of storage facilities) and regional context (in terms of survey data), we may be able to detect different degrees of surplus acquirements and modes of centralization, or potential for redistribution. Some Villa sites are excavated in isolation, so it is an assumption that we have *the* central building (e.g., Sklavokambos). Some sites have been omitted in this discussion, as they are not fully excavated (e.g., Zominthos, Protoria, and Kastelli). Since Figure 8.3 presents central buildings only, it omits settlements that have not (yet) yielded one (e.g., Palaikastro,[98] Pseira, Kommos,[99] Mochlos,[100] and Tylissos[101]).

Moving west to east, we begin with the Mesara, where there was a general decline in site numbers in the Neopalatial period. The Palace at Phaistos was provided with storerooms (just more than 3 per cent of the surviving ground floor), most notably its west magazines. These were designed to hold around 130 pithoi, although the remains of only eleven were found.[102] Its later use, after LM IA, witnessed a dramatic decrease in storage potential.[103] Hitchcock has suggested that storage was undertaken on the first floor of the Palace in the west wing, while the ground floor comprised workrooms.[104] However, the character of the building at the Palace at Phaistos remains overwhelmingly ceremonial with apparently limited and unfulfilled storage potential.[105]

The main storage area of the Villa Reale at Ayia Triada is the north magazines (for both dry goods and liquids) and the south-west quarter, which also included Linear A evidence for wool production. Overall, just more than 40 per cent of the ground floor was set aside for storage, with a substantial number of pithoi found,[106] holding at least 30,000 litres of produce.[107] Other buildings contained substantial storage facilities, such as the Casa Est and the Bastion – these may have been auxiliaries for the Villa Reale. The amount of potential storage space in the Villa Reale is more than three times as much as the Phaistian Palace, and considerably more if its inhabitants also ultimately controlled the contents of other auxiliary buildings. While there are complications with the evidence at Phaistos (the urban context is poorly understood, and much of the Palace has eroded away), the agriculturally rich Mesara region would, potentially, be the most obvious candidate to reveal evidence for palatial redistribution. However, this complex had less storage space then the Palaces at Knossos and Malia. While storage might have been 'outsourced' to Ayia Triada, the texts from there list produce in greater volumes than could be stored centrally. We have good evidence for the storage of agricultural goods in this region, but it is clear that this does not support a simplistic view of redistribution, whereby all produce came into the Palace before being reallocated. But it would not be helpful to deny that redistribution occurred at all, at the least in the form of ceremonial feasting.

The site of Mitropolis-Kannia, further inland, produced the most pithoi from a non-palatial context.[108] With the capacity to contain 23,000 litres, it may have served as an intermediary for the movement of goods. A similar role is likely for Sklavokambos for the Knossian region, located to the north. The north-west storerooms at Sklavokambos were situated next to a veranda, which would have provided a covered, open area for the transactions of staple goods.[109] As transport modes, or even marketplaces, these case studies suggest a form of redistribution.

Around 8.5 per cent of the ground floor space of the Palace at Knossos (with possibly around 518 large pithoi) may have been used for agricultural storage, although the evidence mainly comes from later periods.[110] Estimates must remain vague, but a potential of more than 300,000 litres was stored in Knossos, for example, which could have supported 750–1,000 people annually.[111] In addition to the palatial household itself, this presumably could have maintained a body of craft workers, religious personnel, and so on. Altruism was not therefore the motivation for redistribution. The evidence from the surrounding houses is difficult to assess, but some of the grand mansions appear to have had a comparable proportion (not amount) of space set aside for storage, for example, the House of the Chancel Screen at 8.8 per cent or the Royal Villa at 11 per cent, if the 'Pillar Crypt' was used for storage.[112] Others have yielded little or none, such as the Southeast House or the House of the Frescoes. The picture appears to be of centralization of this activity in the Palace, but not complete monopolization.

The mansion at Nirou Chani revealed both storerooms and at least fifteen large pithoi (6,000–6,750 litres), and mudbrick bins containing carbonized beans and chickpeas (7,200 litres).[113] This gives us tantalizing insights into evidence that would often be poorly preserved or missed. As the building is generally thought to have a cultic function, it may have provided ceremonial feasts (in the court area?). The limited nature of the excavation at Archanes (due to the overlying modern settlement) indicates that the (assumed) central build-ing found here would have had substantial areas for storage, with around 20,000 litres of storage from current information (notably Rooms 32 and 33).[114] This would have provided a surplus beyond a basic household, and, again, the substantial amount of ritual evidence from the site (such as figurines) may indicate redistribution in the form of ceremonial feasting. As at Nirou Chani, the building at Archanes was entered via a Minoan Hall from a court area, and they may deserve a closer comparison.

Vathypetro experienced a decrease in storage from LM IA (Room 10, with a capacity of 6,400–8,000 litres, providing a surplus beyond the needs of a household of five) to LM IB (Rooms 32–4, 40, but few pithoi).[115] While it does not appear to have been a major storage hub, such as Kannia, it was clearly self-sufficient, and could have overseen wider transitions. Little is known of the surrounding settlement. Galatas has revealed (virtually empty) east magazines, and other areas are damaged. Based on current evidence, the (short-lived) Palace is estimated to have had the capacity to hold around 24,000–36,000 litres;[116] this is only about 10 per cent of the Palace at Knossos. We know also from the survey evidence that the surrounding landscape witnessed a significant increase in population, which presumably worked the fields to provide for this institution, for a short period at least. Overall, the storage facilities at sites around Knossos reflect their architectural elaboration and the distribution of elite features.

The (LM IA) Palace at Malia had the potential to hold a high number of the medium-sized pithoi found here (around 546), with nearly 16 per cent of its ground floor assigned to storage.[117] The Palace has west magazines, as well as other rooms in the north-east (apparently with an entrance separate from the grander one) and south-west areas. The east magazines comprise a well-preserved storage area with channels for the spillage of liquids; carbonized grain was also found in the area (Figure 8.2B). Few pithoi were actually found, however. The silos, located to the south-west of the Palace, were possibly accessed from the Palace on the first floor. They were probably palatial institutions, and had a considerable capacity.[118] Urban houses also contained spaces for storage, including some magazines (e.g., Epsilon and Zeta Alpha). This suggests a long-term approach to the organization of elite domestic storage. While the evidence is variable in quality, the proportion of space for storage appears to be less than the Palace (e.g., 4 per cent in Epsilon, and 8.7 per cent in Zeta Alpha),[119] while some have no evidence at all (e.g., Delta Gamma). Including the silos, the Palace had around 1,400 m^2 set aside for storage; therefore, the LM IA Palace appears to have centrally organized agricultural produce, and less so perhaps in LM IB. This may therefore fit the traditional picture of redistribution, but it is notable that the survey evidence indicates a depopulation, and presumably fewer people working the fields.

To the south, the Villa at Myrtos-Pyrgos had 5.6 per cent of its floor space allocated for storage. This is not a great amount, but the surrounding settlement also had limited evidence for storage.[120] However, the Linear A evidence in the Villa includes a reference (PYR 1) to ninety units of wine (or more than 2,500 litres), an amount that could not be physically stored in it. Therefore, its inhabitants appear to have controlled or monitored, in some way, goods not actually stored in the building itself.

Around 6.4 per cent of the semi-palatial structure at Gournia was dedicated to storage. The remains of fifteen large pithoi were found, but it had the capacity to hold eighty. With eighty (roughly 15 per cent of Knossos' 516), it could cater for around 110–50 people annually – well below the town's population, but enough to support a substantial group of workers beyond the household. In contrast, most (forty-nine) of the surrounding houses did not reveal evidence for storage, although twenty-two others did.[121] The 'Palace' could not have served as the sole storage centre, much in the same way that Knossos could not have provided for that entire settlement. Here again, the term 'redistribution' does not need to imply a monopolization of this area of the economy. However, Gournia remains the only site in the Bay of Mirabello area (including Pseira and Mochlos) with a clear central building, and it was presumably a focal point for the entire region. Survey evidence indicates a degree of depopulation in the wider area, so possibly it was not exploited agriculturally to its maximum potential.

The LM IB central building at Makrygialos also stands out in its region. While not very well preserved, it was clearly the seat of a regional author-ity. At 71 m², or 8.8 per cent of the ground floor,[122] it contained more storage than the mansion at Myrtos-Pyrgos to the west, but considerably less than the three nearest Palaces (the semi-Palace at Gournia, Petras, and Zakros). It would only have been able to provide a moderate surplus economically, but this in itself would bear political clout. This example demonstrates again how monumental centres should be contextualized relative to their surroundings, and why, in the Gournian context, its central building may have been perceived as a Palace.

At the Palace at Petras, the storage capacity of the north magazines increases slightly from LM IA to LM IB, when around thirty-six large pithoi were in use; altogether around fifty-one pithoi were discovered from the LM IB building, including those located in the Central Court. Storage was the prime function for around 12 per cent of the ground floor.[123] The storage potential of the two houses excavated nearby is very low. A similar pattern is seen in the western-most Palace, Zakros. The storage capacities of the Palace of Zakros were also considerable, with 5.7 per cent of the space of the Palace set aside for storage, and more than eighty large pithoi found.[124] The pithoi from the town tended to be smaller, and many houses did not reveal evidence for storage at all. However, some town houses had significant capacity for storage as well as agricultural production, such as House B on the Southwest Hill (3,250–4,050 litres). Again, in line with the other Palaces, there is good evidence for concentration, but not full monopolization or total redistribution.

It is clear, in terms of interactions with their surrounding settlements, that the complexes called Palaces are in a league of their own, even though they are not the only buildings with the ability to store a surplus. Yet the Palaces would not have provided for the entire city, even though most urban houses were not self-sufficient. The inhabitants were therefore obtaining supplies outside this centralized mode. Furthermore, the amounts registered in the Linear A documents do not always match the space available in the central buildings. We need to think beyond the traditional Palace-centred redistribution model.[125] As Halstead notes in his discussion of Polanyi, is it not necessary to state that redistribution is entirely centralized spatially, in the terms of the movement of goods and its storage; an administration as sophisticated as the Minoans' allows for decentralized but controlled control of produce. Nor is it necessary to deny the existence of other forms of exchange, such as reciprocity and market forces (without coinage). All may run in parallel, as they do in the modern West – although, rather than progressive taxation, Minoan palatial elites presumably operated with more self-interest.

This discussion has relied considerably on Christakis' work, which, as Halstead points out, 'tells us more about the political than the economic dimension of Minoan political economy'.[126] Pithoi do not need to be filled to the brim to impress onlookers.[127] They were designed to impress, awe, and reassure both the elites and visitors that the economy was under control. The Neopalatial *kouloures* at Malia may be the most striking example of this, located as they are in a depopulated landscape, and with a palatial elite struggling to make its mark.

Ultimately, the Palaces appear to control significant movements of goods. How the Palaces legitimized their mobilization of resources is difficult to determine. Perhaps the elite managed to generate resources under the guise of risk buffering. But how did they convince others? Redistribution is not a purely economic transaction, but deeply embedded in social strategies. Evans believed that religious personnel controlled the economy (a theocracy),[128] and that ritual and storerooms were juxtaposed in Palaces. It has been suggested that harvest festivals may have played an important part of palatial life, when the masses were awed by the generosity of the elite and partook in feasting.[129] Presumably, as in Classical Greece, this was one of the rare times the majority of people could enjoy eating meat.

Great halls have been reconstructed on the Piano Nobile above the west magazines at Knossos, which might have provided the space for great festivals.[130] These halls would have enjoyed views onto the West Court from their windows. There is a similar correlation between the north–east hall above the north–east magazines, although some halls (e.g., the entrance halls and Domestic Quarter) do not appear to be located close to storage areas. It has been suggested that a harvest festival may have been performed at Malia, with the use of the

Neopalatial silos found in the south-west corner of the Palace there.[131] The north magazines may have served the hall in that area, as a banqueting hall. Likewise, the west half of the west wing comprises halls and storage areas, which could have been accessed directly from outside via the west entrance. But these would have been one-off events in the (ritual?) calendar, not the long-term sustenance of the overall town. Chryssoulaki refers to the miniature pithos from the peak sanctuary at Traostalos, which contained seed;[132] this is at the other end of the scale from the monumental facades fronting the palatial magazines.[133] We now turn to a different element of the economy, which was also deeply social and political: the production of prestige goods.

CRAFT PRODUCTION AND SPECIALIZATION

Brumfiel and Earle lay out three different ways in which craft production is controlled: adaptationist, commercial, and political.[134] The first responds to local environmental factors, but may be deterministic and minimalize the role of trade and exchange. The commercial model emphasizes the role of growth, trade, and surplus to support other industries and promote social complexity. In the third model, the elite's control of the economy, including manufacturing, serves their political aims. All three are relevant in the Minoan world. Copper, tin, precious metals, precious stones, and ivory need to be imported into Crete, but the island is well resourced in lesser stones, timber, and clays. As we will see, the juxtaposition of craft production and harbour sites suggests a role for the commercial model in Minoan economics. Finally, the prestige of fine crafts bore clear socio-political impact. Even pottery requires developed technical understanding, and has the potential to carry 'added value'.[135]

Workshops, Work Areas, or General Production

This section focuses on how craft production appears to have been organized spatially.[136] Rarely does as clear an example as the potter's workshop at Zominthos occur.[137] The identification of a workshop is not straightforward, as this term assumes a permanence in terms of use of space and activities. With storage, the architectural shape of magazines can indicate that function, but such standardization does not exist for production. Much work would have been conducted in the open air, under circumstances that have not survived well. Workshops may be on upper floors, for better light, so the remains would be found in fallen, secondary contexts. Benches have been suggested to indicate workshops,[138] but these are often cited as an indication of sanctuaries as well. They are simply useful, flexible, and convenient constructions. Installations such as kilns are an important indication of production. Mostly, however, our evidence consists of finds.

Raw materials, unfinished objects, manufacturing waste or by-products, tools, associated equipment, or the final products have been presented as criteria.[139] Such evidence is not always preserved; for example, manufacturing waste would usually be cleared up or recycled. Unfinished stone vases indicate some involvement in production. For example, the large block of marble found in the south wing of the Palace at Zakros was half-sawn, indicating mid-use, but the area itself appears to be a grand hall (XLIII), so such evidence is difficult to interpret. Likewise, copper ingots represent involvement in production at some level, for example, at Tylissos, the Arkalochori Cave, Knossos, and Poros.[140] This variation in sites indicate that there was no standardization or intense centralization in dealing with these materials.

Isolated tools are difficult to assess, and would presumably be required for day-to-day maintenance as well as craft production. For example, bronze tools were found in the 'Hall of Ceremonies' (XXVIII) in the Palace at Zakros. This may be due to repairs needed during the last days of the Palace.[141] Hoards have been found at palatial sites, such as Knossos[142] and Malia,[143] as well as non-palatial ones, such as Tylissos Building A.[144] These were elite buildings, and the tools may have been valued as much for their materials as their practical use. As tools can move and be stored elsewhere, so can itinerant craftsmen travel across Crete (as well as beyond). The term 'workshop' is perhaps too fixed for our evidence.

Evely prefers the term 'work area' to workshop, as this leaves open the question of how regular the activity was, and does not assume that only one function was performed there.[145] It may be better to approach the evidence in terms of activity systems, rather than focus on identifying specific activities themselves.[146] In other words, the presence of tools indicates engagement in that activity (even if the work was conducted elsewhere).

Even a kitchen is a work area of sorts, but it does not compare with a permanent, formal place for working prestige artefacts such as gold jewellery, involving high-cost raw materials and specialized knowledge. Some areas, such as weaving, cross over the domestic and the elite. Loomweights are widespread, indicating expertise passed down through generations. But the island was also able to produce textiles, for export even, as the New Kingdom Egyptian tombs imply.[147] The textile industry is particularly notable in the later Linear B tablets at Knossos; possibly the island built up a strong reputation for this in the Neopalatial period.

The evidence for bronze-working equipment across the island suggests widespread practice, even if dedicated spaces are difficult to identify. Evely lists the wide distribution of ingots, crucibles, moulds, crucible hearths, furnaces, and sundry objects from a variety of sites, including palatial, coastal, and inland.[148] No particular pattern emerges from this. A similar distribution exists for the working of precious metals, as far as we can tell from the findspots of moulds used in the manufacture of such materials, alongside faience and glass. Evely lists several coastal sites, such as Mochlos, Poros, Palaikastro, and Gournia, but also some inner ones, such as Knossos, Archanes, and Psychro.[149] By grouping according to type of site, we may be able to detect patterns in the economic system. We will explore the evidence according to Palaces, palatial settlements, harbours, and Villas.

There is a long tradition of assuming palatial control over craft specialization, with the further assumption that the work was actually conducted within the Palaces. The application of models such as peer–polity interaction bears the underlying assumption of palatial control over the political economy and these territories.[150] We begin with the evidence for palatial production.

The Palace at Zakros and its immediate surroundings provide the best evidence among the Palaces, for stone-working (eight areas), bronze-working (five areas), ivory and faience-working (probably confined to the Palace), a perfume workshop, and textile work.[151] The upper floor of the west wing provided most of the evidence for stone and bronze-working, and this is where precious raw materials were stored, notably the six copper ingots and three elephant tusks. The south wing was also an industrial area, with stone and bronze-working, and probably ivory-working and a perfume workshop, with weaving and bronze-working done on the upper floor. These spaces were usually quite small, and did not contain distinctive architectural features.

The evidence is less clear from other Palaces, because of later occupation (Knossos had Final Palatial workshops) or due to being discovered relatively empty (Malia and Phaistos). Evidence for stone vase working in XVII 2 in the Palace at Malia includes unfinished vases, but no debris or tools, so it may simply be storage.[152] Evidence for ivory and bone-working in IV 9–10 is likewise problematic.[153] No clear pattern therefore emerges from the Palaces, but Zakros, as the best preserved example, has provided copious evidence.

Even if the workshops were usually located outside the Palaces, this does not indicate a lack of palatial control, particularly in a society with such a sophisticated administration. It is therefore necessary to explore palatial towns as well. Platon argues that professional craftsmen were 'probably economically dependent on the central authority',[154] whether palatial or not. The contrast between Palace and town occurs most notably at Zakros. Here, agricultural production was done in the town, where most of the wine and olive oil-presses and grinding tools were found, but craft specialization was centralized in the Palace.[155]

At Knossos, ivory-working was conducted in the Royal Road North Building, and evidence for stone-making comes from nearby.[156] Likewise, much firmer evidence for craft production comes from outside the Palace at Malia, namely for stone-working in La Maison de la Cave au Pilier, where tools and raw materials were found with complete artefacts, presumably made there.[157] Tentative reasons may be suggested for these variations. The LM IB Zakrian Palace was very new, imposed on a prosperous harbour town: perhaps this sudden establishment required internal production for security reasons. The longer-term institutions at Knossos and Malia may have developed dependent outposts over time.

We need to consider this on another level. If Zakros was indeed a Knossian imposition, as many believe, then it is interesting that the site itself was so productive. For example, it is assumed that high-quality objects, like the Peak Sanctuary Rhyton, were made at the site,[158] so these are local products. Knossian craftsmen could have travelled to Zakros, or there was a general Minoan expertise in craftsmanship, even if stemming from Knossos. The latter scenario weakens the argument that the wide distribution of 'Knossian' goods indicates Knossian political clout.

Craft production was decentralized further, outside the palatial settlements. There appears to be a close relationship between harbours and craft-working. Zakros was of course a harbour town. Recent excavations support the notion that Poros was an intensive manufacturing site, with the discovery of crucibles and tuyères, slag and raw material for bronze-working; tools, raw material, unfinished seal stones and debris for seal-engraving; and raw materials, moulds, tools, and debris for making jewellery and ornaments.[159] As yet, Poros has not yielded evidence for the administrative use of Linear A, which would have supported the hypothesis of close (external) control of production. However, many seal stones were found (beyond those associated with the seal-making workshop, although some of these had been used as well), which could indicate such organization.[160] Dimopoulou argues that there was a 'partial autonomy of these [full-time] craftsmen against the palatial bureaucratic centralization',[161] but the evidence is admittedly ambiguous.

Evans first recognized Poros as a 'flourishing manufacturing, industrial, and artistic centre as well as a port', and compared its relationship with Knossos with that of Piraeus and Athens.[162] It is perhaps because of this belief that we are tempted to place the site, 'in reality a large urban centre' with substantial, well-built houses and rare, rich LM IB burials,[163] in a separate, lesser category from sites like Palaikastro, which is not located near a palatial site. We see again that devising site hierarchies on economic grounds is very problematic.

The semi-Palace at Gournia accommodated some workshop areas on the basement level (Rooms 1, 3, 27) that could be reached directly from the West Court.[164] Several sets of tools were found in town houses, such as the Hill House, Cg and Fd. The northern part of the site, notably Ea and Fh, has been described as the favoured spot for such craftsmen, but the evidence comprises moulds only.[165] Most of the town material comprises evidence for food preparation and consumption. The wine-press installations,[166] the stone basins,[167] and the millstones suggest the processing of staple commodities was an important domestic occupation.

The sandstone quarry at Mochlos may have provided for the Palace at Gournia – there are few quarries of the material on Crete.[168] The LM IB 'Artisans' Quarter' at Mochlos also provides a rich source of information for craft production for 'largely mundane, utilitarian goods that did not serve political needs, but met a general economic demand large enough to support them'.[169] Located on the mainland opposite what has now become an islet (where the main settlement lies), these buildings (A and B) produced work spaces, installations (including kilns), tools, raw materials, debris, and unfinished artefacts.[170] The evidence for domesticity indicates that the workers also lived here. Stone vases were made and weaving was carried out in both buildings, while those living in Building A also worked metal and in Building B pottery. There is limited evidence for the production or storage of agricultural goods, which indicates that they were possibly mainly supported by their craft activities, but with regular access to sustenance from elsewhere.[171] Limited craft production also occurred on the main settlement such as Building C7 (stone vases) and C2 (seal making). Other professions these craftsmen were engaged with would include fishing and sailing/trading.

A similar picture is seen on the island of Pseira. A Late Minoan obsidian workshop probably came from BY, with obsidian debitage or waste products from the area north-east of the Plateia, around Buildings BY and BB.[172] The workshop in BY appears to be a centre for specialized activity and carried out by specialists, probably on a part-time basis.[173] It is possible that some knapping occurred outdoors in the Plateia area near Building BS/BV and BY, where debitage material was also found. Five pieces of partially worked pieces of metal that were intended to be fashioned into finished objects came from the earlier excavations.[174] The island of Chryssi to the south of Crete has also yielded evidence for the intensive crushing of murex shells (for purple dye) in LM IB, probably indicating a strong woollen industry.[175]

Kommos likewise served as a sea gateway to the Mesara, an important harbour town with considerable local investment poured into its structures.[176] The role of trade is obviously considerable; from the MM III–LM III periods, there are at least eighty Cypriot fragments consisting mainly of bowls, jars, and pithoi.[177] The chief items being traded (e.g., metals, grain, oil) may have been ultimately heading to inland sites for further use or processing.[178] However, little of the ceramic evidence travelled further to Ayia Triada or Phaistos. The production of staple goods and essential objects occurred during LM IA, then the monumental Building T was partially abandoned, although agricultural activities (grinding grain) occurred in the North Stoa, and a pottery kiln was built in the South Stoa.[179] The North Stoa was originally painted to imitate marbled stone, and the space subdivided when set aside for grinding in LM IA and possibly metal-working in LM IB.[180] As the Stoas were originally used for gatherings, and potentially of some importance, this would appear to be a marked down-grading in terms of activities. Overall, this important harbour and its associated trade seem to have close relations with the agricultural side of the economy rather than craft production as at Poros. Later occupation has severely damaged our understanding, however.

The link between harbour sites and manufacturing is strong. Transactions involving crafts could potentially contribute to the economy; Earle suggests that taxing traders of these objects generated a surplus.[181] In return, the elite could offer safe passage and harbours. There is no evidence for such an arrangement, but we do not know what the documents, such as in House A at Zakros, stated. Most harbour towns have little or no surviving evidence for Linear A documents; this may point to free commercial exchanges rather than palatial control, but this is not demonstrated.

Not all harbour sites possess much manufacturing evidence. The prosperous coastal town of Palaikastro has limited evidence for this. Building 1 yielded Neopalatial crucibles[182] and Block S produced a piece of lead, two beads, a partly worked piece of Giali obsidian, a cylinder seal, and a mould for the manufacture of glass-paste jewellery.[183] However, the site did not produce substantial evidence for raw materials in copper and ivory as Zakros did, although there was a probable ivory workshop in Block X, where part of elephant tusk and finished pieces were found. Blocks G, E, and N held concentrations of production evidence.[184]

Turning to Villa sites, and bronze-working may have taken place at coastal Nirou Chani and Myrtos Pyrgos. There were pottery workshops at the inland Villa sites of Vathypetro and Zou, but these are not necessarily prestige goods. Evidence for the production of foodstuffs is also present at such sites (e.g., the press at Vathypetro).[185] These were found in a variety of contexts, from Palaces (e.g., MM III Malia), palatial towns (notably Zakros), Villa sites (e.g., Vathypetro) and even a cemetery (Archanes-Phourni). More substantial inland (but apparently non-palatial) sites have also produced evidence for craft production. Archanes-Tourkoyeitonia yielded evidence for stone-working in Area 24, while nearby Xeri Kara has indications that rock-crystal working was undertaken there.[186] In both cases, the evidence comprises unworked or half-worked pieces.

There is little evidence for a strong relationship between workshops and sanctuaries, which contrasts with the later situation on Cyprus.[187] The traditional assumption is that the palatial control of staple goods (and their surpluses) enabled the elite to support craft production and specialization.[188] The term 'specialization' has become a synonym for intense craft production, which can be misleading.[189] However, it conveys the useful sense that professional specialists engaged in craft production with the support of surpluses in other areas – although this may be more complex. There may have been some permanent, centrally organized workshops, as can be seen in the south wing at the Palace at Zakros, but we can also see more part-time, perhaps opportunist work, in certain towns like Gournia and Palaikastro.[190] These people might be primarily farmers, pursuing crafts when time allowed. In the case of the harbour sites, traders, fishermen, and many other professions might be combined with craftsmanship. Soles' detailed exploration of the 'Artisan Quarter' at Mochlos attempts to flesh out the workers, and consider the makeup of the group inhabiting the buildings.[191] Craftsmen may have non-family apprentices living with them, as well as kin.

CONCLUSION

Crete was clearly extensively worked for agricultural and farming purposes, and this produce was, to a certain extent, monitored in the administration. The impact of this intensive farming on settlement patterns is impossible to generalize about, as different trends have been picked up in different parts of Crete. Perhaps most notable is the fall of sites in the areas around Phaistos and Malia, which may be a reflection of the relative weaknesses of these palatial institutions. There is much variation in the archaeological record concerning the storage of staple goods, most clearly indicated by pithoi. Domestic units have evidence for none at all or limited self-sufficiency, although we are lacking information on other kinds of biodegradable containers. Some elite central buildings had very substantial spaces for storage, such as at Ayia Triada, while Building A at Tylissos also had the potential to store large resources, even though it does not appear to have been the only elite residence at the site.

The Palaces were undoubtedly the key storage controllers in the Neopalatial period (assuming that their potential was fulfilled). This is clear despite the fact that a survey of the central buildings on the island reveals much variation. The fact that the Palaces had such potential suggests redistribution, but it is not straightforward to assess whether this was full control, or even if they were the biggest players in a market economy. Linear A tablets indicate the logging of substantial amounts in some cases. This would suggest either redistribution or an unequal market where some parties were able to mobilize disproportionate amounts. Large-scale events involving feasting may support the idea of an ideological control over the masses.

The evidence for craft specialization and the production of elite objects is also hard to ascertain, as workplaces were not necessarily permanent institutions, and the evidence is rather scattered. The Palaces were certainly the main consumers for prestige/ritual objects; one would imagine that they also had an interest in the production of them. The most impressive evidence for production comes from harbour sites, including Zakros. This Palace gives the best evidence for production activities within the complexes themselves. There is a clear pattern of a high level of production at other harbour sites on the island. Taking all the sites such as Poros, Mochlos, and Kommos together suggests a strong link between craft specialization and sea trade.

CHAPTER NINE

WHO WERE THE MINOANS?
SELF-REPRESENTATION AND OTHERS
IN NEOPALATIAL IDENTITY

INTRODUCTION

It is widely recognized that identity is a process, and not a static condition. In fact, this has been understood for some time – John Myers stated that the Greeks were continuously 'becoming' Greek, rather than simply 'being' such, and it is the same for the so-called Minoans.[1] A crucial question here is whether a sense of island-wide Minoan identity can be discerned, loosely mapped onto cultural features and practices that occurred across the island. Setting aside the assumptions behind the label 'Minoan' (see Chapter 2), it remains to explore the widespread distribution of certain (particularly elite) features. Many analyses have been conducted to highlight the regionalism or different socio-political trajectories that materialized across the island during the Neopalatial period.[2] However, it remains the case that the so-called Palaces have been found only on Crete, and that the island is home to an extraordinary concentration of Linear A documents, 'Minoan' architecture, ritual, and art. In addition to the tension between 'Minoan-ness' and regional variation, this chapter revisits the relationship between Minoan and Knossian identity. While there is a clear concentration of a particular culture on Crete, the role of its biggest and best site in producing this apparent *koine* remains unclear, partly because it was such a dynamic and uneven process across time and space.

We approach these issues from several directions. First, we consider representations of the human or anthropomorphic form in a range of media, in order to explore 'Minoan' self-identity in visual culture. It is argued that the human body is observed and objectified, particularly in representations depicting the viewer and the viewed. We then turn to how the Cretans communicated with other worlds. It is part of the human condition to attempt to extend beyond the immediately experienced world, and engage with the spheres of the divine, the dead, and nature. The simple definition of religion as referring to forces that are 'transcendental, supernatural, or at least superhuman' is followed here.[3] This is wide-ranging enough to cover mortuary practices, the dead, and ancestors, but specific enough to cover more than that which is simply 'special'. The mortuary evidence is patchy, to say the least, but this lack of positive evidence may indicate a rejection of any form of ancestor worship, in contrast with the preceding and succeeding periods.

There is more evidence to assess human relations with the divine, although the human form of deities, such as they have been identified, frustrates this study. There appear to be representations of epiphanies and enhanced states of mind, however, which indicate relations with other worlds. Moving to a different area of identity, we consider other worlds beyond the shores of Crete. How were the Minoans perceived by other contemporary civilizations? Did they influence the outside world in any way? These two apparently diverse topics are related through the major role that the sea had in Minoan art and ritual.

DEPICTIONS OF THE HUMAN FORM

'By the 1960s, discussion of "Minoan" material culture had, to a large degree, become discussion of "Minoan art." "Minoan" archaeology of the middle of the 20th century became, like traditional Classical archaeology, largely an archaeology of objects.'[4] Whitley's comment is not an entirely fair appraisal of Minoan studies. Aside from the fact that socio-political interpretations have always been at the forefront of the discipline, the richness of the iconographical record warrants special attention. Neopalatial figural imagery is extremely distinctive, in body shape, posture, and garb. Minoans chose to represent themselves in a particular way, so this should illuminate elements of self-identity.[5]

Neopalatial Minoans have provided us with a rich database of figural imagery; this engagement was innovative, and indicates a new concern with how the body was to be observed and objectified.[6] It has been argued elsewhere that a divide should not be driven between representation and reality, as representation also forms part of the embodied experience and lived practice.[7] Traditionally, art historians have taken representation to be reflective – so image (and language) mirrors reality. At the other extreme, representation is fully intentioned by the subject. In between lies the constructionist approach, where, Hall states, 'things don't *mean*: we *construct* meaning, using representational systems – concepts and signs'.[8] Reality is experienced through the body, while concepts of the body are shaped and articulated through representations.[9] This dynamic relationship between representations and realities allows both material and visual culture a more active and functional role in the production of social identities. Not only do reality and representations have an interdependent connection, but also different modes of representation may indicate or generate different realities.[10] One moves past wall paintings, but may wear, fondle, and stamp seals; in contrast, figurines are arranged, viewed, and possibly handled, while stone vases are used in certain, presumably ritual, occasions.[11]

Elite Visual Culture: Frescoes, Seals, Figurines, and Stone Vases

In contrast to the previous period, Neopalatial Crete has yielded human images and artefacts in a fine range of media, serving an elite (or indeed non-elite) audience. Furthermore, certain types of figural media, such as golden rings and stone vases, appear to be specific to the Neopalatial period, ending at the end of this (arbitrary, architectural) era. This has not only produced a rich database of human imagery, but also allows us to explore how this was worked through in a wide range of media with the various forms of viewing, handling, and engagement that they entail. However, iconographical evidence permits a far lower chronological resolution than the (non-figural) ceramics:[12] for various reasons, it is not possible to securely attach most of the main media discussed here to particular ceramic phases.[13] Indeed, some types (such as wall paintings) continue in style beyond the Neopalatial period. This generalized picture, in turn, has led to the impression that elite iconography is essentially uniform across time and space.[14]

While considerable work has been conducted on reconstructing Minoan frescoes, particularly in terms of composition,[15] chronology,[16] craftsmanship,[17] and connotation, recently they have been considered also as architectural features that one moves among, rather than isolated pieces of art.[18] Most notably, the excellent preservation at the 'Minoanized' site at Akrotiri on Thera provides the opportunity for architectural approaches to wall paintings.[19] The state of preservation on Crete necessitates extensive reconstruction, which has itself at times required radical rethinking. Notable examples are the Knossian Saffron Gatherer, which started life under Evans as a blue boy, before it was understood that the blue signified a monkey,[20] and the Knossian Priest-King also enjoys regular de/re-constructions.[21] Nonetheless, it appears to be the case that Minoan spaces were generously decorated, if they were decorated at all, enabling them to 'envelope the spectator in a total environment', according to Morgan.[22] Human figures, even if smaller than life-size, generally are set at eye level to the actual people moving past them;[23] it is possible, also, that these ghostly images served to direct visitors along set routes.

Figural wall paintings were an innovation of the Neopalatial period,[24] with a particular concentration around Knossos. Wall paintings are very difficult to date, and Evans' original suggestions have often been altered.[25] Knossos is indeed often viewed as 'the birthplace of Aegean wall painting, its techniques and its basic style',[26] and this type of painting continues at the site after LM IB in its 'Mycenaean' period, as well as other sites such as Ayia Triada. Unsurprisingly, therefore, this serves as a further area where the slippage between Knossian/Minoan culture is standard in scholarship. In the Palaces, Neopalatial painted plaster was particularly focused in areas with Minoan Halls, Lustral Basins, and entrances, occurring also in corridors, Palace workshops, and magazines.[27] Certain non-palatial buildings, such as House B1 at Palaikastro and the Villa at Epano Zakros, have mural decoration, although the architectural forms and functions are arguably much less elite than we would expect.[28] It is worth noting how unusual the Cretan case was at the time, in that this iconography was not found just in high-elite contexts (whether palatial or mortuary), but also in private residences in town and country: the rest of the eastern Mediterranean restricted wall paintings to palatial contexts with clear propagandist agendas.[29] Perhaps this is why the artists, techniques, and styles of Neopalatial wall painting travelled as far as they did, to Egypt and the Levant as well as the Aegean. Its focus on nature and an ambiguous female figure was more flexible (and therefore transportable) than the stern ruler-cult that was otherwise the norm.[30]

The function of seals in general can range from bureaucratic, religious, or magical to simply decorative. Seals are usually an inversion of the intended image, which is produced when they are pressed into clay. Metal signet rings also become popular in this period, but these are mostly known from clay impressions in sealing deposits (approximately 200 impressions are known, but only twenty-five to thirty Neopalatial rings survive).[31] Their impressions (sealings) tend to be from administrative, archival contexts, while golden rings have mostly been found in burials. Seals are often complete, although sealings may be fragmentary. Human imagery is proportionally more common on this medium,[32] and female figures are more commonly engraved on them.[33] The main problem with this class of data is establishing provenance; all too often this is lost.[34] Figures are depicted wearing seals, for example, the Cupbearer Fresco,[35] and as 'personal possessions – worn and broken, treasured and copied – seals bring us far closer to the individual than is ordinarily possible in the Aegean Bronze Age'.[36] The ability to impress a personal or office-based marker expands the individual's socio-political footprint. While a personal marker, often with a very practical, administrative function, their images of the human form (around 5–10 per cent of the corpus)[37] may also indicate social attitudes towards it, and, by extension, possibly identity.

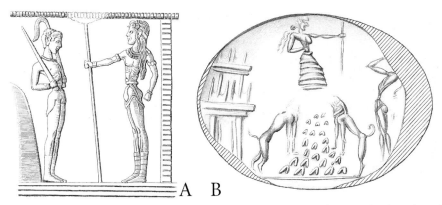

9.1 A) 'Young prince' and officer on Ayia Triada cup, Evans (1928, figure 516); B) Mother of the Mountains sealing, CMS II.8 no. 256 (image courtesy of the CMS Heidelberg).

The lack of life-sized statues is a notable aspect of Minoan culture, with teasing exceptions such as the clay feet from Anemospilia (which may have supported a wooden statue) or the curls of hair from Knossos.[38] This absence marks the island out against Near Eastern cultures, where such objects played a prominent part in rituals. Depending on where they are erected, they may be visible to a large number of people, unlike the life-sized figures in wall paintings (such as the post-Neopalatial Corridor of the Procession Fresco from Knossos).[39] Neopalatial craftspeople produced a wide range of figurines, however, and in a variety of materials – including ivory, gold, bronze, and the cheaper terracotta. These are generally seen to belong in the cultic sphere, and are found in settlements as well as ritual sites.

Unlike paintings or seals, stone vases were objects that were presumably intended to be used in ritual practices. The most common shapes of this kind were rhyta, footed goblets, ewers, and jugs; these were also depicted on other media, such as gold rings and wall paintings.[40] Ritual functions are suggested further by some of the iconography, such as that on the Peak Sanctuary Rhyton from Zakros. The Chieftain Vase from Ayia Triada represents what appears to be a rite of passage, between a youth and older male, and therefore supports a link between drinking and male identity (Figure 9.1A).[41]

The relationship between the body, the person, and, indeed, identity is fluid and dynamic, although the individual body is often, in the modern West, described as indivisible and clearly bounded.[42] Approaches to personhood that are internally divided, along the lines of Strathern's Melanesian 'dividual', are also multiple and extendable.[43] The body's skin is adorned and staged according to context, from clothing, seals, and jewellery to architecture and landscapes. Relations with others extend beyond the skin, such as in gifts, which in turn alter the person within.[44] However, the main challenge archaeologists have in interpreting Neopalatial anthropomorphic images is one of identification, even at the basic level between deities and humans. We will explore anthropomorphic images in general, before considering the relationship between the divine and human sphere in a later section.

Anthropomorphic Imagery

In addition to the distinctiveness of gender roles, the Neopalatial figural ideal is also extremely idiosyncratic. Evans pointed to the realism of Minoan art, such as the relief of an athlete described by Sir William Richmond as 'full of anatomical truth',[45] and elsewhere referred to the 'brilliant naturalism' of Neopalatial art,[46] but it is scarcely naturalistic. The male figures possess an unattainable beauty: hourglass physiques with strikingly narrow waists – the Minoans did not depict deformed individuals, but this shape itself is unnatural. Women were also Barbiefied (both idealized and distorted), with large breasts and swinging hips narrowing into implausible waists (Figure 9.1B). Representations of the human figure are not 'naturalistic' in the sense of 'realistic', and this is a potentially misleading term to use here. The Palaikastro Kouros is of exceptionally high craftsmanship, and deservedly has come to represent the idea of the perfect Minoan youth. Found in an area that yielded ritual equipment, the figurine is also ascribed cultic meaning – and appears to have been deliberately smashed, possibly as an act of iconoclasm.[47]

Several categories and identities were depicted in Minoan art, for example, age, by hairstyle as well as physique.[48] Women and men may be distinguished in wall paintings by skin colour in Neopalatial art (as in many areas of the Mediterranean): men are reddish-brown, while women are white.[49] Alberti has suggested that gender may be more ambiguously depicted: even in the Egyptian context, which influenced the Minoans, these conventions were not always strictly applied.[50] It has also been suggested that the colour-coding may distinguish age or status: the white skin could represent those who spent less time outside (elites) or the young.[51] How and where men and women are depicted is particularly intriguing.

The prominence of women in Neopalatial art is one of the most striking characteristics of the age. Not only are they powerful figures (from position, size, and posture, for example), but there is also a lack of maternal/nurturing and erotic imagery, which comprise the two main 'functions' for women in ancient art.[52] Exceptions to this are very few: a female bronze figurine was found at Makrygialos, possibly with her genitals represented,[53] and schematic representations of women crouching in childbirth are reported from Juktas.[54] There is little full nudity.[55] Sleeved corsets emphasize bare breasts, but they were rarely held, and therefore drawn attention to, as seen in eastern Astarte figurines.[56] These breasts are framed by the clothing, but presented so matter-of-factly that they may be indicative of some kind of status or role rather than a

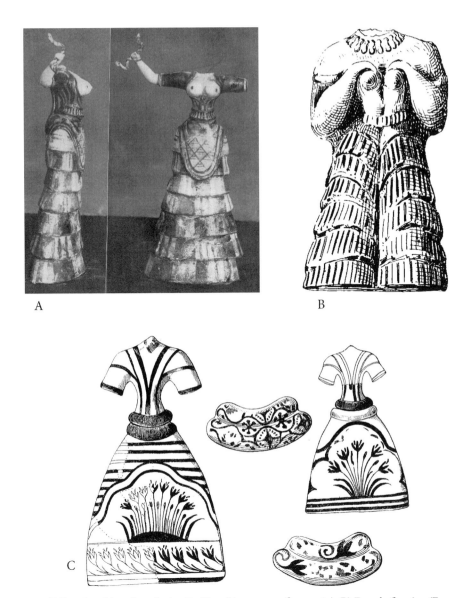

9.2 A) Female with snakes: Snake Goddess (Evans 1921, figure 360); B) Female figurine (Evans 1928, figure 440); C) Models of robes and girdles (Evans 1921, figure 364); all from Knossos. As in Adams 2013, reprinted with permission, © 2013 Institute of Classical Studies University of London, Wiley and Sons.

general allusion to childbearing or sex (Figures 9.2A; see 9.2B: for a rare example of figure holding breasts).[57]

The elite women we see depicted wear full, sometimes flounced, skirts and aprons, and their clothing is marked out in its own right in the iconography – for example, the moulded items of clothing found with the Snake Goddesses (Figure 9.2 C), or the seals and impressions with women carrying garments.[58]

This highly distinctive dress appears significant, serving as a symbol of office or status, possibly involving robing ceremonies.[59] It has been argued that the women's skirts on seals are more important than the figures themselves, and that is why they are given more attention by the engraver.[60] The skirt signifies high status, worn by goddess or human, so they are finely decorated, while the heads are punched. Male figures wear a loincloth and/or belt, while some fuller, older men wear full-length robes: possibly a mark of a particular role such as priesthood.[61]

The suggestion that certain depictions, such as the seated women on the Grandstand Fresco at Knossos, represent a 'matriarchal stage of society' has not been widely accepted.[62] Since Evans, these women have tended to be interpreted as goddesses (or the Goddess in singular),[63] set in the ritual sphere – perhaps partly in the belief that woman were unlikely to have significant 'real-life' roles. Priestesses could have possessed a considerable amount of power and influence, however, especially if there were a substantial overlap between ritual and politics.

Surprisingly, given the wider eastern Mediterranean context, there is little iconographical support for an individual, male ruler.[64] It assumes that art reflects life to use this absence to argue that there was no such ruler, but instead factions jostling for power.[65] There is also a lack of iconographical evidence for this political framework as well. The Linear A evidence sheds little or no light on this matter, while the later Linear B tablets refer to a male *wanax* who was in charge of a complex hierarchical administration.[66] This can in no way be projected back to the Neopalatial period, but the fact that the people of mainland Greece continued to depict strong women reminds us that figural imagery does not necessarily reflect political structure as a simplistic snapshot – and that art and administration may signify different realities.[67]

There is some gender distinction between the media. Only males occur on stone vases, which may have been used on men-only occasions.[68] Figural wall paintings do occur at Cretan sites other than Knossos, but surprisingly few of them. For example, women (not men) occur at Archanes (a woman holding a branch), Ayia Triada (a woman by a 'shrine', a woman kneeling at a baetyl or stone),[69] Pseira (stucco reliefs of two seated women), and further fragments at Chania and Palaikastro. The overall corpus of Cretan Neopalatial wall paintings is too fragmentary to draw clear conclusions, and non-Cretan Akrotiri certainly has men as well as women, but there may have been a deliberate restriction on architectural male imagery outside Knossos.

The Viewer and the Viewed

In the modern world, 'objectification' carries negative overtones, often sexualized, rather than the alternative and more positive process of idealization.

There is a considerable amount of choice regarding how one presents one's body to the world, in terms of both group identity and individualism. As Strathern stated, objectification is 'the manner in which persons and things are construed as having value, that is, are objects of people's subjective regard or of their creation'.[70] But people can have more control over their image and perception, if they have any choice in how they are staged and framed; how one sets out to be objectified is part of one's agency.[71] The value of studying how people in the past themselves objectify the body is clear, but care is needed not to project back our modes of objectification. Both archaeologists and art historians study past remains in the museum context, where 'real' and 'represented' bodies are re-contextualized in a variety of ways.

Scenes of intimacy are few and far between – one exception being the Jewel Fresco from Knossos, where a man is fastening a necklace on a woman (Figure 9.3A).[72] In contrast, there are a number of crowd scenes (again, concentrated at Knossos), observing events that have not always been preserved. The structured, formalized stance of the men bearing ladles on a stone vase fragment suggests such a ceremony (Figure 9.3B). These spectators may be few in number, for example, a woman at a balcony, women at a casement, and the Bull and Spectators Fresco from magazine XIII,[73] or rendered impressionistically as a mass, such as on the Temple or Grandstand Fresco (Figure 9.3 C).[74] This fresco also contains a central band of seated women, much more carefully rendered, with additional (smaller) women standing on platforms at the sides. While it is possible that they are the subjects of the attention of the masses depicted in the upper and lower plains,[75] they are self-absorbed in their own conversation, divorced from the crowds and spectacles occurring around them.[76] Their rejection of the spectacle singles them out, providing a story within the story.

Other media also depict the viewer and the viewed. The gold ring known as the Isopata Ring portrays four women and an additional, smaller, floating figure in the air (Figure 9.4A).[77] An eye appears as a filling motive near the centre of the ring, which reinforces the theme of viewing, whether divine or human.[78] The small figure may be an epiphany of the goddess, but it does not appear to be the figure that three of the women are gesturing towards, who is full-sized and set on a higher plane. Looking at the ring, we are able to see the floating figure that the women in the scene are unable or unwilling to interact with (although one has her arms raised towards it).

On the whole, fresco artists were not interested in depicting frontal faces, which would engage directly with the viewer.[79] One might brush pass a life-size figure on a wall (if, for example, the Corridor of Procession Fresco had Neopalatial precedents),[80] but you would merge in the silent crowd, rather than interacting directly. A rare exception is the necklace on the Jewel Fresco, which consists of a series of frontal male heads (Figure 9.3A). Statues would

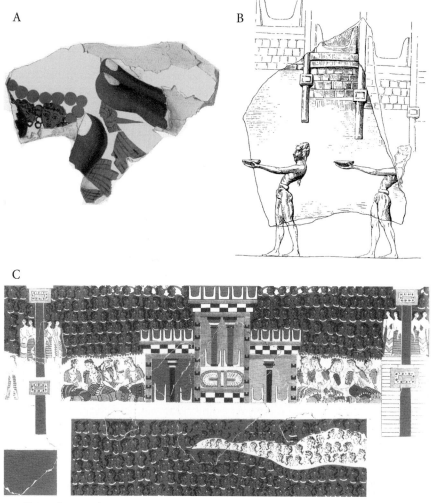

9.3 A) Jewel Fresco from Knossos (Evans 1921, figure 383); B) Men bearing ladles, stone vase fragment from Knossos (Evans 1928, figure 486); C) Grandstand Fresco from Knossos (Evans 1930, Plate XVI). As in Adams 2013, reprinted with permission, © 2013 Institute of Classical Studies University of London, Wiley and Sons.

normally provide the platform for engaging directly with a figural art form, as with many later classical statues.[81] However, these are notably absent in Minoan art, despite the presence of valuable figurines such as the Knossian Snake Goddesses (Figure 9.2A).[82] They may have been dedications, rather than cult statues,[83] but they are assumed to have been ritual and intended for display.[84] Frontal heads on seals and impressions are rare.[85] Assertive eye contact in this manner has been described as a 'focalizer',[86] and, as these objects are indicative of ownership, these figures may have a protective role. In this case, they would not be so much representative of self-identity, but possess an

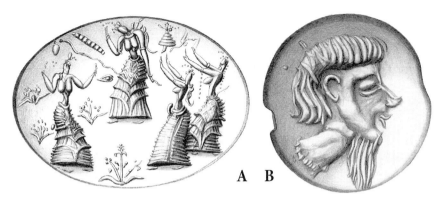

9.4 A) Isopata Ring (CMS II.3, no. 51); B) Male portrait (CMS II.3, no. 13), images courtesy of the CMS Heidelberg.

apotropaic role for the documents/objects stamped, or the frontal face could mean death.[87]

   Nor are there many images that could be described as portraits. The portraits are not necessarily of individuals, but they have certain distinctive features, such as beards.[88] Some bearded males are depicted wearing robes and holding objects such as ritual axes; somewhat stockier than the Minoan youth, they have been interpreted as older, authoritative males, possibly priests (Figure 9.4B). It is notable that these figures tend to have clearly defined facial features, unlike figures with aniconic (featureless) heads such as the females on the Isopata Ring (Figure 9.4A).

OTHER WORLDS

The Mortuary Sphere

Across the eastern Mediterranean during this period, cultures were investing substantial resources in housing their dead, with indications, at times, of ancestor cult. But not, it seems, on Neopalatial Crete, and this is one area where again the island behaves in a very idiosyncratic manner. Furthermore, the people of Protopalatial and Final Palatial Crete buried their dead in a monumental, long-lasting manner: it is just in the Neopalatial period that the Cretans turned away from this standard practice. For example, the island of Pseira has been fully investigated and has not yielded a single tomb. It seems likely that bodies were disposed of in ways that are now undetectable, such as burial at sea.[89] 'Funerary practices serve to create an idealized representation – a "re-presenting" of the individual by others rather than by the man himself', an occasion that can also serve to misrepresent the individual.[90] The rarity of Neopalatial burials, and the fact that they occurred in a relatively sporadic and isolated manner,[91] indicates that Neopalatial socio-political dynamics and identities were not actively played out in the mortuary sphere.[92]

There is some evidence for Neopalatial mortuary practices.[93] Girella has recently provided an analysis of the MM III period, for which, perhaps surprisingly given the overall lack of evidence, a significant amount of regionalism can be detected.[94] Practices continued in the Mesara area, while in central Crete around Knossos practices became much more experimental.[95] Pithos burials and chamber tombs occur, for example, at Knossos,[96] Poros,[97] and in the surrounding landscape.[98] Chamber tombs housed multiple burials, sometimes simply placed on the floor as a group collective, but sometimes the individuals were segregated through placement in pithoi or larnakes. Neopalatial Poros has yielded burials with bronze weapons and boar's tusks helmets; the latter is often associated with the mainland 'Mycenaeans', and, by extension, Homeric accounts of warfare.[99] To the west, Rethymnon yielded some Neopalatial chamber tombs, while to the east, Pachyammos and Sphoungaras possessed MM III pithos burials.[100]

Archanes-Phourni has yielded much Minoan mortuary evidence, but a limited amount for the Neopalatial period. However, the enigmatic MM IIIB–LM IA Building 20 contained human and animal bones as well as a large number of vessels that suggest cooking and feasting.[101] It may have been used for the processing of bodies,[102] or even a burial tumulus.[103] The tomb at Myrtos-Pyrgos has yielded evidence for male burials only, with some evidence for the rearrangement of bones.[104] The deposition of grave goods was unimpressive, with the important exception of the Poros burials, and there is little evidence (e.g., Archanes Building 20) for ongoing rituals and revisits to burials in contrast with other periods. In general, and in contrast to domestic buildings, cemeteries and individual burials were poorly highlighted in the Neopalatial landscape, and not monumental. Furthermore, our understanding is hindered by the lack of representations of death (or sleeping persons) in art, either at the point of death or the funeral process, such as we see in contemporary Egypt, or in Mycenaean Crete, such as the Ayia Triada sarcophagus.[105]

This lack of conspicuousness is important. During the Bronze Age, it has been argued that the self was perceived as fully attached to the body, and would therefore perish with it.[106] This was avoided only by achieving a kind of immortality with a beautiful death,[107] the ultimate 'reaching out' into other worlds. On Neopalatial Crete, even this does not appear to have been a means to immortality. Why, in a period of such high conspicuous consumption, was investment in the mortuary sphere so low? Was mortality and the afterlife less of a material concern? If monumental burial practices are to be associated with times of stress, then this might imply that the Neopalatial period was one of relative stability.[108] However, the site analyses suggest otherwise – this was an exceptionally dynamic period.

Knossos has revealed burials in apparently inhabited structures. The (LM IB) Stratigraphical Museum North Building contained child bones with cut marks; it has been suggested that this indicates not only sacrifice, but also cannibalism.[109] The Minoan Unexplored Mansion contained three LM IA intramural foetus burials and one very young baby.[110] There does appear to be a link between the young and settlement burial here, which could perhaps be extended to a focus on the *future*, rather than the past. If this were the case, then this would be a completely different approach from cultures that did not consider the very young as fully human or persons, and therefore of less social significance (if still emotionally attached). The incorporation of foetuses or young children in Knossian buildings may indicate that concerns about the young and regeneration were of greater relevance than those about the old and ancestors.[111]

Ancestor cult has been a major theme in prehistoric archaeology for a long time. Highlighting the role that ancestors had, or studying the past in the past, reflects the manner in which we ourselves are looking back.[112] Perhaps an archaeology of childhood and descendants should be given equal weight in order to maintain the balance.[113] Viewed as a key part of identity, and perhaps justification for land use in a time before legal ownership, the world of the dead often appears to have played an important part in life. This does not seem to be the case in Neopalatial Crete, and these ancestor cults may have been actively suppressed. Rather than exploring the past in the past, we should perhaps focus on the future in the past; identities can be based as much on intentions and aspirations as on memories.[114] Our backward-looking perspective means that we may easily forget the importance of this, and neglect the myriad intentions, aspirations, and possible outcomes generated and faced by those in the past. Furthermore, our informed hindsight can lead to functionalist explanations of events and processes.[115] Linear narratives should not be depicted as inevitable.[116] There are indeed strong indications that the brave new world of Neopalatial Crete was a very forward-looking era.[117]

Relations with the Divine

While the evidence for strong and marked relations with the dead is lacking, this is not the case for the divine. The intense ritualization of Minoan culture has been noted since the discovery of the civilization, and the ideological grasp that this facilitated for the human elite was likely to have been an important reason why the obvious signs of military might are also generally absent on the island, in contrast with other eastern Mediterranean cultures. The wide distribution of ritual symbolism indicates not just access to this iconography, but also the encouragement of notables to engage with it. This section explores the divine in art – such as we can identify it – and considers the elusive subject of the Minoan belief system, such as whether there was one deity or many.

Sourvinou-Inwood has has been stated that Minoan iconography depicts the interaction between '"this world" of humanity, and "the other world" in which divinities existed',[118] but these boundaries seem fluid.[119] Crowley advocates that figures be referred to as 'humans', rather than defined by role, such as 'priest' or 'priestess'.[120] But since deities also appear to take anthropomorphic form, even the label 'human' may be too specific. Anthropomorphic deities appear not to have been depicted with attributes.[121] We might expect deities to be marked out by size, for example, or in association with exotic and fabulous creatures, such as griffins. There is less 'perspective of importance' in Aegean art than Egyptian, where rulers or gods are larger than others.[122] Even when there is consensus on a scene being 'cultic', a prominent female, for example, may be a goddess, a priestess, or a worshipper (or a combination of these). This is the case in all media, from the faience Snake Goddesses to the ambiguous female figures carrying a quadruped over their shoulder on seals.[123]

Evans promoted the idea of a Mother Goddess figure, borrowing from the art of other cultures.[124] Other scholars followed this interpretation, such as S. Marinatos and N. Platon, who believed that there was a single omnipotent goddess with other minor deities.[125] Cameron's view that there was a fresco programme at the Palace at Knossos centred on a key female deity has had many supporters.[126] Evans saw the power of the Great Mother and Child or Consort as cyclical, dying and reborn annually, with the Mother Goddess later fragmenting into different goddesses of the Greek corpus, such as Aphrodite, Artemis, Cybele, Demeter, and Hera.[127] However, Bronze Age Crete is notably lacking in mother-and-child (kourotrophic) imagery, in contrast with other cultures of the eastern Mediterranean.[128]

It is uncertain whether this was a monotheistic or polytheistic society. Nilsson believed that this was a polytheistic society, albeit with an important Nature Goddess,[129] and N. Marinatos took the line that Minoan religion was polytheistic.[130] It has been suggested that one could deduce whether Minoan religion was monotheistic or polytheistic by analysing the assemblages, i.e., certain tool kits would represent certain deities.[131] However, such an approach fails to recognize the different social statuses of those dedicating the objects.[132] The evidence is ambiguous.

Perhaps the most striking female representations are the so-called Snake Goddesses, from the Temple Repositories in the west wing at the Palace at Knossos.[133] Deliberately deposited with a fine assortment of objects, their label leads to perhaps unfortunate assumptions about their function and meaning.[134] One wears tall cylindrical headwear, akin to a polos, with the Minoan dress of exposed breasts and flared skirt. Snakes coil around her body, arms, and hat. A second figure, dressed in similar costume, holds two snakes, and a cat is

perched on her headwear (with reconstructed head: Figure 9.2A), while fragments of a third also have a snake wrapped around the body. The identification
of these figures as one or more deities is not clear, but if they were, they may
have had a variety of functions: cult image; ritual focal point; or permanent
enactment of a ritual such as robing ceremony.[135] Evans was able to use these
figures to support his Mother Goddess theory only by singling out the first
figure as the goddess, the others as attendants.[136] The artefacts that these
'goddesses' have been found with are mostly those assigned 'ritual' because of
type (such as stone offering tables) or because they are of an uncertain practical
use, such as painted seashells. It is not clear whether these are ritual equipment
or offerings.

Ritualized gesture may help us clarify individuals' roles. The 'gesture of
command', with arm outstretched holding a staff, can be seen on the Master
Impression from Chania or a male figure with lion from the Temple
Repositories, Knossos.[137] Both a male and a female figure have been depicted
standing atop a town or mountain (the Master Impression from Chania and the
Mistress of the Mountains from Knossos: Figure 9.1B). Both share the gesture
of hand on hip and other arm outstretched and holding staff (the male holding
the staff in his right hand and facing left in the impression, the female holding
the staff in her left hand and facing right in the impression). The female is
greeted or worshipped by a male figure, as well as flanked by lions. Some
gestures appear to be a salutation, such as hand held up to forehead as on the
Isopata Ring (Figure 9.4A).[138] Figurines found depicted with this gesture on
peak sanctuaries were presumably intended to represent worshippers rather
than priests, and they are not believed to be cult images.

Cult scenes depicted on seals include processions, offering scenes, and
epiphanies.[139] Scholars have reconstructed two types of Minoan epiphany:
envisioned, whereby the deity is depicted or imagined as present among
humans, and enacted, whereby a human representative stands in for the
deity.[140] Several possible examples come from gold rings, notably the Isopata
Ring (Figure 9.4A) and a ring from Poros.[141] This interpretation is based on the
presence of a small, hovering female figure, which could otherwise be an
attempt to depict perspective. It is notable on both examples that the deity is
smaller than the worshipper – whereas we might expect them to be marked out
as larger than life.[142] The fact that both a male and female figure appears in
epiphany suggests that there was more than one god, at least one from each
sex.[143] Epiphanies may have been enacted. We do not know whether the
Throne Room at Knossos was intended to be the setting of the manifestation
of deities to mortals by sight or presence, or enacted epiphany, a human in
the service and/or guise of the deity, if it were intended for epiphany at all
(Figure 4.1).[144] This ambiguity appears deliberate, signalling a continuum
between this world and the divine, rather than marking a clear separation.

Mythological, exotic, or powerful animals from other worlds may also be set aside humans. This reveals the desire to reach out to other worlds and other realities, particularly when such engagements are life-threatening. Anthropomorphic figures appearing to tame lions, for example, step into otherworldly, unattainable scenarios, while fabulous creatures clearly signal mythological worlds (e.g., CMS II.8 no. 193, which depicts a man in a chariot being drawn by two griffins). This theme is more standardized in the mistress/master of the animals, where a figure is generally seizing a pair of beasts.[145] The 'Zakros Master' was responsible for a variety of imaginary creatures and hybrids.[146] While neither fully human (although some have breasts and some wear dresses) nor deity, their otherworldly qualities are undeniable. A number have frontal animal faces (which may be masks). On the whole, faces are in profile on glyptic, and, if masks, they may represent shamanistic rites.[147] These are highly unusual images in the overall Minoan corpus.

We now turn to the issue of out-of-body or other-world experiences, where bodies seek to cross ordinary boundaries and reach out to parallel realities. This 'ecstatic' state has long been assumed to be part of envisioned epiphany.[148] Here the Isopata Ring can illustrate the remarkable phenomenon of aniconic (or 'faceless') heads in Minoan art (Figure 9.4A). These featureless heads are the result of the punching technique, but it was not the case that the artists were unable to portray this fine detail: they chose not to. Morris suggests that this kind of representation indicates hallucinations or, in other words, the lack of detail signifies an altered state of consciousness.[149] The eyes of the surviving head of a Snake Goddess (or worshipper) appear to stare, perhaps representing a trance-like state, an alternative reality.[150] Drug use could have been a common occurrence,[151] while drinking cups and references to wine in the Linear A tablets indicate the importance of alcohol.[152] Music and regular drumming can also induce other-world experiences.[153] Such altered states of consciousness are more able to engage with other spheres, in particular the divine, if that is what is depicted here.[154]

Neopalatial wall paintings (particularly those outside the Palaces) focus on the natural world. Notable examples of landscape painting occur in Knossian town buildings, such as the House of the Frescoes and the Caravanserai, elite country Villas such as Amnissos, and grander residences, such as Ayia Triada. This strong engagement with nature was not necessarily naturalistic in the sense of realistic; for example, the landscape depicted in the Birds and Monkeys Fresco depicts spring and autumn plants in bloom simultaneously.[155] Seals also often contained nature scenes.[156]

Hunting scenes signal human control over nature and animals,[157] as perhaps also do scenes of bull-leaping and chariot-driving (these include some of the look-alike sealings discussed in Chapter 7: Figure 7.5). The bull is a particularly

Knossian animal,[158] and bull-leaping pushes the boundaries of how people may interact with such creatures.[159] Shapland states that animals had 'a variety of affordances in the Neopalatial period: some afforded hunting and status; other were markers of exotic places'.[160] It is notable that these are elite (ritual?) activities, while domestic animals are not so readily depicted. However, animal figurines deposited at ritual sites may be in lieu of a sacrifice, rather than a request for the safety of herds.[161] 'The "nature-loving Minoans" did not simply observe the world but inscribed, carved and painted the animals they encountered into the fabric of society.'[162]

Was the world of nature blurred at times with the divine sphere? Nature is central to our world and yet also an external force to be reckoned with, and there appears to be a substantial overlap between divine and natural power, a further blurring of worlds that we keep distinct.[163] Minoan religion has been described as a fertility religion on the grounds of the strong iconographical interest in the natural world and animals,[164] and the Minoans have been labelled 'flower lovers'.[165] Many scholars believe that a female divinity held sway over the world of nature.[166] Outside scenes could involve trees, stones (or baetyls), or both.[167] 'Tree cult' (as coined by Evans) is common on gold rings, such as the Minos Ring, one recently found at Poros, and rings from Archanes, Mycenae, and Vapheio.[168] While there is no doubt that there is a series of depictions of tree hugging or 'tugging', the interpretation of these is wide-ranging, from divine epiphany to inspired divination.[169] The 'baetyl cult' is more represented in the iconography than in actual examples.[170] People can engage with 'non-human persons', and objects can be viewed as sentient,[171] albeit not necessarily agents in the human manner.

CRETE AND EXTERNAL RELATIONS

The search for a Minoan identity centred on the island of Crete relies on the underlying assumption that the island's culture was homogeneous, and that it presented a common front to the rest of the world.[172] Islands are taken to be insular, and so the 'people' of Crete are assumed to be a closed, 'pure' ethnicity.[173] This book mainly explores the variability within Neopalatial culture, while recognizing its undeniable distinctiveness. There is clearly a strong island-wide identity during the Neopalatial period, as articulated in certain aspects of the material culture and practices. The bounded unit of an island remains an attractive choice of case study for the researcher, and, indeed, the islanders themselves may have viewed a large island like Crete as the mainland.[174] However, few would now agree with John Evans' view of islands as 'laboratories', entities clinically quarantined from other influences, contacts, and variables.[175] This is at least an unsuitable approach for the Bronze Age. At times, the sea may indeed serve as a barrier, but in the Neopalatial period it clearly acted as a facilitator for travel and a conduit for communication. Such is the flexibility of the relationship between humans and the sea that islands may be stepping stones, hubs, melting pots, and crossroads, all the while bearing very distinct identities.[176]

Whether cultures may be so straightforwardly demarcated is one debated issue, another is whether the spread of such material culture indicates the movement of peoples, a topic that has particular relevance for the Final Palatial period. Traditional accounts follow Wace, who suggested that Mycenaeans arrived and controlled the island through the capital at Knossos.[177] More recently, postcolonial influence on the debate has led to the exploration of other modes of culture contact. It has been argued that practices, such as mortuary ones, can be emulated; these, therefore, do not necessary signify a movement of people.[178] The strongest argument for an influx of mainland Greeks is the introduction of a new language – Greek – however, it has still been contested that new languages can be imposed on administrations.[179] This ambiguity stems from the scholarly desire to draw and distinguish 'real' concrete identities (namely ethnicity) from material culture and language, a highly problematic endeavour. This debate falls beyond the remit of this book, but such striking innovations and introductions in practices, material culture, and language suggest such a strong cultural and psychological shift that the question of whether the movement (or not) of people occurred almost becomes redundant.

For the Neopalatial era, the debate has centred on the nature of Minoan power *outside* the island, particularly in relation to the 'Minoan thalassocracy'.[180] Resistance to the idea of political influence is not mirrored within Crete, where scholars are currently much more willing to accept Knossian influence or control across all or most of the island. Perhaps this is due to a greater willingness to view the sea as a barrier than land.

Archaeologists were able to support references to the Minoan thalassocracy in classical Greek literature when 'Minoan' features were found elsewhere in the Aegean, particularly in the Cyclades.[181] Even excavators in the East were quick to conclude that Aegean potsherds found on their sites signified Minoan involvement.[182] Various 'strings' have been reconstructed, running west to the Greek mainland (via Phylakopi, Akrotiri, and Keos, or via Kythera), or east to Anatolia (via Karpathos, Kasos, Rhodes, Telos, Kos, Kalymnos, and Samos). Ports and the practicalities of sea travel are increasingly well studied.[183] Recent years have produced not only new evidence from various islands, such as Karpathos and Lemnos,[184] and western Asia Minor, such as Teichiussa and Iasos,[185] but also an increasing awareness of the complexities of culture contact.[186] There was not a blanket of Minoan influence across the Aegean – diachronically, for example, Miletus looked much more 'Minoan' in its (MM III–LM IB) Period IV than MBA Period III, whereas Trianda on Rhodes appears more clearly 'Minoan' in LM IA, but more mixed and cosmopolitan in LM IB.[187]

This evidence consists not only of features found at various sites, such as Kythera, Phylakopi, Akrotiri, and Ayia Irini, but also of technologies and the knowhow initially developed on Crete.[188] Evidence for Minoan cult, styles, and administration have been gathered and compared. As ceramic analysis has become increasingly refined, areas of Crete can be pinpointed. For example, the Cretan pottery at Akrotiri is north-central Cretan, with some from the Mesara, Malia, and Mirabello – this mixed origins of the ceramics continues until the LM IA eruption.[189] Further afield on the Anatolian coast, Miletus has yielded evidence for some kind of Cretan outpost.[190] Evidence for imports to and from Cyprus remain surprisingly few, but this appears to increase over the course of the Neopalatial period.[191] Still, few today would deploy the term 'colony' when discussing these sites. Instead, the term 'Versailles effect', which emphasizes local emulation rather than imposed control, is more readily adopted.[192]

It is clear from the iconography that the sea fascinated the Neopalatial Cretans. The painted seashells from the Temple Repositories at Knossos were mentioned earlier, and LM IB Marine Style was an elite ceramic style that took the sea as its inspiration.[193] A model of a boat was found at the ritual site at Traostalos, and fish figurines.[194] Intriguingly, the talismanic seals used clear/green/blue seals for marine depictions, while other red/orange/brown stones were perhaps more set on land – a remarkable attention to detail.[195] These references to marine life in the ritual sphere may indicate that the sea and contact over it was one of the main props to Minoan power.[196] Certainly, the place of the sea and its creatures was another way in which the Minoans (and then Aegeans more widely) were distinctive from other cultures around them.[197] A further Minoan cultural hallmark is the lack of co-occurrence of images and text, while in Egypt and other Eastern societies the two occur hand-in-hand. It is worth emphasizing that the presumably intense maritime contact was celebrated in the iconography, but that the Cretans sought a distinctive culture rather than blindly borrowing.

The means to acquire elite raw materials across the sea was itself a sign of power; ivory, gold, copper, and tin were all imported wholesale for the use of Minoan craftsmen (as indicated by the great stores of elephant tusks and copper ingots, for example, in the Palace of Zakros). Interregional trade was big business in the Mediterranean.[198]

The presence of 'Minoans' far afield is apparent from visual culture. The Bull and Maze fresco from Tell el Dab'a depicts bulls and figures apparently engaging in bull-leaping or 'grappling'. One wears a bracelet and a 'Minoan type seal' around his wrist.[199] The 18th Dynasty occurs after the fall of Avaris, around 1530 BC, and the paintings have been dated to the early part of the this Dynasty.[200] These are probably earlier than the Final Palatial Knossian Taureador paintings,[201] but there was already a clear close association earlier between the Knossian Palace and bull iconography, especially at its entrances.[202] Most importantly, the technique is the same as that developed on Crete.[203] This is the only known example of bull-leaping in paintings from outside the Aegean.[204] A similar influence is detected at Alalakh and Tel Kabri in the Levant. The spread of artistic technique and style is extremely difficult to pin onto ethnic groups, such as 'Minoans' or 'Canaanites';[205] we may, rather, be viewing an artistic, iconographical, ideological, and technological *koine*.[206] Any similarities in style alone do not necessarily require itinerant workers; for example, the import of 'Minoan' textiles may explain the influence.[207] This applies to other media as well – certain Cretan stone vase shapes, such as the blossom bowls, have been found outside Crete.[208]

Important evidence to emerge from Egypt are the male figures in 18th Dynasty tomb paintings at Thebes, described in hieroglyphic inscriptions as the 'Keftiu'. Their clothing is strikingly similar to that depicted in Minoan art, particularly at Knossos. If they were Cretans or Knossians then they appear to be bringing tribute to the pharaoh.[209] This can be seen in various ways, as political parity from the Aegean perspective, generally or as political power over neighbours from the Egyptian one.[210] It has also been suggested that the Keftiu ships mentioned in papyrus 10056 at the British Museum were ships from Crete, and that expertise in ship construction was offered to the Egyptians in this way.[211] The label 'Keftiu' indicates the islanders generally or the Knossians more specifically: possibly from the Egyptian perspective any distinction was of little interest. It cannot, therefore, assist us in terms of the role Knossos had on Crete. Furthermore, this particular evidence dates to after the Neopalatial period, and we should be wary of projecting back this evidence.[212] However, it may suggest that the Cretans were viewed as homogeneous by external contemporaries.

Even with this rich evidence, as Blakolmer states, it remains 'beyond any doubt that the oriental influences and stimuli exerted on Crete outnumber by far the Minoan elements which can be found in the Near East'.[213] However, external influence should not be overblown; Egyptian imports, for example, are surprisingly rare.[214] Most imports of stone vases are Egyptian, forming around 10 per cent of the stone vessels from Knossos, but very rare elsewhere.[215] This suggests a special relationship between Knossos and the south-east Mediterranean (or the eastern Mediterranean, if they came via there), but a complex one, as some Egyptian imports were converted to Cretan shapes.[216] This is a phenomenon that can be seen in other areas as well, such as iconographical motives. For example, the Egyptian Taweret was adopted by Minoan artists, but with notably different form and meaning.[217] Notably, the Egyptian deity had associations with women and childbirth that were not adopted by the Minoans in their Genius, the most 'human' of the hybrid beasts, or even a semi-deity.[218] This apparent rejection of childbirth/maternal connections in Minoan art is one way in which it stands out. Neopalatial Crete was part of an eastern Mediterranean *koine* on one level, but the distinctiveness of the (elite) culture in many different media, and in many different ways, indicates that they were keen to set themselves apart as well. This may have been driven mainly by the Knossian elite, initiating a Minoan pantheon for ideological control.[219]

CONCLUSION

This chapter has explored Neopalatial culture primarily through its art and iconography, in order to highlight its distinctiveness and to explore how people engaged with various 'others'. The Palaces, elite architecture, writing system, and art are concentrated so heavily on the island of Crete that a strong sense of island-wide identity is undeniable. The iconography, which draws heavily on marine life and the natural world, while rejecting the standard ruler cult (including in the form of large statues), is extraordinary in the eastern Mediterranean of the time. The islanders treated their dead in a highly unusual manner as well. This is a culture that did not deploy ancestor cult as was standard at the time, and it has been suggested that it looked forward rather than back. The self-representation of the human form is also very distinctive; the Neopalatial Cretans objectified their bodies in a very specific way. This all points to the presence of a very deliberate expression of identity on an island-wide level. What is more difficult to gauge is the role Knossians had in this. While this cannot be demonstrated on present evidence, the sense is that they were the driving force behind innovations in figural art and promoting them overseas.

CHAPTER TEN

CONCLUSION

THIS BOOK HAS TACKLED A MUCH NARROWER TIMEFRAME THAN
most accounts of the Minoan civilization, which seek explanation
through the long term. One of the great benefits of archaeology is that it
encourages analysis from this wider perspective. However, the wealth of
material from Neopalatial Crete demands and deserves a dedicated study.
Furthermore, a more focused timeframe allows greater consideration of the
lived experience of those in the past, and we can avoid the deterministic and
evolutionistic assumption that understanding the manner of state formation
will explain the state produced. While certain Protopalatial features and practices were continued, they appear to have been appropriated by certain elites
and institutionalized. Indeed, it has been suggested that the Neopalatial Cretans
were very forward-thinking, rejecting high investment in mortuary practices
and allowing certain areas in the landscape (such as Protopalatial peak sanctuaries) and in towns (such as Quartier Mu at Malia) to lie abandoned.[1]

The structure of this book has followed the traditional fields of research,
whether different types of settlements (such as palatial, Villa, or ritual sites), or
different areas (such as administration, the mobilization of resources, or ritual),
or even approaches (such as archaeological or art historical). Gaining a greater
understanding of Neopalatial Crete has required an interdisciplinary approach.
Some contributions that attempt to be holistic end up leaning towards one
direction, such as the political economy, at the expense of others, such as
religion, or vice versa.[2] When the indications appear to be that modern

categories were more fluid in the ancient world, it is preferable to be as open as possible.

This book has presented the evidence in a standardized manner, not only in order to facilitate comparisons within and between types of data and different sites, but also to highlight the importance of context in drawing out the variations within this overall cultural, or 'Minoan', homogeneity. Main areas, such as literacy, administration, communication, redistribution and storage, craft production, the depiction of the human form, and the articulation of identity as set against various 'others', have also been explored on an island-wide basis. This has positioned us to explore certain themes, the most pertinent of which have been: the role of Knossos in island-wide affairs; intra-site organization and different socio-political trajectories; and the role of ritual, particularly in elite social strategies.

THE ROLE OF KNOSSOS: BECOMING 'KNOSSIAN'

Poursat states that: 'These disparities between Minoan sites – decline or renovation – probably reflect the changing interest of Knossos in the management of its cultural and economic influence over Crete rather than competition between local elites.'[3] This statement sums up the two main interpretations of island-wide Neopalatial socio-political structure that scholars advocate. The problem of equifinality here is acute. Neopalatial homogeneity under Knossos has been the narrative promoted since the dawn of Minoan archaeology. Crete's volatile background involved the island being caught between East and West. It was in the interest of the Great Powers and the Cretans to emphasize links with Greece and Europe, and the Europa myth could be usefully harnessed to justify this stance. The distinctive, rich Minoan culture lent justification for the island to be known as the first European civilization, and Europe's first state-level society. States are centralized, according to most definitions, and are assumed to have capitals.[4] Knossos is the strongest contender for such a role, and Arthur Evans was understandably keen to highlight his site.

One of the virtues of the peer–polity interaction model is that it allows for the existence of different, competing political entities within an overall cultural *koine*, or civilization.[5] The term 'peer' can imply a degree of equality between the centres, which is not necessarily the case on Neopalatial Crete, and that each hierarchical polity has a single centre, of the same kind. This again may be questioned when considering regions such as the Bay of Mirabello area. The model is helpful here, with some qualifications. Knossos was biggest and best, and the regional settlement hierarchies varied considerably, as did interactions between sites. However, a consideration of elite social strategies within the broader cultural homogeneity of Neopalatial Crete allows for more localized agency.

While it is fruitful to develop distribution patterns of various types of evidence, equifinality is prevalent in interpretations. For example, the evidence of the 'replica rings', which originate from north-central Crete, presumably the Knossian area, indicate communication between a wide range of sites (in nature, as well as geographical location). However, it is a further interpretative step to claim that this represents Knossian control. Elite features are often assumed to be Knossian in origin, with unclear justification. For example, the Lustral Basin is a more general 'Minoan' feature, and the first known example comes from a Protopalatial non-Knossian, non-Palace context. Knossos may have appropriated the form in the Neopalatial period, and 'branded' it to signal specific Knossian connotations, but this is essentially a hypothesis.[6] Even if it had become a feature that signalled Knossian links in the Neopalatial period, elites from other sites may still have emulated and imitated it, without it representing Knossian control. It is difficult to pin down features that are 'Knossian' as opposed to more generally Minoan. The use of the bull as a symbol is one possible example, but how such a badge might be translated into political power is not yet clear. It is further difficult to reconstruct the motivations behind the presence of objects described as Knossian at other sites. For example, the Bull's Head Rhyton from Zakros was possibly made by a Knossian craftsperson, but the socio-political significance of this evades us.

Traditionally, Knossos has been painted as a force akin to Geertz's portrayal of the Balinese Negara.[7] This 'theatre-state' focuses on the ceremonial and performative foundations of statehood. There is deliberate slippage between capital and state, town and Palace, so that the 'doctrine of the exemplary centre' merged court and state into one glorious performance.[8] The hub was 'not just a center of power, but a standard of civilization'.[9] The slippage between 'Minoan' and 'Knossian' culture and politics, and the emphasis on theatrical performance, is of a similar ilk. However, the range of central places, the variation in the articulation of elitism, and the chronological dynamism all suggest that these two cases are not in fact comparable. The survey evidence demonstrates very different regional trajectories in terms of settlement patterns, and this is matched in the variety of central places. Knossos is deservedly the type-site of Neopalatial Cretan studies, and its special nature also leaves it in a class of its own. However, there is a need for much more attention to local politics, and the aspiration and articulation of power, than is often given.

'Criticism of Knossian control is often based on the unnecessary assumption that it was total, across the whole island if not beyond.'[10] Warren points out that there is likely to have been variation in control, and in the nature of that control. This is correct, and Knossian influence across the island needs to be taken on a case-by-case basis. The Knossian region seems to be the only one with clear second-order centres in central Crete. The Villa sites in the east might play a similar supporting role for the centres located there, but north-central Crete appears to be particularly energized and drawn into a competitive spiral of conspicuous consumption.[11] The concentration of elite architectural features, such as the Minoan Hall and Lustral Basin, is striking in this instance. Beyond this region, however, the evidence for high investment in art and architecture, and evidence for control networks, is concentrated on particular sites, such as Ayia Triada and Zakros. Regional settlement patterns and the type of central places vary enormously across the island. For example, Malia is somewhat isolated, while there is an embarrassment of central places in the Mesara, apparently taking in turns to shine. The Bay of Mirabello area is idiosyncratic: a semi-Palace lies at Gournia and the harbour/production sites at Pseira and Mochlos are clearly prosperous, but not fully engaged in the wider trappings of Minoan elitism. It has, nonetheless, been argued that Pseira was particularly Knossian in outlook; again this rests on aspects of material culture that could indicate other processes at work.

We have explored various sites described as 'Knossian', usually by their excavators. For example, the palatial site of Galatas is located in an area not far from Knossos, and it might be felt unlikely that a Palace would be constructed without the Knossian elite's permission, at least. However, the very short-lived nature of this enterprise might also suggest that this was *not* built with Knossian permission. Later in the Neopalatial period, a Palace was established at the eastern harbour town of Zakros. This possessed certain out-of-date 'Knossian' features, such as a Lustral Basin at an entrance, as well as those still in use at the larger site, such as 'red carpet' paving at the main entrance. The message is therefore confused; the site would indeed be useful for Knossian trade purposes, but a high degree of independence would still be possible for the Zakrian elite taking advantage of this interest – ultimately suggesting interdependency. The palatial form itself is not 'Knossian', as we know from the evidence from the Protopalatial period, so this does not indicate particular Knossian involvement. There is no suggestion that the other eastern Palace at Petras is Knossian.

Another site viewed as Knossian is non-palatial, with a former powerful palatial neighbour – namely, Ayia Triada. The elite features found here are generally Minoan rather than specifically Knossian, but certain aspects, such as the frescoes, have been cited as culturally Knossian, with the implication that they reflect political influence. The idea that Knossian intervention in the region caused the break in use of the Palace at Phaistos is intriguing, and may be supported by the strangely small size of the settlement at Ayia Triada around the very prosperous main buildings: this could have been a luxurious outpost for the Knossian elite. However, this rests on evidence that could reflect emulation or simply itinerant craftspeople. In contrast, it is not suggested that the largest non-palatial site on Crete, Palaikastro, was overly influenced by

Knossos. Indeed, it has been argued that the site's elite articulated resistance to Knossian features in its architecture, although the Minoan Hall is not necessarily an emblem of Knossian identity, and the type of hall found at Palaikastro is also found elsewhere.

Finally, the reference to 'becoming Knossian' in this heading acknowledges the chronological aspects of this study. A model based on peer–polity interaction is widely accepted for Protopalatial Crete. However, the current image of Neopalatial Crete is of an island marching towards the Final Palace centralization under Knossos, as indicated by the Linear B tablets. For example, the previously strong Palaces at Phaistos and Malia appear to have faltered for some of the Neopalatial period at least. The elite at Ayia Triada appears to have taken upon itself the palatial functions, but the role of Knossos in this, if any, remains unclear. The palatial dynamics alone are striking within this period: Palaces were either short lived, as at Phaistos, Zakros, and Galatas, or they changed considerably over the course of the period. Knossian influence and/or control on an island-wide level is likely, therefore, to have been targeted, inconsistent, and subject to change. Simply describing Knossos as some kind of capital shields the actual complexity of the issue.

MODES OF CENTRALIZATION AT THE SITE LEVEL

We have focused on high culture, the elements of the material and visual record that suggest that the islanders desired to present a distinctive identity of 'Minoan-ness'. However, a close, standardized overview indicates how varied the contexts were, in terms of location, type of site, and chronology. We have seen the slippage between 'Minoan' and 'Knossian'; there is also much slippage in the literature between 'elite' and 'palatial'. This occurs even when a feature does not initially come from a palatial context, such as the Lustral Basin, which also occurred in non-palatial contexts in the Neopalatial period. It is clear that 'elite' was a relative and fluid position in Neopalatial Crete; the term needs to be further qualified, and 'palatial' will serve as a useful adjective in certain places.

The assumptions underlying the term 'Palace' are now well understood; perhaps the greater concern may be the application of a single label at all, setting, for example, the Palace against the town. By exploring how the Palaces were approached, we now realize that they were, in lived experience, rather more fragmented entities, and not the homogeneous complexes that a single label implies. You might engage with a small area of the Palace at a given time, and your palatial experience might be delivering foodstuffs, rather than access into the grand halls. Undermining this point is that the Central Courts at the heart of the Palace appear to have served as locales for crowd ceremonies. Another consequence of this, or any, label, is that it leads to the assumption that they functioned the same; in fact, as we have seen, aspects of high culture have a very localized and, at times, idiosyncratic role to play in various regions and at various times.

Perhaps more importantly, the recognition that certain elite features and practices were centralized in the Palaces has led to the belief that the Palaces monopolized them. In some cases, the evidence, as it has survived and been discovered, suggests that this may be the case, such as administrative uses of Linear A at Knossos, or the striking concentration of elite features in the late Neopalatial Palace at Zakros. However, the distributions of the general types of headings explored here are generally spread throughout site and landscape (especially in north-central Crete), so there is no clear monopolization. We return to the problem with the term 'elite' – the residence and location of a political elite may look very different from the distribution of high culture. In the latter case, emulation may be the reason, rather than indications of control.

However, this book has firmly presented Neopalatial Crete as a hierarchical society. No non-palatial building merits direct comparison with its nearest Palace, and, indeed, no Palace can compete with Knossos. Deploying the model of heterarchy in direct contrast to hierarchy is unhelpful, and relies on the assumption that the latter is a static notion consisting only of top-down relations.[12] Stein stated, for example, that 'the co-existence of these non-congruent, and often conflicting, social strategies also forces us to rethink the traditional model of state societies as highly centralized, homogenous, and monolithic political systems'.[13] While fully agreeing that states should not be presented as such, this has not occurred because of the label 'hierarchy', but because of our use of it. Neopalatial Crete contained buildings of varying degrees of prosperity and trajectories over time, implying considerable change existed concerning who was on 'top'. Hierarchies can be as fluid and dynamic as any form of social structure, and it is disingenuous to portray them as simplistic and static, with their central authorities and other tiers somehow possessing less agency than other forms of society.

Centralization may be demonstrated in several areas of Neopalatial Crete, and the different types of centralization and control networks have been a major theme of this book. There is a natural tendency to focus on Palaces in this light, but there were many other types of central building. Furthermore, the second largest site, at Palaikastro, has yet to reveal an obvious central building at all. The mechanisms and modes of centralization are very varied indeed – as are the control networks, such as literacy, administration, and the mobilization of agricultural goods.

Literacy is an important form of control, not only because it enables the monitoring and authorization of goods and labour, but also because it requires a high level of knowledge and training, access to which could be controlled.

It therefore lends a certain prestige and mystification to its users, especially if the vast majority of a society is illiterate. They were controlled by a power that they did not have access to understanding. Examples of the public display of writing support this view (although libation tables deposited at peak sanctuaries could be cast into crevices, suggesting a private display to the deities). It therefore reinforces social differentiation in two different ways: the prestige bestowed by literacy, and the economic and political control enabled by writing.

Other administrative documents, notably seals and sealings, have the potential to authorize transactions. Many of these seal images suggest that even this seemingly mundane procedure had ritual connotations. They also serve as a reminder that centralization need not be indicated physically, on the ground. Administrative documents such as this allow for centralized control, but decentralized spatial distribution. This is the same for the distribution of storage areas for bulky agricultural goods. However, in this case, the palatial contexts are clearly the most generously provided. A key term here is 'redistribution': in economic terms, this is evidence of a successful mode of centralization. Again, if there were events such as harvest festivals, as has been suggested, then this area was also linked to the ritual sphere.

THE ROLE OF RITUAL IN NEOPALATIAL CRETE

Certain control networks, such as administration and the storage of agricultural produce, have been mentioned. One form of control apparently missing from Crete is that of military might: fortifications and other such statements of power. While this situation has been reviewed in recent years, and the hippy image of Minoans as a flower-power society has been eradicated, the lack of military evidence in the material and visual culture is striking, especially in comparison with the rest of the eastern Mediterranean. Was this absence due to and enabled by an overwhelming ideology, embedded in a highly theatrical and performative culture? In contrast, the religious sphere has been a convenient place to deposit all the dominant-looking women: the 'other-worldly' nature of religion relieves them from any everyday, socio-political power. This was not a matriarchy. If it were a theocracy, however, then it is viable that women, perhaps in a priestess role, had a certain amount of influence and authority.

There is a certain contradiction in arguing that ritual was inseparable from secular practices in Neopalatial Crete, and then considering the subject under a separate heading. The difficulties in identifying the figures in Neopalatial iconography (for example: ruler, VIP, priestess, goddess, worshipper) and the fact that certain artefacts are both prestigious and probably additionally ritual (such as decorated stone vases) lend weight to our desire to blur the ritual and secular spheres, but our confusion may be due to our inability to read the signs. It is notable that there is much more consensus on symbols and artefacts that are religious, such as the Horns of Consecration and figurines, than those that are purely secular.

The sense that power relations were fluid in this way is strong, and the ambiguity of terms such as 'Palace-temple' or even 'Priest-King' renders them attractive, especially given the general lack of clear temples and shrines in settlement sites. While obviously loaded, a purely objective term (such as 'central-court compound' or 'figure') may appear less controversial, but they are not necessary any closer to how those in the Neopalatial period perceived these entities – it is difficult to imagine that they viewed them so clinically. It is also a sign of our post-Enlightenment scientific era that such detached labels are considered preferable. Accepting some of Evans' terminology (with due caveats) does not mean that all of his assumptions and conclusions should also be blindly followed. The term 'Pillar Crypt', for example, should probably be abandoned. More importantly, there is a great need to break down his view of Minoan culture as 'singularly continuous and homogeneous'.[14] A contextual approach over space and time of an array of data will move the discipline towards this, but it remains notable that ritual, ritualization, or formulization pervades all aspects of life.

On one level, and for most of this book, references to 'ritual' have involved the evidence for formalized practice in settlements and ritual sites. To a much lesser extent, it has involved the actual interactions with other worlds (Chapter 9): formalized, ceremonial practices need not be religious in nature. A purely ideological approach to ritual may lead to functionalism, neglecting other aspects of the ritual experience, but the role of ritual in asserting authority has been a key theme of this book. The question now is whether this was in fact the key control network for the Neopalatial elites.

'Ritual' is taken to be the formalized processes that serve to bind collective bodies at various scales, from particular groups at a site to the island-wide level, represented, perhaps, by the libation formulae. These ceremonies sanctify cultural identity and foster a sense of belonging with the wider group. In an apparent contraction, they also provide an excellent platform for the negotiation and reinforcement of social differentiation. Special roles and positions can be publicly displayed, which may form part of the justification for socio-political and economic advantages in everyday life. They could also provide the occasion for challenges to authority. The evidence from the miniature frescoes at Knossos would appear to indicate this kind of division, as the crowds are very differently marked from the larger, seated figures. Furthermore, the theme of viewing in Neopalatial art is strong, suggesting that this was con-sidered an important part of social interaction, and where certain social roles could be consolidated. Traditions can be invented and practices can be decommissioned (as appears to be the case with spread of Lustral Basins, followed by many being filled in) in pursuit of these different objectives. Local and chronological variations further complicate a picture based mainly on evidence, such as iconography, that is not always well provenanced or easy to pin down chronologically.

The previous sections have explored various kinds of centralization, whether intra-site or Knossian across the island. Ritual sites should be incorporated, as it is not uncommon for them to mark territory in some way, in addition to serving religious functions. Within some broad generalizations, such as the increased investment and formalization (and institutionalization) of the few peak sanctuaries that continued in use, there is very considerable variation. While the known Neopalatial peak sanctuaries are reasonably fairly distributed across the island, some regions (e.g., Bay of Mirabello) appear not to have one, some (the east) have more than one. They are not all associated with a Palace, as Kophinas and Petsophas indicate (no Palace is known yet at Palaikastro), while the Central Court at Phaistos appears to be pointing towards a ritual cave, not a peak sanctuary.

There is a concentration of ritual caves in the north-central area around the single, rich peak sanctuary at Juktas, which was in turn linked to Knossos: it has been argued that Juktas was a beacon for the wider area.[15] This not only suggests considerable regionalism in the engagement with the ritual landscape, but also perhaps a suppression of peak cult in the area. Skoteino cave lies between Knossos and Malia and could have been a boundary marker; impossible to 'prove', but too important a possibility to disregard. The two great, isolated ritual caves at Ida and Psychro may have served as territorial markers as well as providing powerful locations for the worship of gods; however, their inaccessible location, as with the ritual site at Kato Syme, may have offered politically neutral areas for interactions between the inhabitants of different settlements. Neopalatial Crete is more suggestive of politically neutral locales than ritually neutral ones.[16]

This book has explored in depth a wide range of evidence for a relatively short time period. It has reassessed the long tradition of Minoan scholarship, while being keen not to throw the baby out with the bathwater: Arthur Evans in particular displayed a sensitivity towards interpreting this world that should not be summarily dismissed. The picture is far more complicated than he could ever imagine, however. This is mainly due to the significant increase in the number of settlements excavated, and the additional insights that survey material brings. It is also due to an increase of publications, although much remains unpublished. The messiness of the picture is also due to a greater anthropological awareness of social structures and the dynamism of power relations. Despite the incomplete publications, Neopalatial Crete offers an embarrassment of riches in the sheer quality and quantity of data. It is little wonder that scholars specialize in particular areas or sites, and a good fact that they do. However, this can lead to the wrong kind of fragmentation. Neopalatial Crete is complicated because of the huge variation within certain cultural trends, across time and space: only by developing a coherent narrative can the extent of this be recognized.

NOTES

PREFACE

1. Sakellarakis and Sapouna-Sakellaraki 2010; see also Andreadaki-Vlazaki 2009, 26. This narrative can be traced from Arthur Evans (1921, 24) to Renfrew, via Childe (Schoep and Tomkins 2012, 3).
2. Padgen 2002.
3. Morales 2007, 5–18.
4. Momigliano 2006.
5. E.g., Sakellarakis in discussion after Warren 2009a, 270. Perhaps one fundamental disagreement here is the idea that 'evidence' exists as an objective entity, separate from the questions or interpretations that shape and organize it.

1 INTRODUCTION

1. Evans (1921, 27) states that MM III was specifically the 'Golden Age', 'followed, after a level interval, by a gradual decline'. The 'decline' appears to refer to the LM II overthrow of the Palace at Knossos, which implies that he viewed MM III–LM I as the Golden Age. See also Alexiou (1980, 31) on the Neopalatial era as the 'most brilliant period'.
2. 'Strategies are, according to Bourdieu, the ongoing result of the interaction between the dispositions of the habitus and the constraints and possibilities which are the reality of any given social fact – whether it be cultural consumption, landholding, education or whatever' (Jenkins 1992, 83). See Bourdieu 1977 for the concept of habitus.
3. Rackham and Moody 1996, xi.
4. These are simple, mass-produced, handle-less objects found in a variety of contexts; see Gillis 1990; Wiener 2011.
5. Schoep and Tomkins 2012, 11.
6. Clarke 1968, 12.
7. Platon 1956a, 1966.

8. Rethemiotakis and Warren 2014, 1. They advocate that ceramic periods alone should be deployed, rather than the broader architectural ones; this book would therefore focus on MM III–LM IB rather than the 'Neopalatial' period. It has further been questioned whether the divide between the Prepalatial and Protopalatial periods is so clear-cut (e.g., Schoep 2012). It is now known that there is no single horizon when the Central Court buildings and their associated palatial periods began.
9. Cadogan 2000, 21.
10. The traditional, low chronology dates it to ca. 1530–1520 BC (Warren and Hankey 1989) or ca. 1520 BC (Warren 1998, 328; 1999, 900; 2006; or Warren 2009b for ca. 1530 BC). Wiener (2003, 364, fn. 4) noted that the modified short (low) chronology puts the eruption at ca. 1560–1550 BC, but now follows Warren (e.g., Wiener 2010; 2015a). Manning (1995, 1999), for the high chronology, originally dated it to 1628 BC, based on tree ring dates. Warren (1996, 286; 1998, 328; 1999, 901) makes the point that it is uncertain whether the Theran eruption was responsible for the noted 1628 BC environmental catastrophe (although Baillie 1996, 295, maintains that it is one of the best candidates), in addition to the objection that Manning's higher chronology cannot agree with established Aegean-Egyptian synchronisms. The high chronology has been recently changed to 1645 ± 7 BC based on glass sherds from the Greenland ice sheets (Hammer et al. 2003; Hammer 2005) and on radiocarbon dating (Manning et al. 2002; Manning and Bronk Ramsey 2003).
11. Vitaliano and Vitaliano 1974; Soles and Davaras 1990. Rehak and Younger (1998, 98–100) summarize the known deposits of ash and pumice from Thera. Warren (1999, 894) presents the arguments for the eruption occurring

at the end of LM IA rather than during, although he prefers to place it during LM IA himself (Warren 1999, 894–5).

12. Warren and Hankey 1989, 135–45; Warren 1998, 2010.

13. Manning 1995, 217; Manning et al. 2002; Manning and Brock Ramsey 2003; Kitchen 1996, 2000. Rehak and Younger (1998, 99, Table 1) propose a revised higher chronology. The merits and limitations of radiocarbon dating in Aegean prehistory do not concern us here. See, e.g., Warren 1996; Bietak 2000a; 2003; Macdonald 2001; Wiener 2003. In terms of absolute dating, it is clear that dendrochronology will provide the most secure results when developed (Baillie 1996; Kuniholm 1996, 332–3; Manning 1996, 15, 32; Warren 1996, 288, 1998, 324–5).

14. Warren 1996, 288; Macdonald 2001.

15. Warren 2012a, 264. Betancourt (1998, 293) notes that sites such as Pseira suggest that the length of LM IB must be well over a century. Recent work that prefers to rely on the historical evidence, rather than the contradictory radiocarbon dating, places LM IB at around 1520/1510 BC to 1440/1430 BC (Warren 2006).

16. Morgan (1984, 165) writes that the 'study of iconography frequently has a synchronic rather than diachronic focus: analysis of meaning in structure rather than in sequence'. Krzyszkowska (2005, 321) notes the dangers of attempting to date artefacts such as seals to specific ceramic phases.

17. See Momigliano (1999) for an account of Duncan Mackenzie's life and work.

18. Renfrew 1979; Driessen and Macdonald 1997, 15. Type fossils fix assemblages to certain points of time.

19. Evans 1921, 30.

20. Warren and Hankey (1989, 1) point out that ceramic divisions may bear 'little relation to major factors in the life of the time'.

21. Macdonald and Knappett 2013a on MM III; Brogan and Hallager 2011 on LM IB.

22. E.g., Hatzaki 2013, 37.

23. Betancourt 1985a, 67.

24. Warren and Hankey 1989, 60; Warren 1991, 1999; see also Driessen and Macdonald 1997.

25. Hood (1996), Macdonald (2004), and Betancourt (2013) have preserved Evans' MM IIIB as a distinctive ceramic phase.

26. E.g., Rethemiotakis and Warren 2014.

27. Knappett, Mathioudaki, and Macdonald 2013. This staggered experience of the 'MM III' phase can be witnessed elsewhere at the site, such as the houses to the south-west of the Palace, where two destructions separated three phases of MM III (Macdonald 2013).

28. Macdonald and Knappett (2013b, 1). As the title of their volume, *Intermezzo*, suggests, Macdonald and Knappett present the useful idea that the MM III material is so hard to place in a particular palatial period, precisely because it is an intermediate period. See also Momigliano (2007) for an overview of the Knossian type-site, and particularly Hatzaki 2007a and 2007b.

29. Macdonald and Knappett 2013b, 2.

30. Betancourt 1985a, 117.

31. See Warren (2001) for a review of *The Troubled Island*, which challenges the central thesis; Macdonald (2005, 177–89) has since revised his views, particularly for LM IB Knossos.

32. Driessen and Macdonald 2000; Driessen and MacGillivray 2011. Torrence and Grattan (2002) point out that contemporary social change need not necessarily be *caused* by a natural disaster; however, the effects should not be underestimated (Friedrich and Sigalas 2009; McCoy 2009).

33. Driessen 2002a; Manning and Sewell 2002.

34. Evidence for pumice comes from Pseira (Betancourt 2009), Mochlos (Soles 2009), and Papadiokampos (Brogan and Sofianou 2009), with a likely layer of tephra from the latter.

35. E.g., Driessen and Macdonald (1997, 211) refer to the F40 deposit at Gournia, which are LM IA ceramics in style but in an LM IB context.

36. Brogan 2011, 43.

37. Warren 2015.

38. Brogan and Hallager 2011.

39. Warren 2012a.

40. Warren 2012a.

41. Brogan 2011, 52.

42. Warren 2012a, 263–5. Brogan and Hallager's important volume of 2011 introduces the idea of an LM IC phase, necessitated from the subdivision of LM IB at some sites. More evidence is required before this can be accommodated into syntheses.

43. Hatzaki 2011a, in discussion p. 91.

44. Finley 1968, 17.

45. Lloyd 1990, 54; Jones 1997, 49; Hitchcock 2000, 28.

46. Evans 1921, 13. In basic agreement, Hood (1971, 35) wrote: 'although the civilization of Crete throughout the Bronze Age was basically homogeneous, local difference and divergences of fashion existed in the pottery as they did in other aspects of life such as burial customs.'

47. The assumption prevails from Evans' time that great works of Minoan art originated from the 'School of Knossos' (e.g., Evans 1921, 542–4, on the fish fresco from Phylakopi; Evans 1921, 721, on the Mycenaean Shaft Graves). See Wiener (1984) for the idea of the Versailles Effect, whereby competitive emulation produces a wide distribution of elite features. See also Wiener 1990; Soles 1995; Betancourt 2002; Adams 2006; Shaw 2015. Betancourt (1985a, 140) argues that the 'Special Palatial' ceramic tradition either originated at Knossos or itinerant craftsmen based at Knossos travelled to other sites. Rehak and Younger (1998, 129) suggest that 'as a leader and innovator in artistic production, Knossos was surely the most important Neopalatial center in Crete'.

48. Shaw (2015, 170) argues that Malia was the 'architectural originator' in the Protopalatial period, but still perceives a School of Knossos.

49. Macdonald 2005, 42. See Wiener (2007) for a strong defence of Knossian rule; also Soles (2016, 248): 'Most archaeologists today agree that a unified Minoan state emerged under the control of Knossos in the Neopalatial period, if not before.'

50. E.g., Hallager and Hallager 1995; Warren 1999, 902. See Schoep (1999a, 201–2; 2002a) for discussion and references.

51. Cadogan 1984, 13. See also Evans 1928, 1; Wiener 1990, 150; 2007. Hood (1983, 132) has suggested, on the Egyptian model, that the ruler of Knossos owned other Palaces and great houses elsewhere, and travelled around them.

52. Cherry 1986, 27.

53. Cherry (1986, 25–6) notes five main reasons given for the argument that Knossos controlled the entire island: the lack of fortifications, Minoanization outside Crete, the size and monumentality of Knossos, the very similar sealings found in sites across Crete (see Chapter 7), and the cultural and artistic pre-eminence of Knossos. See also Cherry 1999, 19; Driessen 2001; Palaima 1990, 87–9. See

Cadogan (1994, 1995) for the detection of Protopalatial polities or states.

54. Bennet 1990, 193; at least, this is known for historic periods.

55. Bennet 1990, 209. He points out that, during the Neopalatial period, 'there is nothing in the archaeological record to prove that any one site was in control of the others, although connections among the polities were strong' (Bennet 1990, 199–200), and suggests that these regions were 'clearly defined' (Bennet 1990, 198).

56. Warren 2004; see also Adams 2006.

57. Yoffee 1993, 69–71; see also Knappett 1999.

58. Soles 1995. See also Geertz for a description of the nineteenth-century Balinese theatre state as promoting the 'myth of the exemplary center', where Klungkung's 'orienting image of order was refracted through a series of lesser centers, modelled on it as it had been on Majapakit' (Geertz 1980, 16), although in no way did it reveal 'overall domination by a "single-centered apparatus state" under an absolute despot' (Geertz 1980, 24): Adams 2006, 6. See Pilali-Papasteriou (2004) for a recent discussion of Knossos and theocracy.

59. Recently, Knappett and Schoep (2000) and Schoep (2002a) have suggested that Knossos' cultural dominance was also ideological, and so held a significant political component.

60. Schoep and Knappett (2004) ask whether complexity needs to imply the existence of a central authority, stressing the bottom-up and self-regulating processes in place that produce given kinds of social structure.

61. Warren 2002, 202.

62. Smith's (2003, 103–4) definition of 'complex' is weighted towards the political: 'inequality in access to resources, variability in social roles, differentiation of decision-making bodies, permanence of institutions, and the distribution and flow of symbols, meanings and practices', but a more all-encompassing characterization is advocated here.

63. Chase and Chase (1992) make the distinction between the elite who run the society's institutions, and the distribution of culturally elitist architecture, artefacts, and symbols. The former is frustratingly difficult to reconstruct from archaeology alone, and Neopalatial Crete is no exception to this.

64. Shore 2002, 10–11.

65. Bennett 1961–2; Niemeier 1988; Davis 1995; Koehl 1995.

66. Chase and Chase 1992, 7; Adams 2004a.

67. Evans 1935, 960; Van Effenterre 1980, 327; Marinatos 1986, 1993; Rutkowski 1986; Hallager 1987, 176; Koehl 1995; Hood 1997, 105; Sakellarakis and Sapouna-Sakellaraki 1997, 32.

68. Bell 2007, 278.

69. Adams 2004b, 30.

70. Kertzer 1988; Shore 2002, 2.

71. Cherry 1978, 1986; Peatfield 1987, 1989, 266–7.

72. Soar 2014, 224. See German 2005 for a discussion of performativity and social categories, the performance of an act, and social drama as visible in the iconography.

73. E.g., Morris and Peatfield 2004; 2014; Hamilakis 2013, 161–90: in the case of the latter, it is misleading to suggest that a sensory approach lies in opposition to one that considers how the 'Palaces' (or court-centred buildings) were run and functioned (e.g., p. 166: these 'rather than being centres of political authority, large-scale production of commodities, administration, and subsistence redistribution, seem to be primarily centres of sensorial, communal events, consumption, feasting and drinking, and elaborate performance'). The picture painted by Evans and others after accommodates both approaches.

74. Evans 1921, 447.

75. Nilsson 1950. Nilsson's approach was particularly notable as this was before the 1952 decipherment of Linear B as Greek, therefore distinct from Minoan Linear A. See also Briault 2007a.

76. Evans 1901. It has been argued that, rather than a fanciful reconstruction, Evans was attempting a more scientific presentation that noted the transition from aniconic to anthropomorphic religion in the Minoan world (Harlan 2011). This mirrored Lubbock's evolutionary stages of religious thought (atheism, fetishism, totemism, shamanism, then idolatry or anthropomorphism: Harlan 2011, 218, Table 1; Marinatos 2015, 10–25). See also Goodison 2009; Younger 2009a.

77. Warren (1994, 192–4) notes another area on the south side of the Royal Road with a grandstand; this too could have been used for watching processions (personal correspondence, 22 May 2016).

78. Evans 1928, 578. According to Evans (1928, 579, 585), the steps were seats for 'numerous spectators who could thence look on at sports or religious functions in the area below' or standing room for around 500 people. Graham (1987, 27) stated that these spaces were 'evidently designed for some kind of spectacle or performance'; this could suggest that he envisaged it as the set for the performance rather than the stand for the audience. Driessen (2009) also advocates this sense of ceremony, viewing the causeways as 'red carpets' into the great monuments.

79. Picard (1948, 143–4) referred to the open air ceremonies, while Warren (1990) reconstructed baetylic rituals. Warren (1988) advocated a focus on practice, particularly things done, said or sung, and displayed in order to communicate with deities, also promoting the idea of Minoan epiphany.

80. Bell 2007.

2   THE BACKGROUND TO NEOPALATIAL CRETE

1. McEnroe 2002.

2. Detorakis 1994; Holland 1999; Carabott 2006; see Adams 2010. Perhaps unsurprisingly, Prince George, the High Commissioner, left the job in 1906.

3. Holland 1999, 258.

4. Brown 1986, 38.

5. E.g., Knapp and Antoniadou 1998; Hamilakis 2007; Aronsson and Elgenius 2014.

6. Adams 2010.

7. Cadogan 2000.

8. Brown 2000.

9. Evans 1943; Harden 1983; Brown 1986; Hood 1987. Hazzidakis supported Evans in his endeavour from 1900 onwards. Evans employed both Muslims and Christians at Knossos, a progressive move.

10. Sherratt 2006, 111.

11. Quoted in D'Agata 1994, 7, 14.

12. Simandiraki 2004, 2006; Hamilakis 2006.

13. E.g., the heated debate over the Acropolis/Parthenon marbles now in the British Museum.

14. Simandiraki 2004.

15. Karadimas 2015. See also Moore (2010) for British interest before Evans.

16. Myres 1941, 336; Papadopoulos 2005; Carabott 2006. D'Agata (2010) relates the perception of Knossos through the ages.

17. E.g., Mountjoy 2003.
18. Cadogan 2000, 17–18.
19. From 1904; between 1904 and 1909, Evans exported around 3,500 objects from Knossos (Galanakis 2015, 20).
20. Gardner 1908, x–xi.
21. Adams n.d.
22. Pendlebury 1939.
23. Hood 1958; Hood, Warren, and Cadogan 1964.
24. Peatfield 1990; Tzedakis et al. 1990.
25. Driessen 2001.
26. Bennet 2002, 218.
27. E.g., Hamilakis 2002.
28. *The Times*, 12 June 1899, letter written by Evans and Hogarth promoting the Cretan Exploratory Fund.
29. E.g., Starr 1984, 9; McDonald and Thomas 1990; Fitton 1995, 115; Driessen 2000a, 113; Hamilakis 2006; Gere 2009.
30. Cadogan (2006) makes the important point that Evans generally avoided the term 'The Minoans', keeping it firmly as an adjective. See also Galanakis 2014 (on Evans' quest for the origins of Mycenaean culture).
31. Evans 1921, 1. See also Karadimas and Momigliano 2004.
32. Evans 1921, 3.
33. Burns 2010, 292.
34. Karadimas and Momigliano 2004.
35. See Doumas (2012) for references. The name 'Minoans' may reflect the paradigm of culture history, but there is nothing to be served from 'junking' the term altogether (*pace* Whitley 2006).
36. Marinatos (1993, 40) stated that 'Evans's king was therefore not a secular figure, but a Priest-King in a theocratic society.' More recently, it has been suggested that monasteries of the Middle Ages would be a better analogy (Cadogan 2000, 20). This example indicates how ritualized Minoan Palaces are felt to be.
37. See McEnroe 1995.
38. Schoep 2010.
39. Evans 1912, 278.
40. Evans (1912, 280) believed that the Minoan cult was 'essentially non-Helladic'.
41. Evans 1912, 277; see also Hawes and Boyd Hawes 1922, 2.
42. Evans 1921, 24; see also Childe 1926, 209, although the Minoans 'lacked the vigour for expansion' (see Adams 2010). Momigliano (2006) rightly argues that this role in European history (and, indeed, the

identification of the Minoans as Europeans) is a myth; however, the construction of the history and therefore the identity of modern geopolitical entities is a well-understood process, and this kind of unfounded narrative still carries much weight.
43. Papadopoulos 2005, 88.
44. Papadopoulos 2005, 103; see also Momigliano 2006.
45. Dyson 2006, xi.
46. Adams n.d.
47. Waldstein 1909, 526.
48. Waldstein 1885, 9.
49. Adams n.d.
50. Evans 1921, 1.
51. See Kristiansen and Larsson (2005), but see also Nordquist and Whittaker for a rather critical review; they describe the obsession with origins as one reason why this book is 'strangely old-fashioned' (2007, 82).
52. Said 1978, 3.
53. Evans 1896 (mention of Reinach (1893) on p. 519); Fotiadis 2006.
54. Duchêne 2006.
55. Evans 1921, 3. See Momigliano 2006.
56. Childe 1958, 70. Papadopoulos (2005, 94) places great weight on Evans' and Childe's joint role in helping 'to forge and establish an idealized and robustly 20th-century vision of Europe in prehistory'. Childe was also influenced in Oxford by the classical archaeologist John L. Myres, who was also a friend of Evans': see Brown 1986. While Childe may have been guided by Evans, and studied at Oxford alongside Joan Evans, John's half-sister (Sherratt 1989), whether they explicitly wove together an agreed agenda for European prehistory and identity is less clear. Indeed, Evans' determination to separate the Minoans from the Mycenaeans, and his insistence that neither were Greek, suggests differences in their approaches. Childe saw the Mycenaeans as Indo-European, but appears to have situated Crete as 'the Ancient East', the conduit through which the civilization of the east diffused (Sherratt 2006).
57. Childe 1925, 29.
58. E.g., Evans 1921, 19. He did, however, recognize the role of the East and Egypt in stimulating change in the Early Minoan period (Marinatos 2015, 45–6).
59. See Rethemiotakis and Warren 2014: the point is that, if there is no single destruction

60. See Hamilakis (2002) for a critique of cultural evolution.

61. E.g., Gardner 1908. The intellectual world of the late Victorian era was small, enabling good interaction across disciplinary divides. John Evans, father of Arthur, knew Charles Darwin, for example (Sherratt 2002).

62. Adams n.d.

63. See critique by Cherry (1984, 20–1): 'The underlying notion of historical explanation – one that few archaeologists in other areas would be willing to accept – is essentially that of Collingwood: namely, that understanding of some historical occurrence or process arises merely from the more thorough analysis of antecedent circumstances.'

64. Marinatos (2015, 11–3) argues that Arthur Evans reacted against linear evolutionism, unlike some of his contemporaries, such as Gilbert Murray and Jane Harrison. Recent papers, armed with a far better dataset than Evans had access to, have also argued for a gradualist, incremental model (e.g., Tomkins 2012 on Knossos; Todaro 2012 on Phaistos).

65. Hamilakis' (2002, 6) criticism of Evans' use of the term 'successive stages' in the subtitle to his great work *The Palace of Minos* is unclear in this manner. Archaeologists cannot produce a coherent narrative of this society without conforming to these chronological tools that recognize the linear nature of time, however much experienced temporality may differ (Adams 2007a).

66. Service 1962. Evans himself generated an overarching narrative of growth, flourish, and decline, *contra* Service's model of progression.

67. As highlighted in Schoep 2004.

68. Renfrew 1972, 11.

69. Halstead 1988, 523.

70. E.g., Barrett and Halstead 2004.

71. Watrous 1998, 23.

72. Schoep and Tomkins 2012.

73. Service 1962.

74. Cherry 1978, 411.

75. Cherry 1983a.

76. See Tomkins (2012, 33) for an overview.

77. Furthermore, he argues that 'the continuity in the transition from Prepalatial to Protopalatial Crete must be emphasised' (Renfrew 1972, 98). This tendency continues today (as noted by Whitelaw 2012, 164). The prosperous EC II (Cycladic) culture cannot be drawn upon to help explain the rise of the Cretan Palaces, even if there is some evidence for culture contact between the two areas, although Renfrew (1972, 337) himself notes how 'each area had its own traditions and customs', such as in terms of metallurgy.

78. E.g., Tomkins 2012.

79. Adams 2006, 1–2.

80. Especially since the ground-breaking paper by Cherry 1986; see also Whitelaw forthcoming.

81. Cadogan 1994.

82. Day and Wilson 1998.

83. Knappett 1999; Cadogan 2013a.

84. Whitelaw 2004a.

85. E.g., Renfrew 1972, 297; Van Andel and Runnels 1988.

86. Whitelaw 2012.

87. E.g., Graham 1987. More of a sense of chronological change is given in Cadogan (1976), although the presentation in terms of tours of the Palaces obviously focuses on the later periods of construction.

88. Note Schoep 2004; Shaw 2015, 10–14, table 1.3; see also Schoep 2006. For example, two of the key areas of the Knossian Palace, the Throne Room and the 'Domestic Quarter', possess no evidence for their known form before MM IIIB (Macdonald 2002), although some scholars have projected these forms back to earlier times (Mirie 1979; Günkel-Maschek 2016). *Archaeological Reports* 1987–8, 68, describes the evidence for three phases in the rooms behind the Throne Room. Macdonald (2012, 103–4) points out that the mason's marks from the Throne Room and Lustral Basin areas date to the Protopalatial period, suggesting this early date; see also Shaw (2015, 156–7) on the Lustral Basin.

89. E.g., McEnroe 2010.

90. The evidence from Knossos is patchy: MacGillivray 1998.

91. Manning 2008, 111; after Whitelaw 2000. Whitelaw 2001, 21–7, estimates that Knossos had a population of 11,000 to 14,000; Whitelaw (2004b) 14,000–18,000.

92. Schoep 2004. She argues that similarities between Protopalatial Palaces have been overemphasized.

93. Evans 1921, 203–4; MacGillivray 1994, 46; Macdonald 2005, 56. See also Shaw 2010.

The MM IA Royal Road indicates a central authority perfectly capable of extensive planning: Warren 1994.

94. Tomkins 2012.

95. Macdonald (2012, 83) likewise distinguishes between the history of the monument, the question of whether there was a central authority, and the concentration of particular functions on the Palace.

96. Poursat 1988, 2012; Pelon 1992. The east magazines were used for the storage of liquids, as indicated by the channels running into collector vases to cope with spillage.

97. On three sides of the square were foundations for blocks of seats, somewhat in the manner of the 'Theatral Areas' (see next chapter).

98. Van Effenterre 1980; Poursat 1987.

99. Van Effenterre and Van Effenterre 1969. Actually storage appears to have been a key function in the building.

100. Poursat 1987; 1992, 37–8; Schoep 2002a; 2004.

101. Levi 1976; La Rosa 2010a. See Todaro (2012) and Militello (2012) for recent overviews.

102. See Strasser 1997, and reply by Halstead 1997.

103. Schoep 2004, 252.

104. McEnroe 2010, 52.

105. MacGillivray 1994, 55.

106. E.g., Schoep 2002a.

107. Tsipopoulou 2012a; 2012b; Christakis 2012.

108. Kanta, A. 'The Minoan palatial centre of Monastiraki Amariou in west-central Crete', ICS Ventris Memorial Lecture (15 May 2013).

109. Nowicki 1994.

110. Watrous 2001, 193.

111. Myres 1902–3; Rutkowski 1991.

112. Peatfield 1992.

113. The body parts were originally interpreted as votive phalli, but are now considered to be the arms of female figurines (with bracelets): Peatfield 1992, 74; Morris and Peatfield 2002, 109.

114. Watrous 2001, 195–6.

115. Anastasiadou (2016a) argues that the dividing line sits between Knossos and Malia, with the former part of the Linear A tradition.

116. Schoep 1999a.

117. For example, the noduli: Schoep 1999a.

118. Macdonald and Knappett 2007.

119. Day and Wilson 1998.

120. Soles 1992, 168.

121. Legarra Herrero 2014.

122. Adams 2007a.

123. E.g., Alcock 2002; Van Dyke and Alcock 2003a; Relaki 2012.

124. Lane (2005, 29) points out that the archaeological record may reflect practices more concerned with the 'casting out' of the past than the retrieval or memory of it.

125. Adams 2007a, 411.

126. Brück and Goodman 1999, 7–8. For the Neopalatial period, this may include certain peak sanctuaries or soroi (watch and/or fire-signal post: Panagiotakis, Panagiotaki, and Sarris 2013) that apparently fell out of use.

127. Adams 2007a.

128. E.g., Poursat 1992; Schoep 2002a; 2004.

129. Schoep 2004.

130. It may be the case that the MM III Palace shrank in comparison with its Protopalatial predecessor, such as the erasure of the northwest area. However, this should not detract from the basic continuity of the occupation of the Palace in comparison with shifts occurring in the town.

131. Pelon 1980, 235; 1992, 32–4.

132. Poursat 1966; Gesell 1985, 107.

133. Poursat 1992, 52–3.

134. Adams 2007a, 411.

135. Adams 2007a. The Palace at Phaistos experienced a considerable break in construction during the Neopalatial period, which would clearly have had an impact on those in the settlement and region around. The Protopalatial period at Knossos is less well understood, but see MacGillivray 1998.

136. Gosden and Lock 1998. See also the distinction in Bradley (2002) between the role of distant and recent pasts.

137. The reuse of the Cretan Bronze Age remains by later Greeks serves as a good example: Prent 2005; Adams 2007a, 412.

138. Soles, 235; 2010. See Soles and Davaras (1996, 184–94) for the preliminary report of Building B2.

139. Soles 2010.

140. Conical cups and rhyta, etc. may be present in ritual contexts, but can offer only a very tentative indication of ritual in themselves.

141. Evans 1921, 429; Gesell 1985, 97. The ceremonial use of this area is suggested by the finds, such as the offering stand and ivory sacral knot. While Evans saw no reason to suggest that the cave itself was a cultic focus during the life of the Southeast House, 'it is conceivable that its existence had given some special sanctity to the

spot where the Pillar Room was built' (Evans 1921, 429).

142. Bradley 2002.
143. Herva 2005.

3 ELITE ARCHITECTURE AND ARTEFACTS

1. See Privitera (2008) for a consideration of ritual practice in smaller buildings. For more technical aspects, see Shaw 2009; Devolder 2013.

2. Adams 2004a, 193–4; see also Shaw 2015, 3. In both cases, the term 'Palace' is retained to describe the court-centred buildings; however, there are some discrepancies in the choice of features discussed – for example, we do not consider ascending and parallel stairways in this chapter as Shaw does (see Devolder 2016); see also Driessen (2005a) for upper floors.

3. See, e.g., Rapoport 1990.

4. E.g., Evans (1935, 215) on the House of the High Priest. Among those reacting against this overly simplistic, hierarchical model are Schoep (e.g., 2002b) and Hamilakis (1997–8), in line with more general shifts in anthropological and archaeological thought (e.g., Patterson and Gailey 1987; Brumfiel and Fox 1994; Ehrenreich, Crumley, and Levy 1995; Scarborough, Valdez, and Dunning 2003).

5. Day and Relaki 2002, 227. Brumfiel, one of the first proponents of both terms, considered them in separate works (1994, 1995). See also Driessen (forthcoming) for 'corporate communities'.

6. See Hamilakis (2002) for factions in Minoan Crete; Renfrew and Cherry (1986) for peer–polity interaction.

7. E.g., Kristiansen and Larsson (2005) drew on Marinatos' (1993) work in order to situate the Minoans in a Near Eastern and European narrative whereby theocratic rulership, alongside trade, contributed towards social transformation in Europe during this millennium (Kristiansen and Larsson 2005, 62).

8. McEnroe 2010, 98.

9. See, e.g., Darcque and Van de Moortel 2009.

10. I use the term 'formalization' rather than 'institutionalization', since the latter has connotations that lie strongly towards the political.

11. E.g., Gesell 1985, 26. However, she also states that the presence of a Double Axe is of particular importance.

12. Evans 1921, 427–9, figure 307. Neolithic remains were found in a crevice; see p. 33.

13. Begg 1975, 29; Christakis 1999a, 1999b, 2008; Rehak and Younger 1998, 109. See, e.g., Hatzaki (1996, 36–7) in the case of the pillared rooms in the Little Palace, *contra* Evans (1928, 525–6) and Gesell (1985, 27, 94).

14. E.g., Adams 2004a.

15. Panagiotaki 1999, 241. Marked on Figure 3.2 as 'Central Shrine Area'.

16. E.g., Macdonald 2005, 105.

17. See comment in McEnroe (2010, 77) on Nordfeldt (1987) and Graham (1987, 20).

18. Renfrew 1985, 20; 1994; 2007, 114–15.

19. E.g., Adams 2004b. Darcque and Van de Moortel (2009) call for more neutral language in the discussion of 'special' features and artefacts.

20. Rapoport 1990.

21. Warren 1981a; 1981b.

22. Hitchcock 2000, 46–7; Schoep 2002b, 102–3; Pelon 2002, 111. But see Schoep 2010, where she argues that the term 'Palace-temple' was devised in opposition to the current temple model of the Near East.

23. Schoep 2010. This blurring between religious and secular is followed by others, e.g., Hood 1995. See Bennett 1961–2; Waterhouse 2002 on the 'Priest-King; Boulotis 2008'. Renfrew (1972, 13) wrote: 'not every participant of a civilisation is insulated so effectively as the Minoan prince in his Palace'; see also Renfrew 1972, 366: 'the Palaces, obviously the homes of rich and powerful rulers whom one might well term "kings"'.

24. Macdonald 2005, 90.

25. Hamilakis 2002, 18.

26. Hamilakis 2002.

27. A similar deconstruction of the seemingly innocent term 'house' may be seen in Driessen (2012a) and particularly Warren's (2012b) response to Driessen's paper. This example highlights that English and other languages are much more flexible and ambiguous than they are often portrayed to be: the term 'Palace' can mean many things.

28. E.g., Warren 2002; Niemeier 2009, 13.

29. Driessen 2002b; Schoep 2002b. The suggestion that the term should be replaced by 'regional

center' (Rehak and Younger 1998: 102) fails to distinguish between the Palace itself, the palatial site as a whole, and non-palatial centres, and so is not followed here.

30. Herva 2005.

31. Knappett and Schoep 2000, 365.

32. E.g., Branigan 1983.

33. E.g., Platon 1983. Some, such as Watrous and Hadzi-Vallianou (2004, 291), have argued that religious status, rather than economic control, formed the main basis of Minoan kingship.

34. Halstead 1981, 201.

35. Adams 2004a. In this paper, it was argued that it is important to extract from the data not just the distribution *patterns* of particular types of data, but also the *correlations* among these patterns.

36. Except Neopalatial (and non-palatial) Pseira: Rehak and Younger 1998, 106. The intensive survey confirms this: Betancourt, Davaras, and Hope Simpson (2004, 2005).

37. Preziosi 1983, 138.

38. Driessen 2009.

39. Geertz 1980, 13.

40. Marinatos 1993, 39–40.

41. E.g., Rutkowski 1986, 229.

42. E.g., Marinatos 1993.

43. Architectural summaries of the Palaces can be found elsewhere, e.g., Graham 1987; Hitchcock 2000; Fitton 2002; McEnroe 2010.

44. Trebsche 2009. Function is a social construct, and it is possibly misleading to attach modern mechanisms to ancient evidence.

45. Van Effenterre 1987.

46. Palyvou 2002, 169.

47. Graham 1987.

48. Graham 1987, 73.

49. Shaw 1973. Petras, unusually, falls to the west of true north by ten degrees (Shaw 2015, 22–3).

50. Shaw 1973, 59.

51. Goodison 2004.

52. Shaw 2015, 21–2.

53. McEnroe 2010, 74.

54. E.g., McEnroe 2010, 73.

55. Palyvou 2002, 172–3; see Chapter 9.

56. Palyvou 2002, 170.

57. McEnroe 2010, 84–5.

58. Adams 2007b.

59. See Evans 1930, figure 106 for a section of the elevation by Piet de Jong.

60. Adams 2007b, 365–6.

61. Pelon 1980, 134–5; Van Effenterre 1980, 61–3; Gesell 1985, 105. See Puglisi (2010) for a reconstruction of a kernos cult at Ayia Triada.

62. Tsipopoulou 2007. Gournia also had a somewhat disjointed West Court, standing at just 15 × 5 m, with a baetyl set in the recess of a wall.

63. The West Building has an open space between the covered porch and the Tripartite Shrine (J. W. Shaw 1978, 442–6; Driessen and Sakellarakis 1997), while a further courtyard was situated to the west (Driessen and Sakellarakis 1997, 69).

64. See table in Vansteenhuyse 2002, 247.

65. Rethemiotakis 1997, 37–40, figure 6. See also *Archaeological Reports* (2002–3, 79), for a 'processional way' running along the west facade of the Palace at Galatas.

66. By a structure that was either an altar or the entrance to another building (Driessen and Macdonald 1997, 179).

67. Between the Tripartite Shrine and the columned porch.

68. Sakellarakis and Sapouna-Sakellaraki 1997, 120–9. Furthermore, the 'Theatral Area' at Archanes has been associated with the 'central building', although they lie at some distance apart. A stepped altar and Horns of Consecration were recovered from the Theatral Area.

69. Marinatos 1987; Cucuzza 2011.

70. E.g., Evans (1928, 585) estimated that the eastern stairs could accommodate around 360 standing persons.

71. Graham 1987, 27.

72. Davis 1987; Marinatos 1987.

73. Driessen 2009.

74. Hitchcock and Preziosi 1999, 84–5.

75. McEnroe 2010, 110.

76. The MM II town possessed a 'shrine' and Sanctuary of the Horns. The former (Poursat 1966; Gesell 1985, 107) was a three-roomed building containing libation tables and figurines. The latter (Poursat 1992, 52–3) contained Horns of Consecration and figurines.

77. Pernier and Banti 1951, 104–18. It was common for Neopalatial Palaces to have spaces only accessible from outside, although this is the only clear ritual one (Adams 2007b, 376). The 'shrine' (XVIII) at Malia has been described as a bench sanctuary (Gesell

1985, 106), although the bench was poorly placed to receive votives (Van Effenterre 1980, 446).

78. Driessen 2000b. Fragments of Neopalatial ritual objects were found in the area, but the building is LM III. Hood (1977) has discussed the possible public shrine in areas 24, 38–40, 41–3 of Block Π at Palaikastro on the basis of ritual objects including Bull's Head Rhyta, but the actual architectural context is unclear (Driessen 2000b, 89).

79. Soles 2004, 159.

80. Kaiser 1976, 299–302.

81. Hamilakis 1997–8; 2002.

82. Macdonald 2005, 90; see also Marinatos and Betancourt 1995.

83. Graham 1960, 1961, 1987.

84. Adams 2007b, 371–2. This appears to have been the case in wealthy Roman households (Zanker 1998, 13), and could even be deployed as an intimidation strategy (Trigger 1990, 127; Smith 2003, 235–6).

85. Graham 1959, 1987; Driessen 1982, 1989–90, 1999; Marinatos and Hägg 1986; Nordfeldt 1987; Palyvou 1987; Hitchcock 2000; Letesson 2013.

86. Marinatos and Hägg 1986.

87. Driessen 1982, 1999.

88. Palyvou 1987.

89. Driessen 1982.

90. Adams 2006, 15, figure 8.

91. Adams 2004a.

92. Driessen 1989–90, 21. McEnroe (2010, 98–100) describes the process as 'palatialization'.

93. Graham 1979; but see Begg (1987) for the suggestion that these were not halls.

94. Adams 2004a, 199.

95. The inner hall of the Hall of the Double Axes, for example, was the most private part (Evans 1930, 345).

96. For a summary, see Shaw 2015, 25–30.

97. McEnroe 2010, 77.

98. Graham 1959, 47. See Palyvou (1987) for circulation patterns.

99. Driessen 1982, 56; 2002b, 5.

100. Adams 2007b.

101. Hitchcock 2000, 269; Adams 2007b, 372.

102. The Little Palace at the same site had two halls separated by a large, impluvium-style light-well; the alignment of the three units is the same, but the orientation of the two Minoan Halls lies at right angles.

103. See Gesell (1985, 20–1) for a description of this architectural type; its distinguishing feature is a niche or altar with balustrade at the back of the hall. See Evans (1935, 206, figure 157) for a reconstruction of the example from the House of the High Priest.

104. The excavator has noted a feature reminiscent of the Knossian Chancel Screen Hall at Kastelli, but it is not fully excavated (Rethemiotakis 1997). Similarly, Hall 10 at Archanes has a raised dais in the centre of the north wall (Sakellarakis and Sapouna-Sakellaraki 1997, 101).

105. Fotou 1997, 39.

106. Gesell 1985, 94–5.

107. Evans 1935, 202–15.

108. Macdonald 2005, 115–16. He states that the Lustral Basin was probably filled in at the end of LM IA, but there is no recorded evidence for this. Nor is there any evidence that the unit existed in the Protopalatial Palace; it appears to have been a MM IIIB innovation (Schoep 2004, 249); but see Macdonald 2012, 103–4; Shaw 2015, 156–7.

109. The benches in the room suggest provision for others, although the hierarchy in terms of furniture is clear.

110. Goodison 2004. The sun at the winter solstice would hit the throne, while it would hit the Lustral Basin during the summer solstice. Goodison's views regarding the light entering the throne room may be mirrored by the sensation of emerging from the deep ritual caves into the light (Tyree 2001, 45).

111. Sakellarakis and Sapouna-Sakellaraki 1997, 98–102.

112. Xanthoudides 1922, 7.

113. Adams 2007b, 372.

114. Graham 1961; Van Effenterre 1980, 343–7.

115. Three of its halls are located in the western part of the building. The separation between ceremonial and 'functional' activities in this building is made the more notable by the presence of an entrance to serve each section.

116. See Adams (2004a) for more detailed discussion.

117. Rethemiotakis 2002.

118. Adams 2007b.

119. Reconstructed by Graham 1956.

120. Platon 1971.

121. Graham 1987, 251.

122. Minoan Halls are also found outside this area, including Chania, Phaistos, Ayia Triada, and

Zakros; Lustral Basins are also found at sites such as Chania, Zakros, and Phaistos.

123. Driessen 1982, 57.

124. McEnroe 2010, 98.

125. Palyvou 1987, 198.

126. See Cunningham (2007, 102, figure 11.3) for a photograph of the example from Block B.

127. Driessen 1989–90, 14. The depression in the ground was to collect rainwater (Maison Epsilon) or for a hearth (Galatas). There was no depression in the example at Vathypetro. The hall (15) at Sklavokambos is unusual in that its north-eastern pillar is replaced by the south-western corner of Room 9 (see Figure 7.4). The hall (Figure 7.4, 1) in the north-eastern quarter of Sklavokambos was entered via ashlar pier-and-door doorjambs, but the normal layout in Minoan Halls is that they are *subdivided* by pier-and-door partitions. This is a good example of the idiosyncratic interpretation of a standardized form.

128. Driessen 1999.

129. Platon 1967; Alexiou 1972; Graham 1977, 1987; Gesell 1985; Hitchcock 2000; see also Marinatos (1984, 73–84) for the frescoed example at Akrotiri.

130. Platonos (1990) provides some possibilities, such as the sprinkling of holy water.

131. Graham 1977.

132. A useful summary of previous interpretations is given by Platonos (1990), who emphasizes the ritual use of these units. See also Platon 1967; Rutkowski 1986, 31–5.

133. Evans 1928, 322; Platonos 1990, 154.

134. Evans 1921, 411, 422; 1935, 937; Gesell 1985, 90, 92.

135. Parker Pearson and Richards 1994, 25.

136. Marinatos 1984, 64–5, figure 43.

137. E.g., Marinatos 1984, 74.

138. Marinatos 1984, 74.

139. Marinatos 1984, 81.

140. Marinatos 1984.

141. Platonos 1990. Puglisi (2012) argues that this interpretation can be applied to Cretan examples, along with the suggestion of divine epiphany.

142. Some believe that the 'bathroom' of the so-called Queen's Megaron was a Lustral Basin raised during the Neopalatial period (e.g., McEnroe 2010, 77).

143. That the Throne Room Lustral Basin in the Palace is the least accessible from the outside supports Driessen and Macdonald's argument for increased security in the Palace (Driessen 1995; see Macdonald 2002 for an analysis of different phases in the Palace). Gesell (1985, 24) has suggested that the same body of rites moved from the (MM III) north-west Lustral Basin in the Palace to the one in the Little Palace in LM I and then back to the Palace in the Throne Room example in LM II. However, the Throne Room Lustral Basin may have been much earlier (Niemeier 1987, 163–4).

144. Graham 1987, 267. This example Graham (1987, 268) accepts as used for ritual purposes (as opposed to bathing).

145. Bell 1997.

146. Hatzaki 2005, 75, 199.

147. Driessen and Macdonald 1997, 60.

148. One of the many similarities between Delta Alpha and Zeta Alpha is the location of the Lustral Basin in a central western position, about midway from the south entrance to the buildings.

149. See Driessen (1982) for the suggestion that they were.

150. La Rosa 2002, 90.

151. All such observations regarding the Palace at Galatas must remain preliminary, pending further excavation and publication; in particular, the north wing will shed much light on the nature of the complex (*Archaeological Reports* 2003–4, 78–9).

152. Driessen and Sakellarakis 1997, 70.

153. Gesell (1985, 116–17) suggests that space 7 at Nirou Chani is a remodelled Lustral Basin, and McEnroe (1982, 5) queried its status as a full Lustral Basin. Xanthoudides (1922, 13) believed that this area was a bronze smith's workshop, and this is followed by Fotou (1997), but the evidence for this is unclear.

154. This Lustral Basin is not fully excavated: Sakellarakis and Sapouna-Sakellaraki 1997, 100–1.

155. Driessen 1982.

156. Driessen 1982, 63, fn. 10; Driessen and Macdonald 1997, 59–61. If a floor has been raised, then it can be difficult to establish whether it was originally intended to be a Lustral Basin without tests – see, e.g., the Queen's Megaron in the Palace at Knossos.

157. Platon 1967, 238.

158. Driessen 1982, 39–41.

159. Adams 2007a. If the Lustral Basins were used in relation to chthonic deities, the

160. Graham 1987, 265–8. In this case, the raising of the floor need not imply a change of function (Graham 1987, 256).

161. Alexiou 1972; Platonos 1990, 154. See Driessen and Macdonald (1997, 59–61) for a summary of these changes.

162. Driessen 1982, 63–4, fn. 12; McEnroe 1982, 5. Platonos (1990, 153) does not believe that the Royal Villa at Knossos or the mansions at Nirou Chani and Vathypetro had Lustral Basins, as has been suggested. This hypothesis is problematic in that it is unclear *when* these so-called imitation Lustral Basins were built. If they were early Neopalatial, when most sunken examples appear to have been built, then this would pre-date the raising of the floors of those that they are imitating.

163. In related terms, it has been argued elsewhere that the overall provincial nature of the Malian site should not lead us to assume that time itself was static here, reminiscent of the ahistorical ethnographic present (Adams 2007a).

164. Binford 1981; Murray 1999.

165. Warren 1969, 36.

166. E.g., Adams 2004a.

167. Koehl 1981, 2006.

168. Nilsson (1950, 144) defines the rhyton more specifically as in the form of a head, but it is best to keep it as a reference to the free-flowing nature of the liquid in a variety of shapes.

169. Platon (1971, 125) describes 'low funnel-shaped vessels' found with rhyta in the 'Central Shrine' in the Palace at Zakros, which he suggests served as flowerpots.

170. Brück 1999. For example, Nilsson (1950, 143) states of rhyta that they are 'for the most part of a shape which makes them unfit for practical use …, [which] taken together with other circumstances is a strong argument for the sacral character of these vessels'. This is highly plausible, but ultimately an assumption – Nilsson (1950, 144–6) continues to remark on the potential confusion with objects used in daily life, and notes that the latter could also be votives.

171. Evans 1928, 548; Gesell 1985, 98.

172. Adams 2004b.

173. Verlinden 1984; Rutkowski 1986; Peatfield 1990, 120–2; 1992, 72–4; Sapouna-Sakellaraki 1995; Rethemiotakis 2001 (particularly for Postpalatial figurines); Morris 2009a.

174. Morris and Peatfield 2014.

175. Peatfield 1990, 122, from Davaras 1976, 246.

176. Morris and Peatfield 2002.

177. E.g., Zeimbeki 2004.

178. Peatfield 2016, 490.

179. Adams 2004b, 37.

180. Sakellarakis and Sapouna-Sakellaraki 1997, 506–29.

181. Muhly 1981, 4; this builds on the essential work by Warren (1969).

182. Whittaker 2002.

183. See, e.g., the discussion of bull-leaping, dance, and boxing in Soar (2014). See, however, Shapland (2013) for a rejection of the tendency to set bull-leaping within the ritual sphere.

184. Muhly (1981, 139) states that more than 80 per cent come from ritual sites; more have been found in settlements since 1981, but this figure is notable.

185. Cherry 1986.

186. Muhly 1981, 159.

187. Nilsson 1950, 117. This is in line with his general aim to highlight elements of continuity from the Bronze Age to later periods, when the altar was the focal point.

188. Evans 1901, 135–8. He argued more specifically (p. 137) that they represented the 'actual horns of the sacrificial oxen'. Marinatos (1993, 5) is more restrained in stating that 'the symbolic meaning of the horns is unknown, although the similarity with bulls' horns cannot be entirely fortuitous.'

189. Banou 2008, 32.

190. Evans 1930, 84.

191. Blakolmer 2016, 62–3.

192. Blakolmer 2016, 63.

193. Hazzidakis 1934, 101–3; Banou (2008, 29) refers to other scholars open to this interpretation. Nilsson (1950, 189) argues that it was a symbol in Egypt and a likely influence, but it was a piece of cult equipment on Crete, for the consecration of objects and votives.

194. Poursat 1966, 534; Levi 1976, Tav. 149; Schoep 1994, 192–4, 197. Banou (2008, 32) points out the circularity in that these new 'ritual symbols' are used to confirm the space or model as ritual.

195. E.g., Schoep 1994.

196. Banou 2008, 34. Much of the evidence presented in support of this view postdates the Neopalatial period. Keria also produced clay

examples: E. Kyriakidis, personal correspondence, 4 September 2016.

197. D'Agata 1992, 249. It is obviously difficult to date such objects, but D'Agata places them in the Neopalatial period.

198. D'Agata 1992, 249.

199. Lowe Fri 2011. See also Evely 1993, 41–55. Haysom (2010, 48) suggests that they are also connected to weapons, and also possibly connected to a leadership role in agriculture.

200. Hogarth 1899–1900, 108.

201. Haysom (2010, 43) discusses a sealing each from Ayia Triada, Zakros, and Akrotiri, and a seal from Knossos.

202. Nilsson 1950, 220–1. He refers to the Near Eastern god Teshub, who had attributes of the Double Axe and a lightning bolt.

203. Marinatos 1993, 5. Nilsson (1950, 226–7), while noting that this was a female-only activity (whether goddess or priestess), is still happy to view it as a sacrificial axe. Even if the idea that women should perform sacrifices is too unbelievable, the symbolism of the act does not need to be restricted to those performing it.

204. E.g., Begg 2004; See also Haysom 2014, 81.

205. Seager 1910, 31.

206. Seager 1910, 32. The object was found with a clay bull (Seager 1910, Pl. IX) as well as 'a cover decorated with Double Axes'.

207. See Seager 1910, Pl. VII.

208. E.g., Rutkowski 1986, 229; Marinatos 1993, 5; Hitchcock 2000, 150.

4   PALACES AND THEIR CONTEXT

1. Shaw (2015) focused on Knossos, Malia, and Phaistos. Driessen, Schoep, and Laffineur (2002) rightly question the boundaries of this category, 'Palace', and some sites, such as Archanes and Chania, may be hiding a Palace under their modern towns.

2. Driessen, Schoep, and Laffineur 2002.

3. Poursat 1988, 80.

4. E.g., Moore 1996; Johnson 2002; Saunders 2002; Letesson and Vansteenhuyse 2006; Adams 2007b. See also McMahon 2013.

5. Adams 2007b.

6. Platon 1971, 89. See Adams 2007b. Here, several different categories were assessed in order to define the similarities and differences

between the Palaces of Knossos, Malia, Phaistos, and Zakros. These were: 1) entrances with direct access to the heart of the Palaces, the Central Courts; 2) entrances into other courts; 3) approaches to halls; 4) entrances and purification rites (Lustral Basins); 5) annexes that looked outwards, not penetrating far into the Palace; 6) openings (or windows) where goods could be exchanged. Attention was paid to the impact of the space as well as function.

7. A shift from an emphasis on the monumental and ritual to the everyday and mundane has been advocated; see Gosden 1994; Foxhall 2000, 485.

8. Wilson 1994; 2008, 82.

9. Schoep 2004, 247.

10. Whitelaw 2004b.

11. McEnroe 2010, 78.

12. Macdonald 2002.

13. Mountjoy 1984, 170–1.

14. Macdonald 1990, 88; 2002, 53. See Macdonald (2005) for a revised version of his LM IB 'ghost' or 'ruined' Palace.

15. E.g., Niemeier 1994, 85.

16. Mountjoy 2003; Hatzaki 2007c.

17. Evans 1928, 415–16; Macdonald 2002, 49.

18. Adams 2004a, 198.

19. Hood 2011; Warren 2011.

20. Evans 1927; Graham 1987, 26; Papadopoulos 1997; Hitchcock and Koudounaris 2002.

21. McEnroe 2010, 79; Galanakis (2015) traces Evans' curatorial work at the Ashmolean to his desire to produce an open-air museum at Knossos. Today, it is Evans' concrete reconstructions that require great conservation: Karetsou 2004; Minos and Kavoulaki 2010. See also Marinatos (2015) for a defence of these works and Evans in general.

22. Farnoux (1996, 92–3) on the Throne Room area, view from the Central Court.

23. D'Agata 2010, 57.

24. Myres 1941, 341; Warren 2000, 203; Shaw 2015, 88–91.

25. The role of others (e.g., de Jong) should not be underestimated, but Evans remained the face of the 'campaign' (see reference to de Jong in Papadopoulos 2005, 101).

26. Warren 1994, 201.

27. Driessen 2009.

28. Graham 1960; Hägg 1987.

29. McEnroe 2010, 69.

30. Preziosi 1983, 105.
31. Adams 2007b.
32. This is a modern term, but signals the ability to control and administer both people and things. Evans demonstrated some variability in the term; for example, the 'lodge' at the west entrance was 'evidently the seat of some high official guardian or "Major domus" of the Palace' (Evans 1921, 215).
33. Adams 2007b.
34. Adams 2007b.
35. Adams 2007b, 365–6; note p. 368, figure 6, view up the ramp to the Central Court from the north entrance.
36. Macdonald 2002, 43.
37. Evans (1928, 761) suggested that the north-south corridor was used in processions from Juktas.
38. Evans 1928, 679. See also Hägg 1987; Marinatos 1987; Van Effenterre 1987; Palyvou 2004, 214–15; Adams 2007b, 373–4; Driessen 2009. It appears that, in the Protopalatial period, the west entrance cut straight through the facade into the Palace (Evans 1928, 660–4).
39. Evans (1928, 734–6) took them as being Neopalatial, but this has since been contested: Peterson 1981, 39–40; Immerwahr 1990, 88–90, 174–5; Hood 2000, 203–4. It remains possible that the LM II preserved frescoes followed an earlier programme; repeated layers of the same iconography are attested elsewhere, namely, the bull from the west porch: Immerwahr 1990, 176; see also comment by E. Davis after Hood (2000, 208) and Macdonald (2005, 188).
40. Evans 1928, 720, but see Peterson 1981, 38.
41. Adams 2007b, 374.
42. Hiller 1980; Hitchcock and Koudounaris 2002, 44–5. Evans reconstructed an imposing Protopalatial approach to this area (Evans 1928, figure 75).
43. Evans 1921, 391, figure 282.
44. Evans 1928, 588–96; Begg 1975, 22; Graham 1979, 62–3; Adams 2007b, 376–7.
45. Adams 2004a, 199–200.
46. Hallager and Hallager 1995.
47. Shapland 2013.
48. Adams 2004a, 200.
49. Evans 1930, 397–435; Gesell 1985, 92.
50. E.g., the nodule from the Northeast House: Schoep 1995, 33–4. The relationship to this structure to the Palace is unknown; it may have been some kind of extension.
51. Boskamp 1996.
52. Popham and Gill (1995) note 'earlier deposits', without specifying which phase: compare Gill 1965, 2002.
53. Christakis 1999a, 2004, 2008. Begg (1975, 20) questions whether the Neopalatial magazines were intended to store pithoi, but the later evidence has confused the picture too much for comment.
54. Christakis 2004, 299, after Evans 1905.
55. Christakis 2004, 300.
56. Christakis 2008, 40–3.
57. Hood and Smyth 1981; Whitelaw 2001.
58. E.g., Evans 1928; Hatzaki 1996; Mountjoy 2003.
59. Adams 2004a.
60. Evans 1928, 438–42; Cameron 1968; Godart and Olivier 1982.
61. See Whitelaw (2001) for the floor areas of Minoan houses.
62. Hatzaki 1996, 2005.
63. The publishers (Catling, Catling, and Smyth 1979) dated the later Acropolis House to LM IA, which was naturally followed by subsequent scholars; see Hatzaki (2011b, 254–5) for a re-dating to LM IA and LM IB, with parallels with the Stratigraphical Museum North Building.
64. These two are located to the west of the Palace, while the others hug the Palace on the south side and to the north-east. Too much is unexcavated to draw firm conclusions from this observation, however.
65. Shaw 1971, 21–3. Hogarth's House A had painted stucco, although architecturally it is less grand than the others in this group.
66. Christakis 1999b; 2008.
67. McEnroe 1979, 75–6; 1982, 14.
68. Evans 1928, 623–33; Georgiou 1979.
69. A number of the entries in the plans for my paper comparing Knossos and Malia possess a '??' disclaimer: for example, the prestige artefacts (stone vases) found in the Caravanserai, which are Neopalatial objects found in a later context (so heirlooms). Adams (2004a, 201, figure 4) presents in the key: '??: query over date, location or whether the quality and quantity of artefacts count as an "assemblage" or "concentration"'. No further rationale could be given regarding

each case. Unfortunately, there was insufficient space to allow for individual explanations, and readers have not always noted this kind of qualification (in this case, Hatzaki 2011b, 250, fn. 14). See also Warren 1969, 53 (reference not cited in Hatzaki 2011b, 250, fn. 14) for a similar warning regarding these (MM III-LM I) stone vessels: N.F.C., or no (recorded or published) find context. The decision was taken at this point to include the material, with reservations. It must be recognized that syntheses will, by their nature, be unable to spell out all of the necessary caveats, especially concerning the quality and quantity of the material we have for Neopalatial Crete. The solution for this must not be to avoid the challenge of writing syntheses completely.

70. See Adams 2004a, 207–10.
71. Wall, Musgrave, and Warren 1986.
72. See Adams (2004b) for the distribution of (published) ritual artefacts across the Knossian and Malian landscape.
73. The presence of seals in the Royal Road North Building could indicate the ability to mark goods on behalf of the Palace, or some degree of independence; perhaps, given the ideological link, the former appears more likely.
74. Adams 2004a, 213.
75. Hamilakis 2002; Adams 2004a, 213.
76. See Adams 2006, 27.
77. Adams 2006, 10–12.
78. Adams 2006, 12–14.
79. Adams 2006, 14–16.
80. Adams 2006, 27.
81. Knappett (1999, 638) suggests that, in the case of Neopalatial Crete, there was 'local autonomy in some (economic?) activities coexistent with an overarching (Knossian) control in other (ideological) spheres', but it is yet to be demonstrated that this control was island-wide.
82. Rethemiotakis (2002, 57–8) places the construction of the Palace at MM IIIB/LM IA; this is made earlier in Rethemiotakis and Christakis (2011, 208) to MM IIIA over the MM IB settlement. Rebuilding of the Palace occurred after a MM IIIA destruction. Rethemiotakis and Christakis (2011, 208) state that the gradual abandonment of the Palace occurred before the end of the MM IIIB period.

83. Rethemiotakis 2002, 63.
84. Rethemiotakis and Christakis 2011, 208.
85. Rethemiotakis and Christakis 2011.
86. Whitelaw and Morgan 2009, 94; Rethemiotakis and Christakis 2013. This may follow the pattern of the Knossian grand mansions.
87. In the last period of the Palace (mature LM IA), grinding was practised in the Central Court: Rethemiotakis 2002, 63–4.
88. Rethemiotakis 2012. An early (MM III) model shrine has been found here (Rethemiotakis 2010), which may be compared to that from MM IIIA Gournos Krousonas (not included on map as pre-Neopalatial): Rethemiotakis 2009.
89. Crooks 2013, 20–3 (with photograph figure 16).
90. Rethemiotakis 2010.
91. Rethemiotakis 2002, 57.
92. Rethemiotakis 1999a, 721.
93. Warren 2004; see also Wiener 2007. It might also be suggested that this was a summer Palace for the Knossian elite, but this is a rather anachronistic term.
94. Whitelaw forthcoming.
95. Whitelaw forthcoming; Rethemiotakis 2002, 57.
96. *Archaeological Reports* 1999, 130.
97. Adams 2006, 23.
98. Panagiotakis (2004, 184) suggests that the destruction (rather than the construction) of the Palace at Galatas indicates 'conflict within the Pediada or between Knossos and some Pediada sites' and that it was at this point that 'Knossos extended its political domination over the Pediada'.
99. Rethemiotakis and Christakis 2011, 208; 2013; see Adams 2006, 23–4.
100. *Archaeological Reports* 2006, 107; 2007, 107: the Protopalatial population appears to be low, even though it had increased from the EM period.
101. Haysom 2014, 81.
102. Bennet 2013, 65–6; Christakis, Mavraki-Balanou, and Kastanakis 2015.
103. Van Effenterre (1980, 41–2), but see Pelon (1982, 81) for criticisms of this comparison.
104. Deshayes and Dessenne 1959, 152; Poursat 1988, 67.

105. For an earlier date, see, e.g., Pelon 2005; Driessen 2010, 564; for later, see, e.g., Darcque and Van de Moortel 2001; Poursat 2010; Van de Moortel 2011a; Darcque 2014.

106. Poursat concludes that the buildings fell out of use at the end of LM IB, with the exception of Epsilon, although it might be difficult to distinguish between LM IB and LM II. See Poursat (1988, 67, 76) on whether the end of the Neopalatial period fell in the LM IB or LM II phase.

107. For example, Müller (1990, 923) states that the Neopalatial period is less well represented in the Ayia Varvara area than Protopalatial. However, the area north of Quartier Mu was rich in Neopalatial evidence, including fragments of stone vases (Müller 1991a, 743).

108. Poursat 1988, 80–1. See also Van Effenterre (1980, 77): 'la ville de Mallia tourne le dos à la mer'. Malia was a coastal site, and exploited the sea for fish, but was probably not a major port in the Neopalatial period.

109. Driessen 2010, 565.

110. Adams 2007b.

111. Preziosi 1983.

112. Pelon 1980, 67; Driessen 1995, 76; however, Graham (1987, 44) suggests the south entrance.

113. Adams 2007b, 377.

114. Van Effenterre 1980, 446; Gesell 1985, 106.

115. Gesell 1985, 107.

116. See Adams (2004a) for more detailed discussion.

117. Pelon 1980, 6.

118. Shaw 1971, 23, fn. 4.

119. Crooks 2013, 28–32.

120. Pelon 2002.

121. Warren 1990, 203.

122. Adams 2004a, 205.

123. Baurain and Darcque 1983.

124. Adams 2004a, 206.

125. Schoep 1995, 34–6: these date to the early Neopalatial period.

126. Christakis 2008, 48–50.

127. Van Effenterre 1980, 335. Unlike the case at Knossos and Phaistos, these silos date to the Neopalatial period, rather than the Protopalatial one.

128. Driessen and Macdonald 1997, 185; Pelon 2002, 118. The existence of an upper storey in the south-eastern block at Malia (above the storage) is indicated by the presence of stairs;

what occurred on this upper floor is unclear, however.

129. Christakis 2008, 50.

130. Müller 1991a, 1991b, 1992, 1996, 1998. See also Adams 2004a.

131. Driessen and Macdonald (1997, 186–92) provide a useful overview.

132. Adams 2004a, 210–11.

133. Delta Beta was possibly two separate 'households', one of 200 m² and one of 185 m².

134. Epsilon is unusual in many ways. For example, Space XXXVIII contains a particularly rich and unusual deposit, based around a limestone basin set in the floor (Gesell 1985, 108).

135. Adams 2004a, 210–12.

136. Adams 2004a. While the first examples of these units seem to come from Malia in the Protopalatial period, Knossos appears to have then taken the forms and combined them in a set package.

137. Adams 2004a.

138. Tool assemblages were found in Zeta Alpha, Zeta Gamma, and Delta Beta. Workspaces have been discovered in Zeta Beta, the Maison de la Cave au Pilier (stone carving), and possibly Zeta Alpha and Epsilon (stone carving) (Adams 2004a, 212).

139. Adams 2004a.

140. Adams 2006.

141. Driessen n.d. and www.sarpedon.be; also Jan Driessen's Mycenaean Seminar: 'Excavations at Sissi – exploring Malia's hinterland': 12 February 2013.

142. Ibid.

143. Poursat 1988, 80.

144. Poursat 2010, 264. See also Pelon 1980, 142–3; Van Effenterre 1980, 360.

145. Poursat 2010. He allows for possible independence in MM III when the Palace brought in certain functions once conducted in the town (such as in Quartier Mu).

146. Levi 1976, 237–45; Girella 2001. Levi doubted whether MM IIIB existed as a distinctive phase after his excavations at Phaistos, leading him to suggest that the wider MM III period as established at Knossos was contemporary with the 'III fase protopalaziale' (D'Agata 1989, 96). Banti placed the destruction of the Protopalatial period at the beginning of MM IIIB (La Rosa 2002, 73); La Rosa (2002, 74) states

that the final moment of the First Palace occurs in MM IIIB.

147. Carinci and La Rosa (2013) suggest that this was palatial, while Girella (2011) advocates a non-centralized model.

148. Carinci 1989, 78. This *astraki* was cast with the immediate levelling of the ruins of the MM IIB destruction (La Rosa 2002, 82) as a platform for new construction work before the temporary abandonment. Part of this original fill was later removed.

149. Carinci 1989, 73. Fiandra (1995, 329) has argued that there was 'no break between MM II and LM I, but an intermediate phase during which a great deal of innovation was introduced in MM III, reaching its peak in LM with the life of Palace II'.

150. Alternatively, Carinci (1989, 77) argues that the construction of the Second Palace had already started in MM III, but was interrupted.

151. Carinci 1989; Van de Moortel 2002, 190; Palio 2001a, 267; La Rosa 2002, 80, 89.

152. Driessen and Macdonald 1997.

153. La Rosa 2002, 88.

154. Palio 2001a, 267. Most of the material at Ayia Photini is LM IB, despite the presence of some material that seems to be LM IA (Palio 2001a, 252). Driessen and Macdonald (1997, 198) suggest that Chalara may have been destroyed well before the end of LM IB, and therefore before the Palace and Ayia Triada.

155. Palio 2001a, 243.

156. Pernier and Banti 1951 (half a century after the excavations). Pernier was involved with the excavation (he died 1937), but Banti was not (La Rosa 2001, 2002). Levi 1976; Levi and Carinci 1988.

157. E.g., Beschi et al. 2001. There is no single 'Italian' interpretation of the Neopalatial Palace at Phaistos, and there is no individual as influential as Evans (La Rosa 2001).

158. Karetsou 2001, 11; La Rosa 2001, 27.

159. La Rosa 2001, 35, mentioning Pace 1921. See also Hood 1983.

160. La Rosa 2001, 25.

161. Preziosi 1983, 137.

162. Adams 2007b. Note that this Palace was found relatively empty, so distribution maps of moveable artefacts have not been provided.

163. Preziosi 1983, 127.

164. Pernier and Banti 1951, 41–7, 451.

165. Pernier and Banti 1951, 89–90; Preziosi 1983, 129; Hitchcock 2000, 136. This would lend weight to the suggestion that Room 32 was a porter's lodge, where such transactions could be monitored (Pernier and Banti 1951, 66–7; Adams 2007b, 377).

166. Pernier and Banti 1951, 104–8; Gesell 1985, 127–8.

167. Hitchcock 2000, 73.

168. The stone vases from Rooms 8–11 have been studied by Palio (2001b), who suggests that the use of the libation tables followed Protopalatial tradition, but their typology and the ladle show a strong relationship with the practices occurring on Neopalatial peak sanctuaries. Ferrari and Cucuzza (2004) note that most of the ninety-four kernoi found at Phaistos are Protopalatial rather than Neopalatial.

169. La Rosa (2002) lists the deposits caught in the destruction.

170. La Rosa 2002, 91. See also Carinci (1989, 80), who points out that there is very little evidence for LM III habitation, *contra* Watrous (1984, 132).

171. La Rosa 2002, 90.

172. Watrous 1984, 132.

173. Levi and Carinci 1988, 357.

174. Militello 2001, 167.

175. La Rosa 2002, 92.

176. Christakis 2008, 48.

177. Militello 2002. See also Schoep 1995.

178. E.g., Palio 2001a; 2001c. See Carinci (2001) for the MM III house to the south of the ramp (opposite Corridor 7), which was probably destroyed at the same time as the shrine at Anemospilia (Carinci 2001, 229); there is also Room LXXIX south or south-west of the Palace, the deposit under the geometric Room CC (La Rosa 2002, 88) and Room 103, the LM I pillar hall north-east of the Palace (Levi 1976, 396–9; Driessen and Macdonald 1997, 189).

179. Girella (2011) suggests that there was a 'household ideology' in MM IIIA, when the palatial elite's power was weak and there was a certain decentralization, while the Palace rallied (temporarily) in MM IIIB.

180. Palio 2001a, 243.

181. Palio 2001a, 245, 267.

182. Militello 2002.

183. La Rosa 2002, 92.

184. Levi (1964, 11) states that many storage jars were recovered from here (Christakis 1999a, 153).
185. La Rosa 2002, 95.
186. E.g., La Rosa 2002.
187. La Rosa 2002, 94; see Driessen and Macdonald 1997.
188. Warren 2004.
189. La Rosa 2002, 95.
190. Cunningham 2001.
191. Chryssoulaki and Platon 1987, 77.
192. Shaw 1990, 427.
193. Platon 1971, 40–1.
194. Platon 1971, 247–8.
195. Platon and Gerontakou 2013.
196. Platon 1999a; 2004.
197. Platon 1999a. N. Platon had suggested the existence of an earlier Palace at Zakros, specifically identifying a building investigated under the east wing of the LM IB Palace as one of its wings, but this is unclear (L. Platon 2002, 152).
198. Platon 2011a.
199. There are some intriguing LM IA features found under the east wing, which may indicate a public function, but the west wing has not yielded similar data (Platon 2002, 152–3).
200. Adams 2007b.
201. Platon 1971, 92.
202. Platon 1971, 103.
203. Adams 2007b.
204. Driessen and Macdonald 1997, 238.
205. Adams 2007b.
206. Platon 1971, 83–5.
207. Fragments of tripod offering tables and a terracotta animal figurine were found in the 'Sacred Well', among carbonized material, animal bones, and pottery (Gesell 1985, 140); this is insufficient to demonstrate ritual use. Horns of Consecration were associated with the Spring Chamber, however, which may make a stronger case for ritual use.
208. Platon 1971, 196.
209. Platon 1971, 104.
210. Gesell 1985, 137.
211. Platon 1971, 133–48.
212. Platon 1971, 156.
213. Gesell 1985, 139.
214. Platon 1971, 170.
215. Platon 1971, 179.
216. Platon 1971, 148.
217. Christakis 2008, 52.
218. Driessen and Macdonald 1997, 237.
219. Whitelaw and Morgan 2009, 79.
220. Platon 2002, 152.
221. Platon 2011b.
222. Chryssoulaki and Platon 1987, 78.
223. Platon 2011b.
224. Platon 1988, 43.
225. Platon 1988, 177.
226. Platon 2011b.
227. Tzedakis, Chryssoulaki, Veniéri, and Avgouli 1990; Kriga 2010.
228. Chryssoulaki 1999.
229. E.g., Tsipopoulou 1997, 274.
230. N. Platon 1971, 240; L. Platon 2002, 2004.
231. Platon 2002, 147.
232. Platon 2002, 147.
233. The identification of regional styles, which usually incorporate elements of the local tradition to imported artistic trends, might be a more worthwhile approach.
234. Adams 2007b, 375–6.
235. Adams 2007b.
236. Tsipopoulou 1997, 2012a.
237. Tsipopoulou 2012a, 67.
238. Christakis 2012, 209.
239. Adams 2007b.
240. Cunningham 2001.
241. Cunningham 2001.
242. Tsipopoulou 2012a, 67. In fact, the major discontinuity appears to be after the LM IA destruction rather than the MM IIB one (Tsipopoulou 2002, 140). See also Christakis 2012, 218–19.
243. Tsipopoulou 2002, 137–8.
244. Tsipopoulou 2007.
245. Tsipopoulou 2012a, 55.
246. Christakis 2012, 212.
247. Tsipopoulou 2002; Tsipopoulou and Papacostopoulou 1997.
248. Hallager (2012) adds three Linear A inscriptions.
249. Tsipopoulou 2011.
250. Mavroudi 2011.
251. Mavroudi 2012, 228.
252. Preziosi 1983; Palyvou 2002. Graham's work (e.g., 1987) draws out similarities in Minoan architecture, which has had considerable influence in architectural studies, e.g., McEnroe 2010, 83.
253. Adams 2004a.
254. Adams 2004a.

5   OTHER SETTLEMENTS AND
    REGIONAL GROUPINGS

1. Driessen and Macdonald 1997. This gazetteer remains essential: the sites discussed here are necessarily selective.
2. Evans 1921, 298–9; 1928, 229–39.
3. Schäfer 1991, 113.
4. Excavations are ongoing: see Serpetsidaki 2012.
5. *Archaeological Reports* 1998–9, 117–18.
6. Dimopoulou 2000.
7. Dimopoulou 1999a.
8. Evans 1928, 231–2; Hazzidakis 1934, 73. Pendlebury, Eccles, and Money-Coutts (1932–3 (1935), 92) reported survey evidence for an extensive site.
9. Knoblauch and Niemeier 1992.
10. Schäfer 1991, 113–15.
11. Marinatos 1960, 66.
12. Marinatos 1933, 294–5; Driessen and Macdonald 1997, 134. The Palace at Galatas was left somewhat desolate before the destruction of the Villa of the Lilies, so there is not complete chronological overlap. While other sites lie along this river (Panagiotakis 2003, 2004), it remains highly plausible that the Palace had some access to this port.
13. Gesell 1985, 68.
14. Xanthoudides 1922, 16; Evans 1928, 284–5: 'the Archpriest of the Minoan Cult'; Gesell 1985, 116–18.
15. Graham 1987, 58–9.
16. Xanthoudides 1922, 1; Cadogan 1976, 135, 139–42.
17. Evans 1928, 284–5.
18. Xanthoudides 1919, 63.
19. Xanthoudides 1922, 10–11.
20. Marinatos 1926; Fotou 1997, 41.
21. Xanthoudides 1922, 11; Driessen and Macdonald 1997, 179.
22. Xanthoudides 1919, 63–4; Evans 1928, 281.
23. Xanthoudides 1922, 11; Evans 1928, 284.
24. Gesell 1985, 116.
25. Xanthoudides 1922, 12–13. Evans (1928, 283) also stated that 'the liturgic weapons of the Minoan cult here deposited were for great sanctuaries and imply congregational use in open spaces.'
26. Koehl 1997, 137.
27. Two LM I houses at Daverona containing pithoi and other vases were also excavated, but little is known about these. The famous bronze figurines were recovered to the west of the main three buildings (Hazzidakis 1934, 95).
28. Driessen and Macdonald 1997, 129. Hazzidakis appears to have called LM IB 'LM II'.
29. Shaw 1972, 179; however, Immerwahr (1990, 184) states that they come from Building A.
30. Hitchcock and Preziosi 1997, 60.
31. Gesell 1985, 135. A Double Axe stand also comes from the area, as do animal bones.
32. Two potter's wheels, a sword pommel, a stone hammer, and a bronze axe.
33. See Poblome and Dumon 1987–8; Hitchcock and Preziosi 1997.
34. Gesell 1985, 136.
35. Sakellarakis and Sapouna-Sakellaraki 1997, 55.
36. Sakellarakis and Sapouna-Sakellaraki 1997, 78; however, Driessen and Macdonald (1997, 173) state that it is unclear whether this destruction occurred in the MM III/LM IA or mature LM IA period. The ideograms are identified with wheat, oil, olives, and wine.
37. Sakellarakis and Sapouna-Sakellaraki 1997, 120–9.
38. Driessen and Macdonald 1997, 173.
39. *Archaeological Reports* 2000–1, 126.
40. Evans 1928, 65–6.
41. Sakellarakis and Sapouna-Sakellaraki 1997, 80–2.
42. Sakellarakis and Sapouna-Sakellaraki 1997, 98–101. They draw parallels with the Megaron from the Mycenaean site at Pylos.
43. Sakellarakis and Sapouna-Sakellaraki 1997, 104, 106–10.
44. Driessen and Sakellarakis 1997. Marinatos (1960, 66) suggested that it was planned as a Palace (with north-south orientation), but only the west wing was built.
45. Driessen and Sakellarakis 1997, 68. Elsewhere, all the pottery is said to be LM IA (Driessen and Macdonald 1997, 176).
46. Marinatos 1952, 609; Shaw 1978.
47. Cadogan 1976, 144.
48. Driessen and Sakellarakis 1997, 70.
49. Space 10 was destroyed at the end of the first phase: Christakis 1999a, 158.
50. Adams 2007a, 398–401.
51. Panagiotakis 2004, 182.
52. Rethemiotakis 1997, 45. This has also been suggested for Archanes and Vathypetro.

53. Del Freo 2008, 203–4. This is without parallels, and so was given a different prefix: KAST Wy 1.
54. Vitsila is a further site that was probably a regional centre, but it is too poorly known to be discussed in detail (Evans 1928, 71–3). Evans suggested that this was a 'small Palace, the residence of some local prince or governor'. Marinatos, investigating in the 1950s, found no trace of a court or architecture suggestive of a Palace (Marinatos 1955, 306–9).
55. Adams 2006, 9, figure 3.
56. Evans 1928, 64; Sakellarakis and Sapouna-Sakellaraki 1997, 27.
57. Cunningham and Driessen 2004, 108.
58. Such as Prasa and Xeri Kara, and possibly Zominthos (see Chapter 6), Sklavokambos (see Chapter 7), Galeni, Voni, and Nipiditos: there is no space to discuss them here (see Driessen and Macdonald 1997). Some sites, such as Kroussonas (Dimopoulou 1990), have been assigned to LM I generally, and cannot be narrowed down further at present.
59. See papers in Hägg 1997.
60. Adams 2006.
61. Rethemiotakis 2002, 57–8.
62. Including the Royal Road North Building (Hood 1962, 25–7), the Stratigraphical Museum North Building (Warren 1981b, 1983, 1991), Zeta Alpha (Demargne and Gallet de Santerre 1953, 99–100, Pl. LVII), and the LM IB Building 2 at Galatas (Rethemiotakis 2002, 66–7).
63. Sakellarakis and Sapouna-Sakellaraki 1997.
64. The central building here was destroyed in LM IB (Rethemiotakis 1997, 36).
65. Hazzidakis 1921, 1934. The reference here to LM II means LM IB.
66. The chronological resolution at Gazi is too poor to tell.
67. See, e.g., the Marine Style bucket vase (Xanthoudides 1922, 20, figure 17).
68. Dimopoulou 1999a; 1999b. The settlement was possibly reduced (Driessen and Macdonald 1997, 133).
69. See also Palaioloutra (MM II to LM IIIB): Evely 2010, 189.
70. Chryssoulaki 1997; Kanta 2011a.
71. Kanta and Rocchetti 1989, 326.
72. Andreadaki-Vlazaki 2011, 55–6.
73. Andreadaki-Vlazaki 2002.
74. Andreadaki-Vlazaki 2010, 519. Minoan Halls have also been found at the site, along with ashlar facades, wall paintings, and other trappings of Minoan elitism (Andreadaki-Vlazaki 2009). Chania was the important site of Kydonia, mentioned in the Linear B tablets. Andreadaki-Vlazaki (2005) has also presented the material defined as ritual.
75. Andreadaki-Vlazaki and Hallager (2007) published recent finds.
76. Andreadaki-Vlazaki 2009, 32–43.
77. With seventy-two fragments of clay tablets, 104 small clay discs, twenty-eight faceted clay sealings and fifty-eight simple clay sealings (Andreadaki-Vlazaki 2009, 50).
78. Andreadaki-Vlazaki 2009, 70–7.
79. Andreadaki-Vlazaki 2011, 56–7.
80. Andreadaki-Vlazaki 2010, 521. These activities have been interpreted as ritual (Andreadaki-Vlazaki 2002, 161–3), but we need to await further publication. The ritual nature of similar structures elsewhere (e.g., Kastelli Pediada and Archanes Tourkoyeitonia) is likewise possible but not proven. The platform at Kato Syme is more clearly ritual, but this is a sanctuary.
81. Andreadaki-Vlazaki 2011, 73, but see Warren (88) in discussion following.
82. Watrous and Hadzi-Vallianou 2004, 277.
83. Watrous and Hadzi-Vallianou 2004.
84. Carinci 2003.
85. Watrous and Hadzi-Vallianou 2004, 291–2.
86. Watrous and Hadzi-Vallianou 2004, 297. They point out that a similar pattern may be observed around Gournia.
87. Levi 1959. See Watrous and Hadzi-Vallianou (2004, 295) for other 'Villa' sites of the Mesara.
88. Christakis 1999, 155; 2008, 69–70. This building produced the largest number of pithoi from a non-palatial context: Christakis 2008, 69.
89. Hadzi-Vallianou 2011.
90. Halbherr, Stefani, and Banti 1980. Halbherr died in 1930.
91. La Rosa 2010b. La Rosa (2003) includes very good photographs of early excavations.
92. Cadogan 1976, 104; Watrous 1984.
93. Watrous 1984, 123. Seat of the governor of western Mesara: Alexiou 1980, 34; Palace: Graham 1987, 49–51; Hood 1971, 79; outsized Villa: Halbherr, Stefani, and Banti 1980;

royal summer residence: Halbherr 1903, col. 7.

94. Halbherr, Stefani, and Banti 1980, 233–4.

95. Watrous 1984, 132. He suggests that the reuse of Phaistos after LM IB was responsible for the lack of finds, but this reoccupation was limited, and Ayia Triada was extensively reused too.

96. They presented a rather monolithic view of the Villa, built during LM I and destroyed at the end of the period, with no subdivisions (Halbherr, Stephani, and Banti 1980, 234–5).

97. La Rosa 2002, 72; Carinci 2003. La Rosa (1989, 81) describes a foundation deposit dating to the beginning of the Neopalatial period (MM IIIB–LM IA) in Corridor 74.

98. Carinci 1989, 80. La Rosa (2010b, 499) notes some confusion concerning whether the MM IIIA 'foundation deposit' belongs to this building or a previous one. If it was deposited in an earlier structure, then this would make it possible that the Royal Villa was built in MM IIIB.

99. Girella 2013.

100. La Rosa 1989, 2002; Puglisi 2003: See Plate 1 showing the LM I ceramic deposits (2003, 156–7). See also Monaco and Tortorici 2003.

101. Puglisi 2011. See, however, Mantzourani 2011.

102. La Rosa 1989, 85; Driessen and Macdonald 1997, 204.

103. Driessen and Macdonald 1997.

104. See Puglisi 2003, 192: he refers to Driessen and Macdonald (1997) here, and states that there is no documented evidence for damage caused by the Theran eruption.

105. Puglisi 2003; it also slips into LM II.

106. Evans 1928, 90, 412; Platon 1981, 390; Van Effentere 1985, 179; Graham 1987, 50. See La Rosa (1997) for a thorough overview of previous hypotheses concerning both the nature of the site and its relationship with Phaistos.

107. As suggested by Watrous (1984), but refuted by La Rosa (1997) and Puglisi (2003, 148–50).

108. La Rosa 2010b.

109. Militello 1988.

110. Christakis 2008, 64–6. As a working hypothesis, the containers held around 30,000–33,000 litres.

111. Militello 1998; Puglisi 2003. Puglisi emphasized the religious role of the Villa, assigning ritual and ceremonial functions for the halls.

Furthermore, he suggested that the Casa Est and Casa del Lebete were ritual buildings.

112. Militello 1992, 103. There may be some resemblance to the Chancel Screen Halls at Knossos; furthermore, Militello suggests that the style might suggest some sort of Knossian control, operated partly at least through the ritual sphere (pp. 111–12). This space was considered a bedroom (Halbherr, Stefani, and Banti 1980, 91–5; Watrous 1984, 125).

113. Militello 1992, 2001; Puglisi 2003, 150.

114. Militello 2001, 160.

115. Militello 2001, 165.

116. See La Rosa (2003, 29, figures 14 and 15) for before and after photographs of the reconstructions.

117. Puglisi 2003, 159. Gesell (1985, 74) identified a 'Pillar Crypt' in space 17, but this is unlikely, and the area was found empty (Militello 2001, 161).

118. La Rosa and Militello 1999.

119. Puglisi (2003) nonetheless suggests that it was a cult centre, and also the Casa Est.

120. Christakis 1999, 151. Christakis (2008, 67) suggests that the minimum capacity would have been 3,120–3,600 litres.

121. Driessen and Macdonald 1997, 204. Room 9 contained some pottery with Linear A fragments.

122. La Rosa 2010b, 500.

123. Privitera 2014.

124. Puglisi 2003; a comparison could be made with the Temple Tomb at Knossos.

125. La Rosa 2010b, 501.

126. E.g., Shaw and Shaw 2006a.

127. J. W. Shaw 2004. Many Cypriot sherds were found (Shaw 2002, 108).

128. Shaw 2006a, 19.

129. Shaw 2006b, 30–3. The north facade is the longest-surviving straight ashlar wall at ca. 55.7 m (Shaw 2002, 103).

130. Shaw and Shaw 2006b, 847.

131. E.g., Rutter 2004, 65.

132. Shaw and Shaw 2006b, 848.

133. Shaw 2006a, 28, 59–60; 2006b, 33.

134. Shaw 2002, 102.

135. Shaw et al. 2001; Shaw 2002, 108–9. There is little available evidence for the storage of staples (Christakis 2008, 61).

136. M. C. Shaw 2004.

137. M. C. Shaw 2004, 146.

138. Shaw and Shaw 1985.

139. Shaw (2002, 108–9), in collaboration with La Rosa and Carinci, has presented a diachronic summary of these three sites.

140. Shaw 2002, 109.

141. Shaw 2006b, 35.

142. Shaw and Shaw 2006b, 849.

143. Carinci 2003; La Rosa 2010b, 498.

144. E.g., describing Ayia Triada as the country residence of the Phaistian leader (Halbherr 1903, 7). He reasoned that the proximity of the two sites was comparable to the Epano-Kato split known still today (letter from Halbherr to G. de Sanctis: La Rosa 2003, 61–2).

145. See also Betancourt (1985b, 32), where it is stated that Phaistos was 'the largest and most influential site in southern Crete from MM IB until the end of LM IB' and that the Palace was continually rebuilt throughout.

146. Halbherr, Stefani, and Banti 1980.

147. E.g., Watrous 1984.

148. La Rosa 1985, 50.

149. La Rosa 2002.

150. La Rosa 2010b, 506.

151. Watrous and Hadzi-Vallianou 2004, 297.

152. Watrous 1984, 130. D'Agata (1989, 97) states that Knossian influence would explain why the pottery was different between Phaistos and Ayia Triada, and that the addition of the reed cup in LM IA could be an indication of Knossian identity. It could be, but reading the movement of material culture and/or style in this way is highly problematic.

153. Van de Moortel 2002.

154. Watrous and Hadzi-Vallianou (2004, 298) after Cucuzza (1992).

155. La Rosa 2002, 95.

156. Christakis 2008, 5.

157. Puglisi (2003, 91) states that the Palaces, rather than hierarchical, were integrated in regional systems; however, the 'possibilità' of a Knossian hegemony in LM I is described as 'inevitabile' (Puglisi 2003, 146).

158. Nowicki (2004, 84) notes Neopalatial sites in the area, all with no signs of fortification.

159. Cadogan 1977–8, 2013b.

160. Cadogan 1977–8, 77.

161. Cadogan 1981; 1997, 101; Morpurgo-Davies and Cadogan 1971, 1977. The tubular vessels found here are similar to those from the ritual site of Kato Syme (Warren in discussion to Cadogan 1981).

162. Christakis 1999a, 180; 2008, 84–5. Organic remains of barley, bitter vetch, and Celtic beans were found, and the pithoi had an overall capacity of around 1,350–1,600 litres.

163. For example, Diaskari lies 3 km to the east.

164. Davaras 1997, 118; he described it as a 'small Palace' (Davaras 1985).

165. Mantzourani 2011.

166. Davaras 1997, 120–1. This was around 1.8 × 0.7 m.

167. Christakis 1999a, 197–8.

168. Mantzourani 2011; see also Brogan in discussion after Mantzourani (2011, 305).

169. Mantzourani 2012.

170. Platon 1960a; Vavouranakis 2012.

171. Mandalaki 2011.

172. Soles 2004, 159. See, e.g., Haggis 1995, 1996; Watrous and Blitzer 1999; Hayden 2004; Watrous et al. 2012.

173. Hayden 2004, 118.

174. Hayden 1999; Molloy and Duckworth 2014.

175. Soles and Davaras 1996, 207; Soles 2003a (incorporating comparative data from other Neopalatial farmsteads).

176. Damiani-Indelicato 1984, 47; Watrous and Blitzer 1999. The latter also mention a possible peak sanctuary located during their survey, but the evidence is unclear. The Gournian pottery fabrics suggest that the site had an easterly orientation, towards the Isthmus and away from Vrokastro, but the limitations of this data for reconstructing polities is well understood (Hayden 2004, 119).

177. Watrous 2012a. Obvious parallels may be made between the ship sheds and Building T at Kommos, although the function of the latter is not proven.

178. Watrous 2012a, 522. This is smaller than previous estimates; Soles (1991, 74) estimated it covered as much as 5 ha with a population of around 2,000–3,000, and Watrous before had suggested 4 ha (e.g., Watrous and Heimroth 2011, 204).

179. Boyd Hawes et al. 1908, 24; Annual report for 2011: Gournia Website (accessed 14 July 2014); Watrous 2015, 458. Earlier deposits do of course exist, and Niemeier (1979) discusses the possibility of an LM IA ceramic workshop. However, Watrous and Heimroth (2011) point out that the pottery of LM IB eastern Crete is difficult to compare with central Crete, as the former comprises

two styles, one of which is a continuation of LM IA, and therefore difficult to distinguish (Betancourt 1985a, 137). Most of the town survives as testament to the LM IB destruction; some of this pottery is very late and may be contemporary with LM II in central Crete (Soles 2002, 128).

180. E.g., Boyd Hawes et al. 1908; Cadogan 1976; Preziosi 1983; Graham 1987; Soles 1979, 1991; Fotou 1993. Watrous, its current excavator, deploys the term 'Palace' (Gournia Website: accessed 15 July 2016).

181. E.g., McEnroe 1982; see also Soles 1991, 17–18, fn. 3.

182. Gournia Website (accessed 14 July 2014: see downloadable preliminary report); Watrous 2015.

183. Watrous and Schultz (2012) describe this as a Central Court. The floor was of a cement-like material, not dissimilar to that found at Kommos. Soles (1991) describes this as 'tarazza', a mixture of lime and small pebbles.

184. Soles 1991, 37; Crooks 2013, 23–8.

185. Soles 1983, 43. As the ashlar was structural, its introduction may indicate remodelling rather than simple replacing (Soles 2002, 124). Five areas of the site, including the Palace, have revealed evidence for rebuilding in LM IB (Soles 2002, 123).

186. Around 116 m^2 or 6.4 per cent of the ground floor was dedicated to storage: Christakis 2008, 51.

187. Watrous and Schultz 2012, 62.

188. Soles 1991, 72; 2002, 125.

189. See Watrous and Heimroth (2011) for distribution plans of economic activity.

190. Watrous and Heimroth 2011, 205–6.

191. Watrous and Heimroth 2011, 212.

192. Seager in 1910; Betancourt and Davaras during 1984–92.

193. Betancourt and Hope Simpson 1992; Betancourt 2012. For example, there is evidence for the presence of manure to enrich the soil, and stone and soil dams were built.

194. McEnroe 2001, 14, figure 11; 67, figure 51.

195. Betancourt 2011.

196. Floyd 1995.

197. Floyd 1998, 233. It is not clear how the functional zones of this structure mimic the quarters found in Palaces.

198. Davaras 2001, 87. The emphasis on the religious character of the building reflects his views on Makrygialos (Davaras 1997).

199. Betancourt and Davaras 1988, 211.

200. Hood 1977; Betancourt and Davaras 1998; Shaw 1998. Shaw (1998, 68) points out that relief frescoes of human forms are restricted to the Palace at Knossos and non-palatial buildings, suggesting a special relationship, which 'is likely to have been of a religious and theocratic nature'.

201. Betancourt 2001. Two other rhyta hoards were found at the site: Buildings BQ and BS/BV.

202. Dierckx 1999.

203. Betancourt 1999, 299.

204. Betancourt 2011, 401, 408.

205. Seager 1909, 1912 (mostly on the earlier cemetery); Soles 2003b.

206. Soles 1983.

207. E.g., it has been suggested that obsidian entered Crete from Melos via the site (Carter 2004).

208. Soles and Davaras 1996, 184–94. They describe two spaces as Pillar Crypts; from the upper story of one fell the head of a female figurine, half a clay boat, half a pear-shaped rhyton, and strainers and loomweights (Soles and Davaras 1994, 408). This is an interesting deposit, but not enough to define the space as ritual and the architectural unit as a 'Pillar Crypt'.

209. Soles 2001.

210. Soles 2004, 159.

211. Soles 1997; 2003b, 97: 'independent, nucleated, kin-based, full-time specialists'.

212. Soles 2003b, 99–100.

213. Barnard and Brogan 2003, 107.

214. Barnard and Brogan 2003, 108. They compared their material with the clear LM II Unexplored Mansion ceramics from Knossos. See also Brogan, Smith, and Soles 2002; Soles 2004.

215. Watrous 2012b.

216. Soles 1991.

217. Soles 2002, 128.

218. Betancourt 2004.

219. Betancourt 2004, 22.

220. Hallager and Hallager 1995; Betancourt 2004, 27.

221. E.g., Watrous 2012b.

222. Betancourt 2004, 25.

223. The lack of ritual sites in the region may suggest that Gournia had a weaker ideological hold over neighbouring sites (Chapter 6).

224. Chryssoulaki et al. 1990.

225. Hemingway, MacGillivray, and Sacket 2011, 515. Furthermore, the use of 'MM IIIB/LM IA transition' for the construction of most of the Neopalatial houses excavated in the early stages of fieldwork appears to have gone out of favour (MacGillivray and Driessen 1990, 403).

226. MacGillivray and Sackett 2010, 574.

227. Hemingway, MacGillivray, and Sackett 2011, 522. See, however, Van de Moortel 2011a, who argues that the LM II date for the Palaikastro destruction is unconvincing.

228. Cunningham 2007, 103; see also Cunningham 2001. Eleven buildings in the excavated area had ashlar construction (Cunningham 2007, 99). Palaikastro was able to exploit the nearby quarries at Ta Skaria.

229. MacGillivray and Driessen 1990, 406.

230. Cunningham 2007, 99.

231. Cunningham 2007, 99.

232. Cunningham 2007, 102.

233. Cunningham 2007, 99.

234. This area was originally named 'Block M' in the 1900s; when it was re-investigated in the 1990s, it was called Area 6. The major building in the south-east part was called Building 6. For clarification, Knappett and Cunningham (2012) have reverted to 'Block M', and Building 6 is the Southeast Building.

235. Knappett and Cunningham 2012, 14–15.

236. Driessen 1999.

237. Driessen 1999; Knappett and Cunningham 2012, 2013.

238. Cunningham and Sackett 2009. Some identifications of ritual space are less convincing. For example, Building 4 has a 'Pillar Crypt' – which may simply be a room with a pillar in it. The evidence for food preparation and animal bones do not necessarily indicate ritual practice.

239. Hemingway, MacGillivray, and Sackett 2011, 515, after Koehl 2006, 308–9.

240. MacGillivray, Driessen, and Sackett 2000.

241. MacGillivray and Driessen 1990, 404.

242. MacGillivray and Driessen 1990, 404.

243. Cunningham 2007, 109.

244. Hägg 1997.

245. Tsipopoulou 1997.

246. Platon 1997.

247. Platon 1960b, 1997.

248. Tsipopoulou and Papacostopoulou 1997.

249. Mantzourani and Vavouranakis 2011.

250. Platon 1959; L. Platon 1997.

251. Platon 1971, 45.

252. Platon 1955, 288–93; 1956b, 232–9.

253. Platon 1952, 636–9; 1953, 288–91; 1954, 361–3.

254. Mantzourani, Vavouranakis, and Kanellopoulos 2005.

255. Tsipopoulou and Papacostopoulou 1997.

256. Tsipopoulou 1989.

257. Christakis 2012, 209–10.

258. E.g., Tsipopoulou 2002; Christakis 2012.

259. Cunningham 2001.

260. Tsipopoulou and Papacostopoulou 1997.

261. Cunningham 2001.

262. Sofianou and Brogan 2010; Brogan, Sofianou, and Morrison 2011; Sofianou and Brogan 2012; see also Whitelaw and Morgan 2009, 79–80.

6 THE RITUAL LANDSCAPE AND EXTRA-URBAN SANCTUARIES

1. E.g., Hood 1977; Gesell 1985; Gesell 1987; Hood 1997.

2. Faure (1967) produced further categories, such as a sanctuary with a sacred tree, spring, or baetyl. See Chapter 9 for the iconographical evidence for these practices; identifying where these activities took place is impossible.

3. Warren (in discussion following Karetsou 1981a, 153) points out similarities between peak sanctuary cult and cave cult in terms of the equipment used, and it has been argued that the votive deposits were similar (Watrous 1996, 92–6).

4. Rutkowski and Nowicki 1996, 41: the finds from this context appear to be Protopalatial, however.

5. Nowicki 1994. For example, Peatfield (1992, 66), discussing the lack of ash and other evidence for ritual bonfires, concludes that fires were constructed on none of the smaller, rural, exclusively Protopalatial peak sanctuaries, in contrast with the evidence from the Neopalatial ones. It is implied that lipid analysis of the earth sample from Atsipades will solve the problem for the category as a whole. This extracts data from a specific case to all of its kind, which is problematic (see Warren in discussion of Peatfield 1992, 81).

6. Peatfield and Morris recognized this problem, and one aim of the Atsipades excavation was to emphasize the differences between

(Protopalatial) local and (Neopalatial) 'pala-tial' or institutionalized peak sanctuaries.

7. Myres 1902–3, 356–87. For discussions of peak sanctuaries, see Peatfield 1983, 1987, 1990, 2007, 2009; Cherry 1986; Rutkowski 1988, 1991; Nowicki 1994, 2007, 2012; Watrous 1995; Jones 1999; Briault 2007b; Morris and Peatfield 2014; Haysom 2015. Kyriakidis (2005, 51–4) explains in depth how the known peak sanctuaries are primarily ritual, but this has never really been doubted; the problem is clarifying what evidence is needed to confirm an identification.

8. Evans 1921, 151–9; Peatfield 2009, 251.

9. E.g., Kyriakidis 2005; Briault 2007b; Haysom 2015.

10. Peatfield 2009, 253.

11. But see Peatfield (2007) for a reminder of the journeys made through the landscape as part of the cult in a more phenomenologi-cal approach. His paper also advocates aligning discussions of peak sanctuary topo-graphy with those of sacred caves, as attempted here.

12. Peatfield 1983, 1990, 2009.

13. 'One figurine on top of a mountain does not a peak sanctuary make' (Peatfield 1990, 120). However, as many sites are known only from surface surveys (and very preliminary reports), little evidence may hint at much more to come. See also Briault 2007b.

14. Peatfield 1992, 60.

15. Myres 1902–3, 375–6, Pl. XII 34.

16. Morris and Peatfield 2014. Davaras (2010, 76) describes this interpretation as 'pure theory', but it has convinced most scholars.

17. Recent publications suggest that animal fig-urines are predominantly bovine (Haysom 2015).

18. Peatfield 1983, 274.

19. Nowicki 1994.

20. Chryssoulaki 2001, 62; see also Alexiou 1980, 99.

21. Chryssoulaki 2001, 63.

22. E.g., Tzachili (2003) on Vrysinas; Spiliotop-oulou (2014) on Kophinas. See Girella (2008) for a summary of (mostly MM III) extra-ur-ban sanctuary material relating to feasting.

23. Peatfield 1983, 277; 1990, 126; Rutkowski 1986, 94.

24. He followed N. Platon's lead, and some sites were excavated by Davaras and Alexiou (not fully published). Faure reported on his find-ings in *BCH*, e.g., 1963, 1967, 1969.

25. Peatfield 1983, 1990, 1992, 2009; Rutkowski 1986, 96–8; 1988, 78–98. Watrous (1995) has suggested that peak sanctuaries might be sub-divided into Peatfield's type and Protopalatial 'hilltop shrines' such as Ephendi Christou. Nowicki (2007) has also explored the difficul-ties in identifying this group of sites. For our purposes, most of the confusion concerns Protopalatial examples rather than those active throughout the Neopalatial era.

26. Nowicki 1994; Davaras 2010. A more notable exception is that found at Ayia Kyriaki by Cape Kriou at the far south-west of the island, reported by Nowicki himself (2004). It is notable that (presumably Protopalatial) peak sanctuaries are increasingly being found in the west (Haysom 2015, 97).

27. The Protopalatial extra-urban sanctuaries that are not peak sanctuaries (or caves) form a diverse and poorly understood group (or collection of unique cases). Generally, these sites, such as Piskokephalo and Anemospilia, fell out of use at the end of the Protopalatial period, like the peak sanctuaries; the impor-tant exception is Kato Syme.

28. Modi and Prinias are Protopalatial peak sanc-tuaries that may continue into the Neopalatial period, although the material is limited: Peatfield 1990, 127; Christine Morris and Alan Peatfield, personal communication, 31 August 2016. Nowicki (2012, 146) states the reported ash deposit as the reason for considering Neopalatial use; this does not seem a strong enough one to consider it as such here (see also fn. 5 earlier in this chapter); these sites are present but small on Figure 6.1.

29. Peatfield 1990, 122.

30. Peatfield 1992, 66.

31. Peatfield 2009, 256. For how this has been assumed in the literature, see Alexiou (1980, 80): 'it was the custom to light on these peak-sanctuaries great bonfires which could be seen from a long way off.' Cooking pots from Kophinas have indicated signs of burning, however, and we would expect fires at least in order to prepare food (Spiliotopoulou 2014, 165–6).

32. Tyree 1974. Crete has 3,320 caves (Platon 2013, 156).

33. Faure 1964.

34. Rutkowski 1986, 47. This type of site has much scope for sensory approaches (as noted in Faro 2013; see Tyree 2013 for close consideration of cave environments).

35. Tyree 2013, 179–80.

36. Jones 1999, 5. Protopalatial Anemospilia did not produce figurines (although it contained two clay feet of a statue), and few would deny the ritual nature of this strange site (Sakellarakis and Sakellarakis 1981). The practice there is of such an unusual and distinctive kind (sacrifice?) that ritual seems to be the only explanation.

37. Peatfield 1992, 61.

38. Faure 1964, 189–97.

39. Tyree 1974, 90–1. For example, a high number of weapons might indicate a war god. However, differences in offerings may reflect differences in the dedicators, rather than deities.

40. Renfrew 1985. See Peatfield (1992) on Atsipades; Watrous (1996) on Psychro.

41. Watrous (1996, 73) argues that the mere presence of non-cultic EM pottery at Protopalatial ritual sites cannot be used to demonstrate Prepalatial ritual, but probably represents habitation debris. This same stance could be taken with Neopalatial pottery found at sites definitely used for ritual later on. One site not on Map 6.1 is Aphendis Christou in the Pediada. Some fragmentary libation vessels have been found here, but the nature of the site is poorly known. Tyree (1974, 23) discounted this as a ritual cave; see also Faure 1964, 18; Rutkowski and Nowicki 1996, 50. Other sites that have been considered as sacred but are not here include Milatos (Mirabello), Platyvola (Kydonia), and Kerato/Vigla (Viannos).

42. Brown and Peatfield 1987.

43. The most recent investigation claims cultic use from the Middle Minoan period onwards (Betancourt and Marinatos 1994), but this appears to be based on a small building within the cave and pottery only. Tyree (2013, 176–7) also discounts this example.

44. Stones piled in a ∏ shape are mentioned (Gavrilaki 2010) – function and meaning remain vague. Earlier use is recognized as inhabitation; the Neopalatial pottery is stated as ritual, but the rationale is unclear (Gavrilaki 2010, 658). The large number of cups with a hole in the bottom could have served as rhyta for libations; this is the explanation given at Skoteino (Tyree, Kanta, and Robinson 2008, 181; see also the three large LM IA cylindrical vessels from Zominthos: Whitelaw and Morgan 2009, 98). It is the simple 'presence of a secondary opening that defines a vessel as a rhyton' (Koehl 2006, 5) and the findspot would suggest a 'special' occasion. Tripod cooking pots are reported, as found at Skoteino. These would once have indicated inhabitation rather than ritual, but this seems no longer to be the case (Tyree, Kanta, and Robinson 2008, 180). Many later (e.g., seventh century BC) figurines were found.

45. Marinatos 1950; Rutkowski and Nowicki 1996, 48.

46. Faure 1964, 174.

47. Tyree 2013, 177.

48. It is notable that some scholars have recently accepted a ritual function for sites yielding ceramics only (e.g., Faro 2013). The Kamares Cave produced only pottery, but it is widely considered ritual on account of location (particularly in relation to Phaistos) and inhospitable environment. Platon (2013, 157) expresses doubts concerning the ritual use of this site, but the location tips the balance.

49. Archaeology in Greece Online ID3612 (www.chronique.efa.gr); Haysom 2015, 100.

50. Ritual interpretation: Hazzidakis 1912–13; Marinatos 1935, 215; Tyree 1974; Rutkowski and Nowicki 1996, 25, 75–81. Marinatos (1962) later reinterpreted the site as a metal workshop. Rethemiotakis (1999b) convincingly argued that it was a hoard.

51. Tyree 1974, 29; Rutkowski and Nowicki 1996, 2; Tyree (2013, 177) later recanted.

52. Rethemiotakis 1999b.

53. Platon 2013, 158–9. This site clearly deserves a full re-investigation.

54. N. Platon kept the notebooks for the 1934 excavation (Platon 2013, 158).

55. E.g., Herva 2005.

56. Faure 1972, 402–5.

57. Rethemiotakis 2009.

58. *Archaeological Reports* 2003–4, 79. Rethemiotakis (1997, 61) notes that the south facade of the 'central building' at Kastelli faces the hill with the peak sanctuary.

59. There is clearly some arbitrariness to this division, but this is the cut-off point taken here.

60. See Haysom (2015, 97) for reference to recent discoveries. For example, one, at Mavrou Koryfi, is granted a fleeting mention (Andreadaki-Vlazaki 2004, 35), with no indication of date. A ten-room building has been excavated at Pera Galenoi (Tsivilika and Banou 2000). Evely (2010, 190) describes it as a 'peak sanctuary', without explicit reason given. Furthermore, its date is unclear.

61. Nowicki 2012.

62. The (exceptionally preliminary) references state that the building is MM I (Alexiou 1963, 406; 1966, 322; Faure 1967, 125–6; 1969, 184; Rutkowski 1986, 80; 1988, 81). Driessen and Macdonald (1997, 127) mention early Neopalatial evidence, but this is unclear. Evangelos Kyriakidis is re-examining the material, which indicates MM III as the main period of use (personal communication, 4 September 2016).

63. Rutkowski (1986, 76) states: 'it is thought that sacred buildings first appeared in the sanctuaries at a later stage in their development, that is in MM III, although it is quite possible that most buildings date from an earlier period.' See also Rutkowski (1988, 76) with reference to both Pyrgos and Gonies; both sites were used into the Neopalatial period, but not necessarily throughout (Christine Morris and Alan Peatfield, personal communication, 31 August 2016; Evangelos Kyriakidis, personal communication, 4 September 2016).

64. Christine Morris and Alan Peatfield, personal communication, 31 August 2016. Peatfield lists Pyrgos as Neopalatial (e.g., 1987, 92; 1994, 23, n. 16). The presence of a building and Horns of Consecration has been used to indicate a Neopalatial date (e.g., Peatfield 1989, 396; Driessen and Macdonald 1997, 128). Rutkowski (1989), however, concluded that the building must date to the main period of dedications. Preliminary reports only mention MM I(–II) ceramics (Alexiou 1963, 404–5; Faure 1963, 500–1; 1967, 125; Rutkowski 1988, 87–8. Rutkowski and Nowicki (1984, 184) state MM I and later (not specified).

65. Evangelos Kyriakidis, personal communication, 4 September 2016.

66. Haysom 2014, 82.

67. Watrous 1996.

68. While published preliminarily, these reports are extensive. See Karetsou 1981a; also Karetsou 1974, 1975, 1976, 1977, 1978, 1979, 1980, 1981b, 1984, 1985.

69. Karetsou and Mathioudaki 2012, 90. Alonaki did not yield the figurines normally associated with a cultic building, but did produce five stone ladles and evidence for eating and drinking.

70. Karetsou and Mathioudaki 2012, 103.

71. Karetsou 1974, 1981a. The date of the surrounding wall is unclear; it is possibly Neopalatial or as late as LM III.

72. Karetsou 1975, 1976, 1978.

73. Peatfield 1989, 235; Karetsou 2005. Seal stones were found at Kophinas, but not sealings.

74. Karetsou, Godart, and Olivier 1985.

75. Karetsou and Koehl 2011.

76. Karetsou 1981a, 145.

77. Evans 1921, 66, 761.

78. D'Agata 1992. However, Peatfield (1990, 127) states that Pyrgos is the only site to have produced a fragment of full-sized horns, with miniatures from Petsophas, Prinias, Vrysinas, and Juktas.

79. Hazzidakis 1934, 5.

80. Sakellarakis and Sapouna-Sakellaraki 1997, 68.

81. Myres 1902–3; Faure 1964, 175–6.

82. Marinatos 1950, 250; Faure 1964, 175, fn. 6; Rutkowski 1986, 62, 67. Tyree (1974, 79) suggests that they could be either MM III or LM I.

83. Faure 1963, 500–1; Muhly 1981, 151; Rutkowski and Nowicki 1996, 38. Trapeza Tylissou should not be confused with the earlier peak sanctuary that lies to the south (Pyrgos Tylissos), nor the (earlier) Trapeza cave in Lasithi. Trapeza Tsermiadon was used in the Protopalatial period (Rutkowski and Nowicki 1996, 68–9; Watrous 1996, 61–2).

84. Hazzidakis 1934, 75–6; Faure 1964, 177; Rutkowski and Nowicki 1996, 39. As with so many other ritual sites, this cave warrants further investigation.

85. Tyree et al. 2009.

86. Faure 1964, 164; Rutkowski and Nowicki 1996, 37.

87. Tyree, Kanta and Sphakianakis 2007. More than 850 conical cups and 550 'communion

88. Davaras 1969. The cave also possesses a 'natural altar' (Rutkowski 1986, 48, 55–6).

89. Rethemiotakis (1997, 61) notes that the south facade of the central building at Kastelli faced the peak sanctuary.

90. Rethemiotakis 1985, 297; Whitley 2004, 79.

91. For Psychro: Hogarth 1899–1900; Rutkowski and Nowicki 1996; Watrous 1996, 2004. Nowicki (2013, 158–9) notes two further large Protopalatial and Neopalatial settlements in the Lasithi mountains, at Tzermiado Ayia Anna and Mesa Lasithi Ayioi Apostoloi.

92. Dawkins 1913–14, 2–5; Rutkowski and Nowicki 1996, 8.

93. Jones 1999, 8–9.

94. Watrous 1996, 49.

95. Evans 1897; Hogarth 1899–1900; Watrous 1996, 48–51.

96. Hogarth 1899–1900, 98–9. Rutkowski and Nowicki (1996, 11) state that the altar was covering a crevice, as at Juktas.

97. Cromarty 2008, 56–7.

98. Rethemiotakis 1990.

99. Faure 1964, 160. Tyree (1974, 12–13) dates the gold Double Axe to LM III. However, she states that the three offering receptacles probably date to LM I, 'since there are no stone receptacles from any sacred cave which date after this period'.

100. Rutkowski and Nowicki 1996, 26; Sakellarakis and Sapouna-Sakellaraki 2013.

101. Sakellarakis 1987, 247; Vasilakis 1990, 130.

102. Haysom 2015, 98.

103. Rutkowski (1986, 56) mentions the bones of oxen, goat, sheep, deer, and domestic pig.

104. Rutkowski and Nowicki 1996, 32. Van de Moortel (2006) argues that this was not, in fact, a palatial ware, but made by independent potters and widely available.

105. Dawkins and Laistner 1912–13; Van de Moortel 2006, 2011b.

106. Van de Moortel 2006. It is for this reason that the site is included in the discussion, unlike the examples such as Amnissos.

107. Van de Moortel 2006, 81; 2011b, 308, table 1. Her analysis represents 180 Neopalatial vases. Dawkins and Laistner (1912–13, 9, 26–7) reported that Neopalatial sherds were found in one concentrated point, but Van de Moortel (2006, 85–6) states that they were more widespread (which may indicate a series of separate events).

108. Davaras 1974; Tzachili 2003, 2012; Papadopoulou and Tzachili 2010. See also Faro 2008.

109. Tzachili (2003, 328) states that no traces of built structures are reported.

110. Faro 2008; see also Haysom 2015, 95.

111. Tzachili 2012.

112. Tzachili 2003; Faro 2008, 165.

113. Rutkowski and Nowicki 1996, 42–4.

114. Kourou and Karetsou 1994. Previously, the evidence had been unclear after a survey finding five sherds 'possibly of LM I date', and an LM I stone libation table: Hood and Warren 1966; Warren 1966; also Watrous 1996, 62–3.

115. Rutkowski and Nowicki 1996, 62.

116. The excavators reject the interpretation of a spring sanctuary: Lebessi and Muhly 1987, 111.

117. Lebessi and Muhly 1990, 317.

118. See Muhly (2012) for a terracotta foot model.

119. Lebessi and Muhly 1987, 1990. The lack of Bronze Age terracotta animal figurines is notable, in comparison with other extra-urban sanctuaries (Haysom 2015).

120. Lebessi and Muhly 1990, 334–5.

121. Kanta and Davaras 2011; Kanta 2011b, 84–97.

122. Kanta 2011c, 28; Kanta and Kontopodi 2011, 48–65 (but a number of tripod cooking pots are present). There was probably a route to Kophinas (Kanta 2011c, 29).

123. Kanta 2011c, 29.

124. Therefore not on the peak; this has caused some confusion in the literature. An unexcavated chasm near the peak contains Minoan material, which may be comparable to that at Juktas (Soetens 2009); however, the excavated *temenos* lies lower down.

125. Karetsou 2014, 124.

126. Rethemiotakis 2001, 126–9; 2014. This has led to a suggestion that these represent a male rite of passage, and that the miniature vases (particularly *pitharaki*) signify childhood (Spiliotopoulou 2014).

127. Karetsou 2014.

128. Karetsou 2014, 128.

129. Similarities have been noted with the ceramics from Vrysinas and Juktas (e.g., Haysom 2015, 96).

130. Spiliotopoulou 2014. One sherd with reed decoration indicates LM IA use, while a few others point to LM IB: the evidence is

minimal, however. The site does not, therefore, parallel Vrysinas in chronological terms
as this has clear LM IA evidence (*pace* Haysom
2015, 95–6).

131. Peatfield 1989, 92; Rutkowski 1991.

132. Chryssoulaki 2001.

133. Jones (1999) has collected evidence as it was
known in publications; this is now becoming
out of date.

134. Jones 1999, 77–83.

135. Rutkowski 1986, 47–8. They are also situated
at a similar distance from Kastelli (in terms of
time, not space).

136. Cherry 1986.

137. See critiques in Peatfield 1990.

138. *Pace* Peatfield 1990, 128. The assumption that
the prestige objects found at peak sanctuaries
were made under palatial control is undemonstrated, but the manufacture of such
objects required training and skill and the
acquisition of valuable raw materials.

139. Peatfield 1987, 1990. To claim that peak sanctuaries became institutionalized does not
necessarily presuppose 'that Neopalatial period Crete became politically unified (ultimately, under the sole control of Knossos)':
Cherry in discussion after Peatfield (1992, 83).
Watrous (1996, 74) argues that this occurred
in the Protopalatial period, but only by
arguing that the Linear A inscriptions and
architectural constructions 'appear full
blown in the Protopalatial period'. This does
not appear to be the case.

140. Soetens, Sarris, and Vansteenhuyse 2008, 155.

141. Not only are the criteria by which these are
defined continually being reassessed, but
examples have been found beyond the island,
such as Ayios Georgios (lavishly published by
the Athenian Archaeological Society, e.g.,
Sakellarakis 2013) and Leska (Georgiadis
2012) on Kythera.

142. Warren 2001, 116–17.

143. Moody and Lukermann 1985, 78.

144. Molloy 2012, 88.

145. Molloy 2012, 92.

146. Molloy 2012, 97; see Chryssoulaki (1999, 81)
for date. Later use might include bases for
farmers, workshops, and even a sanctuary
(Karoumes). See Evely (2008, 94) for the
report on Chiromandres, where the
Protopalatial guardhouse was replaced by

a more 'elite' clientele with seal stones and
high-quality pottery.

147. Molloy 2010.

148. Peatfield 1999, 69.

149. Ritual significance is often assumed, they may
have 'simply provided a spectacular display on
the occasion of the holiday' (Alexiou
1980, 110).

150. Krzyszkowska 2005, 139–40. Note that the
Akrotiri sealings date to LM IA.

151. Shapland 2010.

152. E.g., Wiener 2007; 2011, 363; this looks back
to Evans (1928, 79).

153. E.g., Karetsou and Koehl 2011; see also
Haysom 2015, 97.

154. Nowicki (2013, 164) mentions a further peak
sanctuary site on the western fringe of the
Lasithi area, Miliarado Koupa Kastellos, that
may have just tipped into the Neopalatial
period.

155. For example, Karetsou 1981a, 145.
The 'palatial' nature of the finds is unclear
given the presence of such artefacts (such
as inscribed stone libation tables) in non-palatial sites. There may well have been several
workshops, of various degrees of centralization, making the clay figurines (Zeimbeki
2004).

156. Rutkowski 1986, 47–8.

157. Whitelaw 2004b, 155, figure 10.6; Warren
2004, 166. It is often stated that ritual sites
may provide the focal points for the formation
of regional identities (e.g., Schoep and
Tomkins 2012, 23).

158. Bevan 2010, 35, figure 4.

159. De Polignac (1995), but see Hall (1995) for
a criticism of this model.

160. Watrous (1996, 78–81) after de Polignac 1995.
It has become clearer that de Polignac's model
does not work so well for mainland Greece,
although it may do so for colonies, such as
Poseidonia, where space could be treated
more as virgin territory. In the motherland,
sites appear to have been appropriated by
certain poleis after a period of ritual use.
This would support the notion of particular
elites taking over local rituals in the
Neopalatial period.

161. Tyree, Kanta, and Robinson 2008, 184.

162. Rutkowski 1986, 48.

163. Dawkins 1913–14; Watrous 1982.

164. Dawkins 1913–14, 6; Driessen and Macdonald 1997, 194.

165. Dawkins 1913–14; Driessen 2001, 57.

166. Zominthos Fieldnotes for 2015 (accessed 19 August 2015, 13 July 2016). Current evidence suggests LM IA use for both sites.

167. Sakellarakis 1986, 140; 1988, 168; Traunmueller 2011.

168. It took Pendlebury (1939, 7–16) nine hours to reach the Lasithi plain from Knossos, and three and a half hours from Malia to Krasi; however, there is a further fair distance to walk to reach the Lasithi plain and Psychro from Krasi.

169. Watrous 1996, 97.

170. Watrous (2004) also identified some local pottery and that from elsewhere, e.g., eastern Crete.

171. Watrous 2004, 144, table 1 highlights this striking shift.

172. Watrous 2004, 146.

173. Morgan 1990.

174. Whitley 2001, 99, 144. By coincidence, fewer graves are known in the Neopalatial period, in contrast with the Protopalatial picture, where many were wealthy.

175. Rehak and Younger 1998, 142.

176. See also Warren 2002, 202.

7 LITERACY, ADMINISTRATION, AND COMMUNICATION

1. It is only fairly recently that literacy studies have taken a more anthropological turn, exploring how modes of literacy are culturally specific (Street 1993). This is in recognition that modern modes of communication, in terms of both telecommunications and physical transport, are incomparable with those of pre-modern societies. Perhaps most striking is the different levels of literacy across populations.

2. Only Linear A was used as a writing system in the Neopalatial period in contrast with the two (Linear A and Hieroglyphics) in the Protopalatial era.

3. E.g., Stoddart and Whitley 1988; Whittaker 2005.

4. We will not delve too deeply into the semantics of 'administrative'; for some, this implies management rather than mere participation, and so should be used with care (Palaima 1994, 314).

5. Text and image did not share the same space, as in the case of Egyptian Hieroglyphics.

6. Whittaker 2005, 30. On the one hand, see Postgate, Wang, and Wilkinson (1995) for concerns about overemphasizing non-administrative functions of writing. On the other hand, studies attempting to reconstruct societies from undeciphered texts tend to be functionalist, implying that writing was purely utilitarian; this autonomous model has been described as 'dangerously close to technical determinism' (Stoddart and Whitley 1988, 761).

7. Harbsmeier 1986.

8. Palaima 1982; Owens 1999. Examples come from: Phylakopi (Renfrew 1977); Ayia Irini (Caskey 1970); Thera (Doumas 1993); Kythera (Sakellarakis and Olivier 1994); Miletus (Niemeier 1996); Troy (Faure 1996); Tiryns (Olivier 1988); Tel Haror (Oren 1996); Tel Lachish (Finkelberg et al. 1996).

9. Schoep 1999b.

10. E.g., Dimopoulou, Olivier, and Rethemiotakis 1993.

11. E.g., Palaima 1990.

12. Olivier 1986, 378–9; see also Younger n.d. [website].

13. See Begg (2004) for mason's marks; Boskamp (1996) for graffiti on pithoi. Neopalatial mason's marks were incised more lightly than before, with fewer, more standardized types. These included 'Double Axes, stars, gates, branches, tridents, crosses, distaffs, boxes, and bras levés' (Begg 2004, 15).

14. Owens 1996.

15. Begg 2004, 19.

16. Godart and Olivier 1976a, 1976b, 1979, 1982, 1985.

17. Fought 2006. This work is fully aware of the problems in defining 'ethnicity', but provides strong evidence for how language, as a communicative tool, shapes self-identity as well as external categorizations.

18. E.g., Brice 1962; Davis 1968; Patria 1988–9; Finkelberg 1990–1; Brown 1992–3; Renfrew 1998.

19. Bennett 1985; Schoep 2002c, 43–5. The three records of the language of the Keftiu in Egyptian texts are of interest, but, ultimately, of limited value (Kyriakidis 2002).

20. Schoep 2002c, 44. Gordon (1981) supported the Semitic hypothesis, which would render the Linear A language non-Indo-European, whereas Finkelberg (1990–1) argued that it is Luwian and Lycian, which is Indo-European.

21. Schoep 2002c, 157.

22. E.g., Pope 1964; Brice 1969; Best 1976; Gordon 1976.

23. See Nakassis and Pluta (2003) for the suggestion of multidimensional scaling.

24. Schoep 2002c, 9. Hallager (1996, 32) listed the functions of Linear A tablets as: 'inventories, records of deliveries, allotted rations or other economic activities'; see also Uchitel 1994–5; Palmer 1995.

25. Montecchi 2012, 3.

26. More than a quarter of all tablets found at Ayia Triada refer to people (Schoep 2002c, 185).

27. Palmer 1995, 147.

28. The Odos Katre site at Chania is one possible exception, with numerous roundels, sealed documents, and Linear A tablets; the nodules and roundels were possibly kept at different places, but this is unclear as this context is a clearance or fill (Hallager 1996, 50–1 after Papapostolou, Godart, and Olivier 1976). The tablets, in any case, were found across the excavated site. Schoep (1999a, 206) makes pertinent points regarding how the stage of the administrative cycle at which the data was preserved has impacted our understanding.

29. Palmer 1995, 148.

30. Montecchi 2010, 21.

31. Weingarten 1990, 110: the 'Villas' of Amnissos, Epano Zakros, Archanes, Makrygialos, Mitropolis, Nirou Chani, Myrtos Pyrgos, Vathypetro, Achladia, Manares, Tourtouloi and Zou; the towns of Mochlos, Palaikastro and Pseira; the Palaces of Malia and Phaistos. Some of these, such as Archanes and Myrtos-Pyrgos, also had Linear A tablets.

32. E.g., Pini in response to Weingarten (1990, 115).

33. E.g., Warren 2004, 163.

34. Schoep (1999a, 205) is fully aware of the necessary caveats, but suggested that LM IB was less centralized than in LM IA. Krzyszkowska (2005, 191) argues that this rests almost entirely on negative evidence.

35. Accident of preservation is probably also responsible for certain omissions, such as the lack of olives recorded at Chania, or wheat at Zakros (Schoep 1999a, 208). The ideogram for 'person' does not occur at Zakros either.

36. Hallager 1996, 32.

37. Hallager 1996, 32.

38. Morpurgo-Davies and Cadogan 1971, 1977.

39. Cadogan 2008.

40. Weingarten 1990. Hallager (1996, 236) notes its ritual connotations, but refers to this as a 'mini-archive'.

41. Olivier 1986.

42. Palmer 1995, 146; Schoep 1999a, 207–8.

43. Palmer 1995, 149. The mixed commodity tablets are associated with feasting. See Montecchi (2012) on lists of banqueting foodstuffs from Ayia Triada.

44. Schoep 2002c, 188.

45. E.g., Montecchi 2012, 1–2.

46. There is some doubt about this translation, for example, Palmer (1995, 136).

47. Adams 2007a.

48. Schoep 2002c, 142, 178.

49. Schoep 2002c, 115.

50. La Rosa (2010b, 500) states that the value of wheat (or barley?) ranges from three units to a maximum of 1,060 units in tablet HT 102.

51. Palaima 1994, 319.

52. Palaima 1994, 322.

53. Hallager 2002.

54. Watrous 1984, 128–9. He suggests that the 'majority of transactions carried out in the Villas at Ayia Triada was of a voluntary nature and involved a group of people who were to some extent free' (Watrous 1984, 131). The evidence is too slight to establish whether there was slavery in the period.

55. Watrous and Hadzi-Vallianou 2004, 298.

56. La Rosa 2010b, 500.

57. Hallager 1996.

58. Schoep 2002c, 9.

59. Ferioli and Fiandra (1989) offer excellent illustrations showing a range of containers and locks.

60. Schoep 1999a, 206. She contrasts the concentration of single-hole hanging nodules in the north-west section of the Villa at Ayia Triada with the large number of flat-based nodules from House A at Zakros. However, it is possible that both types were used to secure documents, and that the distinction indicates regional preference; hence categorizing according to function here.

61. Krzyszkowska 2005, 156, 192. I am grateful for her demonstration with cigarette foil on this issue: 12 March, 2014.
62. Weingarten 1986, 281.
63. Krzyszkowska 2005, 176.
64. Hallager 1996, 116–18. Hallager comes to the conclusion that this indicates an outgoing movement as it was in the storeroom official's interest to keep a record, whereas it is up to the external individuals to keep a record of what they contribute. However, the Palace may also want to keep a record of goods coming in as confirmation that obligations had been met, while the individual received a docket (nodulus).
65. Boskamp 1996, 112.
66. Hallager 1996, 24.
67. Weingarten 1988.
68. Schoep 1995.
69. Schoep 1995.
70. Schoep 2002c, 24.
71. E.g., at Archanes (Sakellarakis and Sapouna-Sakellaraki 1997, 695–7). There is evidence for seal-engraving at Poros (Dimopoulou 1997, 2000).
72. As such, it may be too simplistic to define this function as 'non-sphragistic' (Younger 1977). Wearing the objects could have facilitated their function as a sealing device, as they were always at hand.
73. Krzyszkowska 2005, 120.
74. Krzyszkowska 2005, 133–4.
75. Hallager 1996, 221.
76. Krzyszkowska 2005, 121: more than 1,800 sealings, with around 500 different seal types.
77. Hallager 1996, 221.
78. Weingarten 2010, 323.
79. For this last possibility, see Touchais et al. 1996, 1306, 1309, figures 261–2. The charioteer scene appears to be as of CMS 11.6 no. 019 and CMS II.6 no. 260 from Ayia Triada and Sklavokambos. The bull-leaping scene from Akrotiri does not appear to be identical to other examples, but it follows the theme.
80. Betts 1967; Hallager 1996, 207–8, table 74.
81. Hallager and Hallager 1995; but see Krzyszkowska 2005, 141.
82. Krzyszkowska (2005, 189) states categorically that there was no such thing as 'replica' rings, and the term should be abandoned. However, there is a tradition of scholarship on these artefacts which uses the term. In some recent scholarship, this group of material has been described as 'look-alikes' (e.g., Bevan 2010; Whitelaw forthcoming); this is not to be confused with the Zakrian group discussed later.
83. Betts 1967, 25.
84. Betts 1967; Schoep 1999a, 213.
85. Pini 2006. As the rings were punched and engraved (Krzyszkowska 2005, 131), they were not mass-produced from moulds. Whether the impression originates from a ring or seal stone, as may be assumed from the label 'replica ring', it is the *image* that authenticates (*pace* Krzyszkowska 2005, 141).
86. See Betts 1967. There are exceptions, e.g., Krzyszkowska 2005, 189: 'even if most high quality signet rings were produced in a Knossian workshop – and for this there is no proof – it does *not* follow that they were used exclusively by Knossian administrators' (her italics).
87. Goren and Panagiotopoulos 2010; Panagiotopoulos, personal communication, 15 April 2014. There was only one exception to this provenance: an example from Ayia Triada. In a passage that strongly questions tight Knossian control, Krzyszkowska (2005, 189) suggests that (concerning the combat scene sealings): 'we can be reasonably confident that the hanging nodules travelled from Ayia Triada to Knossos'; the scientific analyses suggest otherwise. Pini (2006) also offers a refreshing, if perhaps unconvincing, reaction against general assumptions of overall Knossian control.
88. Krzyszkowska (2005, 188) points out that sealings may also travel within museum storerooms.
89. Krzyszkowska 2005, 189.
90. Hallager 1996, 208, table 74.
91. Hallager 1996, 212, 220. Impressions from the so-called replica rings also occur on flat-based nodules, dome-noduli, and two-hole hanging nodules. Hallager points out some examples of the same sealing occurring on different documents, but these are limited in number; for example, KH 20 was found on eight roundels and eight inscribed pendants (Hallager 1996, 215) – these do not serve the same function as flat-based nodules.
92. For example, Hallager (1996, 212) states that the 'replica rings clearly indicate some kind of administrative links between Knossos and other sites on LM IB Crete', later narrowing

93. Goren and Panagiotopoulos 2010, 257.
94. Krzyszkowska 2005, 191.
95. La Rosa 2002, 94.
96. Palaima 1994.
97. But see Militello 1988, 1992.
98. Militello 2002: from the indications given in Halbherr's notebook, HT 6–84, 150, 151 were found in 1903 in the Villa; among these, HT 24 was found in Corridor 9. HT 85–113 and 154a were found in 1904 in Room 7 of the Casa del Lebete. Since HT 1–5 were already discovered in 1902, we have to conclude that the remaining tablets HT 115–17, 119–24, and 129–31, not drawn in the notebook, were found in 1912 in Room 9 of the Casa del Lebete. The archives, located at both ends of the building, recorded incoming goods at its entrances (Watrous and Hadzi-Vallianou 2004, 298).
99. Palaima 1994, 312.
100. Weingarten 1986, 284; 1987.
101. According to the current evidence, and they formed two broad groups in terms of the inscriptions they use: Weingarten 1986; Palaima 1994.
102. Weingarten 1983, 38–44; Hallager 1996, 137–45. Also fifty-nine hanging nodules and five noduli (kept together in a container placed on the first floor): Platon and Brice 1975, 25–6, 35.
103. For a recent treatment, see Anastasiadou 2016b.
104. Weingarten 1990, 108.
105. There are two possible examples from House A. CMS II.7 no. 36 from Zakros may be a similar image to CMS II.6 no. 258 from Sklavokambos, but they are not particularly alike and certainly not from the same ring. CMS II.7 no. 71 from Zakros has been paired with CMS II.8 no. 298 from Ayia Triada, but this provenance is unclear (Krzyszkowska 2005, 188, fn. 93). These examples are not in Figure 7.3.
106. Marinatos 1948; Fotou 1997.
107. Marinatos 1948, 73.
108. Marinatos 1948, 74–5.
109. Fotou 1997, 46–7.
110. Hallager 1996, 70.
111. Gournia Website, accessed 14 July 2014: see downloadable preliminary report.
112. Weingarten 1990, 110.
113. Krzyszkowska 2005, 185.
114. The boundaries of the Gournian Palace are difficult to define; there is the possibility, for example, that Block H to the south was part of the Palace, united on the upper floor (Soles 2002, 125).
115. Christakis 2008.
116. Soles 1991, 75. Outside the sites involved in this discussion, Chania has yielded a high number of roundels, showing a further distinction.
117. Palaima 1994, 312: 24.7 per cent of documents were flat-based nodules.
118. Krzyszkowska 2005, 191.
119. Wiener 1999, 413.
120. Weingarten (1991a, 308); see also Schoep 1999a, 213–17.
121. Pini 2006, 220. Pini urges care in making such associations, but confirms these examples.
122. See review of Krzyszkowska (2005) by Weingarten (2005).
123. Pini 2006, 221.
124. Weingarten 1986, 289. Also, nearly half of the documents from the early Neopalatial Temple Repositories at Knossos are multi-sealed.
125. Weingarten 1989.
126. Hogarth 1900–11; Platon (1971, 28–9) suggested that it was a palatial annex.
127. Wiener 1999, 415.
128. Christakis 1999a, 217.
129. Platon 1988. Six of the thirty town houses contained such winemaking installations, but none was found in the Palace.
130. Platon 1988, 82.
131. Weingarten 1990, 119.
132. Noted by Hogarth (1902), explored by Weingarten (1983); see also Krzyszkowska (2005, 182). Krzyszkowska rejects the term 'look-alike', but they do need some kind of label.
133. Krzyszkowska 2005; Pini 2006.
134. Weingarten 2010, 324.
135. Hallager 1996, 205–6, table 73. The seals used on two-impression nodules were rarely used on three-impression nodules, and vice versa. The same combinations would also occur regularly, and the seals used in these multiple systems were not used individually.
136. Schoep 1999a, 213. This represents a further spatial and temporal abstraction enabled by the development of a complex administrative system.

137. Pini 2006, 224.
138. Wiener 1999.
139. Karetsou, Godart, and Olivier 1985, 144. See also Davis 2014.
140. Warren 1969.
141. Evans 1897, 350–8.
142. Cameron 1965. Inscriptions on stucco have been found only in the Villa Reale at Ayia Triada and in the area of the Taureador Frescoes in the Palace at Knossos, reflecting the poor preservation of frescoes in general.
143. Architectural inscriptions are particularly difficult to date, but could be Neopalatial. Four examples come from a variety of contexts at Knossos (the Palace's north-west entrance, tombs, and town), with one from Malia.
144. Evans (1928, 443) suggested that the Linear A on the frescoes from the House of the Frescoes at Knossos 'may well have been in the nature of religious invocation, talismanic formulae, or others equivalent to the texts on the walls of sacred buildings in later times'.
145. Owens 1996.
146. Forsdyke 1926–7; Alexiou and Brice 1972, 115–16.
147. Xanthoudides 1924, 110; Alexiou and Brice 1976, 19–20.
148. Tsipopoulou, Godart, and Olivier 1982.
149. Pope 1956, 134.
150. For discussion of these libation formulae, see Carratelli 1956–7; Godart and Olivier 1982; Karetsou, Godart, and Olivier 1985; Finkelberg 1990–1; Schoep 1994; Owens 1995; Davis 2014; Karnava 2016. The 'type vessel' IO Za 2 has seven-eight words surviving spread on two lines.
151. Evans 1935, 656.
152. Stoddart and Whitley 1988, 768.
153. Karetsou, Godart, and Olivier 1985, 102. At least 600 libation tables have been found at Syme alone: 0.02 per cent of which were inscribed (Muhly and Olivier 2008, 199–200; they give the proportion of inscribed objects at Juktas as 0.06 on p. 216).
154. Or deliberately broken to prevent later use (Davaras 1981, 3; Peatfield 1990, 128; Schoep 1994, 19).
155. MM III–LM I: Muhly 1981; Schoep 1994, 21. The earliest securely inscribed libation table from a cult place comes from Syme: Muhly and Olivier 2008, 198.
156. Schoep 1994, 22.

157. Karetsou, Godart, and Olivier 1985, 93; Davis 2014.
158. Schoep 1994, 12.
159. See Del Freo (2008, 2012) for recent additions.
160. Gesell 1985, 69.
161. An inscribed ladle was also found at the Ayios Georgios peak sanctuary on Kythera (Sakellarakis and Sapouna-Sakellaraki 1997, 335).
162. Gesell 1985, 69.
163. As observed by Schoep (1994, 20).
164. Karnava 2016, 345.
165. Schoep 1994, 20.
166. According to the regional and site variation in the epigraphical evidence (Schoep 1994, 21).
167. Schoep (2002c, 13) also makes the distinction between the more archaic and elaborate epigraphic writing tradition performed with chisels on artefacts like libation tables, and the pinacological tradition inscribed with a stylus on clay objects. This suggests different intrinsic connotations in terms of grandeur and intended longevity.
168. Muhly (1981, 341) argues that the inscription per se does not suggest that libation tables were 'made to endure', since they were found with uninscribed examples. The fact that most tables were uninscribed does not negate the possibility that those that had inscriptions were intended to both frieze the moment and speak to prosperity – they may represent the general assemblage.
169. Adams 2007a.
170. Adam 2004, 79. She has argued (1990, 132–3) that 'one response to the finitude of our existence is the search for permanence in all that is durable: artefacts, institutions, symbols, rules, and traditions.' See also Van Dyke and Alcock (2003b, 4) for types of strategies that societies employ in order to remember or be remembered.
171. Adam 2004, 81: her italics.
172. Adams 2007a.
173. Schoep 2002c.
174. For example, inscribed libation tables, mostly of uncertain context, have been found in the House of the Frescoes, north of the Palace, 'lower town', and 'Villa Ariadne'.
175. Del Freo (2012) reports two LM I vase inscriptions from Mochlos and Del Freo (2008) an inscribed ring from Poros.

176. As the recently discovered Linear A tablet from Gournia indicates.
177. Schoep 1999a.

8 THE ECONOMY

1. Earle 2002, 8. Feinman's (2004) definition is straightforward to follow: when the economy transcends the domestic mode of production, it requires organization, with possibly hierarchical institutions. It has been suggested that we move from a domestic model to one of the 'house', in the more corporate sense of Shakespeare's Italian plays (Driessen 2005b). It is not clear why this should be less hierarchical than other socio-political models – the households of the Capulets and Montagues were internally pyramidal.
2. Earle 2002, 1. Earle is also, by his own reckoning, a social evolutionist. The 'Bronze Age' societies that form his case studies come from New World archaeology, Hawaiian anthropology, and Danish archaeology. None of these quite fits the Bronze Age societies of the second millennium BC Mediterranean, and it is debatable to what extent we could or should consider vastly separated cultures together on the basis of their technology (bronze). It is further notable that Earle prefers to analyse cultures that belong on the 'chiefdom' rung of his evolutionary ladder, rather than early states as we have on Minoan Crete.
3. Pullen 2010.
4. Petruso 1978.
5. E.g., Michailidou 2003.
6. Michailidou 2003.
7. Studies of Neopalatial political geography, or settlement hierarchies, do not always have space to take full account of the ritual sites, e.g., Bevan and Wilson 2013.
8. Adams 2006, 3.
9. Smith 2003, 153. Even if landownership existed as a concept in Neopalatial Crete, it is difficult to reconstruct who owned it (Schoep 2002c, 190).
10. Cherry (1986, 24) points out that the marked boundaries on his map are 'hypothetical'. Presumably this refers to where they were drawn, rather than whether they were visualized that clearly on the ground as well. It is now well established that the impact of a map with lines drawn for boundaries 'may be more powerful than the scholarly text that accompanies it' (Smith 2005, 832).

11. Modern-day property laws and the legalities of trespass are also reliant on objective territorial measurement, for which we have no evidence in Minoan times (Smith 2005, 834).
12. Pendlebury 1939, 7. He was a particularly swift and robust walker, but his times offer a comparative database. Obviously other journeys may be considerably slower, for example, those involving pack animals. For further Minoan routes, see Evans 1928, 60–92; Sakellarakis and Sapouna-Sakellaraki 1997, 71–3; Panagiotakis 2004.
13. Adams 2006, 7, figure 2.
14. Bevan 2010.
15. Bevan 2010, 31, figures 3a, 3b.
16. The importance of the region is clear in many models, such as Renfrew's (1986) peer–polity interaction, and the regional approach of survey has often been cited in defence of this type of fieldwork (e.g., Cherry 1983b, 385–6).
17. Smith 2005.
18. E.g., Tilley 1994.
19. Cherry 1994, 104. He suggests that those involved in survey are more inclined towards self-criticism than excavators, but this is debatable; see, for example, the excavation at Çatalhöyük.
20. Bintliff 1991; Knapp 1992.
21. Alcock (1991, 422) writes: 'Field walking in the countryside and excavation in the city generate two very different sorts of evidence, demanding two very different processes of inference and interpretation.' She contrasts mainly between town and country, however, rather than between different spatial and chronological narratives.
22. Driessen 2001, 59. See also Todd and Warren 2012. Flood and Soles (2014) note the local responses to water management across the island.
23. Shaw and Shaw 1995; Hope Simpson et al. 1995.
24. Watrous et al. 1993. See also Bredaki, Longo, and Benzi 2012.
25. Watrous, Hadzi-Vallianou, and Blitzer 2004, 294.
26. Whitelaw forthcoming. Ayia Triada provides the most detailed evidence for the amount of the land required to produce the goods listed in the records (Schoep 2002c, 175–99; Christakis 2008, 137).

27. Blackman and Branigan 1975, 34–4; 1977. See Vasilakis and Branigan (2010) for the Odigitria survey.

28. Archaeology in Greece Online: 4,537 (2005); 197 (2006); 266 (2007). See, for example, Voni. The extent of the site at Orphanou Marathia is ca. 0.5 acres, and ashlar blocks have been noted in the field (Rethemiotakis 1999c, 239–41). A second site ca. 2 km east of Voni is substantial (10–12 acres), but badly destroyed by ploughing. The surface finds include various domestic artefacts and an offering table. Warren (2004, 160) suggested that, like Alagni, Voni was dependent on Galatas.

29. Müller 1996, 922–3. See also Müller 1990, 1991a, 1992, 1998.

30. Cunningham and Driessen 2004, 106.

31. Knappett 1999; but see Cadogan 1995, 2013b. Dewolf, Postel, and Van Effenterre (1963) argue that the Lasithi Plain was part of Malian territory in their study of agricultural production and consumption. See Watrous (1982, 16) for a critique of this methodology. See also Warren 2004; Van Effenterre 1980; 1983. It does not appear in the catchment area for Malia in figure 3 (after Whitelaw 2004a). Overall, 'it is open to question, however, whether Malia controlled the Lasithi Plain, although this is likely on the basis of cultural affinities and calculation of productive capacities': Bennet 1990, 195. He notes that historically the Lasithi Plain has been linked to both the easternmost nomos (today) and Herakleion (in the Venetian period). He suggests that the current situation is historically more unusual (Bennet 1990, 209).

32. Watrous 1982, 8.

33. Watrous 1982, 14–15.

34. Watrous 1982, 17.

35. Nowicki 1996, 42–3.

36. Dawkins 1913–14, 5–7.

37. Christakis (2008, 135) suggests the north area of the isthmus and the Asari area.

38. Watrous and Schultz 2012, 55.

39. Watrous 2012b, 279; Watrous and Schultz 2012.

40. Betancourt 1995; Betancourt, Davaras, and Hope Simpson 2004, 2005.

41. Hayden, Moody, and Rackham 1992; Hayden 2004, 118–20; 2005.

42. Watrous and Schultz 2012, 56.

43. Haggis 1996; Hayden 2004, 118. However, the Neopalatial period has produced the first evidence for site ranking (Haggis 1996, 401).

44. Tsipopoulou 1989.

45. Platon 1997; Tsipopoulou and Papacostopoulou 1997.

46. Vokotopoulos 2011a.

47. Vokotopoulos 2011b.

48. Vokotopoulos 2011a.

49. Vokotopoulos 2011b.

50. Platon and Brice 1975. The palatial town was probably supported by sites such as the building at Epano Zakros (Platon 2002).

51. Chryssoulaki et al. 1990.

52. Christakis 2008, 138.

53. Christakis' language reveals this focus (2008, 138): '"Profit margins", trade economics, competition, and the size of the "home market" will all have influenced decision making' (ritual is considered in pp. 139–43).

54. Rackham and Moody 1996, 89. See also the ranking by Branigan (2001, figure 3.1) – the basis on which sites are assigned particular rankings is not always clear: Palaikastro is ranked above palatial Zakros, for example, presumably on the basis of size as well as urban infrastructure such as roads. Branigan is also hesitant to set Knossos apart from the rest.

55. Driessen 2001, 60.

56. E.g., Dickinson 1994, figure 4.22; Branigan 2001, figure 3.1; Bintliff 2012, figure 5.4.

57. E.g., Castleden 1990, figure 22.

58. In addition to regional variation, Kythera may have effectively become 'a part of Crete' in the Neopalatial period, and there is some evidence for a close relationship between inhabitants of Kastri on Kythera and Cretan Knossos: Broodbank 2004, 56, 80. The 'Minoan thalassocracy' is a long-explored phenomenon, e.g., Hägg and Marinatos 1984.

59. Hägg 1997.

60. McEnroe 1982, 3; see also McEnroe 1979.

61. McEnroe 1982.

62. As suggested in Bevan 2010, 30; see also Bevan and Wilson 2013.

63. Smith 2005, 832. Whitelaw (forthcoming) depicts Crete, in both the Protopalatial and Neopalatial periods, without boundaries, although with multiple administrative centres.

64. Adams 2006.

65. One approach that begins 'from the ground' is to chart the spread of set words and phrases as spread across the landscape, which may indicate social interactions. Whitelaw (forthcoming) drew from Nikolaos Kontosopoulos' work on vocabulary differences during the 1960s–1970s, and found that central Crete demonstrated very low levels of differentiation in glossaries, although the mountainous areas of Lasithi and Ida were barriers. In this modern time, Heraklion was the administrative centre of the island within the Greek state and road networks were reasonable, if not as efficient as today; this alone might explain why the eastern Mesara leans towards the Knossian area rather than Phaistos in terms of vocabulary. The impact of modern technological innovations such as radios (telephones and televisions would have been much less common) presumably sets this period apart from the Minoan world, but the intriguing possibility arises that possible political boundaries do not produce social barriers.

66. Adams 2006.

67. Cherry 1986; see also Bevan 2010.

68. Branigan 2001, 48.

69. Whitelaw 2001.

70. Whitelaw forthcoming.

71. Nakassis, Parkinson, and Galaty 2011.

72. Polanyi 1957.

73. Earle 2002, 82.

74. Earle 2011.

75. E.g., Halstead 2004.

76. Nakassis, Parkinson, and Galaty 2011. A criticism here is of the term's vagueness – however, as in other generally used terms (including 'elite'), this ambiguity can prove helpful, *if* the label is then qualified and further defined.

77. Evans (1921, 461–2) suggested three distinct phases, the second of which was broadly MM III, and witnessed the construction of *kaselles* for the storage of goods more valuable than agricultural produce, while in LM I the storage of oil became crucial again. The alterations in the west magazines date to LM IIIA, however (Popham 1970, 53; Christakis 2008, 40–1).

78. Margomenou 2008; Privitera 2014, 442.

79. Renfrew 1972.

80. Halstead 1981. See O'Shea 1981, Moody 1987, Branigan 1988. Moody (1987) argued that agricultural storage moved to the Villas.

81. Halstead 1981, 203; Moody 1987, 236.

82. Christakis 2008 (12–13) points to recent examples of pithoi being sold with houses.

83. Schoep 2002c, 194.

84. Christakis 2008, 121.

85. Christakis 2008, 53.

86. Christakis 2008, 120.

87. Christakis (2008, 114) points to the example of House Fg at Gournia, with no apparent storage facilities but with administrative evidence that could point to regular provisions from elsewhere. Christakis (2008, 139): 'The scenario of exchange of subsistence goods between urban and peripheral groups of not-dependent commoners fits well with the lack of substantial storage facilities observed in most LM IB houses.' Urban inhabitants were expecting trade and exchange to occur on a regular basis.

88. Christakis 2008, 110–11, 114.

89. Christakis 2008, 115.

90. Christakis 2008, 116–17.

91. In the case of the two former, this is based on the allocation of storage space. See also the mansions excavated at Nerokourou and Kastelli Pediada.

92. Christakis 2008, 117.

93. Christakis (2008, 118) distinguishes between sites that were the seat of regional political elites (e.g., Nirou Chani) and those that served as transport hubs for the mobilization of goods (e.g., Sklavokambos). It can in practice be difficult to categorize between the two functions.

94. Christakis 1999a, 1999b, 2008, *contra* Moody 1987. Nor does there appear to be a decentralization of storage in mature LM IA or LM IB as suggested by Driessen and Macdonald (1997, 53).

95. Christakis 2008, 131.

96. Christakis 2008, 53. The standard Malian pithos could take 60–120 litres, while those at Knossos could take up to 500 litres.

97. This analysis is based on the work of Christakis (2008), who treated palatial buildings in a separate chapter.

98. The evidence at Palaikastro is mixed, partly because of the poor recording of the early excavations. Some buildings had substantial

storage space, such as House B with the capacity to store more than 3,000 litres, although most houses appeared to have limited storage (Christakis 2008, 96–7). Building 5 of the modern excavations held a capacity of 1,635–2,100 litres and Building N one of 1,700–2,000 litres, but overall the structures have yielded limited evidence (Christakis 2008, 99–100).

99. At Kommos, Building T served as some kind of civic centre, although the evidence is problematic due to later building. However, the (few) medium-sized pithoi found suggest short-term or limited storage (Christakis 2008, 61).

100. At Mochlos, some houses have no evidence for storage at all, others a considerable amount: House C3 had around 2,000 litres, more than Building B2, which is a possible central building of some kind (Christakis 2008, 90).

101. At Tylissos, Building A had 18 per cent of its ground floor dedicated to storage, with ca. 10–12,000 litres capacity (Christakis 2008, 59–60, 128). Architecturally, Houses B and C appear to have been designed to hold significant numbers of pithoi, but they were found notably empty. House B may have been built as a storage annex for House A, but it yielded just three pithoi, whereas House A has produced far more.

102. Christakis 2008, 47–8. Little is known of the surrounding settlement.

103. Christakis 1999a, 118.

104. Hitchcock 2000, 594.

105. Watrous and Hadzi-Vallianou 2004, 290.

106. Most of which were destroyed in World War II.

107. Christakis 2008, 64–6.

108. Driessen and Macdonald 1997, 206–7; Christakis 2008, 69–70.

109. Marinatos 1948, 74–5; Christakis 1999a, 138.

110. Christakis 2008, 47; also Christakis 2004.

111. Christakis 2008, 120: presumably the Northeast House, which may be a palatial annex, is not included in this figure.

112. Fotou 1997. Christakis (2004, 305) notes how this type of storeroom is known from Roman, Byzantine, and traditional Crete.

113. Xanthoudides 1922, 9; Christakis 2008, 78–9.

114. Christakis 2008, 71–2. Archanes has yielded convincing evidence for the administrative control of storage (Sakellarakis and Sapouna-Sakellaraki 1997, 132–5). The cistern at Archanes indicates centralized or communal water facilities (Evans 1928, 64–7).

115. Christakis 2008, 72–3. Hence to two different figures in Figure 8.3.

116. Christakis 2008, 50. As at Knossos, there is a Linear A inscription on a pithos.

117. Christakis 2008, 48–50.

118. Strasser 1997.

119. Christakis 2008, 82–3. These were also in use in LM IB, which is unclear for the Palace.

120. Christakis 2008, 84–5.

121. Christakis 2008, 51, 85.

122. Christakis 2008, 95.

123. Christakis 2008, 51. Tsipopoulou (2002, 140), following an estimate by Christakis, suggests that the north magazines held around 20,000 litres.

124. Christakis 2008, 52.

125. This is not a new observation. Halstead and O'Shea (1982) and Branigan (1988) argued that the Palaces obtained staples for its household, dependent craftsmen, and ceremonial festivals and feasting; they do not argue that the entire population was dependent on the Palaces.

126. Halstead 2011, 231. Christakis attempts to highlight the importance of domestic units, while having to admit that the evidence from them is low.

127. In fact, Palatial-Style Jars in particular may have been placed on view: Christakis 2006, 128.

128. Evans 1903, 36, 38; 1921, 449–50.

129. E.g., Hallager 1987.

130. Graham 1956; 1987, 114–24. See Begg (1987) for the suggestion that storage also occurred on the upper floor; it may be expected that certain storage areas were needed to provide equipment and so on for such events. Note also that doubt has been thrown on the sacredness of the so-called Central Palace Sanctuary (Chapter 3). The functions of the two 'Pillar Crypts' are extremely difficult to reconstruct, and they may have been used for storage: Christakis 2004, 301.

131. Hitchcock and Preziosi 1999, 79–83. It has recently been argued that feasting and consumption played a major role in MM II Phaistos (Baldacci 2015). The covering over of the *kouloures* at Phaistos and Knossos was

such that it is unlikely that those passing over the West Courts in later years were aware of their existence.

132. Chryssoulaki 2001, 62.

133. E.g., Van Effenterre 1987.

134. Brumfiel and Earle 1987; see Smith 2004 for a review.

135. See Broodbank (2004), for example, for a discussion of the added value of pottery via particular stylistic and technological innovations.

136. For the technological side of craftsmanship, the reader is directed to Evely 1993, 2000.

137. Michaelidis 1993, 17–20.

138. Michaelidis 1993, 33.

139. Platon 1993.

140. Hazzidakis 1921, 56–7; Dimopoulou 1997, 435; Evely 2000, 343–5; *Archaeological Reports* 2001–2, 109–10.

141. Platon 1966, 149.

142. See Evans (1928, 627–33) and Georgiou (1979, 16–28) for the hoards of tools (and other vessels) at Knossos; most notable (in terms of tools) are the hoards in the Northwest House and the South House.

143. See Georgiou (1979, 29–41) for deposits of tools. Most notable are the deposits from Maison Delta Beta, Room 25, 2 in the Palace, and Room 15 in Maison Zeta Gamma (Deshayes and Dessenne 1959, 38, 68). Tools were found throughout the site, for example, in room 5 in Maison Zeta Beta, which is accessed only from the Minoan Hall (Deshayes and Dessenne 1959, 16–17, 68). MM III possible slag was found under the later north-west court (Evely 2000, 338).

144. A few bronze tools were found in Building A, e.g., chisels (Evely 1993, 8, 10) but their dating is unclear.

145. Evely 1988, 398–9; 2000.

146. Rapoport 1990.

147. Evely 1999, 137.

148. Evely 2000, 341.

149. Evely 2000, 405. Note, however, that many dates are 'unknown', and this might not be the Neopalatial picture.

150. Pullen 2010, 4.

151. Platon 1988, 1993; Evely (2000, 341) for bronze-working.

152. Evely 1993, 181.

153. Evely 1993, 244–5.

154. Platon 1988, 427.

155. Chryssoulaki and Platon 1987.

156. Evely 1993, 181, 244.

157. Evely 1993, 181.

158. Platon 1988, 425–6.

159. Dimopoulou 1997, 2004. See also the fine Marine Style ewer from a large rock-cut tomb (Dimopoulou 1999b).

160. Dimopoulou 2000.

161. Dimopoulou 1997, 437.

162. Evans 1928, 238.

163. Dimopoulou 1997, 437; 1999a; Muhly 1992. See Shaw (1978) on an elite fresco fragment.

164. Soles 2002, 124.

165. Evely 2000, 335–8. However, Platon (1988, 311) states that the identification of bronze workshops at Gournia has been based on the discovery of clay crucibles, a number of moulds (in two of the town houses), scrap metal and bronze slag, and bronze tools found together with bronze sheets.

166. Houses Ac, Db, Dd, Fj (Fotou 1993, 60–1, 74–5, 90–1).

167. Houses Ab, Ad, Ba, Bc, Cc, Ck, Eb, Fe, Fi, Fj.

168. Soles 1983.

169. Soles 2003b, 97; also Soles 1997.

170. Soles 2003b.

171. Soles 2003b, 95.

172. See Dierckx (1999) for a critique of 'workshop'. If the identification of this LM I obsidian workshop in Building BY is correct, it is the first one to be identified on Crete during the LBA (as opposed to earlier).

173. Dierckx 1999, 215.

174. Hemingway 1999.

175. Apostolakou, Betancourt, and Brogan 2010.

176. Shaw 2004.

177. Shaw 2002, 108.

178. Shaw 2002, 108.

179. Shaw et al. 2001. Evely (2000, 338–41) mentions also the melting of metals (not smelting) in the area.

180. Shaw 2002, 105.

181. Earle 2011, 242.

182. Evely, Hein, and Nodarou 2012.

183. Platon 1988, 414.

184. Platon 1988, 417.

185. Kopaca and Platon 1993.

186. Sakellarakis and Sapouna-Sakellaraki 1997, 67, 90.

187. For example, sites such as Kition demonstrate a very close spatial relationship between workshops and temples (Knapp 2008, 224–28). Parallels have been drawn (e.g., Soles 2003b, 99), but these serve to emphasize the differences.

188. See Halstead 1989, where the term 'surplus' is explored.

189. Smith 2004, 82.

190. Soles 2003b, 96. As pointed out some time ago, 'some working activities obviously took place . . . for an unspecified amount of time', but not necessarily on a permanent basis and without standardized architecture (Platon 1988, 427).

191. Soles 2003b.

9 WHO WERE THE MINOANS?

1. Myres 1930.

2. For example, Adams 2004a, 2006.

3. Renfrew 1985, 12.

4. Whitley 2006, 61–2.

5. For a recent overview of different types of Minoan identity and bibliography, see Driessen 2015.

6. There is, perhaps surprisingly, little interest in depicting the human form on pottery or as anthropomorphic vessels (Simandiraki-Grimshaw 2013).

7. Adams 2013. This paper argues that objectification can be an active process, on the basis that people have some control at least over their self-image and how they appear to others. This is a different approach to the study of agency and the individual agent, where there is a danger of imposing modern ideas of agency onto the past. It is also different from attempts to reconstruct a person's 'being-in-the-world'; past experiences are evasive. However, we may reconstruct how past notions of the body were portrayed, (re)presented, and objectified.

8. Hall 1997, 25 (original italics). See also McGowan (2011) for ambiguity in Neopalatial seal imagery.

9. Adams 2013, 18.

10. Adams 2013, 18. This is not to suggest that iconography offers snapshots of real life; quite the opposite, we need also to consider how visual imagery may *produce* social realities.

11. Logue 2004. See Blakolmer (2010a, 2012) for a consideration of the interaction between different media.

12. Perhaps surprisingly, painted pottery was not a medium selected for the depiction of figural narrative.

13. Scholars naturally attempt to date these images as closely as possible. For example, on Crete, LM IA provides the heyday of wall paintings (as preserved) with a slight drop in LM IB, while the distribution falls in line with excavated sites (Blakolmer 2000, figures 1, 2). However, the dating of individual frescoes is a contentious subject, especially on the main site of Knossos (see table 1 in Adams 2013).

14. Blakolmer 2010a. Blakolmer (personal correspondence, 30 May 2016) makes the point that there is a remarkable uniformity during MM III–LM I; after this time, we can detect a weaker continuity.

15. E.g., Hägg 1985; Cameron 1987; Kontorli-Papadopoulou 1996; Marinatos 1996.

16. E.g., Hood 2000, 2005.

17. E.g., Shaw 1997.

18. E.g., Blakolmer 2000; papers in Panagiotopoulos and Günkel-Maschek 2012.

19. Palyvou 2000.

20. Morgan 2005, 23.

21. Bennett 1961–2; Coulomb 1979; Niemeier 1988; Sherratt 2000; Waterhouse 2002; Shaw 2004b.

22. Morgan 2005, 24.

23. Palyvou 2000; see Adams 2007b on the Knossian Corridor of the Procession Fresco. While this has been dated as post-Neopalatial, it is possible that it replaced an earlier, similar style.

24. Immerwahr 1990, 50.

25. Hood, however, has generally returned to them. See, e.g., Hood 2000, 2005. See Adams 2013, table 1.

26. Immerwahr 1990, 2.

27. Blakolmer 2000, 397.

28. Blakolmer 2000, 402.

29. Morgan 2005, 21.

30. Blakolmer (2014) links this sudden appearance in the Neopalatial period with the institutionalization of (fewer) peak sanctuaries. He points out that this unique peculiarity is accepted as fact to the extent that it is rarely explicitly addressed; see also Herva 2006a; 2006b; Krzyszkowska 2010.

31. Krzyszkowska 2005, 126.

32. Weingarten 2010, 322.

33. Krzyszkowska 2012.

34. Krzyszkowska 2005, 10, fn. 23, estimates that around half are unprovenanced.

35. Evans 1928, fn. 45, figure 443. Note that this dates to slightly after the Neopalatial period.

36. Krzyszkowska 2005, 23.

37. Krzyszkowska 2005, 137.

38. See Adams 2013. Evans (1930, 522–5) reconstructed this as coming from a female statue 2.8 m high, but Marinatos and Hägg (1983) have argued that these 'locks' belong to several, much smaller statuettes. They argue that the deity appeared in the form of epiphany, rather than cult statue, but one does not exclude the other (Driessen 2000b, 92).

39. Panagiotopoulos 2012, 65.

40. Bevan 2007, 122: here described as 'material mediators between a privileged upper elite group and the divine world'. Uninscribed libation tables found at ritual sites also have an obvious cultic use (Muhly 1981).

41. Koehl 1986; Davis 1995.

42. E.g,. see Fowler 2004, 33; Van Wolputte 2004.

43. Strathern 1988; Busby 1997.

44. Adams 2013, 13.

45. Evans 1930, 506.

46. Evans 1921, 28. He seems to generally use the term in reference to nature, rather than realism; for the former, see Shapland 2010.

47. Driessen 2000b. Such is the attention to anatomical detail such as veins, it has been queried whether the Minoans learned anatomy through dissection, although it is concluded that this is unlikely (Musgrave 2000).

48. E.g., on Thera: Davis 1986; Doumas 2000. See also Simandiraki-Grimshaw 2015.

49. Hood 1985; Doumas 2000; Morgan 2000; Shaw 2004b; Morgan 2005; Chapin 2009.

50. Alberti 2002.

51. Marinatos 1989; 1993, 220.

52. Cadogan 2009; German 2005; Morris 2006; Simandiraki-Grimshaw 2010. Morris (2009b) points out that we are cultured to perceive breasts as either nurturing or erotic, and not both simultaneously. The Temple Repositories include plaques of suckling animals, although it is something of a leap to transfer this role to the Snake Goddesses.

53. Mantzourani 2012.

54. Watrous 1996, 71.

55. Tamvaki 1989.

56. An exception here is the Neopalatial faience figurine found near the early South Propylaeum of the Palace, where the hands hook over the top of the breasts (Figure 9.2B).

57. Adams 2013, 15. Bared breasts was not the universal fashion, as there are examples of clothing that was not cut away in this manner – for example, the sculptured clothing from the Temple Repositories(Figure 9.2C)

58. E.g., CMS II.3 no. 8. See Jones 2015.

59. Morgan 1995, 147–8.

60. Weingarten 2010, 323.

61. Evans (1935, 127–8) suggested that this attire belonged to a priestly class below that of the Priest-King (Marinatos 1993, 127–8), but see Marinatos (2010, 19–23), where they become kings. Davis (1995, 15–17) views them as priests, not kings; they might carry an emblem such as a club (Koehl 1995).

62. Evans 1930, 46; Koehl 1995; Goodison and Morris 1998, 130; Gere 2009. It has been suggested that this was a matrilineal society (Driessen 2012b). This is also impossible to demonstrate either way, and has fewer political ramifications.

63. E.g., Evans (1930, 42) on the women's clothing with designs of sphinxes and griffins, which belonged 'to a figure of the Goddess herself', or a 'holy robe'.

64. Davis 1995.

65. Hamilakis 2002.

66. E.g., Palaima 1995; Duhoux and Morpurgo Davies 2008.

67. Adams 2013.

68. Marinatos (2005) explores the 'expression of male prestige'; see Adams (2013).

69. Militello (1992) interprets this as a scene of the invocation of a deity. See also Jones (2014).

70. Strathern 1988, 176.

71. Adams 2013, 7–8.

72. See Younger 2008 for an alternative interpretation.

73. Evans 1928, 602–3, figures 375, 376; Evans 1921, 527, figure 384.

74. Adams 2013, 8. In the Sacred Grove and Dance Fresco, the standing, reddish figures wear only necklaces and loincloths.

75. Marinatos 1989, 39: they are 'not only watching but *being watched themselves*'.

76. Blakolmer (personal correspondence, 30 May 2016) points out that it may have been the case that no spectacle was represented at all; in this sense, we might imagine

that the crowd served as an audience to the person moving through the building.

77. Rehak 2000 (for the argument that this is not an epiphany scene, but depicts a female rite of passage); Cain 2001; see also Adams 2013, 10.

78. A parallel from Chania shows an eye and an ear (CMS VI no. 278).

79. Morgan 1995.

80. See also the procession on the Grand Staircase, which Cameron (1978, 588) dates to after the MM IIIB destruction. For processional iconography in general, see Blakolmer 2008.

81. E.g., Elsner 2007.

82. See Adams 2013, 10, fn. 52.

83. Blakolmer 2010b.

84. The latter based on their stance and fixed stare (Panagiotaki 1999, 148).

85. E.g., CMS 11.3 no. 33; CMS II.8 no. 217; CMS II.8 no. 218.

86. Kemp 1998.

87. Morgan 1995.

88. See Blakolmer 2007 for the lack of portraits (and narrative) in Minoan art.

89. Suggested by Rehak and Younger 1998, 111.

90. Parker Pearson 1999, 4; see also Adams 2013.

91. Preston 2001. She calculates (with due caveats) that there are around 270 people per generation visible in death for the whole of Crete. She further argues that the elite groups chose not to engage in visible mortuary modes of competition, and that this was a time of experimentation, particularly at Knossos.

92. We are unable, therefore, to reconstruct the 'materiality of performance' as in Mycenaean funerary practices (Boyd 2014).

93. See Rehak and Younger (1998, 110–11) for a summary of Neopalatial burial.

94. Girella 2015; see also Girella 2016.

95. Preston 2013. See also Adams 2007a.

96. At Ailias, Mavro Spelio, and the Temple Tomb area (Preston 2001). In the Mavro Spelio cemetery, a gold signet ring and a silver pin were found, both inscribed with Linear A (Forsdyke 1926–7; Godart and Olivier 1982). See Girella (2015) for the suggestion that this experimentation around Knossos was due, at least in part, to competition with mainland Greeks (but not necessarily the movement of people to Crete). See also Alberti (2013) and Preston (2013) for MM III burial practices at Knossos. Cemeteries were usually established in LM II after something of a lull in mortuary activity (Alberti 2004, 127; Preston 2004a, 138).

97. Dimopoulou 1999b. Only one has, as yet, been fully published (Muhly 1992).

98. E.g., Gazi (Hazzidakis 1921, 60–2; Pendlebury 1939, 176); Episkopi and Stavromenos (Preston 2001; see Adams 2006, figure 1 for map). There are also isolated finds of burials (e.g., at Petrokephalo and Ayios Myron; see Pendlebury, Eccles, and Money-Coutts 1932–3).

99. Dimopoulou 1999b, 2004; Muhly 1992; Dimopoulou-Rethemiotaki 2008, 135. The use of wooden biers in four of the tombs at Poros suggests links with mainland customs (Preston 2001), and this site may be atypical because of the intense external contact.

100. Hall 1912; Seager 1916; Andreadaki-Vlazaki 1987.

101. Sakellarakis and Sapouna-Sakellaraki 1997, 220–1.

102. Preston 2001.

103. Sakellarakis and Sapouna-Sakellaraki 1997, 221.

104. Cadogan 2011.

105. A rare exception is CMS V Suppl. 1B no. 153. Here a Minoan Genius supports the apparently lifeless body of a human figure over its shoulder: this would appear to be a post-Neopalatial context, however (thanks are due to Fritz Blakolmer for pointing this example out).

106. Treherne 1995.

107. Treherne 1995, 122–3.

108. Parker Pearson (1999, 86–7) refers to Childe's point that times of political instability and formative situations were often marked by big funerals.

109. Warren 1981a; Wall et al. 1986. Hughes (1991, 18–24) points out that the evidence as published could also indicate secondary burial and the removal of the remaining soft tissue from mostly decomposed bodies. See Adams 2007a, 413–14.

110. Musgrave 1984; Preston 2001. Note that this building was left unfinished, however, and the main period of occupation lies after the end of the Neopalatial period.

111. Adams 2007a.

112. Van Dyke and Alcock 2003b, 3. See Whitley (2002) for a rather forceful critique of work that emphasizes ancestors.
113. See *Archaeological Review from Cambridge* 13.2 (1994) for a focus on the archaeology of childhood.
114. Alcock focuses on social memories, but also recognizes the role of intentions, or 'active strategies' (2002, 41), which allude to the future. Ingold (1993, 153) vividly states that landscapes are 'pregnant with the past'. See also Munn 1992, 115; Barrett 1994; Gosden 1994, 144; Adams 2007a.
115. Barrett 2004, 17; see Adams 2007a.
116. Lucas 2005, 117. We should attempt to look forward with the actors as with the process of innovation (Torrence and Van der Leeuw 1989).
117. Adams 2007a.
118. Sourvinou-Inwood 1989, 249; see also Morris 2004.
119. Blakolmer 2010b, 37.
120. Crowley 1992, 25–6; also Morgan 1989; Crowley 2008. We know from the Linear B tablets that certain persons had ritual roles (Bendall 2007; Lupack 2008).
121. Blakolmer 2010b.
122. Bietak 2000b, 235; Morgan 2000, 934.
123. Krzyszkowska 2005, 142.
124. Goodison and Morris 1998; Kopaka 2009.
125. Marinatos 1940–1; Platon 1951.
126. Cameron 1987. See also Hägg 1985. This Great Goddess may have been a fusion of diverse chthonic or weather deities (Rutkowski 1986, 64, 87).
127. Evans 1928, 277. This Goddess possessed all of their distinct attributes. Marinatos (2015, 60) suggests that: 'when Evans called the religion monotheistic he did not deny multiple gods but argued instead that the unity of its cosmos was embodied in one principal female deity with many manifestations.' Peatfield (1994) suggested that there was only one Goddess before and during the Neopalatial period, but that her identity then split into several personifications.
128. Budin 2011; see also Kanta and Tzigounaki 2001.
129. Nilsson 1950.
130. Marinatos 1993, 165–6. Goodison and Morris (1998) argued that there were multiple goddesses, rather than a single 'Mother Goddess';

see also Blakolmer (2010b) for arguments for a polytheistic framework.
131. Vernon-Hunt 1988.
132. Marinatos 1993, 124.
133. Panagiotaki 1999.
134. Some have expressed doubt about the existence of anthropomorphic cult images at all: Hägg and Marinatos 1983.
135. Goodison and Morris 1998, 125.
136. Goodison and Morris 1998, 125.
137. CMS II.8 no. 237; CMS V Suppl. 1A no. 142.
138. This gesture is predominant in the Neopalatial period, and is not attested to the Protopalatial era: Tyree 2001, 42.
139. See Krzyszkowska 2005, 142 for examples.
140. E.g., Hägg 1986; Morris and Peatfield 2004.
141. Dimopoulou and Rethemiotakis 2000.
142. As appears to be the case on an example from Archanes Tholos tomb A.
143. Goodison and Morris 1998, 128.
144. See also the Throne Room at Pylos (Lang 1969). It remains unclear whether the so-called Chancel Screen Hall offered a similar stage for epiphanic ritual (Hägg 1986, 56–9).
145. In contrast, no securely dated Neopalatial examples of antithetical compositions of a male or female flanked by animals are known, but this becomes common in LM II–III glyptic (Krzyszkowska 2005, 141, 201, 204).
146. Around half of the 560 sealings in Hogarth's House A depict them: Krzyszkowska 2005, 150.
147. Krzyszkowska 2005, 152. This kind of practice is difficult to reconstruct with the range and nature of evidence at hand here.
148. Morris and Peatfield 2004.
149. Morris 2004; see also Morris and Peatfield 2004. A Cretan ring found on the Greek mainland depicts clear facial features (Elateia T. 62: Krzyszkowska 2005, 305: CMS V Suppl. 2 no. 106); two of the figures are male, in addition to a female and floating figure.
150. Panagiotaki 1999, 97. Note that these figurines were considerably reconstructed by Evans (Bonney 2011).
151. See Morris and Peatfield 2004.
152. Christakis 2010. Certainly wine was very important in the succeeding Mycenaean period (Palmer 1994).

153. Evans 1930, 315.
154. Morris and Peatfield 2004.
155. Chapin 2004, 57.
156. The boundary between images that have been decreed 'talismanic' and those that are 'naturalistic' is blurred. The former style used motifs from the natural world, and no positive evidence supports a talismanic function (Krzyszkowska 2005, 133).
157. E.g., CMS II. 6 no. 37 (from Ayia Triada) and CMS V Suppl. 1A no. 135 (from Chania) (Krzyszkowska 2005, 138–9).
158. Hallager and Hallager 1995. Not all subscribe to the idea that the bull, and bull-leaping scenes, was an emblem of Knossian authority (e.g., Krzyszkowska 2005, 141).
159. Shapland (2013) emphasizes the social significance of this practice, rather than ascribing it to the symbolic (religious) sphere. The two interpretations are not mutually incompatible, however. For accounts of Minoan representations, see, for example, Younger 1995. For Minoan frescoes with bull-leaping outside Crete, see Bietak, Marinatos and Palyvou 2007.
160. Shapland 2010, 124.
161. Watrous 2004, 145.
162. Shapland 2010, 124.
163. However, Shapland (2010) argues that they are two different ontologies.
164. Peatfield 1990, 125.
165. Starr 1984.
166. See, e.g., Morgan 2005, 29; Marinatos (1984) emphasizes the ritual nature of the Akrotiri frescoes. However, Goodison and Morris (1998, 126–8) suggest that the association with the crocus and saffron may indicate an economic power as well.
167. Evans 1901. See more recently Morris 2004; Marinatos 1990; Warren 1990. It is possible that the Minoans believed that gods resided in the mountains. Peatfield (1990, 120) has pointed out that, if this was the case, then the accessibility and intervisibility of peak sanctuaries suggests that human interaction was the focus. Or, rather than viewing the mountain as the home of the god, the emphasis was on the human–divine relationship, the worship and the rituals. Once at the peak sanctuary, however, the ritual may have involved epiphany.
168. Evans 1935, 947–56; Sakellarakis and Sapouna-Sakellaraki 1997, 654–9;

Dimopoulou and Rethemiotakis 2000; CMS I no. 126; CMS I no. 219.
169. Warren 1990; Goodison and Morris 1998, 128; Goodison 2009; Younger 2009a; see Cain 2001 for the difficulties in interpreting such evidence.
170. Warren 1990; Goodison 2009; Younger 2009a.
171. Herva 2006a, 233; 2006b, 591.
172. For example, Wiener (1990, 15) sets a 'unified Crete' against various Cycladic islands.
173. This stems from the Latin word that can also mean 'building block' of flats, with a sense of community and shared living; so a cut-off entity is assumed to be homogeneous within (Constantakopoulou 2007, 3; Adams 2010, 2). See Momigliano (2009) for a convincing attempt to lift the cultural term 'Minoan' from a strictly Cretan base.
174. Doumas 2004; Constantakopoulou 2007, 15.
175. Evans 1973; critiques by Broodbank 2000, 26–7; Constantakopoulou 2007; Rainbird 2007; Knapp 2008. Rainbird (2007, 1) describes the study of islands as 'the study of movement', entailing a fluid archaeology of the sea. Horden and Purcell (2000) rightly emphasize the role of the sea in the Mediterranean; this role is particularly pertinent in the Aegean context (e.g., Broodbank 2000). Other Aegean islands might be more easily accessible from the north-central part of Crete than other areas of the island itself, especially given the dangers of hugging the north coast (Rackham and Moody 1996, 194).
176. Adams 2010.
177. E.g., Popham 1994; Wiener 2015b.
178. E.g., Preston 1999, 2004a, 2004b; Bennet 2008.
179. E.g., Driessen and Langhor 2007.
180. Alexiou 1980, 39–40; Hägg and Marinatos 1984; Broodbank 2004. Niemeier (2009) remains one of the strongest advocates for Cretan supremacy in the Aegean during the Neopalatial period; see also Wiener 1990.
181. Hägg and Marinatos 1984; Niemeier 2009, 18–20. Classical references include Herodotus III 122; Thucydides 1, 4.1.
182. Von Rüden 2014.
183. E.g., Chryssoulaki 2005; Kopaka 2005;
184. Karpathos (Melas 2009); Lemnos (Boulotis 2009).
185. Teichiussa (Voigtländer 2009); Iasos (Momigliano 2009).

186. E.g., Niemeier 2009.
187. Warren 2009a, 265.
188. Knappett and Nikolakopoulou 2008.
189. Nikolakopoulou 2009, 34.
190. Niemeier and Niemeier 1999; Niemeier 2005.
191. Graziadio 2005.
192. Wiener 1984. While scholars are quick to quote Wiener's 'Versailles effect' as cultural influence in contrast to full colonization, Wiener's stance is more accepting of the idea of Minoan (or rather Knossian) control than this – Thera, for example, was probably 'subject to the ultimate authority, perhaps expressed primarily through cult and ritual, of Knossos' (Wiener 1990, 154).
193. Mountjoy 1985. While Marine Style shapes were not made exclusively for ritual, they were present in many probable ritual contexts. See also Vandenabeel 1991; Haysom 2011; Berg 2013; for ship imagery, see Wedde 2000.
194. Chryssoulaki 2001, 61–2.
195. Shapland 2010, 118.
196. Helms (1988) gives a clear account of how the act of interaction itself can enhance social status and therefore one's standing in a community; see also Sherratt and Sherratt 1991.
197. Crowley 1991; 2013, 349.
198. E.g., Knapp 1990.
199. Bietak, Marinatos, and Palyvou 2000, 79. Hood (in discussion to Bietak, Marinatos, and Palyvou 2000, 89) considers this influence to be more likely Syrian than Minoan, or rather, Knossian; the training and influence may also be more international (Morgan in discussion to Bietak, Marinatos, and Palyvou 2000, 90).
200. More specifically, he dates it to the reign of Thutmose III (equivalent to LM IB): Bietak, Marinatos, and Palyvou 2007; see also Bietak 2013.
201. In addition to the slight confusion caused by the change from the date of the earlier Hyskos to later 18th Dynasty periods, it has also been argued that the wall paintings could equate to LM II or later (Shaw 2009, 475; Younger 2009b). Since no definite consensus has been reached, LM IB provides a happy medium.
202. It is further tempting, if unsubstantiated, to link the maze pattern with the labyrinth of myth. Bietak (2005, 89) suggests that this was a symbol of the Knossian Palace. However, it has been pointed out that the practice of superimposing a figural scene over such a pattern is 'un-Minoan' (Shaw 2009, 473).
203. Brysbaert 2002, 2008.
204. Shaw 2009, 473.
205. Von Rüden 2015, 358. Cline (1998a, 209–10) had previously pointed out that the nationality (or, rather, 'ethnicity') of the painters as Minoan was hypothesized rather than proven, in addition to venting some frustration over the change of dates for the wall paintings from the Hyksos occupation of Avaris to the 18th Dynasty. Other scholars continued to argue for a date in the Hyksos period (Niemeier and Niemeier 1998, 85–8: here they suggest that the fragments came from two periods, the late Hyksos and the early 18th Dynasty). See Bietak (2000c) for a rigorous defence of his position, and the Minoan (or 'Knossian') inspiration of the paintings is followed by other scholars (e.g., Shaw 2009; but note that she identifies influence from other cultures as well, so the composition becomes a hybrid one). For our purposes, the date of these wall paintings would seem to be Neopalatial; the difference is whether they are early or late, and associated with the Hyksos or 18th Dynasty regime.
206. Sherratt 1994.
207. Cline 1998a, 210.
208. Warren 1969, 14–17.
209. This association between Cretans and Keftiu has long been recognized: see Hall 1901–2; Wachsman 1987; Rehak 1996. An inscribed statue base from the mortuary temple of Amenhotep III at Kom el-Hetan claims that the Keftiu were subjects under Egyptian rule, but this is fourteenth century (reign 1391–1353 BC). Also, this may be an exaggeration, however – a claim made to enhance local standing (Liverani 1990). Minoan place names have been identified, including Knossos, Phaistos, and Amnissos: Cline 1998b.
210. Panagiotopoulos 2001.
211. Bietak 2010.
212. Cross-dating remains a debated area, but the tombs with Keftiu seem to date between 1480 and 1380 (Panagiotopoulos 2001, 263).
213. Blakolmer 2015, 197. See also Warren 1995.
214. Philips 2006.

215. Warren 1989; Bevan 2007, 124. Warren (1989, 8) concludes that the Neopalatial contexts suggest a 'semi-free merchant model'.
216. Philips 2006, 297; Bevan 2007, 125. Philips cites more than thirty examples of converted vessels, and points out that the Minoan culture is the only one where this practice occurred.
217. Blakolmer 2015. See also Weingarten 1991b.
218. Philips 2008; Blakolmer 2015.
219. Blakolmer 2010b, 2012.

10   CONCLUSION

1. Adams 2007a.
2. E.g., Bevan 2010 and Whitelaw forthcoming.
3. Poursat 2010, 265.
4. Adams 2010.
5. Renfrew and Cherry 1986.
6. We will always be unclear about where features originated and how they influenced other areas. One intriguing case from an earlier period illustrates this. Peatfield refers to Watrous' idea that Cretan peak sanctuaries were imported from the Near East (Peatfield 1992, 123; Watrous 1987). The site of Nahariyah is used to support this idea, but Peatfield points out that its excavator had assumed that the influence had come from Crete, quite the opposite. It is quite common for excavators to look elsewhere for the inspiration for the features found on the sites they are excavating. This helps create an explanatory narrative for what they are finding. This may also explain why excavators are so willing to see the hand of Knossos at 'their' sites.
7. Geertz 1980.
8. Adams 2010.
9. Geertz 1980, 15.
10. Warren 2012a, 266.
11. Adams 2006.
12. Adams 2004a.
13. Stein 1994, 13.
14. Evans 1921, 13.
15. Adams 2004b.
16. The lack of urban shrines (or temples) remains notable, and this is one of the key ways in which Neopalatial Crete stands out from other eastern Mediterranean cultures.

BIBLIOGRAPHY

Adam, B. 1990. *Time and Social Theory.* Cambridge: Polity Press.

Adam, B. 2004. *Time.* Cambridge: Polity Press.

Adams, E. 2004a. 'Power relations in Minoan palatial towns: an analysis of Neopalatial Knossos and Malia.' *Journal of Mediterranean Archaeology* 17: 191–222.

Adams, E. 2004b. 'Power and ritual in Neopalatial Crete: a regional comparison.' *World Archaeology* 36: 26–42.

Adams, E. 2006. 'Social strategies and spatial dynamics in Neopalatial Crete: an analysis of the north-central area.' *American Journal of Archaeology* 110: 1–36.

Adams, E. 2007a. '*Time and Chance*: unravelling temporality in north-central Neopalatial Crete.' *American Journal of Archaeology* 111: 391–421.

Adams, E. 2007b. 'Approaching monuments in the prehistoric built environment: new light on the Minoan palaces.' *Oxford Journal of Archaeology* 26: 359–94.

Adams, E. 2010. 'Centrality, "capitals" and prehistoric cultures: a comparative study of Late Bronze Age Crete and Cyprus.' *Cambridge Classical Journal* 56: 1–46.

Adams, E. 2013. 'Representing, objectifying, and framing the body at Late Bronze Age Knossos.' *Bulletin of the Institute of Classical Studies* 56: 1–25.

Adams, E. n.d. 'From Grand Tour to professionalized archaeology: Britain 1870–1901.' In U. Hansson (ed.), *Classical Archaeology in the Late Nineteenth Century*.

Alberti, B. 2002. 'Gender and the figurative art of Late Bronze Age Knossos.' In Y. Hamilakis (ed.), *Labyrinth Revisited: Rethinking 'Minoan' Archaeology*. Oxford: Oxbow: 98–117.

Alberti, L. 2004. 'The Late Minoan II–IIIA1 warrior graves at Knossos: the burial assemblages.' In G. Cadogan, E. Hatzaki, and A. Vasilakis (eds.), *Knossos: Palace, City, State.* British School at Athens Studies 12. London: British School at Athens: 127–36.

Alberti, L. 2013. 'Middle Minoan III burial customs at Knossos: a *pianissimo intermezzo*?' In C. F. Macdonald and C. Knappett (eds.), *Intermezzo: Intermediacy and Regeneration in Middle Minoan III Palatial Crete*. London: British School at Athens: 47–56.

Alcock, S. 1991. 'Urban survey and the polis of Phlius.' *Hesperia* 60: 421–63.

Alcock, S. 2002. *Archaeologies of the Greek Past: Landscapes, Monuments, and Memories.* Cambridge: Cambridge University Press.

Alexiou, S. 1963. 'I archaiologiki kinisis en Kriti kata ta eti 1961–1963.' *Kretika Chronika* 17: 382–412.

Alexiou, S. 1966. 'I archaiologiki kinisis en Kriti kata to 1966.' *Kretika Chronika* 20: 319–26.

Alexiou, S. 1972. 'Peri ton Minoikon "deksamenon katharmou".' *Kretika Chronika* 24: 414–34.

Alexiou, S. 1980 (4th revised ed.). [Trans. C. Ridley]. *Minoan Civilization.* Herakleion: Kouvidis-Manouras Co.

Alexiou, S. and W. Brice. 1972. 'A silver pin from Mavro Spelio with an inscription in Linear A: Her. Mus. 540.' *Kadmos* 11: 113–24.

Alexiou, S. and W. Brice. 1976. 'A silver pin from Platanos with an inscription in Linear A: Her. Mus. 498.' *Kadmos* 15: 18–27.

Anastasiadou, M. 2016a. 'Drawing the line: seals, script, and regionalism in Protopalatial Crete.' *American Journal of Archaeology* 120: 159–93.

Anastasiadou, M. 2016b. 'Wings, heads, tails: small puzzles at LM I Zakros.' In E. Alram-Stern, F. Blakolmer, S. Deger-Jalkotzy, R. Laffineur, and J. Weilhartner (eds.), *Metaphysis: Ritual, Myth and Symbolism in the Aegean Bronze Age*. Aegaeum 39. Leuven – Liège: Peeters: 79–85.

Andreadaki-Vlazaki, M. 1987. 'Omada neoa-naktorikon aggeion apo ton Stavromeno Rethymnis.' In L. Kastrinaki, G. Orphanou, and N. Giannadakis (eds.), *EILAPINI: Tomos Timitikos gia ton Kathigiti Nikolao Platona*. Herakleion: Demos Herakliou: 55–68.

Andreadaki-Vlazaki, M. 2002. 'Are we approaching the Minoan palace of Khania?' In J. Driessen, I. Schoep, and R. Laffineur (eds.), *Monuments of Minos: Rethinking the Minoan Palaces*. Aegaeum 23. Liège and Austin: Université de Liège, Histoire de l'art et archéologie de la Grèce antique and University of Texas at Austin, Program in Aegean Scripts and Prehistory: 157–66.

Andreadaki-Vlazaki, M. 2004. 'The region of Mylopotamos in antiquity.' In N. Stampolidis (ed.), *Eleutherna: Polis – Acropolis – Necropolis*. Athens: Ministry of Culture, University of Crete, Museum of Cycladic Art: 26–45.

Andreadaki-Vlazaki, M. 2005. 'Cultes et divinités dans la ville minoenne de la Canée. Quelques réflexions.' In I. Bradfer-Burdet, B. Detournay, and R. Laffineur (eds.), *Kris Technitis: L'Artisan Crétois*. Aegaeum 26. Liège and Austin: Université de Liège, Histoire de l'art et archéologie de la Grèce antique and University of Texas at Austin, Program in Aegean Scripts and Prehistory: 17–28.

Andreadaki-Vlazaki, M. 2009. *Khania (Kydonia): A Tour of Sites of Ancient Memory*. [Bilingual with Greek]. Chania: Ministry of Culture and Tourism.

Andreadaki-Vlazaki, M. 2010. 'Khania (Kydonia).' In E. H. Cline (ed.), *The Oxford Handbook of the Bronze Age Aegean (ca. 3000–1000 BC)*. Oxford: Oxford University Press: 518–28.

Andreadaki-Vlazaki, M. 2011. 'LM IB pottery in Khania.' In T. M. Brogan and E. Hallager (eds.), *LM IB Pottery: Relative Chronology and Regional Differences*. Monographs of the Danish Institute at Athens, Volume 11.1. Athens: Danish Institute at Athens: 55–74.

Andreadaki-Vlazaki, M. and E. Hallager. 2007. 'New and unpublished Linear A and Linear B inscriptions from Khania.' *Proceedings of the Danish Institute at Athens* 5: 7–22.

Apostolakou, V., P. P. Betancourt, and T. Brogan. 2010. 'Anaskafikes Erevnes stin Pacheia Ammo kai ti Chrysi Ierapetras.' *Archaiologiko Ergo Kritis* 1: 143–54.

Archaeology in Greece Online: www.chronique.efa.gr.

Aronsson, P. and G. Elgenius (eds.). 2014. *National Museums and Nation-Building in Europe 1750–2010: Mobilization and Legitimacy, Continuity and Change*. London: Routledge.

Baillie, M. 1996. 'The chronology of the Bronze Age 2354 BC to 431 BC.' In K. Randsborg (ed.), *Absolute Chronology: Archaeological Europe 2500–500 BC*. ActaArch 67, ActaArch Supplement I. Copenhagen: Munksgaard: 291–8.

Baldacci, G. 2015. 'The places and the role of consumption in MM II Phaistos.' In S. Cappel, U. Günkel-Maschek, and D. Panagiotopoulos (eds.), *Minoan Archaeology: Perspectives for the 21st Century*. Louvain-la-Neuve: Presses universitaires de Louvain: 95–108.

Banou, E. 2008. 'Minoan "Horns of Consecration" revisited: a symbol of sun worship in Palatial and Post-Palatial Crete?' *Mediterranean Archaeology and Archaeometry* 8: 27–47.

Barnard, K. A. and T. M. Brogan. 2003. *Mochlos IB. Period III. Neopalatial Settlement on the Coast: The Artisans' Quarter and the Farmhouse at Chalinomouri. The Neopalatial Pottery*. Prehistory Monographs 8. Philadelphia, PA: INSTAP Academic Press.

Barrett, J. C. 1994. *Fragments from Antiquity: An Archaeology of Social Life in Britain, 2900–1200 BC*. Oxford: Blackwell.

Barrett, J. C. 2004. 'Temporality and the study of prehistory.' In R. M. Rosen (ed.), *Time and Temporality in the Ancient World*. Philadelphia: University of Pennsylvania Museum of Archaeology and Anthropology: 11–27.

Barrett, J. C. and P. Halstead (eds.). 2004. *The Emergence of Civilisation Revisited*. Oxford: Oxbow Books.

Baurain, C. and P. Darcque. 1983. 'Un triton en pierre à Malia.' *Bulletin de Correspondance Hellénique* 107: 3–73.

Begg, D. 1975. 'Minoan storerooms in the Late Bronze Age.' PhD diss., University of Toronto.

Begg, D. 1987. 'Continuity in the west wing at Knossos.' In R. Hägg and N. Marinatos (eds.), *The Function of the Minoan Palaces*. Skrifter Utgivna av Svenska Institutet I Athen, 4°35. Stockholm: Paul Åströms Förlag: 179–84.

Begg, D. 2004. 'An archaeology of palatial mason's marks on Crete.' In A. Chapin (ed.), *CHARIS: Essays in Honor of Sara Immerwahr*. Hesperia Supp. 33. Princeton, NJ: American School of Classical Studies at Athens: 1–25.

Bell, C. 1997. *Ritual: Perspectives and Dimensions*. New York and Oxford: Oxford University Press.

Bell, C. 2007. 'Defining the need for a definition.' In E. Kyriakidis (ed.), *The Archaeology of Ritual*. Los Angeles: University of California at Los Angeles: 277–88.

Bendall, L. M. 2007. *Economics of Religion in the Mycenaean World: Resources Dedicated to Religion in the Mycenaean Palace Economy*. Oxford: Oxbow Books.

Bennet, J. 1990. 'Knossos in context: comparative perspectives on the Linear B administration of LM II–III Crete.' *American Journal of Archaeology* 94: 193–212.

Bennet, J. 2002. 'Millennial ambiguities.' In Y. Hamilakis (ed.), *Labyrinth Revisited: Rethinking 'Minoan' Archaeology*. Oxford: Oxbow Books: 214–25.

Bennet, J. 2008. 'Now you see it; now you don't! The disappearance of the Linear A script on Crete.' In J. Baines, J. Bennet, and S. Houston (eds.), *The Disappearance of Writing Systems: Perspectives on Literacy and Communication*. London: Equinox: 1–29.

Bennet, J. 2013. 'Crete (prehistoric).' *Archaeological Reports* 2012–13: 56–67.

Bennett, E. L. 1961–2. 'On the use and misuse of the term "priest-king" in Minoan studies.' *Kretika Chronika* 15–16: 327–35.

Bennett, E. L. 1985. 'Linear A houses of cards.' *Cretological Congress*: 47–56.

Berg, I. 2013. 'Marine creatures and the sea in Bronze Age Greece: ambiguities of meaning.' *Journal of Maritime Archaeology* 8: 1–27.

Beschi, L., A. Di Vita, V. La Rosa, G. Pugliese Carratelli, and G. Rizza (eds.). 2001. *I Cento Anni dello Scavo di Festòs*. Atti dei Convegni Lincei 173. Rome: Accademia Nazionale de Lincei.

Best, J. G. P. 1976. 'An analysis of the Linear A tablet HT 12.' *Kadmos* 15: 97–101.

Betancourt, P. P. 1985a. *The History of Minoan Pottery*. Princeton, NJ: Princeton University Press.

Betancourt, P. P. 1985b. 'A Great Minoan Triangle: the changing character of Phaistos, Hagia Triadha, and Kommos during the Middle Minoan IB–Late Minoan III periods.' *Scripta Mediterranea* 6: 31–43.

Betancourt, P. P. 1995. 'Pseira, Crete: the economic base for a Bronze Age town.' In R. Laffineur and W.-D. Niemeier (eds.), *Politeia: Society and State in the Aegean Bronze Age*. Aegaeum 12. Liège and Austin: Université de Liège, Histoire de l'art et archéologie de la Grèce antique and University of Texas at Austin, Program in Aegean Scripts and Prehistory: 163–7.

Betancourt, P. P. 1998. 'The chronology of the Aegean Late Bronze Age: unanswered questions.' In M. S. Balmuth and R. H. Tykot (eds.), *Sardinian and Aegean Chronology: Towards the Resolution of Relative and Absolute Dating in the Mediterranean*. Studies in Sardinian Archaeology 5. Oxford: Oxbow Books: 291–6.

Betancourt, P. P. 1999. 'Summary and discussion of Area B.' In P. P. Betancourt and C. Davaras (eds.), *Pseira IV: Minoan Buildings in Areas B, C, D, and F*. University Museum Monograph 105. Philadelphia: University of Pennsylvania: 297–302.

Betancourt, P. P. 2001. 'The household shrine in the House of the Rhyta at Pseira.' In R. Laffineur and R. Hägg (eds.), *Potnia: Deities and Religion in the Aegean Bronze Age*. Aegaeum 22. Liège and Austin: Université de Liège, Histoire de l'art et archéologie de la Grèce antique and University of Texas at Austin, Program in Aegean Scripts and Prehistory: 145–9.

Betancourt, P. P. 2002. 'Who was in charge of the Palaces?' In J. Driessen, I. Schoep, and R. Laffineur (eds.), *Monuments of Minos: Rethinking the Minoan Palaces*. Aegaeum 23. Liège and Austin: Université de Liège, Histoire de l'art et archéologie de la Grèce antique and University of Texas at Austin, Program in Aegean Scripts and Prehistory: 207–11.

Betancourt, P. P. 2004. 'Pseira and Knossos: the transformation of an East Cretan seaport.' In L. Preston Day, M. S. Mook, and J. D. Muhly (eds.), *Crete Beyond the Palaces: Proceedings of the Crete 2000 Conference*. Prehistory Monographs 10. Philadelphia. PA: INSTAP Academic Press: 21–8.

Betancourt, P. P. 2009. 'Evidence from Pseira for the Santorini eruption.' In D. A. Warburton (ed.), *Time's Up! Dating the Minoan Eruption of Santorini*. Monographs of the Danish Institute at Athens 10. Athens: Danish Institute at Athens: 101–5.

Betancourt, P. P. 2011. 'Pottery at Pseira in LM IB.' In T. M. Brogan and E. Hallager (eds.), *LM IB Pottery: Relative Chronology and Regional Differences*. Monographs of the Danish Institute at Athens 11.2. Athens: Danish Institute at Athens: 401–12.

Betancourt, P. P. 2012. *The Dams and Water Management Systems of Minoan Pseira*. Philadelphia, PA: INSTAP Academic Press.

Betancourt, P. P. 2013. 'Transitional Middle Minoan III–Late Minoan IA pottery at Kommos revisited.' In C. F. Macdonald and C. Knappett (eds.), *Intermezzo: Intermediacy and Regeneration in Middle Minoan III Palatial Crete*. British School at Athens Studies 21. London: British School at Athens: 145–8.

Betancourt, P. P. and C. Davaras. 1988. 'Excavations at Pseira.' *Hesperia* 57: 207–25.

Betancourt, P. P. and C. Davaras. 1998. *Pseira II: Building AC (the Shrine) and other Buildings in Area A*. University Museum Monograph 94. Philadelphia: University of Pennsylvania.

Betancourt, P. P., C. Davaras, and R. Hope Simpson (eds.). 2004. *Pseira: The Pseira Island Survey, Part 1 v. 8*. Philadelphia, PA: INSTAP Academic Press.

Betancourt, P. P., C. Davaras, and R. Hope Simpson (eds.). 2005. *Pseira: The Pseira Island Survey, Part 2 v. 9*. Philadelphia, PA: INSTAP Academic Press.

Betancourt, P. P. and R. Hope Simpson. 1992. 'The agricultural system of Bronze Age Pseira.' *Cretan Studies* 3: 47–54.

Betancourt, P. P. and N. Marinatos. 1994. 'Investigations at the Amnissos Cave.' *American Journal of Archaeology* 98: 306.

Betts, J. M. 1967. 'New light on Minoan bureaucracy.' *Kadmos* 6: 17–40.

Bevan, A. 2007. *Stone Vessels and Values in the Bronze Age Mediterranean*. Cambridge: Cambridge University Press.

Bevan, A. 2010. 'Political geography and palatial Crete.' *Journal of Mediterranean Archaeology* 23: 27–54.

Bevan, A. and A. Wilson. 2013. 'Models of settlement hierarchy based on partial evidence.' *Journal of Archaeological Science* 40: 2415–27.

Bietak, M. 2000a. 'Introduction to this research programme.' In M. Bietak (ed.), *The Synchronisation of Civilisations in the Eastern Mediterranean in the Second Millennium BC: Vol. 1*. Vienna: Österreichischen Akademie de Wissenschaften: 11–12.

Bietak, M. 2000b. 'The mode of representation in Egyptian art in comparison to Aegean Bronze Age art.' In S. Sherratt (ed.), *The Wall Paintings of Thera*. Athens: Thera Foundation: 209–46.

Bietak, M. 2000c. 'Rich beyond the dreams of Avaris: Tell el-Dab'a and the Aegean World: a guide for the perplexed: a response to Eric H. Cline.' *Annual of the British School at Athens* 95: 185–205.

Bietak, M. 2003. 'Science versus archaeology: problems and consequences of high Aegean chronology.' In M. Bietak (ed.), *The Synchronisation of Civilisations in the Eastern Mediterranean in the Second Millennium B.C. II*. Vienna: Österreichischen Akademie der Wissenschaften: 23–33.

Bietak, M. 2005. 'The setting of the Minoan wall paintings at Avaris.' In L. Morgan (ed.), *Aegean Wall Painting: A Tribute to Mark Cameron*. British School at Athens Studies 13. London: British School at Athens: 83–90.

Bietak, M. 2010. 'Minoan presence in the pharaonic naval base of Peru-nefer.' In O. Krzyszkowska (ed.), *Cretan Offerings: Studies in Honour of Peter Warren*. British School at Athens Studies 18. London: British School at Athens: 11–24.

Bietak, M. 2013. 'The impact of Minoan art on Egypt and the Levant: a glimpse of palatial art from the naval base of Peru-nefer at Averis.' In J. Aruz, S. B. Graff, and Y. Rakie (eds.), *Cultures in Context from Mesopotamia to the Mediterranean in the Second Millennium BC*. New York: Metropolitan Museum of Art: 188–99.

Bietak, M., N. Marinatos, and C. Palyvou. 2000. 'The Maze Tableau from Tell el Dab'a.' In S. Sherratt (ed.), *The Wall Paintings of Thera: Vol. 1. Proceedings of the First International Symposium*. Athens: The Thera Foundation: 77–90.

Bietak, M., N. Marinatos, and C. Palyvou. 2007. *Taureador Scenes in Tell El-Dab'a (Avaris) and Knossos*. Denkschriften der Gesamtakademie XLIII. Vienna: Verlag der Österreichischen Akademie der Wissenschaften.

Binford, L. 1981. 'Behavioral archaeology and the "Pompeii Premise".' *Journal of Anthropological Research* 37: 195–208.

Bintliff, J. (ed.). 1991. *The Annales School and Archaeology*. Leicester: Leicester University Press.

Bintliff, J. 2012. *The Complete Archaeology of Greece: From Hunter-Gatherers to the 20th Century A.D.* Oxford: Wiley-Blackwell.

Blackman, D. and K. Branigan. 1975. 'An archaeological survey of the south coast of Crete, between the Ayiofarango and Chrisostomos.' *Annual of the British School at Athens* 70: 17–36.

Blackman, D. and K. Branigan. 1977. 'An archaeological survey of the lower catchment of the Ayiofarango Valley.' *Annual of the British School at Athens* 72: 13–84.

Blakolmer, F. 2000. 'The functions of wall painting and other forms of architectural decoration in the Aegean Bronze Age.' In S. Sherratt (ed.), *The Wall Paintings of Thera: Vol. 1. Proceedings of the First International Symposium*. Athens: The Thera Foundation: 393–412.

Blakolmer, F. 2007. 'The silver battle krater from shaft grave IV at Mycenae: evidence of fighting "heroes" on Minoan Palace walls at Knossos?' In S. Morris and R. Laffineur (eds.), *Epos: Reconsidering Greek Epic and Aegean Bronze Age Archaeology*. Aegaeum 28. Liège and Austin: Université de Liège, Histoire de l'art et archéologie de la Grèce antique and University of Texas at Austin, Program in Aegean Scripts and Prehistory: 213–24.

Blakolmer, F. 2008. 'Processions in Aegean iconography II: who are the participants?' In L. Hitchcock, R. Laffineur, and J. Crowley (eds.), *Dais: The Aegean Feast*. Aegaeum 29. Liège and Austin: Université de Liège, Histoire de l'art et archéologie de la Grèce antique and University of Texas at Austin, Program in Aegean Scripts and Prehistory: 257–68.

Blakolmer, F. 2010a. 'Small is beautiful. The significance of Aegean glyptic for the study of wall paintings, relief frescoes and minor relief arts.' In W. Müller (ed.), *Die Bedeutung derminoischen und mykenischen Glyptik. VI. CMS Beih. 8*. Berlin: Verlag Philipp von Zabern: 91–108.

Blakolmer, F. 2010b. 'A pantheon without attributes? Goddesses and gods in Minoan and Mycenaean iconography.' In J. Mylonopoulos (ed.), *Divine Images and Human Imaginations in Ancient Greece and Rome*. Religions in the Graeco-Roman World 170. Leiden and Boston: Brill.

Blakolmer, F. 2012. 'Image and architecture: reflections of mural iconography in seal images and other art forms of Minoan Crete.' In D. Panagiotopoulos and U. Günkel-Maschek (eds.), *Minoan Realities. Approaches to Images, Architecture and Society in the Aegean Bronze Age*. Aegis 5. Louvain: Presses Universitaires de Louvain: 83–114.

Blakolmer, F. 2014. 'Meaningful landscapes: Minoan "landscape rooms" and peak sanctuaries.' In G. Touchais, R. Laffineur, and F. Rougemont (eds.), *Physis: L'Environnement Naturel et la Relation Homme-Milieu dans le Monde Égéen Protohistorique*. Aegaeum 37. Leuven – Liège: Peeters: 121–9.

Blakolmer, F. 2015. 'The many-faced "Minoan Genius" and his iconographical prototype Taweret. On the character of Near Eastern religious motifs in Neopalatial Crete.' In J. Mynárová, P. Onderka, and P. Pavúk (eds.), *The Crossroads II, or There and Back Again*. Conference at Prague, 15–17 September 2014. Prague: Charles University in Prague: 197–219.

Blakolmer, F. 2016. 'Hierarchy and symbolism of animals and mythical creatures in the Aegean Bronze Age: a statistical and contextual approach.' In E. Alram-Stern, F. Blakolmer, S. Deger-Jalkotzy, R. Laffineur, and J. Weilhartner (eds.), *Metaphysis: Ritual, Myth and Symbolism in the Aegean Bronze Age*. Aegaeum 39. Leuven – Liège: Peeters: 61–8.

Bonney, E. M. 2011. 'Disarming the Snake Goddess: a reconsideration of the faience figurines from the Temple Repositories at Knossos.' *Journal of Mediterranean Archaeology* 24: 171–90.

Boskamp, A. 1996. 'Minoan storage capacities (I): graffiti on pithoi in the palace magazines at Knossos.' *Annual of the British School at Athens* 91: 101–12.

Boulotis, C. 2008. 'From mythical Minos to the search for Cretan kingship.' In *From the Land of the Labyrinth: Minoan Crete, 3000–1100 BC*. Exhibition Catalogue, Onassis Cultural Center, New York [2008]: 44–55.

Boulotis, C. 2009. 'Koukonisi on Lemnos: reflections on the Minoan and Minoanising evidence.' In C. F. Macdonald, E. Hallager, and W.-D. Niemeier (eds.), *The Minoans in the Central, Eastern and Northern Aegean – New Evidence*. Monographs of the Danish Institute at Athens 8. Athens: Danish Institute at Athens: 175–218.

Bourdieu, P. 1977. *Outline of a Theory of Practice*. [Translated by R. Nice.] Cambridge: Cambridge University Press.

Boyd, M. 2014. 'The materiality of performance in Mycenaean funerary practices.' *World Archaeology* 46: 192–205.

Boyd Hawes, H., B. Williams, R. Seager, and E. Hall. 1908. *Gournia, Vasiliki and Other Prehistoric Sites on the Isthmus of Ierapetra, Crete*. Philadelphia, PA: American Exploration Society.

Bradley, R. 2002. *The Past in Prehistoric Societies*. London and New York: Routledge.

Branigan, K. 1983. 'Craft specialization in Minoan Crete.' In O. Krzyszkowska and L. Nixon (eds.), *Minoan Society*. Bristol: Bristol Classical Press: 23–32.

Branigan, K. 1988. 'Social security and the state in Middle Bronze Age Crete.' In R. Laffineur (ed.), *Aegaeum 2*. Liège: Université de Liège, Histoire de l'art et archéologie de la Grèce antique: 11–16.

Branigan, K. 2001. 'Aspects of Minoan urbanism.' in K. Branigan (ed.), *Urbanism in the Aegean Bronze Age*. Sheffield: Sheffield Academic Press: 38–50.

Bredaki, M., F. Longo, and M. Benzi. 2012. 'Phaistos project: preliminary results of the 2009–2010 survey campaigns.' In M. Andrianakis, P. Barthalitou, and I. Tzachili (eds.), *Archaiologiko Ergo Kritis 2*. Rethymnon: Philosophical School of Crete University: 274–87.

Briault, C. 2007a. 'High fidelity or Chinese whispers? Cult symbols and ritual transmission in the Bronze Age Aegean.' *Journal of Mediterranean Archaeology* 20: 239–65.

Briault, C. 2007b. 'Making mountains out of molehills in the Bronze Age Aegean: visibility, ritual kits and the idea of a peak sanctuary.' *World Archaeology* 39: 122–41.

Brice, W. C. 1962. 'Some observations on the Linear A inscriptions.' *Kadmos* 1: 42–8.

Brice, W. C. 1969. 'The Linear A tablets IV 8 and IV 9 from Tylissos.' *Kadmos* 8: 120–30.

Brogan, T. M. 2011. 'Introduction.' In T. M. Brogan and E. Hallager (eds.), *LM IB Pottery: Relative Chronology and Regional Differences*. Monographs of the Danish Institute at Athens 11.1. Athens: Danish Institute at Athens: 39–53.

Brogan, T. M. and E. Hallager (eds.). 2011. *LM IB Pottery: Relative Chronology and Regional Differences*. Monographs of the Danish Institute at Athens 11.1. Danish Institute at Athens, Athens.

Brogan, T. M., R. A. K. Smith, and J. S. Soles. 2002. 'Mycenaeans at Mochlos? Exploring culture and identity in the Late Minoan IB to IIIA1 transition.' *Aegean Archaeology* 6: 89–118.

Brogan, T. M. and C. Sofianou. 2009. 'Papadiokambos: new evidence for the impact of the Theran eruption on the northeast coast of Crete.' In D. A. Warburton (ed.), *Time's Up! Dating the Minoan Eruption of Santorini*. Monographs of the Danish Institute at Athens 10. Athens: Danish Institute at Athens: 117–24.

Brogan, T. M., C. Sofianou, and J. E. Morrison. 2011. 'The LM IB pottery from Papadiokampos: a response to Leonidas Vokotopoulos.' In T. M. Brogan and E. Hallager (eds.), *LM IB Pottery: Relative Chronology and Regional Differences*. Monographs of the Danish Institute at Athens, Volume 11.2. Athens: Danish Institute at Athens: 573–93.

Broodbank, C. 2000. *An Island Archaeology of the Early Cyclades*. Cambridge: Cambridge University Press.

Broodbank, C. 2004. 'Minoanization.' *Proceedings of the Cambridge Philological Society* 50: 46–91.

Brown, A. 1986. 'I propose to begin at Gnossos.' *Annual of the British School at Athens* 81: 37–44.

Brown, A. 2000. 'Evans in Crete before 1900.' In D. Huxley (ed.), *Cretan Quests: British Explorers, Excavators and Historians*. London: British School at Athens: 9–14.

Brown, A. and A. Peatfield. 1987. 'Stous Athropolithous: a Minoan site near Epano Zakro, Sitias.' *Annual of the British School at Athens* 82: 23–33.

Brown, E. L. 1992–3. 'The Linear A signary: tokens of Luvian dialect in Bronze Age Crete.' *Minos* 27–8: 25–54.

Brück, J. 1999. 'Ritual and rationality: some problems of interpretation in European archaeology.' *European Journal of Archaeology* 2: 313–44.

Brück, J. and M. Goodman. 1999. 'Introduction: themes for a critical archaeology of settlement.' In J. Brück and M. Goodman (eds.), *Making Places in the Prehistoric World: Themes in Settlement Archaeology*. London: University College London Press: 1–19.

Brumfiel, E. M. 1994. 'Factional competition and political development in the New World: an introduction.' In E. M. Brumfiel and J. W. Fox (eds.), *Factional Competition and Political Development in the New World*. Cambridge: Cambridge University Press: 3–13.

Brumfiel, E. M. 1995. 'Heterarchy and the analysis of complex societies: comments.' In R. M. Ehrenreich, C. L. Crumley, and J. E. Levy (eds.), *Heterarchy and the Analysis of Complex Societies*. Archaeological Papers of the American Anthropological Association 6. Arlington, VA: American Anthropological Association: 125–31.

Brumfiel, E. M. and T. K. Earle (eds.), 1987. *Specialization, Exchange and Complex Societies*. Cambridge: Cambridge University Press.

Brumfiel, E. M. and J. W. Fox (eds.), 1994. *Factional Competition and Political Development in the New World*. Cambridge: Cambridge University Press.

Brysaert, A. 2002. 'Common craftsmanship in the Aegean and East Mediterranean Bronze Age: preliminary technological evidence with emphasis on the painted plaster from Tell el-Dab'a, Egypt.' *Ägypten und Levante* 12: 95–105.

Brysaert, A. 2008. *The Power of Technology in the Bronze Age Eastern Mediterranean*. London and Oakville: Equinox Publishing Ltd.

Budin, S. L. 2011. *Images of Woman and Child from the Bronze Age: Reconsidering Fertility, Maternity, and Gender in the Ancient World*. Cambridge: Cambridge University Press.

Burns, B. E. 2010. 'Trade.' In E. H. Cline (ed.), *The Oxford Handbook of the Bronze Age Aegean*. Oxford: Oxford University Press: 291–304.

Busby, C. 1997. 'Permeable and partible persons: a comparative analysis of gender and body in south India and Melanesia.' *Journal of the Royal Anthropological Institute* 3, 261–78.

Cadogan, G. 1976. *Palaces of Minoan Crete.* London: Book Club Associates.

Cadogan, G. 1977–8. 'Pyrgos, Crete, 1970–7.' *Journal of Hellenic Studies Archaeological Reports* 24: 70–84.

Cadogan, G. 1981. 'A probable shrine in the country house at Pyrgos.' In R. Hägg and N. Marinatos (eds.), *Sanctuaries and Cults in the Aegean Bronze Age.* Skrifter Utgivna av Svenska Institutet I Athen 4°, 27. Stockholm: Svenska Institutet I Athen: 169–71.

Cadogan, C. 1984. 'A Minoan thalassocracy?' In R. Hägg and N. Marinatos (eds.), *The Minoan Thalassocracy: Myth and Reality.* Skrifter Utgivna av Svenska Institutet I Athen, 4° 35. Stockholm: Svenska Institutet I Athen: 13–15.

Cadogan, G. 1994. 'An Old Palace period Knossos state?' In D. Evely, H. Hughes-Brock, and N. Momigliano (eds.), *Knossos: A Labyrinth of History. Papers Presented in Honour of Sinclair Hood.* Oxford: British School at Athens: 57–68.

Cadogan, G. 1995. 'Mallia and Lasithi: a Palace-state.' *Cretological Congress*: 97–104.

Cadogan, G. 1997. 'The role of the Pyrgos country house in Minoan society.' In R. Hägg (ed.), *Function of the Minoan 'Villa.'* Skrifter Utgivna av Svenska Institutet I Athen 4°, 46. Stockholm: Svenska Institutet I Athen: 99–103.

Cadogan, G. 2000. 'The pioneers: 1900–1914.' In D. Huxley (ed.), *Cretan Quests: British Explorers, Excavators and Historians.* London: British School at Athens: 15–27.

Cadogan, G. 2006. 'From Mycenaean to Minoan: an exercise in myth making.' In P. Darcque, M. Fotiadis, and O. Polychronopoulou (eds.), *Mythos: La Préhistoire égéenne du XIXe au XXIe siècle après J.-C.* Bulletin de Correspondance Hellénique Supplement 46. Athens: École Française d'Athènes: 49–55.

Cadogan, G. 2008. 'A shrine – or shrine treasury – in the country house at Myrtos-Pyrgos.' In C. Gallou, M. Georgiadis, and G. M. Muskett (eds.), *Dioskouroi: Studies Presented to W. G. Cavanagh and C. B. Mee on the Anniversary of their 30-year Joint Contribution to Aegean Archaeology.* Oxford: Archaeopress: 6–14.

Cadogan, G. 2009. 'Gender metaphors of social stratigraphy in pre-Linear B Crete or is "Minoan gynaecocracy" (still) credible?' In K. Kopaka (ed.), *FYLO: Engendering Prehistoric 'Stratigraphies' in the Aegean and the Mediterranean.* Aegaeum 30. Liège and Austin: Université de Liège, Histoire de l'art et archéologie de la Grèce antique and University of Texas at Austin, Program in Aegean Scripts and Prehistory: 225–32.

Cadogan, C. 2011. 'A power house of the dead: the functions and long life of the tomb at Myrtos-Pyrgos.' In J. Murphy (ed.), *Prehistoric Crete: Regional and Diachronic Studies on Mortuary Systems.* Philadelphia. PA: INSTAP Academic Press: 103–17.

Cadogan, 2013a. 'Myrtos and Malia: Middle Minoan entente cordiale? Or unitary state?' *Creta Antica* 14: 105–22.

Cadogan, G. 2013b. 'Where has Middle Minoan III gone? A lack at Myrtos-Pyrgos – and elsewhere? What does it mean?' In C. F. Macdonald and C. Knappett (eds.), *Intermezzo: Intermediacy and Regeneration in Middle Minoan III Palatial Crete.* British School at Athens Studies 21. London: British School at Athens: 179–81.

Cain, C. 2001. 'Dancing in the dark: deconstructing a narrative of epiphany on the Isopata Ring.' *American Journal of Archaeology* 105: 27–49.

Cameron, M. A. S. 1965. 'Four fragments of wall paintings with Linear A inscriptions.' *Kadmos* 4: 7–15.

Cameron, M. A. S. 1968. 'The painted signs on fresco fragments from the "House of the Frescoes".' *Kadmos* 7: 45–64.

Cameron, M. A. S. 1978. 'Theoretical interrelations among Theran, Cretan and Mainland frescoes.' In C. Doumas (ed.), *Thera and the Aegean World I.* London: Thera and the Aegean World: 579–92.

Cameron, M. A. S. 1987. 'The "palatial" thematic system in the Knossos murals. Last notes on the Knossos frescoes.' In R. Hägg and N. Marinatos (eds.), *The Function of the Minoan Palaces.* Skrifter Utgivna av Svenska Institutet

I Athen, 4° 35. Stockholm: Paul Åströms Förlag: 320–8.

Carabott, P. 2006. 'A country in a "state of destitution" labouring under an "unfortunate regime": Crete at the turn of the 20th century (1898–1906).' In Y. Hamilakis and N. Momigliano (eds.), *Archaeology and European Modernity: Producing and Consuming the 'Minoans.'* Padua: Bottega d'Erasmo: 39–53.

Carinci, F. 1989. 'The "III fase protopalaziale" at Phaistos. Some observations.' In R. Laffineur (ed.), *Transition: Le Monde Égéen du Bronze Moyen au Bronze Récent.* Aegaeum 3. Liège: Université de Liège, Histoire de l'art et archéologie de la Grèce antique: 73–80.

Carinci, F. 2001. 'La casa a Sud della Rampa e il Medio Minoico III a Festòs.' In L. Beschi, A. Di Vita, V. La Rosa, G. Pugliese Carratelli, and G. Rizza (eds.), *I Cento Anni dello Scavo di Festòs.* Atti dei Convegni Lincei 173. Rome: Accademia Nazionale de Lincei: 203–38.

Carinci, P. 2003. 'Haghia Triada nel periodo Medio Minoico.' *Creta Antica* 4: 97–144.

Carinci, F. and V. La Rosa. 2013. 'A new Middle Minoan IIIA ceremonial building and the so-called "New Era" at Phaistos.' In C. F. Macdonald and C. Knappett (eds.), *Intermezzo: Intermediacy and Regeneration in Middle Minoan III Palatial Crete.* British School at Athens Studies 21. London: British School at Athens: 107–21.

Carratelli, G. P. 1956–7. 'Sulle epigrafi in lineare A di carattere sacrale.' *Minos* 4–5: 163–73.

Carter, T. 2004. 'Mochlos and Melos: a special relationship? Creating identity and status in Minoan Crete.' In L. Preston Day, M. S. Mook, and J. D. Muhly (eds.), *Crete Beyond the Palaces: Proceedings of the Crete 2000 Conference.* Philadelphia, PA: INSTAP Academic Press: 291–307.

Caskey, J. L. 1970. 'Inscriptions and potter's marks from Ayia Irini in Keos.' *Kadmos* 9: 107–17.

Castleden, R. 1990. *Minoans: Life in Bronze Age Crete.* London and New York: Routledge.

Catling, E., H. Catling, and D. Smyth. 1979. 'Knossos 1975: Middle Minoan III and Late Minoan I houses by the Acropolis.' *Annual of the British School at Athens* 74: 1–80.

Chapin, A. 2004. 'Power, privilege and landscape in Minoan art.' In A. Chapin (ed.), *Charis: Essays in Honor of Sara A. Immerwahr.* Hesperia Supplement 33. Athens: American School of Classical Studies at Athens: 47–64.

Chapin, A. 2009. 'Constructions of male youth and gender in Aegean art: the evidence from Late Bronze Age Crete and Thera'. In K. Kopaka (ed.), *FYLO: Engendering Prehistoric 'Stratigraphies' in the Aegean and the Mediterranean.* Aegaeum 30. Liège and Austin: Université de Liège, Histoire de l'art et archéologie de la Grèce antique and University of Texas at Austin, Program in Aegean Scripts and Prehistory: 175–82.

Chase, A. F. and D. Z. Chase. 1992. 'Mesoamerican elites: assumptions, definitions, and models.' In D. Z. Chase and A. F. Chase (eds.), *Mesoamerican Elites: An Archaeological Assessment.* Norman: University of Oklahoma Press: 3–17.

Cherry, J. F. 1978. 'Generalization and the archaeology of the state.' In D. Green, C. Haselgrove, and M. Spriggs (eds.), *Social Organisation and Settlement: Contributions from Anthropology, Archaeology and Geography.* Oxford: British Archaeological Reports: 411–37.

Cherry, J. F. 1983a. 'Evolution, revolution, and the origins of complex society in Minoan Crete.' In O. Krzyszkowska and L. Nixon (eds.), *Minoan Society.* Bristol: Bristol Classical Press: 33–45.

Cherry, J. F. 1983b. 'Frogs round the pond: perspectives on current archaeological survey projects in the Mediterranean region.' In D. R. Keller and J. W. Rupp (eds.), *Archaeological Survey in the Mediterranean Area.* Oxford: British Archaeological Press: 375–415.

Cherry, J. F. 1984. 'The emergence of the state in the prehistoric Aegean.' In Proceedings of the Cambridge Philological Society 30: 18–48.

Cherry, J. F. 1986. 'Polities and palaces: some problems in Minoan state formation.' In C. Renfrew and J. F. Cherry (eds.), *Peer–Polity Interaction and Socio-political Change.*

Cambridge: Cambridge University Press: 19–45.

Cherry, J. F. 1994. 'Regional survey in the Aegean: "the New Wave" (and after).' In P. N. Kardulias (ed.), *Beyond the Site: Regional Studies in the Aegean Area*. Lanham, MD: University Press of America: 91–112.

Cherry, J. F. 1999. 'Introductory reflections on economies and scale in prehistoric Crete.' In A. Chaniotis (ed.), *From Minoan Farmers to Roman Traders: Sidelights on the Economy of Ancient Crete*. Stuttgart: Franz Steiner Verlag: 17–23.

Childe, G. V. 1925. *The Dawn of European Civilization*. London: Kegan Paul, Trench, Trubner and Co.

Childe, G. V. 1926. *The Aryans: A Study of Indo-European Origins*. New York: Alfred A. Knopf.

Childe, G. V. 1958. 'Retrospective.' *Antiquity* 32: 69–74.

Christakis, K. 1999a. 'Minoan storage jars and their significance for the household subsistence economy of Neopalatial Crete.' PhD diss., University of Bristol.

Christakis, K. 1999b. 'Pithoi and food storage in Neopalatial Crete: a domestic perspective.' *World Archaeology* 31: 1–20.

Christakis, K. 2004. 'Palatial economy and storage in Late Bronze Age Knossos.' In G. Cadogan, E. Hatzaki, and A. Vasilakis (eds.), *Knossos: Palace, City, State*. London: The British School at Athens: 299–309.

Christakis, K. 2006. 'Traditions and trends in the production and consumption of storage containers in Protopalatial and Neopalatial Crete'. In M. H. Wiener, J. L. Warner, J. Polonsky, E. E. Hayes, and C. Macdonald (eds.), *Pottery and Society: The Impact of Recent Studies in Minoan Pottery. Gold Medal Colloquium in Honor of Philip P. Betancourt*. Boston, MA: American Institute of Archaeology: 119–37.

Christakis, K. 2008. *The Politics of Storage: Storage and Sociopolitical Complexity in Neopalatial Crete*. Prehistory Monographs 25. Philadelphia, PA: INSTAP Academic Press.

Christakis, K. 2010. 'A wine offering to the Central Palace Sanctuary at Knossos.' In O. Krzyszkowska (ed.), *Cretan Offerings: Studies in Honour of Peter Warren*. London: British School at Athens: 49–55.

Christakis, K. 2012. 'Petras, Siteia: political, economic and ideological trajectories of a polity.' In M. Tsipopoulou (ed.), *Petras, Siteia – 25 Years of Excavations and Studies*. Monographs of the Danish Institute at Athens 16. Athens: Danish Institute at Athens: 205–17.

Christakis, K., M. Mavraki-Balanou, and A. Kastanakis. 2015. 'Economic and political complexity in the Aposelemis Valley: a preliminary assessment.' *Archaiologiko Ergo Kritis* 3: 293–307.

Chryssoulaki, S. 1997. 'Nerokourou Building I and its place in Neopalatial Crete.' In R. Hägg (ed.), *The Function of the 'Minoan Villa.'* Skrifter Utgivna av Svenska Institutet I Athen, 4°, 46. Stockholm: Svenska Institutet I Athen: 27–32.

Chryssoulaki, S. 1999. 'Minoan roads and guard houses – war regained.' In R. Laffineur (ed.), *Polemos: Le Contexte Guerrier en Égée à l'Âge du Bronze*. Aegaeum 19. Liège and Austin: Université de Liège, Histoire de l'art et archéologie de la Grèce antique and University of Texas at Austin, Program in Aegean Scripts and Prehistory: 75–85.

Chryssoulaki, S. 2001. 'The Traostalos peak sanctuary: aspects of spatial organization.' In R. Laffineur and R. Hägg (eds.), *Potnia: Deities and Religion in the Aegean Bronze Age*. Aegaeum 22. Liège and Austin: Université de Liège, Histoire de l'art et archéologie de la Grèce antique and University of Texas at Austin, Program in Aegean Scripts and Prehistory: 57–66.

Chryssoulaki, S. 2005. 'The imaginary navy of Minoan Crete: rocky coasts and probable harbours.' In R. Laffineur and E. Greco (eds.), *Emporia: Aegeans in the Central and Eastern Mediterranean*. Aegaeum 25. Liège and Austin: Université de Liège, Histoire de l'art et archéologie de la Grèce antique and University of Texas at Austin, Program in Aegean Scripts and Prehistory: 77–90.

Chryssoulaki, S. and L. Platon. 1987. 'Relations between the town and Palace of Zakros.' In R. Hägg and N. Marinatos (eds.), *The Function of the*

Minoan Palaces. Skrifter Utgivna av Svenska Institutet I Athen, 4° 35. Stockholm: Paul Åströms Förlag: 77–84.

Clarke, D. 1968. *Analytical Archaeology*. London: Methuen.

Cline, E. H. 1998a. 'Rich beyond the dreams of Avaris: Tell el-Dab'a and the Aegean World: a guide for the perplexed.' *Annual of the British School at Athens* 93: 199–219.

Cline, E. H. 1998b. 'Amenhotep III, the Aegean, and Anatolia.' In D. O'Connor and E. H. Cline (eds.), *Amenhotep III: Perspectives on His Reign*. Ann Arbor: University of Michigan Press: 236–50.

Cline, E. H., A. Yasur-Landau, and N. Goshen. 2011. 'New fragments of Aegean-style painted plaster from Tel Kabri, Israel.' *American Journal of Archaeology* 115: 245–61.

Constantakopoulou, C. 2007. *The Dance of the Islands: Insularity, Networks, the Athenian Empire and the Aegean World*. Oxford: Oxford University Press.

Coulomb, J. 1979. 'Le "Prince aux Lis" de Knossos reconsideré,' *Bulletin de Correspondance Hellénique* 103: 29–50.

Cromarty, R. J. 2008. *Burning Bulls, Broken Bones: Sacrificial Ritual in the Context of Palace Period Minoan Religion*. Oxford: Archaeopress.

Crooks, S. 2013. *What Are These Queer Stones? Baetyls: Epistemology of a Minoan Fetish*. Oxford: Archaeopress.

Crowley, J. L. 1991. 'Patterns in the sea: insight into the artistic vision of the Aegeans.' In R. Laffineur and L. Basch (eds.), *Thalassa. L'Egée préhistorique et la mer*. Aegaeum 7. Liège and Austin: Université de Liège, Histoire de l'art et archéologie de la Grèce antique and University of Texas at Austin, Program in Aegean Scripts and Prehistory: 219–30.

Crowley, J. L. 1992. 'The icon imperative: rules of composition in Aegean art.' In R. Laffineur and J. Crowley (eds.), *EIKON: Aegean Bronze Age Iconography: Shaping a Methodology*. Aegaeum 8. Liège: Université de Liège, Histoire de l'art et archéologie de la Grèce antique: 23–37.

Crowley, J. L. 2008. 'In honour of the gods – but which gods? Identifying deities in Aegean glyptic.' In L. Hitchcock, R. Laffineur, and J. Crowley (eds.), *Dais: The Aegean Feast*. Aegaeum 29. Liège and Austin: Université de Liège, Histoire de l'art et archéologie de la Grèce antique and University of Texas at Austin, Program in Aegean Scripts and Prehistory: 75–87.

Crowley, J. L. 2013. *The Iconography of Aegean Seals*. Aegaeum 34. Leuven – Liège: Peeters.

Cucuzza, N. 1992. 'Mason's marks at Hagia Triada.' *Sileno* 18: 53–65.

Cucuzza, N. 2011. 'Minoan "Theatral Areas".' *Cretological Congress*: 155–70.

Cunningham, T. 2001. 'Variations on a theme: divergence in settlement patterns and spatial organization in the far east of Crete during the Proto- and Neopalatial periods.' In K. Branigan (ed.), *Urbanism in the Aegean Bronze Age*. Sheffield: Sheffield Academic Press: 72–86.

Cunningham, T. 2007. 'In the shadows of Kastri: an examination of domestic and civic space at Palaikastro (Crete).' In N. Fisher, R. Westgate, and J. Whitley (eds.), *Building Communities: House, Settlement and Society in the Aegean and Beyond*. British School at Athens Studies 15. London: British School at Athens: 99–109.

Cunningham, T. and J. Driessen. 2004. 'Site by site: combining survey and excavation data to chart patterns of socio-political change in Bronze Age Crete.' In S. E. Alcock and J. F. Cherry (eds.), *Side-by-Side Survey: Comparative Regional Studies in the Mediterranean World*. Oxford: Oxbow Books: 101–13.

Cunningham, T. and L. H. Sackett. 2009. 'Does the widespread cult activity at Palaikastro call for a special explanation?' In A. L. D'Agata and A. Van de Moortel (eds.), *Archaeologies of Cult: Essays on Ritual and Cult in Crete in Honor of Geraldine C. Gesell*. Hesperia Suppl. 42. Princeton, NJ: American School of Classical Studies at Athens: 79–97.

D'Agata, A. L. 1989. 'Some MM IIIB/LM IA pottery from Ayia Triada.' In R. Laffineur (ed.), *Transition. Le Monde Égéen du Bronze Moyen au Bronze Recent*. Aegaeum 3. Liège: Université de Liège, Histoire de l'art et archéologie de la Grèce antique: 93–8.

D'Agata, A. L. 1992. 'Late Minoan Crete and Horns of Consecration: a symbol in action.' In R. Laffineur and J. L. Crowley (eds.), *Eikon: Aegean Bronze Age Iconography.* Liège: Université de Liège, Histoire de l'art et archéologie de la Grèce antique: 247–56.

D'Agata, A. L. 1994. 'Sigmund Freud and Aegean archaeology. Mycenaean and Cypriote material from his collection of antiquities.' *Studi Micenei ed Egeo-Anatolici* 34: 7–41.

D'Agata, A. L. 2010. 'The many lives of a ruin: history and metahistory of the Palace of Minos at Knossos.' In O. Krzyszkowska (ed.), *Cretan Offerings: Studies in Honour of Peter Warren.* British School at Athens Studies 18. London: British School at Athens: 57–69.

Damiani-Indelicato, S. 1984. 'Gournia, cité minoenne.' In *Aux Origines de l'Hellénisme. La Crète et Grèce. Hommage à Henri van Effenterre présenté par le Centre G. Glotz.* Publications de Sorbonne: Histoire Ancienne et Médiévale 15. Paris: Université de Paris I Panthéon-Sorbonne: 47–54.

Darcque, P. (ed.) 2014. *Fouilles Exécutées à Malia: Les Abords Nord-Est du Palais I. Les Recherches et l'Histoire du Secteur.* Études Crétoises 35. Athens: French School at Athens.

Darcque, P. and A. Van de Moortel. 2001. 'Late Minoan I architectural phases and ceramic chronology at Malia.' In *Abstracts of the Ninth International Congress of Cretan Studies.* Heraklion: Society of Cretan Historical Studies: 29.

Darcque, P. and A. Van de Moortel. 2009. 'Special, ritual, or cultic: a case study from Malia.' In A. L. D'Agata and A. Van de Moortel (eds.), *Archaeologies of Cult: Essays on Ritual and Cult in Crete in Honor of Geraldine C. Gesell.* Hesperia Suppl. 42. Princeton, NJ: American School of Classical Studies at Athens: 31–41.

Davaras, C. 1969. 'Trois bronzes minoens de Skoteino.' *Bulletin de Correspondance Hellénique* 93: 620–50.

Davaras, C. 1974. 'Anaskafi MM ierou Korifis Vrysina Rethymnis.' *Athens Annals of Archaeology* 7: 210–14.

Davaras, C. 1976. *Guide to Cretan Antiquities.* Park Ridge, NJ: Noyes Press.

Davaras, C. 1981. 'Three new Linear A libation vessel fragments from Petsophas.' *Kadmos* 20: 1–6.

Davaras, C. 1985. 'Architektonika stoicheia tis YM IB epavlis tou Makrygialou.' *Cretological Congress:* 77–92.

Davaras, C. 1997. 'The "Cult-Villa" at Makrygialos.' In R. Hägg (ed.), *The Function of the 'Minoan Villa.'* Skrifter Utgivna av Svenska Institutet I Athen, 4° 46. Stockholm: Svenska Institutet I Athen: 117–35.

Davaras, C. 2001. 'Comments on the Plateia Building.' In J. McEnroe (ed.), *The Architecture of Pseira.* University Museum Monograph 109. Philadelphia: University of Pennsylvania Museum: 79–88.

Davaras, C. 2010. 'One Minoan peak sanctuary less: the case of Thylakas.' In O. Krzyszkowska (ed.), *Cretan Offerings: Studies in Honour of Peter Warren.* British School at Athens Studies 18. London: British School at Athens: 71–87.

Davis, B. 2014. *Minoan Stone Vessels with Linear A Inscriptions.* Aegaeum 36. Leuven – Liège: Peeters.

Davis, E. 1986. 'Youth and age in the Thera frescoes.' *American Journal of Archaeology* 90: 399–406.

Davis, E. 1987. 'The Knossos miniature frescoes and the function of the Central Courts.' In R. Hägg and N. Marinatos (eds.), *The Function of the Minoan Palaces.* Skrifter Utgivna av Svenska Institutet I Athen, 4° 35. Stockholm: Paul Åströms Förlag: 157–61.

Davis, E. 1995. 'Art and politics in the Aegean: the missing ruler.' In R. Laffineur and W.-D. Niemeier (eds.), *Politeia. Society and State in the Aegean Bronze Age.* Aegaeum 12. Liège and Austin: Université de Liège, Histoire de l'art et archéologie de la Grèce antique and University of Texas at Austin, Program in Aegean Scripts and Prehistory: 11–20.

Davis, S. 1968. 'The decipherment of Linear A.' *Studi Micenei ed Egeo-Anatolici* 6: 90–110.

Dawkins, R. M. 1913–14. 'Excavations at Plati in Lasithi, Crete.' *Annual of the British School at Athens* 20: 1–17.

Dawkins, R. M. and M. L. W. Laistner. 1912–13. 'The excavation of the Kamares Cave in Crete.' *Annual of the British School at Athens* 19: 1–34.

Day, P. and M. Relaki. 2002. 'Past factions and present fictions: *Palaces* in the study of Minoan Crete.' In J. Driessen, I. Schoep, and R. Laffineur (eds.), *Monuments of Minos: Rethinking the Minoan Palaces*. Aegaeum 23. Liège and Austin: Université de Liège, Histoire de l'art et archéologie de la Grèce antique and University of Texas at Austin, Program in Aegean Scripts and Prehistory: 217–34.

Day, P. and D. Wilson. 1998. 'Consuming power: Kamares Ware in Protopalatial Knossos.' *Antiquity* 72: 350–8.

Del Freo, M. 2008. 'Rapport 2001–2005 sur les textes en écriture hiéroglyphique crétoise, en linéaire A et en linéaire B.' In A. Sacconi, M. del Freo, L. Godart, and M. Negri (eds.), *Colloquium Romanum atti del XII Colloquio Internazionale di Micenolgia*. Pisa and Rome: Fabrizio Serra Editore: 199–222.

Del Freo, M. 2012. 'Rapport 2006–2010 sur les textes en écriture hiéroglyphique crétoise, en linéaire A et en linéaire B.' In P. Carlier, C. de Lamberterie, M. Egetmeyer, N. Guilleux, F. Rougemont, and J. Zurbach (eds.), *Études Mycéniennes 2010*. Pisa and Rome: Fabrizio Serra Editore: 3–21.

Demargne, P. and H. Gallet de Santerre. 1953. *Fouilles Exécutées à Mallia: Exploration des Maisons et Quartiers d'Habitation (1921–1948): Premier Fascicule*. Études Crétoises IX. Paris: Paul Geuthner.

De Polignac, F. 1995. *Cults, Territory, and the Origins of the Greek City-State*. Chicago. IL: University of Chicago Press.

Deshayes, J. and A. Dessenne. 1959. *Fouilles Exécutées à Mallia: Exploration des Maisons et Quartiers d'Habitation (1948–54), II*. Études Crétoises 11. Paris: Paul Geuthner.

Detorakis, Th. 1994. *History of Crete*. [Translated by J. Davis.] Iraklion: Detorakis Editions.

Devolder, M. 2013. *Construire en Crète Minoenne. Une Approche Énergétique de l'Architecture Néopalatiale*. Aegaeum 35. Leuven – Liège: Peeters.

Devolder, M. 2016. 'Review of J. Shaw, *Elite Minoan Architecture: Its Development at Knossos, Phaistos, and Malia*.' *Bryn Mawr Classical Review* 2016: http://bmcr.brynmawr.edu/2016/2016-01-15.html (accessed 7 June 2016).

Dewolf, Y., F. Postel, and H. van Effenterre. 1963. 'Géographie préhistorique de la region de Mallia.' In H. van Effenterre, M. van Effenterre, and J. Hazzidakis (eds.), *Fouilles Exécutées à Mallia: Étude du Site (1956–1957) et Exploration des Nécropoles (1915–1928)*. Paris: Paul Geuthner: 28–53.

Dickinson, O. 1994. *The Aegean Bronze Age*. Cambridge: Cambridge University Press.

Dierckx, H. 1999. 'The Late Minoan I obsidian workshop at Pseira, Crete.' In P. P. Betancourt, V. Karageorghis, R. Laffineur, and W.-D. Niemeier (eds.), *Meletemata: Studies in Aegean Archaeology Presented to Malcolm H. Wiener as He Enters His 65th Year. Vol. 1*. Aegaeum 20. Liège and Austin: Université de Liège, Histoire de l'art et archéologie de la Grèce antique and University of Texas at Austin, Program in Aegean Scripts and Prehistory: 211–16.

Dimopoulou, N. 1990. 'Krousonas.' *Archaiologikon Deltion* 40 (1985): 297.

Dimopoulou, N. 1997. 'Workshops and craftsmen in the harbour-town of Knossos at Poros-Katsambas.' In R. Laffineur and P. P. Betancourt (eds.), *Techne: Craftsmen, Craftswomen and Craftsmanship in the Aegean Bronze Age*. Aegaeum 16. Liège and Austin: Université de Liège, Histoire de l'art et archéologie de la Grèce antique and University of Texas at Austin, Program in Aegean Scripts and Prehistory: 433–8.

Dimopoulou, N. 1999a. 'The Neopalatial cemetery of the Knossian harbour-town at Poros: mortuary behaviour and social ranking.' In I. Kilian-Dirlmeier and M. Egg (eds.), *Eliten in der Bronzezeit: Ergebnisse zweier Kolloquien in Mainz und Athen*. Monographien des Römisch-Germanischen Zentralmuseums 43. Mainz: Verlag des Römisch-Germanisschen Zentralmuseums in Kommission bei Dr Rudolf Habelt GMBH: 27–36.

Dimopoulou, N. 1999b. 'The Marine Style ewer from Poros.' In P. P. Betancourt, V. Karageorghis, R. Laffineur, and W.-D. Niemeier (eds.), *Meletemata: Studies in Aegean Archaeology Presented to Malcolm Wiener as He Enters His 65th Year*. Aegaeum 20. Liège and Austin: Université de Liège, Histoire de l'art et archéologie de la Grèce antique and University of Texas, Program in Aegean Scripts and Prehistory: 217–26.

Dimopoulou, N. 2000. 'Seals and scarabs from the Minoan port settlement at Poros-Katsambas.' In W. Müller (ed.), *Minoisch-mykenische Glyptik: Stil, Ikonographie, Funktion*. Corpus der Minoischen und Mykenischen Siegal: Beiheft 6. Berlin: Gebr. Mann Verlag: 27–38.

Dimopoulou, N. 2004. 'To epineio tis Knosou ston Poro-Katsamba.' In G. Cadogan, E. Hatzaki, and A. Vasilakis (eds.), *Knossos: Palace, City, State*. British School at Athens Studies 12. London: British School at Athens: 363–80.

Dimopoulou, N., J.-P. Olivier, and G. Rethemiotakis. 1993. 'Une statuette en argile MR IIIA de Poros Irakliou avec inscription en linéaire A.' *Bulletin de Correspondance Hellénique* 117: 501–21.

Dimopoulou, N. and G. Rethemiotakis. 2000. 'The "Sacred Conversation" ring from Poros.' In W. Müller (ed.), *Minoisch-mykenische Glyptik: Stil, Ikonographie, Funktion*. Corpus der Minoischen und Mykenischen Siegal: Beiheft 6. Berlin: Gebr. Mann Verlag: 39–56.

Dimopoulou-Rethemiotaki, N. 2008. 'Community and the individual in death: burial practices in the Neopalatial and Postpalatial periods.' In *From the Land of the Labyrinth: Minoan Crete, 3000–1100 BC*. Exhibition Catalogue, Onassis Cultural Center, New York [2008]: 134–42.

Doumas, C. 1993. 'Thera.' *Ergon*: 83–91.

Doumas, C. 2000. 'Age and gender in the Theran wall paintings.' In S. Sherratt (ed.), *The Wall Paintings of Thera*. Athens: The Thera Foundation: 971–81.

Doumas, C. 2004. 'Aegean islands and islanders.' In J. F. Cherry, C. Scarre, and S. Shennan (eds.), *Explaining Social Change: Studies in Honour of Colin Renfrew*. Cambridge: McDonald Institute for Archaeological Research: 215–26.

Doumas, C. 2012. '*Gaia peripputos:* some thoughts on "Neo-Minoan" mythology.' In E. Mantzourani and P. P. Betancourt (eds.), *Philistor: Studies in Honor of Costis Davaras*. Philadelphia, PA: INSTAP Academic Press: 25–34.

Driessen, J. 1982. 'The Minoan Hall in domestic architecture on Crete: to be in vogue in Late Minoan IA?' *Acta Archaeologica Lovaniensia* 21: 27–92.

Driessen, J. 1989–90. 'The proliferation of Minoan palatial architectural style: 1) Crete.' *Acta Archaeologica Lovaniensia* 28–9: 3–23.

Driessen, J. 1995. 'Observations on the modification of the access systems of Minoan Palaces.' *Aegean Archaeology* 2: 67–85.

Driessen, J. 1999. 'The dismantling of a Minoan Hall at Palaikastro (Knossians go home?).' In P. P. Betancourt, V. Karageorghis, and W.-D. Niemeier (eds.), *Meletemata: Studies in Aegean Archaeology Presented to Malcolm H. Wiener as He Enters His 65th Year*. Liège and Austin: Université de Liège, Histoire de l'art et archéologie de la Grèce antique and University of Texas at Austin, Program in Aegean Scripts and Prehistory: 227–36.

Driessen, J. 2000a. 'The New Palace period.' In D. Huxley (ed.), *Cretan Quests: British Explorers, Excavators and Historians*. London: British School at Athens: 113–28.

Driessen, J. 2000b. 'A Late Minoan IB town shrine in Palaikastro.' In J. A. MacGillivray, J. Driessen, and L. H. Sackett (eds.), *The Palaikastro Kouros: A Minoan Chryselephantine Statuette and Its Aegean Bronze Age Context*. BSA Studies 6. London: British School at Athens: 87–95.

Driessen, J. 2001. 'History and hierarchy. Preliminary observations on the settlement pattern in Minoan Crete.' In K. Branigan (ed.), *Urbanism in the Aegean Bronze Age*. Sheffield: Sheffield Academic Press: 51–71.

Driessen, J. 2002a. 'Towards an archaeology of crisis: defining the long-term impact of the Bronze Age Santorini eruption.' In R.

Torrence and J. Grattan (eds.), *Natural Disasters and Cultural Change*. London and New York: Routledge: 250–63.

Driessen, J. 2002b. '"The King Must Die": some observations on the use of the Minoan court compounds.' In J. Driessen, I. Schoep, and R. Laffineur (eds.), *Monuments of Minos: Rethinking the Minoan Palaces*. Aegaeum 23. Liège and Austin: Université de Liège, Histoire de l'art et archéologie de la Grèce antique and University of Texas at Austin, Program in Aegean Scripts and Prehistory: 1–14.

Driessen, J. 2005a. 'On the use of upper floors in Minoan Neopalatial architecture.' In I. Bradfer-Burdet, B. Detournay, and R. Laffineur (eds.), *Kris Technitis: L'Artisan Crétois*. Aegaeum 26. Liège and Austin: Université de Liège, Histoire de l'art et archéologie de la Grèce antique and University of Texas at Austin, Program in Aegean Scripts and Prehistory: 83–8.

Driessen, J. 2005b. 'Spirit of place. Minoan *houses* as major actors.' In D. Pullen (ed.), *Political Economies of the Aegean Bronze Age*. Oxford and Oakville: Oxbow: 35–65.

Driessen, J. 2009. 'Daidalos' designs and Ariadne's threads: Minoan towns as places of interaction.' In S. Owen and L. Preston (eds.), *Inside the City in the Greek World: Studies of Urbanism from the Bronze Age to the Hellenistic Period*. University of Cambridge Museum of Classical Archaeology Monograph no. 1. Oxford: Oxbow Books: 41–54.

Driessen, J. 2010. 'Malia.' In E. Cline (ed.), *The Oxford Handbook of the Bronze Age Aegean (ca. 3000–1000 BC)*. Oxford: Oxford University Press: 556–70.

Driessen, J. 2012a. 'A matrilocal house society in Pre- and Protopalatial Crete?' In I. Schoep, P. Tomkins, and J. Driessen (eds.), *Back to the Beginning: Reassessing Social and Political Complexity on Crete during the Early and Middle Bronze Age*. Oxford: Oxbow Books: 358–83.

Driessen, J. 2012b. 'Chercher la femme.' In D. Panagiotopoulos and U. Günkel-Maschek (eds.), *Minoan Realities: Approaches to Images,* *Architecture, and Society in the Aegean Bronze Age*. Louvain: UCL Press: 141–63.

Driessen, J. 2015. 'For an archaeology of Minoan society: identifying the principles of social structure.' In S. Cappel, U. Günkel-Maschek, and D. Panagiotopoulos (eds.), *Minoan Archaeology: Perspectives for the 21st Century*. Louvain-la-Neuve: UCL Press: 149–66.

Driessen, J. n.d. *The Kephali at Sissi: A Short Guide to the Excavations*. Download from: www.sarpedon.be/ [February 2013].

Driessen, J. Forthcoming. 'Beyond the collective … The Minoan palace in action.' In M. Relaki and Y. Papadatos (eds.), *Studies in Honour of Keith Branigan*.

Driessen, J. and C. Langhor. 2007. 'Rallying round a Minoan past: the legitimation of power at Knossos during the Late Bronze Age.' In M. L. Galaty and W. A. Parkinson (eds.), *Rethinking Mycenaean Palaces II*. Cotsen Institute Archaeology Monograph 60. Los Angeles, CA: Cotsen Institute of Archaeology, UCLA: 178–89.

Driessen, J. and C. F. Macdonald. 1997. *The Troubled Island: Minoan Crete before and after the Santorini Eruption*. Aegaeum 17. Liège and Austin: Université de Liège, Histoire de l'art et archéologie de la Grèce antique and University of Texas, Program in Aegean Scripts and Prehistory.

Driessen, J. and C. F. Macdonald. 2000. 'The eruption of the Santorini volcano and its effects on Minoan Crete.' In W. J. McGuire, D. R. Griffiths, P. L. Hancock, and I. S. Stewart (eds.), *The Archaeology of Geological Catastrophes*. London: The Geological Society: 81–93.

Driessen, J. and J. A. MacGillivray. 1989. 'The Neopalatial period in East Crete.' In R. Laffineur (ed.), *Transition: Le Monde Égéen du Bronze Moyen au Bronze Récent*. Aegaeum 3. Liège: Université de Liège, Histoire de l'art et archéologie de la Grèce antique: 99–111.

Driessen, J. and J. A. MacGillivray. 2011. 'Swept away in LM IA? Debris deposition in coastal Neopalatial Crete.' *Cretological Congress*: 233–44.

Driessen, J. and J. Sakellarakis. 1997. 'The Vathypetro complex – some observations on its architectural history and function.' In R. Hägg (ed.), *The Function of the 'Minoan Villa.'* Skrifter Utgivna av Svenska Institutet I Athen, 4° 46. Stockholm: Svenska Institutet I Athen: 63–77.

Driessen, J., I. Schoep, and R. Laffineur (eds.). 2002. *Monuments of Minos: Rethinking the Minoan Palaces.* Aegaeum 23. Liège and Austin: Université de Liège, Histoire de l'art et archéologie de la Grèce antique and University of Texas, Program in Aegean Scripts and Prehistory.

Duchêne, H. 2006. 'Salomon Reinach et l'invention de la préhistoire égéenne. Un "Athénien" à l'ombre du minotaure.' In P. Darcque, M. Fotiadis, and O. Polychronopoulou (eds.), *Mythos: La Préhistoire égéenne du XIXe au XXIe siècle après J.-C.* Bulletin de Correspondance Hellénique Suppl. 46. Athens: École Française d'Athènes: 81–96.

Duhoux, Y. and A. Morpurgo Davies (eds.). 2008. *A Companion to Linear B: Mycenaean Greek Texts and Their World. Volume 1,* Louvain-la-Neuve: Peeters.

Dyson, S. L. 2006. *In Pursuit of Ancient Pasts: A History of Classical Archaeology in the Nineteenth and Twentieth Centuries.* New Haven, CT, and London: Yale University Press.

Earle, T. 2002. *Bronze Age Economics: The Beginnings of Political Economies.* Boulder, CO: Westview Press.

Earle, T. 2011. 'Redistribution and the political economy: the evolution of an idea.' *American Journal of Archaeology* 115: 237–44.

Ehrenreich, R. M., C. L. Crumley, and J. E. Levy (eds.). 1995. *Heterarchy and the Analysis of Complex Societies.* Archaeological Papers of the American Anthropological Association 6. Arlington, VA: American Anthropological Association.

Elsner, J. 2007. *Roman Eyes: Visuality and Subjectivity in Art and Text.* Princeton, NJ: Princeton University Press.

Evans, A. J. 1896. 'The Eastern Question in anthropology.' *Nature* 54: 527–35, 906–22.

Evans, A. J. 1897. 'Further discoveries of Cretan and Aegean scripts.' *Journal of Hellenic Studies* 17: 305–57.

Evans, A. J. 1901. 'Mycenaean tree and pillar cult and its Mediterranean relations.' *Journal of Hellenic Studies* 21: 99–204.

Evans, A. J. 1903. 'The Palace of Knossos.' *Annual of the British School at Athens* 9: 1–153.

Evans, A. J. 1905. 'The Palace of Knossos and its dependencies.' *Annual of the British School at Athens* 11: 1–26.

Evans, A. J. 1912. 'The Minoan and Mycenaean element in Hellenic life.' *Journal of Hellenic Studies* 32: 277–97.

Evans, A. J. 1921. *The Palace of Minos at Knossos.* Vol. 1. London: Macmillan.

Evans, A. J. 1927. 'Work of reconstitution in the Palace of Knossos.' *Antiquities Journal* 7: 258–67.

Evans, A. J. 1928. *The Palace of Minos at Knossos.* Vol. 2. London: Macmillan.

Evans, A. J. 1930. *The Palace of Minos at Knossos.* Vol. 3. London: Macmillan.

Evans, A. J. 1935. *The Palace of Minos at Knossos.* Vol. 4. London: Macmillan.

Evans, J. 1943. *Time and Chance. The Story of Arthur Evans and His Forebears.* London and New York: Longmans, Green and Co.

Evans, J. D. 1973. 'Islands as laboratories for the study of culture process.' In C. Renfrew (ed.), *The Explanation of Culture Change: Models in Prehistory.* Pittsburgh, PA: University of Pittsburgh Press: 517–20.

Evely, D. 1988. 'Minoan craftsmen: problems of recognition and definition.' In E. B. French and K. A. Wardle (eds.), *Problems in Greek Prehistory.* Bristol: Bristol Classical Press: 397–415.

Evely, D. 1993. *Minoan Crafts: Tools and Techniques. An Introduction: Volume One.* Studies in Mediterranean Archaeology 92.1. Göteborg: Paul Åströms Förlag.

Evely, D. 1999. *Fresco: A Passport into the Past: Minoan Crete Through the Eyes of Mark Cameron.* Athens: British School at Athens, N. P. Goulandris Foundation – Museum of Cycladic Art.

Evely, D. 2000. *Minoan Crafts: Tools and Techniques: An Introduction. Volume Two.* Studies in Mediterranean Archaeology 92.2. Jonsered: Paul Åströms Förlag.

Evely, D. 2008. 'Crete.' *Archaeological Reports for 2007–2008* 54: 94–112.

Evely, D. 2010. 'Crete.' *Archaeological Reports for 2009–2010* 56: 169–200.

Evely, D., A. Hein, and E. Nodarou. 2012. 'Crucibles from Palaikastro, East Crete: insights into metallurgical technology in the Aegean Late Bronze Age.' *Journal of Archaeological Science* 39: 1821–36.

Farnoux, A. 1996. *Knossos: Searching for the Legendary Palace of King Minos.* New York: Abrams.

Faro, E. 2008. 'Ritual activity and regional dynamics: towards a reinterpretation of Minoan extra-urban ritual space.' PhD diss., University of Michigan.

Faro, E. 2013. 'Caves in the ritual landscape of Minoan Crete.' In F. Mavridis and J. T. Jensen (eds.), *Stable Places and Changing Perceptions: Cave Archaeology in Greece.* Oxford: Archaeopress: 166–75.

Faure, P. 1963. 'Cultes de sommets et cultes de cavernes en Crète.' *Bulletin de Correspondance Hellénique* 87: 193–508.

Faure, P. 1964. *Fonctions des Cavernes Crétoises.* Paris: De Bocard.

Faure, P. 1967. 'Nouvelles recherches sur trois sortes de sanctuaires Crétois.' *Bulletin de Correspondance Hellénique* 91: 114–50.

Faure, P. 1969. 'Sur trois sortes de sanctuaires Crétois.' *Bulletin de Correspondance Hellénique* 93: 174–213.

Faure, P. 1972. 'Cultes populaires dans la Crète antique.' *Bulletin de Correspondance Hellénique* 96: 389–426.

Faure, P. 1996. 'Deux inscriptions en écriture linéaire A découvertes à Troie par Schliemann.' *Cretan Studies* 5: 137–46.

Feinman, G. 2004. 'Archaeology and political economy: setting the stage.' In G. Feinman and L. Nichols (eds.), *Archaeological Perspectives on Political Economies.* Salt Lake City: University of Utah Press: 1–6.

Ferioli, P. and E. Fiandra. 1989. 'The importance of clay sealings in the ancient administration.' In I. Pini (ed.), *Fragen und Probleme der Bronzezeitlichen Ägäischen Glyptik.* CMS Beiheft 3. Berlin: Mann Verlag: 41–53.

Ferrari, C. and N. Cucuzza. 2004. 'I cosiddetti kernoi de Festòs.' *Creta Antica* 5: 53–96.

Fiandra, E. 1995. 'Phaistos between MM II and LM I.' *Cretological Congress*: 329–39.

Finkelberg, M. 1990–1. 'Minoan inscriptions on libation vessels.' *Minos* 25–6: 43–85.

Finkelberg, M., A. Uchitel, and D. Ussishkin. 1996. 'A Linear A inscription from Tel Lachist (Lach ZA 1).' *Tel Aviv* 23: 195–207.

Finley, M. 1968. *Aspects of Antiquity: Discoveries and Controversies.* New York: Viking Press.

Fitton, L. 1995. *The Discovery of the Greek Bronze Age.* London: British Museum Press.

Fitton, L. 2002. *The Minoans.* London: British Museum Press.

Flood, J. and J. S. Soles. 2014. 'Water management in Neopalatial Crete and the development of the Mediterranean dry-season.' In G. Touchais, R. Laffineur, and F. Rougemont (eds.), *Physis: L'Environnement Naturel et la Relation Homme-Milieu dans le Monde Égéen Protohistorique.* Aegaeum 37. Leuven – Liège: Peeters: 79–84.

Floyd, C. 1995. 'Fragments of two pithoi with Linear A inscriptions from Pseira.' *Kadmos* 34: 34–8.

Floyd, C. 1998. *Pseira III: The Plateia Building.* University Museum Monograph 102. Philadelphia: University of Pennsylvania.

Forsdyke, E. J. 1926–7. 'The Mavro Spelio cemetery at Knossos.' *Annual of the British School at Athens* 28: 243–96.

Fotiadis, M. 2006. 'Factual claims in late nineteenth century European prehistory and the descent of a modern discipline's ideology.' *Journal of Social Archaeology* 6: 5–27.

Fotou, V. 1993. *New Light on Gournia: Unknown Documents of the Excavation at Gournia and Other Sites on the Isthmus of Ierapetra by Harriet Ann Boyd.* Aegaeum 9. Liège and Austin: Université de Liège, Histoire de l'art et archéologie de la Grèce antique and

University of Texas at Austin, Program in Aegean Scripts and Prehistory.

Fotou, V. 1997. 'Éléments d'analyse architecturale et la question des fonctions de trois bâtiments "villas": la Royal villa, le "Mégaron" de Nirou et le "Mégaron" de Sklavokampos.' In R. Hägg and N. Marinatos (eds.), *The Function of the 'Minoan Villas.'* Skrifter Utgivna av Svenska Institutet I Athen, 4° 46. Stockholm: Svenska Institutet I Athen: 33–50.

Fought, C. 2006. *Language and Ethnicity.* Cambridge: Cambridge University Press.

Fowler, C. 2004. *The Archaeology of Personhood: An Anthropological Approach.* London and New York: Routledge.

Foxhall, L. 2000. 'The running sands of time: archaeology and the short-term.' *World Archaeology* 31: 484–98.

Friedrich, W. and N. Sigalas. 2009. 'The effects of the Minoan eruption – visible at various archaeological sites on Santorini, Greece.' In D. A. Warburton (ed.), *Time's Up! Dating the Minoan Eruption of Santorini.* Monographs of the Danish Institute at Athens 10. Athens: Danish Institute at Athens: 91–100.

Galanakis, Y. 2014. 'Arthur Evans and the quest for the "origins of Mycenaean culture".' In Y. Galanakis, T. Wilkinson, and J. Bennet (eds.), *Athyrmata: Critical Essays on the Archaeology of the Eastern Mediterranean in Honour of E. Susan Sherratt.* Oxford: Archaeopress: 85–98.

Galanakis, Y. 2015. 'Exhibiting the Minoan past: from Oxford to Knossos.' In S. Cappel, U. Günkel-Maschek, and D. Panagiotopoulos (eds.), *Minoan Archaeology: Perspectives for the 21st Century.* Louvain-la-Neuve: Presses universitaires de Louvain: 17–34.

Gardner, P. 1908. 'Preface.' In A. Michaelis, *A Century of Archaeological Discoveries.* [Translated by B. Kahnweiler.] London: John Murray.

Gavrilaki, I. 2010. 'Oi anaskafes sto spilaio Melidoniou (1987–2008).' *Archaiologiko Ergo Kritis* 1: 657–69.

Geertz, C. 1980. *Negara: The Theatre State in Nineteenth-Century Bali.* Princeton, NJ: Princeton University Press.

Georgiadis, M. 2012. 'Leska: a new peak sanctuary on the island of Kythera.' *Journal of Prehistoric Religion* 23: 7–23.

Georgiou, H. 1979. *The Late Minoan I Destruction of Crete: Metal Groups and Stratigraphic Considerations.* UCLA Institute of Archaeology Monograph 9. Los Angeles: Institute of Archaeology, University of California at Los Angeles.

Gere, C. 2009. *Knossos and the Prophets of Modernity.* Chicago, IL: University of Chicago Press.

German, S. C. 2005. *Performance, Power and the Art of the Aegean Bronze Age.* BAR Int. Ser. 1347. Oxford: Archaeopress.

Gesell, G. C. 1985. *Town, Palace and House Cult in Minoan Crete.* Studies in Mediterranean Archaeology 67. Göteborg: Paul Åströms Förlag.

Gesell, G. C. 1987. 'The Minoan palace and public cult.' In R. Hägg and N. Marinatos (eds.), *The Function of the Minoan Palaces.* Skrifter Utgivna av Svenska Institutet I Athen, 4° 35. Stockholm: Paul Åströms Förlag: 123–7.

Gill, M. A. V. 1965. 'The Knossos sealings: provenance and identification.' *Annuals of the British School at Athens* 60: 58–98.

Gill, M. A. V. 2002. 'The find spots of the sealings.' In M. A. V. Gill, W. Müller, and I. Pini (eds.), Corpus der minoischen und mykenischen Siegel: Band II. Iraklion Archäologisches Museum: Teil 8.1. Die siegelabdrücke von Knossos: Unter Einbeziehung von Funden aus anderen Museen. Mainz am Rhein: Philipp von Zabern: 101–28.

Gillis, C. 1990. *Minoan Conical Cups: Form, Function and Significance.* Göteborg: Paul Åströms Förlag.

Girella, L. 2001. 'Alcune considerazioni in margine al MM III: Archanes e Festòs.' *Creta Antica* 2: 63–76.

Girella, L. 2008. 'Feast in "transition"? An overview of feasting practices during MM III in Crete.' In L. Hitchcock, R. Laffineur, and J. Crowley (eds.), *Dais: The Aegean Feast.*

Aegaeum 29. Liège and Austin: Université de Liège, Histoire de l'art et archéologie de la Grèce antique and University of Texas at Austin, Program in Aegean Scripts and Prehistory: 167–78.

Girella, L. 2011. 'Bridging the gap: the function of houses and residential neighborhoods in Middle Minoan III Phaistos.' In K. T. Glowacki and N. Vogeikoff-Brogan (eds.), *STEGA: The Archaeology of Houses and Households in Ancient Crete.* Hesperia Supplement 44. Princeton, NJ: American School of Classical Studies at Athens: 81–97.

Girella, L. 2013. 'Evidence for Middle Minoan III occupation at Ayia Triada.' In C. F. Macdonald and C. Knappett (eds.), *Intermezzo: Intermediacy and Regeneration in Middle Minoan III Palatial Crete.* British School at Athens Studies 21. London: British School at Athens: 123–35.

Girella, L. 2015. 'When diversity matters: exploring funerary evidence in Middle Minoan III Crete.' *Studi Micenei ed Egeo-Anatolici NS* 1: 117–36.

Girella, L. 2016. 'Aspects of ritual and changes in funerary practices between MM II and LM I on Crete.' In E. Alram-Stern, F. Blakolmer, S. Deger-Jalkotzy, R. Laffineur, and J. Weilhartner (eds.), *Metaphysis: Ritual, Myth and Symbolism in the Aegean Bronze Age.* Aegaeum 39. Leuven – Liège: Peeters: 201–12.

Godart, L. and J.-P. Olivier. 1976a. *Recueil des Inscriptions en Linéaire A. Volume 1. Tablettes éditées avant 1970.* Études Crétoises 21.1. École Française d'Athènes. Paris: Guethner.

Godart, L. and J.-P. Olivier 1976b. *Recueil des Inscriptions en Linéaire A. Volume 2. Nodules, scellés et rondelles édités avant 1970.* Études Crétoises 21.3. École Française d'Athènes. Paris: Guethner.

Godart, L. and J.-P. Olivier 1979. Recueil des Inscriptions en Linéaire A. Volume 3. Tablettes, nodules et roundelles édités en 1975 et 1976. Études Crétoises 21.2. École Française d'Athènes. Paris: Guethner.

Godart, L. and J.-P. Olivier. 1982. *Recueil des Inscriptions en Linéaire A. Volume 4. Autres Documents.* Études Crétoises 21.4. École Française d'Athènes. Paris: Guethner.

Godart, L. and J.-P. Olivier. 1985. *Recueil des Inscriptions en Linéaire A. Volume 5.* Addenda, Corrigenda, Concordances, Index et Planches des Signes. Études Crétoises 21.5. École Française d'Athènes. Paris: Guethner.

Goodison, L. 2004. 'From Tholos tomb to throne room: some considerations of dawn light and directionality in Minoan buildings.' In G. Cadogan, E. Hatzaki, and A. Vasilakis (eds.), *Knossos: Palace, City, State.* British School at Athens Studies 12. London: British School at Athens: 339–50.

Goodison, L. 2009. '"Why all this about oak or stone?": trees and boulders in Minoan religion.' In A. L. D'Agata and A. Van de Moortel (eds.), *Archaeologies of Cult: Essays on Ritual and Cult in Crete in Honor of Geraldine C. Gesell.* Hesperia Suppl. 42. Princeton, NJ: American School of Classical Studies at Athens: 51–7.

Goodison, L. and C. Morris. 1998. 'Beyond the "Great Mother": the sacred world of the Minoans.' In L. Goodison and C. Morris (eds.), *Ancient Goddesses: The Myths and the Evidence.* London: British School at Athens: 113–32.

Gordon, C. H. 1976. 'Further notes on the Hagia Triada tablet no. 31.' *Kadmos* 15: 28–30.

Gordon, C. H. 1981. 'The Semitic language of Minoan Crete.' In Y. L. Arbeitman and A. R. Bomhard (eds.), *Bono Homini Donum: Essays in Historical Linguistics in Honor of J. Alexander Kerns.* Amsterdam: John Benjamins: 761–82.

Goren, Y. and D. Panagiotopoulos. 2010. 'The "Lords of the Rings": an analytical approach to the riddle of the "Knossian replica rings".' *Bulletin of the Institute of Classical Studies* 52: 257–8.

Gosden, C. 1994. *Social Being and Time.* Oxford: Wiley-Blackwell.

Gosden, C. and G. Lock. 1998. 'Prehistoric histories.' *World Archaeology* 30: 2–12.

Gournia Website: www.gournia.org/

Graham, J. W. 1956. 'The Phaistos "Piano Nobile".' *American Journal of Archaeology* 60: 151–7.

Graham, J. W. 1959. 'The Residential Quarter of the Minoan Palace.' *American Journal of Archaeology* 63: 47–52.

Graham, J. W. 1960. 'Windows, recesses, and the Piano Nobile in the Minoan Palaces.' *American Journal of Archaeology* 64: 335–41.

Graham, J. W. 1961. 'The Minoan banquet hall: a study of the blocks north of the Central Court at Phaistos and Mallia.' *American Journal of Archaeology* 65: 165–72.

Graham, J. W. 1977. 'Bathrooms and lustral chambers.' In K. H. Kinzl (ed.), *Greece and the Eastern Mediterranean in Ancient History and Prehistory: Studies Presented to F. Schachermeyr on the Occasion of His Eightieth Birthday*. Berlin and New York: Walter de Gruyter: 110–25.

Graham, J. W. 1979: 'Further notes on Minoan palace architecture: 1. West magazine and upper halls at Knossos and Malia; 2. Access to, and use of, Minoan palace roofs.' *American Journal of Archaeology* 83: 49–69.

Graham, J. W. 1987 [3rd ed.]. *The Palaces of Crete*. Princeton, NJ: Princeton University Press.

Graziadio, G. 2005. 'The relations between the Aegean and Cyprus at the beginning of the Late Bronze Age: an overview of the archaeological evidence.' In R. Laffineur and E. Greco (eds.), *Emporia: Aegeans in the Central and Eastern Mediterranean*. Aegaeum 25, vol. 1. Liège and Austin: Université de Liège, Histoire de l'art et archéologie de la Grèce antique and University of Texas at Austin, Program in Aegean Scripts and Prehistory: 323–35.

Günkel-Maschek, U. 2016. 'Establishing the Minoan "enthroned goddess" in the Neopalatial period: images, architecture, and elitist ambition.' In E. Alram-Stern, F. Blakolmer, S. Deger-Jalkotzy, R. Laffineur, and J. Weilhartner (eds.), *Metaphysis: Ritual, Myth and Symbolism in the Aegean Bronze Age*. Aegaeum 39. Leuven – Liège: Peeters: 255–62.

Hadzi-Vallianou, D. 2011. 'LM IB pottery from the rural Villa of Pitsidia: a response to Jeremy Rutter.' In T. M. Brogan and E. Hallager (eds.), *LM IB Pottery: Relative Chronology and Regional Differences*. Monographs of the Danish Institute at Athens 11.2. Athens: Danish Institute at Athens: 345–77.

Hägg, R. 1985. 'Pictorial programmes in the Minoan Palaces and Villas?' In P. Darque and J. C. Poursat (eds.), *L'Iconographie minoenne*. Bulletin de Correspondance Hellénique Suppl. 11. Athens: École Française d'Athènes: 209–17.

Hägg, R. 1986. 'Die Göttliche Epiphanie in minoischen Ritual.' *Mitteilungen des Deutschen Archäologischen Instituts, Athenische Abteilung* 101: 41–62.

Hägg, R. 1987. 'On the reconstruction of the west façade of the palace at Knossos.' In R. Hägg and N. Marinatos (eds.), *The Function of the Minoan Palaces*. Skrifter Utgivna av Svenska Institutet I Athen, 4° 35. Stockholm: Paul Åströms Förlag: 129–34.

Hägg, R. (ed.). 1997. *The Function of the 'Minoan Villa.'* Skrifter Utgivna av Svenska Institutet I Athen, 4° 46. Stockholm: Paul Åströms Förlag.

Hägg, R. and N. Marinatos. 1983. 'Anthropomorphic cult-images in Minoan Crete?' In O. Krzyszkowska and L. Nixon (eds.), *Minoan Society*. Bristol: Bristol Classical Press: 185–201.

Hägg, R. and N. Marinatos (eds.). 1984. *The Minoan Thalassocracy: Myth and Reality*. Skrifter Utgivna av Svenska Institutet I Athen, 4° 32. Stockholm: Paul Åströms Förlag.

Haggis, D. 1995. 'Archaeological survey at Kavousi, Crete: settlement development in Middle Minoan and Late Minoan I.' *Cretological Congress*: 369–81.

Haggis, D. 1996. 'Archaeological survey at Kavousi, East Crete.' *Hesperia* 65: 373–432.

Halbherr, F. 1903. 'Resti dell'età micenea scoperti ad Haghia Triada presso Phaestos.' *Monumenti Antichi della Reale Accademia dei Lincei* 13: 5–74.

Halbherr, F., E. Stefani, and L. Banti. 1980. 'Haghia Triada nel periodo tardo-palaziale.' *Annuario della Scuola archeologica di Atene e delle Missioni Italiane in Oriente* 55 (N. S. 39: 1977): 5–296.

Hall, E. 1912. *Excavations in Eastern Crete: Sphoungaras*. Philadelphia, PA: The University Museum.

Hall, H. R. 1901–2. 'Keftiu and the peoples of the sea.' *Annual of the British School at Athens* 8: 157–89.

Hall, J. M. 1995. 'How Argive was the "Argive" Heraion? The political and cultic geography of the Argive plain, 900–400 BC.' *American Journal of Archaeology* 99: 577–613.

Hall, J. M. 1997. *Ethnic Identity in Greek Antiquity.* Cambridge: Cambridge University Press.

Hallager, B. and E. Hallager. 1995. 'The Knossian bull – political propaganda in Neopalatial Crete?' In R. Laffineur and W. D. Niemeier (eds.), *Politeia: Society and State in the Aegean Bronze Age.* Aegaeum 12. Liège and Austin: Université de Liège, Histoire de l'art et archéologie de la Grèce antique and University of Texas at Austin, Program in Aegean Scripts and Prehistory: 547–56.

Hallager, E. 1987. 'A "harvest festival room" in the Minoan Palaces? An architectural study of the Pillar Crypt area at Knossos.' In R. Hägg and N. Marinatos (eds.), *The Function of the Minoan Palaces.* Skrifter Utgivna av Svenska Institutet I Athen, 4° 3 5. Stockholm: Paul Åströms Förlag: 169–77.

Hallager, E. 1996. *The Minoan Roundel and other Sealed Documents in the Neopalatial Linear A Administration.* Aegaeum 14. Liège and Austin: Université de Liège, Histoire de l'art et archéologie de la Grèce antique and University of Texas at Austin, Program in Aegean Scripts and Prehistory.

Hallager, E. 2002. 'One Linear A tablet and 45 noduli.' *Creta Antica* 3: 105–9.

Hallager, E. 2012. 'Literacy at Petras and three hitherto unpublished Linear A inscriptions.' In M. Tsipopoulou (ed.), *Petras, Siteia – 25 Years of Excavations and Studies.* Athens: Danish Institute at Athens: 265–76.

Halstead, P. 1981. 'From determinism to uncertainty: social storage and the rise of the Minoan Palace.' In A. Sheridan and G. Bailey (eds.), *Economic Archaeology.* Oxford: Archaeopress: 187–213.

Halstead, P. 1988. 'On redistribution and the origin of Minoan-Mycenaean palatial economies.' In E. French and K. Wardle (eds.), *Problems in Greek Prehistory.* Bristol: Bristol Classical Press: 519–30.

Halstead, P. 1989. 'The economy has a normal surplus: economic stability and social change among early farming communities of Thessaly, Greece'. In P. Halstead and J.

O'Shea (eds.), *Bad Year Economics: Cultural Responses to Risk and Uncertainty.* Cambridge: Cambridge University Press: 68–80.

Halstead, P. 1997. 'Storage and states on prehistoric Crete: a reply to Strasser (JMA 10 [1997] 73–100).' *Journal of Mediterranean Archaeology* 10: 103–7.

Halstead, P. 2004. 'Life after Mediterranean polyculture: the subsistence subsystem and the Emergence of Civilisation revisited.' In J. Barrett and P. Halstead (eds.), *The Emergence of Civilisation Revisited.* Oxford: Oxbow Books: 189–206.

Halstead, P. 2011. 'Redistribution in Aegean palatial societies.' *American Journal of Archaeology* 115: 229–35.

Halstead, P. and J. O'Shea. 1982. 'A friend in need is a friend indeed: social storage and the origins of social ranking.' In C. Renfrew and S. Shennan (eds.), *Ranking, Resource and Exchange. Aspects of the Archaeology of Early European Society.* Cambridge: Cambridge University Press: 92–9.

Hamilakis, Y. 1997–8. 'Consumption patterns, factional competition and political development in Bronze Age Crete.' *Bulletin of the Institute of Classical Studies* 42: 233–4.

Hamilakis, Y. 2002. 'What future for the "Minoan" past? Re-thinking Minoan archaeology.' In Y. Hamilakis (ed.), *Labyrinth Revisited: Rethinking 'Minoan' Archaeology.* Oxford: Oxbow Books: 2–28.

Hamilakis, Y. 2006. 'The colonial, the national, and the local: legacies of the "Minoan" past.' In Y. Hamilakis and N. Momigliano (eds.), *Archaeology and European Modernity: Producing and Consuming the 'Minoans.'* Creta Antica 7. Padua: Bottega d'Erasmo: 145–62.

Hamilakis, Y. 2007. *The Nation and Its Ruins: Antiquity, Archaeology, and National Imagination in Greece.* Oxford: Oxford University Press.

Hamilakis, Y. 2013. *Archaeology of the Senses: Human Experience, Memory, and Affect.* Cambridge: Cambridge University Press.

Hammer, C. 2005. 'The Minoan eruption of Thera occurred in the mid 17th century BC!' Abstract for a Minoan Seminar held 14 April

2005: www.minoanseminar.gr/index.php?option=com_content&view=article&id=48&Itemid=11&lang=en (accessed 2 September 2015).

Hammer, C. U., G. Kurat, P. Hoppe, W. Grum, and H. B. Clausen. 2003. 'Thera eruption date 1645 BC confirmed by new ice core data?' In M. Bietak (ed.), *The Synchronisation of Civilisations in the Eastern Mediterranean in the Second Millennium B.C. II*. Vienna: Österreichischen Akademie der Wissenschaften: 87–94.

Harbsmeier, M. 1986. 'Inventions of writing.' In J. Gledhill, B. Bender, and M. T. Larsen (eds.), *State and Society: The Emergence and Development of Social Hierarchy and Political Centralization*. London and New York: Routledge: 253–78.

Harden, D. B. 1983. *Sir Arthur Evans 1851–1941*. Oxford: Ashmolean Museum.

Harlan, D. 2011. 'The cult of the dead, fetishism, and the genesis of an idea: megalithic monuments and the tree and pillar cult of Arthur J. Evans.' *European Journal of Archaeology* 14: 210–30.

Hatzaki, E. 1996. 'Was the Little Palace at Knossos the "little palace" of Knossos?' In D. Evely, I. Lemos, and S. Sherratt (eds.), *Minotaur and Centaur: Studies in the Archaeology of Crete and Euboea Presented to Mervyn Popham*. British Archaeological Reports International Series 638. Oxford: Archaeopress: 34–45.

Hatzaki, E. 2005. *Knossos: The Little Palace*. British School at Athens Suppl. 38. London: British School at Athens.

Hatzaki, E. 2007a. 'Neopalatial (MM IIIB–LM IB): KS 178, Gypsades Well (Upper Deposit), and SEX North House Groups.' In N. Momigliano (ed.), *Knossos Pottery Handbook: Neolithic and Bronze Age (Minoan)*. British School at Athens Studies 14. London: British School at Athens: 151–96.

Hatzaki, E. 2007b. 'Final Palatial (LM II–LM IIIA2) and Postpalatial (LM IIIB–LM IIIC Early): the MUM south sector, long corridor cists, MUM pits (8, 10–11), Makritikhos "kitchen", MUM north platform pits and SEX southern half groups.' In N. Momigliano (ed.), *Knossos Pottery Handbook: Neolithic and Bronze Age (Minoan)*. British

School at Athens Studies 14. London: British School at Athens: 197–251.

Hatzaki, E. 2007c. 'Review of *Knossos: The South House*, edited by P. A. Mountjoy.' *American Journal of Archaeology* 111: online review.

Hatzaki, E. 2011a. 'From LM IB Marine Style to LM II marine motifs. Stratigraphy, chronology and the social context of a ceramic transformation: a response to Maria Andreadaki-Vlazaki.' In T. M. Brogan and E. Hallager (eds.), *LM IB Pottery: Relative Chronology and Regional Differences*. Monographs of the Danish Institute at Athens 11.1. Athens: Danish Institute at Athens: 75–87.

Hatzaki, E. 2011b. 'Defining "domestic" architecture and "household" assemblages in Late Bronze Age Knossos.' In K. T. Glowacki and N. Vogeikoff-Brogan (eds.), *STEGA: The Archaeology of Houses and Households in Ancient Crete*. Hesperia Supplement 44. Princeton, NJ: American School of Classical Studies at Athens: 247–62.

Hatzaki, E. 2013. 'The end of an *intermezzo* at Knossos: ceramic wares, deposits, and architecture in a social context.' In C. F. Macdonald and C. Knappett (eds.), *Intermezzo: Intermediacy and Regeneration in Middle Minoan III Palatial Crete*. British School at Athens Studies 21. London: British School at Athens: 37–45.

Hayden, B. 1999. 'The coastal settlement of Priniatikos Pyrgos: archaeological evidence, topography, and environment.' In P. P. Betancourt, V. Karageorghis, R. Laffineur, and W.-D. Niemeier (eds.), *Meletemata: Studies in Aegean Archaeology Presented to Malcolm H. Wiener as He Enters His 65th Year*. Vol. II. Aegaeum 20. Liège and Austin: Université de Liège, Histoire de l'art et archéologie de la Grèce antique and University of Texas at Austin, Program in Aegean Scripts and Prehistory: 351–5.

Hayden, B. 2004. *Reports on the Vrokastro Area, Eastern Crete. Vol. 2*. Philadelphia: University of Pennsylvania: Museum of Archaeology and Anthropology.

Hayden, B. 2005. *Reports on the Vrokastro Area, Eastern Crete. Vol. 3. The Vrokastro Regional*

Survey Project: Sites and Pottery. Philadelphia: University of Pennsylvania Museum of Archaeology and Anthropology.

Hayden, B., J. Moody, and O. Rackham. 1992. 'The Vrokastro Survey Project, 1986–1989: research design and preliminary results.' *Hesperia* 61: 293–353.

Haysom, M. 2010. 'The double-axe: a contextual approach to the understanding of a Cretan symbol in the Neopalatial period.' *Oxford Journal of Archaeology* 29: 35–55.

Haysom, M. 2011. 'Fish and ships: Neopalatial seascapes in context.' In G. Vavouranakis (ed.), *The Seascape in Aegean Prehistory.* Monographs of the Danish Institute at Athens 14. Athens: Danish Institute at Athens: 139–60.

Haysom, M. 2014. 'Crete (prehistoric to Hellenistic).' *Archaeological Reports* 2013–14: 81–7.

Haysom, M. 2015. 'Recent research into Minoan extra-urban sanctuaries.' *Archaeological Reports: Archaeology in Greece* 61 (2014–15): 94–103.

Hawes, C. H. and H. Boyd Hawes. 1922 [3rd ed.]. *Crete the Forerunner of Greece.* London: Harper.

Hazzidakis, J. 1912–13. 'An Early Minoan sacred cave at Arkalokhori in Crete.' *Annual of the British School at Athens* 19: 35–47.

Hazzidakis, J. 1921. *Tylissos à l'Époque Minoenne.* Paris: Paul Geuthner.

Hazzidakis, J. 1934. *Les Villas Minoennes de Tylissos.* Études Crétoises 3. Paris: Paul Geuthner.

Helms, M. 1988. *Ulysses' Sail: An Ethnographic Odyssey of Power, Knowledge, and Geographical Distance.* Princeton, NJ: Princeton University Press.

Hemingway, S. 1999. 'Copper and bronze objects from Minoan Pseira.' In P. P. Betancourt, V. Karageorghis, R. Laffineur, and W.-D. Niemeier (eds.), *Meletemata: Studies in Aegean Archaeology Presented to Malcolm H. Wiener as He Enters His 65th Year.* Aegaeum 20. Liège and Austin: Université de Liège, Histoire de l'art et archéologie de la Grèce antique and University of Texas at Austin, Program in Aegean Scripts and Prehistory: 357–9.

Hemingway, S., J. A. MacGillivray, and L. H. Sackett. 2011. 'The LM IB renaissance at post-diluvian pre-Mycenaean Palaikastro.' In T. M. Brogan and E. Hallager (eds.), *LM IB Pottery: Relative Chronology and Regional Differences.* Monographs of the Danish Institute at Athens 11.2. Athens: Danish Institute at Athens: 513–30.

Herva, V.-P. 2005. 'The life of buildings: Minoan building deposits in an ecological perspective.' *Oxford Journal of Archaeology* 24: 215–27.

Herva, V.-P. 2006a. 'Marvels of the system. Art, perception and engagement with the environment in Minoan Crete.' *Archaeological Dialogues* 13: 221–40.

Herva, V.-P. 2006b. 'Flower lovers, after all? Rethinking religion and human–environment relations in Minoan Crete.' *World Archaeology* 38: 586–98.

Hiller, S. 1980. 'The south propylaeum of the palace of Knossos: some reflections on its reconstruction.' *Cretological Congress*: 216–32.

Hitchcock, L. 2000. *Minoan Architecture: A Contextual Analysis.* Studies in Mediterranean Archaeology and Literature, Pocketbook 155. Jonsered: Paul Åströms Förlag.

Hitchcock, L. and P. Koudounaris. 2002. 'Virtual discourse: Arthur Evans and the reconstructions of the Minoan Palace at Knossos.' In Y. Hamilakis (ed.), *Labyrinth Revisited: Rethinking 'Minoan' Archaeology.* Oxford: Oxbow Books: 40–58.

Hitchcock, L. and D. Preziosi. 1997. 'The Knossos Unexplored Mansion and the "villa-annex complex".' In R. Hägg (ed.), *The Function of the 'Minoan Villa.'* Skrifter Utgivna av Svenska Institutet I Athen, 4°46. Stockholm: Paul Åströms Förlag: 51–62.

Hitchcock, L. and D. Preziosi. 1999. *Aegean Art and Architecture.* Oxford: Oxford University Press.

Hogarth, D. G. 1899–1900. 'The Dictaean Cave.' *Annual of the British School at Athens* 6: 94–116.

Hogarth, D. G. 1900–1. 'Excavations at Zakro, Crete.' *Annual of the British School at Athens* 7: 121–49.

Hogarth, D. G. 1902. 'The Zakro sealings.' *Journal of Hellenic Studies* 22: 76–93.

Holland, R. 1999. 'Nationalism, ethnicity and the concert of Europe: the case of the High Commissionership of Prince George of Greece in Crete, 1898–1906.' *Journal of Modern Greek Studies* 17: 253–76.

Hood, S. 1958. *Archaeological Survey of the Knossos Area*. London: British School at Athens.

Hood, S. 1962. 'Archaeology in Greece, 1961–62.' *Archaeological Reports for 1961–62*: 3–31.

Hood, S. 1971. *The Minoans*. New York: Praeger.

Hood, S. 1977. 'Minoan town shrines?' In K. Kinzl (ed.), *Greece and the Eastern Mediterranean in Ancient History and Prehistory*. Berlin and New York: W. de Gruyter: 158–72.

Hood, S. 1983. 'The "country house" and Minoan society.' In O. Krzyszkowska and L. Nixon (eds.), *Minoan Society*. Bristol: Bristol Classical Press: 129–35.

Hood, S. 1985. 'Primitive Minoan artistic convention.' In P. Darcque and J.-C. Poursat (eds.), *L'iconographie minoenne*. Bulletin de Correspondance Hellénique Suppl. 11. Athens: École Française d'Athènes: 21–7.

Hood, S. 1987. 'An early British interest in Knossos.' *Annual of the British School at Athens* 82: 85–94.

Hood, S. 1995. 'The Minoan palace as residence of gods and men.' *Cretological Congress*: 393–407.

Hood, S. 1996. 'Back to basics with Middle Minoan IIIB.' In D. Evely, I. Lemos, and S. Sherratt (eds.), *Minotaur and Centaur: Studies in the Archaeology of Crete and Euboea Presented to Mervyn Popham*. Oxford: Tempus Reparatum: 10–16.

Hood, S. 1997. 'The magico-religious background of the Minoan villa.' In R. Hägg (ed.), *The Function of the 'Minoan Villa.'* Stockholm: Paul Åströms Förlag: 105–16.

Hood, S. 2000. 'Cretan fresco dates.' In S. Sherratt (ed.), *The Wall Paintings of Thera*. Athens: The Thera Foundation: 191–208.

Hood, S. 2005. 'Dating the Knossos frescoes.' In L. Morgan (ed.), *Aegean Wall Painting: A Tribute to Mark Cameron*. British School at Athens Studies 13. London: British School at Athens: 45–81.

Hood, S. 2011. 'Knossos Royal Road: North, LM IB deposits.' In T. Brogan and E. Hallager (eds.), *LM IB Pottery: Relative Chronology and Regional Difference*. Monographs of the Danish Institute at Athens 11. Athens: Danish Institute at Athens: 153–74.

Hood, S. and D. Smyth. 1981. *Archaeological Survey of the Knossos Area*. British School at Athens Supplementary Volume 14. London: British School at Athens.

Hood, S. and P. Warren. 1966. 'Ancient sites in the province of Ayios Vasilios, Crete.' *Annual of the British School at Athens* 61: 163–91.

Hood, S., P. Warren, and G. Cadogan. 1964. 'Travels in Crete, 1962.' *Annual of the British School at Athens* 59: 50–99.

Hope Simpson, R., P. P. Betancourt, P. J. Callaghan, D. K. Harlan, J. W. Hayes, J. W. Shaw, M. C. Shaw, and L. V. Watrous. 1995. 'The archaeological survey of the Kommos area.' In J. W. Shaw and M. C. Shaw (eds.), *Kommos 1: An Excavation on the South Coast of Crete. The Kommos Region and Houses of the Minoan Town. Part 1: The Kommos Region, Ecology, and Minoan Industries*. Princeton, NJ: Princeton University Press: 325–402.

Horden, P. and N. Purcell. 2000. *The Corrupting Sea: A Study of Mediterranean History*. Oxford: Wiley.

Hughes, D. D. 1991. *Human Sacrifice in Ancient Greece*. London and New York: Routledge.

Immerwahr, S. A. 1990. *Aegean Painting in the Bronze Age*. University Park: Pennsylvania State University Press.

Ingold, T. 1993. 'The Temporality of the Landscape.' *World Archaeology* 25: 152–74.

Jenkins, R. 1992. *Pierre Bourdieu*. London and New York: Routledge.

Johnson, M. 2002. *Behind the Castle Gate: From Medieval to Renaissance*. London and New York: Routledge.

Jones, B. 2014. 'Revisiting the figures and landscapes on the frescoes at Hagia Triada.' In G. Touchais, R. Laffineur, and F. Rougemont (eds.), *Physis: L'Environnement Naturel et la Relation Homme-Milieu dans le Monde Égéen Protohistorique*. Aegaeum 37. Leuven – Liège: Peeters: 493–8.

Jones, B. 2015. *Ariadne's Threads: The Construction and Significance of Clothes in the Aegean Bronze Age*. Aegaeum 38. Leuven – Liège: Peeters.

Jones, D. W. 1999. *Peak Sanctuaries and Sacred Caves: Comparison of Artifacts*. Jonsered: Paul Åströms Förlag.

Jones, S. 1997. *The Archaeology of Ethnicity: Constructing Identities in the Past and Present*. London and New York: Routledge.

Kaiser, B. 1976. *Untersuchungen zum minoischen Relief*. Bonn: Habelt.

Kanta, A. 2011a. 'A West Cretan response (Nerokourou) to Lefteris Platon and the LM IB pottery from Zakros.' In T. M. Brogan and E. Hallager (eds.), *LM IB Pottery: Relative Chronology and Regional Differences*. Monographs of the Danish Institute at Athens 11.2. Athens: Danish Institute at Athens: 613–22.

Kanta, A. 2011b. 'Eidolia, Omoiomata.' In A. Kanta and C. Davaras (eds.), *Elouthia Charistiion: To Iero Spilaio tis Eileithyias ston Tsoutsouro*. Heraklion: Dimos Minoa Pediadas: 84–154.

Kanta, A. 2011c. 'I latreia tis eileithyias sto spilaio tou Tsoutsourou.' In A. Kanta and C. Davaras (eds.), *Elouthia Charistiion: To Iero Spilaio tis Eileithyias ston Tsoutsouro*. Heraklion: Dimos Minoa Pediadas: 28–37.

Kanta, A. and C. Davaras (eds.). 2011. *Elouthia Charistiion: To Iero Spilaio tis Eileithyias ston Tsoutsouro*. Heraklion: Dimos Minoa Pediadas.

Kanta, A. and D. Z. Kontopodi. 2011. 'Deigmata tis kerameikis tou spilaiou.' In A. Kanta and C. Davaras (eds.), *Elouthia Charistiion: To Iero Spilaio tis Eileithyias ston Tsoutsouro*. Heraklion: Dimos Minoa Pediadas: 44–79.

Kanta, A. and L. Rocchetti. 1989. 'English summary.' In I. Tzedakis and A. Sacconi (eds.), *Scavi a Nerokourou, Kydonias*. Incunabula Graeca XCI. Rome: Edizioni dell'Ateneo: 293–328.

Kanta, A. and A. Tzigounaki. 2001. 'The character of the Minoan Goddess: new evidence from the area of Amari.' In R. Laffineur and R. Hägg (eds.), *Potnia: Deities and Religion in the Aegean Bronze Age*. Aegaeum 22. Liège and Austin: Université de Liège, Histoire de l'art

et archéologie de la Grèce antique and University of Texas at Austin, Program in Aegean Scripts and Prehistory: 151–7.

Karadimas, N. 2015. 'The unknown past of Minoan archaeology: from the Renaissance until the arrival of Sir Arthur Evans in Crete.' In S. Cappel, U. Günkel-Maschek, and D. Panagiotopoulos (eds.), *Minoan Archaeology: Perspectives for the 21st Century*. Louvain-la-Neuve: Presses universitaires de Louvain: 3–15.

Karadimas, N. and N. Momigliano. 2004. 'On the term "Minoan" before Evans's work in Crete (1894).' *Studi Micenei ed Egeo-Anatolici* 46: 243–58.

Karetsou, A. 1974. 'Ieron Koryfis Yiouchta.' *Praktika tis en Athinais Archaiologikis Etaireias* 1974: 228–39.

Karetsou, A. 1975. 'To Iero Koryfis tou Yiouchta.' *Praktika tis en Athinais Archaiologikis Etaireias* 1975: 330–42.

Karetsou, A. 1976. 'To Iero Koryfis Yiouchta.' *Praktika tis en Athinais Archaiologikis Etaireias* 1976: 408–18.

Karetsou, A. 1977. 'To Iero Koryfis Yiouchta.' *Praktika tis en Athinais Archaiologikis Etaireias* 1977: 419–20.

Karetsou, A. 1978. 'To Iero Koryfis Yiouchta.' *Praktika tis en Athinais Archaiologikis Etaireias* 1978: 232–58.

Karetsou, A. 1979. 'To Iero Koryfis Yiouchta.' *Praktika tis en Athinais Archaiologikis Etaireias* 1979: 280–1.

Karetsou, A. 1980. 'To Iero Koryfis Yiouchta (1979–1980).' *Praktika tis en Athinais Archaiologikis Etaireias* 1980: 337–53.

Karetsou, A. 1981a. 'The peak sanctuary of Mt. Juktas.' In R. Hägg and N. Marinatos (eds.), *Sanctuaries and Cults in the Aegean Bronze Age*. Skrifter Utgivna av Svenska Institutet I Athen, 4° 27. Stockholm: Svenska Institutet I Athen: 137–53.

Karetsou, A. 1981b. 'To Iero Koryfis tou Yiouchta.' *Praktika tis en Athinais Archaiologikis Etaireias* 1981: 405–8.

Karetsou, A. 1984. 'To Iero Koryfis Yiouchta.' *Praktika tis en Athinais Archaiologikis Etaireias* 1984: 600–14.

Karetsou, A. 1985. 'To Iero Koryfis Yiouchta.' *Praktika tis en Athinais Archaiologikis Etaireias* 1985: 286–96.

Karetsou, A. 2001. 'Address.' In L. Beschi, A. Di Vita, V. La Rosa, G. Pugliese Carratelli, and G. Rizza (eds.), *I Cento Anni dello Scavo di Festòs*. Atti dei Convegni Lincei 173. Rome: Accademia Nazionale de Lincei: 11–13.

Karetsou, A. 2004. 'Knossos after Evans: past interventions, present state and future solutions.' In G. Cadogan, E. Hatzaki, and A. Vasilakis (eds.), *Knossos: Palace, City, State.* British School at Athens Studies 12. London: British School at Athens: 547–55.

Karetsou, A. 2005. 'Early sealing evidence and a new "Minoan male portrait" sealstone from the Juktas peak sanctuary.' In M. Perna (ed.), *Studi in Onore di Enrica Fiandra*. Paris: De Boccard: 113–31.

Karetsou, A. 2014. 'Kophinas revisited. The 1990 excavation and the cultic activity.' *Kretika Chronika* 34: 123–46.

Karetsou, A., L. Godart, and J-P. Olivier. 1985. 'Inscriptions en linéaire A du sanctuaire de sommet du mont Iuktas.' *Kadmos* 24: 89–147.

Karetsou, A. and R. Koehl. 2011. 'An enigmatic piece of gold-work from the Juktas peak sanctuary.' In F. Carinci, N. Cucuzza, P. Militello, and O. Palio (eds.), *Kritis Minoidos: Tradizione e Identità Minoica tra Produzione Artigianale, Pratiche Cerimoniali e Memoria del Passato.* Studi di Archeologia Cretese 10. Padova: Bottega d'Erasmo: 207–23.

Karetsou, A. and I. Mathioudaki. 2012. 'The Middle Minoan III Building complex at Alonaki, Juktas.' *Creta Antica* 13: 83–107.

Karnava, A. 2016. 'On sacred vocabulary and religious dedications: the Minoan "libation formula".' In E. Alram-Stern, F. Blakolmer, S. Deger-Jalkotzy, R. Laffineur, and J. Weilhartner (eds.), *Metaphysis: Ritual, Myth and Symbolism in the Aegean Bronze Age.* Aegaeum 39. Leuven – Liège: Peeters: 345–55.

Kemp, W. 1998. 'The work of art and its beholder: the methodology of the aesthetic of reception.' In M. Cheetham, *The Subjects of Art History: Historical Objects in Contemporary Perspectives.* Cambridge: Cambridge University Press: 180–96.

Kertzer, D. 1988. *Ritual, Politics and Power.* New Haven, CT: Yale University Press.

Kitchen, K. A. 1996. 'The historical chronology of ancient Egypt, a current assessment.' In K. Randsborg (ed.), *Absolute Chronology: Archaeological Europe 2500–500 BC.* ActaArch 67, ActaArch Supplementa 1. Copenhagen: Munksgaard: 1–13.

Kitchen, K. A. 2000. 'Regnal and genealogical data of ancient Egypt (Absolute Chronology I): the historical chronology of ancient Egypt, a current assessment.' In M. Bietak (ed.), *The Synchronisation of Civilisations in the Eastern Mediterranean in the Second Millennium BC: Vol. 1.* Vienna: Österreichischen Akademie de Wissenschaften: 39–52.

Knapp, A. B. 1990. 'Entrepreneurship, ethnicity and exchange: Mediterranean inter-island relations in the Late Bronze Age.' *Annual of the British School at Athens* 85: 115–53.

Knapp, A. B. (ed.) 1992. *Archaeology, Annales and Ethnohistory.* Cambridge: Cambridge University Press.

Knapp, A. B. 2008. *Prehistoric and Protohistoric Cyprus: Identity, Insularity and Connectivity.* Oxford: Oxford University Press.

Knapp, A. B. and S. Antoniadou. 1998. 'Archaeology, politics and the cultural heritage of Cyprus.' In L. Meskell (ed.), *Archaeology Under Fire: Nationalism, Politics and Heritage in the Eastern Mediterranean and Middle East.* London and New York: Routledge: 13–43.

Knappett, C. 1999. 'Assessing a polity in Protopalatial Crete: the Malia-Lasithi state.' *American Journal of Archaeology* 103: 615–39.

Knappett, C. and T. Cunningham. 2012. *Palaikastro Block M: The Proto- and Neopalatial Town.* [With contributions by D. Evely, P. Westlake, and M. Bichler.] London: British School at Athens.

Knappett, C. and T. Cunningham. 2013. 'Defining Middle Minoan IIIA and IIIB at Palaikastro.' In C. F. Macdonald and C. Knappett (eds.), *Intermezzo: Intermediacy and Regeneration in Middle Minoan III Palatial*

Crete. British School at Athens Studies 21. London: British School at Athens: 183–95.

Knappett, C., I. Mathioudaki, and C. F. Macdonald. 2013. 'Stratigraphy and ceramic typology in the Middle Minoan III palace at Knossos.' In C. F. Macdonald and C. Knappett (eds.), *Intermezzo: Intermediacy and Regeneration in Middle Minoan III Palatial Crete*. British School at Athens Studies 21. London: British School at Athens: 9–20.

Knappett, C. and I. Nikolakopoulou. 2008. 'Colonialism without colonies? A Bronze Age case study from Akrotiri, Thera.' *Hesperia* 77: 1–42.

Knappett, C. and I. Schoep. 2000. 'Continuity and change in Minoan palatial power.' *Antiquity* 74: 365–71.

Knoblauch, P. and W.-D. Niemeier. 1992. 'Der weg nach Knosos.' In J. Schäfer (ed.), *Amnisos nach den archäologischen, historischen und epigraphischen Zeugnissen des Altertums und der Neuzeit*. Berlin: Gebr. Mann Verlag: 323–8.

Koehl, R. 1981. 'The functions of Aegean Bronze Age Rhyta.' In R. Hägg and N. Marinatos (eds.), *Sanctuaries and Cults in the Aegean Bronze Age*. Skrifter Utgivna av Svenska Institutet I Athen, 4° 27. Stockholm: Svenska Institutet I Athen: 179–88.

Koehl, R. 1986. 'The Chieftain Cup and a Minoan rite of passage.' *Journal of Hellenic Studies* 106: 99–110.

Koehl, R. 1995. 'The nature of Minoan kingship.' In R. Laffineur and W.-D. Niemeier (eds.), *Politeia. Society and State in the Aegean Bronze Age*. Aegaeum 12. Liège and Austin: Université de Liège, Histoire de l'art et archéologie de la Grèce antique and University of Texas at Austin, Program in Aegean Scripts and Prehistory: 23–35.

Koehl, R. 1997. 'The Villas at Ayia Triada and Nirou Chani and the origin of the Cretan andreion.' In R. Hägg (ed.), *The Function of the 'Minoan Villa.'* Skrifter Utgivna av Svenska Institutet I Athen, 4°46. Stockholm: Paul Åströms Förlag: 137–49.

Koehl, R. 2006. *Aegean Bronze Age Rhyta*. Prehistory Monographs 19. Philadelphia, PA: INSTAP Academic Press.

Kontorli-Papadopoulou, L. 1996. *Aegean Frescoes of Religious Character*. Studies in Mediterranean Archaeology 117. Göteborg: Paul Åströms Förlag.

Kopaka, K. 2005. '*Emporia* on the Mediterranean fringe: trading for a living on the small Island of Crete.' In R. Laffineur and E. Greco (eds.), *Emporia: Aegeans in the Central and Eastern Mediterranean*. Aegaeum 25. Liège and Austin: Université de Liège, Histoire de l'art et archéologie de la Grèce antique and University of Texas at Austin, Program in Aegean Scripts and Prehistory: 91–101.

Kopaka, K. 2009. 'Mothers in Aegean stratigraphies? The dawn of ever-continuing engendered life cycles.' In K. Kopaka (ed.), *FYLO: Engendering Prehistoric 'Stratigraphies' in the Aegean and the Mediterranean*. Aegaeum 30. Liège and Austin: Université de Liège, Histoire de l'art et archéologie de la Grèce antique and University of Texas at Austin, Program in Aegean Scripts and Prehistory: 183–95.

Kopaka, K. and L. Platon. 1993. 'LINOI MINOIKOI: Installations minoennes de traitement des produits liquides.' *Bulletin de Correspondance Hellénique* 117: 35–101.

Kourou, N. and A. Karetsou. 1994. 'To iero tou Ermou Kranaiou stin Patso Amariou.' In L. Rocchetti (ed.), *Sybrita. La Valle di Amari fra Bronzo e Ferro*. Incunabula Graeca 96. Rome: Gruppo Editoriale Internazionale: 81–164.

Kriga, D. 2010. 'I YM IB agrepavli stin Epano Zakro: nea stoicheia os pros tin architektoniki morphi kai ti leitourgia tou ktiriou.' *Archaiologiko Ergo Kritis* 1: 155–69.

Kristiansen, K. and T. B. Larsson. 2005. *The Rise of Bronze Age Society: Travels, Transmissions and Transformations*. Cambridge: Cambridge University Press.

Krzyszkowska, O. 2005. *Aegean Seals: An Introduction*. Bulletin of the Institute of Classical Studies Supplement 85. London: Institute of Classical Studies, School of Advanced Study, University of London.

Krzyszkowska, O. 2010. 'Impressions of the natural world: landscape in Aegean glyptic.' In O. Krzyszkowska (ed.), *Cretan Offerings: Studies in*

Honour of Peter Warren. British School at Athens Studies 18. London: British School at Athens: 169–87.

Krzyszkowska, O. 2012. 'Worn to impress? Symbol and status in Aegean glyptic.' In R. Laffineur and M.-L. Nosch (eds.), *Kosmos: Jewellery, Adornment and Textiles in the Aegean Bronze Age.* Aegaeum 33. Liège: Université de Liège, Histoire de l'art et archéologie de la Grèce antique: 739–48.

Kuniholm, P. I. 1996. 'The prehistoric Aegean: dendrochronological progress as of 1995.' In K. Randsborg (ed.), *Absolute Chronology: Archaeological Europe 2500–500 BC.* ActaArch 67, ActaArch Supplementa 1. Copenhagen: Munksgaard: 327–35.

Kyriakidis, E. 2002. 'Indications of the nature of the language of the Keftiw from Egyptian sources.' *Ägypten und Levante* 12: 211–19.

Kyriakidis, E. 2005. *Ritual in the Bronze Age Aegean: The Minoan Peak Sanctuaries.* London: Duckworth.

Lane, P. 2005. 'The material culture of memory.' In W. James and D. Mills (eds.), *The Qualities of Time: Anthropological Approaches.* Association of Social Anthropologists Monographs 41. Oxford and New York: Berg: 19–34.

Lang, M. 1969. *The Palace of Nestor at Pylos in Western Messenia. Vol. II: The Frescoes.* Princeton, NJ: Princeton University Press.

La Rosa, V. 1985. 'Preliminary considerations on the problem of the relationship between Phaistos and Hagia Triadha.' *Scripta Mediterranea* 6: 45–54.

La Rosa, V. 1989. 'Nouvelles données du Bronze moyen au Bronze recent à Haghia Triada.' In R. Laffineur (ed.), *Transition. Le Monde Égéen du Bronze Moyen au Bronze Recent.* Aegaeum 3. Liège: Université de Liège, Histoire de l'art et archéologie de la Grèce antique: 81–92.

La Rosa, V. 1997. 'La "Villa Royale" de Haghia Triada.' In R. Hägg (ed.), *The Function of the 'Minoan Villa.'* Skrifter Utgivna av Svenska Institutet I Athen, 4° 46. Stockholm: Svenska Institutet I Athen: 79–89.

La Rosa, V. 2001. 'La scavo di Festòs nella letteratura archeologica Italiana.' In L. Beschi, A. Di Vita, V. La Rosa, G. Pugliese Carratelli, and G. Rizza (eds.), *I Cento Anni dello Scavo di Festòs.* Atti dei Convegni Lincei 173. Rome: Accademia Nazionale de Lincei: 25–49.

La Rosa, V. 2002. 'Pour une révision préliminaire du second palais de Phaistos.' In J. Driessen, I. Schoep, and R. Laffineur (eds.), *Monuments of Minos: Rethinking the Minoan Palaces.* Aegaeum 23. Liège and Austin: Université de Liège, Histoire de l'art et archéologie de la Grèce antique and University of Texas at Austin, Program in Aegean Scripts and Prehistory: 71–98.

La Rosa, V. 2003. '"Il colle sul quale sorge la chiesa ad ovest è tutto seminato di cocci . . .". Vicende e temi di uno scavo di lungo corso.' *Creta Antica* 4: 11–68.

La Rosa, V. 2010a. 'Phaistos.' In E. Cline (ed.), *The Oxford Handbook of the Bronze Age Aegean (ca. 3000–1000 BC).* Oxford: Oxford University Press: 582–95.

La Rosa, V. 2010b. 'Ayia Triada.' In E. Cline (ed.), *The Oxford Handbook of the Bronze Age Aegean (ca. 3000–1000 BC).* Oxford: Oxford University Press: 495–508.

La Rosa, V. 2010c. 'Oi ergasies tis Italikis Apostolis sti Phaisto kai tin Ayia Triada.' *Archaiologiko Ergo Kritis* 1: 302–10.

La Rosa, V. and P. Militello. 1999. 'Caccia, guerra o rituale? Alcune considerazioni sulle armi minoiche da Festos e Haghia Triada.' In R. Laffineur (ed.), *Polemos: Le Contexte Guerrier en Égée à l'Âge du Bronze.* Aegaeum 19. Liège and Austin: Université de Liège, Histoire de l'art et archéologie de la Grèce antique and University of Texas at Austin, Program in Aegean Scripts and Prehistory: 241–64.

Lebessi, A. and P. Muhly. 1987. 'The sanctuary of Hermes and Aphrodite at Syme, Crete.' *National Geographic Research* 3: 102–12.

Lebessi, A. and P. Muhly. 1990. 'Aspects of Minoan cult. Sacred enclosures. The evidence from the Syme sanctuary (Crete).' *Archäologischer Anzeiger* 1990: 315–36.

Legarra Herrero, B. 2014. *Mortuary Behavior and Social Trajectories in Pre- and Protopalatial Crete.* Philadelphia, PA: INSTAP Academic Press.

Letesson, Q. 2013. 'Minoan Halls: a syntactical geneaology.' *American Journal of Archaeology* 117: 303–51.

Letesson, Q. and K. Vansteenhuyse. 2006. 'Towards an archaeology of perception: "looking" at the Minoan palaces.' *Journal of Mediterranean Archaeology* 19: 91–119.

Levi, D. 1959. 'Cronac d'Arte: la villa rurale Minoica di Gortina.' *Bollettino d'Arte* 44: 237–65.

Levi, D. 1964. *The Recent Excavations at Phaistos.* Studies in Mediterranean Archaeology 11. Lund: Studies in Mediterranean Archaeology.

Levi, D. 1976. *Festòs e la Civiltà Minoica I.* Incunabula Graeca 60. Rome: Edizioni dell'Ateneo.

Levi, D. and F. M. Carinci. 1988. *Festòs e la Civiltà Minoica II.* Incunabula Graeca 77. Rome: Edizioni dell'Ateneo.

Liverani, M. 1990. *Prestige and Interest: International Relations in the Near East ca. 1600–1100 BC.* Padova: Sargon.

Lloyd, J. F. 1990. 'Settlements, dwellings, and painted pottery: a contribution to the history of Minoan Crete in the early Late Bronze Age.' PhD diss., University of New York.

Logue, W. 2004. 'Set in stone: the role of relief-carved stone vessels in Neopalatial Minoan elite propaganda.' *Annual of the British School at Athens* 99: 149–72.

Lowe Fri, M. 2011. *The Minoan Double Axe: An Experimental Study of Production and Use.* BAR Int. Ser. 2303. Oxford: Archaeopress.

Lucas, G. 2005. *The Archaeology of Time.* London and New York: Routledge.

Lupack, S. M. 2008. *The Role of the Religious Sector in the Economy of Late Bronze Age Mycenaean Greece.* BAR Int. Ser. 1858. Oxford: Archaeopress.

Macdonald, C. F. 1990. 'Destruction and construction in the Palace at Knossos: LM IA–B.' In D. A. Hardy and A. C. Renfrew (eds.), *Thera and the Ancient World III. Volume 3: Chronology.* London: The Thera Foundation: 82–8.

Macdonald, C. F. 2001. 'Chronologies of the Thera eruption. Review of *A test of time: the volcano of Thera and the chronology and history of the Aegean and east Mediterranean in the mid-second Millennium B.C.*, by S. Manning.' *American Journal of Archaeology* 105: 527–32.

Macdonald, C. F. 2002. 'The Neopalatial palaces of Knossos.' In J. Driessen, I. Schoep, and R. Laffineur (eds.), *Monuments of Minos: Rethinking the Minoan Palaces.* Aegaeum 23. Liège and Austin: Université de Liège, Histoire de l'art et archéologie de la Grèce antique and University of Texas at Austin, Program in Aegean Scripts and Prehistory: 35–54.

Macdonald, C. F. 2004. 'Ceramic and contextual confusion in the Old and New Palace periods.' In G. Cadogan, E. Hatzaki, and A. Vasilakis (eds.), *Knossos: Palace, City, State.* British School at Athens Studies 12. London: The British School at Athens: 239–51.

Macdonald, C. F. 2005. *Knossos.* London: Folio Society.

Macdonald, C. F. 2012. 'Palatial Knossos: the early years.' In I. Schoep, P. Tomkins, and J. Driessen (eds.), *Back to the Beginning: Reassessing Social and Political Complexity on Crete during the Early and Middle Bronze Age.* Oxford and Oakville: Oxbow Books: 81–113.

Macdonald, C. F. 2013. 'Between Protopalatial houses and Neopalatial mansions: an "intermezzo" southwest of the Palace at Knossos.' In C. F. Macdonald and C. Knappett (eds.), *Intermezzo: Intermediacy and Regeneration in Middle Minoan III Palatial Crete.* British School at Athens Studies 21. London: British School at Athens: 21–30.

Macdonald, C. F. and C. Knappett. 2007. *Knossos: Protopalatial Deposits in Early Magazine A and the South-west Houses.* British School at Athens Supplementary Volume 41. London: British School at Athens.

Macdonald, C. F. and C. Knappett (eds.). 2013a. *Intermezzo: Intermediacy and Regeneration in Middle Minoan III Palatial Crete.* British School at Athens Studies 21. London: British School at Athens.

Macdonald, C. F. and C. Knappett. 2013b. 'Introduction.' In C. F. Macdonald and C. Knappett (eds.), *Intermezzo: Intermediacy and Regeneration in Middle Minoan III Palatial Crete.*

British School at Athens Studies 21. London: British School at Athens: 1–7.

MacGillivray, J. A. 1994. 'The early history of the Palace at Knossos (MM I–II)'. In D. Evely, H. Hughes-Brock, and N. Momigliano (eds.), *Knossos: A Labyrinth of History. Papers Presented in Honour of Sinclair Hood.* London: British School at Athens: 45–55.

MacGillivray, J. A. 1998. *Knossos: Pottery Groups of the Old Palace Period.* British School at Athens Studies 5. London: British School at Athens.

MacGillivray, J. A. and J. Driessen. 1990. 'Minoan settlement at Palaikastro.' In P. Darcque and R. Treuil (eds.), *L'Habitat Égéen Préhistorique.* Bulletin de Correspondance Hellénique Suppl. 19. Athens: École Français d'Athènes: 395–412.

MacGillivray, J., J. Driessen, and L. H. Sackett. 2000. *The Palaikastro Kouros. A Minoan Chryselephantine Statuette and Its Aegean Bronze Age Context.* British School at Athens Studies 6. London: British School at Athens.

MacGillivray, J. A. and L. H. Sackett. 2010. 'Palaikastro.' In E. H. Cline (ed.), *The Oxford Handbook of the Bronze Age Aegean (ca. 3000–1000 BC).* Oxford: Oxford University Press: 571–81.

Mandalaki, S. 2011. 'Pottery from the LM IB building at Skinias.' In T. M. Brogan and E. Hallager (eds.), *LM IB Pottery: Relative Chronology and Regional Differences.* Monographs of the Danish Institute at Athens 11.2. Athens: Danish Institute at Athens: 379–400.

Manning, S. W. 1995. *The Absolute Chronology of the Aegean Early Bronze Age.* Sheffield: Sheffield Academic Press.

Manning, S. W. 1996. 'Dating the Aegean Bronze Age: without, with, and beyond, radiocarbon.' In K. Randsborg (ed.), *Absolute Chronology: Archaeological Europe 2500–500 BC.* ActaArch 67, ActaArch Supplementa 1. Copenhagen: Munksgaard: 15–37.

Manning, S. W. 1999. *A Test of Time: The Volcano of Thera and the Chronology and History of the Aegean and East Mediterranean in the Mid Second Millennium BC.* Oxford: Oxbow Books.

Manning, S. W. 2008. 'Protopalatial Crete: formation of the palaces.' In C. Shelmerdine (ed.), *The Cambridge Companion to the Aegean Bronze Age.* Cambridge: Cambridge University Press: 105–20.

Manning, S. W. and C. Bronk Ramsey. 2003. 'A Late Minoan I–II absolute chronology for the Aegean – combining archaeology with radiocarbon.' In M. Bietak (ed.), *The Synchronisation of Civilisations in the Eastern Mediterranean in the Second Millennium B.C.* Vienna: Österreichischen Akademie der Wissenschaften: 111–33.

Manning, S. W., C. Bronk Ramsey, C. Doumas, T. Marketou, G. Cadogan, and C. L. Pearson. 2002. 'New evidence for an early date for the Aegean Late Bronze Age and Thera eruption.' *Antiquity* 76: 733–44.

Manning, S. W. and D. A. Sewell. 2002. 'Volcanoes and history: a significant relationship? The case of Santorini.' In R. Torrence and J. Grattan (eds.), *Natural Disasters and Cultural Change.* London and New York: Routledge: 264–91.

Mantzourani, E. 2011. 'Makrygialos reloaded: the LM IB pottery: a response to Dario Puglisi.' In T. M. Brogan and E. Hallager (eds.), *LM IB Pottery: Relative Chronology and Regional Differences.* Monographs of the Danish Institute at Athens 11.1. Athens: Danish Institute at Athens: 291–303.

Mantzourani, E. 2012. 'Sexuality or fertility symbol? The bronze figurine from Makrygialos.' In E. Mantzourani and P. P. Betancourt (eds.), *Philistor: Studies in Honor of Costis Davaras.* Philadelphia, PA: INSTAP Academic Press: 105–12.

Mantzourani, E. and G. Vavouranakis. 2011. 'The Minoan villas in East Crete: households or seats of authority? The case of Prophitis Ilias Praisou.' In K. T. Glowacki and N. Vogeikoff-Brogan (eds.), *STEGA: The Archaeology of Houses and Households in Ancient Crete.* Hesperia Supplement 44. Princeton, NJ: American School of Classical Studies at Athens: 125–35.

Mantzourani, E., G. Vavouranakis, and C. Kanellopoulos. 2005. 'The Klimataria-

Manares Building reconsidered.' *American Journal of Archaeology* 109: 743–76.

Margomenou, D. 2008. 'Food storage in prehistoric northern Greece: interrogating complexity at the margins of the "Mycenaean world".' *Journal of Mediterranean Archaeology* 21: 191–212.

Marinatos, N. 1984. *Art and Religion in Thera: Reconstructing a Bronze Age Society*. Athens: Mathioulakis.

Marinatos, N. 1986. *Minoan Sacrificial Ritual: Cult Practice and Symbolism*. Stockholm: Paul Åströms Förlag.

Marinatos, N. 1987. 'Public festivals in the west courts of the palaces.' In R. Hägg and N. Marinatos (eds.), *The Function of the Minoan Palaces*. Skrifter Utgivna av Svenska Institutet I Athen, 4° 35. Stockholm: Paul Åströms Förlag: 135–43.

Marinatos, N. 1989. 'The Minoan harem: the role of eminent women and the Knossos frescoes.' *Dialogues d'histoire ancienne [Hommage à Ettore Lepore]* 15:2: 33–62.

Marinatos, N. 1990. 'The tree, the stone and the pithos: glimpses into a Minoan ritual.' *Aegaeum* 6: 79–92.

Marinatos, N. 1993. *Minoan Religion: Ritual, Image, and Symbol*. Columbia: University of South Carolina Press.

Marinatos, N. 1995. 'Divine kingship in Minoan Crete.' In P. Rehak (ed.), *The Role of the Ruler in the Prehistoric Aegean*. Aegaeum 11. Liège: Université de Liège, Histoire de l'art et archéologie de la Grèce antique: 37–48.

Marinatos, N. 1996. 'The iconographical program of the Palace of Knossos.' In M. Bietak (ed.), *Haus und Palast im Alten Ägypten. House and Palace in Ancient Egypt*. Österreichische Akademie der Wissenschften Denkschriften der Gesamtakademie 14. Wien: Verlag der Österreichischen Akademie der Wissenschaften.

Marinatos, N. 2005. 'The ideals of manhood in Minoan Crete.' In L. Morgan (ed.), *Aegean Wall Painting: A Tribute to Mark Cameron*. British School at Athens Studies 13. London: British School at Athens: 149–58.

Marinatos, N. 2010. *Minoan Kingship and the Solar Goddess: A Near Eastern Koine*. Urbana, Chicago, and Springfield: University of Illinois Press.

Marinatos, N. 2015. *Sir Arthur Evans and Minoan Crete: Creating the Vision of Knossos*. London and New York: I. B. Tauris.

Marinatos, N. and P. P. Betancourt. 1995. 'The Minoan household.' *Cretological Congress*: 591–5.

Marinatos, N. and R. Hägg. 1983. 'Anthropomorphic cult images in Minoan Crete?' In O. Krzyszkowska and L. Nixon (eds.), *Minoan Society*. Bristol: Bristol Classical Press: 185–201.

Marinatos, N. and R. Hägg. 1986. 'On the ceremonial function of the Minoan polythyron.' *Opuscula Atheniensia* 16: 57–73.

Marinatos, S. 1926. 'Anaskafai Nirou Chani Kritis.' *Praktika tis en Athinais Archaiologikis Etaireias* 1926: 141–7.

Marinatos, S. 1933. 'Funde und Forschungen auf Kreta.' *Archäologischer Anzeiger* 48: 287–314.

Marinatos, S. 1935. 'Anaskafai en Kriti: Arkalochori.' *Praktika tis en Athinais Archaiologikis Etaireias* 1935: 212–20.

Marinatos, S. 1940–1. 'The cult of the Cretan caves.' *The Review of Religion*: 425–39.

Marinatos, S. 1948. 'To Minoikon megaron tou Sklavokampou.' *Archaiologika Ephemeris* 1939–41: 69–96.

Marinatos, S. 1950. 'Megaron Vathypetrou.' *Praktika tis en Athinais Archaiologikis Etaireias* 1950: 242–57.

Marinatos, S. 1952. 'Anaskafai en Vathypetro Kritis.' *Praktika tis en Athinais Archaiologikis Etaireias* 1952: 592–610.

Marinatos, S. 1955. 'Anaskafai en Lykasto kai Vathypetro Kritis.' *Praktika tis en Athinais Archaiologikis Etaireias* 1955: 306–10.

Marinatos, S. 1960. *Crete and Mycenae*. [Translated by J. Boardman. With photographs by M. Hirmer.] London: Thames and Hudson.

Marinatos, S. 1962. 'Zur Frage der Grotte von Arkalochori.' *Kadmos* 1: 87–94.

Mavroudi, N. 2011. 'Interpreting domestic space in Neopalatial Crete: a few thoughts on House II at Petras, Sitia.' In K. T. Glowacki and N. Vogeikoff-Brogan (eds.), *STEGA: The Archaeology of Houses and Households in*

Ancient Crete. Hesperia Supplement 44. Princeton, NJ: American School of Classical Studies at Athens: 119–24.

Mavroudi, N. 2012. 'House II.1 at Petras, Siteia: its architectural life.' In M. Tsipopoulou (ed.), *Petras, Siteia – 25 Years of Excavations and Studies.* Monographs of the Danish Institute at Athens 16. Athens: Danish Institute at Athens: 221–33.

McCoy, F. 2009. 'The eruption within the debate about the date.' In D. A. Warburton (ed.), *Time's Up! Dating the Minoan Eruption of Santorini.* Monographs of the Danish Institute at Athens 10. Athens: Danish Institute at Athens: 73–90.

McDonald, W. and C. Thomas. 1990 (second ed.). *Progress into the Past: The Rediscovery of the Mycenaean Civilization.* Bloomington and Indianapolis: Indiana University Press.

McEnroe, J. 1979. 'Minoan house and town arrangement.' PhD diss., University of Toronto.

McEnroe, J. 1982. 'A typology of Minoan Neopalatial houses.' *American Journal of Archaeology* 86: 3–19.

McEnroe, J. 1995. 'Sir Arthur Evans and Edwardian archaeology.' *The Classical Bulletin* 71: 3–18.

McEnroe, J. 2001. 'The architecture of Pseira.' In J. McEnroe (ed.), *The Architecture of Pseira.* University Museum Monograph 109. Philadelphia: University of Pennsylvania Museum: 1–78.

McEnroe, J. C. 2002. 'Cretan questions: politics and archaeology 1898–1913.' In Y. Hamilakis (ed.), *Labyrinth Revisited: Rethinking 'Minoan' Archaeology.* Oxford: Oxbow Books: 59–72.

McEnroe, J. C. 2010. *Architecture of Minoan Crete: Constructing Identity in the Aegean Bronze Age.* Austin: University of Texas Press.

McGowan, E. 2011. *Ambiguity and Minoan Neopalatial Seal Imagery.* Uppsala: Åströms Förlag.

McMahon, A. 2013. 'Space, sound, and light: toward a sensory experience of ancient monumental architecture.' *American Journal of Archaeology* 117: 163–79.

Melas, M. 2009. 'The Afiartis Project: excavations at the Minoan settlement of Fournoi, Karpathos (2001–2004) – a preliminary report.' In C. F. Macdonald, E. Hallager, and W.-D. Niemeier (eds.), *The Minoans in the Central, Eastern and Northern Aegean – New Evidence.* Monographs of the Danish Institute at Athens 8. Athens: Danish Institute at Athens: 59–72.

Michaelidis, P. 1993. 'Potters' workshops in Minoan Crete.' *Studi Micenei ed Egeo-Anatolici* 32: 7–39.

Michailidou, A. 2003. 'Measuring weight and value in Bronze Age economies in the Aegean and the Near East: a discussion on metal axes of no practical use.' In K. Polinger Foster and R. Laffineur (eds.), *Metron: Measuring the Aegean Bronze Age.* Aegaeum 24. Liège and Austin: Université de Liège, Histoire de l'art et archéologie de la Grèce antique and University of Texas at Austin, Program in Aegean Scripts and Prehistory: 301–14.

Militello, P. 1988. 'Riconsiderazioni preliminary sulla documentazione in lineare A da Haghia Triada.' *Sileno* 14: 233–61.

Militello, P. 1992. 'Uno *Hieron* nella villa di Haghia Triada.' *Sileno* 18: 101–13.

Militello, P. 1998. *Haghia Triada I. Gli Affreschi.* Monografie della Scuola Archeologica di Atene e delle Missioni Italiane in Oriente 9. Aldo Ausilio Editore in Padova: Bottega d'Erasmo. Vol. IX.

Militello, P. 2001. 'Gli Affreschi Minoici de Festòs.' *Studi di archeologia cretese* II. Padova: Bottega d'Erasmo: 19–195.

Militello, P. 2002. 'Amministrazione e contabilità a Festòs. II. Il contesto archeologico dei documenti palatini.' *Creta Antica* 3: 51–91.

Militello, P. 2012. 'Emerging authority: a functional analysis of the MM II settlement of Phaistos.' In I. Schoep, P. Tomkins, and J. Driessen (eds.), *Back to the Beginning: Reassessing Social and Political Complexity on Crete during the Early and Middle Bronze Age.* Oxford: Oxbow Books: 236–72.

Minos, N. and M. E. Kavoulaki. 2010. 'Parousiasi tou ergou tou grafeiou Knosou.' *Archaeologiko Ergo Kritis* 1: 108–20.

Mirié, S. 1979. *Das Thronraumareal des Palastes von Knossos: Versuch einer Neuinterpretation seiner Entstehung und seiner Funktion.* Saarbruecker Beiträge zur Altertumskunde 26. Bonn: Habelt.

Molloy, B. 2010. 'Swords and swordsmanship in the Aegean Bronze Age.' *American Journal of Archaeology* 114: 403–28.

Molloy, B. 2012. 'Martial Minoans? War as social process, practice and event in Bronze Age Crete.' *Annual of the British School at Athens* 107: 87–142.

Molloy, B. and C. Duckworth (eds.). 2014. *A Cretan Landscape through Time: Survey, Geoarchaeological Prospection, and Excavation in the Environs of Priniatikos Pyrgos.* Oxford: British Archaeological Reports.

Momigliano, N. 1999. *Duncan Mackenzie: A Cautious Canny Highlander and the Palace of Minos at Knossos.* London: Institute of Classical Studies.

Momigliano, N. 2006. 'Sir Arthur Evans, Greek myths and the Minoans.' In P. Darcque, M. Fotiadis, and O. Polychronopoulou (eds.), *Mythos: La Préhistoire égéenne du XIXe au XXIe siècle après J.-C.* Bulletin de Correspondance Hellénique supplement 46. Athens: École Française d'Athènes: 73–80.

Momigliano, N. (ed.) 2007. *Knossos Pottery Handbook: Neolithic and Bronze Age (Minoan).* British School at Athens Studies 14. London: British School at Athens.

Momigliano, N. 2009. 'Minoans at Iasos?' In C. F. Macdonald, E. Hallager, and W.-D. Niemeier (eds.), *The Minoans in the Central, Eastern and Northern Aegean – New Evidence.* Monographs of the Danish Institute at Athens 8. Athens: Danish Institute at Athens: 121–40.

Monaco, C. and L. Tortorici. 2003. 'Effects of earthquakes on the Minoan "Royal Villa" at Haghia Triada (Crete).' *Creta Antica* 4: 403–17.

Montecchi, B. 2010. 'A classification proposal of Linear A tablets from Haghia Triada in classes and series.' *Kadmos* 49: 11–38.

Montecchi, B. 2012. 'Linear A banqueting lists?' *Kadmos* 51: 1–26.

Moody, J. 1987. 'The Minoan palace as a prestige artifact.' In R. Hägg and N. Marinatos (eds.), *The Function of the Minoan Palaces.* Skrifter Utgivna av Svenska Institutet I Athen, 4° 35. Stockholm: Paul Åströms Förlag: 235–41.

Moody, J. and F. E. Lukermann. 1985. 'Proto-history: the reconstruction of probable worlds.' In N. C. Wilkie and W. D. E. Coulson (eds.), *Contributions to Aegean Archaeology: Studies in Honor of William A. McDonald.* Publications in Ancient Studies 1. Minneapolis: Center for Ancient Studies, University of Minnesota: 61–89.

Moore, D. 2010. *Dawn of Discovery: The Early British Travellers to Crete. Richard Pococke, Robert Pashley and Thomas Spratt, and Their Contribution to the Island's Bronze Age Archaeological Heritage.* Oxford: Archaeopress.

Moore, J. D. 1996: *Architecture and Power in the Ancient Andes: The Archaeology of Public Buildings.* Cambridge: Cambridge University Press.

Morales, H. 2007. *Classical Mythology: A Very Short Introduction.* Oxford: Oxford University Press.

Morgan, C. 1990. *Athletes and Oracles: The Transformation of Olympia and Delphi in the Eighth Century BC.* Cambridge: Cambridge University Press.

Morgan, L. 1984. 'Morphology, syntax and the issue of chronology.' In J. A. MacGillivray and R. L. N. Barber (eds.), *The Prehistoric Cyclades: Contributions to a Workshop on Cycladic Chronology.* Edinburgh: Department of Classical Archaeology, University of Edinburgh: 165–78.

Morgan, L. 1989. 'Ambiguity and interpreta-tion.' In I. Pini (ed.), *Fragen und Probleme der Bronzezeitlichen Ägäischen Glyptik.* CMS Beiheft 3. Berlin: Gebr. Mann Verlag: 145–61.

Morgan, L. 1995. 'Frontal face and the symbo-lism of death in Aegean glyptic.' In W. Müller (ed.), *Sceaux minoens et mycéniens.* CMS Beiheft 5. Berlin: Gebr. Mann Verlag: 135–49.

Morgan, L. 2000. 'Form and meaning in figura-tive painting.' In S. Sherratt (ed.), *The Wall*

Paintings of Thera. Athens: The Thera Foundation: 925–46.

Morgan, L. 2005. 'New discoveries and new ideas in Aegean wall painting.' In L. Morgan (ed.), *Aegean Wall Painting: A Tribute to Mark Cameron.* British School at Athens Studies 13. London: British School at Athens: 21–44.

Morpurgo-Davies, A. and G. Cadogan. 1971. 'A Linear A tablet from Pirgos, Mirtos, Crete.' *Kadmos* 10: 105–9.

Morpurgo-Davies, A. and G. Cadogan. 1977. 'A second Linear A tablet from Pyrgos.' *Kadmos* 16: 7–9.

Morris, C. 2004. '"Art makes visible": an archaeology of the senses in Minoan elite art.' In N. Brodie and C. Hills (eds.), *Material Engagements: Studies in Honour of Colin Renfrew.* Cambridge: Cambridge University Press: 31–44.

Morris, C. 2006. 'From ideologies of motherhood to "collecting mother goddesses".' In Y. Hamilakis and N. Momigliano (eds.), *Archaeology and European Modernity: Producing and Consuming the 'Minoans.'* Creta Antica 7. Padua: Bottega d'Erasmo: 69–78.

Morris, C. 2009a. 'Configuring the individual: bodies of figurines in Minoan Crete.' In A. L. D'Agata and A. Van de Moortel (eds.), *Archaeologies of Cult: Essays on Ritual and Cult in Crete in Honor of Geraldine C. Gesell.* Hesperia Suppl. 42. Princeton, NJ: American School of Classical Studies at Athens: 179–87.

Morris, C. 2009b. 'The iconography of the bared breast in Aegean Bronze Age art.' In K. Kopaka (ed.), *FYLO: Engendering Prehistoric 'Stratigraphies' in the Aegean and the Mediterranean.* Liège and Austin: Université de Liège, Histoire de l'art et archéologie de la Grèce antique and University of Texas at Austin, Program in Aegean Scripts and Prehistory: 243–9.

Morris, C. and A. Peatfield. 2002. 'Feeling through the body: gesture in Cretan Bronze Age religion.' In Y. Hamilakis, M. Pluciennik, and S. Tarlow (eds.), *Thinking Through the Body: Archaeologies of Corporeality.* New York: Springer: 105–20.

Morris, C. and A. Peatfield. 2004. 'Experiencing ritual: shamanic elements in Minoan religion.' In M. Wedde (ed.), *Celebrations. Sanctuaries and the Vestiges of Cult Activity.* Bergen: Åströms Editions: 35–59.

Morris, C. and A. Peatfield. 2014. 'Health and healing on Cretan Bronze Age peak sanctuaries.' In D. Michaelides (ed.), *Medicine and Healing in the Ancient Mediterranean World.* Oxford: Oxbow: 54–63.

Mountjoy, P. 1984. 'The Marine style pottery of LM IB/LH IIA: towards a corpus.' *Annual of the British School at Athens* 79: 161–219.

Mountjoy, P. 1985. 'Ritual associations for LM IB Marine Style vases.' In P. Darque and J. C. Poursat (eds.), *L'Iconographie minoenne.* Bulletin de Correspondance Hellénique Suppl. 11. Athens: École Française d'Athènes: 231–42.

Mountjoy, P. (ed.). 2003. *Knossos: The South House.* British School at Athens Suppl. 34. London: British School at Athens.

Muhly, P. 1981. 'Minoan libation tables.' PhD diss., Bryn Mawr College.

Muhly, P. 1992. *Minoikos Laksevtos Tafos ston Poro Irakleiou (Anaskafes 1967).* Athens: Athens Archaeological Service.

Muhly, P. 2012. 'A terracotta foot model from the Syme sanctuary, Crete.' In E. Mantzourani and P. P. Betancourt (eds.), *Philistor: Studies in Honor of Costis Davaras.* Philadelphia, PA: INSTAP Academic Press: 133–8.

Muhly, P. and J.-P. Olivier. 2008. 'Linear A inscriptions from the Syme Sanctuary, Crete.' *Archaiologiki Ephimeris* 147: 197–223.

Müller, S. 1990. 'Prospection de la plaine de Malia.' *Bulletin de Correspondance Hellénique* 114: 921–30.

Müller, S. 1991a. 'Prospection de la plaine de Malia.' *Bulletin de Correspondance Hellénique* 115: 741–9.

Müller, S. 1991b. 'Routes minoennes en relation avec le site de Malia.' *Bulletin de Correspondance Hellénique* 115: 545–60.

Müller, S. 1992. 'Prospection de la plaine de Malia.' *Bulletin de Correspondance Hellénique* 116: 742–53.

Müller, S. 1996. 'Prospection de la plaine de Malia.' *Bulletin de Correspondance Hellénique* 116: 921–8.

Müller, S. 1998. 'Malia: prospection archéologique de la plaine.' *Bulletin de Correspondance Hellénique* 122: 548–52.

Munn, N. D. 1992. 'The cultural anthropology of time: a critical essay.' *Annual Review of Anthropology* 21: 92–123.

Murray, T. 1999. 'A return to the "Pompeii Premise".' In T. Murray (ed.), *Time and Archaeology*. London: Routledge: 8–27.

Musgrave, J. 1984. 'The human skeletons.' In M. R. Popham (ed.), *The Minoan Unexplored Mansion at Knossos: Vol. 1 Text*. London: British School at Athens and Thames and Hudson: 309–10.

Musgrave, J. 2000. 'The anatomy of a Minoan masterpiece.' In J. A. MacGillivray, J. M. Driessen, and L. H. Sackett (eds.), *The Palaikastro Kouros: A Minoan Chryselephantine Statuette and Its Aegean Bronze Age Context*. British School at Athens Studies 6. London: British School at Athens: 97–101.

Myres, J. L. 1902–3. 'Excavations at Palaikastro II.' *Annuals of the British School at Athens* 9: 356–87.

Myres, J. L. 1930. *Who Were the Greeks?* Berkeley: University of California Press.

Myres, J. L. 1941. 'Sir Arthur Evans: 1851–1941.' *Proceedings of the British Academy* 27: 323–57.

Nakassis, D., W. A. Parkinson, and M. L. Galaty, 2011. 'Redistributive economies from a theoretical and cross-cultural perspective.' *American Journal of Archaeology* 115: 177–84.

Nakassis, D. and K. Pluta. 2003. 'Linear A and multidimensional scaling'. In K. Polinger Foster and R. Laffineur (eds.), *Metron: Measuring the Aegean Bronze Age. Agaeum 24*. Liège and Austin: Université de Liège. Histoire de l'art et archéologie de la Grèce antique and University of Texas at Austin, Program in Aegean Scripts and Prehistory: 335–42.

Niemeier, W.-D. 1979. 'The master of the Gournia octopus stirrup jar and a Late Minoan IA pottery workshop at Gournia exporting to Thera.' *Temple University Aegean Symposium* 4: 18–26.

Niemeier, W.-D. 1987. 'On the function of the "Throne Room" in the Palace at Knossos.' In R. Hägg and N. Marinatos (eds.), *The Function of the Minoan Palaces*. Skrifter Utgivna av Svenska Institutet I Athen, 4°3 5. Stockholm: Paul Åströms Förlag: 163–8.

Niemeier, W.-D. 1988. 'The "Priest-King" Fresco from Knossos. A new reconstruction and interpretation.' In E. French and K. Wardle (eds.), *Problems in Greek Prehistory*. Bristol: Bristol Classical Press: 235–44.

Niemeier, W.-D. 1994. 'Knossos in the New Palace period (MM III–LM IB).' In D. Evely, H. Hughes-Brock and N. Momigliano (eds.), *Knossos: A Labyrinth of History. Papers Presented in Honour of Sinclair Hood*. Oxford: British School at Athens: 71–88.

Niemeier, W.-D. 1996. 'A Linear A inscription from Miletus (MIL Zb 1).' *Kadmos* 35: 87–99.

Niemeier, W.-D. 2005. 'Minoans, Mycenaeans, Hittites, and Ionians in western Asia Minor: new excavations in Bronze Age Miletus-Millawanda.' In A. Villing (ed.), *The Greeks in the East*. British Museum Research Publication 157. London: British Museum: 1–36.

Niemeier, W.-D. 2009. '"Minoanisation" versus "Minoan thalassocrassy" – an introduction.' In C. F. Macdonald, E. Hallager, and W.-D. Niemeier (eds.), *The Minoans in the Central, Eastern and Northern Aegean – New Evidence*. Monographs of the Danish Institute at Athens 8. Athens: Danish Institute at Athens: 11–29.

Niemeier, W.-D. and B. Niemeier. 1998. 'Minoan frescoes in the eastern Mediterranean.' In E. H. Cline and D. Harris-Cline (eds.), *The Aegean and the Orient in the Second Millennium*. Aegaeum 18. Liège and Austin: Université de Liège, Histoire de l'art et archéologie de la Grèce antique and University of Texas at Austin, Program in Aegean Scripts and Prehistory: 69–99.

Niemeier, W.-D. and B. Niemeier. 1999. 'The Minoans of Miletus.' In P. P. Betancourt, V. Karageorghis, R. Laffineur, and W.-D. Niemeier (eds.), *Meletemata: Studies in Aegean Archaeology Presented to Malcolm H. Wiener as*

He Enters His 65th Year. Aegaeum 20. Liège and Austin: Université de Liège, Histoire de l'art et archéologie de la Grèce antique and University of Texas at Austin, Program in Aegean Scripts and Prehistory: 543–54.

Nikolakopoulou, I. 2009. '"Beware Cretans bearing gifts." Tracing the origins of Minoan influence at Akrotiri, Thera.' In C. F. Macdonald, E. Hallager, and W.-D. Niemeier (eds.), *The Minoans in the Central, Eastern and Northern Aegean – New Evidence.* Monographs of the Danish Institute at Athens 8. Athens: Danish Institute at Athens: 31–40.

Nilsson, M. P. 1950 [Second ed.]. *The Minoan-Mycenaean Religion and Its Survival in Greek Religion.* Lund: Gleerup.

Nordfeldt, A. C. 1987. 'Residential quarters and lustral basins.' In R. Hägg and N. Marinatos (eds.), *The Function of the Minoan Palaces.* Skrifter Utgivna av Svenska Institutet I Athen, 4° 35. Stockholm: Paul Åströms Förlag: 187–94.

Nordquist, G. and H. Whittaker. 2007. 'Comments on Kristiansen and Larsson: The Rise of Bronze Age Society. Travels, Transmissions and Transformations.' *Norwegian Archaeological Review* 40: 75–84.

Nowicki, K. 1994. 'Some remarks on the pre- and protopalatial peak sanctuaries in Crete.' *Aegean Archaeology* 1: 31–48.

Nowicki, K. 1996. 'Lasithi (Crete): one hundred years of archaeological research.' *Aegean Archaeology* 3: 27–47.

Nowicki, K. 2004. 'Report on investigations in Greece XI. Studies in 1995–2003.' *Archeologia* 55: 75–100.

Nowicki, K. 2007. 'Some remarks on new peak sanctuaries in Crete: the topography of ritual areas and their relationship with settlements.' *Jahrbuch des Deutschen Archäologischen Instituts* 122: 1–31.

Nowicki, K. 2012. 'East Cretan peak sanctuaries revisited.' In E. Mantzourani and P. P. Betancourt (eds.), *Philistor: Studies in Honor of Costis Davaras.* Philadelphia, PA: INSTAP Academic Press: 139–54.

Nowicki, K. 2013. 'Report on investigations in Greece XIII. Studies in 2011–2013.' *Archeologia* 64: 141–65.

Olivier, J.-P. 1986. 'Cretan writing in the second millennium BC.' *World Archaeology* 17: 377–89.

Olivier, J.-P. 1988. 'Tirynthian Graffiti – Ausgrabungen in Tiryns 1982/83.' *Archäologischer Anzeiger* 1988: 253–68.

Oren, E. 1996. 'Minoan graffito from Tel Haror (Negev, Israel).' *Cretan Studies* 5: 91–118.

O'Shea, J. 1981. 'Coping with scarcity: exchange and social storage.' In A. Sheridan and G. Bailey (eds.), *Economic Archaeology.* Oxford: Archaeopress: 167–86.

Owens, G. 1995. 'Evidence for the Minoan language (1): The Minoan libation formula.' *Cretan Studies* 5: 163–79.

Owens, G. 1996. 'Linear A inscriptions at entrances to buildings.' *Kadmos* 35: 169–71.

Owens, G. 1999. 'Linear A in the Aegean: the further travels of the Minoan script. A study of the 30+ extra-Cretan Minoan inscriptions.' In P. P. Betancourt, V. Karageorghis, R. Laffineur, and W.-D. Niemeier (eds.), *Meletemata: Studies in Aegean Archaeology Presented to Malcolm H. Wiener as He Enters His 65th Year.* Aegaeum 20. Liège and Austin: Université de Liège, Histoire de l'art et archéologie de la Grèce antique and University of Texas at Austin, Program in Aegean Scripts and Prehistory: 583–97.

Pace, B. 1921. 'La monarchia minoica.' *Atti dell'Accademia nazionale dei Lincei: Rendiconti* Series 4 XXIX: 307–16.

Padgen, A. 2002. 'Europe: conceptualising a continent.' In A. Padgen (ed.), *The Idea of Europe. From Antiquity to the European Union.* Cambridge: Cambridge University Press: 33–54.

Palaima, T. 1982. 'Linear A in the Cyclades: the trade and travel of a script.' *Temple University Aegean Symposium* 7: 15–21.

Palaima, T. 1990. 'Origin, development, transition and transformation: the purposes and techniques of administration in Minoan and Mycenaean society.' In T. Palaima (ed.), *Aegean Seals, Sealings and Administration.* Aegaeum 5. Liège: Université de Liège, Histoire de l'art et archéologie de la Grèce antique: 83–104.

Palaima, T. 1994. 'Seal-users and script-users/ nodules and tablets at LM IB Hagia Triada.' In P. Ferioli, E. Fiandra, G. G. Fissore, and M. Frangipane (eds.), *Archives before Writing*. Rome: Centro Internazionale di Ricerche Archeologiche Antropologiche e Storiche: 307–30.

Palaima, T. 1995. 'The nature of the Mycenaean *Wanax*.' In P. Rehak (ed.), *The Role of the Ruler in the Prehistoric Aegean*. Aegaeum 11. Liège and Austin: Université de Liège, Histoire de l'art et archéologie de la Grèce antique and University of Texas at Austin, Program in Aegean Scripts and Prehistory: 119–42.

Palio, O. 2001a. 'Il Tardo Minoico I: la casa di Haghia Photinì.' In L. Beschi, A. Di Vita, V. La Rosa, G. Pugliese Carratelli, and G. Rizza (eds.), *I Cento Anni dello Scavo di Festòs*. Atti dei Convegni Lincei 173. Rome: Accademia Nazionale de Lincei: 243–67.

Palio, O. 2001b. 'I vasi in pietra dai vani 8–11 del palazzo di Festòs.' *Creta Antica* 2: 77–90.

Palio, O. 2001c. *La Casa Tardo Minoico I di Chalara a Festòs. Studi di Archeologia Cretese II*. Padua: Bottega d'Erasmo: 247–420.

Palmer, R. 1994. *Wine in the Mycenaean Palace Economy*. Aegaeum 10. Liège: Université de Liège, Histoire de l'art et archéologie de la Grèce antique.

Palmer, R. 1995. 'Linear A commodities: a comparison of resources.' In R. Laffineur and W.-D. Niemeier (eds.), *Politeia: Society and State in the Aegean Bronze Age*. Aegaeum 12. Liège and Austin: Université de Liège, Histoire de l'art et archéologie de la Grèce antique and University of Texas at Austin, Program in Aegean Scripts and Prehistory: 133–55.

Palyvou, C. 1987. 'Circulatory patterns in Minoan architecture.' R. Hägg and N. Marinatos (eds.), *The Function of the Minoan Palaces*. Skrifter Utgivna av Svenska Institutet I Athen, 4°35. Stockholm: Paul Åströms Förlag: 195–203.

Palyvou, C. 2000. 'Concepts of space in Aegean Bronze Age art and architecture.' In S. Sherratt (ed.), *The Wall Paintings of Thera*. Athens: The Thera Foundation: 413–36.

Palyvou, C. 2002. 'Central Courts: the supremacy of the void.' In J. Driessen, I. Schoep, and R. Laffineur (eds.), *Monuments of Minos: Rethinking the Minoan Palaces*. Aegaeum 23. Liège and Austin: Université de Liège, Histoire de l'art et archéologie de la Grèce antique and University of Texas at Austin, Program in Aegean Scripts and Prehistory: 167–78.

Palyvou, C. 2004. 'Outdoor space in Minoan architecture: community and privacy.' In G. Cadogan, E. Hatzaki, and A. Vasilakis (eds.), *Knossos: Palace, City, State*. British School at Athens Studies 12. London: British School at Athens: 207–18.

Panagiotaki, M. 1999. *The Central Palace Sanctuary at Knossos*. British School at Athens Suppl. 31. London: The British School at Athens.

Panagiotakis, N. 2003. 'L'évolution archéologique de la *Pédiada* (Crète centrale): premier bilan d'une prospection.' *Bulletin de Correspondance Hellénique* 127: 327–430.

Panagiotakis, N. 2004. 'Contacts between Knossos and the Pediada region in central Crete.' In G. Cadogan, E. Hatzaki, and A. Vasilakis (eds.), *Knossos: Palace, City, State*. British School at Athens Studies 12. London: British School at Athens: 177–86.

Panagiotakis, N., M. Panagiotaki, and A. Sarris. 2013. 'Earliest communication system in the Aegean.' *Electryone* 1: 13–27.

Panagiotopoulos, D. 2001. 'Keftiu in context: Theban tomb-paintings as a historical source.' *Oxford Journal of Archaeology* 20: 263–83.

Panagiotopoulos, D. 2012. 'Aegean imagery and the syntax of viewing.' In D. Panagiotopoulos and U. Günkel-Maschek (eds.), *Minoan Realities: Approaches to Images, Architecture, and Society in the Aegean Bronze Age*. Louvain: UCL Press: 63–82.

Panagiotopoulos, D. and U. Günkel-Maschek (eds.) 2012. *Minoan Realities: Approaches to Images, Architecture, and Society in the Aegean Bronze Age*. Louvain: UCL Press.

Papadopoulos, J. K. 1997. 'Knossos.' In M. de la Torre (ed.), *The Conservation of Archaeological*

Sites in the Mediterranean Region. Los Angeles, CA: Getty Conservation Institute: 93–125.

Papadopoulos, J. K. 2005. 'Inventing the Minoans: archaeology, modernity and European identity.' *Journal of Mediterranean Archaeology* 18: 87–149.

Papadopoulou, E. and I. Tzachili. 2010. 'Anaskafi sto iero koryfis tou Vrysina Nomou Rethymnis.' *Archaiologiko Ergo Kritis* 1: 452–63.

Papapostolou, I. A., L. Godart, and J.-P. Olivier. 1976. *I Grammiki A sto Minoïko Archeio ton Chanion*. Incunabula Graeca 62. Rome: Edizioni dell'Ateneo.

Parker Pearson, M. 1999. *The Archaeology of Death and Burial*. Stroud: The History Press.

Parker Pearson, M. and C. Richards. 1994. 'Ordering the world: perceptions of architecture, space and time.' In M. Parker Pearson and C. Richards (eds.), *Architecture and Order: Approaches to Social Space*. London and New York: Routledge: 1–37.

Patria, E. 1988–9. 'The misunderstanding of Linear A.' *Minos* 23–4: 15–38.

Patterson, T. and C. Gailey (eds.). 1987. *Power Relations and State Formation*. Washington, DC: American Anthropological Association.

Peatfield, A. 1983. 'The topography of Minoan peak sanctuaries.' *Annual of the British School at Athens* 78: 273–9.

Peatfield, A. 1987. 'Palace and peak: the political and religious relationship.' In R. Hägg and N. Marinatos (eds.), *The Function of the Minoan Palaces*. Skrifter Utgivna av Svenska Institutet I Athen, 4° 35. Stockholm: Paul Åströms Förlag: 89–93.

Peatfield, A. 1989. 'The peak sanctuaries of Minoan Crete.' PhD diss., University College, London.

Peatfield, A. 1990. 'Minoan peak sanctuaries: history and society.' *Opuscula Atheniensia* 18.8: 117–31.

Peatfield, A. 1992. 'Rural ritual in Bronze Age Crete: The peak sanctuary at Atsipadhes.' *Cambridge Archaeological Journal* 2: 59–87.

Peatfield, A. 1994. 'After the "Big Bang" – what? Or Minoan symbols and shrines beyond palatial collapse.' In S. Alcock and R. Osborne (eds.), *Placing the Gods: Sanctuaries and Sacred Space in Ancient Greece*. Oxford: Oxford University Press: 19–36.

Peatfield, A. 1999. 'The paradox of violence: weaponry and martial art in Minoan Crete.' In R. Laffineur (ed.), *Polemos: Le Contexte Guerrier en Égée à l'Âge du Bronze*. Aegaeum 19. Liège and Austin: Université de Liège, Histoire de l'art et archéologie de la Grèce antique and University of Texas at Austin, Program in Aegean Scripts and Prehistory: 67–74.

Peatfield, A. 2007. 'The dynamics of ritual on Minoan peak sanctuaries.' In D. Barrowclough and C. Malone (eds.), *Cult in Context: Reconsidering Ritual in Archaeology*. Oxford: Oxbow Books: 297–300.

Peatfield, A. 2009. 'The topography of Minoan peak sanctuaries revisited.' In A. L. D'Agata and A. Van de Moortel (eds.), *Archaeologies of Cult: Essays on Ritual and Cult in Crete in Honor of Geraldine C. Gesell*. Hesperia Suppl. 42. Princeton, NJ: American School of Classical Studies at Athens: 251–9.

Peatfield, A. 2016. 'A metaphysical history of Minoan religion.' In E. Alram-Stern, F. Blakolmer, S. Deger-Jalkotzy, R. Laffineur, and J. Weilhartner (eds.), *Metaphysis: Ritual, Myth and Symbolism in the Aegean Bronze Age*. Aegaeum 39. Leuven – Liège: Peeters: 485–94.

Pelon, O. 1980. *Le Palais de Malia V*. Études Crétoises 25. Paris: Paul Geuthner.

Pelon, O. 1982. 'Palais et palais à Malia (Crète).' *Revue des Archéologues et Historiens d'Art de Louvain* 15: 57–81.

Pelon, O. 1992. *Guide de Malia: Le Palais et la Nécropole de Chrysolakkos*. Paris: Paul Geuthner.

Pelon, O. 2002. 'Contribution du palais de Malia à l'étude et à l'interprétation des 'palais' minoens.' In J. Driessen, I. Schoep, and R. Laffineur (eds.), *Monuments of Minos: Rethinking the Minoan Palaces*. Aegaeum 23. Liège and Austin: Université de Liège, Histoire de l'art et archéologie de la Grèce antique and University of Texas, Program in Aegean Scripts and Prehistory: 111–21.

Pelon, O. 2005. 'Les deux destructions du palais de Malia.' In I. Bradfer-Burdet, B. Detournay, and R. Laffineur (eds.), *Kris Technitis: L'Artisan Crétois*. Aegaeum 26. Liège and Austin: Université de Liège, Histoire de l'art et archéologie de la Grèce antique and University of Texas at Austin, Program in Aegean Scripts and Prehistory: 185–97.

Pendlebury, J. 1939. *Archaeology of Crete: An Introduction*. London: Methuen and Co.

Pendlebury, J. D. S., E. Eccles, and M. B. Money-Coutts. 1932–3. 'Journeys in Crete, 1934.' *Annual of the British School at Athens* 33: 80–100.

Pernier, L. and L. Banti. 1951. *Il Palazzo Minoico di Festòs. Scavi e Studi della Missione Archeologica Italiana a Creta dal 1900 al 1950*. Rome: Libreria dello Stato.

Peterson, S. E. 1981. 'Wall painting in the Aegean Bronze Age: the procession frescoes.' PhD diss., University of Minnesota.

Petruso, K. 1978. 'Marks on some Minoan balance weights and their interpretation.' *Kadmos* 17: 26–42.

Philips, J. 2006. 'Why? ... And why not? Minoan reception and perceptions of Egyptian influence.' In E. Czerny, I. Hein, H. Hunger, D. Melman, and A. Schwab (eds.), *Timelines: Studies in Honour of Manfred Bietak: Vol. 2*. Leuven: Uitgeverij Peeters en Departement Oosterse Studies: 293–300.

Philips, J. 2008. *Aegyptiaca on the Island of Crete in Their Chronological Context: A Critical Review I–II*. Vienna: Verlag der Österreichischen Akademie der Wissenschaften.

Picard, C. 1948. *Les Religions Préhelléniques (Crète et Mycènes)*. Paris: Presses Universitaires de France.

Pilali-Papasteriou, A. 2004. 'Knosos kai theokratia.' In G. Cadogan, E. Hatzaki, and A. Vasilakis (eds.), *Knossos: Palace, City, State*. British School at Athens Studies 12. London: British School at Athens: 323–7.

Pini, I. 2006. 'Look-alikes, copies and replicas.' *Cretological Congress*: 219–30.

Platon, L. 1988. 'The workshops and working areas of Minoan Crete: the evidence of the Palace and town of Zakros for a comparative study.' PhD diss., University of Bristol.

Platon, L. 1993. 'Ateliers palatiaux minoens: une nouvelle image.' *Bulletin de Correspondance Hellénique* 67: 103–22.

Platon, L. 1997. 'The Minoan "villa" in eastern Crete: Riza, Akhladia, and Prophetes Elias, Praissos: two different specimens of one category?' In R. Hägg (ed.), *The Function of the 'Minoan Villa.'* Skrifter Utgivna av Svenska Institutet I Athen, 4° 46. Stockholm: Svenska Institutet I Athen: 187–202.

Platon, L. 1999a 'New evidence for the occupation at Zakros before the LM I palace.' In P. P. Betancourt, V. Karageorghis, R. Laffineur, and W. D. Niemeier (eds.), *Meletemata. Studies in Aegean Archaeology Presented to Malcolm H. Wiener as He Enters His 65th Year*. Aegaeum 20. Liège and Austin: Université de Liège, Histoire de l'art et archéologie de la Grèce antique and University of Texas at Austin, Program in Aegean Scripts and Prehistory: 671–82.

Platon, L. 1999b. 'Anupografa "erga technis" sta cheria idioton kata ti neoanaktoriki periodo stin Kriti.' In I. Kilian-Dirlmeier and M. Egg (eds.), *Eliten in der Bronzezeit. Ergebnisse zweier Kolloquien in Mainz und Athen*. Mainz: Römisch-Germanischen Zentralmuseums: 37–50.

Platon, L. 2002. 'The political and cultural influence of the Zakros palace on nearby sites and in a wider context.' In J. Driessen, I. Schoep, and R. Laffineur (eds.), *Monuments of Minos: Rethinking the Minoan Palaces*. Aegaeum 23. Liège and Austin: Université de Liège, Histoire de l'art et archéologie de la Grèce antique and University of Texas at Austin, Program in Aegean Scripts and Prehistory: 144–56.

Platon, L. 2004. 'To Usterominoiko I anaktoro tis Zakrou: mia "Knosos" ekso apo tin Knoso?' In G. Cadogan, E. Hatzaki, and A. Vasilakis (eds.), *Knossos: Palace, City, State*. British School at Athens Studies 12. London: British School at Athens: 381–92.

Platon, L. 2011a. 'Zakros: one or two destructions around the end of the LM IB period.' In T. M. Brogan and E. Hallager (eds.), *LM IB*

Pottery: Relative Chronology and Regional Differences. Monographs of the Danish Institute at Athens 11.2. Athens: Danish Institute at Athens: 595–612.

Platon, L. 2011b. 'Studying the character of the Minoan "Household" within the limits of the Neopalatial settlement of Zakros.' In K. T. Glowacki and N. Vogeikoff-Brogan (eds.), *STEGA: The Archaeology of Houses and Households in Ancient Crete.* Hesperia Supplement 44. Princeton, NJ: American School of Classical Studies at Athens: 151–61.

Platon, L. 2013. 'The uses of caves in Minoan Crete: a diachronic analysis.' In F. Mavridis and J. T. Jensen (eds.), *Stable Places and Changing Perceptions: Cave Archaeology in Greece.* Oxford: Archaeopress: 155–65.

Platon, L. and E. Gerontakou. 2013. 'Middle Minoan III: a "gap" or a "missing link" in the history of the Minoan site of Zakros?' In C. F. Macdonald and C. Knappett (eds.), *Intermezzo: Intermediacy and Regeneration in Middle Minoan III Palatial Crete.* British School at Athens Studies 21. London: British School at Athens: 197–212.

Platon, N. 1951. 'To Ieron Maza (kalou choriou Pediados) kai ta Minoika Iera Koryfis.' *Kretika Chronika* 5: 96–160.

Platon, N. 1952. 'Anaskafai periochis Siteias.' *Praktika tis en Athinais Archaiologikis Etaireias* 1952: 630–48.

Platon, N. 1953. 'Anaskafai eis tin periochin Siteias.' *Praktika tis en Athinais Archaiologikis Etaireias* 1953: 288–97.

Platon, N. 1954. 'Anaskafai periochis Siteias.' *Praktika tis en Athinais Archaiologikis Etaireias* 1954: 361–8.

Platon, N. 1955. 'Anaskafai periochis Siteias.' *Praktika tis en Athinais Archaiologikis Etaireias* 1955: 288–97.

Platon, N. 1956a. 'La chronologie Minoenne.' In Ch. Zervos, *L'Art de la Crète Néolithique et Minoenne.* Paris: Cahiers d'Art: 509–12.

Platon, N. 1956b. 'Anaskafi Minoikis Agroikias eis Zou Siteias.' *Praktika tis en Athinais Archaiologikis Etaireias* 1956: 232–40.

Platon, N. 1959. 'Anaskafi Achladion Siteias.' *Praktika tis en Athinais Archaiologikis Etaireias* 1959: 210–19.

Platon, N. 1960a. 'Anaskafi Chondrou Viannou.' *Praktika tis en Athinais Archaiologikis Etaireias* 1960: 283–9.

Platon, N. 1960b. 'Anaskafai periochis Praisou.' *Praktika tis en Athinais Archaiologikis Etaireias* 1960: 294–307.

Platon, N. 1966. *Crete.* London: Methuen.

Platon, N. 1967. 'Bathrooms and lustral basins in Minoan dwellings.' In W. C. Brice (ed.), *EUROPA: Studien zur Geschichte und Epigraphik der Frühen Aegaeis. Festschrift für Ernst Grumach.* Berlin: Walter de Gruyter: 236–45.

Platon, N. 1971. *Zakros. The Discovery of a Lost Palace of Ancient Crete.* New York: Charles Scribner's Sons.

Platon, N. 1981. *La Civilisation Égéenne.* Paris: Albin Michel.

Platon, N. 1983. 'The Minoan palaces: centres of organization of a theocratic, social and political system.' In O. Krzyszkowska and L. Nixon (eds.), *Minoan Society.* Bristol: Bristol Classical Press: 273–6.

Platon, N. and W. Brice. 1975. *Enepigrafoi Pinakides kai Pithoi Grammikou Sistimatos A ek Zakrou (Inscribed tablets and pithoi of Linear A system from Zakros).* Athens: Athenian Archaeological Service.

Platonos, M. 1990. 'Nees endeikseis yia to problema ton kathartirion deksamenon kai ton loutron sto Minoiko kosmo.' *Cretological Congress* A2: 141–55.

Poblome, J., and C. Dumon. 1987–8. 'A Minoan building program? Some comments on the Unexplored Mansion at Knossos.' *Acta Archaeologica Lovanensia* 26–27: 69–72.

Polanyi, K. 1957. *The Great Transformation: The Political and Economic Origins of Our Time.* [Foreword by Robert M. MacIver.] Boston, MA: Beacon Press.

Pope, M. 1956. 'Cretan axe-heads with Linear A inscriptions.' *Annual of the British School at Athens* 51: 132–5.

Pope, M. 1964. *Aegean Writing and Linear A*. Studies in Mediterranean Archaeology 8. Lund: Paul Åström.

Popham, M. R. 1970. *The Destruction of the Palace at Knossos. Pottery of the Late Minoan IIIA Period*. Studies in Mediterranean Archaeology 12. Göteborg: Paul Åström.

Popham, M. R. 1994. 'Late Minoan II to the end of the Bronze Age.' In D. Evely, H. Hughes-Brock, and N. Momigliano (eds.), *Knossos: A Labyrinth of History. Papers Presented in Honour of Sinclair Hood*. London: British School at Athens: 89–102.

Popham, M. R. and M. A. V. Gill. 1995. *The Latest Sealings from the Palace and Houses at Knossos*. British School at Athens Studies 1. London: British School at Athens.

Postgate, N., T. Wang, and T. Wilkinson. 1995. 'The evidence for early writing: utilitarian or ceremonial?' *Antiquity* 69: 459–80.

Poursat, J.-C. 1966. 'Un sanctuaire du Minoen Moyen II à Malia.' *Bulletin de Correspondance Hellénique* 90: 514–51.

Poursat, J.-C. 1987. 'Town and palace at Malia in the Protopalatial period.' In R. Hägg and N. Marinatos (eds.), *The Function of the Minoan Palaces*. Skrifter Utgivna av Svenska Institutet I Athen, 4°35. Stockholm: Paul Åströms Förlag: 75–6.

Poursat, J.-C. 1988. 'La ville minoenne de Malia: recherches et publications récentes.' *Revue Archéologique*: 61–82.

Poursat, J.-C. 1992. *Guide de Malia. Le Quartier Mu*. Sites et Monuments VII. Paris: École Française d'Athènes.

Poursat, J.-C. 2010. 'Malia: palace, state, city.' In O. Krzyszkowska (ed.), *Cretan Offerings: Studies in Honour of Peter Warren*. British School at Athens Studies 18. London: British School at Athens: 259–67.

Poursat, J.-C. 2012. 'The emergence of elite groups at Protopalatial Malia. A biography of Quartier Mu.' In I. Schoep, P. Tomkins, and J. Driessen (eds.), *Back to the Beginning: Reassessing Social and Political Complexity on Crete during the Early and Middle Bronze Age*. Oxford: Oxbow Books: 177–83.

Prent, M. 2005. *Sanctuaries and Cults in Crete from the Late Minoan IIIC to the Archaic Period: Continuity and Change from Late Minoan IIIB to the Archaic Period*. Leiden: Brill.

Preston, L. 1999. 'Mortuary practices and the negotiation of social identities at LM II Knossos.' *Annual of the British School at Athens* 94: 131–43.

Preston, L. 2001. 'A mortuary approach to cultural interaction and political dynamics on Late Minoan II–IIIB Crete.' PhD diss., University College London.

Preston, L. 2004a. 'Final Palatial Knossos and Postpalatial Crete: a mortuary perspective on political dynamics.' In G. Cadogan, E. Hatzaki, and A. Vasilakis (eds.), *Knossos: Palace, City, State*. British School at Athens Studies 12. London: British School at Athens: 137–45.

Preston, L. 2004b. 'A mortuary perspective on political changes in Late Minoan II–IIIB Crete.' *American Journal of Archaeology* 108: 321–48.

Preston, L. 2013. 'The Middle Minoan III funerary landscape at Knossos.' In C. F. Macdonald and C. Knappett (eds.), *Intermezzo: Intermediacy and Regeneration in Middle Minoan III Palatial Crete*. British School at Athens Studies 21. London: British School at Athens: 57–70.

Preziosi, D. 1983. *Minoan Architectural Design: Formation and Signification*. Berlin: Mouton.

Privitera, S. 2008. *Case e Rituali a Cretan el Period Neopalaziale*. Athens: Scula Archeologica Italiana.

Privitera, S. 2014. 'Long-term grain storage and political economy in Bronze Age Crete: contextualizing Ayia Triada's silo complexes.' *American Journal of Archaeology* 118: 429–49.

Puglisi, D. 2003. 'Haghia Triada nel periodo Tardo Minoico I.' *Creta Antica* 4: 145–98.

Puglisi, D. 2010. 'Dal "vassoio tripodato" al kernos un set di ceramiche TM IA da Haghia Triada e il suo contributo alla conoscenza del rituale Minoico.' *Creta Antica* 11: 45–129.

Puglisi, D. 2011. 'From the end of LM IA to the end of LM IB: the pottery evidence from Hagia Triada.' In T. M. Brogan and E. Hallager (eds.), *LM IB Pottery: Relative*

Chronology and Regional Differences. Monographs of the Danish Institute at Athens 11.1. Athens: Danish Institute at Athens: 267–89.

Puglisi, D. 2012. 'Ritual performances in Minoan Lustral Basins. New observations on an old hypothesis.' *Annuario della Scuola Archeologica di Atene e delle Missioni Italiane in Oriente* 90, N. S. 3.12: 199–211.

Pullen, D. 2010. 'Introduction: political economies of the Aegean Bronze Age.' In D. Pullen (ed.), *Political Economies of the Aegean Bronze Age.* Oxford and Oakville: Oxbow: 1–10.

Rackham, O., and J. Moody. 1996. *The Making of the Cretan Landscape.* Manchester and New York: Manchester University Press.

Rainbird, P. 2007. *The Archaeology of Islands.* Cambridge: Cambridge University Press.

Rapoport, A. 1990. 'Systems of activities and systems of settings.' In S. Kent (ed.), *Domestic Architecture and the Use of Space: An Interdisciplinary Cross-Cultural Study.* Cambridge: Cambridge University Press: 9–20.

Rehak, P. 1996. 'Aegean breechcloths, kilts, and the Keftiu paintings.' *American Journal of Archaeology* 100: 35–51.

Rehak, P. 2000. 'The Isopata Ring and the question of narrative in Neopalatial glyptic.' In W. Müller (ed.), *Minoisch-mykenische Glyptik: Stil, Ikonographie, Funktion.* Corpus der Minoischen und Mykenischen Siegal: Beiheft 6. Berlin: Gebr. Mann Verlag: 269–76.

Rehak, P. and J. G. Younger. 1998. 'Review of Aegean prehistory VII: Neopalatial, Final Palatial and Postpalatial Crete.' *American Journal of Archaeology* 102: 91–173.

Rehak, P. and J. G. Younger 2001. 'Review of Aegean Prehistory VII: Neopalatial, Final Palatial, and Postpalatial Crete.' In T. Cullen (ed.), *Aegean Prehistory: A Review.* Boston: Archaeological Institute of America: 383–473.

Reinach, S. 1893. 'Le mirage oriental.' *L'Anthropologie* 4: 539–78, 699–732.

Relaki, M. 2012. 'The social arenas of tradition. Investigating collective and individual social strategies in the Prepalatial and Protopalatial Mesara.' In I. Schoep, P. Tomkins, and J. Driessen (eds.), *Back to the Beginning: Reassessing Social and Political Complexity on*

Crete during the Early and Middle Bronze Age. Oxford: Oxbow Books: 290–324.

Renfrew, C. 1972. *The Emergence of Civilization: The Cyclades and the Aegean in the Third Millennium B.C.* London: Methuen.

Renfrew, C. 1977. 'A Linear A tablet fragment from Phylakopi in Melos.' *Kadmos* 16: 111–19.

Renfrew, C. 1979. 'Terminology and beyond.' In J. L. Davis and J. F. Cherry (eds.), *Papers in Cycladic Prehistory.* Los Angeles, CA: UCLA Institute of Archaeology: 51–63.

Renfrew, C. 1985. 'The archaeology of cult.' In C. Renfrew (ed.), *The Archaeology of Cult: The Sanctuary of Phylakopi.* London: The British School at Athens: 1–26.

Renfrew, C. 1986. 'Introduction. Peer–polity interaction and socio-political change.' In C. Renfrew and J. F. Cherry (eds.), *Peer–Polity Interaction and Socio-political Change.* Cambridge: Cambridge University Press: 1–18.

Renfrew, C. 1994. 'The archaeology of religion.' In C. Renfrew and E. B. W. Zubrow (eds.), *The Ancient Mind: Elements of Cognitive Archaeology.* Cambridge: Cambridge University Press: 47–54.

Renfrew, C. 1998. 'Word of Minos: the Minoan contribution to Mycenaean Greek and the linguistic geography of the Bronze Age Aegean.' *Cambridge Archaeological Journal* 8: 239–64.

Renfrew, C. 2007. 'The archaeology of ritual, of cult, and of religion.' In E. Kyriakidis (ed.), *The Archaeology of Ritual.* Los Angeles: Cotsen Institute of Archaeology, University of California: 109–22.

Renfrew, C. and J. F. Cherry (eds.). 1986. *Peer–Polity Interaction and Socio-political Change.* Cambridge: Cambridge University Press.

Rethemiotakis, G. 1985. 'Perisylloges-Paradoseis.' *Archaiologikon Deltion* 40B: 297–8.

Rethemiotakis, G. 1990. 'Malia-Luktos. Zitimata archaiologikis topografias tis Eparchias Pediadas.' *Cretological Congress*: 241–8.

Rethemiotakis, G. 1997. 'To Minoiko "kentriko ktirio" sto Kastelli Pediadas.' *Archaiologikon Deltion* 47A (1992): 29–64.

Rethemiotakis, G. 1999a. 'The hearths of the Minoan Palace at Galatas.' In P. P. Betancourt, V. Karageorghis, R. Laffineur, and W.-D. Niemeier (eds.), *Meletemata: Studies in Aegean Archaeology Presented to Malcolm H. Wiener as He Enters His 65th Year*. Aegaeum 20. Liège and Austin: Université de Liège, Histoire de l'art et archéologie de la Grèce antique and University of Texas, Program in Aegean Scripts and Prehistory: 721–7.

Rethemiotakis, G. 1999b. 'To neo Minoiko Anaktoro ston Galata Pediados kai to "Iero Spilaio" Arkalochoriou.' In A. Karetsou (ed.), *Kretes Thalassodromoi*. Herakleion: Synergasia KGEPKA & 13 Ephoreia Byzantinon Archaioteton: 91–111.

Rethemiotakis, G. 1999c. 'Voni.' *Kritiki Estia* 7: 239–41.

Rethemiotakis, G. 2001. *Minoan Clay Figures and Figurines from the Neopalatial to the Subminoan period*. [Translated by A. Doumas.] Athens: The Archaeological Society at Athens.

Rethemiotakis, G. 2002. 'Evidence on social and economic changes at Galatas and Pediada in the New-Palace period.' In J. Driessen, I. Schoep, and R. Laffineur (eds.), *Monuments of Minos: Rethinking the Minoan Palaces*. Aegaeum 23. Liège and Austin: Université de Liège, Histoire de l'art et archéologie de la Grèce antique and University of Texas, Program in Aegean Scripts and Prehistory: 55–70.

Rethemiotakis, G. 2009. 'A Neopalatial shrine model from the Minoan peak sanctuary at Gournos Krousonas.' In A. L. D'Agata and A. Van de Moortel (eds.), *Essays on Ritual and Cult in Crete in Honor of Geraldine C. Gesell*. Hesperia Suppl. 42. Athens: American School of Classical Studies at Athens: 189–99.

Rethemiotakis, G. 2010. 'A shrine-model from Galatas.' In O. Krzyszkowska (ed.), *Cretan Offerings: Studies in Honour of Peter Warren*. British School at Athens Studies 18. London: British School at Athens: 293–302.

Rethemiotakis, G. 2012. 'God save our home: the case of the Horns of Consecration from Galatas.' In E. Mantzourani and P. P. Betancourt (eds.), *Philistor: Studies in Honor of Costis Davaras*. Philadelphia, PA: INSTAP Academic Press: 169–76.

Rethemiotakis, G. 2014. 'Images and semiotics in space: the case of the anthropomorphic figurines from Kophinas.' *Kretika Chronika* 34: 147–62.

Rethemiotakis, G. and K. Christakis. 2011. 'LM I pottery groups from the Palace and the town of Galatas, Pediada.' In T. M. Brogan and E. Hallager (eds.), *LM IB Pottery: Relative Chronology and Regional Differences*. Monographs of the Danish Institute at Athens 11.1. Athens: Danish Institute at Athens: 205–27.

Rethemiotakis, G. and K. Christakis. 2013. 'The Middle Minoan III period at Galatas: pottery and historical implications.' In C. F. Macdonald and C. Knappett (eds.), *Intermezzo: Intermediacy and Regeneration in Middle Minoan III Palatial Crete*. British School at Athens Studies 21. London: British School at Athens: 93–105.

Rethemiotakis, G. and P. M. Warren. 2014. *Knossos: A Middle Minoan III Building in Bougadha Metochi*. British School at Athens Studies 23. London: British School at Athens.

Rutkowski, B. 1986 [second ed.]. *The Cult Places of the Aegean*. New Haven, CT: Yale University Press.

Rutkowski, B. 1988. 'Minoan peak sanctuaries: the topography and architecture.' *Aegaeum* 2: 71–99.

Rutkowski, B. 1989. 'Clay votive sculpture from Pyrgos. Part 1.' *Archeologia* 40: 55–84.

Rutkowski, B. 1991. *Petsofas: A Cretan Peak Sanctuary*. Studies and Monographs in Mediterranean Archaeology and Civilization 1.1. Warsaw: Polish Academy of Sciences.

Rutkowski, B and K. Nowicki. 1984. 'Report on investigations in Greece II. Studies in 1983.' *Archeologia* 35: 178–92.

Rutkowski, B. and K. Nowicki. 1996. *The Psychro Cave and Other Sacred Grottoes in Crete*. Warsaw: Art and Archaeology.

Rutter, J. 2004. 'Ceramic sets in context: one dimension of food preparation and consumption in a Minoan palatial setting.' In P. Halstead and J. Barrett (eds.), *Food, Cuisine and Society in Prehistoric Greece*. Sheffield Studies in Aegean Archaeology 5. Oxford: Oxbow Books: 63–89.

Said, E. W. 1978. *Orientalism*. London: Routledge.

Sakellarakis, Y. 1986. 'Zominthos.' *Ergon*: 139–41.

Sakellarakis, Y. 1987. 'Ekato chronia erevnas sto Idaio Andro.' *Archaeologiai Ephemeris* 1987: 239–63.

Sakellarakis, Y. 1988. 'Zominthos.' *Ergon*: 165–72.

Sakellarakis, Y. 2013. *Kythera: O Ayios Georgios sto Vouno: Minoiki Latreia, Neoteroi Chronoi*. Athens: Athenian Archaeological Society.

Sakellarakis, Y. and J.-P. Olivier. 1994. 'Un vase en pierre avec inscription en linéaire A du sanctuaire de sommet minoen de Cythère.' *Bulletin de Correspondance Hellénique* 118: 343–51.

Sakellarakis, Y. and E. Sakellaraki. 1981. 'Drama of a death in a Minoan Temple.' *National Geographic* 159: 205–23.

Sakellarakis, Y. and E. Sapouna-Sakellaraki. 1997. *Archanes: Minoan Crete in a New Light*. Athens: Ammos Publications: Eleni Nakou Foundation.

Sakellarakis, Y. and E. Sapouna-Sakellaraki. 2010. *Knossos: at the Threshold of European Civilization*. [Translated by C. Macdonald.] Athens: Militos.

Sakellarakis, Y. and E. Sapouna-Sakellaraki. 2013. *To Idaio Andro: Iero kai Mandeio*. Vols. I–III. Athens: Athenais Archaiologiki Etaireia.

Sapouna-Sakellaraki, E. 1995. *Die bronzenen Menschenfiguren auf Kreta und in der Ägäis*. Stuttgart: Franz Steiner Verlag.

Saunders, T. 2002: 'Power relations and social space: a study of the late medieval Archbishop's Palace in Trondheim.' *European Journal of Archaeology* 5: 89–111.

Scarborough, V. L., F. Valdez Jr, and N. P. Dunning (eds.). 2003. *Heterarchy, Political Economy, and the Ancient Maya*. Arizona: University of Arizona Press.

Schäfer, J. 1991. 'Amnisos – harbour-town of Minos?' In R. Laffineur and L. Basch (eds.), *Thalassa: L'Égée Préhistorique et la Mer*. Aegaeum 7. Liège: Université de Liège, Histoire de l'art et archéologie de la Grèce antique: 111–16.

Schoep, I. 1994. 'Ritual, politics and script on Minoan Crete.' *Aegean Archaeology* 1: 7–25.

Schoep, I. 1995. 'Context and chronology of Linear A administrative documents.' *Aegean Archaeology* 2: 29–65.

Schoep, I. 1999a. 'Tablets and territories? Reconstructing Late Minoan IB political geography through undeciphered documents.' *American Journal of Archaeology* 103: 201–21.

Schoep, I. 1999b. 'The origins of writing and administration on Crete.' *Oxford Journal of Archaeology* 18: 265–76.

Schoep, I. 2002a. 'The state of the Minoan palaces or the Minoan Palace-State?' In J. Driessen, I. Schoep, and R. Laffineur (eds.), *Monuments of Minos: Rethinking the Minoan Palaces*. Aegaeum 23. Liège and Austin: Université de Liège, Histoire de l'art et archéologie de la Grèce antique and University of Texas at Austin, Program in Aegean Scripts and Prehistory: 15–33.

Schoep, I. 2002b. 'Social and political organization on Crete in the Protopalatial period. The case of MM II Malia.' *Journal of Mediterranean Archaeology* 15: 101–32.

Schoep, I. 2002c. *The Administration of Neopalatial Crete: A Critical Assessment of the Linear A Tablets and Their Role in the Administrative Process*. Minos Supplement 17. Salamanca: Ediciones Universidad de Salamanca.

Schoep, I. 2004. 'Assessing the role of architecture in conspicuous consumption in the Middle Minoan I–II periods.' *Oxford Journal of Archaeology* 23: 243–69.

Schoep, I. 2006. 'Looking beyond the First Palaces: elites and the agency of power in EM III–MM II Crete.' *American Journal of Archaeology* 110: 37–64.

Schoep, I. 2010. 'The Minoan "Palace-Temple" reconsidered: a critical assessment of the spatial concentration of political, religious and economic power in Bronze Age Crete.' *Journal of Mediterranean Archaeology* 23: 219–43.

Schoep, I. 2012. 'Bridging the divide between the "Prepalatial" and the "Protopalatial" periods?' In I. Schoep, P. Tomkins, and J. Driessen (eds.), *Back to the Beginning:*

Reassessing Social and Political Complexity on Crete during the Early and Middle Bronze Age. Oxford: Oxbow Books: 403–28.

Schoep, I. and C. Knappett. 2004. 'Dual emergence: evolving heterarchy, exploding hierarchy.' In J. C. Barrett and P. Halstead (eds.), *The Emergence of Civilisation Revisited.* Sheffield Studies in Aegean Archaeology 6. Oxford: Oxbow Books: 21–37.

Schoep, I. and P. Tomkins. 2012. 'Back to the beginning for the Early and Middle Bronze Age on Crete.' In I. Schoep, P. Tomkins, and J. Driessen (eds.), *Back to the Beginning: Reassessing Social and Political Complexity on Crete during the Early and Middle Bronze Age.* Oxford and Oakville: Oxbow Books: 1–31.

Seager, R. B. 1909. 'Excavations on the island of Mochlos, Crete, in 1908.' *American Journal of Archaeology* 13: 273–303.

Seager, R. B. 1910. *Excavations on the Island of Pseira, Crete.* Anthropological Publications III. Philadelphia, PA: University Museum.

Seager, R. B. 1912. *Explorations in the Island of Mochlos.* Boston and New York: American School of Classical Studies at Athens.

Seager, R. B. 1916. *The Cemetery of Pachyammos, Crete.* Philadelphia, PA: University Museum.

Serpetsidaki, I. 2012. 'Prosfati anaskafiki erevna ston Poro – Katsamba Irakleiou.' *Archaiologiko Ergo Kritis* 2: 164–72.

Service, E. R. 1962. *Primitive Social Organization: An Evolutionary Perspective.* New York: Random House.

Shapland, A. 2010. 'Wild nature? Human–animal relations on Neopalatial Crete.' *Cambridge Archaeological Journal* 19: 109–27.

Shapland, A. 2013. 'Jumping to conclusions: bull-leaping in Minoan Crete.' *Society and Animals* 21: 194–207.

Shaw, J. W. 1971. 'Minoan architecture: materials and techniques.' *Annuario della Scuola archeologica di Atene e della Missioni italiane in Orientei* 49: 1–256.

Shaw, J. W. 1973. 'The orientation of the Minoan Palaces.' *In Antichità Cretesi: Studi in onore di Doro Levi.* Chronache di Archeologia 12. Catania: University of Catania: 47–59.

Shaw, J. W. 1978. 'Evidence for the Minoan tripartite shrine.' *American Journal of Archaeology* 82: 429–48.

Shaw, J. W. 1990. 'Bronze Age Aegean harbour-sides.' In D. A. Hardy, C. G. Doumas, J. A. Sakellarakis, and P. Warren (eds.), *Thera and the Aegean World III.1: Archaeology.* London: The Thera Foundation: 420–37.

Shaw, J. W. 2002. 'The Minoan palatial establishment at Kommos.' In J. Driessen, I. Schoep, and R. Laffineur (eds.), *Monuments of Minos: Rethinking the Minoan Palaces.* Aegaeum 23. Liège and Austin: Université de Liège, Histoire de l'art et archéologie de la Grèce antique and University of Texas at Austin, Program in Aegean Scripts and Prehistory: 99–110.

Shaw, J. W. 2004. 'Kommos: the sea-gate to southern Crete.' In L. Preston Day, M. S. Mook, and J. D. Muhly (eds.), *Crete beyond the Palaces: Proceedings of the Crete 2000 Conference.* Philadelphia, PA: INSTAP Academic Press: 43–51.

Shaw, J. W. 2006a. 'The architecture and stratigraphy of the civic buildings.' In J. W. Shaw and M. C. Shaw (eds.), *Kommos V: The Monumental Minoan Buildings at Kommos.* Princeton, NJ: Princeton University Press: 1–116.

Shaw, J. W. 2006b. *Kommos: A Minoan Harbor Town and Greek Sanctuary in Southern Crete.* Princeton, NJ: American School of Classical Studies at Athens.

Shaw, J. W. 2009. *Minoan Architecture: Materials and Techniques.* Studi di archeologia Cretese VII. Padova: Bottega D'Erasmo.

Shaw, J. W. 2010. 'Setting in the Palaces of Minoan Crete: a review of how and when.' In O. Krzyszkowska (ed.), *Cretan Offerings: Studies in Honour of Peter Warren.* British School at Athens Studies 18. London: British School at Athens: 303–14.

Shaw, J. W. 2015. *Elite Minoan Architecture: The Development at Knossos, Phaistos, and Malia.* Philadelphia, PA: INSTAP Academic Press.

Shaw, J. W. and M. C. Shaw (eds.). 1985. A Great Minoan Triangle in south central

Crete: Kommos, Hagia Triadha, Phaistos. *Scripta Mediterranea* 6.

Shaw, J. W. and M. C. Shaw (eds.). 1995. *Kommos 1: An Excavation on the South Coast of Crete. The Kommos Region and Houses of the Minoan Town. Part 1: The Kommos Region, Ecology, and Minoan Industries.* Princeton, NJ: Princeton University Press.

Shaw, J. W. and M. C. Shaw (eds.). 2006a. *Kommos V: The Monumental Minoan Buildings at Kommos.* Princeton, NJ: Princeton University Press.

Shaw, J. W. and M. C. Shaw. 2006b. 'Architectural forms and their uses.' In J. Shaw and M. Shaw (eds.), *Kommos V: The Monumental Minoan Buildings at Kommos.* Princeton, NJ: Princeton University Press: 846–54.

Shaw, J., A. Van de Moortel, P. M. Day, and V. Kilikoglou. 2001. *A LM IA Ceramic Kiln in South-Central Crete. Function and Pottery Production.* Hesperia Suppl. 30. Princeton, NJ: American School of Classical Studies at Athens.

Shaw, M. C. 1972. 'The miniature frescoes of Tylissos reconsidered.' *Archäologischer Anzeiger:* 171–88.

Shaw, M. C. 1978. 'A Minoan fresco from Katsamba.' *American Journal of Archaeology* 82: 27–34.

Shaw, M. C. 1997. 'Aegean sponsors and artists: reflections of their roles in the patterns of distribution of themes and representational conventions in the murals.' In R. Laffineur and P. P. Betancourt (eds.), *Techne: Craftsmen, Craftswomen and Craftsmanship in the Aegean Bronze Age.* Aegaeum 16. Liège and Austin: Université de Liège, Histoire de l'art et archéologie de la Grèce antique and University of Texas at Austin, Program in Aegean Scripts and Prehistory: 481–504.

Shaw, M. C. 1998. 'The wall paintings.' In P. P. Betancourt and C. Davaras (eds.), *Pseira II: Building AC (the Shrine) and other Buildings in Area A.* University Museum Monograph 94. Philadelphia: University of Pennsylvania: 55–83.

Shaw, M. C. 2004a. 'Religion at Minoan Kommos.' In L. Preston Day, M. S. Mook, and J. D. Muhly (eds.), *Crete beyond the Palaces: Proceedings of the Crete 2000 Conference.* Philadelphia, PA: INSTAP Academic Press: 137–50.

Shaw, M. C. 2004b. 'The "Priest-King" Fresco from Knossos: man, woman, priest, king, or someone else?' In A. P. Chapin (ed.), *CHARIS: Essays in Honor of Sara A. Immerwahr.* Hesperia Suppl. 33. Athens: American School of Classical Studies at Athens: 65–84.

Shaw, M. C. 2009. 'Review article: A bull-leaping fresco from the Nile Delta and a search for patrons and artists.' *American Journal of Archaeology* 113: 471–7.

Sherratt, A. 1989. 'V. Gordon Childe: archaeology and intellectual history.' *Past and Present* 125: 151–86.

Sherratt, A. 2002. 'Darwin among the archaeologists: the John Evans nexus and the Borneo Caves.' *Antiquity,* 76: 151–7.

Sherratt, A. 2006. 'Crete, Greece and the Orient in the thought of Gordon Childe.' In Y. Hamilakis and N. Momigliano (eds.), *Archaeology and European Modernity: Producing and Consuming the 'Minoans'.* Creta Antica 7. Padua: Bottega d'Erasmo: 107–26.

Sherratt, A. and S. Sherratt. 1991. 'From luxuries to commodities: the nature of Mediterranean Bronze Age trading systems.' In N. Gale (ed.), *Bronze Age Trade in the Eastern Mediterranean.* Studies in Mediterranean Archaeology 90. Göteborg: Paul Åströms Förlag: 351–86.

Sherratt, S. 1994. 'Comment on Ora Negbi, The "Libyan landscape" from Thera: a review of Aegean enterprises overseas in the Late Minoan IA period.' *Journal of Mediterranean Archaeology* 7: 237–40.

Sherratt, S. 2000. *Arthur Evans, Knossos and the Priest-King.* Oxford: Ashmolean Museum.

Shore, C. 2002. 'Introduction: towards an anthropology of elites.' In C. Shore and S. Nugent (eds.), *Elite Cultures: Anthropological Perspectives.* London and New York: Routledge: 1–21.

Simandiraki, A. 2004. 'Minopaidies: the Minoan civilization in Greek primary education.' *World Archaeology* 36: 177–88.

Simandiraki, A. 2006. 'The "Minoan" experience of schoolchildren in Crete.' In Y. Hamilakis and N. Momigliano (eds.), *Archaeology and European Modernity: Producing and Consuming the 'Minoans.'* Creta Antica 7. Padua: Bottega d'Erasmo: 259–74.

Simandiraki-Grimshaw, A. 2010. 'The human body in Minoan religious iconography.' In O. Krzyszkowska (ed.), *Cretan Offerings: Studies in Honour of Peter Warren.* British School at Athens Studies 18. London: British School at Athens: 321–9.

Simandiraki-Grimshaw, A. 2013. 'Anthropomorphic vessels as re-imagined corporealities in Bronze Age Crete.' *Creta Antica* 14: 17–45.

Simandiraki-Grimshaw, A. 2015. 'The body brand and Minoan zonation.' In S. Cappel, U. Günkel-Maschek, and D. Panagiotopoulos (eds.), *Minoan Archaeology: Perspectives for the 21st Century.* Louvain-la-Neuve: Presses universitaires de Louvain: 267–82.

Smith, A. T. 2003: *The Political Landscape: Constellations of Authority in Early Complex Polities.* Berkeley, Los Angeles and London: University of California Press.

Smith, M. E. 2004. 'The archaeology of ancient state economies.' *Annual Review of Anthropology* 33: 73–102.

Smith, M. L. 2005. 'Networks, territories, and the cartography of ancient states.' *Annuals of the Association of American Geographers* 95: 832–49.

Soar, K. 2014. 'Sects and the city: factional ideologies in representations of performance from Bronze Age Crete.' *World Archaeology* 46: 1–18.

Soetens, S. 2009. 'Juktas and Kophinas: two ritual landscapes out of the ordinary.' In A. L. D'Agata and A. Van de Moortel (eds.), *Archaeologies of Cult: Essays on Ritual and Cult in Crete in Honor of Geraldine C. Gesell.* Hesperia Suppl. 42. Princeton, NJ: American School of Classical Studies in Athens: 261–8.

Soetens, S., A. Sarris, and K. Vansteenhuyse. 2008. 'Between peak and palace. Reinterpretation of the Minoan cultural landscape in space and time.' In Y. Facorellis, N. Zacharias, and K. Polikreti (eds.), *Proceedings of the Symposium of the Hellenic Society for Archaeometry.* BAR Int. Series 1746. Oxford: Archaeopress: 153–61.

Sofianou, C. and T. Brogan. 2010. 'Minoikos Oikismos Papadiokampou Siteias.' *Archaiologiko Ergo Kritis* 1: 134–42.

Sofianou, C. and T. Brogan. 2012. 'Papadiokampos and the Siteia Bay in the second millennium BC: exploring patterns of regional hierarchy and exchange in eastern Crete.' In M. Tsipopoulou (ed.), *Petras, Siteia – 25 Years of Excavations and Studies.* Monographs of the Danish Institute at Athens 16. Athens: Danish Institute at Athens: 327–40.

Soles, J. S. 1979. 'Towards a reconstruction of the Palace at Gournia.' In P. P. Betancourt (ed.), *Gournia, Crete. The 75th Anniversary of the Excavations. Temple University Aegean Symposium* 4: 11–17.

Soles, J. S. 1983. 'A Bronze Age quarry in eastern Crete.' *Journal of Field Archaeology* 10: 33–46.

Soles, J. S. 1991. 'The Gournia palace.' *American Journal of Archaeology* 95: 17–78.

Soles, J. S. 1992. *The Prepalatial Cemeteries at Mochlos and Gournia and the House Tombs of Bronze Age Crete.* Hesperia Suppl. 24. Princeton, NJ: American School of Classical Studies at Athens.

Soles, J. S. 1995. 'The functions of a cosmological center: Knossos in Palatial Crete.' In R. Laffineur and W.-D. Niemeier (eds.), *Politeia: Society and State in the Aegean Bronze Age.* Aegaeum 12. Liège and Austin: Université de Liège, Histoire de l'art et archéologie de la Grèce antique and University of Texas, Program in Aegean Scripts and Prehistory: 404–14.

Soles, J. S. 1997. 'A community of craft specialists at Mochlos.' In R. Laffineur and P. P. Betancourt (eds.), *Techne: Craftsmen, Craftswomen and Craftsmanship in the Aegean Bronze Age.* Aegaeum 16. Liège and Austin:

Université de Liège, Histoire de l'art et archéologie de la Grèce antique and University of Texas at Austin, Program in Aegean Scripts and Prehistory: 425–31.

Soles, J. S. 2001. 'Reverence for dead ancestors in prehistoric Crete.' In R. Laffineur and R. Hägg (eds.), *Potnia: Deities and Religion in the Aegean Bronze Age*. Aegaeum 22. Liège and Austin: Université de Liège, Histoire de l'art et archéologie de la Grèce antique and University of Texas at Austin, Program in Aegean Scripts and Prehistory: 229–36.

Soles, J. S. 2002. 'A Central Court at Gournia?' In J. Driessen, I. Schoep, and R. Laffineur (eds.), *Monuments of Minos: Rethinking the Minoan Palaces*. Aegaeum 23. Liège and Austin: Université de Liège, Histoire de l'art et archéologie de la Grèce antique and University of Texas at Austin, Program in Aegean Scripts and Prehistory: 123–32.

Soles, J. S. 2003a. 'Conclusions on Chalinomouri.' In J. S. Soles (ed.), *Mochlos IA. Period III. Neopalatial Settlement on the Coast: The Artisans' Quarter and the Farmhouse at Chalinomouri. The Sites.* Prehistory Monographs 7. Philadelphia, PA: INSTAP Academic Press: 127–34.

Soles, J. S. (ed.) 2003b. 'Conclusions on the Artisans' Quarter.' In J. S. Soles (ed.), *Mochlos IA. Period III. Neopalatial Settlement on the Coast: The Artisans' Quarter and the Farmhouse at Chalinomouri. The Sites.* Prehistory Monographs 7. Philadelphia, PA: INSTAP Academic Press: 91–100.

Soles, J. S. 2004. 'New construction at Mochlos in the LM IB period.' In L. Preston Day, M. S. Mook, and J. D. Moody (eds.), *Crete beyond the Palaces. Proceedings of the Crete 2000 Conference.* Prehistory Monographs 10. Philadelphia, PA: INSTAP Academic Press: 153–62.

Soles, J. S. 2009. 'The impact of the Minoan eruption of Santorini on Mochlos, a small Minoan town on the north coast of Crete.' In D. A. Warburton (ed.), *Time's Up! Dating the Minoan Eruption of Santorini*. Monographs of the Danish Institute at Athens 10. Athens: Danish Institute at Athens: 107–16.

Soles, J. S. 2010. 'Evidence for ancestor worship in Minoan Crete: new finds from Mochlos.' In O. Krzyszkowska (ed.), *Cretan Offerings: Studies in Honour of Peter Warren*. British School at Athens Studies 18. London: British School at Athens: 331–8.

Soles, J. S. 2016. 'Hero, goddess, priestess: new evidence for Minoan religion and social organization.' In E. Alram-Stern, F. Blakolmer, S. Deger-Jalkotzy, R. Laffineur, and J. Weilhartner (eds.), *Metaphysis: Ritual, Myth and Symbolism in the Aegean Bronze Age*. Aegaeum 39. Leuven – Liège: Peeters: 247–53.

Soles, J. S. and C. Davaras. 1990. 'Theran ash in Minoan Crete: new excavations on Mochlos.' In D. A. Hardy with A. C. Renfrew (eds.), *Thera and the Aegean World III.3. Chronology*. London: The Thera Foundation: 89–95.

Soles, J. S. and C. Davaras. 1994. 'Excavations at Mochlos, 1990–1991.' *Hesperia* 63: 391–436.

Soles, J. S. and C. Davaras. 1996. 'Excavations at Mochlos, 1992–1993.' *Hesperia* 65: 175–230.

Sourvinou-Inwood, C. 1989. 'Space in Late Minoan religious scenes in glyptic – some remarks.' In W. Müller (ed.), *Fragen und Probleme der Bronzezeitlichen Ägäischen Glyptik*. Berlin: Mann: 241–57.

Spiliotopoulou, A. 2014. 'Kophinas peak sanctuary. Preliminary results of the pottery study.' *Kretika Chronika* 34: 163–82.

Starr, C. G. 1984. 'Minoan flower lovers.' In R. Hägg (ed.), *The Minoan Thalassocracy: Myth and Reality*. Athens: Svenska Institutet I Athen: 9–12.

Stein, G. 1994. 'Introduction part II: the organizational dynamics of complexity in Greater Mesopotamia.' In G. Stein and M. Rothman (eds.), *Chiefdoms and Early States in the Near East: The Organizational Dynamics of Complexity*. Madison, WI: Prehistory Press: 11–22.

Stoddart, S. and J. Whitley. 1988. 'The social context of literacy in Archaic Greece and Etruria.' *Antiquity* 62: 761–72.

Strasser, T. 1997. 'Storage and states on prehistoric Crete: the function of the koulouras in the First Minoan palaces.' *Journal of Mediterranean Archaeology* 10: 73–100.

Strathern, M. 1988. *The Gender of the Gift: Problems with Women and Problems with Society in Melanesia.* Berkeley, Los Angeles, London: University of California Press.

Street, B. 1993. 'Introduction: the new literacy studies.' In B. Street (ed.), *Cross-Cultural Approaches to Literacy.* Cambridge: Cambridge University Press: 1–21.

Tamvaki, A. 1989. 'The human figure in the Aegean glyptic of the Late Bronze Age: some remarks.' In W. Müller (ed.), *Fragen und Probleme der Bronzezeitlichen Ägäischen Glyptik.* Berlin: Mann: 259–73.

Tilley, C. 1994. *A Phenomenology of Landscape: Places, Paths and Monuments.* Oxford and Providence: Berg.

Todaro, S. 2012. 'Craft production and social practices at Prepalatial Phaistos: the background to the First "Palace".' In I. Schoep, P. Tomkins, and J. Driessen (eds.), *Back to the Beginning: Reassessing Social and Political Complexity on Crete during the Early and Middle Bronze Age.* Oxford: Oxbow Books: 195–235.

Todd, I. and P. Warren. 2012. 'Islandscapes and the built environments: the placing of settlements from village to city state (third to first millennia BC) in Cyprus and Crete.' In G. Cadogan, M. Iacovou, K. Kopaka, and J. Whitely (eds.), *Parallel Lives: Ancient Island Societies in Crete and Cyprus.* British School at Athens Studies 20. London: British School at Athens: 47–59.

Tomkins, P. D. 2012. 'Behind the horizon: reconsidering the genesis and function of the "First Palace" at Knossos (Final Neolithic IV-Middle Minoan IB).' In I. Schoep, P. Tomkins, and J. Driessen (eds.), *Back to the Beginning: Reassessing Social and Political Complexity on Crete during the Early and Middle Bronze Age.* Oxford: Oxbow Books: 32–80.

Torrence, R. and J. Grattan. 2002. 'The archaeology of disasters: past and future trends.' In R. Torrence and J. Grattan (eds.), *Natural Disasters and Cultural Change.* London and New York: Routledge: 1–18.

Torrence, R. and S. E. van der Leeuw. 1989. 'Introduction: what's new about innovation?' In R. Torrence and S. E. van der Leeuw (eds.), *What's New? A Closer Look at the Process of Innovation.* London: Unwin Hyman: 1–15.

Touchais, G., T. Boloti, B. Detournay, S. Huber, A.-P. Touchais, and Y. Varalis. 1996. 'Chronique des fouilles et découvertes archéologiques en Grèce en 1995.' *Bulletin de Correspondance Hellénique* 120: 1109–1349.

Traunmueller, S. 2011. 'The LM I pottery from the ceramic workshop at Zominthos.' In T. M. Brogan and E. Hallager (eds.), *LM IB Pottery: Relative Chronology and Regional Differences.* Monographs of the Danish Institute at Athens 11.1. Athens: Danish Institute at Athens: 93–107.

Trebsche, P. 2009. 'Does form follow function? Towards a methodical interpretation of archaeological building features.' *World Archaeology* 41: 505–19.

Treherne, P. 1995. 'The warrior's beauty: the masculine body and self-identity in Bronze Age Europe.' *Journal of European Archaeology* 3: 105–44.

Trigger, B. G. 1990. 'Monumental architecture: a thermodynamic explanation of symbolic behaviour.' *World Archaeology* 22, 119–32.

Tsipopoulou, M. 1989. *Archaeological Survey at Aghia Photia, Siteia.* Partille: Paul Åström.

Tsipopoulou, M. 1997. 'Palace-centered polities in eastern Crete: Neopalatial Petras and its neighbors.' In W. E. Aufrecht, N. A. Mirau, and S. W. Gauley (eds.), *Urbanism in Antiquity from Mesopotamia to Crete.* Journal for the Study of the Old Testament Suppl. Series 224. Sheffield: Sheffield Academic Press: 263–77.

Tsipopoulou, M. 2002. 'Petras, Siteia: the Palace, the town, the hinterland and the Protopalatial background.' In J. Driessen, I. Schoep, and R. Laffineur (eds.), *Monuments of Minos: Rethinking the Minoan Palaces.* Aegaeum 23. Liège and Austin: Université de Liège, Histoire de l'art et archéologie de la Grèce antique and University of Texas at Austin, Program in Aegean Scripts and Prehistory: 133–44.

Tsipopoulou, M. 2007. 'The Central Court of the Palace at Petras.' In P. P. Betancourt, M. C. Nelson, and H. Williams (eds.), *Krinoi kai Limenes. Studies in Honor of Joseph and Maria Shaw.* Philadelphia, PA: Pennsylvania: 49–59.

Tsipopoulou, M. 2011. 'LM IB Petras: the pottery from Room E in House II.1.' In T. M. Brogan and E. Hallager (eds.), *LM IB Pottery: Relative Chronology and Regional Differences.* Monographs of the Danish Institute at Athens 11.2. Athens: Danish Institute at Athens: 463–98.

Tsipopoulou, M. 2012a. 'Introduction: 25 years of excavations and studies at Petras.' In M. Tsipopoulou (ed.), *Petras, Siteia – 25 Years of Excavations and Studies.* Monographs of the Danish Institute at Athens 16. Athens: Danish Institute at Athens: 45–68.

Tsipopoulou, M. 2012b. 'Becoming palatial in eastern Crete: the case of Petras (Final Neolithic–Middle Minoan IIB).' *Bulletin of the Institute of Classical Studies* 55: 129–32.

Tsipopoulou, M., L. Godart, and J.-P. Olivier. 1982. 'Bol de bronze à base ombiliquée avec inscription en linéaire A de la collection K. et M. Mitsotakis.' *Studi Micenei ed Egeo-Anatolici* 23: 61–73.

Tsipopoulou, M. and A. Papacostopoulou. 1997. '"Villas" and villages in the hinterland of Petras, Siteia.' In R. Hägg (ed.), *The Function of the 'Minoan Villa.'* Skrifter Utgivna av Svenska Institutet I Athen, 4° 46. Stockholm: Svenska Institutet I Athen: 203–17.

Tsivilika, E. and E. Banou. 2000. 'Pera Galinoi.' *Archaeologikon Deltion* 55 B2: 1032–4.

Tyree, E. L. 1974. 'Cretan sacred caves: archaeological evidence.' PhD diss., Missouri, Columbia.

Tyree, E. L. 2001. 'Diachronic changes in Minoan cave cult.' In R. Laffineur and R. Hägg (eds.), *Potnia: Deities and Religion in the Aegean Bronze Age.* Aegaeum 22. Liège and Austin: Université de Liège, Histoire de l'art et archéologie de la Grèce antique and University of Texas, Program in Aegean Scripts and Prehistory: 39–50.

Tyree, E. L. 2013. 'Defining Bronze Age ritual caves in Crete.' In F. Mavridis and J. T. Jensen (eds.), *Stable Places and Changing Perceptions: Cave Archaeology in Greece.* Oxford: Archaeopress: 176–87.

Tyree, L., A. Kanta, and H. Robinson. 2008. 'Evidence for ritual eating and drinking: a view from Skoteino Cave.' In L. Hitchcock, R. Laffineur, and J. Crowley (eds.), *Dais: The Aegean Feast.* Aegaeum 29. Liège and Austin: Université de Liège, Histoire de l'art et archéologie de la Grèce antique and University of Texas at Austin, Program in Aegean Scripts and Prehistory: 179–85.

Tyree, L., A. Kanta, and D. Sphakianakis. 2007. 'The Neopalatial chalice: forms and function in the Cave of Skoteino.' In P. P. Betancourt, M. Nelson, and H. Williams (eds.), *Krinoi kai Limenes: Studies in Honor of Joseph and Maria Shaw.* Philadelphia, PA: INSTAP Academic Press: 277–84.

Tyree, L., F. McCoy, A. Kanta, D. Sphakianakis, A. Stamos, K. Aretaki, and E. Kamilaki. 2009. 'Inferences for use of Skoteino Cave during the Bronze Age and later based on a speleological and environmental study at Skoteino Cave, Crete.' *Aegean Archaeology 2005–2006* 8: 51–63.

Tzachili, I. 2003. 'Quantitative analysis of the pottery from the peak sanctuary at Vrysinas, Rethymnon.' In K. Polinger Foster and R. Laffineur (eds.), *Metron: Measuring the Aegean Bronze Age.* Aegaeum 24. Liège and Austin: Université de Liège, Histoire de l'art et archéologie de la Grèce antique and University of Texas, Program in Aegean Scripts and Prehistory: 327–31.

Tzachili, I. 2012. 'Some particular figurines from the peak sanctuary of Vrysinas, near Rethymnon, Crete.' In E. Mantzourani and P. P. Betancourt (eds.), *Philistor: Studies in Honor of Costis Davaras.* Philadelphia, PA: INSTAP Academic Press: 233–8.

Tzedakis, Y., S. Chryssoulaki, Y. Veniéri and M. Avgouli. 1990. 'Les routes minoennes. Le Poste de Choiromandres et le contrôle des communications.' *Bulletin de Correspondance Hellénique* 114: 43–62.

Uchitel, A. 1994–5. 'Records of conscription, taxation and monthly rations in Linear A archives.' *Minos* 29–30: 77–86.

Van Andel, T. H. and C. N. Runnels. 1988. 'An essay on the "Emergence of Civilization" in the Aegean World.' *Antiquity* 62: 234–47.

Van de Moortel, A. 2002. 'Pottery as a barometer of economic change: from the Protopalatial to the Neopalatial society in Central Crete.' In Y. Hamilakis (ed.), *Labyrinth Revisited: Rethinking 'Minoan' Archaeology*. Oxford: Oxbow: 189–211.

Van de Moortel, A. 2006. 'A re-examination of the pottery from the Kamares Cave.' In M. H. Wiener, J. L. Warner, J. Polonsky, E. E. Hayes, and C. McDonald (eds.), *Pottery and Society: The Impact of Recent Studies in Minoan Pottery. Gold Medal Colloquium in Honor of Philip P. Betancourt*. Boston, MA: American Institute of Archaeology: 73–93.

Van de Moortel, A. 2011a. 'LM IB ceramic phases at Palaikastro and Malia: a response to Seán Hemingway.' In T. Brogan and E. Hallager (eds.), *LM IB Pottery. Relative Chronology and Regional Differences*. Monographs of the Danish Institute at Athens 11. Athens: Danish Institute at Athens: 531–48.

Van de Moortel, A. 2011b. 'The Phaistos Palace and the Kamares Cave: a special relationship.' In W. Gauß, M. Lindblom, A. K. Smith, and J. C. Wright (eds.), *The Cups Are Full: Pottery and Society in the Aegean Bronze Age: Papers Presented to Jeremy B. Rutter on the Occasion of His 65th Birthday*. BAR Int Ser. 2227. Oxford: Archaeopress: 306–18.

Vandenabeele, F. 1991. 'Le monde marin dans les sanctuaires minoens.' In R. Laffineur and L. Basch (eds.), *Thalassa. L'Égée Préhistorique et la Mer*. Aegaeum 7. Liège and Austin: Université de Liège, Histoire de l'art et archéologie de la Grèce antique and University of Texas at Austin, Program in Aegean Scripts and Prehistory: 239–52.

Van Dyke, R. M. and S. E. Alcock (eds.). 2003a. *Archaeologies of Memory*. Oxford: Blackwell.

Van Dyke, R. M. and S. E. Alcock. 2003b. 'Archaeologies of memory: an introduction.' In R. M. van Dyke and S. E. Alcock (eds.), *Archaeologies of Memory*. Oxford: Blackwell: 1–13.

Van Effenterre, H. 1980. *Le Palais de Mallia et la Cité Minoenne. Étude de synthèse, I, II*. Incunabula Graeca 76. Rome: Edizioni dell'Ateneo.

Van Effenterre, H. 1983. 'The economic pattern of a Minoan district: the case of Mallia.' In O. Krzyszkowska and L. Nixon (eds.), *Minoan Society*. Bristol: Bristol Classical Press: 69–74.

Van Effenterre, H. 1985. *La Cité grecque. Des origins à la défaite de Marathon*. Paris: Hachette.

Van Effenterre, H. 1987. 'The function of monumentality in the Minoan Palaces.' In R. Hägg and N. Marinatos (eds.), *The Function of the Minoan Palaces*. Skrifter Utgivna av Svenska Institutet I Athen, 4° 35. Stockholm: Paul Åströms Förlag: 85–7.

Van Effenterre, H. and M. van Effenterre. 1969. *Fouilles exécutées à Mallia. Le Centre Politique 1: L'Agora (1960–1966)*. Études Crétoises 17. Paris: Paul Geuthner.

Vansteenhuyse, K. 2002. 'Minoan courts and ritual competition.' In J. Driessen, I. Schoep, and R. Laffineur (eds.), *Monuments of Minos: Rethinking the Minoan Palaces*. Aegaeum 23. Liège and Austin: Université de Liège, Histoire de l'art et archéologie de la Grèce antique and University of Texas at Austin, Program in Aegean Scripts and Prehistory: 235–48.

Van Wolputte, S. 2004. 'Hang on to your self: of bodies, embodiment, and selves.' *Annual Review of Anthropology* 33: 251–69.

Vasilakis, A. 1990. 'Minoiki kerameiki apo to Idaion Andron.' Cretological Congress A1: 125–34.

Vasilakis, A. and K. Branigan. 2010. *Moni Odigitria: a Prepalatial Cemetery and its Environs in the Asterousia, Southern Crete*. Prehistory Monographs 30. Philadelphia, PA: INSTAP Academic Press.

Vavouranakis, G. 2012. 'The Neopalatial "farm-house" at Kephali Lazana, Chondros Viannou, re-examined.' In E. Mantzourani and P. P. Betancourt (eds.), *Philistor: Studies in Honor of Costis Davaras*. Philadelphia, PA: INSTAP Academic Press: 247–53.

Verlinden, C. 1984. *Les Statuettes Anthropomorphes Crétoises en Bronze et en Plomb, du IIIe Millénaire au VIIe siècle av. J.-C.* Louvain-la-Neuve: Institut supérieur d'archéologie et d'histoire de l'art.

Vernon-Hunt, S. 1988. 'Minoan religion: A comparative analysis of the cult material from a sample of shrine sites in Bronze Age Crete.' PhD Diss., University of Bristol.

Vitaliano, C. J. and D. B. Vitaliano. 1974. 'Volcanic tephra on Crete.' *American Journal of Archaeology* 87: 19–24.

Voigtländer, W. 2009. 'The Bronze Age settlement of Teichiussa.' In C. F. Macdonald, E. Hallager, and W.-D. Niemeier (eds.), *The Minoans in the Central, Eastern and Northern Aegean – New Evidence*. Monographs of the Danish Institute at Athens 8. Athens: Danish Institute at Athens: 111–20.

Vokotopoulos, L. 2011a. 'A view of the Neopalatial countryside: settlement and social organization at Karoumes, eastern Crete.' In K. T. Glowacki and N. Vogeikoff-Brogan (eds.), *STEGA: The Archaeology of Houses and Households in Ancient Crete*. Hesperia Supplement 44. Princeton, NJ: American School of Classical Studies at Athens: 137–49.

Vokotopoulos, L. 2011b. 'Between Palaikastro and Zakros: the pottery from the final Neopalatial horizon of the Sea Guard-House, Karoumes.' In T. M. Brogan and E. Hallager (eds.), *LM IB Pottery: Relative Chronology and Regional Differences*. Monographs of the Danish Institute at Athens 11.2. Athens: Danish Institute at Athens: 553–72.

Von Rüden, C. 2014. 'Beyond the East-West dichotomy in Syrian and Levantine wall paintings.' In B. Brown and M. Feldman (eds.), *Critical Approaches to Near Eastern Art*. Berlin: DeGruyter.

Von Rüden, C. 2015. 'Transmediterranean knowledge and Minoan style reliefs in Tell el Dab'a: an attempt at paradigm shift.' In S. Cappel, U. Günkel-Maschek, and D. Panagiotopoulos (eds.), *Minoan Archaeology: Perspectives for the 21st Century*. Louvain-la-Neuve: Presses universitaires de Louvain: 355–65.

Wachsman, S. 1987. *Aegean in the Theban Tombs*. Leuven: Peeters.

Waldstein, C. 1885. *Essays on the Art of Pheidias*. Cambridge: Cambridge University Press.

Waldstein, C. 1909. 'Classical archaeology and prehistoric archaeology.' In *Fasciculus Joanni Willis Clark Dicatus*. Cambridge: Typis academicis impressus: 517–28.

Wall, S. M., J. H. Musgrave, and P. Warren. 1986. 'Human bones from a Late Minoan IB house at Knossos.' *Annual of the British School at Athens* 81: 333–88.

Warren, P. 1966. 'A stone receptacle from the cave of Hermes Kranaios at Patsos.' *Annual of the British School at Athens* 61: 195–6.

Warren, P. 1969. *Minoan Stone Vases*. Cambridge: Cambridge University Press.

Warren, P. 1981a. 'Minoan Crete and ecstatic religion: preliminary observations on the 1979 excavations at Knossos.' In R. Hägg and N. Marinatos (eds.), *Sanctuaries and Cults in the Aegean Bronze Age*. Skrifter Utgivna av Svenska Institutet I Athen 4°, 27. Stockholm: Svenska Institutet I Athen: 155–67.

Warren, P. 1981b. 'Knossos: Stratigraphical Museum excavations, 1978–1980. Part I.' *Archaeological Reports for 1980–81*: 73–92.

Warren, P. 1983. 'Knossos: Stratigraphical Museum excavations, 1978–82. Part II.' *Archaeological Reports for 1982–83*: 63–87.

Warren, P. 1988. *Minoan Religion as Ritual Action*. Studies in Mediterranean Archaeology 72. Gothenburg: Paul Åström.

Warren, P. 1989. 'Egyptian stone vessels from the city of Knossos: contributions towards Minoan economic and social structure.' *Ariadne* 5 [Festschrift for Stylianos Alexiou]: 1–9.

Warren, P. 1990. 'Of baetyls.' *Opuscula Atheniensia* 18: 192–206.

Warren, P. 1991. 'A new Minoan deposit from Knossos, c.1600 BC, and its wider relations.' *Annual of the British School at Athens* 86: 319–40.

Warren, P. 1994. 'The Minoan roads of Knossos.' In D. Evely, H. Hughes-Brock, and N. Momigliano (eds.), *Knossos: A Labyrinth of History. Papers in Honour of Sinclair Hood*. London: British School at Athens: 189–210.

Warren, P. 1995. 'Minoan Crete and Pharaonic Egypt.' In W. V. Davies and L. Schofield (eds.), *Egypt, the Aegean and the Levant: Interconnections in the Second Millennium B.C.* London: British Museum Press: 1–18.

Warren, P. 1996. 'The Aegean and the limits of radiocarbon dating.' In K. Ransborg, *Absolute Chronology: Archaeological Europe 2500–500 BC.* ActaArch 67, ActaArch Supplement I. Copenhagen: Munksgaard: 283–90.

Warren, P. 1998. 'Aegean Late Bronze 1–2 absolute chronology: some new contributions.' In M. S. Balmuth and R. H. Tykot (eds.), *Sardinian and Aegean Chronology: Towards the Resolution of Relative and Absolute Dating in the Mediterranean.* Studies in Sardinian Archaeology 5. Oxford: Oxbow Books: 323–31.

Warren, P. 1999. 'LM IA: Knossos, Thera, Gournia.' In P. P. Betancourt, V. Karageorghis, R. Laffineur, and W.-D. Niemeier (eds.), *Meletemata: Studies in Aegean Archaeology Presented to Malcolm H. Wiener as He Enters His 65th Year.* Aegaeum 20. Liège and Austin: Université de Liège, Histoire de l'art et archéologie de la Grèce antique and University of Texas, Program in Aegean Scripts and Prehistory: 893–903.

Warren, P. 2000. 'Sir Arthur Evans and his achievement.' *Bulletin of the Institute of Classical Studies* 44: 199–211.

Warren, P. 2001. 'Review of J. Driessen and C. Macdonald, *The troubled island: Minoan Crete before and after the Santorini eruption* (1997).' *American Journal of Archaeology* 105: 115–18.

Warren, P. 2002. 'Political structure in Neopalatial Crete.' In J. Driessen, I. Schoep, and R. Laffineur (eds.), *Monuments of Minos: Rethinking the Minoan Palaces.* Aegaeum 23. Liège and Austin: Université de Liège, Histoire de l'art et archéologie de la Grèce antique and University of Texas, Program in Aegean Scripts and Prehistory: 201–5.

Warren, P. 2004. 'Terra cognita? The territory and boundaries of the early Neopalatial Knossian state.' In G. Cadogan, E. Hatzaki, and A. Vasilakis (eds.), *Knossos: Palace, City, State.* British School at Athens Studies 12. London: British School at Athens: 159–68.

Warren, P. 2006. 'The date of the Thera eruption in relation to Aegean-Egyptian interconnections and the Egyptian historical chronology.' In E. Czerny, I. Hein, H. Hunger, D. Melman, and A. Schwab (eds.), *Timelines: Studies in Honour of Manfred Bietak: Vol. 2.* Leuven: Uitgeverij Peeters en Departement Oosterse Studies: 305–21.

Warren, P. 2009a. "Final summing up" and "General discussion." In C. F. Macdonald, E. Hallager, and W.-D. Niemeier (eds.), *The Minoans in the Central, Eastern and Northern Aegean – New Evidence.* Monographs of the Danish Institute at Athens 8. Athens: Danish Institute at Athens: 263–79.

Warren, P. 2009b. 'The date of the Late Bronze Age eruption of Santorini.' In D. A. Warburton (ed.), *Time's Up! Dating the Minoan Eruption of Santorini.* Monographs of the Danish Institute at Athens 10. Athens: Danish Institute at Athens: 181–6.

Warren, P. 2010. 'The absolute chronology of the Aegean circa 2000 B.C.–1400 B.C. A summary.' In W. Müller (ed.), *Die Bedeutung der minoischen und mykenischen Glyptik: VI. Corpus der Minoischen und Mykenischen Siegel. Beiheft 8.* Verlag Philipp von Zabern: Mainz am Rhein: 383–94.

Warren, P. 2011. 'Late Minoan IB pottery from Knossos: Stratigraphical Museum Excavations, the North Building.' In T. Brogan and E. Hallager (eds.), *LM IB Pottery: Relative Chronology and Regional Difference.* Monographs of the Danish Institute at Athens 11. Athens: Danish Institute at Athens: 193–6.

Warren, P. 2012a. 'The apogee of Minoan civilization: the final Neopalatial period.' In E. Mantzourani and P. P. Betancourt (eds.), *Philistor: Studies in Honor of Costis Davaras.* Philadelphia, PA: INSTAP Academic Press: 255–72.

Warren, P. 2012b. '"Back to the beginning" – an overview.' In I. Schoep, P. Tomkins, and J. Driessen (eds.), *Back to the Beginning: Reassessing Social and Political Complexity on*

Crete during the Early and Middle Bronze Age. Oxford: Oxbow Books: 429–35.

Warren, P. 2015. 'Marine style pottery from Knossos.' In D. Panagiotopoulos, I. Kaiser, and O. Kouka (eds.), *Ein Minoer im Exil: Festschrift für Wolf-Dietrich Niemeier.* Bonn: Verlag Dr. Rudolf Habelt GMBH: 375–88.

Warren, P. and V. Hankey. 1989. *Aegean Bronze Age Chronology.* Bristol: Bristol University Press.

Waterhouse, H. 2002. 'Priest-Kings?' *Cretan Studies* 7: 245–70.

Watrous, L. V. 1982. *Lasithi. A History of a Settlement on a Highland Plain in Crete.* Hesperia Suppl. 18. Princeton, NJ: American School of Classical Studies at Athens.

Watrous, L. V. 1984. 'Ayia Triada: a new perspective on the Minoan Villa.' *American Journal of Archaeology* 88: 123–34.

Watrous, L.V. 1987. 'The role of the Near East in the rise of the Cretan Palaces.' In R. Hägg and N. Marinatos (eds.), *The Function of the Minoan Palaces.* Skrifter Utgivna av Svenska Institutet I Athen, 4°35. Stockholm: Paul Åströms Förlag: 65–70.

Watrous, L. V. 1995. 'Some observations on Minoan peak sanctuaries.' In R. Laffineur and W.-D. Niemeier (eds.), *Politeia: Society and State in the Aegean Bronze Age.* Aegaeum 12. Liège and Austin: Université de Liège, Histoire de l'art et archéologie de la Grèce antique and University of Texas at Austin, Program in Aegean Scripts and Prehistory: 393–403.

Watrous, L. V. 1996. [with a contribution by Y. K. Widenor] *The Cave Sanctuary of Zeus at Psychro: A Study of Extra-urban Sanctuaries in Minoan and Early Iron Age Crete.* Aegaeum 15. Liège and Austin: Université de Liège, Histoire de l'art et archéologie de la Grèce antique and University of Texas at Austin, Program in Aegean Scripts and Prehistory.

Watrous, L. V. 1998. 'Egypt and Crete in the early Middle Bronze Age: a case of trade and cultural diffusion.' In E. H. Cline and D. Cline (eds.), *The Aegean and the Orient in the Second Millennium.* Aegaeum 18. Liège and Austin: Université de Liège, Histoire de l'art et archéologie de la Grèce antique and University of Texas at Austin, Program in Aegean Scripts and Prehistory: 19–28.

Watrous, L. V. 2001. 'Review of Aegean Prehistory III: Crete from earliest prehistory through the Protopalatial period.' In T. Cullen (ed.), *Aegean Prehistory: A Review.* American Journal of Archaeology Suppl. I. Boston, MA: American Journal of Archaeology: 157–223.

Watrous, L. V. 2004. 'New pottery from the Psychro Cave and its implications for Minoan Crete.' *Annual of the British School at Athens* 99: 19–47.

Watrous, L. V. 2012a. 'The harbor complex of the Minoan town at Gournia.' *American Journal of Archaeology* 116: 521–41.

Watrous, L. V. 2012b. 'An overview of secondary state formation on Crete: the Mirabello region during the Bronze Age.' In E. Mantzourani and P. P. Betancourt (eds.), *Philistor: Studies in Honor of Costis Davaras.* Philadelphia, PA: INSTAP Academic Press: 273–82.

Watrous, L. V. (ed.) 2015. 'Excavations at Gournia, 2010–2012.' *Hesperia* 84: 397–465.

Watrous, L. V. and H. Blitzer. 1999. 'The region of Gournia in the Neopalatial period.' In P. P. Betancourt, V. Karageorghis, R. Laffineur, and W.-D. Niemeier (eds.), *Meletemata: Studies in Aegean Archaeology Presented to Malcolm H. Wiener as He Enters His 65th Year, III.* Aegaeum 20. Liège and Austin: Université de Liège, Histoire de l'art et archéologie de la Grèce antique and University of Texas at Austin, Program in Aegean Scripts and Prehistory: 905–9.

Watrous, L. V. and D. Hadzi-Vallianou. 2004. 'Palatial rule and collapse (Middle Minoan IB-Late Minoan IIIB).' In L. V. Watrous, D. Hadzi-Villianou, and H. Blitzer (eds.), *The Plain of Phaistos: Cycles of Social Complexity in the Mesara Region of Crete.* Monumenta Archaeologica 23. Los Angeles, CA: Cotsen Institute of Archaeology at UCLA: 277–304.

Watrous, L. V., D. Hadzi-Vallianou, and H. Blitzer. 2004. *The Plain of Phaistos: Cycles of Social Complexity in the Mesara Region of Crete.*

Monumenta Archaeologica 23. Los Angeles, CA: The Cotsen Institute of Archaeology at UCLA.

Watrous, L. V., D. Hadzi-Vallianou, K. Pope, N. Mourtzas, J. Shay, C. T. Shay, J. Bennet, D. Tsoungarakis, E. Angelomati-Tsoungarakis, C. Vallianos, and H. Blitzer. 1993. 'A survey of the Western Mesara Plain in Crete: preliminary report of the 1984, 1986 and 1987 field seasons.' *Hesperia* 62: 191–248.

Watrous, L. V., D. Haggis, K. Nowicki, N. Vogeikoff-Brogan, and M. Schultz. 2012. *An Archaeological Survey of the Gournia Landscape: A Regional History of the Mirabello Bay, Crete, in Antiquity*. Prehistory Monographs 37. Philadelphia, PA: INSTAP Academic Press.

Watrous, L. V. and A. Heimroth. 2011. 'Household industries of Late Minoan IB Gournia and the socioeconomic status of the town.' In K. T. Glowacki and N. Vogeikoff-Brogan (eds.), *STEGA: The Archaeology of Houses and Households in Ancient Crete*. Hesperia Suppl. 44. Princeton, NJ: American School of Classical Studies at Athens: 199–212.

Watrous, L. V. and M. Schultz. 2012. 'Middle Minoan III–Late Minoan I periods: the rise of a regional state.' In L. V. Watrous, D. Haggis, K. Nowicki, N. Vogeikoff-Brogan, and M. Schultz (eds.), *An Archaeological Survey of the Gournia Landscape: A Regional History of the Mirabello Bay, Crete, in Antiquity*. Prehistory Monographs 37. Philadelphia, PA: INSTAP Academic Press: 51–63.

Wedde, M. 2000. *Towards a Hermeneutics of Aegean Bronze Age Ship Imagery*. Mannheim und Möhnesee: Bibliopolis.

Weingarten, J. 1983. *The Zakro Master and His Place in Prehistory*. Göteborg: Paul Åströms Förlag.

Weingarten, J. 1986. 'The sealing structures of Minoan Crete: MM II Phaistos to the destruction of the palace of Knossos. Part I: the evidence until the LM IB destructions.' *Oxford Journal of Archaeology* 5: 279–98.

Weingarten, J. 1987. 'Seal-use at LM IB Ayia Triada: a Minoan elite in action. I:

Administrative considerations.' *Kadmos* 26: 1–43.

Weingarten, J. 1988. 'The sealing structures of Minoan Crete: MM II Phaistos to the destruction of the palace of Knossos. Part II: the evidence from Knossos until the destruction of the palace.' *Oxford Journal of Archaeology* 7: 1–25.

Weingarten, J. 1989. 'Old and new elements in the seals and sealings of the Temple Repository, Knossos.' In R. Laffineur (ed.), *Transition. Le Monde Égéen du Bronze Moyen au Bronze Recent*. Aegaeum 3. Liège: Université de Liège, Histoire de l'art et archéologie de la Grèce antique: 39–52.

Weingarten, J. 1990. 'Three upheavals in Minoan sealing administration: evidence for radical change.' In T. Palaima (ed.), *Aegean Seals, Sealings and Administration*. Aegaeum 5, Liège: Université de Liège, Histoire de l'art et archéologie de la Grèce antique: 105–20.

Weingarten, J. 1991a. 'Late Bronze Age trade within Crete: the evidence of seals and sealings.' In N. H. Gale (ed.), *Bronze Age Trade in the Mediterranean*. Studies in Mediterranean Archaeology 90. Göteborg: Paul Åströms Förlag: 303–24.

Weingarten, J. 1991b. *The Transformation of Egyptian Taweret into the Minoan Genius: A Study in Cultural Transmission in the Middle Bronze Age*. Studies in Mediterranean Archaeology 88. Partille: Paul Åströms Förlag.

Weingarten, J. 2005. 'Review of O. Krzyszkowska, *Aegean Seals, an Introduction*.' *Studi Micenei ed Egeo-Anatolici* 47: 353–9.

Weingarten, J. 2010. 'Minoan seals and sealings.' In E. H. Cline (ed.), *The Bronze Age Aegean (ca. 3000–1000 BC)*. Oxford: Oxford University Press: 317–28.

Whitelaw, T. 2000. 'Beyond the Palace: a century of investigation in Europe's oldest city.' *Bulletin of the Institute of Classical Studies* 44: 223–6.

Whitelaw, T. 2001. 'From sites to communities: defining the human dimensions of Minoan urbanism.' In K. Branigan (ed.), *Urbanism in the Aegean Bronze Age*. Sheffield: Sheffield Academic Press: 15–37.

Whitelaw, T. 2004a. 'Alternative pathways to complexity in the southern Aegean.' In J. C. Barrett and P. Halstead (eds.), *The Emergence of Civilisation Revisited*. Oxford: Oxbow: 232–56.

Whitelaw, T. 2004b. 'Estimating the population of Neopalatial Knossos.' In G. Cadogan, E. Hatzaki, and A. Vasilakis (eds.), *Knossos: Palace, City, State*. British School at Athens Studies 12. London: British School at Athens: 147–58.

Whitelaw, T. 2012. 'The urbanisation of prehistoric Crete: settlement perspectives on Minoan state formation.' In I. Schoep, P. Tomkins, and J. Driessen (eds.), *Back to the Beginning: Reassessing Social and Political Complexity on Crete during the Early and Middle Bronze Age*. Oxford: Oxbow Books: 114–76.

Whitelaw, T. forthcoming. 'Recognising polities in prehistoric Crete.' In M. Relaki and Y. Papadatos (eds.), *From the Foundation to the Legacy of Minoan Society*. Sheffield Studies in Aegean Archaeology. Oxford: Oxbow Books.

Whitelaw, T. and C. Morgan. 2009. 'Crete.' *Archaeological Reports for 2008–2009* 55: 79–100.

Whitley, J. 2001. *The Archaeology of Ancient Greece*. Cambridge: Cambridge University Press.

Whitley, J. A. 2002. 'Too many ancestors?' *Antiquity* 76: 119–26.

Whitley, J. A. 2004. 'Archaeology in Greece 2003–2004.' *Archaeological Reports*: 1–92.

Whitley, J. A. 2006. 'The Minoans – a Welsh invention? A view from east Crete.' In Y. Hamilakis and N. Momigliano (eds.), *Archaeology and European Modernity: Producing and Consuming the 'Minoans.'* Creta Antica 7. Padua: Bottega d'Erasmo: 55–67.

Whittaker, H. 2002. 'Minoan board games: the function and meaning of stones with depressions (so-called kernoi) from Bronze Age Crete.' *Aegean Archaeology* 6: 73–87.

Whittaker, H. 2005. 'Social and symbolic aspects of Minoan writing.' *European Journal of Archaeology* 8: 29–41.

Wiener, M. 1984. 'Crete and the Cyclades in LM I: the tale of the conical cups.' In R. Hägg and N. Marinatos (eds.), *The Minoan Thalassocracy: Myth and Reality*. Skrifter Utgivna av Svenska

Institutet I Athen, 4° 32. Stockholm: Paul Åströms Förlag. 17–26.

Wiener, M. 1990. 'The isles of Crete? The Minoan Thalassocracy revisited.' In D. A. Hardy, C. G. Doumas, J. A. Sakellarakis, and P. M. Warren (eds.), *Thera and the Aegean World III, Volume One: Archaeology*. London: The Thera Foundation: 128–61.

Wiener, M. 1999. 'Present arms/oars/ingots: searching for evidence of military or maritime administration in LM IB.' In R. Laffineur (ed.), *POLEMOS: Le Contexte Guerrier en Égée à l'âge du Bronze*. Aegaeum 19. Liège and Austin: Université de Liège, Histoire de l'art et archéologie de la Grèce antique and University of Texas at Austin, Program in Aegean Scripts and Prehistory: 411–23.

Wiener, M. 2003. 'Time out: the current impasse in Bronze Age archaeological dating.' In K. P. Foster and R. Laffineur (eds.), *Metron: Measuring the Aegean Bronze Age*. Aegaeum 24. Liège and Austin: Université de Liège, Histoire de l'art et archéologie de la Grèce antique and University of Texas, Program in Aegean Scripts and Prehistory: 363–99.

Wiener, M. 2007. 'Neopalatial Knossos: rule and role.' In P. P. Betancourt, M. Nelson, and H. Williams (eds.), *Krinoi kai Limenes: Studies in Honor of Joseph and Maria Shaw*. Philadelphia, PA: INSTAP Academic Press: 231–40.

Wiener, M. 2010. 'A point in time.' In O. Krzyszkowska (ed.), *Cretan Offerings: Studies in Honour of Peter Warren*. British School at Athens Studies 18. London: British School at Athens: 367–94.

Wiener, M. 2011. 'Conical cups: from mystery to history.' In W. Gauß, M. Lindblom, R. Angus, K. Smith, and J. C. Wright (eds.), *Papers Presented to Jeremy B. Rutter on the Occasion of His 65th Birthday*. Oxford: Archaeopress: 355–68.

Wiener, M. 2015a. 'Dating the Theran eruption: archaeological science versus nonsense science.' In T. Levy, T. Schneider, and W. Propp (eds.), *Israel's Exodus in Transdisciplinary Perspective*. Cham: Springer: 131–43.

Wiener, M. 2015b. 'The Mycenaean conquest of Minoan Crete.' In C. F. Macdonald, E. Hatzaki, and S. Andreou (eds.), *The Great Islands: Studies of Crete and Cyprus Presented to Gerald Cadogan*. Athens: Kapon: 131–42.

Wilson, D. 1994. 'Knossos before the palaces: an overview of the Early Bronze Age (EM I–III).' In D. Evely, H. Hughes-Brock, and N. Momigliano (eds.), *Knossos: A Labyrinth of History: Papers Presented in Honour of Sinclair Hood*. London: British School at Athens: 23–44.

Wilson, D. 2008. 'Early Prepalatial Crete.' In C. Shelmerdine (ed.), *The Cambridge Companion to the Aegean Bronze Age*. Cambridge: Cambridge University Press: 77–104.

Xanthoudidis, S. 1919. 'Anaskafi eis Nirou Chani Kritis.' *Praktika tis en Athinais Archaiologikis Etaireias* 1919: 63–9.

Xanthoudidis, S. 1922. 'Minoikon megaron Nirou.' *Archaiologiki Ephimeris*: 1–25.

Xanthoudidis, S. 1924. *The Vaulted Tombs of Mesara*. London: Hodder and Stoughton.

Yoffee, N. 1993. 'Too many chiefs? (Or, safe texts for the '90s).' In N. Yoffee and A. Sherratt (eds.), *Archaeological Theory: Who Sets the Agenda?* Cambridge: Cambridge University Press: 60–78.

Younger, J. G. 1977. 'Non-sphragistic uses of Minoan-Mycenaean sealstones and rings.' *Kadmos* 16: 141–59.

Younger, J. G. 1995. 'Bronze Age representations of Aegean bull-games, III.' In R. Laffineur and W.-D. Niemeier (eds.), *POLITEIA. Society and State in the Aegean Bronze Age*. Aegaeum 12. Liège and Austin: Université de Liège, Histoire de l'art et archéologie de la Grèce antique and University of Texas at Austin, Program in Aegean Scripts and Prehistory: 507–45.

Younger, J. 2008. 'The Knossos "Jewel Fresco" reconsidered.' In C. Gallou, M. Georgiadis, and G. M. Muskett (eds.), *Dioskouroi: Studies Presented to W. G. Cavanagh and C. B. Mee on the Anniversary of Their 30-year Joint Contribution to Aegean Archaeology*. Oxford: Archaeopress: 76–89.

Younger, J. 2009a. 'Tree tugging and omphalos hugging on Minoan gold rings.' In A. L. D'Agata and A. Van de Moortel (eds.), *Archaeologies of Cult: Essays on Ritual and Cult in Crete in Honor of Geraldine C. Gesell*. Hesperia Suppl. 42. Princeton, NJ: American School of Classical Studies at Athens: 43–9.

Younger, J. 2009b. 'Review article: The bull-leaping scenes from Tell el-Dab'a.' *American Journal of Archaeology* 113: 479–80.

Younger, J. n.d. [website]. http://people.ku.edu/~jyounger/LinearA/

Zanker, P. 1998: *Pompeii: Public and Private Life*. [Translated by D .L. Schneider.] Cambridge, MA: Harvard University Press.

Zeimbeki, M. 2004. 'The organization of votive production and distribution in the peak sanctuaries of state society Crete: a perspective offered by the Juktas clay animal figures.' In G. Cadogan, E. Hatzaki, and A. Vasilakis (eds.), *Knossos: Palace, City, State*. British School at Athens Studies 12. London: British School at Athens: 351–61.

Zominthos Fieldnotes (website): http://interactive.archaeology.org/zominthos

INDEX